SEVENTH EDITION

Child Welfare and Family Services

Policies and Practice

Susan Whitelaw Downs
Wayne State University

Ernestine Moore
Wayne State University

Emily Jean McFadden
Grand Valley State University

Susan M. Michaud
University of Wisconsin–Madison

Lela B. Costin
Late Professor Emeritus, University of Illinois at Urbana–Champaign

Boston ■ New York ■ San Francisco
Mexico City ■ Montreal ■ Toronto ■ London ■ Madrid ■ Munich ■ Paris
Hong Kong ■ Singapore ■ Tokyo ■ Cape Town ■ Sydney

Series Editor: *Patricia Quinlin*
Editorial Assistant: *Annemarie Kennedy*
Marketing Manager: *Taryn Wahlquist*
Editorial-Production Administrator: *Annette Joseph*
Editorial-Production Service: *Omegatype Typography, Inc.*
Manufacturing Buyer: *JoAnne Sweeney*
Composition Buyer: *Linda Cox*
Electronic Composition: *Omegatype Typography, Inc.*
Cover Designer: *Kristina Mose-Libon*

For related titles and support materials, visit our online catalog at www.ablongman.com.

Between the time web site information is gathered and published, some sites may have closed. Also, the transcription of URLs can result in typographical errors. The publisher would appreciate notification where these errors occur so that they may be corrected in subsequent editions.

Library of Congress Cataloging-in-Publication Data

Child welfare and family services : policies and practice / Susan Whitelaw Downs . . . [et al.].—7th ed.
  p. cm.
 Includes bibliographical references and index.
 ISBN 0-205-36007-6
  1. Child welfare—United States. 2. Family services—United States. I. Downs, Susan.

HV741.C4995 2004
362.7'0973—dc21

2003052167

Printed in the United States of America
10 9 8 7 6 5 4 3 2 1   RRD-VA   08 07 06 05 04 03

To my husband, Larry C. Ledebur
S. W. D.

To my mom and the children we serve
E. M.

To my grandchildren, Robin, Justice, Africa, Alema, Danny, Emily,
Elizabeth, Sarah, and Teddy, and to the children of the world
E. J. M.

To child welfare workers and supervisors who care for everyone's children
S. M. M.

To the memory of Laura Kerr Brown
L. B. C.

CONTENTS

v

11 Juvenile Delinquents: The Community's Dilemma   409

12 Professional Responsibilities: Ethics and Advocacy   437

PREFACE

Child Welfare and Family Services: Policies and Practice, Seventh Edition, presents concepts, policies, and practice in the broad field of child and family services. Material has been drawn from research findings, legislation, judicial decisions, professional literature, reports of social work practice, and interviews with practitioners. These sources inform the major subjects of the book: the needs of families and children, the major policies and programs of social services designed for them, and the policy issues that emerge for future planning. Our intent is to provide the student—undergraduate or graduate—with a substantive base of knowledge about policies and practice in family and child services.

The place of child and family services in the curricula of schools of social work has changed in response to broadened concepts of services for children and families within the human service community. In earlier years of social work education, child welfare was narrowly defined as a field of practice dealing mainly with children in the protective service system, in foster care, in institutions, or in the process of adoption. Correspondingly, child welfare courses were self-contained entities in a school's curriculum, combining policy and background knowledge with a large component of practice methods in this specialized field. Today, child welfare services have been redefined as child and family services and include knowledge of the traditional child welfare services as well as a wide range of programs to support families and children and to prevent the need for children's out-of-home care. Because this book addresses policies and programs directed at all children and families, the conceptual framework is appropriate not only for traditionally defined child welfare courses in which the instructor may choose to use the content selectively; it is also especially suitable in the curricula of schools of social work that offer "concentrations" or "specializations" more broadly defined as "services to families, children, and youth." Students in these concentrations are exposed to a range of social services to families and children, organized in a continuum from universal services, through preventive services of various kinds, to the traditional child welfare services. They may be assigned field placements in a variety of agencies serving families and children, including family service agencies, public and private child welfare agencies, child guidance clinics, the courts, and the schools. Students in related concentrations—for example, health and mental health services—for whom knowledge of public policy with respect to families is essential, often elect to enroll in family, child, and youth courses.

The text is designed for use in collaborative educational arrangements between public child welfare agencies and schools of social work. These partnerships evolved in the 1980s and 1990s, supported by state and federal funds to promote the reintegration of public agency practice into BSW and MSW programs. *Child Welfare and Family Services: Policies and Practice* is useful as a reliable reference for new personnel entering employment in child and family social agencies and as a tool for planned staff development programs. In some instances, it can be helpful to citizens in our highly technological society who want to influence the environment in which social services are carried out. Members of the global child welfare community find the text useful in understanding essential principles of child welfare practice, according to the American experience. This book is being used extensively abroad.

Our major objectives are to help the reader do the following:

1. Develop a vital concern for families and children and their potentialities; their cultural diversity; and their experiences in neighborhood, school, and community.
2. Develop an overall orientation to the family as a unit of attention, and to the service concerns of family preservation, kinship care, services to children at risk, continuity of family relationships, and culturally appropriate services.
3. Identify problems necessitating family and child services, see how these problems are related to institutional gaps in the provision of appropriate services, and develop an appreciation for the need for collaboration and integration among service systems.
4. Become familiar with the policies, practices, and goals of current family and child welfare programs and acquire a basis for evaluating them.
5. Learn how services to families and children interact with the larger social and political structures, American cultural values, and global forces and trends, and the profound way these affect the goals and implementation of social policies.
6. Identify some of the salient aspects of social work history that arose in response to rather narrowly conceived social and family–child problems and that still influence family and child welfare programs in this country.
7. Distinguish between family and child welfare practices based on verified knowledge and those based mainly on custom and belief.

This book reflects our conviction that to be effective in today's turbulent world, it is essential that we avoid an overly narrow, categorical view of the welfare of children and their families. Services for children and families must be broadly defined. It would be inaccurate to portray child welfare as a narrow band of traditional services quite apart from the larger societal context in which it finds its energy, focus, and niche. It would be irresponsible to ignore the impact of public welfare and the courts as major influences on the status of children and families.

Full consideration is given to the basic core of child welfare services: services to protect children from neglect and abuse, family preservation services, foster care, adoption, and child advocacy. These topics are discussed with particular attention to continuity of family relationships, kinship care, and efforts to help children reach acceptable levels of health, safety, and educational achievement. We also have striven to highlight the cultural context within which children and families operate. We have been attentive to the need for cultural understanding and for the culturally competent organization of services. We have, thus, infused content on cultural and ethnic issues throughout the text.

In addition, the text includes the legal framework that governs the affairs of children and young persons (an aspect of the family and child welfare system whose importance has burgeoned) as reflected in laws of guardianship and recent United States Supreme Court decisions; the organization and functioning of the juvenile court and family courts; and the sociolegal issues that emerge in matters of poverty, unwed parenting, delinquency, child neglect and abuse, foster care, and adoption.

All the chapters in the seventh edition of *Child Welfare and Family Services: Policies and Practice* have been carefully revised and updated. The case material is drawn generally from our own experiences and that of other practitioners, but as presented here it is entirely fictitious. The chapters also include findings from recent research, important new court decisions and legislation affecting the child and the family, and innovative demonstrations in recent practice with children and families that reflect the renewed commitment to preserve a child's own home and to ensure children's well-being and opportunities for growth and development.

New in this edition is the infusion of content on global issues in child and family services. Child welfare practitioners in the twenty-first century will deal with changes, many not yet foreseen, brought by increasing globalization. The increase in communication, the development of technology, and the accelerated movement of people and ideas around the globe will require that future workers understand child welfare in a global context.

The order of the chapters reflects our preference for providing the student with a beginning understanding of families and of services to families, because this is the primary focus of the book. The first two chapters provide a foundation for the study of family and child welfare, presenting the historical background, an overview of services, and the legal framework for the relationship among children, parents, and the state. The following three chapters emphasize the importance of basic services to children and families, including material on support services to children and families at risk, day care, child development programs, and welfare reform. The last half of the book covers traditional child welfare services, including child protective services, family preservation services, foster care, adoption, and juvenile delinquency. A chapter on juvenile and family courts provides a legal framework for this material. The last chapter addresses the role of social workers in child advocacy and also professional issues in child welfare practice.

The chapters have also been written to stand alone so they can be ordered in a number of different ways to reflect the individual instructor's personal preferences in constructing a family and child services course and teaching outline. In our teaching, we have presented the chapters in differing order for different groups of students. This book is highly adaptable in organization.

At the end of each chapter are questions for individual study and for class discussions as well as selected sources that the instructor can use for lecture–discussion material or that the student can use for independent study. For this edition and the last, we have added two new sections at the end of each chapter: a chapter summary and a list of relevant Internet sites, reflecting the rapid increase in use of the World Wide Web. For additional exploration of ideas, the references at the end of each chapter provide a substantial bibliography of family and child services.

In the course of preparing seven editions of *Child Welfare and Family Services: Policies and Practice,* we have incurred many debts to numerous colleagues and academicians in other disciplines, and to administrators and staff members of public child welfare agencies and professional social workers in other settings, who carry out the demanding work in family and child services. They have directed us to new material and offered criticism and new insights that have been invaluable. We thank Mary Van Dyke, Todd Campbell, and Renee Sutkay, Rock County Human Services, Wisconsin; and Kristin Shook-Slack at the University of Wisconsin–Madison, School of Social Work, for comments and suggestions for Chapter 7. We thank the reviewers of this edition: Monique Busch, Indiana University; Derek Mason, Utah State University; and Martha Roditti, San Francisco State University.

We also thank our universities, Wayne State University, Grand Valley State University, and University of Wisconsin–Madison, for encouragement, resources, and support.

We, her coauthors, would like to acknowledge the contributions of the late Lela B. Costin, the primary author of this text for many years, and its heart and inspiration. The first edition, for which she was the sole author, was published in 1972. With each subsequent edition, her contribution to the education of future professional social workers grew. Wherever we travel, we meet people whose professional child welfare education was formed by her textbook and who continue to use it to guide their practice. Her firm belief that our society must do much better for its children, her keen ability to get to the heart of an issue, her research on child welfare history and policy, her tremendous energy for intellectual projects, and her encouraging mentoring of her coauthors are largely responsible for this book's success. She was a national leader of twentieth-century child welfare practice. We mourn her passing and celebrate her contributions to the field of social work and to the lives of children.

CHAPTER

1

An Introduction to Family and Child Services

In the green years of childhood the young begin their irreversible march into the future with the resolution and sweet calmness of innocence. The march of childhood goes on as long as the human race endures, an affirmation of new hope and the freshness of life that comes with every generation. The message proclaims another chance for mankind.

—United Nations Children's Fund

CHAPTER OUTLINE

Child and family welfare services reflect society's organized conviction about the worth of the child and the family, and the child's rights as a developing person and future citizen. Within the wide range of social welfare and social work, child welfare has a dual role: providing direct services to children and families when serious problems of children and youth are identified, and influencing public policy to improve the lives of all children. To strengthen family life for children is regarded as the primary purpose of child welfare.

The field of practice traditionally known as child welfare has been a dominant and influential force in the development of the social work profession. However, child welfare today as a specialized field of social work practice is vastly more complex than it was in the nineteenth and early twentieth centuries, when our ancestors confidently responded to problems of family functioning by "rescuing" children of poor or neglectful parents and placing them in institutions of one kind or another. Since then, for at least half a century, social changes have impelled child and family agencies to adapt and innovate services. Today's high public concern about the family, traditionally regarded as society's best institution for promoting stability, is showing more clearly the impact of social, industrial, and economic dislocation. Child and family welfare, as a specialized field of social work practice, is now facing challenges to its gradual but respected evolutionary growth as it confronts demands to move beyond the residual, outworn classification of child welfare services and to respond to new, complex family problems.

Some of the effects of rapid social change over the past decades are manifested in alternative family forms and child-rearing patterns, in the greatly accelerated entry of women with very young children into the labor force, in the unprecedented growth of female-headed families, and in increased official reporting of child abuse and neglect. Other developments have heightened concern among the public and professionals in the child welfare system—the phenomenon of children with acquired immune deficiency syndrome (AIDS); children and families who are homeless; the violence perpetrated by a small number of young people that goes beyond the activities usually labeled as "delinquent"; and the heavy damage to parents, children, and adolescents caused by highly increased rates of drug use.

Despite continuing reform efforts to preserve families and reduce the need for out-of-home placement for children, the number of children in foster care remains high. The public has become incensed at the shocking newspaper and television accounts of children who have been terribly abused sexually and physically, or neglected to the point of serious impairment or death, and the apparent inability of the child welfare system to prevent maltreatment or to protect children either in their own families or in substitute care. The anger at maltreating parents and apparent agency unresponsiveness has led to myriad calls for change, including congressional debate on bringing back orphanages for children of substance-abusing parents, class action and civil liability suits against agencies, and grassroots reform efforts to give children more legal standing in court to separate themselves from their parents. All these developments, as well as new federal and state legislation and judicial decisions, have served to give a new face to much of child welfare practice, and to make more urgent the need for competent personnel in the system of child and family social services.

This book, then, is about children. It is about their needs and their problems. It is about our society and its influence on children, and therefore it is also a book about families, governments, agencies, and professionals. It is about what we do *for* children and what we do *to* children. It is also a book about how we can do better for the nation's children.

The welfare of children is dependent on the interaction between them and their environments. It is this focus that places the family at center stage because the family is the most dominant part of a child's environment. The family is the major instrument for providing for the welfare of children. It is the primary social institution in meeting social, education, and health care needs. It is the family that negotiates with a larger environment to see that the child's needs are met. A larger society becomes involved when families are judged incapable of ensuring the child's welfare. This can occur because of the extraordinary needs of a special group of children, such as children with developmental disabilities, which can easily overwhelm family resources. Or it can occur because families, owing to lack of resources or major dysfunction, cannot meet even minimal standards of child care, as in the case of neglected or abused children.

Social work has had a uniquely important role in the connection between children, families, and organized social welfare. The earliest efforts of the profession were devoted to children and families. As Ann Hartman has described it:

> The profession has supported, replaced, taught, rehabilitated, treated, dismantled, abandoned, and embraced the family. To Mary Richmond [practitioner, teacher, and social work theoretician], the family was the central focus of social work's concern. The first professional practice journal was titled *The Family.* . . . The early child guidance workers focused their efforts on helping parents to be better parents, and the child-saving movement sought to rescue children by placing them with families. (1981, p. 7)

Traditionally, child welfare has been at the center of the social work profession. Today, that partnership between child welfare and social work is reflected in the philosophy that the best way to help children is to support, strengthen, and supplement the efforts of families. Laird (1985) has offered this precept for child and family welfare:

> Ecologically oriented child welfare practice attends to, nurtures, and supports the biological family. Further, when it is necessary to substitute for the biological family, such practice dictates that every effort be made to preserve and protect important kinship ties. Intervention in families must be done with great care to avoid actions which could weaken the natural family, sap its vitality and strength, or force it to make difficult costly adjustments. (p. 177)

The Changing American Family

Many observers claim that more changes have occurred in the American family over recent decades than ever before in our nation's history. The changes have led some to pronounce that the American family is breaking down, losing its preeminent position in American society. The more prevalent belief is that the American family is merely adapting to a very different world from the one it experienced earlier. Regardless of the conclusions, few would argue that the last five decades have witnessed major changes in the family.

The U.S. Department of Commerce, Census Bureau, has released figures from the 2000 census, which show that there are now more children under age 18 in the United States than ever before. The total number of children now is 70.4 million, making this the first year that the population of children in the United States has risen above the peak of the baby boom in 1966, when the nation had 69.9 million children. As these children age, the need for services such as health care and schools will increase correspondingly.

The "millennium generation," as the new baby boom is called, looks very different from the previous one, which was fueled by the large number of births following World War II. The current boom was created by immigration as much as by an increase in births to those born in the United States. This generation is more ethnically diverse than any previous one. Minority children (any group except non-Hispanic white) accounted for 36 percent of all children in 2000, compared to 26 percent just twenty years earlier, in 1980. Not all minority groups are growing in relation to the rest of the population, however. African American children comprise 15 percent of the total child population, a percentage that has remained stable since 1980. The greatest increase has been in the percentage of Hispanic children, who can be of any race. Comprising only 9 percent of the child population in 1980, they now account for 16 percent of all American children. They have overtaken African Americans as the largest group of minority children. The number of Asian and Pacific Islander children nearly doubled since 1980, from 2 percent to about 4 percent. Native American children continue to comprise about 1 percent of the population of U.S. children, as they have since 1970. In the 2000 census, for the first time, people could check more than one race; nearly 2 million children are in the "more than one race" category. The diversity of the current generation of children is also evident in statistics on languages they speak at home; in 1999, 5 percent of all school-age children spoke a language other than English at home and had difficulty speaking English. The number of these children doubled in the last twenty years from 1.3 million in 1979 to 2.6 million in 1999 (Russakoff, 1998; Federal Interagency Forum, 2001; O'Hare, 2001). The increasing diversity of American children and families will impel human service agencies to become more adept at offering programs that are congruent with families' cultures and languages.

Even though the number of children is increasing, they represent a smaller portion of the total population than they did in earlier years. From a peak in 1966, when children under age 18 accounted for 36 percent of the population, children today account for only 26 percent of the population, as other age groups increase more rapidly than the under-18 group (Federal Interagency Forum, 2002). This decreasing proportion may result in a loss to children of the government-provided services they need, such as schools, day care, and health care, because there will be fewer households advocating for the needs of children.

Another change within American families is the unprecedented increase in the number of those headed by a single parent. In 1980, 77 percent of children had both parents in the household. Twenty years later, in 2000, only 69 percent lived with two parents; the rest lived with a mother only (22 percent), a father only (4 percent), or neither parent (4 percent). The largest increase in single-parent families occurred during the 1970s and 1980s; since then the increase has been slight (Bryson & Casper, 1998; Federal Interagency Forum, 2002). Children who live in a household with only one parent are at higher risk of poverty and attendant problems.

Along with changes in the number of parents in the home, family structure is becoming more diverse in other ways as well. Small but increasing percentages of children live with grandparents, other relatives, stepparents, adoptive parents, or parent's unmarried partners, with or without their own biological parent(s) in the home. Over 3 million children live with a parent who is cohabiting with either the other parent or another adult. Children who live with neither parent are in a variety of arrangements; about half live with a grand-parent or grandparents, with the rest about evenly divided between homes of relatives and of nonrelatives. Over 500,000 children are in state foster care systems, living in a variety of foster homes, institutions, or group homes (Federal Interagency Forum, 2001).

The age and ethnicity of children are correlated with different types of living arrange-ments. As children get older, they become less likely to live with two parents. About three-fourths of children under age 5 live with two parents, compared to about two-thirds of those in the 15–17 age group (Federal Interagency Forum, 2001). Non-Hispanic white children are much more likely than African American children and somewhat more likely than His-panic children to live with two parents. In 2000, 78 percent of white, non-Hispanic children lived with two parents, compared with 38 percent of black children and 65 percent of chil-dren of Hispanic origin (Federal Interagency Forum, 2002).

Related to the increase in single-parent families is the decision by increasing numbers of young people to delay marriage. Young men and women are much less likely to marry in their teens and early twenties than they were in the 1960s. Today, the median age at first mar-riage is 27 for men and 25 for women (Saluter, 1994). One result of this has been an increase in the proportion of children born to unmarried parents. Between 1980 and 1994, the birth rate of unmarried women (number of births per thousand women age 15–44 in the population) in-creased sharply, from twenty-nine to forty-seven per thousand. The sharpest increase was among women in their late teens and twenties. Since 1994 the birth rate to unmarried women of childbearing age has stabilized, at about forty-five births per thousand. However, it has sta-bilized at a high rate, particularly for certain age groups. In 1999, nearly two-thirds of women under age 25 having their first baby were not married (Federal Interagency Forum, 2001).

The increased participation of mothers in the labor force is another distinguishing feature of family life today. Impelled by the trend toward single parenthood, the women's rights movement, and the state of the economy, more women, especially women with chil-dren, entered or reentered the labor force in the 1970s than ever before in U.S. history. The trend has continued. Today, 65 percent of mothers with children under age 6 and 78 percent of mothers with children ages 6 to 13 are in the labor force. Very troubling is the fact that only a minority of these children have safe, affordable, quality child care (*CDF facts about child care in America,* 1998). (See Chapter 5.)

The last four decades have witnessed a large migration of people from northern urban areas to the South and West. There has also been a shift of people from large cities to medium- and small-sized areas. Even with these trends, however, most children and youth continue to live in or near a city. Further, the majority of urban nonwhite children live in central cities, while the majority of white children live in suburbs. Yet larger numbers of white than nonwhite children live in central cities. This latter statement illustrates the para-dox of numbers versus proportions.

Problems of Children and Young Persons

Millions of American children are living and growing up under economic, social, or psycho-logical conditions that hinder their development and their future prospects. Among the most serious problems of many American children are poverty, violence, and extremely deprived home environments, which may lead to their removal from home and placement in the nation's foster care system. These children may have serious health problems and lack access to medical care. They are also more likely than other children to fail at school if they lack educational support at home and attend poor schools.

Being Poor Means Being at Risk

Poverty is a condition that afflicts about 16 percent of American families with children (Federal Interagency Forum, 2002). The lack of sufficient means to live decently may grow out of parents' mental or physical illness or disability, low educational levels and lack of marketable skills, or a lack of access to employment because of poor job skills or transportation difficulties.

Regardless of the cause, for children being poor means that the odds are stacked against them developmentally. Poor children have more health problems. They face a higher risk of death; have a higher risk of infant mortality; and are more likely to die from disease, accident, drowning, or fire. Poor children are more likely to have stunted physical or intellectual growth. The environments in which many poor children live include toxic waste contamination and high levels of lead poisoning, which can cause brain damage and behavior problems (Bearer, 1995; Children's Defense Fund, 1997). Poverty and unemployment are strongly related to child maltreatment, which Garbarino (1992) calls "certainly the bottom line when it comes to indicators of child welfare and family functioning" (p. 27).

In some areas, the poor have been clustered together in public housing complexes or inner-city neighborhoods where a variety of factors, including racism, lack of jobs, poor schools, and lack of social and community services, have combined to exacerbate the physical effects of poverty with a systematic pattern of deprivation. Children in crowded inner cities usually have only the street as a place for play, where they are often at the mercy of hostilities and violence. Safe areas to play may be similarly lacking in isolated rural areas. Growing up in such communities, these children may never be able to overcome their developmental disadvantages to become successful in the competitive American economy.

> *He's scared and crying bad; stopped wanting to go to school 'cause of the shooting. (A mother in a dangerous neighborhood—The Ounce of Prevention Fund, 1993)*

Because of larger social and economic changes, the condition of childhood poverty today is often experienced as a state of deprivation in the midst of material affluence. During the past two decades, society has become increasingly polarized; while the top 20 percent of American families have grown richer, the bottom 20 percent have experienced a decline in income. Social isolation, alienation, low self-esteem, and other social and psychosocial problems are exacerbated by the condition of deprivation and feeling excluded from mainstream society. (See Chapter 5.)

Homelessness.   Homelessness is a devastating experience for parents and children. By the time they have lost their home and entered a shelter, family members already have experienced stressful events they could not control. A family's homeless status brings a clear risk for child development. Family life is disrupted, children's schooling is interfered with, physical and emotional health may be damaged, and family members could be separated (Ziesemer, Marcoux, & Marwell, 1994).

Attempting to assess the magnitude of homeless families and children, census takers have been confronted with numerous definitional and methodological issues. However, a 1996 survey of mayors in twenty-nine cities found that families with children make up 38 percent of the homeless population. Particularly alarming was the finding that families with children make up the fastest-growing homeless group (Masten, 1992; Bernstine, 1997).

> *Davonte returned from the bathroom and slumped against his mother. "I'm cold," he murmured. "I want to go home."*
>
> *There was a pause. It was unclear where, exactly he meant: the apartment where they lived until October, whose contents . . . were in storage? The East River Family Center, their first and favorite placement, where they'd had a Christmas tree and opened presents before they'd been deemed ineligible and had to vacate the premises? Or some primal notion we all carry around in our minds of a comfortable place that is our own, where we can retreat to safety?*
>
> *"Are you sleepy?" [the mother] asked her son.*
>
> *"Yeah."*
>
> *"Well, we don't have a home," she said. "Isn't that sad?" (Egan, 2002, p. 32)*

Negative Peer Influence, Violence, and Substance Abuse

As children age, they become susceptible to a variety of developmental risks to their health and to their social and intellectual development. Millions of youth confront a lack of opportunity to develop useful skills and find satisfying employment. Noting this situation and its consequences, Currie (1982) wrote: "As long as we continue to trap many young people in a low wage, unstable and generally unrewarding sector of the economy, increasing their stake in 'straight life' will be impossible" (p. 25).

Many of these problems in large part reflect the failure of communities and the public schools to educate young people in ways that are relevant to the complexity of life today and that generate a level of competence vital to successful social functioning and individual well-being. For many school children and youth, the result is a diminishing desire to learn, an inability to adapt to change, confusion about life goals, alienation from school and community, and antagonistic attitudes toward a society that has not solved its problems of war, poverty, unemployment, drugs, and racism.

As children get older, peer influences become more important, and friends can influence each other in a positive or negative way. Peers are more influential on today's youth than in the past for a variety of reasons. Adult authority today is weaker, and there is less consensus on the core values and behaviors that should be transmitted to youth. Young people are spending greater amounts of time with each other as society in general becomes more age-segregated and they have more freedom in directing their own lives. The mass media and the entertainment industry expose youth to a broader range of experiences and behavior than formerly, and youth fads are often amplified and glorified in the media (Zill & Nord, 1994).

Parents, teachers, social workers, and other professionals have had to face a lack of knowledge about how to help youth with the growing problem of alcohol and drug usage. Young people throughout the population experiment with all kinds of available drugs. The problems have appeared most noticeably among suburban upper-middle-class youth and among lower-class young people of various racial and ethnic backgrounds. The growth in the numbers of young addicts and the increase in numbers of teenagers who die as a result illustrate the widespread danger of drug use.

A particularly poignant result of the drug epidemic is evidenced in the rising number of infants born addicted to drugs. Their low birth weight and other health problems make them susceptible to developmental delays and at increased risk of abuse and neglect.

The AIDS Epidemic.   Another tragic risk for children and families is the AIDS epidemic. The numbers of children with AIDS is growing; each year there are approximately 2,000 new cases of AIDS among infants. The problem is particularly acute in African American and Latino communities; 94 percent of HIV-infected children are members of these ethnic groups. Women are especially vulnerable to infection, either through sexual contact with an infected person or through intravenous injection of drugs. It was estimated that between 125,000 and 150,000 children would be orphaned by the AIDS epidemic by the early twenty-first century (Stein, 1998). Children and families afflicted with AIDS make special demands on the social service system. (See Chapter 9.)

Youth Violence.   The drug epidemic has brought in its wake a wave of violence that engulfs children, young people, and residents of entire communities, as victims or as offenders or both. Although media accounts of youth violence have fanned fears of a coming wave of juvenile "superpredators," the truth is that young people are ten times more likely to be the victims of violence than to be arrested for it (Children's Defense Fund, 1997).

After a decade of large increases in youth violence, juvenile arrests for violent crimes have fallen, although the rate is still quite high. In one national survey, 20 percent of adolescents reported having engaged in one violent incident by the time they were 18 years of age. Although no community or ethnic group is immune, youth violence is particularly prevalent in urban neighborhoods characterized by high levels of male unemployment, extreme poverty, social disorganization, poor schools, gang activity, and families who have engaged in criminal activity and who engage in violent acts with each other (Rhodes, 2000). (See Chapter 11.) Most of the increase in violent crime affecting juveniles as either victims or perpetrators involves guns. As the Children's Defense Fund (1997) points out:

> Because juveniles have increasingly easy access to guns, what formerly would have been a fist fight or knife fight, or a serious act of delinquency, now too often involves a gun and is far more likely to result in death or a homicide arrest.

In 1997, 4,223 children and teenagers were killed by guns. That number does not include the number of children who were injured or permanently maimed by firearms. On average, 12 American children were killed each day by guns in that year (Office of Juvenile Justice and Delinquency Prevention, 2000).

Children of Vulnerable Families

For many families who seek help on behalf of their children, the presenting problem centers on functioning within the family and conflict in the parent–child relationship or between husband and wife. Some parents are immature and overwhelmed with new or overdemanding responsibilities; others are poorly equipped with the knowledge they need to give good care to children and maintain family balance. Despite greater availability of birth control, many parents lack the help they want to plan the size of their families and to use contraception effectively.

Some children's problems stem from their birth to teenage parents who are themselves immature, highly vulnerable to discontinued schooling, and lacking the knowledge of how to care for their children as well as the financial means to do so. (See Chapter 3.)

Children are frequently brought to the attention of social agencies because of complaints that they are neglected or abused by their parents or other caretakers. The incidence of these reports has increased greatly since the reporting laws were established in the 1970s, currently reaching a level of about 3 million a year (U.S. Department of Health and Human Services, 2002). Federal funding and leadership have been inadequate to address the need for child protection. The solution to the problem of how to protect these children, yet maintain the family, continues to be elusive in too many cases. Some of these children must be enabled to live away from their own parents in foster homes or institutions, though many others can remain at home safely if sufficient supportive services are available to their families. (See Chapters 7, 8, and 9.)

The experience of out-of-home placement exposes children to the wrenching emotional trauma of separation from familiar family members, home, school, and neighborhood. In addition, they may be vulnerable to confusion over guardianship. The juvenile court, the public child welfare agency, the foster parents, and the parents all have legally sanctioned rights and responsibilities to the child, but these interests may be conflicting, overlapping, and not well defined. Children are often left with the powerless feeling that those who decide where they will live and other important life issues are remote strangers. (See Chapters 2 and 6.)

The approximately 131,000 children who are in the public child welfare system waiting for adoption face special vulnerabilities and the disregard of their individual rights (Children's Bureau, 2002). They are without an adult protector, guide, or advocate. Their duly appointed guardian is an officer of the state or an administrator of a large child care agency. This practice fixes responsibility for the child but denies the child an opportunity for an ongoing personal relationship with his or her guardian. Adoption has been shown to be a successful solution for children who need new homes and loving, responsible parents, but there are thousands who grow older as children of the state, waiting for adoptive parents who do not materialize. (See Chapter 10.)

All these problems directly affect the well-being of the nation's children and are appropriate for attention by family and child agencies. Child welfare as a field of social work practice deals with only a small portion of the nation's children; the wider range of family and child service agencies addresses a larger segment, mainly through offering various preventive and supportive services. In spite of these services, many children and families need help that is not available at all or that is insufficient to improve their situation.

Measuring the Well-Being of America's Children

In 1997, the federal government created the Interagency Forum on Child and Family Statistics, whose mission it is to collect data on children and youth from various governmental and other data sources, and "to improve the reporting and dissemination of information on the status of children to policy community and the general public" (Federal Interagency Forum, 2002, p. i). Each year, the Forum issues a report on the most recent, most reliable official statistics that gives a profile of the strengths and difficulties confronting the nation's children. Twenty-four key indicators are used, chosen to represent a broad range of important aspects of children's lives that are necessary to meet their basic needs for safety, education, health, and an environment that offers consistent nurturing, stimulation, and opportunities for growth. Comparisons of current statistics with those of earlier years are provided to show improvement or decline on a given indicator. These reports provide the best available profile of the overall well-being of children in the United States. They can be considered a "national scorecard" on how we are doing as a nation in creating a healthy and safe society for children. They may also help policy makers establish priorities and track progress toward policy goals for children.

Table 1.1 provides a list of the indicators included in the annual series of reports (Federal Interagency Forum, 2002). Overall, the trends point to some improvement in the lives of children since the early 1990s. The following is a sample of the findings from the report for 2000.

- Child poverty has declined since 1993, from a high of 22 percent to 16 percent in 2000.
- The proportion of young children with good diets increased from 21 percent to 27 percent.
- Infant mortality declined significantly, to a rate of seven deaths per thousand live births in 1999.
- The birth rate for adolescents, twenty-seven births per one thousand females in 2000, has dropped by one-third since 1991.
- The youth violent crime offending rate dropped 67 percent between 1993 and 2000, when the rate was seventeen violent crimes per thousand youth.
- Between 1999 and 2001, the percentage of children ages 2 to 5 who were read to daily by an adult increased from 54 percent to 58 percent.

These trends, while promising, must be accepted with caution until longer-term trends can be tracked. It should be noted also that even with current improvements, some indicators show a still unacceptably low condition, such as the low percentage of children eating a healthy diet and the high percentage of children living in poverty. The infant mortality rate, though declining, is still higher than those of other industrialized countries. Those concerned with the condition of children will watch with interest and concern as these reports

TABLE 1.1   Indicators of Child Well-Being

Economic Security
Child poverty and family income
Secure parental employment
Housing problems
Food security and diet quality
Access to health care

Health Care
General health status
Activity limitation
Childhood immunization
Low birth weight
Infant mortality
Child mortality
Adolescent mortality
Adolescent births

Behavior and Social Environment
Regular cigarette smoking
Alcohol use
Illicit drug use
Youth victims of serious crimes
Youth perpetrators of violent crimes

Education
Family reading to young children
Early childhood care and education
Mathematics and reading achievement
High school academic coursetaking
High school completion
Youth neither enrolled in school nor working
Higher education

Special Feature
Children of at least one foreign-born parent

Source: Federal Interagency Forum on Child and Family Statistics (2002), *America's children: Key national indicators of well-being* (Washington, DC: U.S. Government Printing Office).

provide an increasingly comprehensive picture over time of changes in the well-being of U.S. children.

Historical Highlights of Services to Families and Children

The history of family and child welfare policy shows distinct, although sometimes overlapping, organized efforts to improve the welfare of children and the development of social services for them and their parents.

Indenture and "Outdoor Relief"

In the early years of this nation, individuals who could not maintain themselves or their families were considered the responsibility of the local township. Some children were mentally retarded; some were physically handicapped. Some were orphaned by epidemics and other disasters. Some showed incorrigible behavior. The methods of treatment within a community, however, were simple. The youngest children who required support by the town were "farmed out" to the lowest bidder—a family that agreed to give care to the child for a small, regular sum of money or goods. Others were often sent to live in the dreary, unsanitary almshouses with the adult misfits of the town—the mentally ill, the mentally deficient, lawbreakers, and the aged and infirm.

Able-bodied, older children were usually indentured; that is, placed under contract with a citizen of the town who agreed to maintain the child and teach him or her a trade or other gainful occupation in return for the profit from the child's labor. This was a favored practice, as everyone's labor was needed during the development of the new country. With the beginning of the Industrial Revolution, indenture became less feasible and by 1875 had almost completely disappeared (Folks, 1911). Despite some cases of cruel masters, indentured children, on the whole, were more fortunate than were children in almshouses. In that sense, indenture was seen as a forward step in child care (Thurston, 1930).

Another choice, termed *outdoor relief* and managed by the local poor law authority, was to give meager aid to dependent children in their own homes. This approach was poorly administered and the least accepted form of care (Abbott, 1938). Nevertheless, public outdoor relief provided aid to more dependent children than did all other special forms of protecting children. (A current form of outdoor relief is seen in today's Temporary Assistance for Needy Families program.)

Children's Institutions and the Growth of Voluntary Agencies

Gradually, society realized that children need a different type of care from adults and more "security" than was provided by a master under a contract of indenture. Many of the earliest institutions for children were sponsored not by government but by private child-caring agencies. To a large extent, these private or voluntary agencies had their beginnings in the desire of people to fulfill neighborly obligations. Orphanages were a response of the community to disasters that left children without parents (Downs & Sherraden, 1983). Concerned citizens would then undertake to organize a group of people to care for the children in need. Examples include the Ursuline Convent in New Orleans, which in 1729 undertook the care of ten girls who had been orphaned by Indian wars; an asylum for the care and education of destitute girls, established in Baltimore in 1799 by St. Paul's Church; and institutions in various states called Protestant Orphan Asylums, which came into being to care for children orphaned in the cholera epidemics of the 1830s. Many of these institutions later became child-placing agencies, extending their care of children into foster homes in the communities or taking on other community activities.

The latter half of the nineteenth century brought an era of "child-saving" activities. The intent was to save children from conditions of crime, vice, and poverty found in urban areas where slums were crowded with poor, European immigrants. The Children's Aid Societies, found first in the cities of the Eastern seaboard, took many children into care and placed them in free foster homes (Cook, 1995; Nelson, 1995). An example is the Children's Aid Society of New York City, founded in 1853 by the Reverend Charles Loring Brace, who organized a massive program that resettled nearly 100,000 children from eastern cities in free foster homes in midwestern and southern states.

In addition to the intent of the new voluntary agencies to protect harmless children orphaned by disaster or to save others from a life of crime and moral degradation, a third concern was protection of children from neglect and cruelty. Where laws existed for the protection of children from cruelty and abuse, they were poorly enforced. The New York Society for the Prevention of Cruelty to Children (NYSPCC)—the first of its sort—was formed in 1875 to rescue children from cruelty and inhumane treatment and to bring about enforcement of existing laws and passage of new laws.

Still another kind of voluntary agency established in the nineteenth century pioneered in many kinds of service to families and children. Settlement houses such as Jane Addams's famous Hull House in Chicago and Lillian Wald's Henry Street Settlement in New York were notable examples. Founded with broad aims and open to all the inhabitants of the neighborhood, they focused on the needs of families and the preservation and enhancement of human dignity, skill, and values. They were attuned to the social forces that buffeted poor people, most of whom were immigrants of various nationalities and religions. These early settlement houses demonstrated new services for families and children and worked steadfastly for social reform and for strengthening local communities as environments for families.

African American Children.   Slavery is a shocking and terrible part of American history. According to some estimates, between 1686 and 1786 approximately 2 million African people were forcibly taken from their homes; about 250,000 of them became slaves in America. Slavery as an institution was established to meet the need for cheap labor, particularly in the South. The economy of the North was also deeply implicated through its involvement in transporting slaves in its shipping industry. In addition to slaves, some Africans came to America during earliest colonial days as explorers and servants.

During the time of slavery and beyond, the family was the major and often only system of child welfare for African American children. In the North, African American children were excluded from most orphanages (Smith & Merkel-Holguin, 1995). A notable exception was the Philadelphia Association for the Care of Colored Children, a Quaker shelter for African American children founded in 1822. It was burned down by a white mob in 1838.

After the Civil War, limited progress was made in providing for needy African American children through the efforts of African Americans. They worked though mutual aid groups such as churches and benevolent organizations, some of which formed cooperative arrangements with white philanthropists and governmental sponsors. For example, the Virginia Industrial School for Colored Girls, founded in 1915, was maintained by the Virginian Federation of Colored Women's Clubs with an arrangement for interracial cooperation (Peebles-Wilkins, 1995). African American children were not fully integrated into the public child welfare system until after World War II (Billingsley & Giovannoni, 1972).

State Boards of Charities

During the latter part of the nineteenth century, states had begun to assume responsibility for certain classes of the poor—those the towns, parishes, and other local units of government were unwilling or unable to care for. Children, too, began to benefit from this assumption of responsibility by the state. Specialized state institutions were established: "reform" schools and training schools for children who were blind, deaf, or mentally deficient (Sherraden & Downs, 1984). This increased activity underscored the need for a central agency at the state level to coordinate the administration of the welfare programs that local governments had been unable to finance or administer. Massachusetts, in 1863, was the first state to establish such a central agency, the State Board of Charities, for the supervision of all state charities.

Federal Government Involvement

The federal government was long reluctant to become involved with child and family welfare because of concern that it would violate *states'* rights, as social welfare is considered primarily the domain of state and local government. Even more significant in the opposition to federal action was the fear of invasion of *family* rights. Traditionally, the right and the responsibility for raising children had been held by parents; the government's role was confined to local matters and protection. As one senator in 1919 framed the situation, "The homes of the country are best protected through the local government" and not by a "federal nursery that shall pass upon the wisdom of the mothers and fathers of the land" (Heyburn, 1919, p. 189). This emphasis on family rights, conceptualized as the essential, basic civil right to conceive and raise one's children without governmental interference, has continued to influence development of federal policy (Garwood, Phillips, Hartman, & Zigler, 1989).

Federal Policy on Native American Families.   An exception to the general principle of nonintervention into family life was the role of the federal government in breaking up Native American families. As described in Chapters 3 and 6, during the early twentieth century, federal policy toward Native Americans was to encourage the dissolution of Indian culture and the incorporation of Indians into mainstream American life. As part of this policy, Native American children were removed from their families and placed in Indian boarding schools, where they were required to give up their language and culture, and where they lost ties to their families, who were far away on reservations. The Indian Child Welfare Act of 1978 has put safeguards in place to prevent the loss of Indian children to their culture.

Growth of Federal Programs.   Despite the opposition to federal involvement in families, inequities among the states and the lives of children were apparent. Initial steps to address the problems nationally were indirect—the founding of the Children's Bureau and the first White House Conference of 1912. Significantly, each endeavor was oriented toward wide dissemination of information, not the delivery of much-needed services to families. The Great Depression of the 1930s made it clear that government intervention was essential to help many persons and families cope with various overwhelming problems. Under the Social Security Act of 1935, the federal government established the financial assistance program known as Aid to Dependent Children (ADC), which served far more families and children than any other federal program. Since 1996, that program has become Temporary Assistance for Needy Families (TANF) and has changed substantially. (See Chapter 5.) The act also established a federal role in child welfare services through Title IV-B.

The social climate of the 1960s fostered a significant expansion of the federal role in numerous facets of life for children and families; an array of programs was created. Federal and state joint efforts produced extensive legislation on such crucial problems as public assistance, civil rights, housing, and employment. In the 1970s, dissatisfaction began to be heard about the size of the federal government and some of its decisions. A more conservative view of the role of federal government prevailed. Since then, there have been fewer new services for children, and overall federal spending for children's programs has eroded from budget cuts and inflation (Garwood et al., 1989).

Public policy toward families and children during the last quarter of the twentieth century was characterized by conflicting ideological trends. The perceived worsening of the condition of children and families led to calls for a comprehensive, concerted national effort on their behalf. However, concerns about the suitability and feasibility of expanded governmental involvement prevented a consensus from forming to support such a comprehensive vision. Currently, most family policy is directed toward only one aspect of family life: economic security. Public policy in relation to the family as a unit has been neglected because of the lack of agreement about the scope of governmental involvement with families and a reluctance to interfere with their "privacy."

Public Policies for Families and Children

Social policy has received enormous public attention in recent years. Books and television debate social policy issues such as the need to change the financial structure of health care insurance, including public insurance such as Medicare and Medicaid, welfare reform, the role of government in encouraging marriage, and federal support for social services offered under religious auspices. Furthermore, there is vigorous debate on which level of government is best suited to implement public policy, as responsibility is shifting from the federal level to state governments, and from public to nonprofit and for-profit agencies and organizations (Ewalt, Freeman, Kirk, & Poole, 1997).

In the study of family and child welfare, we are primarily concerned with the impact of *public social policy* on the child and on family life developed by government through its judicial, legislative, and executive branches. Figure 1.1 shows these branches of government, and the names of the governmental bodies in each branch at the federal, state, and local levels. Together these entities make and implement most of the public social policy in the United States.

As used here, social policy refers to official decisions about social issues or a broad principle of operation for carrying out a specific aspect of the social welfare system. Policies define such matters as the nature of the services or aid, who shall receive service, what the standards of practice shall be, and specific principles and procedures for carrying out a social welfare program.

Residual versus Developmental View of Social Welfare

The residual conception of social welfare emphasizes the provision of programs and services for people only after the primary group that usually functions has broken down. Services are provided in relation to an underlying assumption (although often denied or unacknowledged) that normal families—adequate and competent families—do not need help. Such an assumption influences legislative and administrative decisions. As a result, the policy directions for a particular service often reflect restrictive and inconsistent attitudes, and negative views of people and their circumstances. Frequently services have been provided only after the family

FIGURE 1.1   Sources of Policy by Level and Branch of Government

BRANCH / LEVEL	LEGISLATIVE	EXECUTIVE	JUDICIAL
FEDERAL	U.S. Congress	President Department of Health and Human Services Other Departments	U.S. Supreme Court
STATE	State Legislature	Governor Department of Social Services Other Departments	State Supreme Court
LOCAL	City Council County Board of Commissioners School Board	Mayor County Executive School Superintendent	Family Court Juvenile Court District Circuit Court

has endured hardship and trouble and the community has stood by while the family in crisis disintegrates.

By contrast, an "institutional" or "developmental" conception of social welfare holds that many "normal" and adequate families in today's complex, technological society have common human needs and require help at various times; therefore, services for children and families, in addition to being protective and therapeutic, should also be preventive and supportive, easily available without stigma. They should provide social supports necessary to help families meet the social realities of the present patterns of family and community living. This conception includes social inventions to support, reinforce, and enhance family functioning, available to *all* people, not only those who are in some way a casualty of modern life and in need of protective or therapeutic services. Kahn (1965) has termed these kinds of social services "social utilities" to emphasize the notion of the user as citizen rather than client or patient.

In the field of family and child welfare, the distinction between residual and developmental services is seen in the contrast between preventive services and traditional child welfare services. Preventive services, including family support programs and day care, are developmental services offered widely in the community on a voluntary basis. (See Chapters 3 and 4.) Traditional child welfare services, such as child protective services and foster care, are interventions offered only after the family system has broken down and are therefore classified as residual services.

Families and Government

Traditionally, the family has been viewed in America as an inappropriate target for government planning and intervention except under the most compelling circumstances. Family policy issues raise fears, unresolved reluctance, and serious division within a population that has been wary of change in the relations of the family and the state. To some extent, the reluctance of government to intervene in family life has given way to a perspective that encourages public involvement under certain conditions. When family dysfunction touches enough families, public or quasi-public efforts are initiated to fulfill the economic, physical, or emotional needs of the individuals affected.

There are at least two reasons for this changing perspective. First, the changes taking place in American families, noted earlier in this chapter, have brought to many a growing fear that the family as an institution is breaking down. The declining role of the parent and the inevitably increasing role of the state have led to expectations in some quarters that the essential concerns of the family will be reflected in effective public social policy. Proponents for a more visible family policy believe that the importance of parental affection and a full parent–child relationship is not to be minimized, but neither is a positive role for government in the welfare of the child and his or her family.

A second reason for the change in perspective has been the realization that virtually all governmental actions directly or indirectly affect families. Varying state and federal programs have an impact on family life even though family concerns were not a reason for the intervention or directly considered in the formulation of the policies. For example, the globalization of the economy can affect drastically the ability of workers to find good-paying manufacturing jobs in the United States, and therefore also affects the well-being of families who depend for their livelihood on those workers. Similarly, if the government acts ineffectively to prevent the pollution of lake waters by the discharge of industrial waste, already scarce recreational areas that are important to family life are lost. Some urban renewal programs have cleared unsightly and overcrowded areas of a city and constructed modern buildings, but in doing so they have ignored the established patterns of neighborhood life that had lifelong importance to some families. This more comprehensive view of the relationship between government actions and the family has led to interest in evaluating new government laws and regulations before passage for their effects on family well-being.

This is not to say that government can replace families or do what good families can do in nurturing and socializing children into useful adulthood. But by testing its policies of taxation, energy, trade, transportation, housing, education, and income security for their effects on family life, government can add to the stability of the family—the unit of society this country still depends on for its basic child-rearing tasks.

The debate over government involvement with families has shifted from whether it should occur to how and when it should occur. The debate becomes most intense when it is focused, not in the abstract, but on a specific problem or proposal. For example, abortion and contraception, public policies regarding same-sex domestic partners, and the rights and responsibilities of unmarried fathers have developed proponents and opponents who can be equally vociferous. The lack of unanimity has contributed to the fragmented and erratic nature of American policy toward families and reflects, in part, the impossibility of mandating a comprehensive family policy in our pluralistic society.

The struggle to find a balance between governmental and family responsibility in promoting the welfare of children is evident in the debates over welfare reform, day care, the advisability of governmental policy to promote marriage, and health care for children (Skolnick, 1997). The 1996 welfare reform law, called the Personal Responsibility and

Work Opportunity Reconciliation Act, changed the program known as Aid to Dependent Children to Temporary Assistance for Needy Families. As the name of the act implies, the emphasis has shifted from a program of governmental aid to an emphasis on parental work as a means to support children. Linked to this new emphasis is increased federal responsibility for the enforcement of child support laws and for financing day care and health care for the children of poor working parents, though it is not clear that governmental support in these areas will be even minimally adequate (Hagen & Davis, 1997). (See Chapter 5.)

Behind much of the new emphasis on family responsibility is a changing assumption about the causes of poverty. Since the New Deal, the assumption was that large economic changes, outside the control of individuals, were the main cause of poverty. However, that view has now changed to one that places primary responsibility for poverty on behavioral choices that are in the control of individuals. As Kamerman (1997) observed:

> In a process that has been under way for several decades, the problem of poverty has been largely redefined by some groups in Congress and elsewhere in society from an unfortunate condition resulting from external social and economic factors to a problem that results mostly from the immoral and irresponsible behavior of individuals. And the solution has been transformed, for those who hold such views, from a search for effective social policies to an emphasis on individual change. (pp. 167–168)

Devolution

Federal spending on social policy increased during the three decades after World War II, as did federal regulation of these funds that would be spent at the state and local level. Federal involvement increased at least in part because of growing skepticism that the states would allocate federal funds fairly and effectively. There was particular concern that the southern states would discriminate against African Americans. However, it would be a mistake to overestimate the extent of federal power in social welfare policy during these decades. Most federal funds continued to be administered through state and local agencies.

During the 1990s, there was a movement to return more authority for social policy to the states, where it rested during the nineteenth century and in the twentieth century until the New Deal of the 1930s. The hope is that smaller units of government, closer to those the programs are designed to serve, will offer more flexible, efficient, and targeted programs. It is further expected that state and local governments can form partnerships with nonprofit agencies and community organizations to better tailor programs to the needs and cultural values of local families (Weil, 1997). Those who remember the discriminatory, erratic, and extremely meager condition of many state welfare programs before the federal government became involved are concerned that any "devolution" to state-level units of government will result in a major setback to the well-being of children and families (Kamerman, 1997). (See Chapter 5.)

Child and Family Services

Principles of Child and Family Services

Child and family welfare practice and policy are guided by certain overarching principles. *A major principle of the field of child welfare and family services is that a safe and perma-*

nent home is the best environment for children. Children are dependent, immature individuals who require care, protection, and guidance to survive and flourish. They need certain kinds of care in order to move gradually toward assumption of adult roles in society. The Casey Outcomes and Decision-Making Project (1998) has defined children's needs as "the opportunity to grow and develop in an environment which provides consistent nurture, support, and stimulation. Practice and research in child development have documented that families can usually best provide the consistent nurturing environment, and secure, uninterrupted relationships with caring adults, that are necessary for child well-being" (p. 4).

A second major principle concerns child safety. Children need to grow up in environments free of physical, sexual, and emotional abuse. They need to have the basic necessities of food, clothing, and shelter, and personal relationships with loving, attentive caregivers.

A major dilemma for the child welfare field is what to do when these two principles collide. Families enter the child welfare system because their ability to provide a safe environment for their children has been called into question. How can we as professionals take action that is congruent both with the principle that children do best when growing up in families and also with the principle that they need to be free from abuse and neglect?

One solution to this dilemma involves another principle of child and family services. *As the needs of children can best be met by families, a third major principle of family and child services is that they should work to strengthen and support family functioning.* Families deserve strong support from the community to help them provide an adequate environment for their children, including access to medical care, decent housing, and a minimally adequate income. Child and family services are offered to the family based on their needs and whether the family is voluntarily seeking help, is receiving child protective services, or has children in foster care. The term *wraparound services* refers to the effort to provide families who are struggling to provide a safe, nurturing environment with whatever community services they need to prevent separate placement of their children. These services are also provided to achieve family reunification, if it has been necessary to remove the children from the home. Whether a child is at home or in foster care, the family is entitled in either case to receive parent education, supportive counseling, help with housing and employment, drug or mental health treatment, and other services, depending on their needs. The provision of family support and preservation services is one way that child welfare and family services can reconcile the needs of children both for family life and for freedom from physical, sexual, and emotional abuse and from neglect.

A fourth major principle of family and child services is that placement decisions should respect the children's needs for family continuity. If children need to be separated from families, the focus should be on maintaining continuity of the children's emotional attachments to family (McFadden & Downs, 1995). Kinship networks can play an important part in maintaining this continuity. If safety concerns require that children be placed temporarily away from biological parents, the children are likely to feel more comfortable about the move if they are going to relatives they know, if they are moving with their siblings, or if they are remaining in their neighborhoods where they can stay in touch with friends, teachers, and relatives. Even for children who must be permanently separated from their parents, planning must focus on maintaining continuity of the child's attachments—for example, through permanent placement with relatives or foster parents already known to the child or through maintaining a connection to the biological parents in an "open adoption" arrangement.

These four principles guide the organization and delivery of all types of social services to families and children, and lead logically to the formation of program goals and desired outcomes of services. Types of child welfare services and their outcomes are discussed in the following sections.

Classification of Services

Services to families and children traditionally have been classified into four major groups: preventive and supportive, protective, foster care, and adoption services. These categories reflect the historical development of child and family services and their varying legal mandates.

■ *Preventive and supportive services* are available to families to support and strengthen family life, to promote the healthy development of children and adults, to reduce risks to children, and to help families maintain connections with community institutions such as schools, welfare, and the workplace. Depending on the type of service offered, these services may be called therapeutic, preventive, or supportive. (See Chapters 3, 4, and 5.)

■ *Protective services* are for families who have fallen below a minimally sufficient level of child rearing and whose children therefore suffer from abuse or neglect. Services include investigation of the family's situation and help in improving family life so that the children can remain safely in the home. (See Chapters 6, 7, and 8.)

■ *Foster care services* are for families who temporarily cannot maintain a minimally sufficient child-rearing environment in the home. While children are in foster care, the focus is on helping parents to improve their life situation so that children can be returned to them safely. Children may be placed with relatives, called "kinship care," in a foster family, in a group home, or in a children's institution. They are helped to cope with the separation and to adjust to their new living situation. Arranging visitation to help family members maintain connection with one another and planning for reunifcation as early as possible are important aspects of foster care services. (See Chapter 9.)

■ *Adoption services* are available to children in need of a new, permanent family because their biological parents have relinquished them for adoption or had their parental rights permanently terminated in court. Helping the child (if older) grieve for the loss of his or her biological family and adjust to the new family are key adoption services. Adoption services provide support to the adoptive family and the biological family. (See Chapter 10.)

Preventive and supportive services differ from the other three service categories—protective services, foster care, and adoption—in a number of ways. Protective services, foster care, and adoption are traditionally considered the elements making up the domain of child welfare services. Government, through regulation, funding, and the legal system, defines much of the framework within which these services are offered. Families usually do not seek out protective services and foster care services voluntarily; the agencies, through their legally established mandates, require the family's participation when its ability to maintain a minimally sufficient environment for children is in serious question. The families in these service systems come disproportionately from the poorest and most vulnerable segments of the population.

Preventive and supportive services, in contrast, are a loosely grouped category comprising a number of disparate programs and approaches offered in a variety of community settings. Their purposes are to prevent child maltreatment and strengthen families. (See Chapter 3.)

Pyramid of Services

The Children's Defense Fund has developed a framework called the Pyramid of Services, which places services in a continuum of increasing intensity, reflecting the needs of the family (see Figure 1.2). Services needed by all families, such as schools, health care, and

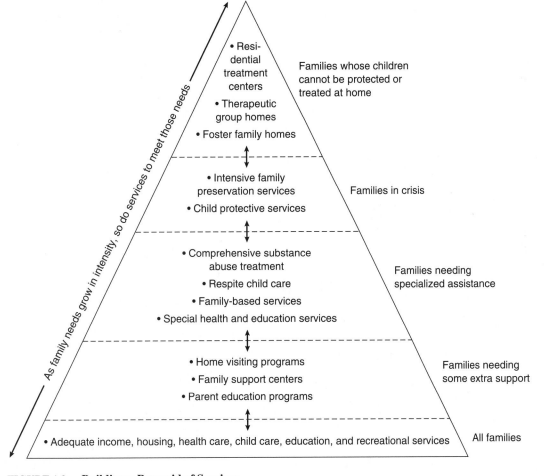

FIGURE 1.2   Building a Pyramid of Services

Sources: Children's Defense Fund (1993, December), Family support, *CDF Reports, 15,* p. 7. Reprinted with permission of Children's Defense Fund.

recreational facilities, are at the base of the pyramid, reflecting their status as widely available services. Families needing some extra support from time to time, often during family transitions such as divorce, birth, or death, or during other periods of stress, may need such services as a home visitor or parent education programs. Other families may also need a more specialized level of assistance, for such serious threats to family functioning as substance abuse, the physical or intellectual impairment of family members, or domestic violence. All of these services at the lower half of the pyramid are included in the category described earlier of preventive and supportive services and should be widely available in the community on a voluntary basis to families.

Services at the upper end of the pyramid include the traditional child welfare services of child protection and foster care, for families who are in crisis and for families whose children cannot be protected and treated at home. They are needed by a relatively small number of families. They are of high intensity, in that the parents are expected to be highly involved in the treatment process, and require more professional time and other resources than do less intensive services.

Child Welfare Outcomes

Increasingly, funding sources and society at large expect child welfare and family services providers to be accountable for the outcomes of the services they offer. Recent federal laws, regulations, and policies require that agencies justify their financing through demonstrating that their programs meet certain identified, measurable goals (Sahonchik, 2000). However, in the experience of many agencies, it seems that the outcomes of service are somewhat ambiguous, not entirely in the control of the agency, and in any case hard to measure. Agencies are challenged to conceptualize and formulate a clear vision of what they hope to achieve in their various programs and interventions, and to develop objective ways to track progress toward meeting these goals.

The Casey Outcomes and Decision-Making Project (1998) has pointed out that outcome-based research and evaluation have the potential to improve child welfare services significantly, as they provide a feedback loop showing how certain types of interventions are working or not working, and provide an empirical base to guide program innovation. In the coming years, child welfare practitioners can expect to conduct their work within a framework formed by specific articulation of guiding principles, clearly stated goals, and measurable outcomes of services.

In 2000, the federal government, through the Children's Bureau, initiated reviews of publicly financed child and family services in each state (Children's Bureau, 2000). The primary goals of these comprehensive, large-scale reviews of state child welfare systems are to improve child welfare services and to achieve certain identified outcomes for families and children who receive these services. Table 1.2 shows the outcomes identified for the state child welfare services, with certain performance items that have been identified as necessary for the outcome to be achieved. The table shows that the primary outcomes expected of state child welfare programs are child safety, permanency, continuity of family relationships, and enhanced child well-being. For many state child welfare agencies, achieving these outcomes will require much greater funding, improved training of staff, and other improvements to the overall system.

TABLE 1.2   Outcomes for Children in the Public Child Welfare System

Safety Outcome 1: Children are, first and foremost, protected from abuse and neglect.

Safety Outcome 2: Children are safely maintained in their homes whenever possible and appropriate.

Permanency Outcome 1: Children have permanency and stability in their living situations.

Permanency Outcome 2: The continuity of family relationships and connections is preserved for children.

Child Well-Being Outcome 1: Families have enhanced capacity to provide for their children's needs.

Child Well-Being Outcome 2: Children receive appropriate services to meet their educational needs.

Child Well-Being Outcome 3: Children receive adequate services to meet their physical and mental health needs.

Source: Children's Bureau (2000), *Child and family services reviews state team training* (Washington, DC: U.S. Government Printing Office).

Culturally Competent Family and Child Services

The majority of the families involved with the formal child welfare system (supportive and protective, foster care, and adoption services) and the juvenile justice systems are members of cultural groups of color, particularly African Americans, Native Americans, and Hispanics or Latino Americans (the fourth major group, Asian/Pacific Islanders, is not overrepresented in these systems) (Leashore, Chipungu, & Everett, 1991). Yet the majority of workers and administrators are white, and the agencies and organizations within the child welfare system are based on models formulated by various European cultures. In past decades, service systems to families and children often were not culturally responsive and sometimes were actually destructive to the cultural values of various ethnic groups (McPhatter, 1997).

Examples of inattention to cultural issues in child welfare include setting standards for foster and adoptive families that have the effect of excluding poor families, including many families of color; directing youth of color into the juvenile justice system while generally referring white youth to the mental health system; misinterpreting parents' behavior and therefore erroneously assuming that they wish to harm or neglect their children; and failing to reach out in a cooperative and mutually respectful spirit to communities of color, leaving them excluded from planning and decision-making processes regarding agency policies and structures.

Cultural groups of color are overrepresented in the child welfare system for a number of historical and continuing social and economic reasons. The long history of oppression of African Americans through slavery and the Jim Crow laws created enormous strains on family life, prevented parents from earning a decent living, withheld education, and left entire communities in terror of organized, systematic violence against them. Native Americans suffered enormous losses during the conquest of North America by European cultures and underwent further cultural destruction by forced assimilation policies. Hispanic or Latino Americans have, like the other groups, suffered overt as well as covert discrimination and racism, and have been hampered by language barriers. The difficulties these groups have faced in the United States have caused disruptions in family life that result in disproportionate numbers of their children needing child welfare services. Unfortunately, the children and families have suffered from discrimination and insensitive treatment in this service system as well, leading to further family and community problems.

NASW Standards for Cultural Competence in Social Work Practice

Cultural competence has been defined as "a set of congruent behaviors, attitudes, policies, and structures which come together in a system, agency, or among professionals and enables that system, agency, or those professionals to work effectively in the context of cultural differences" (Cross, 1988, p. 1). This definition emphasizes that cultural competency needs to be ingrained into the administrative structure and procedures of an organization and also needs to be a part of each social worker's personal set of beliefs and skills. The definition makes the point that cultural competency is not simply "the right thing to do," but is essential to effective provision of services.

The National Association of Social Workers recently formulated Standards for Cultural Competence in Social Work Practice (NASW, 2001) with the intent of helping individuals and agencies to develop high levels of cultural competence so that they can respond more appropriately to diverse clients and communities. The standards identify guidelines for cultural competence in aspects of professional social work practice and administration, including social work values, ethics, self-awareness, professional knowledge base, social work skills, and service delivery. Five of the ten standards are reproduced below.

1. *Ethics and Values.* Social workers shall function in accordance with the values, ethics, and standards of the profession, recognizing how personal and professional values may conflict with or accommodate the needs of diverse clients.
2. *Self-Awareness.* Social workers shall develop an understanding of their own personal and cultural values and beliefs as a first step in appreciating the importance of multicultural identities in the lives of people.
3. *Cross-Cultural Knowledge.* Social workers shall have and continue to develop specialized knowledge and understanding about the history, traditions, values, family systems, and artistic expressions of major client groups served.
4. *Cross-Cultural Skills.* Social workers shall use appropriate methodological approaches, skills, and techniques that reflect the workers' understanding of the role of culture in the helping process.
5. *Service Delivery.* Social workers shall be knowledgeable about and skillful in the use of services available in the community and broader society and be able to make appropriate referrals for their diverse clients. (NASW, 2001)

Infused throughout this book are discussions and examples of cultural competency in child and family welfare practice such as kinship care and family group conferencing (Chapter 8); same race and interethnic adoption (Chapter 10); differential effects of major public programs such as income security, child protective services, and juvenile justice on children and families of different ethnic groups (Chapters 5, 7, and 11); and many other program examples, analyses, and research reports. The following example shows how an advocacy organization worked collaboratively with an inner-city community to develop a local branch in their neighborhood.

Program Example: Organizing Urban Families for Children's Mental Health

The Federation of Families for Children's Mental Health is an association of local organizations for parent empowerment and advocacy in the nation's mental health system. Wishing to expand its organization into minority communities, the federation is developing materials for families of color who have a child with serious mental health problems. The goals are to introduce members of diverse communities to the services available from a variety of national, state, and local resources and to "build the necessary trust of people of color involved in local organizations with the hope that they might choose to affiliate themselves formally with the Federation as a local chapter" (Huff & Telesford, 1994, p. 10). The federation organized focus groups in various communities in order to obtain the advice of families of color on the types of materials they would like the federation to develop. Initially, federation planners "were shocked to learn how little we actually knew about the difficulties families experience—difficulties that limit their opportunities to access and participate in the activities of organizations such as the Federation" (Huff & Telesford, 1994, p. 10).

The federation identified community leaders through churches, schools, public housing resident councils, Head Start programs, and other centers. Working with these leaders, they learned to respect the geographical boundaries of the neighborhood as understood by the residents. Meetings were held within those boundaries in locations accessible to the target participants by walking or public transportation; meeting times were scheduled for late afternoon, because families, apprehensive about criminal activity, were afraid to be out after dark. Transportation was provided as needed. The federation publicized the meetings by telephone and mail delivery, and also posted flyers announcing meetings in laundromats, clinics, churches, grocery stores, public transportation stops, and day care centers. "We have learned not to ask people, 'What's your address?' or 'What's your phone number?' Instead, we ask, 'Do you have an address or telephone number?' 'Are there ways we can get in touch with you?' " (Huff & Telesford, 1994, p. 10). Federation members sent flyers home with children after school and made public service announcements on the local radio. As incentives, the flyers announced that child care and food would be provided at the meetings. Follow-up meetings were held less than a month apart in order to sustain momentum.

The federation members learned not to be discouraged by the difficulties in organizing parents in some very poor neighborhoods. Only after the challenges of reaching families and reducing barriers to attending meetings were addressed could the work begin of empowering parents to be advocates for their children's mental health needs.

The Organization of Services

Family and child services usually are provided under the auspices of a social welfare agency—a formal organization existing to serve children and their families and sanctioned by society. Some of the agencies offer a variety of services to families and children; others are specialized in that they offer fewer services or even only one.

Social welfare agencies providing services to children and their families are identified by various names, usually "child welfare agencies" or "family service agencies." Until recently, child welfare services and family services were conceptually and organizationally separate despite their common professional knowledge and principles. According to Meyer (1985), the separation resulted in "a dysfunctional structure of services for both families and children" (p. 109). To understand how this separation came about, she cites the late nineteenth-century child-saving history of child welfare with its focus, not on maintaining intact families, but rather on child placement as a way to protect children from their parents, who were perceived by child-savers as inadequate or harmful. Another factor reinforcing separateness was the founding of two national organizations in the early twentieth century—the Child Welfare League of America and the Family Service Association of America—two bodies that traditionally have not found ways to join forces effectively. In addition, the fragmentation of federal funding in family and children's legislation worked to keep the fields of child welfare and family services apart. The current focus on family support to prevent abuse and neglect, and family preservation services to prevent foster care, now are resulting in a long-needed integration of child welfare services and family services. However, the transition to a fully integrated service system is not complete, and, in many communities, the work of family service agencies remains quite separate from that of child welfare agencies.

The organization offering the social services may be a "public" agency, or the services may be given under private auspices by a "voluntary" (nonprofit) agency or as a "proprietary" (for-profit) venture. Although both public and voluntary agencies are committed to broad, common goals in behalf of children, there are significant differences between the two forms of organization. Each has its separate legal base and means of financing its work; there are also differences in the underlying philosophy and in the groups of children served. Proprietary services for children differ considerably from both public and voluntary child welfare services.

Child welfare agencies come in all shapes and sizes. Some agencies may employ only two to five people and provide a specialized service, such as family treatment or adoption home placements. Some of the smaller agencies will have a few professionals and many volunteers or paraprofessionals, like those in family support programs or in big brother and big sister programs.

Mental health centers, child guidance clinics, family service agencies, and youth service bureaus may all be midsize agencies. These types of agencies are more likely to provide several child welfare services. For example, mental health centers may provide psychological assessment, family therapy, individual counseling, group work, and perhaps consultation to schools and the juvenile court. Family service agencies may provide parenting education groupwork, and a variety of treatment options. These agencies would typically employ between eight and fifty people.

At the most complex end of the continuum are the large state child welfare agencies. They may employ thousands of people responsible for providing a wide range of services, geographically dispersed throughout the state. The budgets of such organizations can reach hundreds of millions of dollars a year. These state agencies have been delegated public responsibility for the protection and care of children and authority over life-determining de-cisions for children and families who come under their mandate.

Public Child Welfare Services

The public child welfare agency is established by the passage of law—a particular statute that defines the agency's responsibilities for providing a welfare service for children and their families. Public welfare services for children and families are financed by taxation—federal, state, or local, or some combination of these sources. Most federal expenditures for children are made by or channeled through some unit of the Department of Health and Human Services (HHS). Federal funds provide a significant proportion of the total expenditures for children's programs, particularly in such programs as public assistance, Medicaid, Head Start, foster care, and maternal and child health services.

The primary responsibility for administering public child welfare services rests on the states and their regional and local subdivisions. The principle of local responsibility is well entrenched in the history of social welfare. Local and state influences have always been strong in child welfare programs because children and their families are closely linked to other concerns that traditionally have been regarded as the responsibility of the various states. For example, marriage, divorce, guardianship, custody, adoption, juvenile delinquency, and treatment of the mentally ill are all principally matters for legislation by the separate states.

Voluntary Family and Child Agencies

A voluntary (nonprofit) child and family welfare agency receives its authorization from a group of responsible citizens who undertake to assume responsibility for a defined and limited part of a community's social services for families and children. These agencies may form a corporate body and obtain a legal charter by showing that a need for a particular service exists and that a group of citizens is ready to support the activity. Some of these interested citizens are selected to serve as members of a board of directors with certain policy-making and advisory responsibilities in relation to a professional social work staff. The voluntary agency that provides out-of-home care of children is usually subject to the regulatory authority of the state and must establish its eligibility for a license certifying that it meets certain standards of child care. Voluntary agencies, if they meet certain standards, may be accredited by national organizations such as the Council on Accreditation (COA). As these agencies become connected to managed care systems, their operation is also subject to policy and oversight by managed care coordinating organizations.

In theory, voluntary welfare agencies are financed completely by voluntary contributions from citizens. However, the practice of channeling public tax monies to voluntary agencies has a long history. During the twentieth century the practice has grown of a public agency paying a private agency for services to children and families. Private agencies typically provide family preservation services, parent education and family support, foster care, and adoption services under purchase-of-service agreements with the state. Purchase-of-care arrangements raise complicated issues of agency autonomy in service planning and delivery, and in categories of clients served. If purchase of care is employed as a means of financing a community's social services for children, it should be carried out within a framework of community planning if it is to further the welfare of children and their families.

Faith-Based Initiatives.   Many child and family agencies started under religious auspices, to serve the needs of new immigrant groups arriving in America. Immigration and its attendant problems of disease, poverty, and social isolation caused many families to split apart or cease to function as protective and nurturing environments for family members, leaving the children abused, neglected, orphaned, or abandoned. Churches and synagogues acted on the needs they saw around them by organizing service programs, such as orphanages, foster care programs, and food and shelter programs. The names of many voluntary agencies reflect their faith-based beginnings, even if they are no longer closely connected with a religious denomination; Protestant Children's Home, Jewish Family Services, Catholic Social Services, and St. Francis Home for Boys are just a few examples of names of agencies identifying their denominational roots. As indicated earlier, during the twentieth century, many, though not all, child welfare agencies begun under religious auspices formed partnerships with public child welfare agencies. In accepting governmental funding to provide services, these agencies also agreed to run secular programs and not use the money to convert people. Also, they could not discriminate on the basis of religion in accepting clients for service or in hiring staff.

In the welfare reform legislation of the 1990s, Congress added "Charitable Choice" to the welfare bill, which gives religious congregations the right to compete with other charities for government funds without giving up their religious character. In 2002, President Bush initiated his program, Faith-Based and Community Initiatives, to support the work of faith-based social services (White House, 2002). This action has spurred debate on the advisability of providing federal funds directly to faith-based organizations. Proponents believe that the new initiative would simply level the playing field so that faith-based organizations could compete on equal footing with secular agencies for public dollars. They also believe that a religious or spiritual framework might enhance social services, at least in some areas, such as in hospice programs, substance abuse treatment centers, and teen pregnancy programs. Opponents fear erosion of the principle of the separation of church and state, and a return of the days when people could be denied basic services based on their religion, ethnicity, or race. This debate has raised a host of issues on how government can reconcile, in its policies, two competing and compelling principles: nondiscrimination and equal access to needed services and programs, on the one hand, and respect for and support of ethnic (and religious) diversity, on the other (De Vita & Wilson, 2001).

Proprietary Child Welfare Services

Purchase of child welfare services is sometimes contracted between a public agency and a *proprietary for-profit* agency. For-profit contracting occurs mainly in the provision of child care for working parents (Smith, 1989, p. 297). Very large numbers of other children have care arranged and carried out for them independent of any social welfare agency. Some families have found their own homemaker to bring into the home during periods of crisis and the mothers' absence. Some parents find a foster home and make arrangements for others to care for their children. Many children are placed in adoptive homes without the planning or supervision of a social welfare agency; this is very often arranged by an attorney for a fee or by other intermediaries.

Not enough is known about the quality of care and the experiences of children through these various independent arrangements. Some such children suffer poor quality of care, instability, and even abuse. However, some parents, particularly those with initiative, sound judgment, and financial resources, have been able to make satisfactory, independent arrangements for some aspects of their children's care.

Interagency Partnerships

A major barrier to more effective services to vulnerable families and children has been the way that social services are compartmentalized into separate organizations, each one responsible for providing only one service. For example, child welfare agencies traditionally have been responsible for investigating abuse and neglect and for placing children in out-of-home care; mental health agencies have provided inpatient and outpatient services to children with identified mental health problems; the juvenile justice system has provided correctional facilities and services; and the schools and the health care system have offered specific educational or health care services. Yet these organizations tend to serve the same children and families. The fragmentation of services is confusing for families, causes many to "fall through the cracks" and not get the service they need from any source, and is wasteful of resources. The following case shows a family in need of coordinated services.

> Mike is a fifth-grade boy, eleven years of age. He does not have a father at home. As far as is known, he has no contact with his father. Mike's mother is sickly and is generally homebound. He has an older sister who stays with him along with her boyfriend and a baby. Mike's older brother is in reform school. At the beginning of the year he was identified as a child who "gets into trouble and seldom finishes or does his homework." Mike responded by saying, "I don't care about school and my work is too hard." Mike follows peers who delight in disrupting classroom activities; he never smiles, and when things get too stressful, breaks into tears with no sound. (Bruner, 1991, p. 4)

Mike's family needs economic assistance, social support, and psychological assistance as well as educational help for Mike. However, our current service delivery system is structured into separate services with specific eligibility guidelines and bureaucratic regulations about what kinds of services it can offer and to whom. Mike and his family may get help but it is likely to be offered by different service providers working for different agencies and to be confusing for the family. Fragmented services to families like Mike's can also be very expensive: reform school, psychological assessment and counseling for the brother, welfare assistance, and Medicaid for the family may cost the state tens of thousands of dollars annually but not result in an integrated plan to help the family.

Recognizing the problems caused by uncoordinated service systems, state governments and local communities are making efforts to increase the level of cooperation and collaboration among agencies.

Program Example: Child Welfare and Community Mental Health

One area in which closer collaboration is greatly needed is between the child welfare and mental health systems. The children and families served by these systems are virtually indistinguishable. Knitzer and Yelton (1990) describe one highly successful collaboration as follows:

> The potentially most significant new efforts to help troubled children and adolescents involve comprehensive reforms . . . to the overall service delivery system. Perhaps the best example of this approach was developed in Ventura County, California. The Ventura County Board of Supervisors decided in 1985 to target an all-out effort on children who were likely to be placed out of home through child welfare, mental health, juvenile justice, or special education agencies. The county has used a $2 million state grant to supplement existing services with a day treatment program, therapeutic foster homes, and most recently a family preservation program. A strong case management program was also developed with mental health as the lead agency, and a series of inter-agency agreements was promulgated. Data suggest that county juvenile justice recidivism rates are down, the number of children in psychiatric hospitals has decreased, and . . . group home costs have been reduced by 13 percent. (pp. 29, 30)

Interagency partnerships can begin at different levels and through different procedures. A key to successful cooperation is strong leadership. "Someone, either by mandate or by predilection, must want collaboration to happen—and must have the clout to engage other agencies" (Knitzer & Yelton, 1990, p. 32). At the same time that administrative arrangements are made to promote cooperation, workers at the direct service level must also be committed to building bridges to workers in other agencies. Ultimately, integration of funding streams, though challenging to accomplish, would link services to families more holistically.

Trends and Issues

Child Welfare in a Global Context

We are fast approaching the time when child welfare practice will take place in not only a national context but also a global one. As the boundaries separating nations become more permeable, due to rapidly improving technology, communications, and travel, information about children and children's services from every part of the globe becomes available to us here. This new perspective influences the way we understand our own service system, our assumptions about child rearing in families, and our ideas about the appropriate role of government in the lives of families and children. The preface to the recently published *Child Abuse: A Global Perspective* observes that as we "learn more about our counterparts in other countries, they become real to us, and our worldview cannot help but change. We will think of others as we think of those we know" (Schwartz-Kenney, McCauley, & Epstein, 2001).

We can no longer ignore children in faraway lands who are living in horrific conditions. Daily on our TV screens and in our newspapers we learn of the hopeless plight of millions of children worldwide, their lives destroyed by war, poverty, famine, and disease, particularly HIV/AIDS. The sexual exploitation of children through pornography and sexual slavery, both here and abroad, has been made much easier by new communication technologies, such as the World Wide Web, and seems almost impossible to deter. With the fall of the iron curtain in 1989, we discovered the plight of more than a million orphans languishing in institutions in Central and Eastern Europe. The late Princess Diana helped make the world aware that land mines claim the life and limbs of untold numbers of innocent children. Many people in the United States are also uncomfortably aware that the consumer products they buy may have been made by the labor of children in developing countries.

The increased movement of people across national boundaries has affected social workers in their own communities. Children and their families from many countries seek asylum from the traumas of their homeland, or simply more opportunity and a better life in the United States; as they settle in communities across the country, they become part of our personal and perhaps also our professional lives. Children of other cultures, many with limited English language skills, are arriving in our schools, health clinics, day care centers, and recreation programs, requiring staff to develop culturally competent service approaches (Pipher, 2002). The field of international adoption is expanding, as U.S. families adopt children from other countries in increasing numbers. The child welfare community has been challenged to offer help effectively for adoptive families struggling with a thicket of adoption policies, and to develop postadoption counseling approaches for traumatized children and their adoptive families (Pasztor & McFadden, 2001).

Social workers and policy makers, as they learn more about child welfare practices and policies in other countries, are gaining new perspectives on policies and programs from abroad that hold promise for benefiting children here. The New Zealand Maori model of family decision making for the culturally sensitive protection of a family's children has been successfully exported to the United States. Information about the role of siblings in Africa in caring for AIDS orphans has helped us to "discover" siblings, often overlooked in child welfare services here, as a possible resource in maintaining family continuity for children who must be separated from their parents. In Canada, policies and practices have been developed to help immigrant children from war-ravaged countries find opportunities for healing and hope in a new homeland (Pasztor & McFadden, 2001).

Information on governmental policies and the condition of children in many other countries also is making us aware that we are doing a mediocre job, at best, on many measures of child well-being. Other countries have a very different understanding from ours on the role of government in providing to children basic social services, health care, and child care while their parents work. We are learning that strong supports for children's development will lead to better outcomes for children, thereby improving prospects for our nation's future (Child Trends, no date; Clearinghouse on International Developments in Child, Youth and Family Policies, 2001). The United States is also involved in international legal initiatives for the protection of children. The Hague Convention on Intercountry Adoption is an international treaty regulating the adoption of children across national boundaries. The United Nations Convention on the Rights of the Child is designed to protect and preserve the individual rights and basic human needs of children. The United States continues to be one of only two countries in the United Nations that has not ratified this treaty (the other is Somalia).

Information on children, families, and governments in other countries can give us new perspectives on service approaches and policies here, and renew our commitment to advocating for more resources to meet the needs of American children.

The Increasing Complexity of Family and Child Welfare Practice

As a specialized field of social work practice, child welfare is now being challenged to move beyond the residual, outworn classification of child welfare services and to respond to new, complex family problems. New forces are impelling change. Society's expectations for child welfare have increased. It is no longer enough to rescue children from unsuitable home situations; the child welfare system is expected to provide a relatively high level of care and to plan appropriately for the children's future. A number of legal reforms over the past four decades have increased accountability and reduced autonomy in agencies. Workers are required to work within a clear legal and policy framework. The sometimes competing goals of protecting children and preserving families have resulted in widely publicized reviews of agency decisions that have been proven by subsequent events to be bad judgments.

At the same time that child welfare has fallen under closer public scrutiny, the deteriorating condition of many children and families has presented new challenges to the system. The poverty, isolation, violence, and fractured family life experienced by many children have increased demands on the child welfare system. The disease of HIV/AIDS, in particular, has created a new group of orphans who need care and planning assistance from the child welfare system.

It is no longer possible for child welfare to remain a relatively small service system addressing the needs of a limited number of children who require out-of-home care or protective services. The problems of families and children demand that the child welfare system broaden its scope and diversify its practice approaches into a wider arena of family and child services. The child welfare system must forge new relationships with families, with neighborhoods and communities, and with other organizations in the service delivery system.

In tandem with the increasing array of problems in child welfare and the services to address them, professional responsibilities also have become more complex in the past few decades. Issues of professional malpractice and liability and concerns about the scope and limits of confidentiality have influenced practice both directly and indirectly. New mandates increasingly require social workers to understand complicated protocols for risk management, to warn others of threats made about them, to conduct forensic investigations, and to testify competently in judicial proceedings. These heavy responsibilities and expectations have not been matched by sufficient training, leaving workers exposed to legal and other difficulties. (See Chapter 12.)

The social work profession and child welfare practice have a long, shared history. Social work has been the predominant discipline in the field of child welfare services. Starting in the 1970s, however, child welfare and social work as a profession diverged. Changes within the child welfare system weakened its status and the effectiveness of its services. The growth in the number of very difficult cases and the downgrading of positions by reclassifying them from professional to nonprofessional, accompanied by declining salaries, caused a decline in the number of professional staff (Kamerman & Kahn, 1989). Unfortunately, at the same time that child welfare was being perceived as less professional than other social work fields, the work was becoming increasingly complex, requiring higher levels of skill than ever before, as discussed in the previous paragraphs. These developments encouraged renewed collaboration between public child welfare and social work education. Federal child welfare training monies have become available to finance special child welfare courses of study in schools of social work at both the BSW and MSW levels, for students who are current or future child welfare workers (Zlotnick, 1997).

Community Approaches to Family and Child Welfare

It is widely recognized that the communities in which children are raised influence their development. Families do not raise their children in isolation but in communities that, for better or worse, also affect how children grow to maturity. Some of the ways that communities affect children are through the quality of their schools, parks, and recreation facilities; their provisions for public safety; the economic opportunities that exist; the availability of positive adult role models and mentors; and the residents' values of citizenship and norms of socialized behavior. The importance of the community in children's development is captured in the phrase, "It takes a village to raise a child." The profession of social work, recognizing that the functioning of families depends on their social environment, has a long history of working to improve community life. The settlement houses at the turn of the century are only one example of organized efforts to increase community cohesion, to provide more resources for families in a community setting, and to organize focused advocacy efforts to improve neighborhood conditions.

It is also recognized that the failures of children are concentrated geographically and ethnically. Many of the children in the United States who are not prepared for successful, productive adult lives inhabit highly distressed and socially deprived neighborhoods. Recently, there has been renewed interest in community-level interventions in order to make these communities a more positive environment for children.

Bruner (1996) calls for a comprehensive vision of family and child welfare that would recreate the current fragmented service system into a holistic, dynamic program of renewal functioning at the neighborhood level. In the long run, he contends, improving neighborhoods will be a more effective and less expensive way to improve outcomes for children than our current system of categorical services for different types of child and family problems.

Another approach to connecting child welfare more closely with communities is the effort to involve residents and grassroots organizations more directly with the child welfare service system. Federal and state funding, as well as philanthropic foundations, have encouraged child welfare agencies to develop more permeable boundaries and to establish community partnerships. These efforts have borne fruit in the form of family support programs and intensive family preservation services, which attempt to strengthen families by coordinating an array of local services.

Recently, the concept of partnership between child welfare and community services has been expanded to include the idea of community responsibility for child safety, involving child protective service collaborations with local entities (White, 2000). The rationale for this initiative is that remote bureaucracies such as child protective services cannot do the whole job of keeping children safe. Ultimately, families and communities must also be mobilized in cooperative arrangements with child protective services to achieve this goal. Public child welfare agencies are just beginning to experiment with ways to share responsibility for child protection with communities. Farrow (1998) has identified some early demonstration efforts. One approach is to outstation child protection staff in schools or other neighborhood settings, as part of teams with other community workers. CPS workers may "walk the streets, get to know neighborhood residents before problems occur, and are familiar with each neighborhood's assets and resources" (Farrow, 1998, p. 12).

The idea that communities themselves have resources that have been insufficiently mobilized is an appealing one, and the new approaches described in the preceding paragraph show promise for strengthening child protective services through partnerships. However, there are reasons to be cautious about the ability of communities harrowed by substance abuse, poverty, unemployment, and violence to solve seemingly intractable child welfare problems. Wattenberg (1998) points out that "the conflicting views of the community as the source of problems or the location of solutions have not been reconciled" (p. 15) and that some communities lack the capacity to deliver social services. She notes that in some neighborhoods, there is reluctance to intervene directly to "confront, chastise or even offer help to a child" for fear of retribution from parents. In these areas, an anonymous call to child protective services may be the limit of what can be expected in neighborly responsibility for children's welfare. Another barrier is the belief of some community-based organizations that they will be tainted and stigmatized if it becomes known that they are cooperating with child protective services, a governmental agency that is viewed with suspicion by many residents in inner-city neighborhoods.

The community partnership concept is a work in progress. At this early stage, it is important to assess neighborhoods individually and carefully for their capacity to be hospitable environments for young families. So far, we have had the most experience with community-based programs whose focus is on promoting family strengths and preventing maltreatment. Much less is known about the potential for community collaborations with child protective services.

Chapter Summary

Child and family welfare services are concerned with providing direct services to children and families in which serious problems are identified, and also with influencing public policy to improve the lives of all children. To strengthen family life for children is regarded as the primary purpose of child welfare. Many observers claim that more changes have occurred in American families over recent decades than ever before in our nation's history. The 2000 census found that there are more children in the United States than ever before and that our child population is becoming much more diverse, with Hispanic children the fastest-growing ethnic group. Increasingly, children are living in families other than the traditional two-parent model, such as single-parent households, three-generation households, and stepfamilies. Children face many risks in today's society, with poverty being a pervasive condition that puts children in jeopardy of unfortunate developmental outcomes. Many children's lives are shadowed by violence and substance abuse. About 3 million children are reported to authorities for abuse and neglect each year; many of these children will end up in the nation's foster care system and face an uncertain future. National data on children's well-being show that the overall condition of children in this country may be improving, but too many children still face serious obstacles to healthy growth and development.

The history of child welfare services shows that until the twentieth century, the care of destitute, neglected, and abused children was the domain of private, charitable organizations. Many children received no protection from cruel families or the problems associated with disease, immigration, child labor, and crowded, inner-city tenement living. State and federal programs for children began early in the twentieth century, but has never reached a funding level sufficient to meet the needs of vulnerable children.

Social policy toward families and children may be categorized as residual, directed at the resolution of problems after they arise, or developmental, which holds that even well-functioning families need help from time to time and offers preventive services to anyone who needs them. Most child welfare services are in the category of residual services, because they are intended to ameliorate, and not to prevent, serious problems in families' care of children. Traditionally, family policy in the United States has reflected the reluctance for government to become involved in family life. In a diverse society, there is often intense disagreement about what form family policy should take, and many people believe that family life should be private and free from government intervention. The most prominent governmental policy affecting families is public welfare and attendant policies involving child support by absent parents and public support for day care while parents work.

Child and family services are guided by principles emphasizing the need for children to live in families and also to be free from physical neglect and abuse and sexual abuse. If children are not safe at home, child welfare services operate under the principle of supporting the family through intensive rehabilitation services; if the child must be removed for his or her own safety, family continuity is the principle guiding placement decisions, with relatives or others who have a relationship with the child given preference for placement. Child welfare services may be classified as preventive and supportive, protective, foster care and kinship care, and adoption. Agencies are now often required to identify outcomes by which their services can be measured and evaluated; it is important for programs to identify outcomes that are appropriate to the type of service they are offering. There is increased awareness of the importance of culturally competent services, to serve effectively children and families of diverse ethnic backgrounds. Child welfare agencies vary in size and auspices; common types are large, publicly financed state child welfare bureaucracies, and smaller private agencies that undertake a specialized function such as foster care, often under purchase-of-service agreements with the state agency. The complex problems of children and families often require the help of multiple service systems; child welfare agencies are forming partnerships with mental health organizations and substance abuse and domestic violence centers to coordinate services to a family.

Child welfare as a field of social work practice continues to grow and change in response to forces in the society, which forms its context. We are becoming more aware of and interconnected to the global child welfare community as technology and advances in communication reduce the boundaries between countries and cultures. Child welfare services are becoming increasingly complex; families and children coming into the system have more difficult and intractable problems than ever before; federal policy mandates require that agencies work within strict guidelines to achieve outcomes, but are not given enough resources to do the job. Child welfare agencies are also trying to form linkages with local communities, to find innovative ways to protect children through neighborhood-based interventions.

FOR STUDY AND DISCUSSION

1. Contact your state public child welfare agency to find out the status of the federal Children's Bureau Child and Family Services Review for your state. What are the identified strengths and weaknesses of your state's child welfare program? What plans have been developed to improve the state's performance in attaining the outcomes listed in Table 1.2?

2. Learn about the background of a social agency in your area. When was it founded? Is it public or private? Was it started by a religious organization? If so, what are its links to that organization today? What are its funding sources? What are the main components and goals of its programs? Has the service mission changed over time?

3. Delineate services that should be included in a comprehensive system of services for families and children, by identifying the problems that face children and families today.

4. Assess the cultural competency of this textbook. How well does it exemplify the values, knowledge, and skills of cultural competency set out in the NASW standards? How might it be improved?

5. Undertake a project in global child welfare. For example, study an aspect of child welfare in another country and identify implications for improving child welfare service delivery in this country. Or, learn more about children and families who have emigrated from another country to your community. What difficulties are they facing in adjusting to a new country and culture, and how might the human service and educational systems in your community be more responsive to their needs?

6. Learn about the Bush administration's Marriage Initiative. Conduct a debate in class on whether it will be effective in encouraging American citizens to marry. Do you think that government has a legitimate role to play in people's decisions to marry or stay single?

FOR ADDITIONAL STUDY

Ewalt, P. L., Freeman, E. M., Kirk, S. A., & Poole, D. L. (1997). *Social policy: Reform, research, and practice.* Washington, DC: NASW Press.

Haveman, R., & Wolfe, B. (1995). *Succeeding generations: On the effects of investments in children.* Thousand Oaks, CA: Russell Sage Foundation.

Hutchinson, J., & Sudia, C. (2002). *Failed child welfare policy.* Lanham, MD: University Press of America.

Jackson, S., & Brissett-Chapman, S. (Eds.). (1997, January–February). *Child Welfare Special Issue: Perspectives on Serving African-American Children, Youth, and Families, 76*(1).

Kozol, J. (2001). *Ordinary resurrections.* New York: Perennial HarperCollins.

McFadden, E., & Pasztor, E. (Eds.). (2001). *Child Welfare Special Issue: International Issues in Child Welfare, 80*(5).

Ortega, R. M., Guillean, C., & Najera, L. G. (1996). *Latinos and child welfare/Latinos y et bienestar del Nino, voces de la communidad.* Ann Arbor: University of Michigan School of Social Work.

Schorr, L. (1997). *Common purpose.* New York: Doubleday.

Stein, T. J. (1998). *The social welfare of women and children with HIV and AIDS.* New York: Oxford University Press.

INTERNET SEARCH TERMS

Child outcomes	Social services
Child welfare	Social welfare
Family policy	

INTERNET SITES

Administration for Children and Families (ACF). Within the Department of Health and Human Services (DHHS), the ACF is responsible for federal programs that promote the economic and social well-being of families, children, and communities. Programs described at this web site include welfare, foster care, adoption, family preservation, child protection, Head Start, child care, child support enforcement, services to youth, programs to strengthen communities, and special programs for such populations as the developmentally disabled, refugees, and Native Americans.
www.acf.dhhs.gov

Children's Defense Fund. This advocacy organization is for children in America who cannot vote, lobby, or speak for themselves. It pays particular attention to the needs of poor and minority children and those with disabilities. The web site offers current information on federal policy initiatives and encourages citizen involvement in the policy process.
www.childrensdefense.org

Child Trends. Child Trends is a nonpartisan research organization dedicated to improving the lives of children by conducting research and providing science-based information to improve the decisions, programs, and policies that affect children. In advancing this mission, Child Trends collects and analyzes data; conducts, synthesizes, and disseminates research; designs and evaluates programs; and develops and tests promising approaches to research in the field. The Child Trends Data Bank is a one-stop shop for the latest national trends and research on over seventy key indicators of child and youth well-being, with new indicators added each month.
www.childtrends.org

Child Welfare League of America. This is the nation's oldest and largest membership-based child welfare organization. It is an association of almost 1,000 public and private nonprofit child welfare agencies. The web site lists the services offered to members and provides advocacy information concerning current policy proposals of the federal government.
www.cwla.org

Clearinghouse on International Developments in Child, Youth and Family Policies. The web site of this organization is a venue for those wanting information about international developments in child, youth, and family policies. The web site provides cross-national, comparative information on policies, programs, benefits, and services in twenty-three advanced industrialized countries to address child, youth, and family needs.
www.childpolicyintl.org

Federal Interagency Forum on Child and Family Statistics. This web site offers easy access to federal and state statistics and reports on children and their families, including population and family characteristics, economic security, health, behavior and social environment, and education. Reports of the Federal Interagency Forum on Child and Family Statistics include *America's Children: Key National Indicators of Well-Being,* the annual federal monitoring report on the status of the nation's children.
www.childstats.gov

Kids Count. A project of the Annie E. Casey Foundation, this is a national and state-by-state effort to track the status of children in the United States. The annual *Kids Count Data Book* uses the best available data to measure the educational, social, economic, and physical well-being of children.
www.aecf.org/aeckids.htm

Welfare Information Network. This is a foundation-funded project to help states and communities obtain the information, policy analysis, and technical assistance they need to develop and implement welfare reforms. It has a clearinghouse of welfare reform–related information, including special web sites on teenage parenting, child support, and all aspects of child welfare. The site includes summaries of federal legislation concerning families and children. It provides links to related organizations, policy analysis research centers, state agencies, and technical assistance resources, including "best practices" projects. The following site is devoted specifically to child welfare issues.
www.welfareinfo.org/childwelf.htm

REFERENCES

Abbott, C. (1938). *The child and the state, vol. 1.* Chicago: University of Chicago Press.

Barbaro, F. (1979). The case against family policy. *Social Work, 24*(6), 447–456.

Bearer, C. F. (1995). Environmental health hazards: How children are different from adults. *The Future of Children, 5*(2), 11–26.

Bernstine, N. (1997). Housing and homelessness. *The state of America's children: Yearbook, 1997.* Washington, DC: Children's Defense Fund.

Billingsley, A., & Giovannoni, J. M. (1972). *Children of the storm: Black children and American child welfare.* New York: Harcourt Brace Jovanovich.

Briar, K. H., Hansen, V. H., & Harris, N. (Eds.). (1992). *New partnerships: Proceedings from the National Public Child Welfare Training Symposium, 1991.* Miami: Florida International University.

Bruner, C. (1991). *Thinking collaboratively: Ten questions and answers to help policy makers improve children's services.* Washington, DC: Education and Human Services Consortium.

Bruner, C. (1996). *Realizing a vision for children, families, and neighborhoods.* Des Moines, IA: National Center for Service Integration.

Bryson, K., & Casper, L. M. (1998, April). *Household and family characteristics: March, 1997.* (Current Population Reports, P20–509, U.S. Department of Commerce, Census Bureau). Washington, DC: U.S. Government Printing Office.

Casey Outcomes and Decision-Making Project. (1998). *Assessing outcomes in child welfare services: Principles, concepts, and a framework of core outcome indicators.* Englewood, CO: American Humane Association. Available: www.caseyoutcomes.org.

CDF facts about child care in America. (1998, March 10). [Online]. Available: www.childrensdefense. org/cc_facts.html [1998, May].

Child Trends. (no date). The Kids Count international data sheet. Available: www.childtrends.org.

Children's Bureau. (2000). *The AFCARS report.* Washington, DC: U.S. Department of Health and Human Services. Available: www.acf.hhs.gov/programs/cb/publications/afcars/report7.htm.

Children's Defense Fund. (1997). *The state of America's children: Yearbook, 1997.* Washington, DC: Children's Defense Fund.

Clearinghouse on International Developments in Child, Youth and Family Policies. (2001). *New 12 country study reveals substantial gaps in U.S. early childhood education and care policies.* New York: Columbia University. Available: www.childpolicyintl. org.

Cook, J. F. (1995). A history of placing-out: The orphan trains. *Child Welfare, 74*(1), 181–200.

Council on Social Work Education. (1992). *Social work education and public human services: Developing partnerships.* Washington, DC: Council on Social Work Education.

Cross, T. L. (1988). Services to minority population: Cultural competence continuum. *Focal point, 3*(1), 1–4. [Bulletin of the Research and Training Center on Family Support and Children's Mental Health, Portland State University, Regional Research Institute for Human Services, Portland, OR].

Currie, E. (1982). Fighting crime. *Working Papers, 9*(4).

De Vita, C., & Wilson, S. (2001). *Faith-based initiatives: Sacred deeds and secular dollars. Emerging issues in philanthropy seminar series.* Washington, DC: The Urban Institute.

Downs, S. W., & Sherraden, M. (1983). The orphan asylum in the nineteenth century. *Social Service Review, 57*(2), 272–290.

Egan, J. (2002, March 24). To be young and homeless. *New York Times Magazine,* pp. 32–37 ff.

Ewalt, P. L., Freeman, E. M., Kirk, S. A., & Poole, D. L. (1997). *Social policy: Reform, research, and practice.* Washington, DC: NASW Press.

Farrow, F. (1998). Community responsibility for protecting children: What does it mean now, what can it mean in the future? *The Prevention Report, 1998*(1), 11–13.

Federal Interagency Forum on Child and Family Statistics. (2001). *America's children: Key national indicators of well-being.* Washington, DC: U.S. Government Printing Office.

Federal Interagency Forum on Child and Family Statistics. (2002). *America's children: Key national indicators of well-being.* Washington, DC: U.S. Government Printing Office.

Folks, H. (1911). *The care of destitute, neglected, and delinquent children.* New York: Macmillan.

Garbarino, J. (1992). The meaning of poverty in the world of children. *American Behavioral Scientist, 35*(2), 220–237.

Garwood, S. G., Phillips, D., Hartman, A., & Zigler, E. G. (1989, February). As the pendulum swings:

Federal policy programs for children. *American Psychologist, 434–440.*

Hagen, J. L., & Davis, L. V. (1997). Mothers' views on child care under the JOBS program and implications for welfare reform. In P. L. Ewalt, E. M. Freeman, S. A. Kirk, & D. L. Poole (Eds.), *Social policy: Reform, research and practice* (pp. 280–296). Washington, DC: NASW Press.

Hartman, A. (1981). The family: A central focus for practice. *Social Work, 26*(1).

Heyburn, I. (1919). *The congressional record* (Senate). Washington, DC: U.S. Government Printing Office, p. 189.

Huff, B., & Telesford, M. C. (1994). Outreach efforts to involve families of color in the Federation of Families for Children's Mental Health. *Focal Point, 8*(2), 10–12. [Bulletin of the Research and Training Center to Improve Services for Seriously Emotionally Handicapped Children and Their Families, Portland State University, Regional Research Institute for Human Services, Portland, OR].

Jackson, S., & Brissett-Chapman, S. (Eds.). (1997). *Child Welfare Special Issue: Perspectives on Serving African-American Children, Youth, and Families, 76*(1).

Kadushin, A. (1987). Child welfare services. In *Encyclopedia of social work* (18th ed.) (pp. 265–275). Washington, DC: National Association of Social Workers.

Kahn, A. J. (1965). The societal context of social work practice. *Social Work, 10*(4), 145–155.

Kamerman, S. B. (1997). The new politics of child and family policies. In P. L. Ewalt, E. M. Freeman, S. A. Kirk, & D. L. Poole (Eds.), *Social policy: Reform, research and practice* (pp. 167–183). Washington, DC: NASW Press.

Kamerman, S. B., & Kahn, A. J. (1989). *Social services for children, youth and families in the United States.* New York: Columbia University School of Social Work, Annie E. Casey Foundation.

Knitzer, J., & Yelton, S. (1990). Collaborations between child welfare and mental health. *Public Welfare, 48*(2), 24–33.

Laird, J. (1985). An ecological approach to child welfare. In C. Germaine (Ed.), *Social work practice: People and environments.* New York: Columbia University Press.

Leashore, B. R., Chipungu, S. S., & Everett, J. E. (1991). *Child welfare: An afrocentric perspective.* New Brunswick, NJ: Rutgers University Press.

Lieberman, A., Russell, M., & Hornby, H. (1989). *National survey of child welfare workers.* Portland, ME: University of Southern Maine, National Resource Center for Management and Administration.

Masten, A. S. (1992). Homeless children in the United States: Mark of a nation at risk. *Current Directions in Psychological Science, 1*(2), 41–44.

McFadden, E. J., Berns, D. A., & Downs, S. W. (1995). *Partnerships in developing graduate curriculum competencies: The Michigan experience.* Unpublished manuscript.

McFadden, E. J., & Downs, S. W. (1995). Family continuity: The new paradigm in permanence planning. *Community Alternatives: International Journal of Family Care, 7*(1), 44.

McPhatter, A. R. (1997). Cultural competence in child welfare: What is it? How do we achieve it? What happens without it? *Child Welfare, 76*(1), 255–278.

Melaville, A. I., & Blank, M. J. (1991). *What it takes: Structuring interagency partnerships to connect children and families with comprehensive services.* Washington, DC: Education and Human Services Consortium.

Meyer, C. H. (1984). Can foster care be saved? *Social Work, 29*(6), 499.

Meyer, C. H. (1985). The institutional context of child welfare. In J. Laird & A. Hartman (Eds.), *Handbook of child welfare.* New York: Macmillan.

Monthly vital statistics report. (1995, March 22), *43*(9).

National Association of Social Workers. (2001). *NASW standards for cultural competence in social work practice.* Washington, DC: National Association of Social Workers.

National Center for Child Abuse and Neglect. (2001). *Child abuse and neglect state statutes elements.* Washington, DC: U.S. Government Printing Office.

Nelson, K. (1995). The child welfare response to youth violence and homelessness in the nineteenth century. *Child Welfare, 74*(1), 56–70.

Office of Juvenile Justice and Delinquency Prevention. (2000, March). 1999 National Report Series: Kids and guns. *Juvenile Justice Bulletin.*

O'Hare, W. (2001). *The child population: First data from the 2000 census.* Seattle, WA: The Annie E. Casey Foundation and the Population Reference Bureau.

Ounce of Prevention Fund. (1993). *Beethoven's Fifth: The first five years of the center for successful child development.* Chicago: Ounce of Prevention Fund.

Pasztor, E., & McFadden, J. (2001). Global perspectives on child welfare. *Child Welfare, 80*(5), 487–496.

Peebles-Wilkins, W. (1995). Janie Porter Barrett and the Virginia Industrial School for Colored Girls: Community response to the needs of African-American children. *Child Welfare, 74*(1), 143–161.

Petit, M. R., & Curtis, P. A. (1997). *Child abuse and neglect: A look at the states.* Washington, DC: CWLA Press.

Pheatt, M., Douglas, B., Wilson, L., Brook, J., & Berry, M. (2000). Family preservation under managed care: Current practices and future directions. *Family Preservation Journal, 5*(1), 21–40.

Pipher, M. (2002). *The middle of everywhere: The world's refugees come to our town.* New York: Harcourt.

Rhodes, R. (2000). What causes brutality? *Children's Voice, 9*(2), 10–11.

Russakoff, D. (1998, September 28). Birth of a new boom. *Washington Post, National Weekly Edition,* p. 6.

Sahonchik, K. (2000, Summer). Using outcomes data in decision making. *Managing Care: A Newsletter of the National Child Welfare Resource Center for Organizational Improvement, 3*(1), 1–8.

Saluter, A. F. (1994). *Marital and living arrangements: March, 1993.* (Current Population Reports, P20-478, U.S. Department of Commerce, Census Bureau). Washington, DC: U.S. Government Printing Office.

Schwartz-Kenney, B. M., McCauley, M., & Epstein, M. A. (Eds.). (2001). *Child abuse: A global view.* Westport, CT: Greenwood Press.

Sherraden, M., & Downs, S. W. (1984). Institutions for juvenile delinquency in historical perspective. *Children and Youth Services Review, 6*(3), 155–173.

Skolnick, A. (1997, May–June). State of the debate, family values: The sequel. *The American Prospect (32),* 86–94. Available: http://epn.org/prospect/32/32skolfs.html.

Smith, E. P., & Merkel-Holguin, L. (1995). From family duty to family policy: The evolution of kinship care. *Child Welfare, 74*(1), 200–216.

Smith, S. R. (1989). The changing politics of child welfare services: New roles for the government and the nonprofit sectors. *Child Welfare, 68*(3), 289–299.

Stein, T. J. (1998). *The social welfare of women and children with HIV and AIDS.* New York: Oxford University Press.

Steiner, G. Y. (1981). *The futility of family policy.* Washington, DC: The Brookings Institution.

Terpstra, J. (1993). *Reprofessionalizing child welfare.* Concept paper circulated from the U.S. Children's Bureau.

Thurston, H. W. (1930). *The dependent child.* New York: Columbia University Press.

U.S. Department of Health and Human Services. (2002). *Child maltreatment 2000: Reports from the states to the National Child Abuse and Neglect Data System.* Washington, DC: U.S. Government Printing Office.

U.S. General Accounting Office. (1998, October). *Child welfare: Early experiences implementing a managed care approach.* [GAO/HEHS-99-8)]. Washington, DC: U.S. Government Printing Office.

Wattenberg, E. (1998). Are communities the problem or the solution for high-risk families and children? *The Prevention Report, 1998*(1), 14–17.

Weil, M. (1997). Community building: Community practice. In P. L. Ewalt, E. M. Freeman, S. A. Kirk, & D. L. Poole (Eds.), *Social policy: Reform, research, and practice* (pp. 35–61). Washington, DC: NASW Press.

White, A. (2000). Strengthening communities: A family-centered strategy in Jacksonville, Florida. *Best Practice, National Child Welfare Resource Center for Family-Centered Practice, 1*(2), 4–8.

White House Faith-Based and Community Initiatives. (2002). *Guidance to faith-based and community organizations on partnering with the federal government.* Washington, DC: U.S. Government Printing Office. Available: www.fbci.gov/faith.

Ziesemer, C., Marcoux, L., & Marwell, B. E. (1994). Homeless children: Are they different from other low-income children? *Social Work, 39*(6), 658–668.

Zill, N., & Nord, C. W. (1994). *Running in place: How American families are faring in a changing economy and an individualistic society.* Washington, DC: Child Trends, Inc.

Zlotnick, J. L. (1997). *Preparing the workforce for family-centered practice: Social work education and public human services partnerships.* Alexandria, VA: Council on Social Work Education.

2 Rights and Responsibilities of Parents, Children, and Government

The child is not the mere creature of the State; those who nurture him and direct his destiny have the right, coupled with the high duty, to recognize and prepare him for additional obligations.

—*Pierce v. Society of Sisters*, 1925, p. 535

CHAPTER OUTLINE

Case Example

Joshua DeShaney was born in 1979. His parents divorced in 1980 and his father was granted custody. In January 1982 the father's second wife reported that the father had hit the child causing marks. The Winnebago County Department of Social Services (DSS) interviewed the father, who denied the charges. DSS closed the case. In January 1983 Joshua was admitted to a local hospital with multiple bruises and abrasions. The examining physician filed a suspected child abuse report with DSS. DSS obtained a court order to keep Joshua hospitalized until a multidisciplinary team could review the case. Three days later, the team decided that there was insufficient evidence of child abuse to pursue continuing court jurisdiction. They recommended some measures to protect Joshua, which his father voluntarily agreed to. Joshua was returned to his father. A month later, Joshua was treated in an emergency room for "suspicious injuries." A report to DSS was made. The caseworker investigated, concluded that there was no basis for court action, and continued to make monthly visits under the voluntary arrangement; she documented these visits and her suspicions that someone in the home was physically abusing Joshua. Nothing else was done. In November 1983, Joshua was treated again for suspicious injuries. The caseworker visited the home, but did not see Joshua because the father told her he was too sick to see her. In March 1984, Joshua was badly beaten and fell into a life-threatening coma. Joshua suffered brain injuries so severe that he was expected to spend the rest of his life confined to an institution. His father was tried and convicted of child abuse.

Joshua's mother and guardian ad litem brought a suit against DSS, alleging that DSS violated his constitutional rights (Fourteenth Amendment: deprivation of liberty without due process) "by failing to intervene to protect him against a risk of violence at his father's hands of which they knew or should have known" (*DeShaney v. Winnebago County DSS*, 1989, p. 193). The Court concluded that the state had not violated Joshua DeShaney's constitutional rights in failing to protect him from his father's abuse. The Court stated:

> nothing in the language of the Due Process Clause itself requires the State to protect the life, liberty, and property of its citizens against invasion by private actors. The Clause is phrased as a limitation on the State's power to act, not as a guarantee of certain minimal levels of safety and security. It forbids the State itself to deprive individuals of life, liberty, or property without "due process of law," but its language cannot fairly be extended to impose an affirmative obligation on the State to ensure that those interests do not come to harm through other means. (Ibid., p. 195)

While finding that there was no constitutional violation, the Court held open the possibility of liability of the state under state law. It concluded:

> It may well be that, by voluntarily undertaking to protect Joshua against a danger it concededly played no part in creating, the State acquired a duty under state tort law to provide him with adequate protection against that danger. . . . A State may, through its courts and legislatures, impose such affirmative duties of care and protection upon its agents as it wishes. (*DeShaney v. Winnebago County DSS*, 1989, p. 201)

Introduction

Child welfare practice is rooted in a legal environment that seeks to balance the interests of child, parents, and the government (federal and state). It is an area that requires understanding the interplay of the federal and state legislative, executive, and judicial systems. This chapter provides a basic overview of that legal environment.

Historical Context

A discussion of the historical context of the three entities whose interests are to be balanced— parent, child, and government—is necessary to understanding how we got to where we are now and to projecting where we might go in the future. In our society, historically and presently, the primary right and responsibility of caring for children rests with their parents.

Until the onset of the nineteenth century, parents were afforded almost absolute autonomy, privacy, and independence in carrying out their parental responsibilities unless they committed some criminal act against the child. During the nineteenth century, the government began to impose certain restrictions on parental rights related to child labor and education. Religious organizations and other reformers began to take an interest in the basic care, or lack thereof, of children and to establish orphanages and boarding homes for children found to be destitute, abandoned, or wayward. In 1899, the first juvenile court was established in Illinois to address the abuse, neglect, and delinquency of children (Kramer, 2002).

The early twentieth century saw the beginning of federal involvement, with the first White House Conference on Children in 1909 and establishment of the Children's Bureau in 1912. These actions signaled the beginning of federal leadership in developing legislation and programs to promote the general well-being and protection of children throughout the country.

Policy and Legal Context

Legal ramifications of the parent–child relationship are demanding more and more attention from social workers engaged in the spectrum of child protection services: prevention, protection, family preservation, foster care, guardianship, custody, adoption, and juvenile justice. Various public constituencies, often with different values and philosophies, want to and do participate in the development of public social policy that is generally codified; that is, written down, in federal or state laws that form the basis of administrative rules and policies for agencies delegated the responsibilities to carry out the requirements of the laws. Some advocates for the family favor policy reaffirming the traditional presumption that parents will act in their child's best interests, and support legislation that safeguards the rights of parents by imposing stringent legal procedures to justify governmental intrusion into the family's autonomy. Other child and family advocates place greater emphasis on policy that advocates the legal rights of children as distinct from those of their parents. Most child and family advocates prefer an approach to intervention to remedy or alleviate family problems that represents the least intrusive intervention necessary to ensure that the harm or threatened harm to the child is removed. Chapter 12 provides more detail on the role of advocacy in the development of social policy. Chapters 1, 3, 4, 5, 6, 7, 8, 9, 10, and 11 provide detailed reviews of specific federal legislation impacting child welfare policy and practice.

The legal framework for child welfare practice is rooted in federal and state laws (constitutions, statutes, ordinances) that regulate parent, child, and government interrelationships; the administrative rules and agency policies promulgated to carry out these laws; and the judicial and administrative decisions applying the laws to specific cases. Every state now has laws covering the basic areas of child welfare practice, protecting children from the certain acts of commission or omission by their parents, guardians, or caretakers; addressing the status offender and the juvenile offender/delinquent; establishing the conditions and procedures for legal guardianship; establishing conditions and procedures for emancipation; and establishing the procedures for adoption. In addition, every state has laws that regulate matters that the child welfare professional frequently encounters, such as education, medical treatment, consent for abortion, treatment for sexually transmitted diseases, mental health treatment, and substance abuse treatment. The scope of this text is such that each cannot be discussed in detail. You are encouraged to obtain and review copies of the applicable statutes within the state where you practice. It is important to note that not every state law on a similar matter is the same. Subsequent chapters highlight some of these statutory variances and expound on the practice implications.

Constitutional Overlay

The states and the federal government, under the police powers, have the right and responsibility to enact laws to promote public safety, peace, morals, and general societal welfare that regulate the behaviors of its citizenry, but the scope of authority of those police powers is limited by the constitutional privileges afforded to the citizenry. A basic principle of U.S. law (broadly speaking, "law" includes constitutions, statutes, ordinances, rules, regulations, and policies) is that actions of the legislative or executive branches at the state and federal level must not violate rights and privileges provided under the Constitution of the United States (*Lawton v. Steele,* 1893). Coupled with that basic principle is another; namely, the courts do not "case find." Someone (an aggrieved person, that is, a person who thinks his or her rights have been violated, or a person acting on behalf of the aggrieved party) must present a "controversy" to the court via the method prescribed in court rules, usually a petition or complaint. Once presented with a petition or complaint, the courts can determine whether the facts in the case are such that a violation of the law, including the Constitution, has occurred. In the area of parent, child, and government interrelations, the interpretation of the constitutional rights of parents and children vis-à-vis one another, independently and in relation to the state and federal government, is unfolding. Because the Supreme Court of the United States, the Court, has the final decision as to whether a particular law (federal, state, or local), as applied to a specific set of facts, is constitutional or not, several decisions of that Court with respect to parents, children, and governmental interests and rights within the context of child welfare practice are discussed here and in subsequent chapters. This gives us a framework for understanding the decisional climate in which states must operate as they enact laws and practices affecting child welfare.

Before beginning that discussion, however, a brief overview of the mechanics of the Supreme Court, its decision-making process, and the usual mechanism by which cases come before the Supreme Court may help you understand the case decisions. The **nine justices** are appointed for life by the president with the consent of the Senate. The **decision** (also known as the **holding** or **ruling,** depending on the nature of the decision) of the majority is the decision of the Court. The **majority opinion** has the greatest weight and the more justices included in the majority the stronger the decision. When there is agreement on the decision but differences in the reasoning—that is, the legal explanation—one or more **minority opinions** or **concurring opinions** are written. Any justice who disagrees with the court's decision writes a **dissenting opinion.** Although this opinion holds no authority, it frequently provides food for thought for legislators and lawyers (Pratt, 1993).

The process by which the Supreme Court usually comes to hear cases involving parent, child, and state interests is as an appeal of a federal court decision that claims the action (that is, a particular statute or administrative rule, policy, or practice) of the state agent violated the constitutional rights of the person. Constitutional protections against states' actions are granted under the due process or equal protection clauses of the Fourteenth Amendment of the Constitution of the United States. Section 1 of the Fourteenth Amendment states:

> All persons born or naturalized in the United States and subject to the jurisdiction thereof, are citizens of the United States and of the State wherein they reside. No State shall make or enforce any law which shall abridge the privileges or immunities of citizens of the United States; nor shall any State deprive any person of life, liberty, or property, without due process of law; nor deny to any person within its jurisdiction the equal protection of the laws.

The Supreme Court justices, by vote, determine which cases will be heard by the Court, a process known as *writ of certiorari.*

The decisions and reasoning of the Supreme Court in the area of parent, child, and state rights, responsibilities, and interests are complex and at first glance contradictory. However, with careful review and analyses of the difference in the legal questions being asked, the laws or rules being applied, and the facts of the specific cases, the decisions become more cogent. A fundamental reason for the variances is that Supreme Court decisions interpret the public policy that frames the often conflicting needs and goals of parents, children, and society. Some of these cases are weighted in the direction of reinforcing the rights of parents in the upbringing of their children. Some clearly extend legal rights to minors; others limit rights they would have but for their status as minors. In all cases the influences and interests of society are apparent.

The justices have clearly said that the child, merely on account of his or her minority status, is not beyond the protection of the Constitution: "Whatever may be their precise impact, neither the Fourteenth Amendment nor the Bill of Rights is for adults alone" (*In re Gault,* 1967, p. 13). In some cases the Court has concluded that the child's right to due process is the same as that of an adult, particularly in matters of threat to liberty or property interests (*In re Gault,* 1967; *Tinker v. Des Moines Independent Community School District,* 1969). But also it has rejected "the uncritical assumption that the constitutional rights of children are indistinguishable from those of adults," or that under the law children can never be treated differently from adults (*Bellotti v. Baird,* 1979, p. 633). The challenge facing the Court is one of achieving a just and workable balance in parent–child–society conflicts.

U.S. Supreme Court cases not only reveal the rights of parents and their offspring but also the Court's view of children—their needs, protections, and capabilities. The justices have offered three principles that guide their reasoning and justify the conclusion that the constitutional rights of children cannot be unequivocally equated with those of adults: "the peculiar vulnerability of children; their inability to make critical decisions in an informed, mature manner; and the importance of the parental role in child-rearing" (*Bellotti v. Baird,* 1979, p. 623). In the words of former Justice Felix Frankfurter, "Children have a very special place in life which law should reflect. Legal theories and their phrasing in other cases readily leads to fallacious reasoning if uncritically transferred to determination of a State's duty toward children" (*May v. Anderson,* 1953, p. 536).

It follows that although children are generally protected by the same constitutional guarantees as adults, the state is allowed to adjust its legal system to accord with children's vulnerability and the unique role of the family; constitutional principles must be applied flexibly and sensitively to the special needs of children and parents. Given this framework for legal reasoning in relation to child rights, the ambivalence perceived by child advocates (that is, a dichotomy of rights bestowed and rights denied) becomes more understandable, if not fully acceptable, to proponents of expanded and inclusive constitutional protections for children.

Rights and Responsibilities of Parents

In our society the primary right and responsibility of caring for children rests with their parents. Differences are accepted and valued as part of our way of life. Parents have the right of natural guardianship by the fact that the child was born to or legally adopted by them. In situations in which a child is born to unwed parents, the mother automatically assumes natural guardianship rights and responsibilities. The unwed (also known as putative) father must follow the law and procedures legislated by each state to establish paternity and acquire care, custody, support, and visitation (now commonly called "parenting time") rights. Parents determine the living pattern and the standards of everyday conduct that influence the developing personality of the child. They can determine religion and may affect basic ethical values of the child. They influence the kind and extent of the child's education, the decision as to vocation, and the level of adult achievement. The quality of health care the child receives depends not only on the availability of health services in a particular community but also on the extent of the parents' knowledge and the choices made by them when medical care is needed.

The responsibilities of parenthood include (1) financial support—meeting the child's money needs in a society that looks with disfavor on economic dependency and the inability of parents to keep the family economically self-supporting; (2) the provision of physical care—keeping the child safe from harm and injury and giving attention to his or her physical condition and health needs; (3) emotional care—for many parents a nebulous and poorly defined concept, carrying connotations of responsibility without knowledge of ways to meet it; and (4) a range of other parental duties, such as giving guidance and supervision to the young child as well as to the adolescent, promoting the growth of self-discipline, and setting forth clear parental and societal expectations that are adapted to the individual child's pace and ability. In addition, the right of parents to make certain major decisions for the child—for example, consent to medical care, to enlistment in the armed forces, and to marriage—is also a serious responsibility.

Decisions Reinforcing Parental Rights

Parental rights to make decisions about various aspects of their children's lives have been reinforced in several Supreme Court decisions. The following discussion summarizes the most relevant decisions. The format used in this discussion is to summarize the state law being challenged; to then state the issue before the Court, that is, the alleged constitutional violation(s); and to state the relevant facts, the rule of law as applied to the case facts and the holding of the Court. Further, in each instance, specific quotations from the decisions are given to show the rationale for the Court's decision.

Pierce v. Society of Sisters, 1925.   The Oregon Compulsory Education Act required parents of children between the ages of 8 and 16 years to send them to public schools. Two private schools brought action on behalf of themselves and the parents of children attending their schools claiming that this act deprived them of property interests and deprived the parents of their right to direct the religious upbringing of their children. The Court held that a state could not require parents to send their children to public schools only. The Court stated:

> Under the doctrine of Meyer v. Nebraska, 262 U.S. 390, we think it entirely plain that the Act of 1922 unreasonably interferes with the liberty of parents and guardians to direct the upbringing and education of children under their control. As often heretofore pointed out, rights guaranteed by the Constitution may not be abridged by legislation which has no reasonable relation to some purpose within the competence of the State. The fundamental theory of liberty upon which all governments in this Union repose excludes any general power of the State to standardize its children by forcing them to accept instruction from public teachers only. The child is not the mere creature of the State; those who nurture him and direct his destiny have the right, coupled with the high duty, to recognize and prepare him for additional obligations. (*Pierce v. Society of Sisters,* 1925, pp. 534–535)

Wisconsin v. Yoder, 1972. Wisconsin required parents to send their children to either public or private school until the age of 16 years. Amish parents refused to send their 14- and 15-year-old children to school after completion of the eighth grade because they believed it to be contrary to their religion. The Court stated:

> The record strongly indicates that accommodating the religious objections of the Amish by forgoing one, or at most two, additional years of compulsory education will not impair the physical and mental health of the child, or result in an inability to be self-supporting or to discharge the duties and responsibilities of citizenship, or in any other way materially distract from the welfare of society. (*Wisconsin v. Yoder,* 1972, p. 234)

Justice Douglas stated *in dissent:*

> On this important and vital matter of education, I think the children should be entitled to be heard. While the parents, absent dissent, normally speak for the entire family, the education of the child is a matter on which the child will often have decided views. . . . It is the student's judgment, not his parents, that is essential if we are to give full meaning to what we have said about the Bill of Rights and of the rights of students to be masters of their own destiny. (Ibid., pp. 244–245)

Palmore v. Sidoti, 1984. This case involved a child-custody decision. These types of cases are extremely rare before the Supreme Court. Two Caucasian parents divorced when their child was 3 years old. Custody was given to the mother. She subsequently cohabitated with and married a Negro. The father petitioned for custody on the basis of "changed conditions." A Florida court awarded custody to the father based on a counselor's recommendation for the change in custody because "the wife has chosen for herself and for her child, a life-style unacceptable to the father and to society. . . . The child is, or at school age will be subject to environmental pressures not of her choice" (*Palmore v. Sidoti,* 1984, p. 431).

The Supreme Court stated:

> It would ignore reality to suggest that racial and ethnic prejudices do not exist or that all manifestations of those prejudices have been eliminated. . . . The question, however, is

whether the reality of private biases and the possible injury they might inflict are permissible considerations for removal of an infant child from the custody of its natural mother. We have little difficulty in concluding that they are not. The Constitution cannot control such prejudices but neither can it tolerate them. (Ibid., p. 433)

The Supreme Court repeatedly has emphasized the guiding role of parents in the upbringing of their children and the responsibility of parents to "inculcate and pass down many of our most cherished values, moral and cultural" (*Wisconsin v. Yoder,* 1972, p. 233). This "unique role" of the family, the Court has said, entitles biological parents to substantive due process protections and, although not without disagreement among the justices, justifies limitations on the freedom of minors.

Parham v. J. R., 1979.   A long-awaited Supreme Court decision was made in this case challenging the rights of parents to institutionalize their children for mental health treatment and of the state to institutionalize its wards (that is, children under its supervision and/or in its custody) without due process procedures on behalf of the child. Georgia's law, in relevant part, stated:

> The superintendent of any facility may receive for observation and diagnosis any individual under 18 years of age for whom such application is made by his parent or guardian. If found to show evidence of mental illness and to be suitable for treatment, such person may be given care and treatment at such facility and such person may be detained by such facility for such period and under such conditions as may be authorized by law. (Ga. Code Section 88-503.1)
>
> The superintendent of the facility shall discharge any voluntary patient who has recovered from his mental illness or who has sufficiently improved that the superintendent determines that hospitalization of the patient is no longer desirable. (Ga. Code Section 88-503.2)

J. R. was a neglected child who was removed from his natural parents at 3 months and placed in seven different foster homes prior to admission to the state hospital at 7 years of age on request of the Department of Family and Children Services. He was assessed to be borderline retarded with an unsocialized, aggressive reaction of childhood and suitable for admission and treatment. His case was reviewed periodically. Unsuccessful efforts were made to place him in foster homes during the hospitalization.

On these facts, the Supreme Court concluded that the traditional presumption that natural bonds of affection lead parents to act in the best interests of their children should apply. Parents should retain a substantial if not the dominant role in the decision to voluntarily commit their children to an institution. Furthermore, Georgia law provided for informal medical review thirty days after admission to state hospitals, and the Court underscored as protection to the child the authority of doctors to make medical judgments. Thus the decision reinforced not only the authority of parents and agents of the state over children, but also the authority of the medical profession in confining children for medical treatment.

Justice Brennan, concurring in part and dissenting in part, noted that even under ideal circumstances, psychiatric diagnosis and decisions about therapy are uncertain; that when a child is institutionalized by his or her parents, there has already been a break in family autonomy; and that parental authority should not stand in the way of a child's constitutional rights. Further, children held in mental hospitals are "not only deprived of physical liberty; they are also deprived of friends, family, and community, and at risk of stigma as well. They live in unnatural surroundings under the continuous and detailed control of strangers" (*Parham v. J. R.,* 1979, p. 632). Brennan questioned the traditional presumption that parents will act in their child's best interests when making commitment decisions and said "a child who has been ousted from his family has even greater need for an independent advocate" (Ibid., p. 631).

Santosky v. Kramer, 1982.   The New York law provided that a child could be declared permanently neglected using a "fair preponderance of the evidence" standard, and on the basis of that declaration, the court could permanently terminate parental rights.

    The Santoskys had lost custody of three children on petitions filed by the local Department of Social Services alleging neglect of the oldest child, physical abuse of the second child, and "immediate removal necessary to avoid imminent danger to his life or health" of the third child within three days of birth. The children were placed in foster care, where they remained for about five years before the petition to terminate parental rights.

    While the Santosky children were in foster care, the Department of Social Services offered the parents training by a mother's aide, a nutritional aide, and a public health nurse and counseling at a family planning clinic. In addition, psychiatric treatment and vocational training were offered to the father and counseling at a family service center to the mother. Eventually the department filed a termination petition stating that the parents' response to their efforts was "marginal at best": They wholly disregarded some of the available services and used others only sporadically. Infrequent visits between parents and children had been "at best superficial and devoid of any real emotional content" (*Santosky v. Kramer,* 1982, p. 751). The New York Family Court terminated parental rights. The parents appealed, alleging that the New York statute under which the termination of their rights occurred violated the due process clause of the Fourteenth Amendment. Without expressing any opinion on the merits, the Court held that the appropriate question before them was "What is the standard of proof that should be used in termination of parental rights proceedings?" The justices, in a five-to-four decision, ruled that the due process clause of the Fourteenth Amendment demands more than "a fair preponderance of the evidence" before terminating irrevocably the parent–child relationship. Allegations must be supported by at least "clear and convincing evidence."

    The Court stated:

> A majority of the States has concluded that a "clear and convincing evidence" standard of proof strikes a fair balance between the rights of the natural parents and the States' legitimate concerns. We hold that such a standard adequately conveys to the factfinder the level of subjective certainty about his factual conclusions necessary to satisfy due process. We further hold that determination of the precise burden equal to or greater than that standard is a matter of state law left to state legislatures and state courts. (*Santosky v. Kramer,* 1982, p. 769)

Troxel v. Granville, 2000.   This case involves third-party visitation rights over the objection of the parent. The Troxels were paternal grandparents to two children whose mother was Granville. Granville and the children's father, who were not married, ended their relationship in June 1991. The father lived with his parents, the Troxels, until he committed suicide in May 1993. During the time he resided with his parents, the children visited in the Troxels' home each weekend. After his death, the Troxels continued to see the children regularly. In October 1993, Granville told them she wished to limit their visitation to one visit per month.

The Troxels filled a petition in December 1993 requesting two weekends of overnight visitation per month and two weeks of visitation each summer. The state of Washington's statute at Section 26.10.160(3) states, "any person may petition for visitation rights at any time including, but not limited to, custody proceedings. The court may grant such visitation rights whenever visitation may serve the best interests of the child whether or not there has been any change of circumstances." Granville did not object to all visitation. However, she asked the court to limit the visitation to one day per month. The Washington Superior Court entered an order in 1995 granting visitation one weekend per month, one week during the summer, and four hours on both of the petitioning grandparents' birthdays (*Troxel v. Granville,* 2000, p. 61).

Granville appealed to the Washington Court of Appeals. Because there were no written findings of facts and conclusions of law, the Washington Court of Appeals remanded the case to the Superior Court. The Superior Court, in its written opinion, found that visitation was in the children's best interests because the Troxels were part of a large, loving family located in the area and provided the children access to cousins and music. The Washington Court of Appeals reversed the lower court's visitation order and dismissed the Troxels' petition for visitation stating that nonparents lacked standing to seek visitation under the statute unless a custody action was pending. The Washington Supreme Court granted the Troxels' petition for review and affirmed the decision. However, it disagreed with the rationale for the decision, that is, that they lacked standing to seek visitation under the statute. The Washington Supreme Court found that the Troxels had "standing to seek visitation irrespective of whether a custody action was pending" (Ibid., p. 62). The Washington Supreme Court held that the statute "unconstitutionally infringes on the fundamental right of parents to rear their children" (Ibid., p. 63).

The Supreme Court of the United States framed the issue before it as "we are asked to decide whether Section 26.10.160930, as applied to Tommie Granville and her family violates the Federal Constitution" (Ibid., p. 65). It stated, "the interest of parents in the care, custody, and control of their children—is perhaps the oldest of the fundamental liberty interests recognized by this Court" (Ibid., p. 65). In its opinion, it recounted the precedent established in this area in the cases discussed previously in this chapter and concluded:

> In light of this extensive precedent, it cannot now be doubted that the Due Process Clause of the Fourteenth Amendment protects the fundamental right of parents to make decisions concerning the care, custody, and control of their children. (Ibid., p. 67)

The Court held the Washington statute to be "breathtakingly broad" and, as applied in the current case, unconstitutional because it "violated her due process right to make decisions concerning the care, custody, and control of her daughters" (Ibid., p. 75). In the opinion of the Court, the Washington statute permitted the judge sole discretion to determine what was in the best interest of the children without any finding of parental unfitness. Justice O'Connor, writing for the Court, said,

> In an ideal world, parents might always seek to cultivate the bonds between grandparents and their grandchildren. Needless to say, however, our world is far from perfect, and in it the decision whether such an intergenerational relationship would be beneficial in any specific case is for the parent to make in the first instance. And, if a fit parent's decision of the kind

at issue here becomes subject to judicial review, the court must accord at least some special weight to the parent's own determination. (Ibid., p. 70)

The opinion goes on to state:

> We do not consider the primary constitutional question passed on by the Washington Supreme Court—whether the Due Process Clause requires all nonparental visitation statutes to include a showing of harm or potential harm to the child as a condition precedent to granting visitation. We do not, and need not, define today the precise scope of the parental due process right in the visitation context. In this respect, we agree with Justice Kennedy that the constitutionality of any standard for awarding visitation turns on the specific manner in which that standard is applied and that the constitutional protections in this area are best "elaborated with care." (dissenting opinion at 101) Because much state-court adjudication in this context occurs on a case-by-case basis, we would be hesitant to hold that specific nonparental visitation statutes violate the Due Process Clause as a per se matter. (Ibid., p. 73)

Justice Stevens, in a *dissenting opinion,* states,

> A parent's rights with respect to her child have thus never been regarded as absolute, but rather are limited by the existence of actual, developed relationship with a child, and are tied to the presence or absence of some embodiment of family. These limitations have arisen, not simply out of the definition of parenthood itself, but because of this Court's assumption that a parent's interests in a child must be balanced against the State's long-recognized interests as parens patriae, . . . , and, critically, the child's own complementary interest in preserving relationships that serve her welfare and protection. . . . While this Court has not yet had occasion to elucidate the nature of a child's liberty interests in preserving established familial or family-like bonds, . . . , it seems to me extremely likely that, to the extent parents and families have fundamental liberty interests in preserving such intimate relationships, so, too, do children have these interests, and so, too, must their interests be balanced in the equation. At a minimum, our prior cases recognizing that children are, generally speaking, constitutionally protected actors require this Court reject any suggestion that when it comes to parental rights, children as so much as chattel. . . . The constitutional protection against arbitrary state interference with parental rights should not be extended to prevent the States from protecting children against the arbitrary exercise of parental authority that is not in fact motivated by an interest in the welfare of the child. (Ibid., p. 88)

His dissenting opinion concludes,

> It seems clear to me that the Due Process Clause of the Fourteenth Amendment leaves room for States to consider the impact on the child of possibly arbitrary parental decisions that neither serve nor are motivated by the best interests of the child. (Ibid., p. 89)

So, based on the *Troxel* decision, the answer to the question, "What are the constitutionally permitted circumstances under which a court may grant third-party visitation over the objection of the parent?" is "It depends." What we can be certain of is that all fifty states who had grandparent or other third-party visitation statutes at the time of the *Troxel* decision have reviewed those statutes to ensure that they are not "breathtakingly broad" and that they protect the due process rights of parents by affording greater weight to the parent's decision provided there has been no finding of unfitness of the parent. Justice Stevens's dissent, while it offers no legal weight, does broadcast a message to states that their statutes can, and perhaps should, also include protections for the liberty interests of children in maintaining relationships with third parties carefully balanced in relation to the parents' liberty interest in their care, custody, and control.

Ferguson v. City of Charleston, 2001. At issue in this case was the constitutionality of a policy developed by a Charleston public hospital, in cooperation with law enforcement. This policy provided, among other things, that the hospital would order urine drug screens on women suspected of using cocaine, report women who tested positive for cocaine to the local police, and refer them for substance abuse treatment services. The record is not clear as to the specificity of consent to testing for drug use, if any, required by the women.

Ten women who received obstetrical care at the hospital were arrested. They challenged the validity of the policy stating "warrantless and nonconsensual drug tests conducted for criminal investigatory purposes were unconstitutional searches." The city of Charleston argued that the women had consented to medical treatment and, if that consent was insufficient for reporting their positive results to the police, that there existed a non-law-enforcement purpose—that is, providing appropriate medical treatment to the pregnant woman, the fetus, and the child at birth. The case was submitted to a jury in the District Court. The jury found that there had been consent. The women appealed stating that the evidence was not sufficient to support the jury's finding that they had consented. The Court of Appeals for the Fourth Circuit affirmed the decision of the District Court, but without addressing the question of consent. Rather, their decision relied on Supreme Court cases recognizing "special needs" circumstances that might abrogate the need for consent and/or warrants under the Fourth Amendment, the second argument advanced by the City.

The Supreme Court granted certiorari. The Court framed the issue before it as

> whether the interest in using the threat of criminal sanctions to deter pregnant women from using cocaine can justify a departure from the general rule that an official nonconsensual search is unconstitutional if not authorized by a valid search warrant. (*Ferguson v. City of Charleston,* 2001, p. 1)

The Court reversed the Fourth Circuit and remanded the case for a decision on the consent issue. Its decision distinguished the *Ferguson* case from its previous "special needs" case decisions, on which the Fourth Circuit relied, stating

> Because the hospital seeks to justify its authority to conduct drug tests and to turn the results over to law enforcement agents without the knowledge or consent of the patients, this case differs from the four previous cases in which we have considered whether comparable drug tests "fit within the closely guarded category of constitutionally permissible suspicionless searches." . . .
>
> In each of those cases, we employed a balancing test that weighed the intrusion on the individual's interest in privacy against the "special needs" that supported the program. As an initial matter, we note that the invasion of privacy in this case is far more substantial than in those cases. In the previous four cases, there was no misunderstanding about the purpose of the test or the potential use of the test results, and there were protections against the dissemination of the results to third parties. The use of an adverse test result to disqualify one from eligibility for a particular benefit, such as a promotion or an opportunity to participate in an extracurricular activity, involves a less serious intrusion on privacy than the unauthorized

dissemination of such results to third parties. The reasonable expectation of privacy enjoyed by the typical patient undergoing diagnostic tests in a hospital is that the results of those tests will not be shared with nonmedical personnel without her consent. . . .

In each of those earlier cases, the "special need" that was advanced as a justification for the absence of a warrant or individualized suspicion was one divorced from the State's general interest in law enforcement. . . . In this case, however, the central and indispensable feature of the policy from its inception was the use of law enforcement to coerce the patients into substance abuse treatment. This fact distinguishes this case from circumstances in which physicians or psychologists, in the course of ordinary medical procedures aimed at helping the patient herself, come across information that under rules of law or ethics is subject to reporting requirements, which no one has challenged here. (Ibid., pp. 9–13)

In summary, the Supreme Court decisions have established that parents have full right to choose to send their child to a public or a private school; to refuse to adhere to compulsory school attendance statutes when they can show that compliance is in violation of their religious beliefs; to institutionalize their child for mental health treatment provided there are appropriate assessment, evaluation, and periodic reviews that support the need for the institutionalization; to have a clear and convincing standard of proof applied in proceedings to terminate their parental rights; to have their decisions about third-party visitations with their child given weight in the courts; and to be free from warrantless or nonconsensual drug screenings during pregnancy.

Parental Rights of the Unwed Father

Within recent decades the unwed father has gained legal recognition of some aspects of parental rights to his nonmarital child. A chain of U.S. Supreme Court cases has established that the father must have developed a significant and personal relationship with his nonmarital child to warrant constitutional protection in adoption proceedings. To date, the fact of biological relationship alone between father and nonmarital child does not merit protection. Unwed fathers must "grasp the opportunity" of their biological connection to their child to form an actual parenting relationship. What is protected, then, is a "liberty interest" in a "developed parent–child relationship resulting from the father's shouldering significant responsibility with respect to daily supervision, education, protection and care of his child that has been recognized as an interest with due process safeguard" (Gitlin, 1987, p. 2).

Stanley v. Illinois, 1972.   Illinois law provided that the state could assume custody of children of married parents, divorced parents, and unmarried mothers only after a hearing and proof of neglect. The children of unmarried fathers, however, are declared dependent children, that is, children who have no surviving parent or guardian. Furthermore, Illinois law stated "parent means the father and mother of a legitimate child, or the survivor of them, or the natural mother of an illegitimate child, and includes any adoptive parent" (*Stanley v. Illinois,* 1972, p. 650). Under a dependency proceeding, the state is required only to show that the father was not married to the mother and need not prove unfitness, as required for married mothers and fathers or unmarried mothers.

Stanley was an unwed father who had lived with the mother of his children, provided some financial support, and served in the parental role. After the death of the mother, the children were declared dependent and made wards of the state without any hearing to determine

Stanley's fitness. Stanley was excluded from a voice in the state's effort to place his children in adoptive homes. He appealed, alleging that the Illinois law deprived him and other unwed fathers of due process and equal protection rights granted by the Fourteenth Amendment.

The Court stated:

> The private interest here, that of a man in the children he has sired and raised, undeniably warrants deference and, absent a powerful countervailing interest, protection. It is plain that the interest of the parent in the companionship, care, custody, and management of his or her children comes to this Court with a momentum for respect lacking when appeal is made to liberties which derive merely from shifting economic arrangements.
>
> But we are here not asked to evaluate the legitimacy of the state ends, rather, to determine whether the means used to achieve these ends are constitutionally defensible. What is the State interest in separating children from fathers without a hearing designed to determine if the father is unfit in a particular disputed case? We observe that the State registers no gain toward its declared goals when it separates children from the custody of fit parents. Indeed if Stanley is a fit father, the State spites its own articulated goals when it needlessly separates him from his family.
>
> The State's interest in caring for Stanley's children is *de minimis* if Stanley is shown to be a fit father. It insists on presuming rather than proving Stanley's unfitness solely because it is more convenient to presume than to prove. Under the Due Process Clause that advantage is insufficient to justify refusing a father a hearing when the issue at stake is the dismemberment of his family. . . . We have concluded that all Illinois parents are constitutionally entitled to a hearing on their fitness before their children are removed from their custody. It follows that denying such a hearing to Stanley and those like him while granting it to other Illinois parents is inescapably contrary to the Equal Protection Clause. (Ibid., pp. 652–658)

Quilloin v. Walcott, 1978. Georgia law provided both parents' consent to the adoption of a child born in wedlock, whereas only the mother's consent was required for the adoption of an illegitimate child, that is, a child born out of wedlock. The law further provided that the father could acquire veto rights over the adoption if he had legitimated the child through marriage to the child's mother or acknowledgment of paternity.

Quilloin, the father, had never exercised custody over his child nor assumed any significant responsibility for the child's daily care, protection, supervision, or education. For eleven years he had not availed himself of the opportunity under Georgia law to legitimate his nonmarital child and thus gain full parental rights. He petitioned to block the adoption of the child by the mother's husband after the mother had consented and the husband filed a petition to adopt. He did not seek custody or object to the child continuing to live with the mother and her husband. The child had resided with and been parented by the mother's husband for almost nine years. The Georgia courts conducted a trial on his petitions stating "these matters are being tried . . . to allow the biological father . . . a right to be heard with respect to any issue or other thing upon which he desire(s) to be heard, including his fitness as a parent . . ." (Ibid., p. 250). Based on the findings at the trial, the Georgia courts concluded that the adoption was "in the child's best interests" and that granting either legitimation or visitation rights would not be in the child's best interests. On that basis it found that Quilloin had no right to object to the adoption. Quilloin appealed, alleging that the Georgia law as applied violated the equal protection and due process clauses of the Fourteenth Amendment. He contended that he should be entitled to the same power to veto the adoption as the unwed mother and married or divorced parents.

The Court stated, "*Stanley* left unresolved the degree of protection a State must afford to the rights of an unwed father in a situation, such as that presented here, in which the countervailing interests are more substantial" (Ibid., p. 248). It further determined the issue before it to be "Whether, in the circumstances of this case and in light of the authority granted by Georgia law to married fathers, appellant's (Quilloin's) interests were adequately protected by a 'best interests of the child' standard" (Ibid., p. 254).

The Court responded:

> We have little doubt that the Due Process Clause would be offended if a State were to attempt to force the breakup of a natural family, over the objections of the parents and their children, without some showing of unfitness and for the sole reason that to do so was thought to be in the children's best interest. . . . But this is not a case in which the unwed father at any time had, or sought, actual or legal custody of his child. Nor is this a case in which the proposed adoption would place the child with a new set of parents with whom the child had never before lived. Rather, the result of the adoption in this case is to give full recognition to a family unit already in existence, a result desired by all concerned, except appellant. Whatever might be required in other situations, we cannot say that the State was required in this situation to find anything more than that the adoption, and denial of legitimation, were in the "best interests of the child." (Ibid., p. 255)

The Court found no violation of the equal protection clause. It stated:

> We think appellant's interests are readily distinguishable from those of a separated or divorced father, and accordingly believe that the State could permissibly give appellant less veto authority than it provides to a married father. . . . He has never exercised actual or legal custody over his child, and thus has never shouldered any significant responsibility with respect to the daily supervision, education, protection, or care of the child. Appellant does not complain of his exemption from these responsibilities and, indeed, he does not even now seek custody of his child. In contrast, legal custody of children is, of course, a central aspect of the marital relationship, and even a father whose marriage has broken apart will have borne full responsibility for the rearing of his children during the period of the marriage. (*Quilloin v. Walcott,* 1978, p. 256)

Caban v. Mohammed, 1979. New York law provided that an unwed mother, but not an unwed father, could block the adoption of a child by withholding consent.

Caban lived with the mother and their two children, his name appeared on the birth certificates of the children, he had contributed to their support, and, even after the mother left with the children to marry another man, he continued to see them frequently. The mother's new husband subsequently sought to adopt the children with the mother's consent but without the consent of the biological father.

Caban petitioned to block the adoption on the basis that the New York law violated the equal protection clause of the Fourteenth Amendment because it bore no substantial relation to an important state interest. The Court stated:

> The State's interest in providing for the well being of illegitimate children is an important one. We do not question that the best interests of such children often may require their adoption into new families who will give them the stability of a normal, two-parent home. Moreover, adoption will remove the stigma under which illegitimate children suffer. But the

unquestioned right of the State to further these desirable ends by legislation is not in itself sufficient to justify the gender-based distinction of § 111. Rather, under the relevant cases applying the Equal Protection Clause it must be shown that the distinction is structured reasonable to further these ends. . . . Such a statutory classification must be reasonable, not arbitrary, and must rest upon some ground of difference having a fair and substantial relation to the object of the legislation, so that all persons similarly circumstanced shall be treated alike. . . . We find that the distinction in § 111 between unmarried mothers and unmarried fathers, as illustrated by this case, does not bear a substantial relation to the State's interest in providing adoptive homes for its illegitimate children. (*Caban v. Mohammed,* 1979, p. 391)

The effect of New York's classification is to discriminate against unwed fathers even when their identity is known and they have manifested a significant paternal interest in the child. The facts of this case illustrated the harshness of classifying unwed fathers as being invariably less qualified and entitled than mothers to exercise a concerned judgment as to the fate of their children. . . . We conclude that this undifferentiated distinction between unwed mothers and unwed fathers, applicable in all circumstances where adoption of a child of theirs is at issue, does not bear a substantial relationship to the State's asserted interests. (Ibid., p. 394)

In summary, uncertainty still persists as to the scope of constitutional protections of the rights of the unwed father with respect to his nonmarital children. However, the Supreme Court decisions have established that unwed fathers have the right to be notified and to be heard when the matter of termination of parental rights and adoption of their illegitimate child is concerned, and, if they have had a substantial relationship with their child, they have a right to a "determination of fitness" equal to that afforded married parents or unmarried mothers before their children can be taken from them. Many states have statutes and procedural rules that further clarify the rights of unwed fathers. As long as these laws and rules afford the unwed father the protections of notice and opportunity to be heard, and they support a legitimate state interest without discrimination on the basis of race or gender, they will most likely pass constitutional challenges.

Decisions Limiting Parental Rights

The Supreme Court has also issued decisions in which the rights of parents in the choices affecting their children were limited. For the most part, this line of cases recognizes that children have rights separate from their parents and that the states have interests in protecting those rights.

Prince v. Massachusetts, 1944. Massachusetts law prohibited children under 12 years of age from selling newspapers, magazines, and periodicals in public places. Further, it was unlawful for any parent or guardian to permit a minor to engage in such behavior. The aunt of a 9-year-old girl gave her Jehovah's Witness magazines to distribute on the streets at 5 cents per copy. The aunt was convicted of violating the law. Her appeal alleged that the Massachusetts law violated the free exercise of religion provision in the First Amendment. The Supreme Court stated:

The state's authority over children's activities is broader than over like adult activities. . . . What may be wholly permissible for adults therefore may not be so for children, either with or without their parents' presence. . . . Parents may be free to become martyrs themselves. But it does not follow that they are free, in identical circumstances, to make martyrs of their children before they have reached the age of full and legal discretion when they can make that choice for themselves. . . . We think that with reference to the public proclaiming of religion, upon the streets and in other similar public places, the power of the state to control the conduct of children reaches beyond the scope of its authority over adults, as is true in the case of other freedoms, and the rightful boundary of its power has not been crossed in this case. (*Prince v. Massachusetts,* 1944, pp. 168–170)

Baltimore City Department of Social Services v. Bouknight, 1990. The Fifth Amendment of the Constitution provides, in part, that "no person shall be compelled in any criminal case to be a witness against himself, nor be deprived of life, liberty, or property, without due process of law." Bouknight was the mother of an adjudicated abused child who was in her custody under the supervision of Baltimore City Department of Social Services (BCDSS). A petition was filed to return the child to foster care based on the mother's failure to follow the court-ordered treatment plan. She refused to produce the child. The court held her in contempt and ordered her imprisoned until she produced the child or revealed to the court his whereabouts. She appealed this order claiming that it violated her Fifth Amendment rights. The Court of Appeals of Maryland found that the contempt order unconstitutionally compelled Bouknight to admit through the act of production "a measure of continuing control and dominion over Maurice's person" in circumstances in which "Bouknight had a reasonable apprehension that she will be prosecuted." BCDSS appealed. The Supreme Court reversed the judgment of the Maryland Court of Appeals, stating:

> Once Maurice was adjudicated a child in need of assistance, his care and safety became the particular object of the State's regulatory interests. . . . By accepting care of Maurice subject to the custodial order's conditions . . . Bouknight submitted to the routine operation of the regulatory system and agreed to hold Maurice in a manner consonant with the State's regulatory interests and subject to inspection by BCDSS. (*Baltimore City Department of Social Services v. Bouknight,* 1990, p. 559)

In summary, the Supreme Court has supported the states, allowing them greater authority than parents in the regulation and enforcement of child labor (the age at which children can work, the types of jobs or labor they can perform, the hours they can work, etc.) and child protection.

Parental Authority and the Reproductive Rights of Minors

No issue of child, parent, and society rights and responsibilities has attracted and sustained more controversy than the question of the minor's right to control his or her own reproductive capacities by access to contraception or abortion.

Roe v. Wade, 1973. This well-known case gave constitutional protection to the right of women to choose abortion early in pregnancy and the right of the state to regulate the termination of pregnancy after "viability of the fetus," that is, "when the life of the unborn child may be continued indefinitely outside the womb by natural or artificial life supportive systems" (*Roe v. Wade,* 1973, p. 163).

Planned Parenthood of Central Missouri v. Danforth, 1976. A Missouri statute required the written consent of a parent or person *in loco parentis* for an abortion during the first twelve weeks of pregnancy of an unmarried woman under the age of 18 years unless there was a certification by a physician that abortion was necessary to preserve the life of the mother. The Court found the statute unconstitutional and stated:

> . . . the State may not impose a blanket provision, such as § 3 (4), requiring the consent of a parent or person *in loco parentis* as a condition for abortion of an unmarried minor during the first 12 weeks of her pregnancy. Just as with the requirement of consent from the spouse, so here, the State does not have the constitutional authority to give a third party an absolute, and possibly arbitrary, veto over the decision of the physician and his patient to terminate the patient's pregnancy, regardless of the reason for withholding the consent. Constitutional rights do not mature and come into being magically only when one attains the state-defined age of majority. Minors, as well as adults, are protected by the Constitution and possess constitutional rights. . . . The Court indeed, however, long has recognized that the State has somewhat broader authority to regulate the activities of children than of adults. . . . It remains, then, to examine whether there is any significant state interest in conditioning an abortion on the consent of a parent or person in loco parentis that is not present in the case of an adult. (*Planned Parenthood of Central Missouri v. Danforth,* 1976, pp. 74–75)

The Court went on to discuss the argument that the state's interest was in safeguarding the family unit and the parent's authority. It concluded that an absolute veto power did nothing to safeguard the family unit or the parent's authority. The Court stated clearly that this opinion did not preclude state regulation of abortion decision making for minors; rather it precluded a state statute that provided absolute veto power over that decision to a parent or person *in loco parentis.*

Bellotti v. Baird, 1979.   A Massachusetts's statute required a pregnant unmarried minor to have the consent of her parent or the permission of a judge of a state court of general jurisdiction before she could obtain an abortion. Massachusetts passed this statute after the *Danforth* decision and provided an alternative procedure—that is, the permission of a judge—to ensure that the parent did not have absolute veto authority over the unmarried minor's abortion decision. The Court affirmed the desirability of fostering parental involvement in a minor's large decisions and noted that deference to parents may be appropriate with respect to a range of choices facing a minor. However, the Court stated:

> Although it satisfies constitutional standards in large part, § 12S falls short of them in two respects: First, it permits judicial authorization for an abortion to be withheld from a minor who is found by the superior court to be mature and fully competent to make this decision independently. Second, it requires parental consultation or notification in every instance, without affording the pregnant minor an opportunity to receive an independent judicial determination that she is mature enough to consent or that an abortion would be in her best interests. (*Bellotti v. Baird,* 1979, p. 651)

After the Court decisions discussed above, some states sought to maintain parental involvement in unmarried minors' abortion decisions by enacting legislation that mandated *notice* to parents, rather than consent.

H. L. v. Matheson, 1981.   A Utah law required a physician to notify, if possible, the parents or guardians of a minor on whom the physician intended to perform an abortion. Neither parents nor judges had veto power over the minor's abortion decision. Her physician had advised a 15-year-old pregnant girl, living with her parents, that an abortion would be in her best medical interests. Because of the criminal liability involved, he refused to perform the abortion without notifying her parents. The girl argued that this notification requirement restricted her right to privacy to obtain an abortion and to enter into a doctor–patient relationship. The Court upheld the law and stated:

> That the requirement of notice to parents may inhibit some minors from seeking abortions is not a valid basis to void the statute as applied to appellant and the class properly before us. The Constitution does not compel a state to fine-tune its statutes so as to encourage or facilitate abortions. To the contrary, state action "encouraging childbirth except in the most urgent circumstances" is "rationally related to the legitimate governmental objective of protecting potential life." . . . As applied to the class properly before us, the statute plainly serves important state interests, is narrowly drawn to protect only those interests, and does not violate any guarantees of the Constitution. (*H. L. v. Matheson,* 1981, p. 413)

Ohio v. Akron Center for Reproductive Health, 1990.   An Ohio law required a physician or other person contemplating performing an abortion on a pregnant unmarried person under the age of 18 to notify at least one parent or to have a judge's order permitting the minor to consent to the abortion (a judicial bypass). To secure a judicial bypass order, the minor was required to present "clear and convincing proof that she has sufficient maturity and information to make the abortion decision herself, that one of her parents has engaged in a pattern of physical, emotional, or sexual abuse against her, or that notice is not in her best interests" (*Ohio v. Akron Center for Reproductive Health,* 1990, p. 502). The Court, after much discussion of the compatibility of the Ohio statute with the requirements imposed by the prior decisions of the Court on the issues of parental consent and parental notification, stated, "It would deny all dignity to the family to say that the State cannot take this reasonable step in regulating its health professions to ensure that, in most cases, a young woman will receive guidance and understanding from a parent" (Ibid., p. 520).

Hodgson v. Minnesota, 1990.   The Court held unconstitutional the section of Minnesota law requiring physicians or their agent to notify both parents of an unmarried person under the age of 18 years of the intent to perform an abortion and to wait 48 hours before carrying out the procedure, while holding constitutional that section of the law that provided for judicial bypass to two-parent notification when the minor could establish that she was mature and capable of giving informed consent, that she was the victim of parental abuse or neglect, or that it was in her best interests to have an abortion without notice to one or both of her parents and the judge authorized the physician to perform the abortion. In holding the two-parent notification provision unconstitutional, the Court stated:

> It is equally clear that the requirement that both parents be notified, whether or not both wish to be notified or have assumed responsibility for the upbringing of the child, does not reasonably further any legitimate state interest. The usual justification for a parental consent or

notification provision is that it supports the authority of a parent who is presumed to act in the minor's best interest and thereby assures that the minor's decision to terminate her pregnancy is knowing, intelligent, and deliberate. To the extent that such an interest is legitimate, it would be fully served by a requirement the minor notify one parent who can then seek the counsel of his or her mate or any other party, when such advice and support is deemed necessary to help the child make a difficult decision. . . . Not only does the two-parent notification fail to serve any state interest with respect to functioning families, it disserves the state interest in protecting and assisting the minor with respect to dysfunctional families. (*Hodgson v. Minnesota,* 1990, p. 450)

Carey v. Population Services International, 1977.   A New York statute prohibited the sale and distribution of nonprescription contraceptives to minors under the age of 16 years. In its decision to strike down the statute, the Court stated that "the right to privacy in connection with decisions affecting procreation extends to minors as well as to adults" and that inhibiting minors' privacy rights was valid only to serve "a significant state interest," one that would not be present in the case of an adult. There was substantial doubt, the Court said, that limiting access to contraception would in fact act as a meaningful deterrent to sexual activity among the young, as had been contended (*Carey v. Population Services International,* 1977, pp. 693–694).

The decision did not abate the controversy. Congress subsequently amended Title X of the Public Health Service Act that governed the federal funding of family planning services. The statutory amendment required that such federally funded programs encourage "family participation" in the provision of contraceptive services "to the extent practical." The Reagan administration, through the secretary of Health and Human Services, stated its intent to implement the amendment by requiring federally funded family planning programs to notify the parents of "unemancipated minors" who sought contraceptive services. Criticism and support for the proposed regulations came from many sides. The rules were amended to provide that

> A project is not required to comply with paragraph (a)(12)(i)(A) [the parental notification provision] of this section where the project director or clinic head (when specifically so designated by the project director) determines that notification will result in physical harm to the minor by a parent or guardian. 42 CFR 59.5 (a)(12)(i)(B).

Several lawsuits were filed even after this amendment to the rules. The Court of Appeals of the District of Columbia enjoined the implementation of these rules in *Planned Parenthood of America, Inc. v. Heckler,* 719 F.2d 650 (1983). Thus the parental notification provisions never went into effect.

The area of parental authority over the reproductive rights of minors has been and continues to be surrounded in controversial debate. The Supreme Court decisions have established that minors have the right to receive contraceptive services without parental permission; that they have a right to abortions; that their parents or persons acting *in loco parentis* may not have an absolute veto power over their decision to have an abortion; and that they have a right to an independent judicial determination that they are mature enough to make a decision to have an abortion or that an abortion is in their best interests. However, the Court has not precluded states from enacting legislation requiring or permitting notification to a parent of the minor's decision to have an abortion by the medical professional who will perform the abortion.

Rights and Responsibilities of Children

Constitutional Rights

An essential question in any formulation of family social policy is the extent to which children have their own rights and interests independent of their parents, with a claim to their recognition and enforcement. The common law, on which the American legal system is based, provided limited freedom to children because "they needed to be protected against their own actions, while society, in addition, needs to be protected from their 'untutored' behavior" (Nurcombe & Partlett, 1994). The evolution of children's rights in America is divided into four periods: prenineteenth century, 1800 to 1900, 1900 to 1967, and 1967 forward. Prior to the nineteenth century, children were considered their parents' property to do with as they saw fit. In the nineteenth century, with industrialization and urbanization leading to neglect, abandonment, and exploitation of children, benevolent laws and institutions were established to offer protection to children. In the early years of the twentieth century, juvenile courts and the attitude of benevolent oversight of orphaned, abandoned, neglected, abused, and delinquent children predominated. *In re Gault* and *Kent v. United States,* decided by the U.S. Supreme Court in 1966, marked the beginning of the children's legal rights era (Kramer, 2002).

Although the U.S. Constitution makes no reference to children per se, U.S. Supreme Court decisions have afforded children the protections enumerated in the First, Fourth, Fifth, Sixth, Eighth, and Fourteenth Amendments (Jacobs, 1995). The reproductive rights cases, presented in the Rights and Responsibilities of Parents section, provide a framework for understanding the Court's perspectives on balancing the interests of children's privacy rights and parents' rights to decide matters affecting their children within the constitutional context. In this section, we present those case decisions that focus specifically on children's due process and equal protection rights within the scope of child welfare practice areas, through discussions of Supreme Court decisions.

Brieland and Lemmon (1985) observed that "laws dealing with youths are characterized by paradoxes and inconsistencies" (p. 15). These paradoxes and inconsistencies are explained by the balancing of interests present in all legislation and case decisions involving children's rights: The interests of the family (privacy and autonomy), the child (self-determination, privacy, and autonomy), and the state (*parens patriae*) must be addressed in every case brought before the Court. Each decision rests on how the Court resolves the fundamental interests being attacked.

The juvenile court system's procedures for handling delinquency matters sparked the children's rights under the Constitution era. What had been designed as a benevolent system to handle child abuse, neglect, and delinquency so as to protect children from the trauma of the adult legal system was found to be constitutionally deficient.

Kent v. United States, 1966.   A District of Columbia law provided that a person 16 years of age or older charged with an offense that would be a felony if committed by an adult could be waived to the adult court for trial after a full investigation by the juvenile judge.

Kent was charged with robbery, rape, and breaking and entering. He was waived. He challenged the waiver on the grounds that he was not afforded a hearing, no reasons for the waiver were provided to him, and his lawyer was denied access to his records. The Court held that under the due process clause, a juvenile was entitled to a hearing, full access to records and reports used by the court in arriving at its decision, and a statement of the reason for the juvenile court's decision.

In re Gault, 1967.   Gault was a 15-year-old charged with making a lewd telephone call to a neighbor. He was on probation at the time of the call. He was arrested without notification to his parents, detained, not provided counsel, and never afforded a formal hearing. He was found delinquent and committed to the state training school until the age of majority. He challenged the proceedings. The Court, in reversing the decision of the Arizona Supreme Court, established the due process requirements for juvenile delinquency hearings: (1) notice of sufficient detail to mount a defense; (2) right to be represented by counsel and, if necessary, right to court-appointed and -paid counsel if child and parents could not afford counsel; (3) privilege against self-incrimination; and (4) right to review evidence and cross-examine witnesses. Justice Fortas made two statements in this decision that challenged the basic foundation of the juvenile court system and signaled the scope of constitutional protections for juveniles:

> . . . neither the Fourteenth Amendment nor the Bill of Rights is for adults alone. (*In re Gault,* 1967, p. 13)
>
> . . . juvenile court history has again demonstrated that unbridled discretion, however benevolently motivated, is frequently a poor substitute for principle and procedure. (Ibid., p. 18)

In re Winship, 1970.   Winship was a 12-year-old charged with stealing. He was adjudicated delinquent. The Court held that the standard of proof in a delinquency case is "beyond a reasonable doubt," the same standard required in adult criminal proceedings. The Court stated:

> The constitutional safeguard of proof beyond a reasonable doubt is as much required during the adjudicatory stage of a delinquency proceeding as are those constitutional safeguards applied in Gault. (*In re Winship,* 1970, p. 363)

McKeiver v. Pennsylvania, 1971.   McKeiver was a 16-year-old charged with robbery, larceny, and receiving stolen property. He was denied a jury trial, adjudicated, and placed on probation. He challenged the denial of a jury trial. The Court held that the fundamental fairness standard in fact-finding procedures for juvenile proceedings as developed by *Gault* and *Winship* did not require a jury trial: "One cannot say that in our legal system the jury is a necessary component of accurate fact-finding" (*McKeiver v. Pennsylvania,* 1971, p. 543). A signal of the willingness of the Court to maintain some of the informalities of the juvenile court system is found in the words of Justice Blackmun:

> If the formalities of the criminal adjudicative process are to be superimposed upon the juvenile court system there is little need for its separate existence. Perhaps that ultimate disillu-

sionment will come one day, but for the moment we are disinclined to give impetus to it. (Ibid., p. 551)

Breed v. Jones, 1975. Jones was a 17-year-old charged with armed robbery. The juvenile court found that he had committed the crime and then determined that he was not suitable for treatment in the juvenile system. It turned him over for prosecution in the adult system. Jones appealed, claiming that this was a violation of the double jeopardy clause of the Fifth Amendment and the due process and equal protection clauses of the Fourteenth Amendment. The double jeopardy clause provides that a state may not bring a person charged with a criminal offense to trial more than once for the same crime. The issue before the Supreme Court was whether the prosecution of Jones as an adult, after the juvenile court had found he had committed the crime, violated the Fifth and Fourteenth Amendments. The Court held that a transfer to adult court for prosecution after an adjudication of delinquency in the juvenile court violates the Fifth Amendment protection against double jeopardy.

> We conclude that respondent was put in jeopardy at the adjudicatory hearing. Jeopardy attached when respondent was "put to trial before the trier of the facts" . . . that is, when the Juvenile Court, as the trier of the facts, began to hear evidence. (*Breed v. Jones,* 1975, p. 531)

In addressing the issue of juvenile court waivers—that is, transfer of its jurisdictional authority in a particular case to the adult system—the Court held that the state must determine whether to handle the case in the juvenile or the adult system prior to engaging in any proceedings that might result in an adjudication. In essence, where the state's statute required the juvenile court to determine if a case is to be waived or not, it must utilize a process to make that determination without requiring evidence sufficient for an adjudication.

Fare v. Michael C., 1979. Michael was a 16-year-old charged with murder. He was taken into custody and advised of his rights under *Miranda* (specifically, the right to an attorney and the right to remain silent). He asked to see his probation officer. The request was denied. He provided information about the murder. When he was charged with the murder, he sought to have the information he provided to police suppressed because it had been obtained in violation of his *Miranda* rights in that his request to see his probation officer constituted a request to remain silent. The Court held that a juvenile's request to speak with his probation officer does not constitute a per se request to remain silent nor is it tantamount to a request for an attorney, because the probation officer "does not fulfill the important role in protecting the rights of the accused juvenile that an attorney plays" (*Fare v. Michael C.,* 1979, pp. 723–724).

Eddings v. Oklahoma, 1982. Eddings was a 16-year-old youth tried as an adult for first-degree murder. He was convicted and sentenced to death. Oklahoma law provided for presentation of evidence of "mitigating circumstances." Eddings offered that he had a history of beatings by his father and of serious emotional disturbance. The judge refused to consider this evidence in mitigation. The Court vacated the death sentence and held that the Eighth and Fourteenth Amendments required individualized consideration of mitigating circumstances in capital cases. It is important to note that the Court did not say that a death penalty could not be imposed, only that the trial judge must consider and weigh all mitigating evidence.

Schall v. Martin, 1984.   New York law authorizes pretrial detention of an accused juvenile delinquent on a finding that there is a serious risk that the youth might commit another offense if not detained pending trial. Martin, a 14-year-old, was arrested for first-degree robbery, second-degree assault, and criminal possession of a weapon. He was detained overnight after lying about where he lived. A hearing was held the following day on a delinquency petition. He was ordered detained pending trial. Five days later a probable cause hearing was held and probable cause was found to exist for all charges. Within fifteen days of the original detention, Martin was adjudicated delinquent and placed on two years' probation. Martin, as well as other juveniles similarly detained, challenged the New York law as violative of the due process and equal protection clauses of the Fourteenth Amendment. The Court's balancing dilemma is quite evident in this discussion from the opinion:

> There is no doubt that the Due Process Clause is applicable in juvenile proceedings. "The problem," we have stressed "is to ascertain the precise impact of the due process requirement upon such proceedings." . . . We have held that certain basic constitutional protections enjoyed by adults accused of crimes also apply to juveniles. . . . But the Constitution does not mandate elimination of all differences in the treatment of juveniles. . . . The State has "a *parens patriae* interest in preserving and promoting the welfare of the child," . . . which makes a juvenile proceeding fundamentally different from an adult criminal trial. We have tried, therefore, to strike a balance—to respect the "informality" and "flexibility" that characterize juvenile proceedings . . . and yet ensure that such proceedings comport with the "fundamental fairness" demanded by the due process clause.
>
> . . . The question before us is whether preventive detention of juveniles pursuant to 320.5(3)(b) is compatible with the "fundamental fairness" required by due process. (*Schall v. Martin,* 1984, p. 263)

The Court held that the referenced statute was not invalid under the due process clause of the Fourteenth Amendment "given the regulatory purpose for the detention and the procedural protections that precede its imposition" (Ibid., p. 281).

Thompson v. Oklahoma, 1988.   Oklahoma law provided that juveniles charged with serious offenses could be tried and sentenced as adults. Thompson was a 15-year-old charged with murder. He was tried as an adult, convicted, and sentenced to death. The question addressed by the Court was whether the "execution of that sentence would violate the constitutional prohibition against the infliction of 'cruel and unusual punishments' because petitioner was only 15 years old at the time of his offense" (*Thompson v. Oklahoma,* 1988, pp. 818–819). The Court, in holding that it would violate the Constitution, stated:

> The authors of the Eighth Amendment drafted a categorical prohibition against the infliction of cruel and unusual punishments, but they made no attempt to define the contours of that category. They delegated that task to future generations of judges who have been guided by the "evolving standards of decency that mark the progress of a maturing society." . . . In performing that task the Court has reviewed the work product of state legislatures and sentencing juries, and has carefully considered the reasons why a civilized society may accept or

reject the death penalty in certain types of cases. Thus, in confronting the question whether the youth of the defendant—more specifically, the fact that he was less than 16 years old at the time of his offense—is sufficient reason for denying the State the power to sentence him to death, we first review relevant legislative enactments, then refer to jury determinations, and finally explain why these indicators of contemporary standards of decency confirm our judgment that such a young person is not capable of acting with the degree of culpability that can justify the ultimate penalty. (Ibid., pp. 821–823)

Stanford v. Kentucky, 1989, and Wilkins v. Missouri, 1989.   Stanford was 17 years and 4 months old when he committed a murder in Kentucky. The juvenile court transferred him for trial as an adult under Kentucky law. He was convicted and sentenced to death. Wilkins was 16 years and 6 months old when he committed murder in Missouri. He was also tried as an adult, convicted, and sentenced to death. The issue before the Court in both cases was whether the imposition of the death sentence for a 16- or 17-year-old constituted cruel and unusual punishment under the Eighth Amendment. The Court held that it did not. It distinguished this decision from that in *Thompson* by finding that, in reviewing state legislative actions and jury decisions as objective indicia of the evolving standards of what constitutes cruel and unusual punishment,

we discern neither a historical nor a modern societal consensus forbidding the imposition of capital punishment on any person who murders at 16 or 17 years of age. Accordingly, we conclude that such punishment does not offend the Eighth Amendment's prohibition against cruel and unusual punishment. (Ibid., p. 380)

On October 21, 2002, the Court denied a petition for writ of habeas corpus in this matter (*In Re Kevin Nigel Stanford,* 537 U.S. (2002); No. 01-10009. Decided October 21, 2002). Stanford asked the court to hold that his execution would be unconstitutional because he was under the age of 18 when he committed the offense. By denying the requested writ, the Court again affirmed its earlier decision that it was not cruel and unusual punishment under the Eighth Amendment to sentence a juvenile to death. This current decision was a 5–4 decision as was the 1989 Stanford decision. Justice Stevens, joined by Justices Souter, Ginsberg, and Breyer, dissented in the October 2002 decision. They argued that given the 2002 Court decision in which it held that it was cruel and unusual punishment to apply the death penalty to mentally retarded persons (*Atkins v. Virginia,* 2002), the Stanford matter should be reconsidered because "the reasons supporting that holding, with one exception, apply with equal or greater force to the execution of juvenile offenders" (Ibid., p. 1). The exception identified was the difference in the number of states that prohibit the execution of juveniles and those that prohibit the execution of persons with mental retardation. The two reasons cited in *Atkins* that Justice Stevens thought applicable to juveniles, though not stated in the dissent, related to decreased capacities in the areas of reasoning, judgment, and control of impulses and the potential for these diminished capacities to impact negatively the reliability and fairness of the capital proceedings.

In summary, then, for juveniles charged with delinquent/criminal offenses, the Court has clearly established that they must be afforded due process rights equal to those afforded adults; that the states can, provided the fundamental fairness tests are met, maintain some flexibility and informality in its juvenile court processes to ensure the benevolent treatment of juveniles; and that juveniles can be sentenced to death. We discuss these decisions in more detail in Chapter 11.

Most states extended by legislation or court rules the principles of fundamental fairness developed by the line of delinquency case decisions to child abuse and neglect matters (Saltzman & Proch, 2000).

State Interventions to Protect Children's Independent Rights

The states, acknowledging that children's rights and interests might be different from those of parents, have provided for appointment of a guardian *ad litem* or emancipation process.

Guardian **Ad Litem.**   Recognizing the particular vulnerabilities of children and the potential for conflicting interests between the child's interests and the parent's interests, all states provide for appointment of a guardian *ad litem* to serve in a particular litigation to which a minor is a party for the purpose of representing and protecting that child's interests.

A 1992 Florida circuit court ruling, which attracted nationwide interest, concerned the rights of children to bring legal actions without the assistance of a guardian *ad litem,* or "next friend." While the news media promoted the story as "child divorces his own parents," this was a termination of parental rights under Florida's law for such actions. It was the first widely reported case in the United States in which parental rights were ended as the result of a legal action brought by a child rather than by a state agency or an adult. The circumstances were these: Gregory K. had lived in foster homes most of his life. In the last eight years he had lived with his birth mother for only seven months. At the time of the trial, Gregory was living with foster parents who hoped to adopt him, as Gregory also wished to happen. In asking the court to end the parental rights of his biological mother, Gregory took the stand and, in more than an hour of questioning, described how she had long neglected, abused, and abandoned him. He asked the juvenile court to allow him to be adopted by his current foster parents, who had cared for him for the last year.

Gregory's birth father was ready to relinquish his parental rights if the foster parents were allowed to adopt Gregory. His mother had a long history of serious behavioral problems that made it highly improbable she could provide the care Gregory needed. Her claim for Gregory was based on the rights of natural families over any other interest. When the foster parents had made known their desire to adopt, the state was planning to return Gregory to his mother, a factor that led Gregory's foster father to talk with him about the possibility of Gregory himself taking legal action that would free him to choose adoption by his foster parents. As Gregory's situation became clearer, the state changed its position and favored Gregory's adoption by his foster parents. The judge terminated the mother's parental rights and allowed Gregory's foster parents to adopt him.

It is generally agreed that Gregory K.'s case established a significant legal precedent: that a child has the same constitutional rights as adults to due process, equal protection, privacy, access to the courts, and the right to life, liberty, and the pursuit of happiness. In 1993, a Florida appellate court held that Gregory did not have the capacity to bring the action independently (Russ, 1993, p. 366). The Florida Supreme Court declined to review the appellate decision. The present state of the law was that children, through guardians *ad litem* or next friend, had long had the right to bring legal actions, including action to terminate parental rights. Thus, a child, whose child welfare agent is not pursuing or who refuses to file a petition for termination of parental rights, must request that an adult do so for him or her.

Emancipation.   Partial or complete "emancipation" is a means by which in some instances a young person can be legally released from parental custody and control and thereafter be considered an adult for most purposes. Although state statutes vary, criteria used frequently to justify an action of emancipation are that the youth is living separately from parents, is self-supporting, has joined the military, or is married. Emancipation empowers a minor to transact business such as buying or selling property, suing or being sued, enlisting in the military, and consenting to medical, psychological, or social work services (Horowitz & Davidson, 1984, p. 152).

The doctrine of emancipation is not new; it existed in common law times. Traditionally, however, the courts declared a minor emancipated only in particular cases involving individual circumstances distinct from those that might be more generally found among youth. To the extent that emancipation cases commonly involved minors in the 18 to 21 age group, the overall significance of the emancipation doctrine was diminished by the adoption of 18 rather than 21 as the age of majority. In more recent years, legislation in some states has allowed persons under 18 years of age to petition the court for a determination of emancipation. A typical example appears in the California Civil Code, which permits "a child fourteen or older to petition the court for emancipation on a showing that the child lives separately and apart from the parents with the parents' consent and is self-supporting. . . . The petition is granted if the court finds the information contained in it to be true and that emancipation would not be adverse to the child's best interest" (Davis & Schwartz, 1987, p. 40).

Rights and Responsibilities of Government

Recognition of the government's role in intervening in the autonomy of the family was slow to develop. This role is being further defined and limited by the decisional law (that is, the Court decisions discussed earlier) involving the balancing of interests cases. Many of the Court cases served to clarify the permissible scope of governmental intrusion and the procedures requisite to ensuring that those intrusions did not violate the rights of parent or child or both. While the cases have been discussed in the context of parent or child rights, it is important to note that the cases were before the Court because of a challenge that a specific state law or procedure violated a protection granted under the U.S. Constitution. In other words, the state, via its laws, was attempting to balance the rights of child, parent, and state. The aggrieved party challenged the state's conclusion as to what the balance should be and asked the Supreme Court, the final voice on the constitutionality of a specific law, to review the state's conclusion. Thus each case discussed earlier is in fact an exploration of the permissible scope of governmental action under its police powers and *parens patriae* authority (Myers, 1992, p. 26).

Federal and State Government Interests

The government's interest in protecting children from harm and protecting society from the delinquent acts of children is rooted in the principle of *parens patriae,* which translated literally, means "father of the country." Under this principle, the state is required to ensure that children (and other persons under disability) receive proper care from their parents or guardians and, if a child is deprived of appropriate parental care, control, and oversight, to exercise its police powers and assume parental authority over the child (*Chapsky v. Wood,* 1902; *Prince v. Massachusetts,* 1944; Nurcombe & Partlett, 1994). In *New York v. Ferber* (1982) the Court stated that the state's interest in protecting children from abuse and neglect is "an objective of surpassing importance" (p. 757).

This authority is the basis for all governmental legislation regulating the parent–child relationship, the scope of the child's independent rights and responsibilities, and the relationship of society to the child. For example, the government, through state and federal laws, plays significant roles in altering the parenting relationships:

- If the parents are unwed, state laws are invoked to establish paternity.
- If the parents separate or divorce, state child custody laws are invoked to determine custody, parenting time (visitation), and support.
- If the parents are temporarily unable to care for the child, state guardianship laws are invoked to provide for voluntary transfer of guardianship or state child abuse and neglect or juvenile delinquency laws are invoked to provide for court wardship due to dependency, abuse, neglect, or delinquency (involuntary action).
- If parents are found to be unable or unwilling to remedy the situation that necessitated involuntary action, then state termination of parental rights of child emancipation laws are invoked to permanently terminate their rights and responsibilities (emancipation or termination of parental rights).
- If new parents are found, state adoption laws are invoked to legally establish a new parenting relationship with all the rights, privileges, and duties afforded biological parents.

The specifics of the legislation impacting these areas of family life are discussed in more detail in subsequent chapters.

In addition, state and federal legislation regulates the rights of minors in many areas: child labor (hours and types of jobs a child can work), mandatory education (ages for school attendance, discipline in public schools, search and seizure guidelines), medical treatment consent (age at which a child can give consent or types/duration of treatments to which a child can consent without parental notification), sexual exploitation/child pornography, marriage (minimum age, permissions required, prerequisites to receiving license), freedom of movement (curfews, access to shopping centers), and alcohol and drug use (age for sale and purchase).

What are the state's responsibilities once it has undertaken to provide a service or offer a protection? In *DeShaney,* the case discussed at the beginning of this chapter, the Court, while holding that there was no constitutional right to protection from the abusive acts of the parent (a private party), did state that there may be basis for action under the state statute governing child abuse and neglect. Thus the question to be asked is not, "Were Joshua's constitutional rights violated when the state failed to protect him from continuing abusive acts by his father?" but "Did the State fail to follow its own laws, regulations, policies, and procedures, and, if so, did this failure lead to Joshua's harm?" This is the fundamental question for any examination of the broader question, "Once the state has undertaken a responsibility, what is its liability when it fails to carry out that responsibility in the manner proscribed by it?"

In *Suter v. Artist M.* (1992), the Court held that private parties could not bring a case to enforce the "reasonable efforts" provisions of the Adoption Assistance and Child Welfare Act of 1980. This decision is discussed in detail in Chapter 9. It is interesting to note that the Court let stand the lower court opinion. That opinion permitted private parties to seek and receive enforcement of the procedural requirements (completion and periodic review of case plans) of the Act while stating that there was no right to force agencies to provide specific services as part of the case plans (*Suter v. Artist M.,* 1992).

Native Americans. The government has a special relationship with Native Americans because of the sovereignty granted to tribes through many treaties and agreements. The specific protections depend on the legal issues involved and the unique legal relationships created by treaties, agreements, and special legislation (Getches, Rosenfelt, & Wilkinson, 1979). The Indian Child Welfare Act of 1978 (ICWA) frames child welfare practice for an "Indian child." "Indian child" is defined as "any unmarried person who is under age eighteen and is either (a) a member of an Indian tribe or (b) is eligible for membership in an Indian tribe and is the biological child of a member of an Indian tribe" (25 USC 1606). ICWA provides that the tribe has first right to address—that is, exclusive jurisdiction—child welfare issues for children meeting the definition and provides specific procedures to ensure compliance by the states with U.S. policy as stated in the Act "to protect the best interests of Indian children and to promote the stability and security of Indian tribes and families." Specifics of the Act are discussed in subsequent chapters.

The Supreme Court has decided one case involving ICWA. In *Mississippi Band of Choctaw Indians v. Holyfield* (1989), the Court held that ICWA clearly intended that the tribes would have exclusive jurisdiction over custody proceedings involving an Indian child who resides or is domiciled within a tribe's reservation. Two babies were born 200 miles from the reservation to parents who were enrolled members of the Mississippi Band of Choctaw Indians. The parents voluntarily released the children for adoption. The tribe challenged the jurisdiction of the state courts. The Court found that the mother was domiciled on the reservation; the children's domicile is determined by that of the parents or, in this case, by the mother because the children were born of unwed parents. The intent of ICWA was to preserve the integrity of the tribes by reducing the number of unnecessary removals of Indian children; thus "Congress could not have intended to enact a rule of domicile that would permit individual reservation-domiciled tribal members to defeat the tribe's exclusive jurisdiction by the simple expedient of giving birth and placing the child for adoption off the reservation" (Ibid., p. 35).

The federal government's influence in child welfare and juvenile justice manifests through the states' acceptance of federal funds to implement programs. The acceptance of federal funds includes the commitment to implement federal statutory requirements or administrative guidelines with respect to the funding. Box 2.1 summarizes the most significant statutory requirements and administrative guidelines currently in effect. In addition, they are discussed further in Chapters 1, 3, 4, 5, 7, 8, 9, 10, and 11.

BOX **2.1**

Major Federal Legislation for Child Welfare and Juvenile Justice Services

This chart outlines the major provisions of these statutes as amended through December 2002.

Name of Legislation and Citation	Major Provisions of Legislation as Amended through December 2002
Child Abuse Prevention and Treatment Act of 1974 (CAPTA) P.L. 93-247	■ Defines child maltreatment ■ Establishes National Center on Child Abuse and Neglect in HHS-ACYF to serve as clearinghouse for the development and transmittal of information on child protection research and demonstration programs; to provide technical assistance to states; to allocate federal funds for child abuse and neglect (CAN); and to coordinate federal CAN activities ■ Authorizes grants to the states for child protection programming ■ Ties receipt of funds by the states to the states' passing reporting laws with immunity provisions; mandated reporters; and public education initiatives
The Indian Child Welfare Act of 1978 (ICWA) P.L. 95-608	■ Defines "Indian child" ■ Provides that tribes have exclusive jurisdiction over child welfare issues involving an "Indian child" ■ Provides specific procedures to ensure compliance by the states
Adoption and Safe Families Act of 1997 (ASFA) P.L. 105-89 (amended significant provisions of the Adoption Assistance and Child Welfare Act of 1980)	■ Clarifies that health and safety of child is paramount ■ Specifies certain offenses against the child or a sibling for which "reasonable efforts" to prevent removal is unnecessary ■ Expands the required court oversight ■ Requires permanency hearings within twelve months of out-of-home placement and initiation of termination of parental rights proceeding whereby child is in care for fifteen of last twenty-two months except if child is with relative, there is a compelling reason that TPR is not in best interests, or agency has not provided services in care plan ■ Sanctions concurrent planning, i.e., planning for return home and other permanent placement at same time ■ Reaffirms reasonable efforts and reunification philosophy expressed under AACWA of 1980 ■ Promotes timely adoptions through provisions of incentives and funds postadoption services ■ Requires developments and implementation of performance standards

Name of Legislation and Citation	Major Provisions of Legislation as Amended through December 2002
Mutiethnic Placement Act of 1994 P.L. 103-382 as amended by the Interethnic Placement Provisions of 1996	■ Prohibits the delay or denial of foster home or adoption placement on the basis of the race, color, or national origin of the child or the potential foster or adoptive parent
Foster Care Independence Act/John H. Chafee Foster Care Independence Program of 1999 (FCIA/Chafee) P.L. 106-169 (replaced the former Title IV-E Independent Living Program)	■ Provides flexible funding to states to develop and implement independent living services to all foster care children expected "to remain in foster care until age 18" irrespective of age ■ Provides funding for "room and board" to youth who have left care and are less than 21 years old ■ Allows Medicare coverage of former foster children through 21 years ■ Encourages youth and community participation in programming
Juvenile Justice and Delinquency Prevention Act of 1974 (JJDPA) P.L. 93-415 as amended by P.L. 107-273 (2002)	■ Diverts minor offenders ■ Separates juvenile offenders from adult offenders in detention ■ Places status offenders in secure detention facilities only if they have violated a court order and secure detention is found to be the only way to contain them ■ Establishes the Office of Juvenile Justice and Delinquency Prevention (OJJDP) ■ Requires compliance as condition for states to receive federal funding for prevention and treatment services ■ Mandates sharing of case information between child abuse and neglect and juvenile delinquency service systems

The United Nations Convention on the Rights of the Child

The United Nations Convention on the Rights of the Child, the Convention, is a treaty containing fifty-four articles with legally enforceable norms with respect to child protection and well-being. It was adopted by the United Nations' General Assembly on November 20, 1989, and became effective with ratification by the first nations in September 1990. The United States and Somalia remain the only two nations that have not ratified the United Nations Convention on the Rights of the Child as of this writing. One hundred and ninety-one nations have signed the Convention. The United States' basic objections to the ratification of the Convention is that it becomes a treaty with all of the intricacies of international law, most of the core principles have been adopted in state legislation and Supreme Court decisions, and some of the provisions are outside the scope of authority of the federal government in our federal-state system (Hodgkin & Newell, 2002).

Trends and Issues

States' Responsibility to Children with Whom It Has Entered into a Special Relationship

The *DeShaney* decision raised the issue of what state actions constitute violations of the constitutional rights of children whom it has undertaken to protect. While that decision addressed the state's protective role for children remaining in their own homes and found no constitutional rights were violated, there is growing interest in defining the scope of the state's responsibility for protecting children placed in out-of-home care under the supervision of the state. The Supreme Court has yet to hear a case on this issue. However, several U.S. Court of Appeals decisions have been issued. These essentially find the state has entered into a special relationship with these children and therefore there are constitutional rights issues and responsibility for abuse or neglect of children by foster parents, residential facility staff, and others with whom it has placed children (*Doe v. New York City Department of Social Services,* 1987; *Walker v. Ledbetter,* 1987). Each such infraction requires a careful examination of the individual state's law—including agency policies and procedures—to determine the actual lapse in care required before liability ensues.

While *Suter* appears to have foreclosed states' responsibility to provide comprehensive services to meet the "reasonable efforts" requirements, advocates are attempting to utilize the procedural requirements to challenge states' inadequacies in service provisions. Thus as time passes, we may see greater legal responsibility imposed on the state once it has entered into special relationships with children, neither to do further harm nor to permit those under its authority to perform their duties inadequately. Termination of parental rights cases occurring after the implementation of the Adoption and Safe Families Act (ASFA) of 1997 are worth watching over the next five years to determine how the courts will decide due process challenges to the terminations required by the expedited time frames for termination in ASFA coupled with the lack of availability or timeliness of appropriate services.

Children with Emotional Disabilities

A problem that continues to exist in many states concerns children with serious emotional disabilities that require costly and intensive special treatment at residential centers. In many instances, states refuse to provide for the expensive treatment of these children unless the parents relinquish legal custody, generally through child abuse and neglect proceedings, voluntary relinquishment of parental rights acquired through birth or adoption, or disrupting nonfinalized adoptions.

These children's parents are not necessarily characteristic of those who come to the attention of child protective agencies following reports of child neglect and abuse. "They may be birth parents or adoptive parents—unquestionably involved in providing the best for [their children] but who most often seek a foster home or a special treatment facility when they reach the limits of their physical endurance and financial resources" (Stubbee, 1990, p. 1). These are children with emotional disabilities so severe and/or unpredictable that they are not able to be safely maintained in home and community environments with any degree of stability. These are the children for whom the state mental health systems have abrogated responsibility for provision of services and shifted responsibility to the child welfare system. The child welfare system, in many states, is required to provide mental health treatment services to the child and parent through the same mental health system that in effect "dumped" them into the child welfare system.

The issue of inadequate mental health treatment services for children (and their parents) already in out-of-home care due to neglect, abuse, or delinquency also continues to pose great challenges for most states as they debate whether their child welfare, juvenile justice, or mental health service agencies are primarily responsible for providing the necessary services. Many of these children and parents do not meet state mental health codes definitions for conditions eligible for treatment through the mental health services system; that is, they do not have developmental disabilities, mental illnesses, or emotional disturbances that meet the definitions of serious, chronic, or disabilities occurring before a certain age and expected to last indefinitely. Meanwhile, the children remain inappropriately serviced and, some might say, suffer greater harm at the hands of the systems that ostensibly are designed to protect them from harm. Again, ASFA requirements, the Federal Child and Family Services Reviews, and postadoption services expansion may encourage greater action on the part of states to correct this thirty-year problem by implementing systems more appropriate to meeting the mental health needs of children in out-of-home care and their parents.

Custody in Same-Sex Relationships

The awarding of custody whereby one parent is engaged in a same-sex relationship or the approval for foster care or adoption by gay and lesbian persons engaged in same-sex relationships continues to be hotly debated. Judicial prejudice against homosexual parents in child custody cases remains despite the fact that the child's best interests standard is the overriding one for all states. Most of the contested cases have involved actions by fathers to obtain custody from their former spouses who are now living in lesbian relationships. The contemporary trend is to "assess, case by case, whether parental eccentricities preclude adequate child care" (Nurcombe & Partlett, 1994, p. 108); but even so, the courts do not seem to stray far from considerations of "the stigma"; "the influence on the child's own sexuality"; "the effect on the child's morals"; and "the homosexual parent as criminal for violating state sodomy laws" analyses (Seidel, 1994). Foster care and adoption agencies appear to favor a "don't ask, don't tell" approach. When confronted openly with the issue, they are hesitant to place foster children in these homes but less hesitant to complete adoption placements. Some suggest the former is out of fear of potential suits from birth parents or the children placed with these parents (Jacobs, 1995). While many state courts continue to address the issue, no case has been brought to the Supreme Court. The American Academy of Pediatrics issued a policy statement, *Coparent or Second-Parent Adoption by Same-Sex Parents,* in February 2002. In essence, the Academy supports legislative and legal efforts to provide for the adoption of a child by the second parent or coparent in same-sex relationships. The impact of this statement by this highly regarded organization on the court decisions should be watched in the coming years.

Chapter Summary

This chapter focused on the current state of U.S. Supreme Court decisional law with respect to balancing the interests of child, parent, and state within the context of the U.S. Constitution.

The Court's decisions result from challenges to state actions (legislation or administrative rules), which the aggrieved parties contend go beyond legitimate state interest in regulating the conduct of its citizens and/or substantially impede a constitutional guarantee without compelling state interest. The Court's decisions appear somewhat contradictory at first glance; however, with careful analysis, they become less so.

The current balance says that the state has the right and responsibility to regulate the behavior of parents regarding their children where that parental behavior causes harm or potential harm, interferes with the privacy rights of mature minors as related to medical treatments including abortion, and to promote the general welfare of its citizens. Although great deference in the responsibility of raising children remains with the parents and although children have not been granted the full, absolute protections of the Constitution granted to adults, the Court clearly acknowledges that children are citizens entitled to the protections of the Constitution in their own right, but those protections need to be tempered on the basis of developmental capacities and childhood status within the family context.

FOR STUDY AND DISCUSSION

1. Reconcile the Supreme Court's decisions on duties, rights, and limitations on parents' rights of care, custody, and control of their children.

2. Read in its entirety one of the U.S. Supreme Court decisions discussed in the text. Then, with other students, analyze the line of reasoning used by the majority and minority justices. How does such reasoning square with your own conception of a just balance in parent, child, and society rights and responsibilities?

3. Why is it important that the juvenile court system provides due process in delinquency and child abuse and neglect matters?

4. Should age be a factor in determining whether the death penalty is cruel and unusual punishment? Why or why not?

5. What are the requirements in your state for parents to obtain needed treatment for their emotionally impaired children? Are there circumstances under which they need to relinquish custody solely for the purpose of getting access to treatment?

FOR ADDITIONAL STUDY

Bell, J. L. (2001). Prohibiting adoption by same-sex couples: Is it in the "best interest of the child"? *Drake Law Review, 49*(2), 345.

Friedman, S. E. (1992). *The law of parent–child relationships: A handbook.* Chicago: American Bar Association.

Gregory, J. D. (2002). Family privacy and the custody and visitation rights of adult outsiders. *Family Law Quarterly, 36*(1), 163.

Humm, S. R., Ort, B. A., Anbari, M. M., Lader, W. S., & Biel, W. S. (Eds.). (1994). *Child, parent and state law and policy reader.* Philadelphia: Temple University Press.

Madden, R. G. (1998). *Legal issues in social work, counseling, and mental health.* Thousand Oaks: Sage Publications, Inc.

Mechanic, D. (1999). *Mental health and social policy: The emergence of managed care.* Boston: Allyn & Bacon.

National Council of Juvenile Judges. (1998). Child custody rights of homosexual parents. *NCJJ Snapshot, 3*(10).

Pardeck, J. T. (2002). *Children's rights: Policy and practice.* New York: The Haworth Social Work Practice Press.

Schacter, J. S. (2000). Constructing families in a democracy: Courts, legislatures, and second parents adoption. *Chicago Kent Law Review, 75,* 933.

Tomaine, S. (2001). Troxel v. Granville: Protecting fundamental parental rights while recognizing changes in the American family. *Catholic University Law Review, 50,* 731.

United Nations. (1989). *Convention on the rights of the child.* New York: United Nations.

Ziegler, E. F., Kagan, S. L., & Hall, N. W. (Eds.). (1996). *Children, families and government: Preparing for the twenty-first century.* Cambridge: Cambridge University Press.

INTERNET SEARCH TERMS

Rights of children
Rights of parents

INTERNET SITES

The following sites provide a range of information and access to statutes, case decisions, and agency regulations.

Juvenile Justice Clearinghouse.
www.fsu.edu/~crimdo/jjclearinghouse/jjclearinghouse.html

National Center on Child Abuse and Neglect Clearinghouse.
www.calib.com/nccanch

National Child Welfare Resource Center on Legal and Judicial Issues.
www.abanet.org/child/rclji

Office of Juvenile Justice and Delinquency Prevention.
www.ncjrs.org/ojjhome.html

United States Congress.
thomas.loc.gov

U.S. Department of Health and Human Services.
www.os.dhhs.gov

United States Supreme Court.
www.uscourts.gov

REFERENCES

Cases

Baltimore City Department of Social Services v. Bouknight, 493 U.S. (1990)

Bellotti v. Baird, 428 U.S. 132 (1979)

Breed v. Jones, 421 U.S. 519 (1975)

Caban v. Mohammed, 441 U.S. 380 (1979)

Carey v. Population Services International, 431 U.S. 678 (1977)

Chapsky v. Wood, 185 U.S. 373 (1902)

DeShaney v. Winnebago County Department of Social Services, 489 U.S. 189 (1989)

Doe v. New York City Department of Social Services, 670 F.Supp. 1145 (S.D.N.Y. 1987)

Eddings v. Oklahoma, 455 U.S. 104 (1982)

Fare v. Michael C., 442 U.S. 707 (1979)

Ferguson v. City of Charleston, 532 U.S. 67 (2001)

H. L. v. Matheson, 450 U.S. 398 (1981)

Hodgson v. Minnesota, 497 U.S. 417 (1990)

In re Gault, 387 U.S. 1 (1967)

In re Kevin Nigel Stanford, 537 U.S. _____ (2002)

In re Winship, 397 U.S. 358 (1970)

Kent v. United States, 383 U.S. 541 (1966)

Lawton v. Steele, 1893

May v. Anderson, 345 U.S. 528 (1953)

McKeiver v. Pennsylvania, 403 U.S. 528 (1971)

Meyer v. Nebraska, 262 U.S. 390 (1923)

Mississippi Band of Choctaw Indians v. Holyfield, 490 U.S. 30 (1989)

New York v. Ferber, 458 U.S. 747 (1982)

Ohio v. Akron Center for Reproductive Health, 497 U.S. 502 (1990)

Palmore v. Sidoti, 466 U.S. 429 (1984)

Parham v. J. R., 442 U.S. 584 (1979)

Pierce v. Society of Sisters, 268 U.S. 510 (1925)

Planned Parenthood of America, Inc. v. Heckler, 719 F.2d 650 (1983)

Planned Parenthood of Central Missouri v. Danforth, 428 U.S. 52 (1976)

Prince v. Massachusetts, 321 U.S. 158 (1944)

Quilloin v. Walcott, 434 U.S. 246 (1978)

Roe v. Wade, 410 U.S. 160 (1973)

Santosky v. Kramer, 455 U.S. 745 (1982)

Schall v. Martin, 467 U.S. 253 (1984)

Stanford v. Kentucky, 492 U.S. 361 (1989)

Stanley v. Illinois, 405 U.S. 645 (1972)

Suter v. Artist M., (1992)

Thompson v. Oklahoma, 487 U.S. 815 (1988)

Tinker v. Des Moines Independent Community School District, 393 U.S. 503 (1969)

Troxel v. Granville, 530 U.S. 57 (2000)

Walker v. Ledbetter, 818 F.2d 791 (11th C.R. 1987)

Wilkins v. Missouri, 492 U.S. 361 (1989)

Wisconsin v. Yoder, 406 U.S. 205 (1972)

Constitution and Statutes

U.S. Constitution

The Adoption and Safe Families Act of 1997, P.L. 105-89

Child Abuse Prevention and Treatment Act, 42 U.S.C. § 5101 (1974)

The Federal Adoption Assistance and Foster Care Act of 1980, P.L. 96-272

The Foster Care Independence Act/John H. Chafee Foster Care Independence Program of 1999, P.L. 106-169

Indian Child Welfare Act, 25 U.S.C. § 1901 (1978)

The Indian Child Welfare Act of 1978, P.L. 95-608

The Juvenile Justice Delinquency Prevention Act of 1974, P.L. 93-415 as amended through P.L. 107-273

The Multiethnic Placement Act of 1994, P.L. 103-382 as amended by the Interethnic Placement Provisions of 1996 in the Small Business Job Protection Act of 1996, P.L. 104-188

Books, Chapters, and Articles

Brieland, D., & Lemmon, J. A. (1985). *Social work and the law* (4th ed.). St. Paul: West Publishing.

Davis, S. M., & Schwartz, M. D. (1987). *Children's rights and the law.* Lexington, MA: Lexington Books/D.C. Heath.

Getches, D. H., Rosenfelt, D. M., & Wilkinson, C. F. (1979). *Cases and materials on federal Indian law.* St. Paul: West.

Gitlin, H. J. (1987, November 3). The rights of fathers of illegitimate children. *Chicago Daily Bulletin,* pp. 2, 20.

Hodgkin, R., & Newell, P. (2002). *Implementation handbook for the convention on the rights of the child.* New York: UNICEF.

Horowitz, R. M., & Davidson, H. A. (Eds.). (1984). *Legal rights of children.* Colorado Springs: Shepard's/McGraw-Hill.

Jacobs, T. A. (1995, supp. 1997). *Children and the law: Rights and obligations.* St. Paul: West.

Kramer, D. T. (2002). *Legal rights of children* (2nd ed.). Colorado Springs: Shepard's/McGraw-Hill.

Myers, J. E. B. (1992). *Legal issues in child abuse and neglect.* Newbury Park, CA: Sage.

Nurcombe, B., & Partlett, D. F. (1994). *Child mental health and the law.* New York: Free Press.

Pratt, D. V. (1993). *Legal writing: A systemic approach* (2nd ed.). St. Paul: West.

Russ, G. H. (1993, Fall). Through the eyes of a child, "Gregory K.": A child's right to be heard. *Family Law Quarterly, 27*(3).

Saltzman, A., & Proch, K. (2000). *Law in social work practice.* Chicago: Nelson-Hall.

Seidel, A. I. (1994). Custody denials to parents in same-sex relationships: An equal protection analysis. In S. R. Humm, B. A. Ort, M. M. Anbari, W. S. Lader, & W. S. Biel (Eds.), *Child, parent & state law and policy reader* (pp. 51–67). Philadelphia: Temple University Press.

Stubbee, B. (1990). Relinquishing custody: Continuing the dialogue. *Focal Point, 4*(2), 1–2.

3

Services to Prevent Maltreatment and Support Families

The little world of childhood with its familiar surroundings is a model of the greater world. The more intensively the family has stamped its character upon the child, the more it will tend to feel and see its earlier miniature world again in the bigger world of adult life.

—Carl Gustav Jung

Mitakuye oyasin. (We are all related.)

—Oglala Lakota Sioux

CHAPTER OUTLINE

Case Example: Reaching Out to a Family at Risk for Child Maltreatment

This case shows a family support worker in Hawaii's Healthy Start program reaching out to an overburdened mother just home from the hospital with a new baby.

Jane is a poor Hawaiian woman in her early thirties who lives in a community where the disparities between rich and poor are extreme. When the Healthy Start program first came into contact with Jane, she had just given birth to twins, leaving Jane with four children under the age of 3. Because Jane had no phone, Healthy Start home visitor Evelyn went to Jane's home to meet Jane, an introduction that took three months to complete.

Each week for twelve weeks, Evelyn stood outside Jane's door hoping to speak to her. While Evelyn waited patiently, a typical scene would ensue: Jane and her partner could be heard shouting and yelling, the older children sobbing, and the twin babies screaming, looking for attention amid the confusion. When the older children stared out the window at Evelyn, the fighting seemed to escalate. Evelyn worried about what to do, but stuck with a gut feeling that if she persisted with the family she could make contact.

When Jane finally did let Evelyn in, Evelyn learned something that surprised her about her earlier visits. Jane told her that although she was afraid to let this strange woman into her commotion-filled home, she also felt soothed by her presence.

This was the start of trust-building between Evelyn and Jane, which was necessary to begin work on Jane's many needs. Jane's family had no family doctor and no concept of preventive medicine. Evelyn soon discovered that Jane had used the drug "ice" (methamphetamine) while pregnant with her first two children and that extended family members sold the drug on the streets. Two months after giving birth to the twins, Jane was pregnant with a fifth child. In another ten months, she would become pregnant again.

Over a period of months, Evelyn and Jane set some initial goals for their work together: finding an acceptable means of birth control, developing an understanding and commitment to well-care (i.e., preventive health care) for her children, finding programs to help her become drug-free, and establishing a stable home.

In three years of work and weekly visits with Jane, Evelyn feels that the family has made important headway. The older children have been enrolled in kindergarten and Head Start respectively; the twins have started in a special program for children with developmental delays; and the newest baby has received consistent medical care since birth and shows no signs of delay. Most importantly, Jane's approach to her children's health and development has changed. No longer are emergencies the only time her children come into contact with a doctor. All six of her children receive regular health checkups from a local physician. Jane actively seeks out programs and activities for them as well. Instead of sending her children to school alone, Jane now walks them there and even volunteers at her son's Head Start program.

Jane's attitude toward Evelyn has transformed as well. Jane calls Evelyn every other day from a pay phone and talks openly about her daily problems. Although Jane's situation isn't altogether rosy—she has recently lost her housing and lives in a hut on the beach—Jane and Evelyn continue to work at the problem one step at a time. Jane thinks differently now about what she can do to help her children get off to the right start. (Adapted from Charles Bruner and Judy Langford Carter, *Family Support and Education: A Holistic Approach to School Readiness.* Denver and Washington, DC: National Conference of State Legislatures, 1991. Reprinted with the permission of National Conference of State Legislators.)

Twenty years ago this family might have been sent home from the hospital with no follow-up services, until, as seems likely, the parents' care of the children deteriorated to the point that someone made a referral to child protective services. The children probably would have been placed in foster care. The prevention services described in this chapter are an effort to intervene early in the lives of families, before the home situation becomes untenable, so that children can safely remain with their parents.

A description of the Hawaiian Healthy Start Program is located in this chapter, in the Family Support Services section.

Need for Preventive and Family Support Services

For most of the twentieth century, professionals in the human services recognized the importance of strengthening families to prevent child abuse and neglect. Yet efforts to conceptualize and develop social services to preserve, strengthen, and enhance family life and the quality of the child's environment have lagged. Society's reliance on the family for essential nurturance and guidance of the nation's children has not been accompanied by necessary changes in social and economic policies and preventive social provisions. As a result, social agencies tend to be overwhelmed with demands from families and children in crisis. (See Chapters 7, 8, and 9.)

Many parents cannot provide an environment conducive to the positive functioning of their children. The kinds of problems they face are numerous and may vary widely in their characteristics, duration, and degree of gravity. Their causes and symptoms are interrelated and frequently overlapping.

Continuing Constraints on Parental Capabilities

Many children are denied constructive experiences and opportunities because of inadequate parental care.

1. For many parents, the overriding problem is *poverty* and all its accompaniments (see Chapters 1 and 5); poor health; low educational levels; unemployment or underemployment; substandard housing; discrimination; lack of playgrounds, libraries, and other public facilities; loneliness; alienation from the mainstream of society; and individual depression and lack of hope.

2. *Single parents* may be overwhelmed with total responsibility for home management, rearing children, and earning the family income. There may be a lack of adequate adult models of both sexes, insufficient financial and emotional support, difficulties in visiting arrangements by the absent parent, or trauma to other members if the parent's absence is due to death.

3. In some families, the problems are exemplified by *interpersonal conflicts between family members.* Marital conflict may threaten family unity or endanger a child's emotional balance. In other instances, there is conflict or a lack of satisfying relationships between a parent and a particular child, or among siblings.

4. *Parents with serious behavior problems* may cause deleterious conditions within a family and impair a child's chance to develop normally. At all socioeconomic levels a parent may steal or lie, have destructive attitudes that affect success in employment, be addicted to drugs or alcohol, or be sexually exploitive or aggressively hostile. In recent years a long-standing pattern has been documented—violence in marriage—that has proved difficult to interrupt and modify. Some parents are struggling with unresolved issues from their own childhoods, such as sexual abuse, which impede their functioning as parents.

5. Many persons, including teenage parents, have been poorly prepared for parental responsibilities and show *family management problems*—for example, inability to obtain and keep appropriate housing, to organize and execute housekeeping tasks, to get children to school regularly and on time, or to protect them from health hazards. Parents frequently have not learned successful methods of child rearing, and their ignorance is reflected in damaging methods of discipline or supervision. They may be unprepared for the responsibility of planning and controlling family size, and may have difficulty in seeking or using contraceptive methods. Inadequate preparation for parenthood, resulting in dissatisfactions in the parental role, may stem from psychological problems of adjustment to the requirements, rewards, and penalties of parenthood.

Behaviors Centered in Children

Physical and mental conditions and behavior in children often constitute a problem toward which services are directed:

1. Some children, including premature and low birth-weight infants, may have *special needs* as a result of mental or physical disabling conditions, severe emotional disturbances, or chronic illness. They often experience parental rejection, feelings of inferiority, isolation from other children, lack of normal play, or separation from parents in order to receive treatment or education. A lack of appropriate treatment resources and social services compounds their problems and generates new ones for them, their parents, and the community.

2. Some children who are without easily observable or serious physical or mental impairment nevertheless show symptoms of *disturbed functioning or development.* These symptoms may reflect trouble in parent–child relationships or in other aspects of home or community life. In turn, the disturbed behavior and other troublesome symptoms may produce new inabilities to function successfully on the part of both the children and their parents.

Community Characteristics

Many of the supports traditionally available to families from extended family systems and neighborhood or village life are lacking in modern society. Today, conditions within a community, a state, or the nation often are unfavorable to family life and infringe on the needs and rights of children and youth. The mobility of many families, precipitated by the vagaries of the job market, have placed them far from close relatives and friends who would otherwise be available to them at times of family stress. The increasing employment of women has left some neighborhoods nearly empty of adults during the day. In some inner-city neighborhoods, families feel they must remain behind locked doors to be safe. Neighbors distrust rather than help one another, and children cannot freely roam the neighborhood. The loss of traditional neighborhood and extended family supports has increased the pressure on the nuclear family to meet the needs of all family members and has deprived them of the companionship, help, and comfort that all families need to raise children effectively.

Formal social services are often far removed from the day-to-day needs of families. Many are available only after a crisis occurs, reflecting the historical trend toward offering *residual* rather than *developmental* services (see Chapter 1). Overlapping and restrictive eligibility regulations and bureaucratic procedures also limit access of families to traditional social services. The mismatch between public social service requirements and the needs of families has given impetus to a variety of preventive and supportive services that offer flexible, easily accessible services with a holistic service approach, close to the family's home.

The Many Faces of Family Life

The "traditional" family form—two married parents caring for children born within their marriage, with the father as the essential wage earner and the mother the chief child caretaker in the home—was for many years considered the norm. Today, however, relatively few children live in a traditional family. Variety and diversity characterize current family forms; children may live with two parents, one parent, a parent and a stepparent or the parent's partner, or with grandparents and other relatives, with or without their own parents present. Some family forms carry additional demands or have needs and problems that become intensified, making access to supportive and preventive social services even more essential.

Single-Parent Families

One of the most remarkable demographic trends is the large increase in the number of American children living with one parent, usually the mother. Families headed by women do not constitute a new phenomenon, having been present throughout history. Nevertheless, the acceleration in the number of such families and awareness of the problems that many of them face have attracted national concern. The needs of single-parent families are not markedly different from those of all other families. At the same time, because of the responsibility of single parents to carry out the duties of child care and family decision making without a marital partner, and because of the high probability that family income will be limited, normal needs and problems may become harder to deal with (Schmitz, 1995; Jung, 1996).

Children in divorced families may face a number of special challenges. A study by McLanahan and Sandefur (1994) found that, other things being equal, teenagers who spent part of their childhood apart from their biological father were twice as likely to drop out of high school, twice as likely to become parents themselves before age 20, and one and a half times as likely to be idle in their late teens and early twenties. One explanation for the difficulties of children of divorce has already been mentioned—the great drop in income often following divorce, which may require that a family move to a less desirable location and leave behind school friends and helpful neighbors. Children may find that parents have less time for them after divorce. Although many fathers do remain involved with their children, the reality for many families is a "disappearing father," one who absents himself from his children emotionally and financially (Furstenberg & Harris, 1990, p. 4). The remaining parent, usually the mother, though physically present, may have difficulty shouldering all the responsibilities of single parenthood. Children of divorced parents often have experienced parental conflict, and numerous studies have shown that conflict between parents affects children negatively. They may blame themselves for the deterioration in their parents' relationship (Amato, 1993). No one explanation is sufficient to explain the various adjustments children may make following divorce, and it seems likely that a combination of factors is at play, including both increased stress and loss of former supports and resources (Wallerstein & Blakeslee, 1996; Emery, 1999; Hetherington, 1999; Thompson & Amato, 1999).

A few children face the extreme risk of abduction, if they have become pawns in bitter quarrels between divorcing parents. The number of abductions is increasing, due to the higher rate of divorce and the greater ease of cross-country travel. The practice is pervasive and found among all social classes and racial groups. The need is very great for more professional services to parents considering divorce to help them understand the consequences and reach a custody decision that each can accept, one that is the best alternative for the child. In recent years social workers in some family and child social agencies and in court services have been providing such help.

Families with Lesbian or Gay Parents

Homosexuality, though it has always existed, has until recently been an unacknowledged phenomenon in our society. With increasing openness about sexual orientation, lesbian and gay families are slowly becoming more visible in the community. Social workers in child welfare are being called on more frequently than in the past for advice and guidance in relation to families headed by lesbian or gay parents, particularly in matters of child custody and in planning services for these families.

In a more socially tolerant climate brought about by changes in sex mores and in the rights of women, homosexuals' need for secrecy about themselves has been reduced, particularly in urban areas. Homosexual parents now find more support for their sexual identification. However, this support is often elusive. For example, some states now have laws stating that homosexuality cannot be used as a basis for custody decisions, but in other states parents who openly identify themselves as lesbian or gay are presumed to be unfit as parents (Patterson, 1992). (See Chapters 2 and 10.) Underlying these attitudes is a series of largely untested stereotyped beliefs: (1) The child reared in a homosexual home will lack traditional role models and will be more likely than others to become gay or lesbian; (2) the child will be harmed by the stigma that attaches to the parent and inevitably extends to the child; (3) the child is at risk of sexual abuse by the parent or the parent's friends; and (4) homosexuality will compete with and undermine the provision of parental care, thus impairing the child's overall growth and development (Patterson, 1992). Behind these fears is a view of homosexuality as indicative of an inherent pathology that would dominate all other aspects of family interaction.

Research over the past twenty years has failed to support any of these assumptions and shown no differences overall between the adjustment and well-being of children in lesbian or gay families versus those in other types of families (Patterson, 1992). The difficulties that lesbian and gay families face are not caused by homosexuality per se but rather by the stigma associated with homosexuality in American society. The widespread view is that "it is good to be a mother, but it is bad to be a lesbian" (Levy, 1992, p. 23). One area of concern is the issue of disclosure of the parent's sexual orientation to the children. It is generally agreed that it is preferable to tell children at a young age of their parent's homosexuality. It is better for the child to hear the disclosure from a parent, who can explain the situation to the child in a caring and loving way, than for the child to hear of it first from relatives, neighbors, or schoolmates, who may have prejudicial interpretations (Gartrell et al., 2000; Morgan, 2000).

Although it is neither desirable nor practically feasible for the parent not to tell the child but remain in hiding to the world at large, there are potential negative consequences to leading an openly lesbian or gay existence, including discrimination in jobs, housing, and child custody decisions (Lott-Whitehead & Tully, 1993).

Social workers can play a significant role in helping lesbian and gay parents decide to come out, as they weigh the value of living without secrecy with concerns about losing child custody and discrimination. Social workers can also help these parents devise strategies for disclosing their sexual orientation to their children and their families of origin. Support groups for parents and children may be helpful in building self-esteem and creating mutual aid networks. Advocacy for all family members may be necessary with schools, the legal system, and other traditional service systems (O'Dell, 2000).

Stepparent Families

The current high rate of divorce followed by a new marriage has resulted in a major and no longer unusual phenomenon: the family made up of children and one or two stepparents. These families are variously termed *remarried, reconstituted,* or *blended* families. Their composition varies and can include a stepmother with no children married to a man with children, a stepfather with no children married to a woman with children, or a man with children married to a woman with children. Although stepfamilies undoubtedly have unique challenges, many researchers and practitioners today no longer view these units as inherently problematic. The prevailing perception is that they represent a normative family form.

Visher and Visher (1990) have identified the challenges and tasks of creating a successful stepfamily. These tasks are of two types: the "in-house tasks" involve "the challenge of moving from an absence of emotional connections between people, now living under the same roof, to a sense of belonging to a group of individuals who feel connected to one another" (p. 4); there are also "supra-family relationships," in which the challenge is to maintain meaningful connections between the newly formed stepfamily and the households of the children's other parents and close relatives. Successful stepfamilies are those that have dealt successfully with these challenges. Visher and Visher (1990) identify the following characteristics of these families: Losses have been mourned; expectations are realistic; there is a strong, unified couple; constructive rituals are established; satisfactory step relationships have formed; and the separate households cooperate.

Stepparents are required to cope with complicated and emotionally demanding situations. When there are not others with whom to share these challenges, tensions persist for stepparent family members. Sometimes the primary service need is for marital counseling with individual couples. In numerous instances, however, the primary need of stepparents and their children is an opportunity to share their feelings and experiences with other stepparents and stepchildren.

Early Childbearing and the Family

Historically, teenage pregnancy was a problem left to parents, schools, faith communities, and social service agencies. But starting in the 1970s, the old concern about unwed mothers expanded into an explosive controversy about teenage sexuality and teenage parenting. The issues involved—adolescent sexual intercourse, contraception, abortion, sexually transmitted diseases and HIV/AIDS, substance abuse, adoption, race, family structure, child support, and welfare dependency—evoke impassioned conflicts of value and ideology.

The enormous increase in systematic study of the subject since the 1970s is an outgrowth of a highly publicized belief that the nation is confronted with a dangerous "epidemic" of teenage pregnancies. It is curious that during most of the past forty years, while interest in the problem increased dramatically, births to teenagers were actually declining. A major cause for the increased public attention has been the *great increase in the percentage of teenage births to parents who are not married.*

There have been both positive and negative outcomes from this concern about a teenage pregnancy epidemic. Positively, it has increased public awareness and acceptance of the need for contraceptive services and education about sexuality for adolescents, and has stimulated federal funds for such services and for research. Negatively, however, the "crisis" approach has been sexist in its focus on the problem-laden, sexually active female; it has directed attention away from the more fundamental social and economic problems that warp the lives of so many teenagers, especially if they are black or come from low-income backgrounds.

In 2001, there were forty-six births per thousand teen girls aged 15 to 19. After a steady decline from 1950 to the mid-1980s, the teen birth rate rose by 24 percent from 1986 to 1991. From 1991 to 2001, it fell steadily with an overall decline of 26 percent, thus reversing the earlier increase. The largest decline since 1991 was for African American teenagers, which has fallen by 36 percent. Hispanic teen birth rates declined 14 percent between 1994 and 2001. However, the teen birth rates for African American and Hispanic young women are still higher than for other racial groups; Hispanic teens now have the highest birth rate (Martin et al., 2002). Explanations for this reduction include better access to sex education and other teenage pregnancy programs, abstinence, increased contraceptive use, fear of HIV/AIDS and other sexually transmitted diseases, and abortion. It should be noted that the abortion rate among teenagers has also declined, suggesting that abstinence and contraception are increasingly important factors.

Although the recent decline is encouraging, there are reasons to be concerned about the teen birth rate: (1) The United States has the highest rates of teen pregnancy and birth in the Western industrialized world. (2) More than four out of ten young women become pregnant at least once before they reach the age of 20—nearly 1 million a year. Most of these pregnancies are unintended and most are to unmarried teens. (3) The younger a teenager becomes sexually active, the more likely she is to have had unwanted or involuntary sex (Moore & Driscoll, 1997).

In considering the consequences of teenage parenting, it must be kept in mind that underlying factors that were present in the lives of these new parents prior to pregnancy, notably poverty, living in a single-parent family, and minority ethnicity, may also be present afterward. Nevertheless, many years of research have documented that the teenager who becomes a parent is vulnerable to a range of risks to herself and to her child as well. Teen mothers are less likely to complete school and more likely to need public assistance. The children of teen mothers are more likely to have lower birth weights, to perform poorly in school, and are at greater risk of abuse and neglect. Sons of teen mothers are more likely to end up in prison, and daughters of teen mothers are more likely to become teen mothers themselves (Butler, 1992; Maynard, 1996; O'Dell, 2001).

The welfare reform law, the Personal Responsibility and Work Opportunity Reconciliation Act of 1996, contains several provisions intended to discourage out-of-wedlock births and adolescent childbearing. Minor teen parents are required to live in an adult-supervised setting and to stay in school in order to receive benefits. States are required to submit plans for establishing pregnancy prevention programs and for educating the public on statutory rape. Bonuses are available to states that reduce out-of-wedlock births and abortion among the general population, and states may also get grants to provide abstinence education. States are encouraged to develop special voluntary paternity procedures for teens (Barkan, 1996; Mayden & Brooks, 1996). However, the relationship of welfare policies and the behavioral choices of teenagers is not clear; studies attempting to ascertain whether the availability of welfare contributes to teenage pregnancy have obtained inconclusive results (Allen & Pittman, 1986).

Culturally Diverse Families

The effectiveness of family support services depends in large measure on the extent to which the services have been planned and offered within the context of a family's own cultural, racial, and ethnic identity. Family and child services focus on family functioning and child-rearing practices. Any group's cultural or ethnic identity is most clearly reflected within the family. Whether the services offered are based on an understanding of ethnically determined behaviors and cultural differences will be a potent influence on whether they are used. Ethnicity is significant in determining how different groups define normality and social competence. The way in which a family addresses a particular situation reveals the practical strategies it has developed over time to manage many aspects of daily life. However, the usefulness of these strategies may not be readily understood by a social worker who is charged with assessing family functioning but is unfamiliar with the culture (Cross, 1996; Schiele, 1996).

As suggested by the NASW Standards for Cultural Competence in Social Work Practice presented in Chapter 1, family support programs must address cultural issues at all levels of the organization. Individuals of the same race or ethnicity as the families being served should be included among the professional, paraprofessional, and volunteer participants in a family support program. This practice is essential to an accurate interpretation of community norms and of the ways ethnicity affects a family's lifestyle and child-rearing practices. Having members of the service team who share the family's culture facilitates recruitment and empathetic communication and understanding, and gives credibility to the services being offered. Program materials such as flyers, handouts, crafts, and videos should reflect the ethnic background of participants. Decisions about the kinds of services to offer, scheduling, and overall approach will be more successful if they are made using knowledge from those closely connected to the community (Choi, 2001; Hurdle, 2002).

Immigrant Families

At the beginning of the twenty-first century, this country is experiencing another great wave of immigration, paralleling the former "era of immigration" that occurred in the early years of the twentieth century. During the 1990s, there were more immigrants in the United States than ever before in its history. The increase in immigration has been very rapid. In 1970, 10 million persons in the United States were foreign born, less than 5 percent of the population. By 2000, there were 30 million foreign born, comprising 11 percent of the population. This phenomenon has raised many questions: Can we accommodate all who are coming? How are the immigrants and their children faring? How will it change the country? (Fix & Passel, 2001).

Who are the immigrants? In 2001, there were over 1 million immigrants in the United States. They came from every continent on the globe: 38 percent from North and Central America and the Caribbean (19 percent from Mexico); 33 percent from Asia (particularly India, China, the Philippines, and Vietnam); 16 percent from Europe (currently many from Bosnia-Herzegovina or the former Soviet Republics); 5 percent from Africa; and nearly 7 percent from South America. Immigrants fall into various immigration status categories: In 2000, 30 percent were naturalized citizens, 30 percent were legal aliens, 28 percent were undocumented aliens, and 10 percent were in other categories (U.S. Department of Justice, 2003).

Immigrant families are found in every part of the United States although they are concentrated in six states: California, New York, Florida, Texas, Illinois, and New Jersey, with very large concentrations in New York City and Los Angeles (U.S. Department of Justice, 2003).

Children are a large part of the immigration population. Children of immigrants are the fastest-growing segment of the U.S. population under age 18; one in five children in this country is the child of an immigrant, and one in four poor children is the child of an immigrant. Most of these children were born in the United States and are U.S. natives. This gives rise to another important fact about immigrant families: Most noncitizen families are mixed, with at least one noncitizen parent and a citizen child (Fix & Passel, 2001).

The Urban Institute recently reported on the well-being of children in immigrant families, including both children born abroad and in the United States. The study reported that even though children of immigrants are more likely to live in two-parent families than are children of native-born Americans, they are more likely to be poor. They are more likely than children of natives to have health problems and behavioral problems but are doing about as well in school as are children of native-born parents. They and their families tend to have less access to health and mental health services (Reardon-Anderson, Capps, & Fix, 2002).

Immigrant families are in a process of cultural transition regarding their language, religion, education, and lifestyle. A number of factors affect the way that they experience this process, including the reasons for immigration, the availability of support systems, the structure of the family, and the degree of harmony between the home culture and the new one (Landau, 1982). According to Landau (1982), these factors interact with one another to create situations that may require social service intervention; for example, a family that experienced a very stressful immigration and has very few supports in this country may become very isolated and possibly dysfunctional. One common area of stress is the differential rate of assimilation of different family members. Landau emphasizes that "recognition of transitional conflict is the key to helping families in cultural transition" (p. 556). Sibling rivalry, marital stress, and particularly intergenerational conflicts can be understood as stemming from different adjustments to the culture of the host country.

Interventions with immigrant families require a high level of cultural competence and ideally are conducted by social workers who are of the same cultural background or who are immersed in its traditions and speak the language. See the description of a multiservice center for Chinese immigrant families, in this chapter, for one example of a culturally specific social service program. However, social workers in many settings, including those in the child welfare system, are likely to come into contact with immigrant children and their families, and will need to develop skills of cultural competency in order to intervene effectively.

African American Families

Among American families that are African American, great diversity exists. Country of origin, level of acculturation, religion, and socioeconomic status combine to create families that differ in lifestyle and values (Black, 1996). However, all black families in the United States share the experience of color discrimination. Racism and oppression too often have prevented African Americans from moving into the mainstream of American life. The strengths of black families are credited with helping those of African American descent to advance in education, income, and employment, despite the almost overwhelming obstacle of discrimination. As a group, African American families value kinship ties and mutual help, work, and educational attainment (Nobles, 1988; Billingsley, 1992; Hill, 1997).

> *If we are going to serve Black children and families, we have to understand how Blacks are simultaneously like every family in this country, like some other families, and like no other family at all. The professional helping person has to be able to assess at what point they are dealing with universalities and at what point they are dealing with unique issues. (Solomon, 1985, p. 10)*

Three aspects of black family and community life that have helped African Americans survive in the United States are role flexibility of family members, the extended family support system, and the church. Black parents are able to take on a range of roles within the family, regardless of gender; fathers and mothers both expect to work outside the home and to care for children and the home, although women do seem to assume more responsibility for child rearing. This flexibility helped black families to survive the undermining of the male role as family provider, caused by discriminatory employment practices (Hines & Boyd-Franklin, 1996).

The concept of role sharing extends to children as well as grandparents and other extended family members, who may take instrumental and affective roles in the family. Freeman (1990) cites the advantages and potential difficulties for children of role sharing in the family. "Such patterns tend to broaden each child's role network and teach him or her responsibility for others in the 'group'—those within the same cultural context. In assessment, however, distinctions must be made between these normative cultural expectations within black families, and dysfunctional circumstances involving child neglect" (Freeman, 1990, p. 58).

Social workers and other professionals especially need an understanding of the extended family ties found in black communities. Here, the definition of "family" includes extended family members and perhaps also close family friends. Extended family networks operate informal exchange systems of mutual help, sharing resources of various kinds, such as material goods, transportation, and child care. Relatives often live near each other and help raise their nieces, nephews, and grandchildren. "Informal adoption" is not unusual, in which children are raised by close family members other than their parents (Billingsley, 1992). These arrangements take place outside the formal child welfare system; usually, the family turns to the public child protection system only after the resources of the extended family have attempted to resolve the problem. The child welfare system is a "last resort" for the family, if extended family strengths are insufficient to maintain an adequate level of protection for the child (Mosley-Howard & Evans, 2000; Barnes, 2001).

African American families are complex, and power in the family may reside with relatives, such as grandparents, who are key decision makers in issues affecting their children and grandchildren (Hunter, 1997). Social workers may find that these significant family members do not necessarily present themselves to the agency, yet ignoring them risks jeopardizing the planned interventions with the family. These influential family members are usually best identified and included in the treatment plan if sessions with the social worker are held in the family home.

The black church has been the predominant cultural institution of Americans of African descent. During slavery and the Jim Crow era the church was a source of strength, consolation, and community solidarity. In today's world, the church continues to be a strong source of cohesiveness in African American communities. Churches offer social support in times of family crisis and offer age-related activities for all family members. Groups for the enhancement of personal and family development, day care centers, and support groups for people suffering from various physical and psychological difficulties are offered through the churches. Innovative programs are being developed in many churches to help adolescent boys make the transition to manhood, through sports, recreation, opportunities for exchanges with adult role models, and group sessions devoted to health, spirituality, family life, and the special problems of black men (Haight, 1998).

Hispanic/Latino Families

The diverse groups in the United States who are known as "Hispanic" or "Latino" share a common link to Latin America, the Spanish language, and certain religious and cultural values. Within this unity of background, there is great variation. The majority is of Mexican or Chicano origin, many of whom are not immigrants but original settlers in lands later conquered by the United States and now comprising the southwestern portion of the nation.

Smaller percentages of Hispanic/Latino persons in America are immigrants from Puerto Rico, Cuba, and Central and South America.

Hispanic Americans are the fastest-growing ethnic group in the United States, and, according to the 2000 census data, are now also the largest (O'Hare, 2001). The great increase in population is due largely to immigration, particularly from Mexico and among Central Americans fleeing economic and political turmoil (Ortiz, 1995).

Hispanic/Latino groups share a history of exploitation and oppression, conquest and defeat. In Latin America as in the United States, white European groups held power and gained control of the land while oppressing indigenous populations. Although liberation movements have been successful in some parts of Latin America, the social and economic effects of civil war and ongoing oppression have caused many people from these countries to look to the United States as a place to achieve security and economic stability (Garcia-Preto, 1996).

However, once in the United States, Latin American immigrants frequently encounter prejudice and oppression based on their language, traditions, and color. They may see themselves as placed at the bottom of the social ladder. Recent proposed and enacted legislation penalizing illegal and, in some cases, legal immigrants have increased the sense of alienation among Hispanic groups. They may perceive the dominant Anglo culture as cold, competitive, and hostile to their own culture, which they see as warmer, more family oriented, and more respectful of individual dignity (Padilla, 1997).

Poverty is a way of life for many persons of Hispanic background, although most Hispanic families have an adult who is working or looking for work. A major factor in the pervasive poverty of Hispanic families, in spite of high levels of work, is the low level of educational attainment; other factors are recent immigration and the lack of English language ability (Zambrana, Silva-Palacios, & Powell, 1992; Aponte, 1993).

Social workers involved with Hispanic families need to learn about the specific cultural attributes of those families, because much diversity exists among those who are identified as Hispanic or Latino, depending on the country of origin. However, some commonalties have been identified for Hispanic/Latino families in general. Familism is a characteristic strongly emphasized in discussions of Latino family life—the family as a central source of emotional support through close bonds not only with immediate family members but also with grandparents, aunts, uncles, cousins, and family friends (Garcia-Preto, 1996). Grandparents are influential in the lives of children, less as authority figures than as sources of love and nurturance. Extended family networks offer much needed social support to Hispanic families, especially those who are recent immigrants and have left other supports behind. Many Hispanic families prefer to live close to extended family members. Support may take the form of economic or other instrumental help, and also of socioemotional interaction.

Extended family systems include not only blood relatives but also other persons close to the family such as *compadres* (godparents) and *hijos de crianza* (adopted children, whose adoption may not have been legalized), as described by Garcia-Preto (1996). *Compadrazco* (godparenthood) is a system of ritual kinship with binding, mutual obligations for economic assistance, encouragement, and even personal correction. *Hijos de crianza* refers to the practice of transferring children from one nuclear family to another within the extended system in times of crisis. Relatives assume responsibility as if the children were their own and "do not view the practice as neglectful" (p. 151).

Although the concepts of *machismo* and *marianismo,* terms describing prescribed sex roles for men and women, may reflect a general organizing framework for relations between the sexes, the reality is much more complicated than these terms suggest. The mother in Mexican American family life is critically important in intrafamily relationships despite the common characterization of the father as the unquestioned authority in the family. Family decision making is often either a joint process of both parents or primarily the job of the mother. Vega (1990) points to the flexibility and adaptability of Hispanic families to meet changing social conditions, with the result that families may differ greatly on how closely they adhere to traditional gender roles.

For Hispanic women, joining the labor force is not necessarily a sign of personal autonomy or liberation from the family. If the family is poor, the mother may work out of economic necessity and quit when the family has achieved economic stability. Thus the status of being employed may reflect positively on men, but for women, it may reflect the family's vulnerability (Vega, 1990).

Hispanic families seen by social workers usually want help in improving their lives. They may have special concerns for the safety of their children, as the poor neighborhoods in which they often live are plagued by violence, disease, and low educational attainment. They may be grieving for losses associated with immigration, and, if here illegally, may have extremely serious problems in accessing needed health and social services. Adolescents may feel a conflict between values and expectations at home and the allure of popular culture. Garcia-Preto recommends that social workers help Hispanic families reflect on cultural contrasts and on the positives and negatives of each culture. "The metaphor of building bridges to connect the world they come from to the world they live in now helps them to take what is needed from both. Validating the positives in their culture is essential to help Latinos rid themselves of shame, regain their dignity, make connections, and have a sense of community" (Garcia-Preto, 1996, p. 153; Bean, Perry, & Bedell, 2001).

> *We are bilingual, bicultural, and by ourselves. How do we retain our assets, how do we contribute to society at large in a synergy that makes us all more? (Mario J. Aranda)*

Native American Families

After centuries of decline, the population of Native Americans in the United States is again increasing. The introduction of modern medical services in rural areas has helped lower infant mortality rates, and improved adaptations to modern living have increased somewhat the longevity of adults.

The term *Indian* can be defined in many ways, such as having a certain percentage of Indian blood as established by the Federal Register of the United States, enrollment in a recognized tribe, community recognition, and self-declaration, the method used by the Census Bureau. Each Indian nation sets its own criteria for membership. Over half of those declaring themselves to be Indian live in urban areas. There is a wide range of cultural identification; at one end of the spectrum are those who claim Indian heritage because of an Indian ancestor; at the other end are those born on reservations who speak native languages as well as English (Sutton & Broken Nose, 1996). Native Americans differ from other ethnic "minority" groups in that the federal government and some state governments have specific legal rights and responsibilities toward them, including tribal recognition and issues of tribal sovereignty (Weaver, 1998).

Traditional Indian culture was diverse, with an estimated 200 different nations at the time of first European contact in the 1600s. In spite of much variation, it is broadly true that each nation provided natural systems to safeguard children and promote their healthy development. Children were raised in an extended family environment that included three or more generations; separate households of cousins, aunts, and uncles; and nonrelatives who became incorporated into the family. Aunts, uncles, and grandparents had specific roles and responsibilities in regard to the family's children and were also ready to help if the parents became overburdened, become incapacitated, or died. Children could form bonds to several parental figures who offered affection, education in proper behavior, and various role models (Sutton & Broken Nose, 1996). Spiritual beliefs reinforced the value of children as a special gift from the Creator (Cross, 1986).

The conquest of America by Western immigrants drastically altered tribal life. The loss of land separated families so that the extended family system could no longer provide a nurturing environment for children. Adults lost their traditional occupations and their ability to be role models as competent providers. Women's domestic skills made it easier for them than for Indian men to find work in the economy of the dominant culture, both on and off the reservation. The massive unemployment of Indian men has resulted in an increase of single-mother families. Alcohol, introduced by early explorers to Native American cultures with no social context to control its use, has plagued Indian families. For Indian and non-Indian families alike, alcoholism is associated with higher rates of family problems, child maltreatment, and developmental disabilities. Native Americans have a shared background of being a people subject to policies that had the effect of genocide, resulting in the devastation of an entire people and their civilization (DuBray & Sanders, 1999).

Native American families historically have been at great risk of family breakup because of government programs and policies. Indian boarding schools, established in the late nineteenth century by the Bureau of Indian Affairs, were designed to "separate a child from his reservation and family, strip him of his tribal lore and mores, force the complete abandonment of his native language, and prepare him in such a way that he would never return to his people" (*Indian Education,* 1969). Consequently, Indian children were often forcibly removed from their homes, given English names, required to speak English, and in many instances not allowed to return home. A devastating effect of this program was that young people grew up with no experience of family life and no parental role models to guide their own efforts to establish families after they were grown and had left the schools (Tafoya & Del Vecchio, 1996). Some children suffered abuse in these institutions, which offered them only negative patterns of childrearing.

Through the years, Indian children continued to be at highest risk of out-of-home placement of children in any racial or cultural group in the country, with placement rates reported to be twenty times higher than that of white children (Johnson, 1981). Many non-Indian foster and adoptive families provided loving and caring homes, but the children were inevitably deprived of the opportunities needed to incorporate their cultural heritage into their personal identity. By the 1970s, it is estimated that a quarter of all Indian children were not living with their families but were in boarding schools or in foster or adoptive homes (Johnson, 1981). This great loss of Indian children to their cultural heritage gave impetus to the passage of the Indian Child Welfare Act of 1978, federal legislation intended to restore and preserve Indian families (Bending, 1997).

In spite of adversity, Indian culture and Indian families endure. Present-day Indians are survivors who have learned to adapt to an alien culture. Many urban Indian families are coping and managing successfully. A study of Indian women in rural North Dakota who were affiliated with Head Start found that their family and personal relationships were characterized by mutual respect and helpfulness. The women were optimistic and courageous, and were "certain they could make plans work" (Light & Martin, 1986).

In recent years, the interest of government and industry has focused on certain tribes that own land rich in energy and other natural resources. Resource development and other entrepreneurial activity such as the development of casinos on Indian lands is changing social and economic conditions of life on reservations, and may result in greater economic and political power for Native American groups in relation to the dominant society.

Framework for Preventive and Family Support Services

Evidence has accumulated that in many cases the abuse and neglect of children could have been prevented if prompt and supportive services had been directed to the problems in the child's own family (MacLeod & Nelson, 2000). This awareness has led to an intensified interest in developing more and better services to protect children in their own homes from abuse and neglect. *Preventive services* and *family support services* are terms covering a wide range of programs aimed at preventing abuse and neglect and strengthening family functioning. They comprise a very loosely defined category of services, which may include a variety of approaches.

In this chapter, the term *preventive services* refers to any program that has as its main goal the prevention of child maltreatment. The term *family support services* refers to a type of preventive program specifically intended to support family functioning. Family support programs are a widely used and significant component of preventive services in the area of child protection.

Educational approaches are also useful in deterring child abuse and neglect, such as educational programs for children to prevent teen pregnancy or child sexual abuse. Preventive and family support programs may target a community, in an effort to make the area more family friendly and to encourage civic advocacy regarding the quality and availability of city services and schools. They may also involve improving linkages between service systems, to better identify families at risk of child abuse and neglect and offer services to ameliorate the problems, before a referral to child protective services becomes necessary.

Participation in prevention and family support programs is usually voluntary. These programs are intended for either the entire community or certain groups identified as "at risk," such as teenage parents and their children. Programs for parents who have been ordered by the court to improve family functioning in order to retain or resume custody of their children have mandatory participation and are usually more intense and focused on specific, serious problems and behaviors of parents. (These programs are discussed in Chapters 7, 8, and 9.)

Although preventive and family support services vary widely in approach, population served, level of intensity, community auspices, professional disciplines involved, and specific program components, they share a focus on preventing child maltreatment and improving overall quality of life and developmental outcomes of children. They also share certain attributes and theoretical foundations.

Attributes of Preventive Services

Martin Bloom (1996) has defined *prevention* as "coordinated actions seeking to prevent predictable problems, to protect existing states of health and healthy functioning, and to promote desired potentialities in individuals and groups in their physical and sociocultural settings over time" (p. 2). Preventive services are designed to ensure conditions in families and communities that reduce overall risks of social distress and offer opportunity for normal maturation of children and effective social functioning of all family members. The primary aim is to prevent situations from becoming unfavorable or hazardous to the well-being of children. Preventive services operate on the belief that prevention of problems is more humane and more effective than is offering services after a crisis has occurred.

Preventive services are *oriented to the future.* In child protection, their purpose is to prevent abuse and neglect, rather than to combat or cope with the effects of maltreatment after it has occurred, as is true of protective or therapeutic services. (See Chapters 7 and 8.) Because they are services offered in advance of harm to the child, they contain an essential component of teaching and learning in relation to recognized and accepted norms of family life. They utilize educational techniques not only in delivering services to families but also in teaching the community about the possible injurious influences in family life that can be prevented.

Preventive services are *grounded in the ecological perspective.* Bloom (1996) defines this perspective as the understanding "that each element in a given situation is ultimately related to every other element, often in an interactive way. . . . [O]ne chooses what to do based on an analysis of all potentially relevant and interactive ingredients, the entire array of components in the ecology of the problem" (p. 5). The causes and correlates of child abuse and neglect are best understood with an ecological perspective, identifying parental, child, and community factors that, in combination, may lead to child maltreatment. (See Chapter 7.) Correspondingly, services to prevent maltreatment must also address some or all of the range of possible factors involved in abuse and neglect, including parental characteristics, child characteristics, support systems, community resources and supports or their absence, and the sociocultural values and conditions that surround the family.

Preventive services often use a helping philosophy emphasizing *empowerment.* This refers to a process of personal development in which individuals become increasingly aware of their strengths and abilities, build competency and self-esteem, and take steps to make positive changes in their family relationships and other immediate environments. Programs with an empowerment perspective are based on the fundamental idea that all persons have strengths but may need a supportive environment to realize them. These programs differ markedly from deficit models of helping, in which the deficiencies of clients are first identified and then a treatment, therapy, or educational program is supplied to address the defined area of weakness in the client's functioning (Bronfenbrenner, 1987; Cochran, 1993; Early & GlenMaye, 2000; Rose, 2000).

Prevention programs attempt not only to prevent negative outcomes, such as child abuse and neglect, but also to enhance participants' quality of life by taking a *developmental approach* to service delivery. The effort is not only to reduce the risk of child maltreatment but also to improve the overall quality of family life. Prevention and family support programs may offer or refer family members to developmentally enriched preschool programs, recreational and tutorial programs for school-age children and adolescents, and adult education and other personal development programs for adults. Through program activities, participants are offered opportunities to identify talents and possibilities within themselves and to find ways to use them that improve the quality of their lives.

Attachment Theory

Attachment theory provides a foundation for understanding the importance of relationships in attaining healthy developmental outcomes. A central tenet of attachment theory is that a strong attachment, reinforced by affectional bonds, is central to the personality development of infants and affects their ability to maintain healthy family relationships throughout life. It is also important in developing cognitive ability in children and may even determine the shape and functioning of the brain. Attachment starts with the loving relationship that infants first develop with their primary caretaker, usually the mother, and then grows over time to include other family members and a wider circle of relatives and friends. (The discussion that follows is based largely on an article by Patricia Van Horn, in the journal *The Source,* 1999.)

John Bowlby (1980), the leading figure in the development of attachment theory, has suggested that the need for infants to attach themselves to a parenting figure is deeply rooted in the biological drive for species survival. An infant needs the protection of adults in order to survive. He or she ensures that protection by developing a set of attachment behaviors that are linked to a reciprocal set of caregiving behaviors by an adult. The attachment system, in which the developing infant and the primary caretaker need and want to remain close to each other, is a fundamental part of our genetic heritage.

Attachment theory directs our attention to the caregiver as well as to the infant. The infant's need to attach is matched by the responsiveness of the primary adult. Together, through building a repertoire of reciprocal interactions, they create a strong psychological bond. The kinds of caretaking behaviors that the adult brings to the relationship are fundamental to the quality of the attachment that develops.

Attachment behaviors change as a child develops. A baby who is hungry or in need of attention will show signs of wanting to bring the caregiver close by crying, reaching out, or clinging. Toddlers may follow the caregiver and have a pattern of leaving the caregiver briefly to explore the world, then returning and reestablishing a sense of security. Older children have cognitive understandings of separations and rely less on the physical presence of the caregiver than on mental representations that provide needed security.

The need for attachment continues throughout life, as people develop intimate relationships. These bonds are built on the early experiences a child has with attachment to the caregiver. Ainsworth (1989, cited in Van Horn, 1999) identified the following qualities of a strong affectional bond, which apply to relationships between adults as well as between a child and an adult:

- It is persistent, not transitory.
- It involves a particular person, who is not interchangeable with another.
- It involves a relationship that is emotionally significant.

- The individual wishes to maintain contact with the person to whom he or she is attached.
- The individual feels sadness or distress if separated from the person to whom he or she is attached.
- The individual seeks comfort and security in the relationship.

Ainsworth (1978, cited in Van Horn, 1999) has identified different patterns of attachment between young children and their primary caregiver: securely attached, avoidant, and resistant. *Securely attached* babies actively seek out contact with their mothers. Babies showing *avoidant behavior,* in contrast, try to avoid the mother by such behaviors as refusing eye contact and ignoring her after she returns from a separation. They may prefer to be comforted by a stranger rather than their mother. *Resistant babies* alternate between seeking contact and pushing the mother away. They may prefer a stranger for comfort, but may also appear angry with both the stranger and the mother. Main and Solomon (1990, cited in Van Horn, 1999) have added another category: babies who show *disorganized/disoriented behavior.* These babies may act frightened of the caregiver or confused by her. Studies have linked disorganized/disoriented behavior in infants to mother's abuse of alcohol and to intimate partner violence (Lyons-Ruth, Connell, Zoll, & Stahl, 1987; Steiner, Zeanah, Stuber, Ash, & Angell, 1994; both cited in Van Horn, 1999).

These different styles of attachment may reflect different ideas the child has developed about himself or herself and about the trustworthiness and comfort available in the world. Developmental theorists call these ideas "internal working models" (George, 1996). For example, a securely attached baby may see himself or herself as worthy of being loved and also have a sense of self-efficacy, that he or she can make things happen in the world. Conversely, an avoidant child, who has received inconsistent or insensitive caregiving, may see himself or herself as unworthy and the world as unpredictable. The baby may believe that he or she is powerless to make the world respond to his or her needs.

Securely attached children as they grow older demonstrate self-confidence, competence, and a growing independence from caretakers. Children with attachment disorders may be more aggressive (particularly boys) or more dependent and passive (particularly girls). Serious attachment disorders involve emotional withdrawal from relationships or indiscriminate behavior in which superficial attachments may be sought with a number of different adults.

It is important to remember that the building of affectional bonds is an interactive process between two people. The mother does not have total responsibility for the quality of the attachment between her and her infant. Infants have varying temperaments; those with temperaments categorized as "slow to warm up" or "difficult" may present challenges to the adult caretaker trying to create a strong affectional bond (Greenberg, 1999). An ecological perspective directs attention not only to the mother's caretaking behaviors but also to the child's temperament and, in addition, to the quality of the environment in which the attachment process is taking place. Supportive family members, sufficient material resources, and lack of stress are very important environmental qualities in promoting secure attachments.

Attachment theory has obvious and significant implications for child welfare and family services. It directs our attention to prevention and early intervention strategies, because attachment begins in infancy and has long-lasting developmental repercussions. The home visiting and family support programs described in this chapter have, as part of their theoretical base, a focus on assessing attachment between mothers and their infants and young children, and offering environmental supports to strengthen it. Day care policy and programs also must take account of the importance of strong affectional bonds between children and a primary caretaker.

Family preservation services, as will be seen in Chapter 8, are premised on the understanding that children need secure and permanent attachments, with the implication that services should be directed at maintaining the family where possible, if the child is safe with the family. Family continuity, as a child welfare goal, suggests that placement decisions be made to protect as much as possible the attachments children have to siblings, extended family, or substitute caretakers, and discourages placement choices that will disrupt relationships already formed. As described in Chapters 9 and 10, the very disturbed behavior of some older children in foster and adoptive homes is related to their earlier experiences of attachment.

Difficulties in attachment may be amenable to therapeutic interventions. Many of the treatment interventions described in Chapters 9 and 10 to help parents and children cope are directed at resolving, strengthening, and protecting their attachments to one another, and to helping the avoidant child begin to trust the world and risk trying once again to develop attachments with adults.

Social Learning Theory

Social learning theory attempts to explain how people think and learn, and what factors determine their behavior. According to this theory, a fundamental learning mechanism is operant conditioning, through which we learn the consequences that follow behavior. We tend to repeat behavior that results in positive consequences and stop behavior that tends to produce negative results. Other people can affect our behavior through positive or negative reinforcement. Another mechanism for learning is through imitation and modeling the behavior of others. Children seem to have strong imitative skills and learn to behave like those around them.

Albert Bandura (1976), the main architect of social learning theory, emphasized that learning does not occur in a vacuum; rather it is the result of complex interactions among the individual's attitudes, skills, expectations, and knowledge, and the environment that may encourage or discourage different types of behavior. Social learning theory emphasizes that learning is an active process; as we learn new information, we actively engage in evaluating it, organizing it in terms of other information we have, and applying it to different situations. It addresses not only the acquisition of intellectual knowledge and physical skills but also the development of ideas about our own competence and self-worth, about what we can expect from others, and about how much we can influence our environment.

Many problems of children and adults are the consequences, according to this theory, of failure to learn or distortions in learning. Interventions may use respondent conditioning to change behavior, offering positive or negative consequences for different behavioral choices. They may also use imitation or modeling, by offering the learner opportunities to learn by example. Through a complex process, individuals may learn to incorporate many intangible qualities of another person, including their approach to life, values, and goals, into their own behavioral repertoires and their understanding of themselves and the world.

The following list identifies key elements of social learning theory that are relevant to the design of prevention and family support programs, and examples of how each element might be applied. (This material is partly based on information from the Resource Center for Adolescent Pregnancy Prevention, no date.)

- People have expectations about the consequences of their behavior. Application: Provide information on the likely consequences of different courses of action.
- People learn by observing others. Application: Identify positive role models; discuss the experiences others have had.
- People can change their behavior by learning new skills and gaining knowledge. Application: Provide opportunities to gain new skills.
- People can become more self-confident through persuasion, encouragement, and succeeding at making changes one small step at a time. Application: Point out strengths; help people set limited, sequential goals.
- The environment influences people's behavior, and in turn, people influence the environment in which they live. Application: Help people develop strategies for changing their environments; advocate for clients.
- People are likely to increase behavior that gets rewarded and decrease behavior that is punished or discouraged. Application: Provide incentives, rewards, praise, and encouragement; decrease negative responses.

Social learning theory is widely used in social work practice, and interventions based on social learning theory have demonstrated their success through numerous evaluations (Thyer, 1994). Its fundamental tenets link easily with such prevention concepts as empowerment, early intervention, and orientation to the future. "By viewing client problems as arising from past and/or present environmental learning experiences and as a function of various physical, social, and psychological resources, an inherently nonpathological, respectful, and optimistic perspective arises from which to promote positive changes" (Thyer, 1994, p. 146). Social learning theory is also congruent with cultural competence, because it emphasizes individual assessments and does not make global assumptions (stereotypes) about people based on race or skin color (Thyer, 1994).

Parenting education classes use this theory extensively to help parents change their own behavior and also to change the behavior of their children and the way that family members interact with one another. The preventive programs for children and adolescents described in this chapter are based wholly or mainly on tenets of this theory.

Social learning theory is also used extensively in programs to help families and children recover from the effects of abuse and neglect. Intensive family preservation services (Chapter 8) and many of the child interventions used in treatment foster care, group home care, and residential treatment programs (Chapter 9) rely heavily on social learning theory and other closely related theories (cognitive-behavioral, behavior modification) in structuring their programs.

An Ecological Model: Prevention of Maltreatment of Children with Disabilities

The ecological perspective provides a useful framework for linking information about the causes and correlates of child maltreatment with strategies for prevention. The following example uses an ecological framework for organizing information about one group of at-risk children, those with developmental disabilities.

Many of the factors in maltreatment are the same for all children, with or without disabilities, so the example also provides a general overview of an ecological approach to prevention. The example in Figure 3.1 shows that effective prevention of child maltreatment

FIGURE 3.1   An Ecological Model for Preventing Maltreatment of Children with Disabilities

Society

Risk Factors: Attitudes, beliefs, and myths about children with disabilities

- Societal "devaluation" of children with disabilities.
- Segregation of children with disabilities reinforcing perceptions of difference, which, in turn, influence attitudes about the acceptability of violence.
- Interaction: Child may internalize negative societal attitudes about him or her and feel less worthy of being treated respectfully.

Prevention Strategies

- Public awareness campaigns on the extent of the problem.
- Coordination and cross-training of different professionals to increase awareness and identification of maltreatment.
- Reduce segregation of children with disabilities.

Family

Risk Factors

- Parental attitudes, such as viewing the child as "different," being embarrassed by the child, feeling anger at the child for not being the "normal" child they wanted.
- Disruptions in early bonding and attachment process.
- Increased stress due to special caretaking demands.
- Interaction: Child may seem unresponsive or unaffectionate, making bonding difficult.
- Interaction: Child may have needs for caretaking beyond the material or emotional capacity of the parents to meet, making child neglect or abuse more likely.

Prevention Strategies

- Family support services to increase parental knowledge of child, strengthen parenting skills, improve coping skills, reduce isolation, and improve access to resources.
- Linkage with school case management services through the Individualized Family Service Plan.
- Parent-to-parent group support.

Child

Risk Factors

Note: Some factors refer to people's response to the disability, not to inherent factors in the child him- or herself. Although some feel that any reference to child characteristics is "victim blaming," it is important to be aware of characteristics that make children more vulnerable, in conjunction with a constellation of other factors.

- Child may not know when behavior is wrong or inappropriate.
- Child may have physical limitations that prevent him or her from communicating or defending self.
- Children with emotional and behavioral disorders are most at risk for abuse and neglect, followed by children with speech/language impairments, mental retardation, and health impairments.

Prevention Strategies

- Prevention programs appropriate for children with different types of disabilities.

Institutional or Nonfamilial Maltreatment

Risk Factors

- Extreme power and control inequities, detachment from the children, isolation of children, clustering of children risking bullying by other children, an abusive subculture in the institution.

Prevention Strategies

- Improved agency policies and procedures: careful screening of job applicants, training in positive behavior management techniques, effective staff/client ratios, reasonable expectations of staff, strong supervision and support, explicit commitment to child protection.
- Families should get to know and be involved with nonfamilial caretakers. Discuss abuse awareness with the child.

Source: National Clearinghouse for Child Abuse and Neglect (2001, February), *In Focus: The risk and prevention of maltreatment of children with disabilities* (The Administration for Children and Families).

requires interventions at many levels of a child's environment and that factors interact and work in combination to increase risk. Attachment theory and social learning theory help explain how various factors in the child's environment work to increase risk, which leads logically to various prevention strategies. Some of the material for this ecological analysis comes from the National Clearinghouse for Child Abuse and Neglect (2001).

Family Support Services

Family support services is a term covering a wide range of programs aimed at preventing abuse and neglect and strengthening family functioning. These programs can be helpful to all families, as they offer expert consultation on child health, child management, and family relationships, as well as social support and information on resources. However, they may be particularly useful to families with identified risk factors for child abuse and neglect: teenage parents; families affected by substance abuse or domestic violence; and families who face special challenges in family life due to single parenthood, physical or mental limitations of family members, poverty, social isolation, language barriers, or other impediments to family wellness.

Family support programs operate in many different kinds of communities and settings. Some are free-standing; others are under the auspices of hospitals, day care centers, faith communities, social service agencies, or universities. Services may take place through home visiting, at a center, or both in combination. Home visiting, if it is a part of the service, usually begins prenatally and continues through the child's infancy. Center programs tend to fit well with the needs of families with preschoolers, particularly if the program offers a preschool experience for children concurrently with the parental group sessions.

Typical program components include life skills training and parent education, developmentally appropriate experiences for children, parent–child and group activities, crisis intervention, and information and referral (Family Resource Coalition, no date). These programs attempt to create an atmosphere that parents and children find comfortable for exploring new ways of relating to each other, to professionals, and to other families.

In 1993, the federal government took a major step forward in addressing the need for family support services with the passage of the Family Preservation and Support Services Act. The Act defined family support services as

> primarily community based preventive activities designed to alleviate stress and promote parental competencies and behaviors that will increase the ability of families to successfully nurture their children; enable families to use other resources and opportunities available in the community; and create supportive networks to enhance child-rearing abilities of parents and help compensate for the increased social isolation and vulnerability of families. (*Highlights,* 1994, p. 1)

In this legislation family *support* services and family *preservation* services are differentiated; family support services are preventive services available on a voluntary basis to a wide range of families, whereas family preservation services are remedial, intended for families who have already abused or neglected their children and need more intensive services in order to preserve their families and prevent foster care. Family preservation services are the subject of Chapter 8 in this text.

Home Visiting: Hawaii's Healthy Start Program

The case example at the beginning of this chapter is from Hawaii's Healthy Start Program, a service to promote child health and development in newborns of families at risk for abuse or neglect. Begun in 1985 as a demonstration project, it has inspired national and international adaptations and is currently being replicated in many sites by Healthy Families America.

Families are first identified at the hospital when the mother gives birth. They are screened for risk factors, such as a history of unstable housing, substance abuse, depression, parent's abuse as a child, late or no prenatal care, less than high school education, poverty, and unemployment. Because the program has resources for a limited number of families, only families with several risk factors are accepted. About 15 percent of reviewed families are considered as at risk; over 90 percent of those choose to participate in the program.

The trained paraprofessional home visitors are members of the community. They are close to the families served in social and cultural background and can approach the families in the helpful, nonthreatening way of a concerned neighbor or extended family member. Workers carry caseloads of twenty-five families and initially visit families weekly.

At the beginning, the workers and families often must cope with crises in housing, employment, or substance abuse. During this early period, workers also try to get the families established in using the medical system for preventive health care, encouraging them to keep regularly scheduled well-baby and immunization appointments rather than waiting for medical emergencies.

Over time, as the family's situation stabilizes, the family begins to set goals and define its own level of participation. After a trusting relationship has been established with the worker, the focus may turn to parent–child relationships, child development, parenting skills, family planning, and relationships between adult partners. A child development specialist is available to visit the family concerning developmental issues of children. A male worker may visit the father to discuss the male role in the family. Gradually, the home visitor may decrease the visits to once a month. Group activities are also available to families and participation is encouraged. Families may remain in the program until the youngest child is 5 years old and ready to enter school.

A rigorous outcome evaluation of the project is currently underway; preliminary results on two years of program operation suggest that outcomes vary with local adaptations of the program. No overall statistically significant benefits have been identified, but some individual programs are showing positive change in families. The evaluators conclude that home visiting programs should be monitored for faithfulness to the original model (Duggan et al., 1999).

Family Support Programs for Teen Parents

Family support programs for teen parents are needed because of the documented deficits in development that often occur in the teen parents and in their children (Butler, 1992). Early intervention is key, because the longer the teen parent takes to learn adequate parenting skills and to create a supportive environment, the greater the risk to her child. Family support programs for teen parents are similar to other types of family support programs, but according to the Family Resource Coalition (no date), they may have special emphases reflective of the parent's adolescent stage of development:

- emphasis on strong teen–staff relationships that are accepting yet firm and that foster high levels of trust
- awareness of and sensitivity to the cultural milieu in which teens live, including understanding of kinship and extended family systems and of community norms
- focus on teens' visions of the future, while working incrementally to attain skills needed for current goals and an improved sense of control
- provision of long-term support starting during pregnancy
- coordination of services with health, education, and economic resources
- opportunities for peers to share and validate their experience (p. 4)

One example of a family support program for teenagers is the New Futures School, an alternative school in the Albuquerque public school system. It provides educational, health, counseling, parenting education, and child care services to pregnant and parenting teens. The clientele include Latino, Caucasian, African American, and Native American adolescents. The goals of the program are to assist parents in completing their education, making informed decisions, having healthy pregnancies and healthy families, and being responsible parents (which may sometimes mean releasing the child for adoption). Through a comprehensive array of services, the program provides an environment that links teen parents' needs for an education and for the social experiences of adolescence with the developmental tasks they need to master to become competent parents and productive adults (Family Resource Coalition, no date).

Special Services for Pregnant and Parenting Teens

Sexual Abuse.   An additional program focus concerns the relationship of sexual abuse to teen pregnancy. It is usually assumed that teen pregnancies are the result of voluntary sexual encounters between the teen mother and her teenage boyfriend. However, evidence is mounting that for some pregnant teenagers, particularly younger ones, the pregnancy may be the result of sexual abuse. The perpetrator is usually a family member or known to the family. Legal, health, and social work professionals working with teen parents must be aware of the possibility that the pregnancy may have been the result of forced intercourse, make referrals to child protective services as appropriate, and offer services for survivors of sexual abuse as well as family support services (Mayden, 1997; Moore & Driscoll, 1997). (See Chapter 7.)

The Decision to Parent or Choose Adoption.   The number of infants relinquished for adoption has sharply declined in the past 30 years. Currently only about 5 percent of children of teenage mothers are released, in contrast to 19 percent in the early 1970s (Lewin, 1992). Changes in society's acceptance of single mothers and increased employment opportunities for women make the decision to be a single parent more feasible than in earlier times.

Research shows that teenagers who choose to relinquish their child for adoption tend to have the most to lose by teenage parenthood. They are likely to be in school, to have parents who went to college, and to have aspirations for college or other personal achievement goals. In contrast, characteristics associated with deciding to keep the baby include living in poverty and dropping out of high school (Bachrach, 1986).

The ability of the mother to weigh alternatives wisely and think through the consequences may also affect her decision to place or parent. In the past, some agencies and caseworkers have been reluctant to broach the subject of adoption with pregnant teenagers under the principle of client self-determination or because they were unprepared to counsel teenagers on the difficult issues of grief and loss inherent in a plan of relinquishment. The Infant Adoption Awareness Training Program was passed by Congress in 2000. The purpose of the program is to develop a training program for health care professionals designed to increase their knowledge of adoption and their capacity to counsel adoption along with other options with persons who have unintended or unwanted pregnancies (Children's Bureau, no date). Social workers can help pregnant teenagers weigh the burdens and benefits of keeping or placing the child, and imagine the future for themselves and the child given different decisions about adoption (Cervera, 1993). It is important to give teenagers "psychic space" to weigh alternatives and consider possibilities, and to keep the focus on reality issues. Some programs have had success with involving teenagers who have already made different decisions about keeping or placing, to facilitate clarification and discussion on these difficult issues. (See Chapter 10.)

Family Support Programs in Economically Deprived Communities

Family support services depend for their success on acceptance by the local community. Ironically, the low-income neighborhoods in which family support programs are most needed are also the places where they will take the longest to become established. A unique feature of this program model is that relatively large expenditures of time must be allocated to start-up tasks that build credibility. Experience has shown that it may take a year or more for a family support program to become a trusted, integrated component of the community.

Residents in poor communities often have attitudinal and other barriers to participation. They may have learned to distrust new programs because they have seen so many come and go over the years, after raising everyone's expectations for improvements that never materialized. In many low-income areas, the only parenting services known to residents are those that abusive and neglectful parents are mandated to attend, so family programs have become stigmatized as punishment for "bad" parents. Another problem is that people who have experienced multiple failures in school, work, and personal relationships may feel that they cannot be helped. Parents may believe that parenting "comes naturally" and is not a skill that can be taught (Downs, 1997). Many have had no positive experiences with social service systems and have no expectations that such encounters can be helpful.

Recruitment.   For all of these reasons, recruitment of families requires careful strategizing and expenditure of program resources. Flyers, posters, and radio ads tend to attract mainly people who already know that family support services could be beneficial. For other potential participants, additional approaches are necessary, such as door-to-door canvassing, recruitment in welfare and health clinic waiting rooms, and the endorsement of community leaders, such as pastors, teachers, and housing project leadership councils. Offering small incentives, such as snacks or food coupons, to newcomers gives tangible evidence that the program cares about participants. Community baby showers have been used as recruiting devices; for these, area merchants and charitable organizations donate baby supplies. Child care and transportation are necessary components of some programs. Family support programs located in a host setting, such as a community center, health clinic, or school, often have more success than stand-alone centers because they have easier access to potential participants (Downs & Walker, 1996).

Assertive Outreach.   Family support programs attempt to improve family and individual functioning but also to prevent child maltreatment. Unfortunately, families most at risk may be the least likely to participate initially. It is a mistake to believe that if families who know about the program will not come, then nothing more can be done unless the situation warrants a report to Child Protective Services. There is room to maneuver between totally voluntary participation and forced participation through the child protection system. *Assertive outreach* is the term given to focused, persistent, yet respectful recruitment efforts targeted to needy but reluctant families. In general, if the program offers families a tangible benefit and does not label them *dysfunctional,* they eventually can be recruited. As the case example at the beginning of this chapter shows, the family visitor had to make many visits to the family's home before she was finally admitted into the house. However, eventually she was able to win the family's trust (Downs & Nahan, 1990).

Advocacy and Cultural Competency.   Family support programs in poor communities need to offer ongoing advocacy on behalf of the families in the program. Family support is not enough in communities that lack basic public services, have ineffective schools, and are dangerous. Advocacy must occur both in helping individual families access services and in helping groups of residents work for change in their neighborhoods. These efforts give credibility to the programs and address the reality that the risk factors for many of the residents lie outside of the family.

   Cultural competency needs to occur at all levels of the program. Successful family support programs are comprised mainly of staff of the same ethnic or racial group as the families served. The foods, music, holidays, celebrations, and beliefs about parenting and family life of participants' cultures are infused into all areas of the program. Languages other than English may be used.

Assessment of Family Support Programs

Family support programs have proliferated in the last two decades, outpacing the development of research and evaluation studies that could guide and shape them. Family support programs present challenges to rigorous evaluation designs. The development of instruments suitable for measuring changes in parenting has lagged. Rigid designs requiring pre- and posttests and comparison groups are difficult to implement without disrupting the voluntary, empowering qualities of the programs and are financially beyond the reach of most programs. Sometimes, funding imperatives require that evaluation take place before the programs have had enough time to become fully established.

In spite of these difficulties, several recent reviews of research have pointed to modest but measurable effects of family support programs (Weiss & Halpern, 1990; Powell, 1994; MacLeod & Nelson, 2000). Parents have been shown to increase their knowledge of child development and their skills in managing their children's behavior. Studies of comprehensive programs have shown effects on parents' general coping ability and personal development, such as returning to school or taking other steps toward economic self-sufficiency. Infants have shown improvements in developmental tests. Home visiting programs have demonstrated fewer low birth-weight babies, fewer reported cases of child abuse and neglect, and higher rates of immunizations (Olds et al., 1998).

Because of the wide range of program designs, generalizing about overall program effects is difficult. However, there is enough evidence from research to conclude that family support programs can have a positive impact on the quality of family life and reduce the likelihood of child maltreatment.

Social Work Roles in Family Support

The role of professional social work in maltreatment prevention and family support programs is not clearly defined. Social workers are the dominant profession in the therapeutic approaches to individuals, families, and groups that are described later in this chapter. However, many of these services are not available to or used by families most at risk of maltreatment, and generally speaking they have not been conceptualized primarily as programs to prevent child maltreatment. Nonetheless, they are well established in most communities and provide a strong line of defense in preventing the kinds of family dysfunction that may lead to child maltreatment.

Family support programs have a very different focus and history from traditional individual, family, and group work approaches in social work, though they share some of the same knowledge and theory base. They grew largely out of grassroots initiatives to offer help to families in underserved inner-city communities, and staff have come from a variety of disciplines, including health care, education, and early childhood development. Many of the front-line staff are paraprofessionals. As these programs become better established, social workers are increasingly involved as administrators, program planners, evaluators, group work facilitators, community organizers, consulting therapists, and direct service providers in these programs. The programs are inherently multidisciplinary, so successful social workers in these settings have good teamwork and collaboration skills; interpersonal practice skills of assessment, treatment planning, and engagement, with individuals and groups; and community organizing and advocacy skills as well.

Other Approaches to Strengthening Families

Besides family support programs, a range of social services is available to support family life.

Therapeutic Services.   Therapeutic services stem from the identification of a serious problem, the development of an assessment, and the engagement of an individual or group in a course of social treatment whose goal is to stimulate change from maladaptive functioning to more adaptive behavior. People may seek these therapeutic services on their own initiative or be strongly encouraged to seek help; in any case, in varying ways and degrees they acknowledge a problem and choose to engage themselves in the treatment process. Typical examples are the casework treatment of a seriously emotionally disturbed boy or girl, the group work treatment of a number of children with similar handicapping behavior problems, the treatment of a mentally ill parent in an outpatient facility or hospital setting, and therapy based on the interaction of family members as a vital part of both the cause and the treatment of family problems. Therapeutic services are essential for the deeply troubled family or the seriously upset young person. These services are specialized and relatively well developed among the agencies offering family and child services; however, such services are too frequently not available in communities where children and families most need them.

Casework with Individual Parents.   A principal method in family and child services is working with individual parents. A commonly used approach is one that is strength based and solution focused. In this approach, the social worker and parent together usually arrive at an assessment early in the intervention process, emphasizing the issues the parent wishes to address and identifying strengths the parent brings to the plan for resolving them. Through helping the parent identify the problem causing stress in the family, understand some of its roots, and recognize the feelings and behaviors the problem produces, the social worker hopes to enable the parent (and indirectly other family members) to act more effectively. Social workers may lend strong emotional support to parents. They may offer interpretations of the parents' feelings and behaviors to help them gain insight into the behaviors that affect all family members.

Individual and Group Work with Children.   Many children can best be helped by participating directly in the modification of their troubling behavior, in which case a social worker may give therapy to the individual child. Social workers blend theories and techniques in various ways to help children reach certain developmental goals, learn about themselves and the world around them, utilize opportunities, meet an unexpected crisis, or resolve a conflict that impairs their social functioning. Both social-cognitive theory and ego psychology are used as the basis for planning interventions.

Group work is an increasingly common approach used in working with children. Groups may take place at schools or social service agencies and have been used successfully with children as young as 4 or 5. Groups are commonly organized around an experience children share, such as having a substance-affected family member, living in a divorced family, suffering abuse or neglect, or having adjustment difficulties at school. Many groups for children have both an educational and a therapeutic purpose, encouraging children to learn new ways of coping and also to explore feelings in a safe environment.

Family Therapy.   In its various forms, family therapy is based on the view that family life is a system of relationships between people. Family therapy may provide several advantages: attention to each individual member as well as the family as a whole; an opportunity for the reenactment of crucial themes within a family and a broader and more balanced diagnostic view of the strengths and weaknesses in the family; a reduction of the pressure on a single family member, particularly a child, who may have been singled out by other family members as their special problem; and an increase in the probability that improvement in a child's behavior and direction of growth will be sustained by changes and adaptations of family interaction patterns (Hartman & Laird, 1983).

Prevention Programs for Children and Adolescents

In contrast to family support programs, which are targeted to both parents and children, some prevention efforts are focused solely or mainly on children.

Sexual Abuse Prevention Programs

Sexual abuse prevention programs have become a very common strategy to reduce the risk of sexual abuse to children, both in this country and abroad. Most of these programs are offered through the schools. Finkelhor and Dziuba-Leatherman (1995, in Rispens, Aleman, & Goudena, 1997) estimate that about two-thirds of American school children will participate at some time in a school-based sexual abuse prevention program. The intent of these programs is to empower children to an extent that will enable them to exercise more control over what happens to them in an often unfriendly world.

A number of programs are available for educators. One common curriculum, developed and widely used in Atlanta, Georgia, is Good-Touch/Bad-Touch. This curriculum is designed for children from preschool through the sixth grade and focuses on knowledge and skills to help children protect themselves from abuse. Included is information on what abuse is, body safety rules, and strategies the child can use if threatened or harmed. The intent is not to provide sex education, but to prevent violence. Specific objectives are

- To give children language and information about abuse that is positive, nonthreatening, and practical;
- To teach children their body is their own;
- To teach children they can say "NO" to abuse;
- To help children identify people who can help if there is a problem with abuse/sexual abuse, bullying, or other situations that make them feel uncomfortable or give them an "uh-oh feeling." (Good-Touch/Bad-Touch, no date)

Sexual abuse prevention programs have been criticized for inadvertently giving children the understanding that they bear most of the responsibility for protecting themselves from adult behaviors that adults themselves do not understand sufficiently and find abhorrent. Another criticism is that teaching "good touches," "bad touches," "private zones," and skepticism of strangers is a simplistic approach. Most sexual abuse of children goes on in the child's own home and involves someone he or she has been led to trust. Critics question how much empowerment a young child can maintain in such situations (Costin, 1985; Reppucci & Haugaard, 1989).

Defenders have argued that sex offenders often gravitate toward children who seem vulnerable, and that they may be less likely to victimize a child who has participated in such a program. Such children would tend to be suspicious of adults who wanted special "alone time" with them or offered "special relationships" that needed to be kept secret from others. Children who have been exposed to a sexual abuse program, it is thought, might be less likely targets for sexual offenders in the first place, even if they were not able to thwart an attack once attempted.

During the last two decades, the evidence from evaluations has consistently shown that these programs are effective in teaching self-protection concepts and skills, even for children younger than 5 years old, and that, although retention decreases over time, children's retention is at a satisfactory level (Rispens et al., 1997). Currently, research is addressing more complicated questions including whether children are able to transfer skills learned to a real-life situation, the extent to which the programs reduce sexual abuse, and the presence of undesirable side effects, such as increasing fearfulness in children. A recent retrospective study, in which college women completed survey questionnaires on their experiences with sex abuse prevention programs and with sexual abuse, found that "young women who had not participated in a school prevention program in childhood were about twice as likely to have experienced child sexual abuse as those who had participated in a program" (Gibson & Leitenberg, 2000). Future research is needed to clarify further the benefits and possible risks of these programs.

Teenage Pregnancy Prevention Programs

In contrast to earlier decades, when teenage pregnancy was seen as a manifestation of maternal pathology, today services related to teenage pregnancy usually take an ecological approach to understanding parenthood. Teenage pregnancy is seen as a complex phenomenon with multiple causes such as social and economic conditions; cultural attitudes about early parenthood, family, school and peer influences; and developmental and psychological issues related to individual teenagers.

Public concern about the costs and consequences of teenage pregnancy has led to increased interest in developing effective programs to prevent teenagers from becoming parents. The welfare reform legislation of 1996 contains funds for grants to states to develop pregnancy prevention programs. See the earlier section Early Childbearing and the Family.

During the past twenty-five years, extensive research on teenage pregnancy has identified promising practices that have been shown to reduce sexual activity or pregnancy among teenagers (Ooms & Herendeen, 1990; Kirby, 2001). Kirby (2001), in his review of research on promising practices, categorizes pregnancy prevention programs as falling into one of three types:

- those that focus on knowledge and skills about sex and sexual behavior, including abstinence programs, sex education programs, and clinics that offer access to condoms and other contraceptives
- those that focus on a broader range of risk factors, such as detachment from school, work, and other social institutions, lack of positive relationships with adults, and disadvantaged families and communities. These programs include service learning and other youth development programs
- those that address both reproductive health and youth development

Sex Education and Clinic Programs.   Sex education programs often use social learning theory as the foundation of the curriculum, with a focus on gaining knowledge about the advantages of abstinence, the consequences of sexual intercourse including pregnancy, the dangers of sexually transmitted diseases and HIV/AIDS and how they are spread, and biological concepts of reproduction and contraception. The programs give students an opportunity to practice communication, negotiation and refusal skills, and other behavioral aspects of sexual health. They also incorporate discussions on social pressure, cultural attitudes about teen sexuality, and media messages about sexuality. Some programs, connected to clinics, provide access to health services including condoms and other contraceptives.

Many curricula and program models exist for sex education programs in schools, health clinics, and other settings. *Reducing the Risk: Building Skills to Prevent Pregnancy, HIV and STD* is a widely used and well-established curriculum. It contains sixteen lessons for middle school students. Based on social learning and cognitive-behavioral theories, it emphasizes knowledge and skill objectives regarding sexual choices and consequences (Kirby, Barth, Leland, & Fetro, 1991). A new curriculum, *Be Proud! Be Responsible!,* is designed for small groups of inner-city youth, in school or community settings. In addition to the approaches discussed earlier, this curriculum also addresses specific cultural issues for inner-city youth. Its curriculum includes information on how sexually transmitted diseases and HIV/AIDS have affected inner-city communities, and the importance of protecting the community as a motivation for changing behavior. Recognizing the confusion and shame that surround much adolescent sexuality, the curriculum emphasizes the theme of making proud and responsible sexual choices (Select Media, no date). Kirby (2001) found that successful programs deliver a consistent message about abstinence from sexual activity and, if abstinence is not the choice, using condoms or other contraceptives.

In reviewing the research on sex education programs, Kirby (2001) found that some well-developed curricula can have measurable, positive outcomes, such as delaying the onset of intercourse, increasing condom or other contraceptive use, and preventing teen pregnancy. Programs offering access to contraceptives have increased the use of contraceptives and thereby decreased the occasions of unprotected sex. Critics of sex education programs, and especially of school-based clinics, believe that their presence encourages youth to engage in sexual activity that they would not do if the services were unavailable. However, for both the sex education programs and those that include a clinic component offering condoms and other contraceptives, Kirby (2001) found no evidence from published research that they hasten the onset of sex or increase sexual activity among participants.

Youth Development Programs. Studies have shown linkages among dropping out of school, delinquency, substance abuse, and teen pregnancy, indicating that unprotected sexual activity is part of a cluster of high-risk behaviors. Youth development programs try to reduce risky behavior through exposure to careers, community service, remedial education, and job counseling. Service learning programs include voluntary service by teens in the community (tutoring, working in nursing homes or day care centers, fixing up parks); they usually have a component of discussion and reflection concurrently with the service activity, which may also include writing in journals. Kirby (2001) found that these programs "may have the strongest evidence of any intervention that they reduce actual teen pregnancy rates while the youth are participating in the program" (p. 14). It is not clear why they are so successful, but possibilities include

> participants develop relationships with program facilitators, they gain a sense of autonomy and feel more competent in their relationships with peers and adults, and they feel empow-

ered by the knowledge that they can make a difference in the lives of others. All such factors, in turn, may help increase teenagers' motivation to avoid pregnancy. In addition, participating in supervised activities—especially after school—may simply reduce the opportunities teens have to engage in risky behavior, including unprotected sex. (p. 14)

Other youth development programs, such as the Job Corps, with more of a vocational focus, did not achieve these same pregnancy prevention outcomes.

Some programs address both sex education and youth development simultaneously. One very comprehensive (and very expensive) such program is the Children's Aid Society—Carrera Program. This long-term program offers participants family life and sex education, tutoring, assistance with college entrance exams and college applications, work-related activities, help with establishing bank accounts, self-expression through the arts and sports, and comprehensive health care including mental health services. It has found positive impact on sexual and contraceptive behavior on girls that lasts as long as three years. However, the program did not reduce sexual risk taking among boys (Kirby, 2001).

Current research on outcomes of pregnancy prevention programs shows encouraging results. Several different kinds of approaches are achieving positive outcomes. Kirby (2001) cautions, however, that it is important for program planners to replicate faithfully the program components of models that have been shown to be effective, to attain similar successful outcomes.

Community Approaches

The programs described in this section illustrate some of the many ways that community factors influence the treatment children receive at home. Some of these programs are not conceptualized as "prevention" but as "developmental" programs to strengthen family functioning. Although the programs described here vary widely in the community elements involved, program design, populations served, and goals, they are alike in demonstrating that strengthening communities and strengthening the linkages between service systems are important components of efforts to reduce harm to children and strengthen families. They illustrate the ecological principle that family interaction patterns and individual functioning are affected by the environments in which families live.

Multiservice Centers for Chinese Immigrant Families

Though not focused primarily on preventing child maltreatment, multipurpose centers located in immigrant communities are included here because they exemplify the developmental, family strengthening approach that is a characteristic of family support programs. For many recently arrived immigrant families, they may be the only formal social services that are available or perceived as acceptable. They are a potential resource for the identification of problem situations and resolving them within a context familiar to the children and their parents, thus avoiding potentially confusing and threatening encounters with child protective services.

Multiservice centers for new immigrants build on the American settlement house tradition. Settlement houses were founded in the late nineteenth century to address an emerging problem: the dislocation and lack of support felt by families who had recently immigrated to U.S. cities from their rural homes in the United States or Europe. These families lacked the extended family and neighborly supports that had been available in their previous communities. They also faced special stressors of immigration: family breakup, exploitation by landlords and employers, unsafe living conditions, language barriers, and lack of political power, which meant that local politicians often ignored their neighborhoods.

A major function of the settlement houses was to work toward better living conditions for urban slum dwellers through political activism. Settlement house workers and local residents were effective in securing better street lighting, garbage pickup, and police protection. Settlement houses also helped families to adapt to their new life situation and to create a sense of community through mutual support. English language classes, political and discussion groups, sewing and child care classes, employment referrals, and recreational and arts programs drawing on the cultural traditions of participants were among the services commonly offered.

The settlement house model has contributed substantially to the development of prevention and family support programs. Although they did not use the term, founders of settlement houses such as Jane Addams took an "ecological approach" to services. Settlement houses were among the first social service programs to recognize that the neighborhood influenced the way families functioned and to develop interventions at the neighborhood as well as the family and individual levels. Settlement houses were also a model for organizing and delivering services to all members of a community, not targeting services only to those previously identified as needing special help. Further, they showed how professionals could work with local residents so that they would be empowered to take action on their own behalf (Addams, 1909; Wald, 1915; Husock, 1992).

An updated version of the settlement house model is the multiservice centers for recently arrived Chinese immigrants. They exist in three major U.S. cities: Los Angeles, New York, and Chicago. Developed over the past two decades, they provide a practice model for culturally competent and integrated service delivery. Asian Americans are a fast-growing minority group in the United States, the majority of whom are from China. About 70 percent of the Chinese in this country are foreign-born, first-generation immigrants. Many have settled in the city's "Chinatown," which have become among the most prominent ethnic enclaves in American cities (Chow, 1999).

Chow (1999) has described the service approach of these centers. It is developmental and preventive, and is designed to meet "the normative needs of the population rather than the few who are having problems" (p. 72). The centers are part of the community, where people can drop in and relax. The prevention focus is seen in the range of services offered. According to Chow (1999),

> [Most] recent immigrants arrived as whole families. Therefore, the entire family, not just the individual, is in need of services. It is not unusual, for example, to see parents attending English lessons and job training, their younger child attending the day care center, their teenage child going to the after school program, and their elderly parents drinking tea and playing chess next door in a senior citizens' center. Involving the entire family also helps in the early discovery of potential problems, thereby strengthening the center's primary prevention focus. (p. 74)

The after-school programs for youth "teach Chinese culture, so that ethnic identity and solidarity can be developed and maintained. These programs are successful in involving at-risk youths in healthy activities in a safe environment" (p. 72).

Cultural competence is another important aspect of these centers. According to Chow (1999), "frontline staff and workers are bilingual. . . . From the front entrance where the receptionists sit, to the intake workers, to the professionals, the centers are full of the sights and sounds familiar to service users. Art work, posters, brochures, displays, as well as background music, all fit into the cultural context" (p. 77). The Chinese cultural ideals of harmony and cooperation are reflected in the management structure of the centers. The focus is on teamwork and boundary spanning roles (p. 75).

Empowerment strategies help residents learn to be effective advocates for the needs of their community. Chow (1999) points out that for many recent Chinese immigrants, political activism is a new experience; part of the acculturation process is to learn the responsibilities and rights of citizenship. The centers offer help with voter registration, census counts, citizenship classes, and fund-raising events for local politicians (p. 75).

Using TANF Dollars to Prevent Child Maltreatment

El Paso County, Colorado, has developed an innovative approach to the prevention of child maltreatment. As part of an overall reorganization to link the public assistance (TANF) and public child welfare service systems, the county has moved responsibility for child maltreatment prevention from the child welfare department to public assistance. The rationale for this was the following: (1) Poverty is the overriding factor in referrals to child protective services. (2) Traditional prevention programs, involving counseling, therapy, parenting skills, and drug therapy, were not enough to keep children safe; many parents could not participate in these prevention programs for economic reasons, including lack of transportation, child care, housing, or other poverty-related issues. (3) Even middle-class families might need financial assistance in order to protect their children, for example, if a sexually abusing stepfather has also been the financial support of the family.

Using resources saved through the declining caseloads that came from welfare reform, El Paso County was able to increase programs to support families. Program innovations include having a staff member from the local Prevention of Domestic Violence bureau located in the welfare office to serve as a resource to staff and to help families; increased resources for many types of child care; extra support for teen parents on TANF; employment and support services for foster children aging out of foster care, to help them become productive members of the community and responsible parents; joint training initiatives for public assistance and child welfare staff; and community partnerships with faith-based and other community agencies for mentoring and employment services. The county has also used TANF funds creatively to help families already in the child welfare system through increased support for kinship providers and including TANF workers in intensive family preservation services.

As a result of these and other strategies, El Paso County has experienced a decline in the foster care population and in child protective services intake, and has increased the well-being of children and families. The leaders of this innovation believe that it is important to challenge the status quo and try new ways to use public resources to help families. "Policymakers, agencies, communities and families design and build our systems and our society. The question remains: will we design, consolidate, and build a system that meets the needs of our children and families?" (Berns, 2001).

Community Awareness Campaigns

Public health social marketing campaigns to prevent drinking and driving, smoking, and HIV/AIDS, have been a model for child maltreatment initiatives directed at the entire community. For example, a current campaign to prevent shaken baby syndrome has produced bumper stickers and billboards admonishing, "Never Never Shake a Baby!" Several of the prevention web sites listed at the end of this chapter have information for organizing public information initiatives in local communities.

Most sexual abuse prevention programs focus on teaching children how to avoid sexual abuse (see Sexual Abuse Prevention Programs section). Vermont has initiated an innovative campaign, called STOP IT NOW!, that addresses child sexual abuse as a public health issue. It uses social marketing and public education to emphasize the responsibility of adults for prevention. A help line for adults with questions about or experience of sexual abuse and for social agencies seeking information about sexual abuse is available. Linkages with the legal system allow self-disclosed offenders to seek treatment within the framework of the criminal code on court processing of alleged perpetrators.

The program was evaluated in 1997 by surveying sex offender treatment programs and state attorney's offices to assess self-reported abuse by adults and adolescents. During a two-year period, fifty persons self-reported sexual abuse through the influence of the campaign, including thirty-nine adolescents who entered treatment as a result of a parent soliciting help. The evaluation found that community factors were critical to the program's success. Vermont has sufficient quantity of sex offender treatment programs to guarantee a place for anyone who enters the legal system, has accessible media markets, and has a coalition of victim and abuser treatment organizations that supported the initiative. The Centers for Disease Control recommends more evaluations of the efficacy of public information campaigns to prevent child abuse, and suggests that "a collaborative effort between public health officials, sex offender treatment providers, and the criminal justice system in the model of STOP IT NOW! may benefit the well being of children" (Centers for Disease Control, 2001).

Fatherhood Programs

The high level of interest in services to fathers reflects research showing that children whose fathers are positively involved with them tend to have higher levels of functioning and are more likely to receive child financial support (Child Trends, no date; Salovitz, 2002). These findings increase concern about the trend toward fatherless families. Additionally, an increasing number of fathers are raising children alone (National Center for Children in Poverty, 1997). The problem of the "disappearing father" must be addressed at a number of levels, including improving preventive and supportive services to fathers, facilitating paternity establishment procedures, assisting low-income and low-skill fathers to find employment, and improving child support enforcement procedures.

Social services, often explicitly or implicitly directed mainly at women and children, are challenged to find ways of reconnecting fathers to their families (Miller, 1997). The Fatherhood Project of New York City has identified that articulating clear expectations for fatherhood is a first step toward changing the practices of social agencies that have discouraged father participation and toward reengaging fathers with their family. This project publicizes that a father who behaves responsibly toward his family does the following: He waits to make a baby until he can support the child emotionally and financially; he establishes paternity; he shares parenting with the mother; and he shares with the mother ongoing financial responsibility for the child (Levine & Pitt, 1995, p. 5). Family support programs can promote father involvement by including both parents in activities, providing opportunities for fathers to network with each other, and being sensitive to the shame fathers may feel if unemployed, emphasizing their role as emotional nurturers as well as financial providers.

Establishing Paternity.   Important benefits accrue to children for whom paternity has been established. These benefits include financial support and eligibility for benefits such as Social Security and health insurance. Although young unmarried fathers may have little income to contribute to their newborn children, their ability to contribute increases over time. Psychologically, paternity establishment gives children a stronger sense of their identity and the security that comes from having been "claimed" by both parents. Early establishment of paternity can strengthen the bond the father has with the child and encourage a pattern of responsible parenting. In spite of the benefits of establishing paternity, many children are without this protection. Estimates are that only about a third of children born out of wedlock have had paternity established legally (Wattenberg, Brewer, & Resnick, 1991). Disincentives to establishing paternity include fear of becoming involved with the "system" and bureaucratic hurdles to accomplishing the paperwork involved.

Growing evidence suggests that the best time to establish paternity is at birth. This capitalizes on the "glow of the moment"; most fathers are present at the birth of their child and find it a moving experience. Some states have had good results when they simplified their paternity establishment procedures and enabled hospital staff to distribute paternity papers and encourage new parents to complete them (Pearson & Thoennes, 1996).

Child Support.   For many fathers, failure to pay child support is related to their low earnings level or unemployment. A recent demonstration project, the Parents' Fair Share, involving seven sites and two thousand participants, showed that comprehensive job placement and skill-building services increased only modestly the extent of child support payments made by these low-earning, low-skill fathers. The National Association of Child Advocates recommends that, until programs for noncustodial fathers demonstrate more substantial benefits to children's well-being, they should not replace more traditional means of providing public support for children. More experimentation with innovative approaches to strengthening families through interventions with noncustodial, low-income fathers is needed (Feeley, 2000).

Trends and Issues

Controversy over Corporal Punishment

Prevention programs aimed at parents offer instruction on parenting practices that will increase the likelihood of good developmental outcomes and reduce the risk of child maltreatment. There is substantial agreement among parents, educators, other professionals, and researchers on many of these practices, such as the importance of communication and mutual respect, and the concept of "authoritative parenting," which combines parental warmth with the willingness to set limits on children's behavior (Maccoby & Martin, 1983; Steinberg, Elman, & Mounts, 1989). These and similar concepts guide and inform much of the curriculum of parent education programs. Research has shown that they increase the odds of creating good developmental outcomes in children.

However, there are areas of disagreement on optimal or acceptable parenting practices. One major disagreement concerns the acceptability of corporal punishment. Murray Straus (2000), a nationally known researcher on family violence, defines corporal punishment as: "the use of physical force with the intention of causing a child to experience pain, but not injury, for the purpose of correction or control of the child's behavior. This includes spanking on the buttocks and slapping a child's hand for touching a forbidden or dangerous object" (p. 1110). He points out that discussion of the acceptability of CP (corporal punishment) is curiously missing from discussions of maltreatment prevention. For example, *Child Abuse & Neglect,* a major scholarly journal on maltreatment, in a special issue called "A National Call to Action: Working Toward Elimination of Child Maltreatment" (1999), did not include discussion of elimination of CP in any of its nine articles. National surveys find that CP is widespread; a 1995 Gallup survey found that 94 percent of parents reported using CP and 35 percent hit infants, making its omission from the public debate quite troubling (Straus & Stewart, 1999). Straus cites a number of highly respected research studies that have linked CP both with negative developmental outcomes and with increased risk of child maltreatment.

In seeking for answers to the question of why the elimination of CP is not on the prevention agenda, in spite of its link to child maltreatment, Straus (2000) dismisses two common arguments for tolerating CP. To the argument that most parents who use CP do not abuse their children, he retorts that the same can be said of poverty, as most poor parents do not maltreat their children, yet everyone thinks that eliminating poverty would go a long way in reducing child maltreatment. Another common argument is that we cannot take away CP as a parental tool without first giving parents alternatives for managing children's behavior. Straus's response is that in other areas of interpersonal violence, such as spousal abuse, we are clear as a society that the behavior should stop regardless of whether the abuser knows alternative ways of handling conflict and disagreement.

Straus (2000) argues that the main reason that CP has not been targeted in prevention efforts is that CP raises deeply contradictory feelings. Many people believe that it is best to avoid CP, while at the same time believing that it is justified in some instances, or that it should be available as a "last resort." This position is held by many child protection agencies, which do not consider physical punishment of children as cause for substantiated abuse if they are done in the context of "reasonable discipline." (See Chapter 7.) Straus sees this position as inconsistent: "It is just as contradictory as being against slapping a spouse for misbehavior, while also believing that a slap may sometimes be necessary, and is harmless if done in moderation by a loving partner" (p. 1113).

Straus (2000) urges an all-out public media campaign against CP, because of its pervasiveness in American society and its proven link to poor developmental outcomes and child maltreatment. As part of this campaign, he suggests that it be called "hitting" and "physically attacking." He suggests that words in more common use, such as *spanking, whooping,* and *licking,* should be avoided because they suggest that "hitting children may be an approved disciplinary strategy" (p. 1113).

Child Maltreatment Prevention and the Schools

For at least three decades, there has been recognition that closer linkages between schools and child welfare agencies would improve services to children and families (Barth, 1985). Human service programs have been conducting innovative school-based and school-linked services for many years. As Landsman (2001), points out: "As a universal point of access for children, youth, and families, schools are increasingly being recognized as potential sites for innovation in attempts to tackle some of the vexing challenges facing youth, families, and communities today" (p. 1).

Schools are involved in both maltreatment prevention and family support efforts. There are a number of examples of school-linked prevention efforts. The schools have been a primary source of reports of child maltreatment to child protection agencies (see Chapter 7) and educators are mandatory reporters in every state. As described in Chapter 1, child protection agencies are experimenting with placing CPS workers in the schools, to work collaboratively with school personnel on prevention and early identification of abuse and neglect. Prevention efforts aimed at children are often conducted in schools, such as the sexual abuse prevention and teen pregnancy prevention programs discussed earlier in this chapter. After-school programs frequently include elements aimed at prevention of delinquency, substance abuse, and other unhealthy behaviors.

Increasingly, family support and family development programs are linked to the schools. Blank and Melaville (1999) report that there are 5,000 school-based family support programs currently in existence. These programs are characterized by the strong partnerships they form with the school, including sharing of resources and expertise, and mutual responsibility for being accountable for outcomes.

The School of the Twenty-first Century concept was developed by Edward Zigler, one of the principal architects of Head Start. The concept eliminates the distinctions among family support, child care, and education, recognizing that learning begins at birth and occurs in all settings. The comprehensive program envisioned by this concept includes parent outreach and education, preschool programs, before- and after-school programs, health education services, networks for child care providers, and strong parental support and involvement. This model of family support and prevention is currently being implemented in a number of communities across the country, although it has not yet received a comprehensive evaluation (Weisberg, 2001). Although various initiatives linking schools, maltreatment prevention, and family support show promise and are increasing in number, the potential for collaboration between child welfare and school service systems has not yet been realized. A major challenge for the new century is to find productive ways of collaboration for two of the major public service systems for children and families, the schools and the child welfare system (Dupper & Evans, 1996).

Chapter Summary

Services to prevent maltreatment and support families are based on the principle that all families need help from time to time in order to fulfill their societal function of promoting the well-being and development of all family members. Some families face special stresses from a combination of factors: parental problems, such as teen parenthood or substance abuse; special conditions of children, such as developmental disabilities or low birth weight; and insufficient supports and resources in the extended family and community. Families of color and gay and lesbian families may face special stresses because of societal oppression and discrimination.

The United States has lagged behind other Western countries in establishing preventive and supportive services to parents, so many families do not get help until the home situation has become dangerous to children and a referral to child protective services becomes necessary. However, since the early 1990s, there has been increased interest in establishing supportive programs for families.

Preventive and family support services are oriented to the future, use an ecological perspective, emphasize empowerment, and take a developmental approach. Attachment theory and social learning theory provide a conceptual foundation for many preventive approaches.

Family support programs have the dual function of preventing maltreatment and improving family life. Services may be offered through home visits, centers, or both, and are offered to both parents and (usually) preschool children. Services may include parenting education on child management and child health, developmental services for parents, preschool programs for infants, referral and linkage to other services, assessment, and advocacy. Traditional social work services, including casework, group work, and service to children are not usually considered to be family support services but are also very helpful in preventing child maltreatment and supporting families.

Another type of prevention program focuses directly on children, attempting to empower them to develop healthy, safe habits. Sexual abuse prevention programs attempt to teach children to avoid sexual abuse. Teen pregnancy prevention programs offer education on sexual issues and try to help teens make healthy choices and implement them in daily life. Some youth development programs, though not focusing directly on pregnancy prevention, are nonetheless very successful in preventing pregnancy.

Community approaches to prevention reflect the understanding that the environment affects maltreatment of children and family well-being. Many different types of prevention programs exist: Examples given in this chapter are multiservice centers for new immigrant families; using public welfare dollars and programs to prevent maltreatment; public health information campaigns; and programs to encourage responsible, involved fatherhood.

A controversial issue in the field of maltreatment prevention is the acceptability of corporal punishment in child management. From the point of view of community organization an linking human service systems, it is important to try to strengthen linkages between schools and the child welfare system, and to make use of the opportunities this collaboration provides for prevention and family support.

FOR STUDY AND DISCUSSION

1. Individually or as a class, select a population at risk for child maltreatment (e.g., children of teen parents, children of substance abusing parents), and conduct an ecological assessment such as that presented in Figure 3.1, listing risk factors and possible prevention strategies at the community, family, and child levels.

2. For an ethnic or racial group with which you are familiar, consider the group's definition of family,

its child-rearing patterns, and the family roles. How would you design a culturally competent family support program for this group?

3. What are the arrangements for establishing paternity in your state? Which agencies or courts are responsible? Are parents routinely counseled on paternity establishment at the hospital? Do procedures and practices work to encourage or discourage voluntary avowal of paternity?

4. Visit a sexual abuse prevention program or a teen pregnancy prevention program, and report to the class your impressions. What were the themes covered? Did the program seem to use a social learning theory approach? How were the participants responding?

5. Visit a family support program. Learn the auspices under which it operates, funding sources, program goals, types of families served, range of services offered, and eligibility requirements, if any. Assess the benefits you see to the program and ways it could improve. Find out the results of any evaluations of the program. If possible, interview staff and participating families.

FOR ADDITIONAL STUDY

Bloom, M. (1996). *Primary prevention practices.* Thousand Oaks, CA: Sage.

Center for the Future of Children. (1999). *The future of children: Home visiting, recent program evaluations, 9*(1).

Dunst, C., Trivette, C., & Deal, A. (Eds.). (1994). *Supporting and strengthening families, Vol. I: Methods, strategies, and practices.* Cambridge, MA: Brookline Books.

Family Resource Coalition. (1996). *Guidelines for family support practice.* Chicago: Author.

Levine, J. A., & Pitt, E. W. (1995). *New expectations: Community strategies for responsible fatherhood.* New York: Families and Work Institute.

McGoldrick, M., Giordano, J., & Pearce, J. K. (1996). *Ethnicity and family therapy* (2nd ed.). New York: Guilford Press.

INTERNET SEARCH TERMS

Children at risk

Child therapy

Teen pregnancy

INTERNET SITES

Child Abuse Prevention Web Site.   This site, sponsored by the National Clearinghouse on Child Abuse and Neglect Information, offers information on prevention-related issues, resources for communities planning prevention activities, special resources on such topics as shaken baby syndrome and maltreatment of children with disabilities, and information on emerging practices in abuse and neglect prevention.

www.calib.com/nccanch/prevmnth/ welcome/index.cfm

Family Support America.   This site promotes family support as the nationally recognized movement to strengthen and support families. The web site provides information on program models, evaluation studies and designs, policy and advocacy initiatives, upcoming events, and publications and products.

www.familysupportamerica.org

National Campaign to Prevent Teen Pregnancy. The Campaign is a nonprofit, nonpartisan initiative supported mainly by private donations with a goal to reduce the teen pregnancy rate by one-third between 1996 and 2005. The site is a rich source of information for local campaigns directed at teenagers and communities, and has extensive research and statistical reports available.

www.teenpregnancy.org

National Fatherhood Initiative. This engages in educational, public information, and technical assistance initiatives to encourage involved, responsible, committed fathers. It serves all demographic groups, including traditionally underserved and high-risk groups.

www.fatherhood.org

National Indian Child Welfare Association. This site is a source of comprehensive information on American Indian child welfare.

www.nicwa.org

National Resource Center for Family Centered Practice. Located at the School of Social Work, University of Iowa, the Center promotes family-centered, culturally responsive practice across human service systems. The web site offers online publications and other information on prevention and family support.

www.uiowa.edu/-nrcfcp

Prevent Child Abuse America. The goals of this organization are of building awareness, providing edu-

cation, and inspiring hope to everyone involved in the effort to prevent the abuse and neglect of children. The organization has chapters in thirty-nine states and provides them with leadership and support for local abuse prevention campaigns. The web site has useful materials and resources, particularly for public information initiatives.

www.preventchildabuse.org

Resource Center for Adolescent Pregnancy Prevention. This is an online resource for educators of pregnancy prevention programs.

www.etr.org/recapp/about.htm

Welfare Information Network: Teen Parents. The Welfare Information Network offers up-to-date policy information on issues relating to welfare reform. A special section of its web site is devoted to policies concerning teen pregnancy and parenthood.

www.financeprojectinfo.org

REFERENCES

Addams, J. (1909). *The spirit of youth and the city streets.* New York: Macmillan.

Ainsworth, M. (1989). Attachments beyond infancy. *American Psychologist, 44,* 709–716 (cited in Van Horn, 1999).

Ainsworth, M., Bichar, M., Waters, E., & Wall, S. (1978). *Patterns of attachment: A psychological study of the strange situation.* Hillsale, NJ: Erlbaum (cited in Van Horn, 1999).

Allen, M., & Pittman, K. (1986). *Welfare and teen pregnancy: What do we know? What do we do?* Washington, DC: Children's Defense Fund, Adolescent Pregnancy Prevention Clearinghouse.

Altshuler, S. (2003). From barriers to successful collaboration: Public schools and child welfare working together. *Social Work, 48*(1), 52–63.

Amato, P. R. (1993). Children's adjustment to divorce: Theories, hypotheses, and empirical support. *Journal of Marriage and the Family, 55*(1), 23–28.

Aponte, R. (1993). Hispanic families in poverty: Diversity, context, and interpretation. *Families in Society, 74*(9), 527–537.

Bachrach, C. A. (1986). Adoption plans, adopted children and adoptive mothers. *Journal of Marriage and the Family, 48,* 243–253.

Bandura, A. (1976). *Social learning theory.* Englewood Cliffs, NJ: Prentice-Hall.

Barkan, S. (1996, December). *Teen parent provisions in the new law.* Washington, DC: Center for Law and Social Policy. Available: www.handsnet.org/handsnet2/welfarereform/Articles/art.849902466.html [1997, September].

Barnes, S. L. (2001). Stressors and strengths: A practical examination of nuclear, single-parent, and augmented African American families. *Families in Society, 82*(5), 449–460.

Barth, R. (1985). Collaboration between child welfare and school social work services. *Social Work in Education, 8*(1), 32–47.

Bean, R. A., Perry, B. J., & Bedell, T. M. (2001). Developing culturally competent marriage and family therapists: Guidelines for working with Hispanic families. *Journal of Marital and Family Therapy, 27*(1), 43–54.

Bending, R. L. (1997). Training child welfare workers to meet the requirements of the Indian Child Welfare Act. *Journal of Multicultural Social Work, 5*(3–4), 151–164.

Berns, D. (2001). Addressing poverty issues in child welfare: Effective use of TANF as a prevention resource. In Alvin L. Sallee, Hal A. Lawson, & Katharine Briar-Lawson (Eds.), *Innovative practices with vulnerable children and families*. Dubuque, IA: Eddie Bowers.

Billingsley, A. (1992). *Climbing Jacob's ladder: The enduring legacy of African-American families*. New York: Simon & Schuster.

Black, L. (1996). Families of African origin: An overview. In M. McGoldrick, J. Giordano, & J. Pearce (Eds.), *Ethnicity and family therapy* (2nd ed.) (pp. 57–65). New York: Guilford Press.

Blank, M., & Melaville, A. (1999). Creating family-supportive schools: Taking the first steps. *Family Support, 18*(3), 37–40.

Bloom, M. (1996). *Primary prevention practices*. Thousand Oaks, CA: Sage.

Bowlby, J. (1980). *Attachment and loss, vol. 3: Loss*. New York: Basic Books.

Bronfenbrenner, U. (1987). Foreword. In S. L. Kagan, D. R. Powell, B. Weissbourd, & E. F. Zigler (Eds.), *America's family support programs: Perspectives and prospects*. New Haven, CT: Yale University Press.

Bruner, C., & Carter, J. L. (1991, November). *Family support and education: A holistic approach to school readiness. Network Briefs*. Denver and Washington, DC: National Conference of State Legislatures.

Butler, A. C. (1992, March). The changing economic consequences of teenage childbearing. *Social Service Review*, 1–31.

Centers for Disease Control. (2001, February 9). Evaluation of a child sexual abuse prevention program. *MMWR Weekly*, Available: www.stopitnow.com.

Cervera, N. J. (1993). Decision making for pregnant adolescents: Applying reasoned action theory to research and treatment. *Families in Society: The Journal of Contemporary Human Services, 74*(6), 355–365.

Child Trends. (no date). What do fathers contribute to children's well-being? *Child Trends Research Brief*. Available: www.childtrends.org.

Children's Bureau. (no date). *Infant adoption awareness training program*. Available: www.acf.dhhs.gov/programs/cb.htm.

Choi, N. G. (2001). Social work practice with the Asian American elderly. *Journal of Gerontological Social Work, 36*(1–2), 1–3.

Chow, J. (1999). Multiservice centers in Chinese American immigrant communities: Practice, principles, and challenges. *Social Work, 44*(1), 70–81.

Cochran, M. (1993). Parent empowerment: Developing a conceptual framework. *Family Science Review, 5*(1–2), 81–92.

Costin, L. (1985). Protective behaviors. *Social Work in Education, 7*(4), 210–211.

Cross, T. L. (1986). Drawing on cultural tradition in Indian child welfare practice. *Social Casework, 67*, 283–289.

Cross, T. L. (1996, Spring). Developing a knowledge base to support cultural competence. *The Prevention Report*, 2–5.

Downs, S. W. (1997). Parenting pioneers and parenting teams: Strengthening extended family ties in family support programs. *Family Preservation Journal, 2*(1), 33–46.

Downs, S. W., & Nahan, N. (1990, Fall). Mixing clients and other neighborhood families: Neighborhood family support centers offer services plus peer support. *Public Welfare, 48*(4), 26–33.

Downs, S. W., & Walker, D. (1996, June–July). Family support while you wait: The waiting room approach. *Zero to Three, 16*(6), 25–32.

DuBray, W., & Sanders, A. (1999). Interactions between American Indian ethnicity and health care. *Journal of Health and Social Policy, 10*(4), 67–84.

Duggan, A., McFarlane, E., Windham, A., Rohde, C., Salkever, D., Fuddy, L., Rosenberg, L., Buchbinder, S., & Sia, C. (1999). Evaluation of Hawaii's Healthy Start Program. *The Future of Children: Home Visiting, Recent Program Evaluations, 9*(1), 66–90.

Dupper, D. R., & Evans, S. (1996). From bandaids and putting out fires to prevention. *Social Work in Education, 18*(3), 186–192.

Early, T. J., & GlenMaye, L. F. (2000). Valuing families: Social work practice with families from a strengths perspective. *Social Work, 45*(2), 118–130.

Emery, R. E. (1999). *Marriage, divorce, and children's adjustment* (2nd ed.). Thousand Oaks, CA: Sage.

Family Resource Coalition. (no date). *Family support programs and teen parents.* Available: www.ericeece.org [1998, July].

Feeley, T. (2000, February). Low-income noncustodial fathers: A child advocate's guide to helping them contribute to the support of their children. *Issue Brief.* National Association of Child Advocates.

Finkelhor, D., & Dzuiba-Leatherman, J. (1995). Victimization prevention programs: A national survey of children's exposure and reactions. *Child Abuse & Neglect, 19,* 129–139.

Fix, M., & Passel, J. (2001). *U.S. immigrants at the beginning of the 21st century.* Washington, DC: The Urban Institute.

Freeman, E. M. (1990). The black family's life cycle: Operationalizing a strengths perspective. In S. M. L. Logan, E. M. Freeman, & R. G. McRoy (Eds.), *Social work practice with black families* (pp. 55–72). White Plains, NY: Longman.

Furstenberg, F. F., & Harris, K. M. (1990, April). *The disappearing father? Divorce and the waning significance of biological parenthood.* Paper presented at the Albany Conference on Demographic Perspectives on the American Family: Patterns and Prospects.

Garcia-Preto, N. (1996). Latino families: An overview. In M. McGoldrick, J. Giordano, & J. Pearce (Eds.), *Ethnicity and family therapy* (2nd ed.) (pp. 141–154). New York: Guilford Press.

Gartrell, N., Banks, A., Reed, N., Hamilton, J., Rodas, C., & Deck, A. (2000). The national lesbian family study. *American Journal of Orthopsychiatry, 70*(4), 542–548.

George, C. (1996). A representational perspective of child abuse and prevention: Internal working models of attachment and caregiving. *Child Abuse & Neglect, 20*(5), 411–424.

Gibson, L., & Leitenberg, H. (2000). Child sexual abuse prevention programs: Do they decrease the occurrence of child sexual abuse? *Child Abuse & Neglect, 24*(9), 1115–1125.

Gomby, D., Culross, P., & Behrmann, R. (1999). Home visiting: Recent program evaluations—Analysis and recommendations. *The Future of Children: Home Visiting, Recent Program Evaluations, 9*(1), 4–26.

Good-Touch/Bad-Touch. (no date). *About good-touch/bad-touch.* Available: www.goodtouchbadtouch.com.

Greenberg, M. (1999). Attachment and psychopathology in childhood. In J. Cassidy & P. R. Shaver (Eds.), *Handbook of attachment: Theory, research, and clinical applications* (pp. 469–490). New York: Guilford Press.

Haight, W. L. (1998). "Gathering the spirit" at First Baptist Church: Spirituality as a protective factor in the lives of African-American children. *Social Work, 43*(3), 213–221.

Hartman, A., & Laird, J. (1983). *Family centered social work practice.* New York: Free Press.

Hetherington, E. M. (1999). *Coping with divorce, single parenting, and remarriage: A risk and resiliency perspective.* Mahwah, NJ: Lawrence Erlbaum.

Highlights from the family preservation and support services program instruction. (1994, January). Washington, DC: U.S. Department of Health and Human Services.

Hill, R. B. (1997, Spring). Supporting African-American families: Dispelling myths, building on strengths. *Children's Voice, 2*(3), 4–7.

Hines, P. M., & Boyd-Franklin, N. (1996). African-American families. In M. McGoldrick, J. Giordano, & J. Pearce (Eds.), *Ethnicity and family therapy* (2nd ed.) (pp. 66–84). New York: Guilford Press.

Hunter, A. G. (1997). Counting on grandmothers: Black mothers' and fathers' reliance on grandmothers for parenting support. *Journal of Family Issues, 18*(3), 251–269.

Hurdle, D. E. (2002). Native Hawaiian traditional healing: Culturally based interventions for social work practice. *Social Work, 47*(2), 183–192.

Husock, H. (1992, Fall). Bring back the settlement house. *The Public Interest, 109,* 53–72.

Indian education: A national tragedy: A national challenge. (1969). Washington, DC: Committee on Labor and Public Welfare, Special Subcommittee on Indian Education; U.S. Senate, 91st Cong., 1st Sess.

Johnson, B. B. (1981). The Indian Child Welfare Act of 1978: Implications for practice. *Child Welfare, 60*(7), 435–446.

Jung, M. (1996). Family-centered practice with single parent families. *Families in Society, 77*(9), 583–590.

Kirby, D. (2001). *Emerging answers: Research findings on programs to reduce teen pregnancy (Summary).* Washington, DC: National Campaign to Prevent Teen Pregnancy.

Kirby, D., Barth, R., Leland, N., & Fetro, J. (1991). Reducing the risk: Impact of a new curriculum on sexual risk-taking. *Family Planning Perspectives, 23*(6), 253–263.

Koser, G. (Ed.). (1996). *From communities to capitols: State experiences with family support.* Chicago: Family Resource Coalition.

Landau, J. (1982). Therapy with families in cultural transition. In M. McGoldrick, J. Pearce, & J. Giordano (Eds.), *Ethnicity and family therapy.* New York: Guilford Press.

Landsman, M. (2001). Schools in partnership with families and communities. *The Prevention Report, 2001*(1).

Levine, J. A., & Pitt, E. W. (1995). *New expectations: Community strategies for responsible fatherhood.* New York: Families and Work Institute.

Levy, E. F. (1992). Strengthening the coping resources of lesbian families. *Families in Society: The Journal of Contemporary Human Services,* 23–31.

Lewin, T. (1992, February 27). Sharp decline found in number of children up for adoption. *New York Times,* p. 10.

Light, H. K., & Martin, R. E. (1986). American Indian families. *Journal of American Indian Education, 26*(1), 1–5.

Lott-Whitehead, L., & Tully, C. T. (1993). The family lives of lesbian mothers. *Smith College Studies in Social Work, 63*(3), 265–280.

Lyons-Ruth, K., Connell, D., Zoll, D., & Stahl, J. (1987). Infants at social risk: Relations among infant maltreatment, maternal behavior, and infant attachment behavior. *Developmental Psychology, 23,* 223–232 (cited in Van Horn, 1999).

Maccoby, E., & Martin, J. (1983). Socialization in the context of the family: Parent–child interaction. In E. M. Hetherington (Ed.), *Handbook of child psychology, vol. 4: Socialization, personality, and social development* (4th ed.).

MacLeod, J., & Nelson, G. (2000). Programs for the promotion of family wellness and the prevention of child maltreatment: A meta-analytic review. *Child Abuse & Neglect, 24*(9), 1127–1149.

Main, M., & Solomon, J. (1990). Procedures for identifying infants as disorganized/disoriented during the Ainsworth Strange Situation. In M. T. Greenberg, D. Cicchetti, & E. M. Cummings (Eds.), *Attachment in the preschool years* (pp. 121–160). Chicago: University of Chicago Press (cited in Van Horn, 1999).

Martin, J. A., Hamilton, B. E., Ventura, S. J., Menacker, F., Park, M. M., & Sutton, P. D. (2002). Births: Final data for 2001. *National Vital Statistics Reports, 51*(2).

Mayden, B. (1997). Child sexual abuse: Teen pregnancy's silent partner. In *Adolescent sexuality, pregnancy, and parenting: Selected readings* (pp. 57–60). Washington, DC: Child Welfare League of America.

Mayden, B., & Brooks, T. R. (1996). *Welfare reform and teen parents.* Washington, DC: Child Welfare League of America.

Maynard, R. A. (Ed.). (1996). *Kids having kids: A Robin Hood Foundation special report on the costs of adolescent childbearing.* New York: Robin Hood Foundation.

McLanahan, S., & Sandefur, G. (1994). *Growing up with a single parent: What hurts, what helps.* Cambridge, MA: Harvard University Press.

Miller, D. B. (1997). Adolescent fathers: What we know and what we need to know. *Child and Adolescent Social Work Journal, 14*(1), 55–69.

Moore, K. A., & Driscoll, A. (1997). Partners, predators, peers, protectors: Males and teen pregnancy. In *Not just for girls: The roles of boys and men in teen pregnancy* (pp. 5–10). Washington, DC: National Campaign to Prevent Teen Pregnancy.

Morgan, K. (2000). Mother—not mother. *The Family Therapy Networker, 24*(1), 54–59.

Mosley-Howard, G. S., & Evans, C. B. (2000). Relationships and contemporary experiences of the African American family: An ethnographic study. *Journal of Black Studies, 30*(3), 428–452.

National Center for Children in Poverty. (1997, Summer). Study maps state strategies to spur responsible fatherhood. *News and Issues, 7*(1), 1–2.

National Clearinghouse for Child Abuse and Neglect. (2001, February). *In focus: The risk and prevention of maltreatment of children with disabilities.* Available: www.calib.com/nccanch/prevmnth/actions/risk.cfm.

Nobles, W. G. (1988). American family life: An instrument of culture. In H. P. McAdoo (Ed.), *Black Families* (2nd ed.) (pp. 44–53). Beverly Hills, CA: Sage.

O'Connell, A. (1993). Voices from the heart: The developmental impact of a mother's lesbianism on her adolescent children. *Smith College Studies in Social Work, 63*(3), 281–299.

O'Dell, K. (2001, July). Reducing out-of-wedlock childbearing through pregnancy prevention. *Welfare Information Network Issue Notes, 5*(10). [Online]. Available: www.welfareinfo.org/reducingwedlock issuenote.htm [2003, January 27].

O'Dell, S. (2000). Psychotherapy with gay and lesbian families. *Clinical Social Work Journal 28*(2), 171–182.

O'Hare, W. (2001). *The child population: First data from the 2000 Census.* The Annie E. Casey Foundation and the Population Reference Bureau.

Olds, D., Perritt, L. M., Robinson, L., Henderson, C., Ekemode, J., Kitzman, H., Cole, B., & Powers, J. (1998). Reducing risks for antisocial behavior with a program of prenatal and early childhood home visitation. *Journal of Community Psychology, 26*(1), 65–83.

Ooms, T., & Herendeen, L. (1990). Teenage pregnancy programs: What have we learned? *Background briefing report and meeting highlights: Family Impact Seminar.* Washington, DC: American Association for Marriage and the Family.

Orrego, M. E. (1994–1995). Introduction to this issue. *Family Resource Coalition Report, 13*(3–4), 3–4.

Ortiz, V. (1995). The diversity of Latino families. In R. E. Zambrana (Ed.), *Understanding Latino families* (pp. 18–39). Thousand Oaks: Sage.

Padilla, Y. C. (1997). Immigrant policy: Issues for social work practice. *Social Work, 42*(6), 595–606.

Patterson, C. J. (1992). Children of lesbian and gay parents. *Child Development, 63,* 1025–1042.

Pearson, J., & Thoennes, N. (1996, Summer). Acknowledging paternity in hospital settings. *Public Welfare, 54,* 44–51.

Powell, D. R. (1994). Evaluating family support programs: Are we making progress? In S. L. Kagan & B. Weissbourd (Eds.), *Putting families first: America's family support movement and the challenge of change* (pp. 441–470). San Francisco: Jossey-Bass.

Reardon-Anderson, J., Capps, R., & Fix, M. (2002). *The health and well-being of children in immigrant families.* The Urban Institute. Available: www.urban.org/urf.cfm?ID=310584 [2003, February 7].

Reppucci, N., & Haugaard, J. (1989). Prevention of child sexual abuse: Myth and reality. *American Psychologist, 44*(10), 1266–1275.

Resource Center for Adolescent Pregnancy Prevention. (no date). Social learning theory's major concepts. ETR Associates. Available: www.etr.org.

Rispens, J., Aleman, A., & Goudena, P. (1997). Prevention of child sexual abuse victimization: A meta-analysis of school programs. *Child Abuse & Neglect, 21*(10), 975–987.

Rose, S. M. (2000). Reflections on empowerment-based practice. *Social Work, 45*(5), 403–412.

Salovitz, B. (2002, February). Reintroducing dad into the family equation. In *Making a difference that matters.* Duluth, GA: Child Welfare Institute.

Schiele, J. H. (1996). Afrocentricity: An emerging paradigm in social work practice. *Social Work, 41*(3), 284–294.

Schmitz, C. L. (1995). Reframing the dialogue on female-headed single parent families. *AFFILIA, 10*(4), 426–441.

Schorr, L. (1991). *Successful programs and the bureaucratic dilemma: Current deliberations.* New York: National Center for Children in Poverty.

Select Media. (no date). *Be proud! Be responsible!* Available: www.selectmedia.org.

Solomon, B. B. (1985). Assessment, service, and black families. In S. S. Gray, A. Hartman, & E. S. Saalberg (Eds.), *Empowering the black family* (pp. 9–20). Ann Arbor: University of Michigan, National Child Welfare Training Center.

Steinberg, L., Elman, J., & Mounts, N. (1989). Authoritative parenting, psychosocial maturity, and academic success among adolescents. *Child Development, 60,* 1424–1436.

Steiner, H., Zeanah, C., Stuber, M., Ash, P., & Angell, R. (1994). The hidden faces of trauma: An update on child psychiatric traumatology. *Scientific Proceedings of the Annual Meeting of the American Academy of Child and Adolescent Psychiatry, 31* (cited in Van Horn, 1999).

Straus, M. (2000). Corporal punishment and primary prevention of physical abuse. *Child Abuse & Neglect, 24*(9), 1109–1114.

Straus, M., & Stewart, J. (1999). Corporal punishment by American parents: National data on prevalence, chronicity, severity, and duration, in relation to child and family characteristics. *Clinical Child and Family Psychology Review, 2,* 55–70.

Sutton, C. T., & Broken Nose, M. A. (1996). American Indian families: An overview. In M. McGoldrick, J. Giordano, & J. Pearce (Eds.), *Ethnicity and family therapy* (2nd ed.) (pp. 57–65). New York: Guilford Press.

Tafoya, N., & Del Vecchio, A. (1996). Back to the future: An examination of the Native American holocaust experience. In M. McGoldrick, J. Giordano, & J. Pearce (Eds.), *Ethnicity and family therapy* (2nd ed.) (pp. 45–54). New York: Guilford Press.

Thompson, R. A., & Amato, P. R. (Eds.). (1999). *The postdivorce family: Children, parenting, and society.* Thousand Oaks, CA: Sage.

Thyer, B. (1994). Social learning theory: Empirical applications to culturally diverse practice. In R. Greene (Ed.), *Human behavior theory: A diversity framework.* Hawthorne, NY: Aldine de Gruyter.

U.S. Department of Justice. (2003). *2001 statistical yearbook of the Immigration and Naturalization Service.* Washington, DC: U.S. Government Printing Office.

Van Horn, P. (1999). Understanding attachment disorders in infants and young children. *The Source, 9*(3), 1ff. National Abandoned Infants Resource Center.

Vega, W. A. (1990). Hispanic families in the 1980s: A decade of research. *Journal of Marriage and the Family, 52*(1), 1015–1024.

Visher, E. B., & Visher, J. S. (1990). Dynamics of successful stepfamilies. *Journal of Divorce & Remarriage, 14*(1), 3–12.

Wald, L. D. (1915). *The house on Henry Street.* New York: Henry Holt.

Walker, J. S. (2001). Caregivers' views on the cultural appropriateness of services for children with emotional or behavioral disorders. *Journal of Child and Family Studies, 10*(3), 315–331.

Wallerstein, J. S., & Blakeslee, S. (1996). *Second chances: Men, women, and children a decade after divorce.* Boston: Houghton Mifflin.

Wattenberg, E., Brewer, R., & Resnick, M. (1991). Executive summary of a study of paternity decisions: Perspectives from young mothers and young fathers. Minneapolis: Center for Urban and Regional Affairs, University of Minnesota.

Weaver, H. (1998). Indigenous people in a multicultural society: Unique issues for human services. *Social Work, 43*(3), 203–211.

Weisberg, C. (2001). The school of the 21st century. *The Prevention Report, 2001*(1), 4.

Weiss, H. (1990). *Innovative models to guide family support and education policy in the 1990s: An analysis of four pioneering state programs.* Cambridge, MA: Harvard Family Research Project, Harvard Graduate School of Education.

Weiss, H., & Halpern, R. (1990). *Community-based family support and education programs: Something old or something new?* New York: National Center for Children in Poverty, Columbia University.

Zambrana, R. E., Silva-Palacios, V., & Powell, D. (1992). Parenting concerns, family support systems, and life problems in Mexican-origin women: A comparison by nativity. *Journal of Community Psychology, 20*(4), 276–288.

4 Supporting Families with Day Care and Child Development Programs

There was a child went forth every day,
And the first object he look'd on, that object he became,
And that object became part of him for the day or a certain part of the day,
Or for many years or stretching cycles of years.

—Walt Whitman

CHAPTER OUTLINE

Case Example: A Neighborhood Day Care Network

The following case example shows a community-based approach to day care that helps providers offer good-quality care in their homes. This fictional case is a composite of similar family day care networks being developed across the country. It illustrates the importance of community organization in developing good day care options in low-income neighborhoods.

Elisa Hernandez is a day care coordinator at the Casa del Barrio, a community agency for economic and social development, located in a low-income Puerto Rican neighborhood in a large city. A community organizer, she became concerned about the lack of day care in her neighborhood about six years ago. Many of her neighbors are young families, often headed by the mother, who work at low-paying jobs in other areas of town. As welfare became stricter about requiring mothers to work, even if they had infants and toddlers to care for, the shortage of day care slots in the local neighborhood became severe. The only day care center in the area that would accept the low welfare reimbursement rates was always full. Besides, it took only children who were toilet trained and it did not offer evening or weekend services, when many of the mothers worked.

Ms. Hernandez called together a committee consisting of current family day care providers, working parents, and representatives of Head Start, the schools, the public health department, and the public day care licensing department. The group decided to focus on increasing family day care in the area, which would provide scheduling flexibility to parents, be reasonable in cost, and offer parents, many of whom had limited English language skills, caregivers who spoke Spanish and were part of the Puerto Rican culture. An initial grant from a foundation gave the group resources to begin recruiting and training family day care providers, and to offer ongoing support to them. In order to find women who would be capable day care providers, Ms. Hernandez asked people in the area for names of women whom the neighbors trusted to do baby-sitting and who were considered to know a lot about children. She visited each of these women to get better acquainted and to invite them to an informational meeting.

The Family Day Care Program now has thirty family day care providers serving from seventy to eighty children. The program accepts infants and preschoolers, and older siblings who may come before and after school. Some providers offer care in the evenings and on weekends. Most speak Spanish as well as English.

Training is a major aspect of the program's success. Before caring for any children, providers receive training in how licensing works in the state and get help completing the licensing forms, which are not available in Spanish. They also receive information on the food program available from the state and learn other basics about running a small day care business from their homes. Ms. Hernandez learned that many women who were interested in providing day care had been discouraged because they didn't know how to cope with the red tape involved; she now guides them through this process. She also talks with the potential providers realistically about the rates welfare will pay for day care and how much the provider can expect to earn.

Within the first three months of taking children, providers also receive training in early childhood development, nutrition, health, and child abuse and neglect. Further training is also available in early childhood education. In addition to training, the program offers providers the free use of baby furniture and toys for six months, and can help providers install smoke detectors and make other minor improvements to meet licensing requirements.

During the last few years, due in part to welfare reform, more money has been available from the state to improve day care quality. The program was able to access these funds to hire a full-time, bilingual early childhood education teacher, who has been successful in increasing the skills of the providers. She visits each home at least once a month, bringing books and other learning materials. She shows the providers how to use them and consults on any special issues with the children. She helps the parents and providers keep track of the children's immunizations, and she refers children as needed to early screening programs for possible developmental problems.

The providers have developed a support group that meets monthly in members' homes. They share ideas and concerns, and often have guest speakers. Ms. Hernandez believes that these monthly meetings and the training help the providers to develop a sense of professionalism, as they begin to think of themselves less as "baby-sitters" and more as child care specialists with knowledge of how children grow and develop and of the community service system for children. Providers have learned to identify potential problems in child development and to refer parents to Head Start, the food stamp program, and adult education classes. As one provider observed, "People have always come to me to talk about their kids. The difference is now I know many different ideas to tell them, and not just based on my own experience."

The services offered to providers have also created program stability; few providers quit, so children experience long-term continuity of care. Parents are comfortable with the program; they know that their children are cared for in homes that are connected to the social service system, and that the providers have been screened and trained. Overall, the program has been able to improve the early childhood experiences of numerous children with working parents in the neighborhood, at relatively modest cost, through developing a cadre of dedicated, skilled family day care providers. Unfortunately, neither this day care program nor most others are able to offer day care providers with a decent income. However, for some women, it is a reasonable alternative to outside employment.

Introduction

With most mothers at work some part of each day, the question of what happens to the children has become an issue of intense national interest. Highly publicized stories of children left in dangerous situations while their parents, oblivious to the problem, were at work, have received widespread coverage in the press. This concern reflects the anxiety parents feel about having to juggle home and work responsibilities, and their worries about whether, by working outside the home, they are shortchanging their children of the care they need, or even jeopardizing their safety (Vobejda & Davis, 1997; Lewin, 2002). The fact that day care is in the national spotlight indicates that, after decades of ignoring the reality that many children were being cared for by people other than their parents, the country is beginning to address the issue of what happens to children in a society organized around parental employment outside the home.

Unlike most industrialized countries, the United States has lagged in establishing government-assisted arrangements for the daytime care of children of working parents. Reasons for this long delay come from a host of conflicting values in American society about the appropriate role of women as workers and mothers, and about the responsibility of government to participate in what many consider to be the "private sphere" of family life (Cherlin, 1998). The high cost of quality child care, the cultural diversity of U.S. families, and the controversy over the effects of day care on children's growth and development have also inhibited the establishment of comprehensive federal policy on children's daytime care and development.

> *Failing to respond to the past century and a half's change in work means that we are failing to meet the essential needs of children and adults in the United States. The gaps in caregiving do not exist because parents work or even because they work hard. The gaps are formed by social conditions that never adapted to the changes in where and how parents work. (Heymann, 2000)*

Today, however, a variety of social forces have created a national consensus on the need for a more comprehensive approach to the nation's child care needs. Sheila B. Kamerman has identified the following reasons for increased national interest in child care (Kamerman, 2001, p. 259):

- Widespread awareness that school readiness depends on the experiences of children during their infancy and preschool years, and that a good start in life is important to future success and the avoidance of negative outcomes for children
- The idea developed by economists that investing in the development of children, who are the "human capital" of the nation's future, is sound economic policy
- Research of developmental psychologists, which shows that early childhood programs can significantly benefit children
- Recent brain research, which underlines the importance of early childhood to the development of the brain
- The increased and apparently irreversible movement of women, including mothers of young children, into the workforce
- Welfare reform, as enacted in the Personal Responsibility and Work Opportunity Reconciliation Act, enacted in 1996, which requires mothers to work

Parents from all regions and levels of income are concerned about child care and are demanding programs that offer not only nurturance, safety, and affordability but also experiences that advance early childhood development (Children's Defense Fund, March 12, 2002). Economists, business leaders, and government officials now view child care as an issue affecting the economic and social well-being of the country as a whole (Newman et al., 2000). The increasing political power of women has also played a part in moving child care from the private sphere of family life to the public arena. The elevation of child care to a national policy issue was reflected in the convening of a White House Conference on Child Care in 1997.

> *[P]eople in this country have to be able to succeed at work and at home in raising their children. And if we put people in the position of essentially having to choose one over the other, our country is going to be profoundly weakened. Obviously, if people are worried sick about their children, and they fail at work, it's not just individual firms, it's the economic fabric and strength of the country that is weakened. Far more important, if people fail at home, they have failed in our most important job, and our most solemn responsibility. (W. Clinton, 1997)*

In spite of increased interest in and concern about child care, advocates for children and working families point out that many gaps exist in providing suitable daytime care for the nation's children. The quality of care that children receive is a major concern (Helburn et al., 1995). This problem becomes even more urgent when considered in light of recent scientific findings that the experiences of children in their earliest years affect how well they will learn for their entire lifetime. Former First Lady Hillary Rodham Clinton pointed out that "With 45% of our children under the age of one in day care regularly, the issue of quality has tremendous bearing not just on individual lives, but on the future of our nation" (H. Clinton, 1997). Too many families have choices severely limited by what is available and affordable in their community (Cherlin, 1998). National attention is also focusing on making it easier for parents who want to do so to stay home with their children for some period of time.

Child Care as a Child Welfare Service

Child care is usually considered only in the context of maternal employment. However, child care also has potential as a child welfare service, to strengthen vulnerable families and to prevent abuse, neglect, and the necessity for foster care placement for children. This potential has not been fully developed, partly because child care services are often administered by organizations outside the traditional child welfare service spectrum, and necessary linkages between service systems have not been made (Hershfield, 1995; Roditti, 1995).

Families Needing Specialized Assistance.   Families who have characteristics that put them at risk for child maltreatment may need many types of specialized assistance, including access to child care. For example, children whose parents are in a substance abuse treatment program can benefit from child care that offers them a safe environment and developmentally appropriate experiences while their parents are working at overcoming their addiction. Similarly, children of teen parents who are in good-quality day care settings may receive the developmental stimulation and oversight on their healthy growth and development that their young mothers are not ready to provide.

Respite care and crisis nurseries are also a valuable supplemental resource for families needing specialized assistance. Respite care is provided in some communities to families who have a child with disabilities or to families at risk of child abuse and neglect (ARCH, 1994).

Many children with *serious emotional problems* have parents who can continue to care for them in their homes if proper therapy is provided and if the parents have periods of respite from demanding caretaking duties. Day treatment centers for emotionally disturbed children are a useful alternative to outpatient therapy or full-time residential treatment.

Children of migrant farm workers are vulnerable to serious physical, social, and emotional deprivation. Because their parents have no way of caring for them while the parents are working in the fields, these children may spend their days in hazardous conditions of care. Sometimes they stay in parked cars or buses near the fields with only very occasional attention from adults, or they may be left in the camps under the supervision of an elderly, incapacitated member of the family or with the oldest child—perhaps only 6 or 7 years of age. Community child care centers are needed for infants and preschoolers to get the nutrition and intellectual stimulation they need to achieve success at school.

Families in Crisis.   For families who have abused or neglected their children and are at risk of losing them to foster care, child care services can help the family remain together while ensuring the child's safety. Such services allow a child to live at home while spending the day under the care of a trained child care provider, who can supplement the parent's minimally adequate care with developmentally enriching experiences and also can be a "first line of defense" in monitoring risky home situations. At the same time, child care services can provide needed respite to overburdened parents; the children receive appropriate daytime care while the parent attempts to resolve the serious problems that precipitated the child abuse and neglect. Homelessness, mental or physical illness, and mental retardation are among the family situations in which specialized day care services would be an appropriate middle-ground intervention between leaving children in a poorly functioning family with agency supervision and removing them from their homes entirely.

Changing Patterns of Work and Family

Working mothers are not new in America. Well before the Industrial Revolution of the nineteenth century, mothers worked many hours a day in their homes and on farms to produce goods and services that supplemented the family's income. This essential work often resulted in as much divided attention to children as occurs now among many mothers employed more formally outside their homes. Viewed against this background, the high rate of maternal employment today is not a radically new phenomenon, but an old one modified by new occupations and changed work locale, relationships, and rewards.

> *We decided to come back here because there were supposed to be jobs, but he couldn't find anything. So we decided I better go back to work—I haven't worked since we were married, but I'm a telephone operator and I knew I could get a job—but first we had to find a baby-sitter for Shelley. We didn't like the idea—she's two—but then. . . . (Family day care user—Collins & Watson, 1976, p. 4)*

The most urgent reason that women have entered the labor force in the past and continue to do so today is that like men, they feel a strong pressure to earn money. Women who enter the labor force almost universally do so out of necessity of one kind or another. Historic advances in science and technology have brought about an unprecedented growth and change in the national economy.

For growing numbers of women, an equally compelling reason for working is that, just as in the case of men, work is central to their identities. More women than ever before subscribe to and take for granted the aims and principles of the organized women's movement—women as individual human beings, rather than persons treated collectively without recognition of their interests and capabilities (Orenstein, 1998). Women are entering and deriving satisfaction from a wide range of jobs at all levels of occupations previously viewed as suitable only for men. It should be noted, though, that the wage gap persists: In 1999, white women received approximately 72 percent and black women, 65 percent, of the average wage earned by men (Office of the Equal Opportunity Ombudsman, no date). The increased likelihood of divorce or widowhood impels women to develop their own economic security through work, rather than rely solely on their husbands.

Although the pattern is changing, women still bear most of the responsibility for housework and child care. Since women first entered industrial work more than a century ago, the way in which work is organized has been a stress factor in family life. Recognition that the "second shift" is a constant in the lives of many American women, and concerns about the quality of care children receive while parents are working, have led to increased interest in better coordinating work and family life. The Family and Medical Leave Act of 1993 gives parents time off from work to care for a new baby or ill child. Some advocates are also urging shorter workweeks for both men and women and other policies that would allow a parent to stay home for a period of time.

Sharing the Costs of Care

The Child Care Crunch

Child care is a costly expense for many American families. The Children's Defense Fund (1998) describes the problem: "Full-day care easily costs $4,000 to $10,000 a year—at least as much as college tuition at a university. Yet, half of America's families with young children earn less than $35,000 a year. A family with both parents working full-time at the minimum wage earns only $21,400 a year." According to the most recent available federal statistics, families with preschoolers who required day care in 1993 paid an average of $74 a week (Casper, 1995).

For poor families, child care costs are especially burdensome. Poor families who pay for care spend about 18 percent of their income on child care for preschoolers, compared to 7 percent for the nation's wealthier families (Casper, 1995). Figure 4.1 shows the percentage of income spent by women of different income categories on child care.

In spite of the large percentage they spend on day care, poor families spend less in actual dollars than do wealthier families. The poorest working families spend less than $50 on average a week for child care, whereas the wealthiest families spend $92 a week. See Figure 4.2. Quality of care is related to cost. Recent research showing that the later learning ability of children depends on the quality of care they receive as infants and preschoolers underscores the importance of ensuring high-quality child care for all children (Barnett, 1995). Women with low earning capacity cannot support their families and pay for child care on their earnings alone. Advocates for children are concerned that without governmental assistance, poor children will be relegated to substandard day care facilities that will not provide the needed emotional, social, physical, and cognitive experiences to help them do well in school and become productive adults (Giannarelli & Barsimantov, 2000).

Federal Legislation

Parents, businesses, and federal, state, and local governments all contribute to the payment for child care in the United States. The federal role in funding child care changed drastically in the early 1990s as a result of legislation increasing the federal contribution. In 1997, the federal government spent about $10 billion on the three largest federal child care pro-

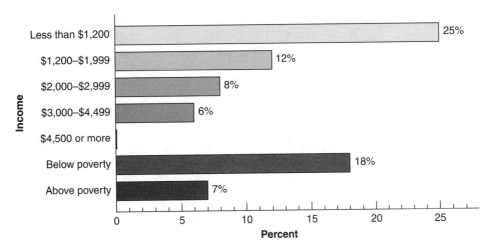

FIGURE 4.1   Percent of Monthly Family Income Spent on Child Care by Family Income and Poverty Status*

*Limited to families with a preschooler.

Source: L. M. Casper (1995), *What does it cost to mind our preschoolers?* Current Population Reports, P-70, no. 52. U.S. Department of Commerce, Census Bureau (Washington, DC: U.S. Government Printing Office).

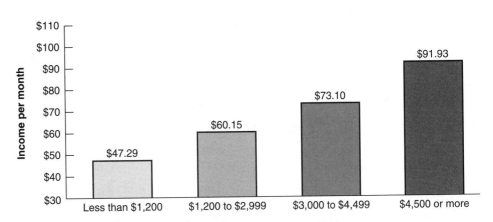

FIGURE 4.2   Weekly Payment for Child Care by Monthly Family Income

Source: L. M. Casper (1996), *Who's minding our preshoolers?* Current Population Reports, P-70, no. 53. U.S. Department of Commerce, Census Bureau (Washington, DC: U.S. Government Printing Office).

grams: the Child Care Development Block Grant; Head Start; and the Dependent Care Tax Credit (Shalala, 1997).

■ *Child Care Development Block Grant* provides funds to states for child care subsidies for low-income families, including those in welfare-to-work programs, and for improving the quality and supply of child care. Federal funding for child care subsidies increased substantially from 1996 to 1998; in 1998 the Child Care Development Fund was $5.2 billion (Cabrera, Hutchens, & Peters, 2002). Recently, government funding for this essential program has decreased, creating concern about the adequacy of day care arrangements for young children of mothers working their way off welfare.

- *Head Start* is a federally and locally financed early childhood development program for low-income children. In 1997, the federal share of this program's costs was $4 billion. This program is described in another section of this chapter.
- *Dependent Care Tax Credit* helps families reduce their child care costs by allowing them to deduct a portion of these costs from their federal tax obligation. An important limitation of this program is that it helps only families who earn enough to pay federal taxes. Those earning too little to pay taxes do not get any help from this program on their child care expenses. In 1997, the federal cost of this program was $2.5 billion.

In addition to these programs, numerous smaller funding streams funnel resources to specific populations, such as children with disabilities and Native American children.

The Family and Medical Leave Act

The Family and Medical Leave Act was signed into law by President Clinton in 1993, the culmination of seven years of lobbying by child advocacy groups. It addresses the needs of families for both job security and caregiving. The law requires employers of fifty or more workers to grant employees who work twenty-five or more hours per week, up to twelve weeks of unpaid leave a year, for the birth or adoption of a child, for the care of a seriously ill child or other family member, or for a serious illness of their own. Although the leave is unpaid, employers do have to provide health benefits during the leave. Because part-time workers and workers in small businesses are exempt, only about half the nation's workers are covered by the law. In spite of this limitation, the law is a milestone toward the goal of making work more compatible with family life for American workers and their children, and puts the United States in the company of other industrialized countries, most of which have provisions for leave following childbirth and for child care emergencies.

Day Care Regulation

Although varying in form, today all states have statutory provisions for the regulation of day care for children. The intent of these regulations is to safeguard children from harm and prevent ills that might befall them from poor care and supervision. Regulation is an action of the government to bring an activity in the private sector (in this case the places where and means by which children are cared for outside their own homes) under the control of constituted authority and to require compliance with agreed-on expectations (Gazan, 1998).

> *Licensing is one of the activities affecting the standard of care that children receive. . . . Its mission is to require services in which the safety and well-being of children are givens. (Terpstra, 1989, p. 442)*

Appropriate and well-enforced licensing and regulatory standards are important strategies in assuring quality in day care. Remember, however, that licensing rules represent minimum baseline requirements below which no program may operate. They do not provide a guarantee that day care will be of high quality. States, not the federal government, make and enforce regulations for day care. The states vary considerably in their day care licensing provisions; as the findings of studies by the Children's Foundation (2002), which periodically surveys the states on their licensing provisions for day care centers and family day care homes, have verified.

All states do require that day care centers be licensed. Despite many differences, state day care regulations are fairly uniform in the areas they address. Most specify the amount of space that must be available to each child and also define fire and other building safety requirements. Providers may be required to pass health examinations; more and more states are also requiring criminal background checks. Most states require that the providers have certain levels of education and specify required child–adult ratios.

Special Issues in Day Care Regulation

In recent years a number of states have begun to consider and evaluate different ways of regulating family day care. Licensing, the traditional form of regulation, requires that a state agency reviews applications, inspects the day care centers and homes, approves the license, and regularly monitors the centers and homes. This arrangement has proved very costly, and states have not traditionally allocated sufficient resources to provide sound, ongoing assessments of day care homes. Concern has grown about the high costs of licensing day care homes in view of the limited safeguards achieved for children.

Most private day care homes are not regulated at all. Most states exempt various categories of day care providers from regulation; for example, some states exempt homes caring for three or fewer children, or those caring for the children of relatives. States may require only homes that are receiving public funds, such as those caring for the children of welfare recipients, to be regulated (Galinsky, Howes, Kontos, & Shinn, 1994). Many day care providers simply do not comply with the law, if they find the process of licensing burdensome and intrusive. Some providers do not become licensed because they want to avoid paying taxes on their income.

For all these reasons, only a small proportion of day care homes actually caring for children are brought to the attention of licensing agencies. In fact, if licensing authorities actively undertook to study and evaluate all the homes now giving care to unrelated children, the endeavor would be beyond the capacities of administrative departments as now constituted. This is in contrast to day care centers that by their nature are more easily identified in a community and brought under the jurisdiction of a licensing statute.

Registration: An Alternative to Licensing

Many states are now considering "registration" as an alternative to traditional licensing. This approach to regulation operates as follows: Persons giving family day care to one or a small number of children are required to make this fact known to the state's regulatory agency—that is, to register the day care operation and report the names of children being cared for. The regulatory agency is then responsible for supplying the child care provider with a statement of the mandatory forms to be completed for registration, and other literature deemed to be helpful to anyone caring for young children. Day care providers are instructed to review the requirements carefully, assess their own degree of compliance, and report the degree of conformity to the regulatory agency. In addition, they must supply the parents of the children they care for with a copy of the mandatory requirements and the means by which complaints can be made to the regulatory agency. After registration, day care providers are given access to consultative resources for improving their child care endeavors. The regulatory agency also makes inspection visits to randomly selected registered day care homes to determine whether substantial conformity to standards does in fact exist and, when necessary, to help day care providers overcome obstacles to meeting standards.

Advantages to family day care of registration over licensing include these: (1) Regulatory staff members are free to concentrate on problem homes rather than on routine inspections; (2) parents have a greater role in evaluating day care homes; and (3) family day care becomes more socially visible, increasing the feasibility of measuring its extent and evaluating and strengthening its characteristics.

Working Parents' Child Care Arrangements

Families at the beginning of the twenty-first century are dynamic and changing. Their needs for child care are increasing, and they are demanding change in the child care system. Today, most mothers with dependent children are working outside the home, including 65 percent of mothers with children under age 6, and 78 percent of mothers with children ages 6 to 13 (Bachu & O'Connell, 2000). Welfare recipients are required to work, go to school, or participate in job training, and they need child care to meet these demands. Also fueling the demand for child care is the desire of many parents to provide some form of early educational experience to prepare their children for school.

The large number of working mothers means that every day millions of children are in child care of some sort. Sixty percent of all preschoolers, or about 13 million children, are in some form of day care or early childhood educational program. Millions more school-age children are in after-school and summer activity programs (Smith, 2000). These figures clearly show that "other-than-mother" care is now normative, rather than the exception, for children in the United States. How then are the nation's children of working parents distributed among the different child care arrangements?

The 1999 National Survey of America's Families (NSAF) collected information on child care arrangements while the adults most responsible for the children's care (usually the mothers) were working. Currently, these are the most recent national data available on child care arrangements of the children of working families in the United States. The NSAF researchers state that their survey is "representative of the noninstituionalized, civilian population of persons under age 65 in the nation as a whole" and in the thirteen states specifically surveyed (Sonenstein, Gates, Schmidt, & Bolshun, 2002, p. 2).

Child Care Arrangements for Preschoolers

According to the NSAF survey, parents themselves cared for over a quarter of the preschool children with employed parents. Relatives, such as grandparents, and day care centers were each responsible for another quarter of the preschool age children of working parents. Family day care providers cared for 14 percent of these children, and nannies who come to the family's home cared for 4 percent. Nannies would be the preferred option for many parents, especially parents of infants, but this is too expensive for most families (Casper, 1996).

Child Care Arrangements for School-Age Children

The NSAF survey found that 45 percent of the 5-year-olds in the United States who had working primary caretakers were in kindergarten or first grade in 1999. For some kindergarten-age children, school provided all of their needs for care while their parents were at work, but over three-quarters of the children were in a day care arrangement, either instead of or in addition to school. "These arrangements included child care centers, before and after school programs, family child care providers, babysitters, and relatives" (Sonenstein et al., 2002, p. 3). Compared with younger children, 5-year-olds were more likely to be in centers and were less likely to be cared for by relatives.

The NSAF survey found that as children get older, they spend less time in child care settings outside of school. About half of children ages 6 to 12 with an employed primary caretaker were in some type of child care arrangement besides school, usually care by relatives (23 percent). Children also attended before- and after-school programs (15 percent) and family day care settings (7 percent). About 10 percent of the children cared for themselves. The rest were children whose parents were able to arrange their work schedules to provide child care coverage or who pieced together care on an irregular basis.

The NSAF survey researchers also looked at differences in child care arrangements according to family structure and family income. They found that, among parents of preschoolers or school-age children, single-parent families were more likely to use either child care centers or care by relatives than were two-parent families. Two-parent families were more likely to use parental care while the other parent was at work. These differences were true for both higher-income and lower-income families.

Day Care Programs

Family Day Care

Made up of many different arrangements between parents and the caretakers of their children, family day care is the most complex system of child care in the country. Family day care defies simple description because it is so varied. Ways of categorizing family day care include whether the home is licensed/regulated and how many children it is allowed to care for. By far the majority of day care homes are not regulated or licensed; a smaller percentage have some kind of oversight through regulation or licensing by the state, and a still smaller percentage are regulated homes linked to a day care network (Hofferth, 1996). The case example at the beginning of this chapter describes such a network. Day care homes may care for one to six children; licensed group day care homes may care for up to twelve children. Most providers work alone, although some homes have helpers.

Family day care offers several advantages to parents and children. It is relatively easy to locate, because day care homes are dispersed widely in neighborhoods across the country.

Parents can often find day care close to home, which minimizes transportation problems. The arrangements parents make with the providers often can accommodate special situations, such as a parent's unusual work schedule or special needs of the children. It is less expensive than other forms of care. Parents are likely to form a close, personal relationship with the provider, which may continue even after the child leaves care. For children, day care offers the stimulation of playing with other children and relating to nonfamily adults within the comfort and safety of a home setting.

The major disadvantage of family day care is the lack of accountability. Day care homes are private; after dropping off the child, the parent does not know what goes on in the home. The vast majority of providers are not licensed or regulated, and are not part of a network of providers. They operate independently and are unsupervised. They are unlikely to offer educational activities and usually do not have the training to provide ongoing, planned experiences for the children to promote their cognitive development. Another disadvantage is that the day care homes are inherently unstable and are often short lived. An illness in the family or other event can cause the provider to quit offering care. The quality of care in day care homes varies a great deal. "They offer experiences for the child ranging from concerned and competent care by an involved and happy care provider to neglectful or even abusive care by a depressed and isolated woman who believes she has no marketable skills but needs the money and so takes in babies" (Clarke-Stewart, 1993, p. 45).

Day Care Centers

As with day care homes, there is tremendous variety among day care centers, making general descriptions inadequate. A center may offer care for a few as 15 children or as many as 300, though on average there are about 60 children per center. Children are usually divided into classes based on age; the average size of these groups is 7 for infants, 10 for toddlers, and 14 for preschoolers. Most children in day care centers are 3 or 4 years old. The teachers are usually young women who have attended college (Hofferth, 1996).

Compared with day care homes, day care centers have several advantages. They are more stable and are publicly accountable through licensing and other regulations. They stay open even if staff are sick or go on vacation. Usually, staff have some training in child development and are likely to offer educational activities to children. Children have opportunities to play with other children in a safe environment that may be rich in stimulating games and activities. Their major disadvantages are that they may be farther from home than day care homes located in the immediate neighborhood, and they are often less flexible in hours or in taking sick children than are day care homes. Day care centers may seem large and impersonal to children; poor or mediocre centers often are not sufficiently attentive to the needs and abilities of individual children. Children may not have a close connection with a caring adult who knows them well.

After-School Care

How school-age children spend their after-school time has become a matter of increasing interest to parents, community leaders, researchers, and policy makers. The large number of school-age children with working parents has increased concern about after-school supervision. It is widely acknowledged that many school children ages 6 to 12 are only loosely supervised in a piecemeal pattern of care by older siblings, neighbors, relatives, and parents themselves, interspersed with periods of self-care. Children age 13 and older are frequently left to fend for themselves after-school hours. Instead of being an opportunity for constructive involvement with adult mentors, for activities promoting academic success, and for enriching leisure time activities, after-school hours are too often spent in nonproductive and possibly dangerous ways (de Kanter, Williams, Cohen, & Stonehill, 2000; Newman, Fox, Flynn, & Christeson, 2000).

Children and young teenagers left unsupervised are also more likely to be involved in crime. The after-school hours from 3 P.M. to 6 P.M. are hours when children are most likely to be victims or perpetrators of violent crime, to be in car crashes, to experiment with drugs and cigarettes, to engage in sexual intercourse with resultant pregnancies, and to become hooked on violent video games, which are now thought to be a training ground for violent behavior (Newman et al., 2000). These destructive activities may have devastating consequences for the communities in which the children live as well as for the children themselves. Recognition of the harm that often comes from too much unsupervised time has led to an increase in organized after-school programs.

Evaluations of several model after-school programs have shown that good programs work to reduce crime, keep children safe, and help them learn to be successful in school and in relating constructively to others. For example, the Opportunities Industrialization Centers' Quantum Opportunities Program, operating in four cities, randomly selected high school freshmen whose families received public assistance to participate in an after-school program. The program offered opportunities in academics, community service, personal development, and monetary incentives to encourage healthy life choices, including high school graduation. Results of the evaluation showed that boys participating in the program were only one-sixth as likely to be convicted of a crime during high school as boys who did not participate. Encouraging results have also been found in other programs with a variety of auspices and program models, such as Boys and Girls Clubs, Big Brothers/Big Sisters, the Police Athletic League, and the Cooperative Extension Service of Wisconsin (Newman et al., 2000).

In assessing the results of many program evaluations, the staff of the advocacy group Fight Crime: Invest in Kids identified two major effects of these programs. The "safe haven and control effect" refers to the immediate effect of moving children from unsupervised or gang-related activity to a setting with responsible adults, interesting and wholesome activities, developmental opportunities, and guidance in managing peer and adult relationships. The programs offer a safe haven from the streets and an attractive alternative to crime and other undesirable activity. The "values and skill effect" refers to long-term benefits of the programs, in helping children learn to succeed academically, and the importance of personal responsibility, hard work, and respect for others. Personal relationships with adult mentors are vital to the transmission of these desirable "values and skills." Participation in community service activities gives children an opportunity to experience the satisfaction of helping others (Newman et al., 2000).

In spite of a widely acknowledged need for after-school programs, a recent survey shows that in 1997, programs were meeting as little as 20 percent of existing need (U.S. General Accounting Office, 1997). The federal government, local school districts, social service agencies, and a variety of national and regional foundations have been working to increase the opportunities for youngsters to have constructive and safe after-school experiences while their parents are at work (de Kanter et al., 2000). However, the need remains greatest in low-income areas, both rural and urban, where shortages of available slots in after-school programs are critical. Research shows that children in low-income areas are most at risk for criminal behavior in after-school hours and for thwarted adult lives; these children stand to benefit most from well-designed after-school enrichment programs and are among the least likely to get them (Newman et al., 2000).

Day Care Networks in Low-Income Communities

The organization of family day care homes into "day care systems" is a relatively recent development that has significant implications for child care planning and programming (Kisker et al., 1990; Out-of-School Time, 1997). Although these homes are only a small proportion of all day care homes, they are representative of a growing trend more important than their numbers suggest. The U.S. Congress, in enacting the Child Care and Development Block Grant of 1990, called on governors to designate a state lead agency to act as a convener and coordinator for organizing various day care constituencies into an overarching day care system.

As the case example at the beginning of the chapter shows, day care networks are systems that link family day care providers in a geographical area with each other and with professional support and consultation. They are usually organized by established agencies, such as schools, health departments, departments of social services, community-based organizations, or early childhood development and child care services. They improve the quality and supply of family day care in an area by recruiting, screening, training, and offering ongoing support and technical assistance to family day care providers and by linking the providers and the children they care for to other needed services in the community.

Providers in day care systems are also more likely to remain stable than are other providers, because the system can provide supports that help the provider function better. The system can offer referrals of new families and consultation on fee schedules, taxes, and other business issues. It provides training and opportunities for providers to interact with one another. Expert consultation can help providers manage situations relating to children or their families. Backup care is available if the provider is temporarily unable to care for children. Day care systems can alleviate such problems with family day care as lack of accountability, instability of provider homes, lack of training, and insufficient attention to children's developmental needs. At the same time, day care systems maintain all the advantages of family day care, such as flexibility, home atmosphere, and the close personal connections that can occur between provider and parent (Sugarman, 1991; Larner & Chaudry, 1993).

As Larner (1994) points out, family day care may be especially well suited to low-income families because it is close to home, flexible, small in scale, relatively affordable, and gives the parents the choice of who will care for their child, particularly regarding cultural and language compatibility. It also provides low-income women with the opportunity to earn a living at home while providing day care, although subsidies are required to supplement what the parents can pay for care.

Child Care Choices and Consumer Education

With *parent empowerment* becoming a watchword for services to families, it is not surprising that parents are increasingly taking responsibility for making informed choices about what kinds of child care their children receive. Recent federal legislation on day care reinforces this trend toward empowerment, requiring that parents have choices regarding the care their children receive under federal programs. This is in contrast to earlier policy, which required that low-income parents use care in specific centers or day care homes. Current legislation is based on consumer subsidies, in which parents have vouchers that can be applied to various child care possibilities. Some states require that programs help parents become informed consumers of child care by providing information about licensing regulations and about the child care options available in their area.

A number of guides are available to parents to help them assess the suitability of various day care environments for their children. Parents who have consulted published guides, who have developed criteria and expectations about the kind of care they want, and who have plenty of time to search for care increase their chances of finding appropriate day care for the children. It is just as important to stay involved after the child is placed. Forming alliances with the day care staff, visiting on a drop-in basis, talking with the child about his or her day, and asking questions about confusing situations are important ways for parents to continually monitor their children's progress in day care.

The caregiver is the key to day care quality. Children do best when the caregivers are actively engaged with the children, when they think of themselves as professionals and not just "baby-sitters," when they have received training in child development and early childhood education, and when they are part of a network of providers that offers ongoing support and training.

Recent Research on Child Care

The Effect of Child Care on Infants

Economic and social changes in the past several decades have influenced a major change in the care of young children. Today, the majority of children under age 3 with working parents spend a portion of each week in nonparental child care. "This fact of contemporary life represents a dramatic reapportioning of the care of young children from parents to others, starting in the first few months of life" (Phillips & Adams, 2001). This change in the child care environment experienced by many American children has given rise to an intense debate on the effects of nonparental care on child development (Stolberg, 2001; Lewin, 2002; Waldfogel, Brooks-Gunn, & Han, 2002). This debate reflects the public's awareness of the vulnerability of infants and their utter dependence on others for their care. Further, infants are thought to be particularly susceptible to environmental influences, which may have long-term effects on the child's development. This view of the importance of infancy in shaping the future is reflected in the popular adage, "As the twig is bent, so grows the tree."

Recently the debate about the effect of day care on young children has moved beyond global questions about whether child care is good or bad, and now focuses on how the different aspects of child care affect children's development in the early years. It is important to know about the qualities of day care that tend to help or hinder healthy development.

Results of a major research project conducted by the National Institute of Child Health and Human Development (NICHD) have been released to the public on an ongoing basis since 1997 (updates are available online at http://public.rti.org/secc). The longitudinal study began in 1991 by enrolling more than 1,300 families and their children from 10 locales across the country. The researchers have followed the children from the time of enrollment, when they were 1 month old or less up to the present time. The children are now in middle school. The families are diverse in ethnicity, income, family structure, maternal employment status, type and quality of child care, and length of time children spent in care. The study design takes into account the effects of other influences on children's development such as family economic status, mother's psychological well-being and intelligence, and infant sex and temperament. The research design makes it likely that findings on the children reflect the effects of day care on them, rather than the effects of these other influences (National Institutes of Health, 1997).

The analysis so far focuses on cognitive development. The main finding is that child care need not be harmful to very young children *if it is high quality*. "The most striking aspect of these results from the early child care study is that children are not being placed at a disadvantage in terms of cognitive development if they have high-quality day care in their first three years," said NICHD Director Duane Alexander (National Institutes of Health, 1997, p. 1). The study researchers found that children whose caregivers spoke to them frequently, asked them questions, and responded to their vocalizations were likely to have greater language abilities as they grew older than did children whose caregivers did not give them this type of attention. Another important finding was that, although the quality of the care made a difference in the child's language development, home influences were still much more important.

A more recent analysis, based on new, longitudinal data of the children, has reported more disturbing findings, indicating that maternal employment may adversely affect the cognitive development of white (but not black) children, compared to those whose mothers did not work outside the home during the first year of life (Waldfogel et al., 2002).

In summarizing the results of the NICHD as well as other research, Phillips and Adams (2001) point out that the story these studies tell is complex, with "overlapping impacts that diverse child care settings and home situations have on children" (p. 35). The public can expect confusing and seemingly contradictory findings from research in the near future, as studies look narrowly at specific aspects of maternal employment and child care, and their effects on child development. Phillips and Adams (2001) identify the following key points in summarizing the results of this line of research so far:

- Early exposure to child care can foster children's learning and enhance their lives, or it can leave them at risk for troubled relationships. The outcome that results depends largely on the quality of the child care setting.
- Responsive caregivers who surround children with language, warmth, and a chance to learn are the key to good outcomes. Other quality attributes (like training and staff-to-child ratios) matter because they foster positive caregiving.
- Diversity and variability are hallmarks of the American child care supply. Both "wonderful and woeful" care can be found in all types of child care but, overall, settings where quality is compromised are distressingly common.
- Children whose families are not buoyed by good incomes or government supports are the group most often exposed to poor-quality care. (p. 35)

The authors call on government, communities, foundations, and businesses to play a larger role in helping parents find good-quality care for infants and toddlers.

Given that quality is the most important single factor in determining the effect of a day care experience on children, we turn now to explore in more detail the findings of research on day care quality.

The Importance of Quality

The study just described points out the importance of quality of care in assessing the effect of day care on infants. It is discouraging, then, to learn from other recent research that overall the care provided in the nation's child care centers is mediocre and not of the high quality needed to optimize children's development (Dwyer, Chait, & McKee, 2000). The poor quality of child care is particularly prevalent in low-income neighborhoods. The National Research Council (2000) published a synthesis of research, which warns that many children from low-income families are in child care programs "of such low quality that learning and development . . . may even be jeopardized" (p. 1).

A comprehensive study, the Cost, Quality, and Child Outcomes study, collected data in 1993 through visits to fifty nonprofit and fifty for-profit randomly chosen centers in four states: California, Colorado, Connecticut, and North Carolina. Data collectors conducted interviews and distributed questionnaires to center directors, teachers, and parents and observed classrooms in each center. Data were also collected on the 826 children from the visited classrooms (Helburn et al., 1995).

The main finding of the study was that the level of quality at most child care centers in the United States does not meet children's needs for safety, warm relationships, and learning. Fifty-eight percent of the centers fell in the area of the scale from 3 to under 5, which the researchers labeled "mediocre." Another 28 percent of the centers fell below even this mediocre level. Thus, only 14 percent of the centers were rated as "good" or "excellent" and were considered developmentally appropriate by the researchers.

Of particular concern was the quality of center care for infants and toddlers. Of the classrooms serving these age groups, only 8 percent offered "good" or "excellent" quality, while 40 percent rated less than "minimal." The data collectors point out that "[b]abies in poor-quality rooms are vulnerable to more illness because basic sanitary conditions are not met for diapering and feeding; are endangered because of safety problems that exist in the room; miss warm, supportive relationships with adults; and lose out on learning because they lack books and toys required for physical and intellectual growth" (Helburn et al., 1995, p. 3).

The researchers found that good-quality child care was related to such factors as higher staff-to-child ratios and teacher education, specialized training, and wages. States with higher licensing standards had fewer poor-quality centers. The auspices of the center also was related to quality; those operated by public schools, universities, or public agencies, by employers at the work site, or by organizations using public funding that required them to adhere to higher standards were likely to provide higher quality care than other centers. These centers were likely to have more donated resources and subsidies that helped increase the funding available for child care. Centers dependent mainly on parent fees, on the other hand, had fewer resources and, overall, lower quality of care.

This important study confirms that the care children receive in many centers in the United States is not helping them develop cognitively and emotionally, and is not preparing them to enter school fully ready to learn. It also confirms that the costs of child care are high, and that parent fees alone cannot provide sufficient resources to ensure high-quality care. The study's findings strongly suggest that subsidies, from foundations, employers, and the government, are needed in addition to parent fees to ensure that an adequate level of care is offered to all children needing child care in the United States.

Sexual Abuse in Day Care

Although sexual abuse in day care has probably been going on for a long time, the Mc-Martin Preschool case in California galvanized the issue for the general public during the 1980s. The case had characteristics that fed public fears: The preschool was located in a prosperous suburb, dispelling notions that "it can't happen here"; the facility was well established and trusted; and the teachers, who seemed to be typical day care providers, were accused of having abused hundreds of 3- and 4-year-olds with terrifying and bizarre rituals. After six and a half years of legal activity, the jury finally acquitted the defendants on most of the charges and deadlocked on others because of questions about the credibility of the child witnesses. The McMartin case undermined confidence that children could be safely left with day care providers. Hundreds of other cases were also uncovered around the country in the wake of the McMartin case publicity.

A government-funded national investigation of sexual abuse in day care, conducted from 1983 to 1985, found that the risk of sexual abuse in day care is about 5.5 children sexually abused for every 10,000 children enrolled. Although any sexual abuse is a matter of serious concern, it is important to keep these figures in perspective. Children are more at risk of sexual abuse in their own homes, with an estimated incidence of about 9 per 10,000 children (Finkelhor, Williams, & Burns, 1988).

The study findings give guidance to parents, day care centers, licensing agencies, and the child welfare and criminal justice systems investigating and prosecuting these cases on how to increase the protection of children in day care. About two-thirds of the abuse took place around toileting, in the bathroom, suggesting that day care centers become more alert to who is taking children to the bathroom and also decrease the amount of private or enclosed spaces in the bathroom. Many children were threatened or coerced into not disclosing the abuse. In half the cases, children did not disclose for a month or more. Finkelhor and colleagues strongly recommend that parents make sure their preschool children understand there are no secrets in day care, and that anything that happens there can be told safely to parents. Day care staff need to be more alert to the possibility that abuse can occur and to be informed frequently of the necessity of reporting suspected abuse to child protective services. Over half the perpetrators were neither owners nor part of the professional staff; they were aides, volunteers, family members of the staff, bus drivers, or janitors. This finding suggests more diligence in monitoring who has unsupervised access to the children. Although most of the abusers were men, women made up a surprising 40 percent of the perpetrators; allegations against female staff should not be dismissed without investigation.

Parents should be free to drop in to the center at any time and to have access to all parts of the facility. Law enforcement and child protective services should form collaborative relationships that allow for a coordinated, comprehensive investigation, and should make special efforts to keep parents informed about the progress of the case.

Developmental Programs for Families with Young Children

Throughout the United States, a large and growing number of programs exist to enhance the development of young children; the intent is for these children to be ready developmentally to start school and move forward on the path to becoming productive, self-sufficient adults. Middle-class families now routinely enroll their preschoolers in developmental programs, convinced that the experiences the children receive there will help them prepare for school. Publicly funded programs attempt to offer some of these same opportunities to lower-income children, who may have even greater need. Since the 1960s, with the founding of Head Start, legislators, policy makers, parents, and professionals in child development and child welfare have focused attention on making preschool programs available for children of poor families, who frequently lack access to high-quality early education programs.

The need for these programs is widely recognized. Too often children who are reared without stimulating home environments and who have not received supplemental preschool education find when they start school that they are already behind their peers in mastering skills necessary to succeed in school. Children may become discouraged and fall further and further behind, a pattern that encourages feelings of failure and dropping out early. Children who are not successful in school are at high risk for adjustment difficulties in adolescence, including juvenile delinquency, early teenage pregnancy, and abuse of drugs and alcohol.

Developmental programs for young children may be offered under a variety of auspices, including various levels of government, school districts, health and social service agencies, universities, grassroots community organizations, or a combination of sponsors.

Head Start: A Federal–Community Partnership

A major assumption of public responsibility for children's daytime programs came about through Project Head Start (U.S. Office of Education and Office of Economic Opportunity, 1966). A critical factor in the founding of Head Start was the "war on poverty" in the administration of President Lyndon Johnson. Head Start is intended to give preschool children from economically disadvantaged backgrounds child development services to prepare them to enter first grade ready to learn, with the social and cognitive skills needed to be successful in school (Zill, Resnick, McKey, Clark, & Connell, 1998).

Emphasis is placed on working with all aspects of a child's environment, including the family and the community. The comprehensive program aims to improve children's physical health and abilities through medical assessment and remedial health programs; help with their emotional and social development by encouraging qualities such as self-confidence, expectation of success, spontaneity, curiosity, and self-discipline; improve their mental processes with particular attention to conceptual and verbal skills; and strengthen the child–parent relationship.

Parents are encouraged to participate in every phase of developing and administering the program. Many work as teachers' aides and in other nonprofessional capacities. Parenting education courses have taught parents how to improve the home environment and help young children "learn to learn" at home.

Head Start is administered by the Administration for Children, Youth and Families (ACYF) in the U.S. Department of Health and Human Services. Grants to operate Head Start programs are awarded to local public and nonprofit agencies, Indian tribes, and school systems. As the major federal program providing developmental services to low-income preschoolers, the scope of federal involvement is large; in fiscal year 2001, the federal budget included over $6 billion for Head Start programs, which served nearly 1 million children, mainly from very-low-income families. Two-thirds of Head Start children are of minority ethnicity, and about 13 percent have disabilities (Administration for Children and Families, 2002).

In 1994 the U.S. Congress established the Early Head Start program for low-income pregnant mothers and families with infants and toddlers. This program supplements Head Start, which is mainly for 3- and 4-year-olds. There are currently 650 Early Head Start programs serving children under age 3. Like Head Start, Early Head Start provides comprehensive services for family and child development and also encourages ongoing training for staff, many of whom are Head Start parents, and the development of community resources for young children (Paulsell, Kisker, Love, & Raikes, 2000).

Does Head Start Have Lasting Effects?

Head Start has been a source of pride for the country for many years. It has held its popularity even as other programs from the 1960s have failed to reach their early promise and have lost funding. Head Start has been considered a sound investment in the nation's children and a cost-effective way of reducing school dropout and social failure of poor children. However, over the years, various studies have given mixed results on the long-term benefits of Head Start participation (Haskins, 1989). These studies exhibited methodological limitations and could not provide a comprehensive picture of Head Start's effectiveness. Therefore, during the 1990s, Head Start undertook a major, ongoing research program—the Head Start Program Performance Measures Initiative—to identify the program's strengths and weaknesses and provide guidelines for attaining high-quality operations. Because the study design calls for tracking children over time, findings on long-term benefits are not yet available. Prelimary findings are encouraging, however, suggesting that Head Start programs are consistently offering good-quality programs. The study rated most Head Start classrooms as "good," with small class size (average about 14 children) and good child–staff ratios (average about one to six). The study reported that most Head Start teachers had at least some college education. The graduates of Head Start demonstrated many skills associated with school readiness, including cognitive skills, such as identifying colors, and social and behavioral skills, such as using free time constructively and following the teacher's directions. Importantly, the study found that program quality is linked to child performance, reinforcing the point made by other researchers and policy makers advocating for the need to develop, and find a way to pay for, high-quality programs for children (see earlier sections of this chapter) (Zill et al., 1998).

Although it will be several years before this study can provide information on the long-term benefits of the Head Start participants, another study offers insights into the possible effects of a high-quality preschool program. The Perry Preschool Project, a program similar in some ways to Head Start, has conducted a longitudinal investigation of the children it served in the 1960s to see how they have fared later in life. The results of this follow-up study have shown that the Perry graduates derived many benefits, including reduced grade retention, welfare usage, and crime, and increased school completion and employment rates. A cost–benefit analysis reported that for every dollar spent on the program, taxpayers saved $7 on reduced need for social programs by the time the children reached age 27 (Berreuta-Clement, Schweinhart, Barnett, Epstein, & Weikart, 1984; Schweinhart, Barnes, & Weikart, 1993).

Early development programs cannot guarantee success in life. The Perry Preschool Project graduates, though they were likely to be more successful than their peers who did not attend preschool, nonetheless were less successful than children from middle- and upper-income families. A reasonable conclusion of the effects of early childhood programs is that "they cannot overpower the effects of poor living conditions, inadequate nutrition and heath care, negative role models, and substandard schools. But good programs can prepare children for school and possibly help them develop better coping and adaptation skills that will enable better life outcomes, albeit not perfect ones" (Zigler & Styfco, 1994, p. 129). In addition to benefits to children, Head Start has helped numerous parents and had a positive effect on their communities. Thousands of parents obtain training and jobs through Head Start each year and may go on to further their education and become employed.

State and Local Programs

Although Head Start is the major national program offering developmental services to young children, a wide range of local initiatives with similar goals and program components also exist, giving a diversity of program models tailored to fit regional and ethnic conditions. For example, Avance, started in a housing project in San Antonio, Texas, in the 1970s, offers developmental programs to preschoolers and adult education, employment services, and family life education to their parents. Many of the families have limited English language skills, and the program caters to the language and cultural characteristics of the families served (Johnson, Walker, & Rodriguez, 1991).

The Parents as Teachers program is an example of state government involvement in early childhood education for poor families. This program began in Missouri in 1981, intended to demonstrate the benefits of a high-quality parent education and family support program to strengthen parents' skills and enhance their children's development from birth to age 3. This program model incorporates regular home visits, as well as group activities for both children and parents. Evaluations consistently showed that the program resulted in improved language and social development of children, and appeared to reduce the likelihood of participating families being reported for child abuse and neglect. The program, known as

PAT, is now being implemented in 2,000 program sites in forty-eight states and abroad (Pfannestiel, Lambson, & Yarnell, 1991; Promising Practices: Parents as Teachers, no date).

Historical Development of Day Care

A review of the development of *day nurseries* and *nursery schools* casts light on some of the problems in evolving a comprehensive approach to programs for children's daytime care and development. Formally organized daytime programs have existed in two parts—child care as a philanthropic undertaking, chiefly under social work auspices, and nursery schools as a form of preschool education. Despite their common elements, these two institutional approaches generally developed quite separately and have served different groups and classes of children.

Child Welfare Day Care

The Early Day Nurseries.   The first program for the daytime care of young children in this country began in Philadelphia in 1798. This first "charitable nursery" was sponsored by a group of Quaker women, and its initial goal was to increase productivity of working mothers in the "spinning room" (Michel, 1988). Another goal soon emerged—to attend to the education and welfare of the children. Early day nurseries were modeled on the French crèche, a form of care for children of working mothers founded in Paris in 1844. The crèche was a response to the rapidly expanding employment of women in factories. In addition, in France, it was used as a weapon against the problem of infant mortality. Mothers of infants nursed their babies in the factory crèches and were taught methods of hygienic child care. French crèches were considered important enough to receive official recognition by an imperial decree in 1862. Regulations were issued to specify the conditions under which they could open and the standards that had to be met to receive a government subsidy.

The early day nurseries in America lacked this kind of official attention. They were usually sponsored by a church, a settlement house, or sometimes a voluntary social agency. Their purposes were to prevent child neglect during a mother's working hours and to eliminate the need to place children of destitute parents in institutions. They served an underprivileged group, handicapped by family problems. The emphasis was on physical care. Children were fed, often inadequately, and guarded from only the most obvious dangers. Provision for cleanliness and medical care was a common lack. The public generally was unconcerned about the nurseries. For information on the history of early day nurseries, see Forest (1927), Beer (1938), and Lundberg (1947).

Day Care Services.   By the 1930s the social work profession somewhat more agreed that day care, although still very insufficiently provided, was an essential part of a child welfare program. Emphasis was placed on the provision of social casework as a means of strengthening family life for the child in day care. Efforts were made to differentiate day care, as a child welfare service, from nursery schools, as a form of preschool education. Day care was regarded as a sharing of child-rearing responsibilities with parents, a way of keeping families together or helping them maintain an adequate level of child care. Consequently, day care agencies usually applied some test of economic or social need before making the service available to parents.

Preschool Education

Nursery schools in the United States were an outgrowth of early twentieth-century progress in such fields as biology, medicine, psychology, and psychiatry, which led to scientific interest in early childhood and a new awareness of the importance of the preschool years. As a consequence of early experiments in preschool education, the nursery school developed as a "normal" service to be used without stigma even though, like day care, it was conceived as an educational and social supplement to the home. Undoubtedly the origin of nursery schools in America, developed from the beginning as a resource for middle- and upper-class families, has contributed to their acceptance and perceived desirability.

Assumption of Public Responsibility

The WPA Program.   There was a major expansion in day care during the Depression of the 1930s, when the federal government made funds available to the states for the establishment of nursery schools for the children of low-income parents. This action was part of the Works Progress Administration (WPA) program, and its immediate purpose was to provide employment for unemployed teachers, nurses, nutritionists, clerical workers, cooks, and janitors.

The Lanham Act.   As economic conditions improved and fewer teachers were unemployed, it appeared that the public day care program would be ended. But as the United States became involved in World War II, defense industries mushroomed. Many children were exposed to instability in family and community life as their parents moved to overcrowded new communities to which they were attracted by wartime employment. The Children's Bureau began to receive reports of less-than-adequate child care situations in various communities with a concentration in the defense industries. These reports told of children who were left alone, locked in parked cars, or expected to shift for themselves or adjust to other unsatisfactory child care arrangements while their mothers worked.

> *During the war years, you were more concerned with trying to compensate for the lack of a family with the father gone and the mother working. These children were in there from sometimes—when the mother lifted them over the fence to me and I lifted them back at 6 o'clock at night and they hadn't seen their parents or home and went to bed very soon after that. (WPA day care center director—Langlois, 1989, p. 30)*

Pressure mounted for a continuation of public financing for day care, this time for children whose mothers were being drawn into the national defense effort. Under the Lanham Act of 1941, federal funds were made available to the states to establish day care facilities for the children of working mothers in war-impacted communities. At the peak of the program in 1944, about 115,000 children were enrolled in nursery schools and day care centers receiving federal funds, most of them sponsored by schools (Pedgeon, 1953; Farmer, 1969).

Federal funds were withdrawn in 1946, at the end of the war, with resulting difficulties for many families. Most programs disappeared. Some people believed that maternal employment would cease to exist on any substantial scale with the end of the war. There was a widespread view that mothers should not be encouraged to leave their children and work during the day. In some communities the expanding school population required all the available classroom space and other educational resources. There also was underlying disagreement or confusion as to whether daytime programs were a continuing responsibility of welfare or education.

The loss in public day care facilities following the end of World War II was serious. For example, although Chicago had had twenty-three centers operating during the war, there were no programs of public day care early in 1965. The same was true of Detroit, although during World War II there had been eighty centers in that city supported by Lanham Act funds. The dismantling of the day care infrastructure built during the 1940s had long-term consequences for public child welfare services in this country. While many European countries expanded their day care facilities after the end of the war, the United States, which had the beginnings of a professionally sound, developmentally appropriate system, allowed its to collapse.

Heightened Interest for Child Care in the 1960s.   Various social, economic, and political forces in the 1960s removed day care from the periphery of social services for children and back into the forefront of public attention. For example, scientific interest in how a child's intelligence develops and in the social and psychological factors in the intellectual functioning of poor children led to research into preschool curriculum development and evaluation. As a result, enriched experimental nursery school programs were developed as university researchers investigated the area of early childhood education in search of reliable methods of compensatory training. Head Start was a product of this new recognition of the long-term effects of early childhood educational experiences. By a series of amendments to the Social Security Act in 1962, day care was defined as a public child welfare service.

The history of day care in the United States contains two major themes: (1) the separation of day care into two streams—day care as a service to the poor while their mothers were at work, and early childhood education, in the form of nursery schools primarily for children of the middle class; and (2) the reluctance of the federal government and American society to subsidize day care for working mothers, largely due to ambivalence about the role of women and concerns about government involvement in family life. These tensions and contradictions are still apparent in the way day care services are conceptualized, funded, and implemented in this country.

Trends and Issues

Welfare Reform and Child Care Subsidies

Changes in the welfare law are affecting many families with young children. (See Chapter 5.) Before the 1996 changes in welfare, families with children under age 3 were exempt from work requirements. Now, families with children under the age of 1 year may be required to work; Michigan, for example, requires parents of children 3 months old or older to work. Under the new TANF law, more mothers need child care, particularly for very young children. These low-income parents often experience the "day care crunch" described elsewhere in this chapter; their low incomes cannot cover the costs of day care.

Recognizing this problem, subsidies to help parents pay for child care were part welfare reform legislation. Federal funding for child care subsidies increased substantially from 1996 to 1998, when it reached $5.2 billion. However, states have great flexibility in how they use federal subsidy dollars and how much they draw down, depending on the state-specific work requirements of their welfare programs. In spite of overall increases in subsidies for child care, only about 14 percent of the 14.7 million children eligible for subsidies actually receive them. The reasons for this low usage rate are not clearly understood, but probably include administrative complexity and lack of information about availability of subsidies.

Another problem is the availability of good-quality care of the type needed by low-income mothers with young children. Many mothers find that informal care offered by relatives and (usually) unlicensed family day care providers is more suited to their needs than center care. Informal care in family homes is more likely to be affordable, available during their work hours, which may include evenings and weekends, and conveniently located. However, center care, which must be licensed, may be of better quality. The problem of availability versus quality is serious, as the quality of the care children receive when young affects their future development.

As this book goes to press, most states and the federal government are experiencing large budget deficits. Lawmakers may be tempted to shortchange funding for child care. This would be a serious mistake because it would exacerbate the difficulties many children from poor families already face in preparing for school. Short-term budget savings from underfunding day care for welfare and other low-income mothers, which may force children into substandard care, could result in increased federal expenses for remedial programs later on, to compensate for the lack of developmental enrichment in earlier day care experiences (Blum, 1994; Cabrera, Hutchens, & Peters, 2002).

Child Care Workers: High Skills Needed—Low Wages Offered

The issue of quality versus cost is encompassing, and it cloaks other matters of importance. One of the most significant of these has to do with the status and roles of women in the provision of day care. Women constitute virtually all the caregiving personnel in the day care industry in this country. As a class of essential workers, they are underpaid and have access to few government work benefits taken for granted by other wage earners (Whitebrook & Phillips, 1999).

Thus we find a large labor force of women who are essential to the economy as well as to the families of working parents. Yet these caregivers are grossly underpaid and denied benefits common to other workers. Child care workers earned an average of $6.12 an hour in 1996. The pay for preschool teachers, many of whom have bachelor's or master's degrees, averaged $7.80. These figures compare to $10.35 for all workers. People taking care of zoo animals earn $2,500 more on average than child care workers (Rally 'Round the Kids, 1993; Kids Count, 1998). Furthermore, the fact that additional training in child-related fields and experience in child care brings no rewards in earnings suggests that the government and the public still subscribe to the sexist notion that "since child care is women's work it is not worth paying for" (*Children at the Center,* 1979, pp. 21–22).

The devalued perception of child care staff with its low pay and demanding working conditions has led to high rates of turnover in child care. Research has shown that staff are a key component of good child care. A study based on classroom observations and testing of children at over 200 child care centers in five geographically dispersed metropolitan areas established that link. Children in centers with persistently high rates of turnover among caregivers, when compared with children at centers with low rates of staff turnover, were found to be less competent in language and social development. The high rates of turnover were found to be directly related to pay and working conditions (Lewin, 1989).

What must not be overlooked is that the lack of government subsidies for child care maintains the existence of an exploited underclass of women performing child care work that is essential to the economy and to the well-being of the nation's families. The lack of public attention to this injustice unfairly places two groups of women with opposing needs in confrontation with each other (Franks, 1998). Working mothers who must pay for day care usually feel financial pressures, as do their caretaking substitutes. If problems of the women purchasing care are lessened by lowering prices, the caregiving women suffer. On the other hand, if the caregivers are paid at higher levels, mothers in the labor force may find it no longer feasible to continue to work outside their homes. Responsibility for this dilemma does not belong to either set of working women. Instead it reflects a vacuum of leadership at the national level in efforts to develop a more effective and fair resolution of the issue of day care cost (Bergmann, 2001).

Day Care in the U.S. Military: Lessons Learned

Day care services provided by the military to U.S. service personnel was mediocre, at best, until recently. Day care was a low-priority issue during the years when the military services were made up primarily of young, single, male draftees. With the advent of the volunteer military in 1972, personnel were more likely to be career-minded married people, including many women. Recognizing that military readiness depended in part on stable and high-quality care for children while their soldier parents were at work, the U.S. Department of Defense set about transforming the day care services available to its personnel. With the passage of the Military Child Care Act of 1989, resources became available to improve day care dramatically for the children of military staff.

Today, the military runs what is essentially the largest employer-sponsored day care program in the country. The lessons learned from the improvements to military day care can be applied to parallel efforts in civilian life. As Nancy Duff Campbell, one of the researchers of a major study of the transformations in military day care observed, "If the U.S. military can do an about-face and dramatically improve its child care system in a relatively short period of time, there is great hope for improving child care across the United States. The lessons learned from this example should be applied to expand access to high quality, affordable child care for everyone" (National Women's Law Center, 2000, p. 1).

The report of the study of military day care, entitled *Be All That We Can Be: Lessons from the Military for Improving Our Nation's Child Care System* (Campbell, Appelbaum, Martinson, & Martin, 2000), identifies specific ways the military accomplished major improvements, with implications for initiatives to improve the quality and availability of care in every state. These lessons include the following:

- Create a comprehensive system. The military built a system linking centers, family day care providers, schools, and information and referral services, to provide coverage for children of different ages, including before- and after-school care. A single point of entry at each location helps parents learn what is available and to tailor a day care plan to the family's needs.
- Set high standards and enforce them. The military developed basic standards, including health, safety, staff–child ratios, staff training, and other issues, and rigorously enforces them. Enforcement includes at least four unannounced inspections to each site per year.
- Use accreditation. The report says that 95 percent of military child care centers are accredited by the National Association for the Education of Young Children, compared with only 8 percent of civilian centers.
- Provide and require staff training. All military day care staff receive preservice and ongoing training, and their compensation is linked to training milestones. Entry-level wages for military day care staff is $8 an hour, increasing to $10 after core training, compared to $5 to $7 an hour, on average, in most states. A result of these personnel policies is greatly reduced staff turnover, which remains a huge obstacle to quality care in the civilian sector.
- Make day care affordable. Fees for day care are on a sliding scale based on family income, and subsidies are provided to day care homes to help keep fees to parents affordable. On average, military families pay 25 percent less per week than do civilian families for day care. Following this example, state governments should greatly increase the public resources allocated to day care.
- Expand availability. The military made a conscious decision to improve quality before vastly expanding the number of day care slots available. It estimates that it now meets about 58 percent of need, with a plan to meet 80 percent of need by 2005. No state provides quality, subsidized care to anywhere near half of its families needing care.
- Allocate significant resources to day care. This obvious point needs to be emphasized, because massive improvements to the day care system that the military accomplished require large financial commitments from state and federal governments. Appropriations for military day care have increased greatly, from about $90 million before the enactment of the Military Child Care Act to $352 million in 2000.

The future health and strength of our nation depends on an able workforce strongly supported by a high-quality child care system. States should be strongly encouraged to follow the model laid out by the military in improving day care services (Campbell et al., 2000; National Women's Law Center, 2000; Campbell, 2001).

Chapter Summary

Care for children during the hours that their parents work, long a concern within the private realm of the family, has emerged as a major public policy issue as well. Welfare reform has given impetus to the movement to increase government involvement in funding and planning children's daytime care. Sensational stories from the news and entertainment media, showing children left with abusive or careless baby-sitters, have reflected the anxieties of parents about leaving their children while they work. Recent research documenting the mediocre quality of many day care centers, combined with research showing the importance of high-quality day care for children's development, have given strong empirical support to efforts to improve conditions under which children are cared for during the day. High-quality care may be expensive and beyond the reach of many working families. Although federal and state support for day care has increased, greater government involvement is needed to reduce the number of children in mediocre or poor care. In addition to cost, other barriers to finding good care include lack of day care resources in the area, and lack of day care for children of parents working nights and weekends.

Families in which parents work and children are in day care have become prevalent in American society. Today, about 60 percent of all preschoolers, or 13 million children, are in some form of day care or early childhood development program. In addition to day care for children of working mothers, day care may also be provided as a child welfare service, offering specialized and respite care to abusive and neglectful families as an alternative to placement of children in foster care. Day care arrangements include care by relatives, family day care, offered in the caregiver's home, in-home caregivers, and day care centers. Much day care is unregulated, particularly family day care, and little is known about what kind of experiences children have during the time they are with the day care provider. Most school-age children are in school during the hours that their parents work, but many children spend time alone, without adult supervision, during the week.

A promising approach to improving quality and accessibility at relative low cost are day care networks. These programs, located in schools, other child development centers, or social or community agencies, offer information and referral services to parents, and recruit and train day care providers. By offering ongoing support to providers, they increase the number of day care homes in an area and help improve the skills of providers in promoting children's intellectual, social, and physical development. Another approach to improving care is to offer consumer education to parents on how to find good care and on the importance of staying involved in the day care program. The importance of parental involvement is highlighted by the cases of child abuse in day care; these deplorable situations have illustrated that parents need to encourage children to talk about their day care experiences and to visit the day care facilities as often as possible.

Child development programs, such as Head Start, have as their primary goal the enhancement of preschool age children's development so that they will enter school ready to learn. These programs focus on the family, as well as the children, and work to help parents become more effective at promoting their children's cognitive, social, and physical development. They are based on a large body of research showing the importance of parents as the child's first and most important teacher.

FOR STUDY AND DISCUSSION

1. Discuss why child care personnel remain so poorly paid although they are essential to the economy and to family life. What values within the economy and the status of women come together to maintain this inequity?

2. Look further into the concept of neighborhood day care networks. Are there any in your community? Identify the benefits and barriers to implementation to be derived from this form of organization.

3. What have been some of the effects or influences of the historical separation between day nurseries and nursery schools? What were the positive accomplishments of public nursery school and day care programs under WPA and the Lanham Act? What explanation can you advance for the failure of these two large public programs to lead to a comprehensive provision of programs for the daytime care and development of children?

4. Propose a variety of arrangements that could be made to serve school-age "self-care" children who need outside-of-school supervision and guidance. Is there such a service in your community? Could you bring one about?

5. Visit a child care center in your community to learn its purpose, the population of children that it serves, its means of financing its operations, its staffing pattern, and the focus of its programs. What evidence is there that the program plays a responsible role in a community network of quality daytime programs?

FOR ADDITIONAL STUDY

Besharov, D. J. (Ed.). (1996). *Enhancing early childhood programs: Burdens and opportunities.* Washington, DC: CWLA Press and American Enterprise Institute.

Blau, D. M. (2001). *The child care problem: An economic analysis.* Thousand Oaks, CA: Sage.

Center for the Future of Children. (2001). *The future of children: Caring for infants and toddlers, 11*(1). The David and Lucile Packard Foundation. Available: www.futureofchildren.org.

Heymann, J. (2000). *The widening gap: Why America's working families are in jeopardy and what can be done about it.* New York: Basic Books.

Kamerman, S. B. (Ed.). (2001). *Early childhood education and care: International perspectives.* New York: The Institute for Child and Family Policy at Columbia University.

Larner, M. (1994). *In the neighborhood: Programs that strengthen family daycare for low-income families.* New York: Columbia University School of Public Health, National Center for Children in Poverty.

Lombardi, J. (2002). *Time to care: Redesigning child care to promote education, support families, and build communities.* Philadelphia: Temple University Press.

National Institute of Child Health and Human Development. (no date). *The NICHD Study of Early Child Care.* Available: www.nih.gov/nichd/html/lpublications.html.

INTERNET SEARCH TERMS

Day care
Maternal employment
Preschool
School readiness

INTERNET SITES

National Child Care Information Center. The Center is part of the Children's Bureau, U.S. Department of Health and Human Services. It disseminates child care information in response to requests from states,

territories and tribes, policy makers, parents, programs, organizations, providers and the public. The Center also publishes the *Child Care Bulletin* six times a year.
www.nccic.org

National Institute of Child Health and Human Development. The NICHD administers a multidisciplinary program of research, research training, and public information, nationally and within its own facilities, on prenatal development as well as maternal, child, and family health. The web site offers access to NICHD publications.
www.nich.nih.gov

National Network for Child Care. This nonprofit, educational organization affiliated with the Cooperative Extension programs of state universities attempts to increase and strengthen the quality of nonparental care environments using the expertise of Cooperative Extension's nationwide dissemination system. It offers an email listserv for communication on day care, support and assistance to day care providers and users, and a newsletter. The web site is an Internet source of over a thousand publications and resources related to child care. Publications are research based and reviewed.
www.nncc.org

REFERENCES

Administration for Children and Families. (2002). *2002 Head Start fact sheet.* Washington, DC: U.S. Department of Health and Human Services. [Online]. Available: www2.acf.dhhs.gov/programs/hsb/research/02_hsfs.htm [2002, September 4].

Annie E. Casey Foundation. (2002). Family child care. *Child care you can count on.* Available: www.aeacf.org/publications/child/fam.htm [2002, July 25].

ARCH. (1994). *Respite: Prevention, preservation and family support.* Chapel Hill, NC: Access to Respite Care and Help, ARCH National Resource Center for Crisis Nurseries and Respite Services.

Bachu, A., & O'Connell, M. (2000, September). *Fertility of American women.* (Current Population Reports, P20-526. U.S. Department of Commerce, Census Bureau.) Washington, DC: U.S. Government Printing Office.

Barnett, W. S. (1995). Long-term effects of early childhood programs on cognitive and school outcomes. *The Future of Children: Long Term Outcomes of Early Childhood Programs, 5*(3), 25–50.

Beer, E. S. (1938). *The day nursery.* New York: Dutton.

Bergmann, B. R. (2001, January 1–15). Decent child care at decent wages. *The American Prospect: Children and Families,* 8–9.

Berreuta-Clement, J. R., Schweinhart, L. J., Barnett, W. S., Epstein, A. S., & Weikart, D. P. (1984). *Changed lives: The effects of the Perry Preschool Program on youths through age 19.* Ypsilanti, MI: High/Scope Press.

Blum, B. (1994). Children and welfare reform. *National Center for Children in Poverty. News and Issues. 4*(3), 4–6.

Cabrera, N., Hutchens, R., & Peters, H. E. (2002). From welfare to child care. *Poverty Research News, 6*(2), 11–13.

Campbell, N. D. (2001, January). Child care: All that it can be? *Children's Voice, 10*(1), 16–18.

Campbell, N. D., Appelbaum, J. C., Martinson, K., & Martin, E. (2000, April). *Be all that we can be: Lessons from the military for improving our nation's child care system.* Washington, DC: National Women's Law Center.

Casper, L. M. (1995). *What does it cost to mind our preschoolers?* (Current Population Reports, P-70, no. 52. U.S. Department of Commerce, Census Bureau.) Washington, DC: U.S. Government Printing Office.

Casper, L. M. (1996). *Who's minding our preschoolers?* (Current Population Reports, P-70, no. 53. U.S. Department of Commerce, Census Bureau.) Washington, DC: U.S. Government Printing Office.

Casper, L. M., Hawkins, M., & O'Connell, M. (1994). *Who's minding the kids?* (Current Population Reports, Series P70-36. U.S. Department of Commerce, Census Bureau.) Washington, DC: U.S. Government Printing Office.

Chavez, L. (1987, July). Women's movement, its ideals accepted, faces subtler issues. *New York Times,* p. 8.

Cherlin, A. J. (1998, April 5). By the numbers. *New York Times Magazine,* pp. 39–41.

Children at the center: Final report of the national day care study, executive summary. (1979). Cambridge, MA: Abt Associates.

Children's Defense Fund. (1998, March). *Facts about child care in America.* Available: www.childrensdefense.org [1998, May].

Children's Defense Fund. (2002, March 12). *Child care now! Polls indicate widespread support for increased investments in child care.* Available: www.childrensdefense.org [2002, February].

Children's Defense Fund. (2002). *Low-income families bear the burden of state child care cutbacks.* Washington, DC: Author.

Children's Foundation. (2002). *Family child care licensing study.* Washington, DC: Author.

Clarke-Stewart, A. (1993). *Daycare.* Cambridge: Harvard University Press.

Clinton, H. (1997, September–October). Remarks by First Lady Hillary Rodham Clinton. *Child Care Bulletin, Issue 17.* Available: http://Ericps.ed.uiuc.edu/nccic [1997, November].

Clinton, W. (1997, September–October). Remarks by President Bill Clinton. *Child Care Bulletin, Issue 17.* Available: http://Ericps.ed.uiuc.edu/nccic [1997, November].

Collins, A. H., & Watson, E. L. (1976). *Family day care.* Boston: Beacon Press.

De Kanter, A., Williams, R., Cohen, G., & Stonehill, R. (2000). *21st century community learning centers: Providing quality afterschool learning opportunities for America's families.* Washington, DC: U.S. Department of Education. Available: www.ed.gov/pubs/ProvidingQualityAfterschoolLearning/title.html [2002, July 23].

Dwyer, C., Chait, R., & McKee, P. (2000). *Building strong foundations for early learning: Guide to high-quality early childhood education programs.* Washington, DC: U.S. Department of Education, Planning and Evaluation Service.

Farmer, J. (1969). *Senate hearings on Head Start Child Development Act* (Pt. 1, 91st Cong., 1st Sess.).

Finkelhor, D., Williams, L. M., & Burns, N. (1988). *Nursery crimes: Sexual abuse in day care.* Newbury Park, CA: Sage.

Forest, I. (1927). *Pre-school education: A historical and critical study.* New York: Macmillan.

Franks, L. (1998, April 5). The auxiliary mother: An uneasy alliance. *New York Times Magazine,* pp. 70–73.

Galinsky, E., Howes, C., Kontos, S., & Shinn, M. (1994). *The study of children in family child care and relative care: Highlights of findings.* New York: Families and Work Institute.

Gazan, H. S. (1998, April 3). *Regulation: An imperative for ensuring quality child care.* Paper presented at the Yale University Bush Center in Child Development and Social Policy. New York: Foundation for Child Development.

Giannarelli, L., & Barsimantov, J. (2000). *Child care expenses of America's families.* Occasional Paper No. 40. Washington, DC: The Urban Institute.

Haskins, R. (1989). Beyond metaphor: The efficacy of early childhood education. *American Psychologist, 44,* 274–282.

Helburn, S., Culkin, M. L., Howes, C., Bryant, C., Clifford, R., Cryer, D., Peisner-Feinberg, E., & Kagan, S. L. (1995). *Cost, quality, and child outcomes in child care centers: Public report.* Denver: University of Colorado at Denver, Department of Economics.

Hershfield, B. (1995, Fall). The role of child care in strengthening and supporting vulnerable families. *The Prevention Report.* Iowa City: National Resource Center for Family Centered Practice, University of Iowa, 2–4.

Heymann, J. (2000). *The widening gap: Why America's working families are in jeopardy and what can be done about it?* New York: Basic Books.

Hofferth, S. (1996). Child care in the United States today. *The Future of Children: Financing Child Care, 6*(2), 41–61.

Hunt, J. M. (1969). Black genes—white environment. *Transaction, 6*(7), 20–21.

Johnson, D. L., & Walker, T. (1991). *Final report of an evaluation of the Avance Parent Educaton and Family Support Program.* San Antonio: Avance.

Johnson, D. L., Walker, T., & Rodriguez, G. (1991). *Enhancing the vocational prospects of low-income Hispanic mothers: Results of a family support program.* Paper presented at the biennial meeting of the Society for Research in Child Development, April 18–20, Seattle.

Kagan, S. L., & Glennon, T. (1982). Considering proprietary child care. In E. F. Zigler & E. W. Gordon (Eds.), *Day care: Scientific and social policy issues.* Boston: Auburn House.

Kamerman, S. B. (Ed.). (2001). *Early childhood education and care: International perspectives.* New York: Institute for Child and Family Policy at Columbia University.

Kids Count 1998 Data Online. (1998). *Profile for the United States: Child care indicators.* Available: www.aecf.org [1998, October].

Kisker, E. E., Hofferth, S. L., Phillips, D. A., & Farquahar, E. (1991). *A profile of child care settings: Early education and care in 1990.* Washington, DC: U.S. Government Printing Office.

Langlois, J. (1989). *Serving children then and now: An oral history of early childhood education and day care in metropolitan Detroit.* Detroit: Wayne State University.

Larner, M. (1994). *In the neighborhood: Programs that strengthen family daycare for low-income families.* New York: National Center for Children in Poverty, Columbia University.

Larner, M., & Chaudry, N. (1993). *Promoting professionalism through family day care networks.* New York: Columbia University School of Public Health, National Center for Children in Poverty.

Lewin, T. (1989, October 18). Study finds high turnover in child care workers. *New York Times,* p. 9.

Lewin, T. (2001, October 19). More mothers of babies under 1 are staying home. *New York Times,* p. A13.

Lewin, T. (2002, July 21). A child study is a peek. It's not the whole picture. *New York Times,* p. WK4.

Long, T. J., & Long, L. (1983). *Handbook for latchkey children and their parents.* New York: Arbor House.

Lundberg, E. O. (1947). *Unto the least of these: Social services for children.* New York: Appleton-Century-Crofts.

Michel, S. (1988, January). *The nineteenth-century origins of the American child care policy.* Unpublished paper, Women's Studies, History and Literature, Howard University, Washington, DC.

National Institutes of Health. (1997, April 3). *Results of NICHD study of early child care reported at Society for Research in Child Development meeting.* Available: www.nih.gov/news/pr/apr97/nichd-03.htm [1998, March].

National Research Council. (2000). *Eager to learn: Educating our preschoolers.* Executive summary. Washington, DC: National Academy Press.

National Women's Law Center. (2000, May 16). *Military provides model for child care reforms, new NWLC report concludes.* Available: www.nwlc.org [2002, October 1].

Newman, S., Brazelton, T. B., Zigler, E., Sherman, L. W., Bratton, W., Sanders, J., & Christeson, W. (2000). *America's child care crisis: A crime prevention tragedy.* Washington, DC: Fight Crime: Invest in Kids.

Newman, S., Fox, J. A., Flynn, E. A., & Christeson, W. (2000). *America's after-school choice: The prime time for juvenile crime, or youth enrichment and achievement.* Fight Crime: Invest in Kids. Available: www.fightcrime.org.

Office of the Equal Opportunity Ombudsman. (no date). *Pay Equity Guide FACTsheet—Wage differences.* Available: www.jamombud.se.

Orenstein, P. (1998, April 5). The working mother. *New York Times Magazine,* pp. 42–48.

Ounce of Prevention Fund. (1993). *Beethoven's Fifth: The first five years of the Center for Successful Child Development.* Chicago: Author.

Out-of-school time. (1997, September–October). *Child Care Bulletin, 17.* 2 pages. Available: http://Ericps.ed.uiuc.edu/nccic [1997, November].

Paulsell, D., Kisker, E., Love, J., & Raikes, H. (2000). *Leading the way: Characteristics and early experiences of selected Early Head Start Programs, Executive Summary, Volumes I, II, and III.* The Commissioner's Office of Research and Evaluation and the Head Start Bureau, Administration on Children, Youth and Families. Washington, DC: U.S. Department of Health and Human Services.

Pedgeon, M. (1953). *Employed mothers and child care.* Bulletin 246. Washington, DC: Women's Bureau.

Pfannestiel, J., Lambson, T., & Yarnell, V. (1991). *Second wave study of the Parents as Teachers program.* St. Louis: Parents as Teachers National Center, Inc.

Phillips, D., & Adams, G. (2001, Spring–Summer). Caring for infants and toddlers. *The Future of Children,* 35–51.

Promising practices: Parents as teachers. (no date). Available: www.welfareinfo.org/pat.htm [2002, September 4].

Rally 'round the kids. (1993, April 21). *Detroit Free Press,* p. E1.

Roditti, M. G. (1995). Child day care: A key building block of family support and family preservation programs. *Child Welfare, 74*(6), 1043–1068.

Rodriguez, G. (1989). *Avance family support and education programs.* Hearing before the House Select Committee on Children, Youth, and Families.

101st Cong., 1st Sess. Washington, DC: U.S. Government Printing Office.

Schweinhart, L. J., Barnes, H. V., & Weikart, D. P. (1993). *Significant benefits: The High/Scope Perry Preschool Study through age 27.* (Monographs of the High/Scope Educational Research Foundation, No. 10.) Ypsilanti, MI: High/Scope Press.

Shalala, D. (1997, October). Remarks by Secretary Donna E. Shalala, DHHS. *Child Care Bulletin, Issue 17.* Available: http://Ericps.ed.uiuc.edu/nccic [1997, November].

Smith, K. (2000). *Who's minding the kids? Child care arrangements: Fall 1995.* (Current Population Reports P70-70. U.S. Department of Commerce, Census Bureau.) Washington, DC: U.S. Government Printing Office.

Sonenstein, F. L., Gates, G. J., Schmidt, S., & Bolshun, N. (2002). *Primary child care arrangements of employed parents: Findings from the 1999 National Survey of America's Families.* Assessing the New Federalism: Occasional Paper Number 59. Washington, DC: The Urban Institute.

Stolberg, S. G. (2001, April 22). Science, studies and motherhood. *New York Times,* p. WK3.

Stoney, L., & Greenberg, M. H. (1996). The financing of child care: Current and emerging trends. *The Future of Children, 6*(2), 83–102.

Sugarman, J. (1991). *Building early childhood systems: A resource handbook.* Washington, DC: Child Welfare League of America.

Terpstra, J. (1989). Day care standards and licensing. *Child Welfare, 68*(4), 437–442.

U.S. General Accounting Office. (1997, May). *Welfare reform: Implications of increased work participation for child care.* Washington, DC: Author.

U.S. Office of Education and the Office of Economic Opportunity. (1966). *Education: An answer to poverty.* Washington, DC: U.S. Government Printing Office.

Vobejda, B., & Davis, P. (1997, November). Keeping an eye on the hand that rocks the cradle. *Washington Post National Weekly Edition,* p. 30.

Waldfogel, J., Brooks-Gunn, J., & Han, W. (2002, March–April). Early maternal employment's effects on children. *Poverty Research News, 6*(2), The newsletter of the Northwestern University/ University of Chicago Joint Center for Poverty Research.

Westinghouse Learning Corporation. (1969, April). *The impact of Head Start: An evaluation of the effects of Head Start experience on children's cognitive and affective development.* Athens: Ohio University.

Whitebrook, M., & Phillips, D. (1999). Child care employment: Implications for women's self sufficiency and for child development. *The Foundation for Child Development Working Paper Series.* New York: Foundation for Child Development.

Willer, B., Hoffereth, S. L., Kisker, E. E., Divine-Hawkins, P., Farquahar, E., & Glandtz, F. B. (1991). *The demand and supply of child care in 1990: Joint findings from the "National child care survey 1990" and "A profile of child care settings."* Washington, DC: National Association for the Education of Young Children.

Women's Bureau. (1990). *Facts on working women.* (No. 90-2). Washington, DC: U.S. Department of Labor.

Zigler, E., & Styfco, S. J. (1994). *Head Start and beyond: A national plan for extended childhood intervention.* New Haven: Yale University Press.

Zill, N., Resnick, G., McKey, R., Clark, C., & Connell, D. (1998). *Head Start program performance measures, Second progress report.* Research, Demonstration and Evaluation Branch and the Head Start Bureau, Administration on Children, Youth and Families. Washington, DC: U.S. Department of Health and Human Services.

5

Family Income Security*

A caring society is one where people need not lose their dignity if they fall ill or fall on hard times or simply grow old; where each child is encouraged to fulfill his or her talents; and where people can live like human beings . . .

—John R. Short, as cited in Mulroy (1995)

CHAPTER OUTLINE

*By Dr. Alma H. Young, Coleman A. Young Professor of Urban Affairs, and Dean, College of Urban, Labor and Metropolitan Affairs (CULMA), Wayne State University. Dr. Young was educated at Radcliffe College (B.A. 1969), Columbia University (M.S. 1970), and the Massachusetts Institute of Technology (Ph.D. 1978). Her areas of research include women and children in poverty and the political economy of urban development.

Case Example: Welfare Reform Creates
Hard Choices for Mothers

Denise Jordan, a 34-year-old mother of three children, is a former welfare recipient who now has a government job in Washington, D.C., which she likes. Her oldest daughter is childless and in the Army. Her middle daughter, Kyisha, is 15 years old, with a sickly 9-month-old son, and pregnant again. Her youngest child is Kimberly, a bright 7-year-old, with an optimistic view of her future.

Denise Jordan is now faced with several major decisions, made more poignant given the recent changes in the federal welfare system. Before 1996, if a teenage girl became pregnant, she could establish her own household and begin collecting welfare benefits. Under the 1996 law, to collect welfare benefits, a teenage girl must live with her parents or guardians. If the family has too much income, then the girl gets no benefits. Denise Jordan makes too much for her family to receive benefits. Thus Denise Jordan is faced with a dilemma—how to get child care assistance for Kyisha's babies.

Does she leave her full-time job, which she has gotten after years of being on welfare and working part-time jobs? If she does, then her family would be back on public assistance and qualify for benefits, including child care assistance for Kyisha's babies. Does she keep her job, but ask Kyisha to drop out of school and take care of her babies, thus saving the child care cost of about $800 a month, which would be half of Denise's take-home monthly salary?

Does Denise take a second job in the evenings in order to make the additional money necessary to cover child care costs? If she does, then she will not be available to help Kyisha take care of her babies in the evenings or help her 7-year-old when she comes home from school. In the neighborhood where Denise lives, she knows that keeping children occupied after school is extremely important.

I have felt myself a strong woman, but now I feel my spirit breaking. (Denise Jordan, in Boo, 1997)

After not being able to talk Kyisha into an abortion or into putting the baby, once born, up for adoption or in foster care, Denise ponders other options for Kyisha. She could put her out on the street, but the child is too "slow" to make it on her own. She could encourage Kyisha and her boyfriend to marry, but she knows that is not likely given his limited resources. Even so, the boyfriend maintains an occasional presence in the family. In the end, after the second baby is born, Denise decides to keep her government job, not look for an additional evening job because the children need her presence more than the extra earnings, and ask Kyisha to drop out of school to take care of her babies. Denise hates to see Kyisha so trapped, but she hopes that life will be better for 7-year-old Kimberly (Boo, 1997).

This case study, taken from a *Washington Post* article, conveys some of the private costs borne by those who leave welfare for work, and the dilemmas faced by the poor and the near-poor in the United States. This country has a history of dividing the poor into the deserving and the undeserving (Katz, 1986), with the undeserving seen as not worthy of assistance, whether from public or private sources. To be considered deserving, the poor must prove their worthiness, generally through the kinds of behaviors that they exhibit (e.g., being willing to work, being capable of maintaining strong families, and being willing to make short-term sacrifices for long-term gains).

Much of the current debate about welfare reform centers on how to get the poor to exhibit "proper" behaviors, with the assumption being that if they do so, they will no longer be poor. The federal welfare reform legislation passed in 1996, the Personal Responsibility and Work Opportunity Reconciliation Act (PRWORA), linked personal responsibility with work, and ended the country's sixty-year program that entitled poor people to public assistance.

Poverty in the United States

What Is Poverty?

Although many families in the United States feel financial pressure, some families experience serious difficulties in providing basic needs to their family members. These families are considered poor. The federal government measures the extent of poverty in the United States and regularly issues reports through the U.S. Census Bureau. The basis for measuring poverty in this country is the government's Poverty Line Index, which attempts to classify families as being above or below an income level required to maintain a minimally adequate standard of living for families of different sizes. Poverty, then, refers to those families with cash incomes falling below the official U.S. poverty line. In 2001, the poverty line for a family with two parents and two children was $17,960, and for a family with one parent and two children it was $14,259 (Proctor & Dalaker, 2002). Based on the government's definition, a total of 32.9 million people lived in poor families in 2001, which represents 11.7 percent of the population (Proctor & Dalaker, 2002). The poverty rate for the nation as a whole has been declining slightly in recent years, though it increased slightly from 2000 to 2001 (see Figure 5.1).

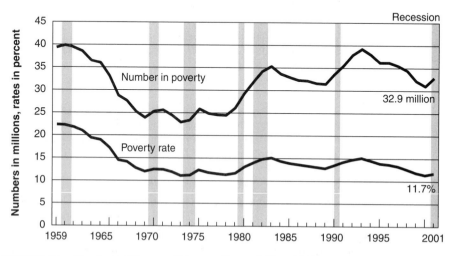

FIGURE 5.1   Number of Poor and Poverty Rate: 1959 to 2001

Note: The data points represent the midpoints of the respective years. The latest recession began in March 2001.

Source: U.S. Census Bureau, Current Population Surveys, 1960–2002, Annual Demographic Supplements.

There are a number of points that need to be kept in mind when using the Poverty Line Index (Blank, 1997). First, the poverty line is not one number, but a series of numbers developed for families of different sizes. The calculations were devised in the mid-1960s and have not been adjusted for changes in spending patterns over the past forty years. Second, poverty is based on the income of the family, not the individual. An individual is poor if the income of his or her family (those with whom he or she resides) is below the official poverty line for that size family. Third, there are no provisions for noncash assistance programs such as food stamps and Medicaid, which have grown in size since the 1960s. Fourth, there is no adjustment for differences in the cost of living across regions of the United States or between rural and urban areas. Finally, the poverty numbers do not give any indication of the intensity of poverty; people are considered as either poor or not poor.

Who Are the Poor?

Many of our conceptions of who is poor in the United States are based on stereotypes. The truth is, the poor are a heterogeneous group of individuals. Some of the poor are more visible than others, especially the poor who live in concentrated areas of central cities, in places of deteriorating housing and in stagnant economies. Others are almost invisible, such as the children of the working poor.

Who is poor changes over time. In the 1960s, the concern was with the high rate of poverty among the elderly. As a result of federal programs, their rate of poverty has dropped sharply, from approximately 30 percent in 1965 to about 10 percent in 2001 (see Figure 5.2). However, poverty among children under 18 declined from a high of 27 percent in 1960 to about 14 percent in 1969, but then began to climb upward in the 1970s. The poverty rate for

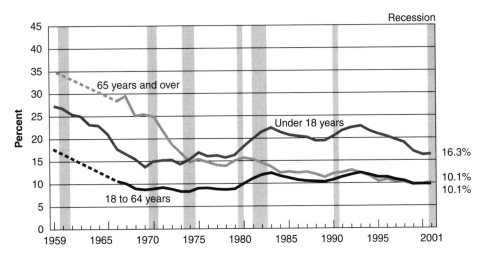

FIGURE 5.2   Poverty Rates by Age: 1959 to 2001

Note: The data points represent the midpoints of the respective years. The latest recession began in March 2001. Data for people 18 to 64 and 65 and older are not available from 1960 to 1965.

Source: U.S. Census Bureau, Current Population Surveys, 1960–2002, Annual Demographic Supplements.

children peaked at 23 percent in the early 1990s, but by 2001 had dropped to about 16 percent. About 11.7 million children are poor today. Children represent a disproportionate share of the poor population; they are only one-fourth of the total U.S. population but comprise 36 percent of the poor population. Children under age 6 are especially likely to live in poor families; in 2001, over 18 percent of children in this age group were poor (U.S. Census Bureau, 2002).

If we look at the distribution of poverty among different races and ethnic groups, we see a disproportionate number of poor among people of color. In 2001, the poverty rate for non-Hispanic whites was about 8 percent, 23 percent for African Americans, 25 percent for American Indians and Alaska Natives, and 10 percent for Asians and Pacific Islanders. For Hispanics, who may be of any race, the poverty rate was 21 percent. Even though the poverty rate for non-Hispanic whites was lower than that for any other group, over 46 percent of the poor were non-Hispanic white (Proctor & Dalaker, 2002). Figure 5.3 shows trends in poverty rates by race and Hispanic origin, from 1959 to 2001. Data for American Indian and Alaska natives are not included on the figure, because the annual population surveys used to generate the data do not produce reliable enough estimates of these relatively small populations. Poverty estimates for these groups are based on three-year averages. Figure 5.3 shows that the poverty rates for African Americans has declined substantially since 1959, and that the trend has also been generally downward for Asian and Pacific Islanders and for whites. The trend for Hispanics, who can be of any race, has fluctuated over time, reflecting changes in immigration patterns.

With the growth of immigration to the United States, the U.S. Census is tracking poverty among U.S. residents who were born elsewhere, both naturalized citizens and noncitizens. Among naturalized citizens, about 10 percent were poor in 2001, slightly less than the

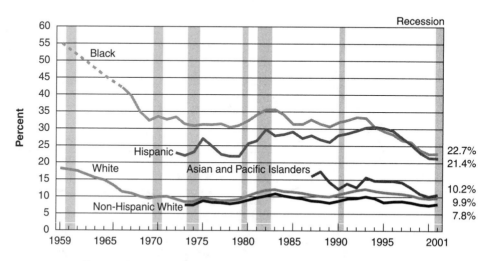

FIGURE 5.3   Poverty Rates by Race and Hispanic Origin: 1959 to 2001

Note: The data points represent the midpoints of the respective years. The latest recession began in March 2001. Data for Blacks are not available from 1960 to 1965. Data for the other race and Hispanic origin groups are shown from the first year available. Hispanics may be of any race.

Source: U.S. Census Bureau, Current Population Surveys, 1960–2002, Annual Demographic Supplements.

percent of the total population in the United States who were poor (11.7 percent). Nonciti-zens, however, were more likely to be poor; the poverty rate among this group was about 20 percent (Proctor & Dalaker, 2002).

Along with race, ethnicity, and citizenship status, family structure is also related to poverty rate. Single-parent families are more likely to be poor than two-parent families. In 2001, about 5 percent of married-couple families were poor, compared to 26 percent of fe-male householders with no spouse present and 13 percent of male householders with no spouse present. African American and Hispanic families headed by a woman were most likely to be poor (35 percent and 37 percent, respectively) (Proctor & Dalaker, 2002).

How long someone has lived in poverty is another concern. Those who have been poor for a relatively short period of time might face fewer disadvantages than those who have been poor for longer periods of time. According to recent research, of those in poverty, about half have experienced poverty for less than three years (Blank, 1997). This suggests that many people cycle off poverty fairly quickly, and that poverty for them is a temporary condition, caused, for example, by a period of unemployment or, for a young person, a period of getting established in the work world. However, about 7 percent of those who are poor have been in that condition for ten or more years. Compared to whites, African Americans are more likely to experience long-term poverty. Long-term poverty is especially detrimental to the physical, social, and cognitive development of children. Blank (1997) reports that, if we look only at younger children, less than 3 percent of white children were poor for ten or more years, while over 30 percent of the African American children were poor for that period.

Along with the length of time in poverty, the depth of poverty is also of interest, be-cause the depth of deprivation in which children are raised is thought to affect their devel-opmental attainments and their risk of many types of harm. The U.S. Census Bureau defines people as "severely poor" if they have incomes that are less than half of the poverty thresh-old. Thus, a family consisting of a single mother with two children was "poor" in 2001 if their income was below $14,259 (see earlier discussion), but would be considered "severely poor" if their income were below half that, or $7,130. In 2001, the number of severely poor people rose to 4.8 percent (13.4 million) from 4.5 percent (12.6 million) in 2000. The se-verely poor represented 41 percent of the poor population (Proctor & Dalaker, 2002).

Also of interest is the number of "near poor" whose incomes are just above the pov-erty line. Many families in this category, though not poor according to the poverty line threshold, live in circumstances that represent substantial developmental risks to children. The U.S. Census Bureau defines the near poor as those whose incomes are between the pov-erty line and 125 percent of the poverty line. About 12 million people were in this category in 2001, over and above the 32.9 million officially classified as "poor."

What Causes Poverty?

The link between poverty and work seems clear: Those who work experience less poverty than those who do not (Blank, 1997). Full-time employment seems the most likely way to move out of poverty, yet many poor adults do not work full time. There are a number of ex-planations offered as to why they do not. According to some, the poor do not work because they are not motivated to do so (Murray, 1984). Thus one motivation for the Personal Re-sponsibility and Work Opportunity Reconciliation Act (PRWORA) of 1996 was to encourage people to work and penalize those who do not. Others believe that the poor do not work because of structural constraints—either because of the changing nature of work, the location of jobs, or domestic responsibilities (Wilson, 1987; Mulroy, 1995).

Blank (1997) reminds us, though, that we must be careful in suggesting that people are poor because they do not work. In 2001, 38 percent of poor people age 16 and older worked during the year, although most did not work full time throughout the year. Even full-time year-round employment does not guarantee freedom from poverty, however; nearly 12 percent of poor people in 2001 were full-time workers who held a job year-round. Thus, work is an important factor in determining who is poor but other factors are also involved in creating poverty.

Some suggest that the changing economy and the structural impediments to work explain why families enter poverty. In the past thirty years, a number of changes have occurred in the U.S. economy that make it difficult for many families to maintain a decent standard of living. One major change has been the stagnation in wages; in contrast to the quarter century following World War II, when wages increased rapidly, during the past twenty years they have risen much less rapidly. Hardest hit have been young men, aged 16 to 24. In recent years, as the economy has expanded (and with it, the number of jobs created), wages have still declined. This is especially troubling because of the long-held assumption that economic growth leads to a reduction in poverty. These wage losses are related to fundamental changes in the American economy:

- loss of manufacturing jobs due to foreign competition, automation, and the transfer of jobs by U.S. companies to overseas factories
- growth of jobs in the service industry, which tend to pay less than manufacturing jobs, have fewer fringe benefits, and are less secure
- recent technological changes that affect the skill level needed by American workers and the stability of American firms

A compounding factor is the eroded value of the minimum wage. The minimum wage held constant between 1981 and 1989, despite the continuing rise in the cost of living. The minimum wage was raised in 1990, from $3.35 to $3.80 per hour (Stout, 1996). Since then, Congress has raised the minimum wage periodically, most recently in 1997. The current level of the federal minimum wage is $5.15 per hour.

These changes in the U.S. economy have been most detrimental to low-skilled, poorly educated workers, especially young men. As their wages have declined, young men have also worked fewer hours. In response to the stagnation of male wage rates, women have entered the labor force in larger numbers to supplement the family income. Women seem to have been less affected by declining wages. For many women, wages have risen dramatically, at least partly due to increasing job opportunities for women. (See Chapter 4.) The exception is among women who have dropped out of high school; they have experienced a significant decline in wages in the last twenty years and their earnings remain far below those of similarly skilled men. Nor have job opportunities increased for poorly skilled women, as they have for most other women. These women continue to face a narrow range of jobs, with low wages and few job-related benefits, just as they have in the past (Blank, 1997). Many women also continue to work in part-time jobs, often because they have child care and other domestic duties to fulfill (Edin & Lein, 1997).

> *Women with limited education and skills continue to have "access to bad jobs at bad wages." (Blank, 1997, p. 64)*

Even though in most American families with children both parents now work outside the home, their standard of living has not improved. Although family incomes are higher in two-earner than in one-earner families, the larger economic changes described earlier have limited sharply the financial gains to working parents. To make matters worse, the effort to maintain a stable income through increasing work has added stressors at home, as parents try to meet both work and family commitments. With less time for family life, parents are hard pressed to provide the level of nurturing and supervision of children that they would prefer to do. This juggling of child care and paid work becomes especially difficult for single mothers who are poor.

Background of the TANF Programs

For families who need financial help but are not insured or are insufficiently insured through Social Security, unemployment insurance, or other insurance programs, our country provides a system of public assistance. The term *public assistance* refers to tax-supported programs of financial aid to individuals and families based on established need. Temporary Assistance for Needy Families (TANF) is the largest public assistance program serving families with children. TANF is a cooperative program between federal and state governments for the purpose of maintaining income to families in which children have been deprived of parental support for such reasons as the parent's death, continued absence from the home, mental or physical incapacity, and unemployment. The intent has been to provide financial assistance when a family has no income or insufficient income and to do so in ways that will enable children to remain in their own homes, where they can be reared by at least one of their parents or by relatives. The program is financed by a sharing of costs between the federal and state governments. As a step toward achieving a valid basis for evaluation of the TANF program as a method of assuring income security for needy families, a review of the background of the program and its original philosophy will be useful.

Mothers' Pensions

Activity on the part of social reformers of the early 1900s and resolutions of the first White House Conference on the Care of Dependent Children in 1909 highlighted concern about poor children who lost their own homes because of their parents' inability to support them. At this time there was a new awareness of the importance of a child's own home and his or her need for family life experiences that found expression in the following resolution of the conference:

> Home life is the highest and finest product of civilization. It is the great molding force of mind and of character. Children should not be deprived of it except for urgent and compelling reasons. . . . Except in unusual circumstances, the home should not be broken up for reasons of poverty. (*Proceedings,* 1909, pp. 9–10)

Reaction against old methods of public outdoor relief (assistance to persons living in their own homes rather than in institutions) contributed to support for a new and special form of financial aid for mothers. Public relief, when it was given, reluctantly, consisted mostly of coal or grocery orders or emergency medical care. Another impetus to preserve the child's own home through the payment of public funds to mothers of dependent children was a reaction to the institutionalization of young children. Not only was there concern over children's loss of their home; public officials also realized that paying for children to live in an institution was costlier than furnishing a small amount of aid to them in their own home. The increasing legislation among states to prohibit or regulate child labor and the passage of compulsory school attendance laws were additional factors leading to the passage of mothers' pension laws. A child of 9 or 10 years of age was no longer free to quit school and go to work in factories and mines to help his or her widowed mother feed and care for younger brothers and sisters.

Mothers' pension laws were not passed without controversy, however. Much of the controversy was rooted in the fear that a family program of public assistance would not be restricted to "worthy" parents; mothers of "poor character" might also claim its help. Inherent in the controversy was a reluctance to enact any legislation that would appear to relieve fathers of responsibility for their children's support. It was feared that the substance of family life would be seriously weakened, and irresponsibility and immorality would be encouraged.

Nevertheless, there was support for the concept of public responsibility for aid to needy children, popular distaste for the practice of removing children from their own homes for reasons of poverty, and belief that honest, efficient, and service-oriented public welfare could be created. Illinois passed the first statewide mother's pension law in 1911. By ten years later, forty states had enacted such laws.

In most locales, only mothers who were deemed "worthy" were eligible to receive assistance. Mothers were screened on the basis of their morality and whether they kept "suitable homes" for their children. Most of the recipients were widows. Less frequently, divorced, deserted, or separated mothers, or mothers whose husbands were incapacitated or physically disabled, were deemed eligible. Most questionable of all were unmarried mothers. In addition, mothers considered to be worthy and fit usually turned out to be white; only about 3 percent of recipients were African American.

The mothers' pension programs provided a model for a state-supported humanitarian effort on behalf of dependent children and reflected a growing commitment to the concept of public responsibility. But the program also left unresolved the complicated administrative problems of shared state and local responsibility and complicating, ambivalent attitudes about suitable homes.

Aid to Families with Dependent Children

When the Social Security Act was passed in 1935, mothers' pensions were replaced by Aid to Dependent Children (ADC). The Act required that all states implement the program. As is clear from its name, ADC did not provide for mothers directly but only for their children. Coverage for mothers was introduced in 1950. In 1962 ADC was renamed Aid to Families with Dependent Children (AFDC) to reflect its new purpose of strengthening families. Initially the program was limited to single parents, but in 1961 the program was expanded in approximately half the states to include unemployed parents (AFDC-UP), thus providing aid to families with an unemployed male head. The 1988 Family Support Act required that AFDC-UP be implemented in all states by 1994 (Mink, 1998).

ADC and later AFDC established a federal role in child and family welfare. The federal government had long been reluctant to become involved with these matters out of concern that this would violate the rights of states and families. However, inequities among the states were apparent, and the Great Depression of the 1930s made it clear that the intervention of the federal government was essential to ameliorate the severe poverty in which many families lived. Thus, under the Social Security Act of 1935, the federal government established a cooperative program between itself and the states.

In 1995, AFDC served 4,873,398 families a year (U.S. Department of Health and Human Services, 1998). Even with the large numbers aided by AFDC, not all poor children were in families receiving public assistance. Furthermore, most families who were aided by AFDC payments were provided with income still well below the poverty level. The great bulk of the AFDC caseload was made up of families headed by a woman, always among the most vulnerable to poverty.

The public increasingly viewed AFDC with suspicion and disappointment, and from time to time it came under bitter attack. Concern was high that the existing AFDC program had an unintentional consequence of discouraging work by enabling recipients to subsist on welfare payments. Although at least half of all AFDC recipients remain on welfare only temporarily, others were caught in a pattern of continuing dependency, and the public perception was that their children too would grow up without the ability to become self-sufficient workers.

In their efforts to find a means to break this "cycle of dependency," several states created demonstration work programs. Studies of several state programs showed a promising level of success, leading to a belief that such demonstration programs benefited welfare recipients and that the programs could eventually pay for themselves.

A social factor that contributed heavily to the new consensus on welfare was that, women having for some time been entering the workforce in large numbers, a new norm of family life was in place, and welfare mothers who stayed home with their children seemed to be out of step with reality.

In 1988 Congress passed the Family Support Act, the intent of which was to enable the states to help poor families leave welfare and become self-sufficient. The Act required AFDC recipients to participate in education, job training, and work programs.

The political climate is not a friendly one for poor women on relief. (Kingfisher, 1996, p. 22)

The Family Support Act of 1988 reflected the country's shifting views of welfare and work. The Act incorporated the principle of parental responsibility by strengthening child support enforcement and by emphasizing work and employment training for parents. It also made AFDC available for two-parent families so that families would not have to separate in order to become eligible for aid. It increased the commitment of the state to the goal of family self-sufficiency through the guarantee of child care and Medicaid for twelve months after the parent left welfare for work.

Temporary Assistance for Needy Families

In the years after the passage of the Family Support Act, momentum increased for further welfare reforms to link welfare benefits to approved parental behaviors of work and family responsibility. Donna Shalala, secretary of the Department of Health and Human Services (HHS), described the welfare reform strategy of the Clinton administration as being "based on a simple point: welfare must be a temporary, transitional program that builds on core American values—work, family, opportunity, and responsibility" (Shalala, 1993, p. 5).

The nation's governors also lobbied to have more power devolved to the states. Devolution reflects the changing federal–state relationship in which the federal government gives greater flexibility to the states to determine the social agenda, and the states in turn assume more responsibility for the design and administration of social programs. Congress incorporated this idea when it dramatically transformed the social safety net for low-income families with the 1996 passage of the Personal Responsibility and Work Opportunity Reconciliation Act (PRWORA). PRWORA eliminated the sixty-one-year-old AFDC program and replaced it with a block grant to states to establish the Temporary Assistance for Needy Families (TANF) program.

Emphasis on Work

TANF emphasizes short-term, employment-related assistance (Pavetti, 1997). Families are eligible to receive TANF assistance for only sixty months in their lifetime. TANF recipients are also required to perform community service after receiving assistance for two months. They must work once they are determined to be job ready or after receiving assistance for twenty-four months. States can set shorter time limits for work participation. To ensure that state TANF programs emphasize work, PRWORA requires states to meet steadily increasing work participation rates in order to receive their full TANF allocation. Because TANF is so prescriptive in the area of work participation, families must quickly find employment or other sources of support.

Approaches Differ by State

Under PRWORA, there is no longer one national model of welfare provision. Within very general guidelines, as stated earlier, states have now been given the flexibility to design welfare programs that respond to their political and economic needs. Even before TANF was passed, thirty-seven states, through waivers from the Department of Health and Human Services, had enacted major welfare reforms. Since TANF, every state has passed a comprehensive welfare program that is work based. Almost every state has adopted time limits, although there is some variation in the limits set. The majority of states have adopted lifetime limits, most sixty months; six states have set shorter lifetime limits. A few states have set "periodic time limits" that allow recipients to return to the welfare rolls after being off for a certain period of time. For instance, in Ohio a family can receive a total of thirty-six cumulative months of benefits and then, unless it gets a hardship exemption, it must wait twenty-four months to reapply (Tweedle, 1998).

Most states have expanded their income disregards; that is, they have increased the amount of money that recipients can earn without losing eligibility for some benefits. Connecticut and Indiana, for example, allow recipients to earn up to the federal poverty threshold before they lose benefits. Other states have increased the percentage of earnings that are disregarded from determining the family's benefits. In Massachusetts, families can keep more than half their earnings and still get benefits (Tweedle, 1998). Many states allow recipients to build assets and still be eligible for assistance. These assets include the value of a car, or monies in individual development accounts, which recipients can open in order to save for education, starting a business, or buying a home.

More than twenty states have enacted family caps, which limit the amount of increase in benefits that families that have additional children while on welfare can receive. South Carolina allows the increase only in vouchers for the child's expense or the mother's education and training expenses. About 40 percent of the states provide diversion payments. These are lump sums to prospective recipients to cover expenses that would prevent them from working (e.g., buying a car so that they have transportation to work, or for emergency shelter). Finally, fourteen states provide lower benefits for recipients who moved into the state during the preceding year. In most of these states, applicants receive the benefit level from their former state for twelve months if it is lower (Tweedle, 1998).

Other Income Programs for Families with Children

TANF, like AFDC before it, provides cash income to poor families. The federal government also provides other kinds of assistance to families in need. When PRWORA was passed in 1996, it affected the way some of these resources would be dispensed.

SSI and Social Security

Enacted in 1972, Supplemental Security Income (SSI) provides assistance to elderly or disabled persons who are below certain income levels. For the elderly, it supplements Social Security and pension income if the amount they receive in retirement benefits is insufficient. For those who are medically certified as physically or mentally unable to work, it provides a source of income. Because SSI is strict in its certification guidelines, only those with considerable physical or mental disabilities can qualify for the program.

Unlike AFDC and now TANF, SSI is a federally designed program with a standard set of national benefits. A single individual living alone with no other income can receive a maximum of $545 per month, no matter where that person lives in the United States. Support decreases for those who live with others. Benefit amounts in SSI are calculated in the same way that AFDC benefits were: Maximum benefits go to those with no other source of income.

The 1996 welfare reform act toughens the definition of disability and requires reviews of children's disabilities every three years. The 1996 legislation also made legal immigrants ineligible for SSI and food stamps until they become citizens. Those legal immigrants who have worked for at least ten years were exempted from all benefit restrictions. The Balanced Budget Act of 1997 restored SSI and derivative Medicaid benefits to all elderly and disabled immigrants receiving SSI at the time PRWORA was enacted, and to all legal immigrants who were in the United States on the date of enactment and who become disabled in the future. The budget also restores additional benefits to refugees and expands the group of immigrants treated as refugees for the purposes of welfare assistance. The Welfare Reform

Act draws lines more sharply than before among classes of immigrants in the United States and devolves more of immigration policy to the states. For instance, states must now police benefit programs to ensure that unauthorized immigrants do not receive benefits (Fix & Tumlin, 1997).

Earned Income Tax Credit

The Earned Income Tax Credit (EITC) was passed by Congress in 1975 to offset the Social Security taxes paid by low-income families. The credit is available only to working poor people and is intended to encourage work by supplementing the income of low-wage earners. EITC is the fastest-growing antipoverty program in the country and has wide bipartisan support. It was a relatively small program until it was expanded in 1993 under the Clinton administration. In 1994, more than 18 million families received benefits, for a total cost of nearly $10 billion.

The EITC operates in a way that is almost the opposite of a cash grant program like AFDC. The EITC pays nothing if an individual does not work. As an individual earns income, the EITC provides about a thirty-cent supplement for every dollar earned (Blank, 1997). Income increases faster than earnings as workers at very low wages increase their hours of work. For workers who earn more, generally between $11,000 and $29,000, there is some concern that the EITC may not be as helpful, because the amount of the benefit declines as earnings increase. The actual amount received depends on the number of children the family has and its earnings. To receive the EITC supplement, families must file a tax return, even if their incomes are so low that they do not owe income taxes. Thus a family whose EITC is greater than its tax obligation will receive a check from the government after their tax return has been filed. EITC is a cost-effective way for the government to support poor families.

In a recent study, the National Center for Children in Poverty found that the EITC has had a significant impact on driving down young-child poverty rates. Without the EITC, the 1996 young-child poverty rate would have been 23 percent higher. In contrast, the report found no substantial evidence that state welfare reform efforts contributed to lowering the young-child poverty rate from 1993 to 1996, a period during which forty-three states made significant welfare changes. While over one-third of the children living in mother-only families experienced poverty if their mothers worked only part time, those with single mothers working full time still had poverty rates nearly three times as high as those in "traditional" two-parent families—those with the father working full time and the mother not working (17 percent to 6 percent, respectively) (National Center for Children in Poverty, 1998). EITC is likely to become even more important as an antipoverty measure as larger numbers of single mothers enter the labor market.

Child Support Enforcement

In the past, governmental efforts to enforce child support payments have been applied mostly to welfare families headed by women, although the problem of adequate child support from absent fathers is pervasive throughout the country. Many custodial parents (usually women) are not awarded child support payments at all, and others do not receive the amount to which they are legally entitled (Mulroy, 1995). In 1975 the federal government began to make systematic efforts to address child support enforcement, and has increased these enforcement provisions periodically ever since. However, support payments on behalf of children are still at very low levels, reflecting three decades of federal ineffectiveness.

The TANF legislation strengthens child support and paternity establishment provisions. States are now mandated to have a process in place for voluntary paternity acknowledgment and to establish paternity for 90 percent of all births to unmarried women. For custodial parents receiving TANF, the federal government has returned discretion in setting policy to the states. States now make decisions regarding cooperation requirements of the parent applying for TANF in determining paternity and locating the noncustodial parent. States may suspend professional and recreational licenses of individuals owing past due child support. Finally, states may establish procedures for imposing work activity requirements on noncustodial parents who were past due in child support (*A Comparison of Selected Key Provisions,* 1996; Institute for Research on Poverty, 2000). For information on innovative programs to establish paternity and encourage child support, see Chapter 3.

Why do many noncustodial parents fail to meet their child support obligations? Several reasons have been identified. First, the lower the noncustodial parent's income, the less likely it is that the noncustodial parent will pay. Second, noncustodial parents whose support orders represent a higher proportion of their income than that prescribed by federal guidelines are less likely to pay. Third, those who have visitation rights or joint custody are more likely to pay. Finally, we know that noncustodial parents are more likely to pay if the support orders are diligently enforced by the courts.

Medicaid and CHIP

The federal program designed to address the health needs of the poor is Medicaid. Under the 1996 welfare reform act, states must provide Medicaid to persons who would have been eligible for AFDC under the prior law. Medicaid transition benefits also remain in force but can be terminated if adults refuse to work. In most states, the children of sanctioned parents are still eligible for Medicaid. Because states now have to maintain dual eligibility systems (one for TANF and one for Medicaid), the federal government established a fund to reimburse states for increased administrative costs.

After much clamoring by advocates and policy specialists that the Personal Responsibility and Work Opportunity Reconciliation Act of 1996 did not provide enough protection to children who were without medical coverage, Congress made some corrections in its 1997 Reconciliation Act. That legislation allocated $47 billion over the next five years to allow states to expand health insurance coverage to a larger group of uninsured children. States can provide this added protection either through the Medicaid program or through separate state initiatives, called the Children Health Insurance Program (CHIP) (Currie, 1996). States must contribute 70 percent of what they would have contributed under the matching provisions of the Medicaid program. The result is that states can get federal money to expand health insurance coverage at a very favorable match rate.

What is the effect on children? A longitudinal study found that when children are covered by Medicaid they are more likely to have visited a doctor in the past six months (Currie,

1996). The study found that the expansion of Medicaid led to improved quality of care for children, as measured by the fraction of health care visits that took place in doctor's offices rather than in hospital outpatient clinics or emergency rooms (Currie, 1996).

Assessment of Welfare Reform

As this book goes to press, the U.S. Congress is preparing to reauthorize the welfare reform act that was originally passed in 1996 (PRWORA). During the six and a half years between original passage and reauthorization (March 2003), scholars have studied changes in welfare caseloads and the extent to which these changes could be attributed to welfare reform or to other factors.

The main finding is that welfare caseloads have plummeted. The number of families receiving AFDC or TANF fell by 57 percent from January 1994 to January 2001. The sharpest decline has been among young mothers (age 18–24) with young children (Corbett, 2002). However, not everyone who goes off welfare stays off. Loprest (2002, as cited in Weil, 2002) found that among those who left welfare between 1997 and 1999, 22 percent were back on the rolls when interviewed in 1999.

More welfare recipients are now working. A goal of welfare reform was to encourage recipients to replace welfare income with earned income. Loprest (2002, as cited in Weil, 2002) found that in 1999, 32 percent of welfare recipients reported some kind of paid work, up from 22 percent in 1997. Even among recipients who face high obstacles to working, such as those with very limited education and work skills, those caring for a disabled child, those in poor physical and mental health, and those with poor English language skills, the percentage who are working has increased, from 5 percent to 20 percent between 1997 and 1999 (Zedlewski & Alderson, 2001, cited in Weil, 2002).

Many of those leaving welfare for work are earning low wages. The median wage for former welfare recipients in 1999 was only $7.15 an hour (and remember, half of those leaving were earning less than this), and the jobs they take have few benefits, such as health care and personal leave time.

One in seven of those leaving welfare has no visible means of support. Follow-up of these recipients indicate that they are not living with a wage earner and are not receiving disability benefits. The several hundred thousand families with children in this category remain a major policy concern, because they may be faring very poorly (Weil, 2002).

States are doing more to make work pay. One of the major goals of welfare reform was to make working more desirable than welfare assistance, through allowing families to keep more of their earned income without docking their welfare benefit, and also providing other supports and income supplements to the income from wages. In compliance with this goal, states are spending less on welfare benefits but more on supporting work through child care and other assistance. States vary considerably in how much they spend to support the work effort of recipients; some states are spending as little as 25 percent of the welfare budget on actual cash grants to families, with the rest allocated to child care, transportation, and other activities to support work (Weil, 2002).

Welfare reform may affect different ethnic and racial groups differently. Aspects of welfare reform create an environment in which discrimination against people of color may occur. Welfare reform has returned much discretion to the states, to implement programs as they see fit. Individual welfare offices may have discretion in the supports and services they provide, in the expectations they place on clients, and on imposing sanctions for noncompliance. Because welfare recipients now are expected to enter the labor market, they are affected by differential rewards for different levels of education, training, work experience, and by possible discriminatory practices. A recent study by Finegold and Staveteig (2002, as cited in Weil, 2002) found that a larger proportion of African Americans than whites have left welfare because of administrative reasons. This and other findings give reason for watchful concern in the implementation of welfare reform policies among different racial groups. Immigrants, who were targeted in the welfare reform act with a number of very restrictive new policies, have responded to the "chilling effect" of these policies by leaving welfare or failing to apply. Not only have legal permanent-resident aliens left welfare, but there is also evidence that refugees, a group that should have been unaffected by the PRWORA's provisions, are also declining in welfare participation.

There is debate on the extent to which these changes noted are due to changes in the welfare program brought about by PRWORA in 1996 or are due to other changes in the economy. During the first several years of welfare reform, the economy was in a period of growth, which made it possible for people who were usually unemployed to find work. Other federal legislation during this time expanded supports for the working poor who were not on welfare, including child care, Medicaid, and the Earned Income Tax Credit. These programs also had an effect on people's decision to leave welfare for work, quite apart from changes in the structure of the welfare program itself (Besharov, 2000). Most observers are prepared to declare that welfare reform appears to be a success at this point, in that more people are working and leaving the rolls, with no major increase in homelessness and other social problems. As welfare reform continues, further research will be needed to track changes in the work behavior and the well-being of the poor over time.

Welfare Reform and Child Well-Being

President Bush has proposed that the overall goal of TANF should be "to increase flexibility of states in operating a program *designed to improve the well-being of children . . .*" (Laracy, 2002). If adopted, the focus of welfare programs and policies would change from reducing dependence and encouraging work to improving developmental outcomes of the nation's poor children. President Bush's suggestion acknowledges the large body of research on the negative effects of poverty on children's development and their future life chances.

Welfare policy in this country has always had significant implications for the well-being of children, and the Personal Responsibility and Work Opportunity Reconciliation Act (PRWORA) is no exception. Various researchers have analyzed the Act and, based on the findings of earlier research on welfare-to-work programs, identified key provisions that have significant implications for children.

Time Limits and Employment Requirements

The law places a sixty-month lifetime limit on welfare receipt, although some states have even stricter time limits. States exempt some families from the sixty-month limit because of specific hardships. However, some families and children have lost financial assistance entirely because of the parent's failure to comply with this requirement.

The legislation requires participation in work-related activities, as defined by each state, within twenty-four months of receiving assistance. Findings from earlier studies suggest that children fare slightly better or about the same on measures of development when their mothers are employed than when they are not. This may be due to the better mental health of employed mothers, or it may be due to the infusion of needed economic resources. However, some studies suggest negative outcomes for children when employment is initiated during the first year of a child's life. This is significant, given that under PRWORA, some states are requiring mothers whose infants are as young as newborn to three months to go to work. Studies also show that outcomes for children vary according to maternal wage level and the quality of the home environment (which may decline when the mother goes out to work).

The day care setting in which children stay while their parents work also has a large influence on children's development and well-being. Under the new law, states have flexibility regarding child care funding and child care assistance eligibility guidelines. States vary in the degree to which they use federal money for child care to provide subsidies, increase the supply of child care, assist parents in finding child care, and strengthen regulation and monitoring of licensed child care. (See Chapter 4.)

Children with Special Needs and Immigrant Children

Under PRWORA, an estimated quarter million children with behavioral disorders and learning disabilities who received Supplemental Security Income (SSI) are no longer eligible for benefits. In addition, adult welfare recipients in the families of many of these children are subject to work requirements. Likewise, children of legal immigrants who are no longer eligible for food stamps under PRWORA may experience diminished family resources. Some states provide supplemental funds or emergency benefits for such families, but others do not, and these families have to provide for themselves.

Teenage and Nonmarital Childbearing

The legislation requires teenage welfare recipients to attend school and live with their parents or other responsible adults. The Act also allows states to institute a "family cap" that denies additional benefits to families in which more children were born while the families are receiving assistance. States that succeed in reducing nonmarital births receive monetary bonuses.

Recent trends indicate that the teen birth rate has declined significantly. (See Chapter 3.) However, the extent to which welfare reform is responsible for this decline is not known. Other factors, including increased awareness of sexually transmitted diseases, may also influence teenage sexual behavior. The requirement that teen parents attend school, sometimes called "Learnfare," may be having a positive impact. Early research indicates that this provision may improve a teen parent's enrollment, grade completion, and chances of receiving a high school equivalency diploma (Greenberg et al., 2002).

Welfare Reform and Kinship Care

The case example at the beginning of this chapter highlighted the important role of grandparents in assuring children's well-being. TANF and its predecessor, Aid to Families with Dependent Children, allows grandparents and other nonparental caretakers to receive "child only" grants for children in their homes if their parents could not care for them. With over 2 million children now living with grandparents or other relatives with no parent present, the specific provisions for financially supporting children's placements with relatives is increasingly significant (U.S. Census Bureau, 2000). Although many of these families do not receive public aid of any kind, about half a million children live in homes of relatives that receive TANF child only grants. The relatives with whom the child is living do not have to comply with work requirements, unless they are also receiving TANF for themselves. However, the child only grants are quite small in most states and generally do not cover the costs of caring for the child. There is concern that some otherwise highly suitable relatives are unable to care for children because they simply cannot afford it. Relatives may have the option of becoming licensed foster parents for the children, and thus receive a much higher level of reimbursement, but this option is available only if the child has been maltreated, and if the relative is willing and able to meet the state's requirements for foster parent licensing. (See Chapter 8.)

Overall, initial research on the effects of welfare reform on children suggests that moving parents from welfare to work may be a good start to improving children's well-being. Further, the potential exists to use savings in welfare made possible by TANF to fund more preventive and support services for families. An innovative program in El Paso County, Colorado, that takes this approach is described in Chapter 3. However, further efforts are needed to improve outcomes for poor children. Shields and Behrman (2002) recommend the following improvements to current welfare policy:

- Support services should be available to families even after the parent is established in a job. Parents need help in attaining job advancement, which may include the need for additional training or education. Income supplements to the parents' wages may be necessary over an extended period of time in order to ensure that children have the resources necessary for healthy development. Single mothers should have more flexibility in accepting part-time employment and should be able to maintain eligibility for financial assistance over time, in order to combine work and family demands successfully.
- More services should be available to fathers of children on public assistance to help them find and keep work, advance their careers, and contribute to healthy family functioning.
- Day care and after-school programs need to be expanded and the overall quality improved, if children are to benefit from their parent's employment outside the home. (See Chapter 4.)

Welfare reform will be a success when it has moved children and their families out of poverty. Sufficient material resources are essential to attaining healthy, positive developmental outcomes in children. If welfare succeeds only in moving people from inadequate public assistance to low-paying jobs, leaving them as poor as they were before, it cannot claim success in improving the lives of poor children.

Trends and Issues

Welfare Reform: Challenging Populations

In 1997, Pavetti, Olson, Nightingale, and Duke reported that 90 percent of welfare recipients experienced at least one of the following barriers to employment: low basic skills, substance abuse, depression, had a child with a chronic illness or disability, or had a physical health condition themselves. In 2002, Loprest found that of the recipients who left welfare between 1997 and 1999, 22 percent were back on the rolls. The long-term recipients, that is, those continuously on welfare for two years, and the returners, that is those who had left welfare but returned, shared these characteristics: poor physical or mental health and less high school education. Early in the welfare reform process, it was recognized that poor physical or mental health of the parent of the child would be a major barrier to sustained employment. Approximately 40 percent of the states' TANF recipients had multiple barriers to employment in 1997. States initially focused their attention on those with the fewest barriers to employment. Early on, caseloads were screened to determine whether any of those with physical or mental disabilities might qualify for Supplemental Security Income and, if so, to refer them for SSI. In 1999, approximately 40 percent of the TANF recipients had multiple barriers to employment, no change from 1997. However, of those persons receiving TANF support, 20 percent with multiple barriers were working some hours, up from 5 percent in 1997 (Weil, 2002).

Most states began to consider the more extensive support systems that would be required to transition persons with multiple barriers, with poor physical or mental health being one barrier, from welfare to work who did not qualify for SSI. These recipients require extensive coordination between mental health systems, vocational rehabilitation systems, and TANF systems. The significant increase in recipients with multiple barriers who are working but still eligible for welfare benefits, is indicative that these populations can be gainfully employed. Given both their personal characteristics and the current economic environment, a modified policy may be more appropriate: namely, part-time employment with ongoing TANF benefits along with continuing mental and physical health supports (particularly continuing health insurance benefits for adults).

Persons with substance abuse issues are another group of recipients who initially offered challenges. Many states initiated drug screening programs for applicants and recipients to detect drug use/abuse and make referrals to drug abuse treatment services early in the TANF cycle. After some legal challenges, these policies were found legally acceptable so long as they were implemented to detect a service need and provide treatment and not to deny services. Another strategy was to carefully assess the impact of the parents' substance abuse on child safety. Many cases of parental substance abuse were referred to children's protective services. Some cases resulted in voluntary placement of the children with relatives. Others resulted in abuse and neglect petitions with placement of the children in foster care. Many TANF cases were closed to substance-using and -abusing parents and many child only cases were opened with relatives as grantees when the parents failed to participate in the required substance abuse treatment programming. Some advocates are concerned that these parents will be lost to the systems of service and continue their downward spirals. Insufficient substance abuse services is as much of a challenge for the TANF system as it is for the child welfare system.

Persons in domestic violence situations are another group of recipients who offer unique challenges. Initially, some advocates argued that this group of recipients should be granted waivers or deferrals from the work requirements due to concerns about safety. However, others argued that they should not be categorically denied the opportunity to participate in programs that would increase their capacity for economic independence. Most states implemented employment protocols including screening for domestic violence in all cases. Services were offered to those who had domestic violence issues. After assessment, victims of violence could obtain a temporary deferral if it were determined necessary for safety or they could be immediately referred for work activities. Joint client–recipient decision making in individual cases appears to be the most beneficial approach to these challenging cases because there is no uniform face to domestic violence and its impact on employability.

Perhaps the greatest challenge to welfare reform in the coming years is not the people and their characteristics, but the state of the economy.

Chapter Summary

According to federal government calculations, about 12 percent of the U.S. population is poor. The poor are a heterogeneous group, but poverty is especially prevalent among children under 18 and among households headed by African American and Hispanic females. Poverty figures are highest for children under 6 years old who live in female-headed households. Poverty is caused in large measure by a number of changes in the U.S. economy that make it difficult for families to maintain a decent standard of living, including wage stagnation and a declining need for male workers with few skills and limited education.

Before the Great Depression, providing for the poor was mainly the responsibility of local and state governments. From 1935 until recently, the federal government, in partnership with the states, provided a safety net to eligible poor families with children through the Aid to Families with Dependent Children (AFDC) program. AFDC was a means-tested program that required applicants, mainly single mothers and their children, to meet federal and state criteria of eligibility in order to receive benefits. The AFDC program was increasingly viewed with suspicion, and concern grew that the existing program discouraged work by enabling recipients to subsist on welfare payments.

By the mid-1980s, a number of states began demonstration programs among targeted groups of welfare recipients. In 1988 Congress passed the Family Support Act, which required AFDC recipients to participate in education, job-training, and work programs. The professed intent was to help poor persons leave welfare and become self-sufficient.

Welfare benefits were further linked to approved parental behaviors when, in 1996, Congress passed the Personal Responsibility and Work Opportunity Reconciliation Act (PRWORA). PRWORA eliminated the AFDC program and replaced it with block grants to states to establish Temporary Assistance for Needy Families (TANF) programs. PRWORA places emphasis on work and leaves states responsible for designing and implementing their welfare programs.

TANF, like AFDC before it, provides cash income to poor families. The federal government also provides other kinds of assistance to families in need. These noncash resources include tax credits, food stamps, medical benefits, and child care subsidies. PRWORA affects the way some of these noncash resources are dispensed. For example, Medicaid can be terminated if adults refuse to work, although in most states the children of parents who have been terminated are still eligible for Medicaid.

FOR STUDY AND DISCUSSION

1. Identify five nonprofit organizations in your community that provide resources to the poor. What kinds of resources do they provide? Where do their funds come from?

2. Ask a representative of a welfare rights organization in your community how women and their families are faring under the 1996 welfare reform act.

3. Review the history of public assistance in this country. Identify the premises of major programs, from mothers' pensions through the Personal Responsibility and Work Opportunity Reconciliation Act of 1996. What are the similarities? What are the differences?

4. Talk with a welfare worker (generally called a case worker) and a current or former welfare recipient about why women go on welfare. Identify any similarities and differences in the reasons they give you.

5. Identify two major employers in your community. Ask the employers about the kinds of entry-level jobs their companies provide. What skills and attitudes do they expect of entry-level employees? How much do they pay entry-level employees?

FOR ADDITIONAL STUDY

Blank, R. M. (1997). *It takes a nation: A new agenda for fighting poverty.* New York: Russell Sage Foundation and Princeton, NJ: Princeton University Press.

Duncan, G., & Chase-Lansdale, L. (Eds.). (2002). *For better and for worse: Welfare reform and the well-being of children and families.* Thousand Oaks, CA: Sage.

Ehrenreich, B. (2001). *Nickel and dimed.* New York: Metropolitan Books.

Garfinkel, I., McLanahan, S., Meyer, D., & Seltzer, J. (Eds.). (2001). *Fathers under fire: The revolution in child support enforcement.* Thousand Oaks, CA: Sage.

Katz, M. B. (1986). *In the shadow of the poorhouse: A social history of welfare in America.* New York: Basic Books.

Mink, G. (1998). *Welfare's end.* Ithaca, NY: Cornell University Press.

Shirk, M., Bennett, N., & Aber, J. (1999). *Lives on the line: American families and the struggle to make ends meet.* Boulder, CO: Westview Press.

Zaslow, M., Tout, K., Botsko, C., & Moore, K. (1998). *Welfare reform and children: Potential implications.* Washington, DC: The Urban Institute.

INTERNET SEARCH TERMS

Child poverty

Poverty

Welfare reform

INTERNET SITES

Administration for Children and Families. The Administration for Children and Families is a division of the U.S. Department of Health and Human Services. The web site provides technical information and statistical data in regards to welfare reform.

www.acf.dhhs.gov

Children's Defense Fund. The Children's Defense Fund is committed to the well-being of children. The web site provides helpful information about children and welfare reform but focuses mainly on statistics related to the state of children in the United States.

www.childrensdefense.org

Child Trends, Inc. Child Trends, Inc. is a nonprofit organization dedicated to research focused on children, youth, and families. The web site offers comprehensive data on how welfare reform affects children.

www.childtrends

Institute for Women Policy Research. The Institute for Women Policy Research was established to research policies that impact women. A portion of the web site covers welfare reform and contains information on domestic violence, reproduction, education, and issues that impact women in relation to welfare reform. The site also provides an online forum for interested individuals to discuss welfare reform.

www.iwpr.org

National Center for Children in Poverty. The NCCP promotes policies and programs that work to reduce child poverty. The web site provides statistics about children, along with information on how welfare reform affects children.

www.cpmcnet.columbia.edu/dept/nccp

Urban Institute: Assessing the New Federalism. The Urban Institute provides extensive information on social and economic issues. "Assessing the New Federalism" is the Urban Institute's project examining welfare reform. In addition to information about all aspects of welfare reform, the site offers thorough and extensive research related specifically to families and children. The web site also has a database with information about the efforts of each state in addressing welfare reform.

http://newfederalism.urban.org

Welfare Information Network. The Welfare Information Network is a foundation-sponsored web site with extensive information on all aspects of welfare reform, including policies regarding immigrants, child support, teenage parenting, welfare-to-work programs, TANF, domestic violence, and child welfare.

www.welfareinfo.org

REFERENCES

Abramovitz, M. (1988). *Regulating the lives of women: Social welfare policy from colonial times to the present.* Boston: South End Press.

American Federation of State, County and Municipal Employees. (1998, July). *Thinking creatively about welfare-to-work job creation.* Unpublished manuscript.

Besharov, D. (2000, Summer). Welfare reform: Four years later. *The Public Interest.* Available: www.welfareacademy.org/pubs.

Blank, R. M. (1997). *It takes a nation: A new agenda for fighting poverty.* New York: Russell Sage Foundation and Princeton, NJ: Princeton University Press.

Boo, K. (1997, October 19). Painful choices: Denise Jordan is off welfare and loves her job, but what about her daughter? *Washington Post,* p. A1.

A comparison of selected key provisions of the welfare reform reconciliation act of 1996 with current law. (1996). Washington, DC: The Urban Institute. Available: www.urban.org/welfare/WRCA96.htm.

Corbett, T. (2002). The new face of welfare: From income transfers to social assistance? *Focus,* 22(1), 3–10. Publication of the University of Wisconsin–Madison Institute for Research on Poverty.

Currie, J. (1996, May). The effects of welfare on child outcomes: What we know and what we need to know. Paper prepared for National Academy of Sciences meeting.

DeBord, K., Canu, R., & Kerpelman, J. (2000). Understanding a work–family fit for single parents moving from welfare to work. *Social Work, 45*(4), 313–324.

DeParle, J. (1997, December 30). Tougher welfare limits bring surprising results. *Washington Post,* p. A1.

DeParle, J. (1998, July 27). Shrinking welfare rolls leave record high share of minorities. *New York Times,* p. A1+.

Edin, K., & Lein, L. (1997). *Making ends meet: How single mothers survive welfare and low-wage work.* New York: Russell Sage Foundation.

Finegold, K., & Staveteig, S. (2002). Race, ethnicity, and welfare reform. In Alan Weil and Kenneth Finegold (Eds.), *Welfare reform: The next act* (pp. 203–223). Washington, DC: The Urban Institute. As cited in Weil, 2002.

Fix, M. E., & Tumlin, K. (1997). *Welfare reform and the devolution of immigrant policy.* Washington, DC: The Urban Institute.

Gallagher, L., Jerome, M., Gallagher, K. P., Schreiber, S., & Watson, K. (1998). *One year after federal welfare reform: A description of state temporary assistance for needy families (TANF) decisions as of October 1997.* Occasional Paper Number 6. Washington, DC: The Urban Institute.

Greenberg, M., Levin-Epstein, J., Hutson, R., Ooms, T., Schumacher, R., Turetsky, V., & Engstrom, D. (2002, Winter–Spring). The 1996 welfare law: Key elements and reauthorization issues affecting children. *The Future of Children, 12*(1), 27–57.

Harris, J. F. (1998, May 28). Clinton extols his welfare policies. *Washington Post,* p. A15.

Herr, T., & Halpern, R. (1991). *Changing what counts: Rethinking the journey out of welfare.* Evanston, IL: Northwestern University. Project Match, Center for Urban Affairs and Policy Research.

Institute for Research on Poverty. (2000, Spring). Child support enforcement policy and low-income families. *Focus, 21*(1), 1–4.

Katz, M. B. (1986). *In the shadow of the poorhouse: A social history of welfare in America.* New York: Basic Books.

Kingfisher, C. P. (1996). *Women in the American welfare trap.* Philadelphia: University of Pennsylvania Press.

Knitzer, J., & Page, S. (1998). *Map and track: State initiatives for young children and families.* New York: National Center for Children in Poverty.

Laracy, M. (2002). Making TANF work better for children. *News & Issues, 12*(2). New York: Columbia University, National Center for Children in Poverty.

Long, S. K., & Clark, S. J. (1997). *The new child care block grant: State funding choices and their implications.* The Urban Institute. Available: www.newfederalism.urban.org/html/anf_a12.htm.

Loprest, P. (2002). Making the transition from welfare to work: Successes but continuing concerns. In Alan Weil and Kenneth Finegold (Eds.), *Welfare reform: the next act* (pp. 17–31). Washington, DC: The Urban Institute. As cited in Weil, 2002.

Mathews, J. (1990, May 18). Working off welfare: Study sees treasuries in major beneficiaries. *Washington Post,* p. A4.

Mink, G. (1998). *Welfare's end.* Ithaca, NY: Cornell University Press.

Miranne, K. B., & Young, A. H. (1998). Women "reading the world": Challenging welfare reform in Wisconsin. *Journal of Sociology & Social Welfare, 25,* 155–176.

Mulroy, E. A. (1995). *The new uprooted: Single mothers in urban life.* New York: Auburn House.

Murray, C. (1984). *Losing ground: American social policy, 1950–1980.* New York: Basic Books.

National Center for Children in Poverty. (1998, Spring). Poverty rates remain high despite the booming economy. *News and Issues, 3.*

Pavetti, L. (1997, July). *How much more can they work? Setting realistic expectations for welfare mothers.* The Urban Institute. [Annie E. Casey Foundation]. Available: www.urban.org/welfare/howmuch.htm.

Pavetti, L., Olson, K., Nightingale, D., & Duke, A. (1997). *Welfare-to-work options for families facing personal and family challenges: Rationale and program strategies.* The Urban Institute. Available: www.urban.org/welfare/pave1197.html.

Pear, R. (1998, September 26). Americans lacking health insurance put at 16 percent. *New York Times,* p. A1+.

Proceedings of the conference on the care of dependent children. (1909, January 25–26). 60th Cong., 2nd. Sess., S. Doc. No. 721. Washington, DC: U.S. Government Printing Office.

Proctor, B. D., & Dalaker, J. (2002). *Poverty in the United States: 2001.* (Current Population Reports, P60-219. U.S. Department of Commerce, Census Bureau.) Washington, DC: U.S. Government Printing Office.

Regenstein, M., & Meyer, J. A. (1998, July). *Job prospects for welfare recipients: Employers speak out.* The Urban Institute. Available: www.newfederalism.urban.org/html/occ10.htm.

Seefeldt, K. S., Pavetti, L., Maguire, K., & Kirby, G. (1998). Income support and social services for low-income people in Michigan. *State Reports.* Washington, DC: The Urban Institute.

Shalala, D. (1993). Welfare reform: A priority for the Clinton administration. *Children Today, 27,* 4–6.

Shields, M., & Behrman, R. (2002, Winter–Spring). Children and welfare reform: Analysis and recommendations. *The Future of Children, 12*(1), 5–25.

Stout, H. (1996, August 21). Clinton signs measure raising minimum wage. *Wall Street Journal,* p. 3.

Tweedle, J. (1998, January). Building a foundation for change in welfare. *State Legislatures,* 26–35.

U.S. Census Bureau. (1998, March). *Poverty and health statistics.* Washington, DC: Branch/HHES Division. Current Population Survey.

U.S. Census Bureau. (2000, March). *America's families and living arrangements.* (Current Population Reports. U.S. Department of Commerce, Census Bureau.) Washington, DC: U.S. Government Printing Office.

U.S. Census Bureau. (2002). *Poverty in the United States: 2001.* (Current Population Reports. U.S. Department of Commerce, Census Bureau.) Washington, DC: U.S. Government Printing Office.

U.S. Department of Health and Human Services. (1998). *Temporary assistance for needy families, 1936–1998.* HHS Administration for Children and Families. Available: www.acf.dhhs.gov/news/stats/369/htm.

Vobejda, B., & Haveman, J. (1998, August 12). States' welfare shift: Stop it before it starts. *Washington Post,* p. A1+.

Vobejda, B., & Jeter, J. (1997, September 1). And now comes the hard part. *Washington Post National Weekly,* p. 22.

Waller, M. (1997). *Welfare-to-work and child care: A survey of the ten big states.* Democratic Legislative Committee. Available: www.dlcppi.org/texts/social/ccare.htm.

Weil, A. (2002, May). Ten things everyone should know about welfare reform. *New Federalism.* Series A, no. A52. Washington, DC: The Urban Institute.

Weir, M., Orloff, A. S., & Skocpol, T. (Eds.). (1988). *The politics of social policy in the United States.* Princeton, NJ: Princeton University Press.

Wertheimer, R., & Moore, K. (1998). *Childbearing by teens: Links to welfare reform.* Washington, DC: The Urban Institute.

Wilson, W. J. (1987). *The truly disadvantaged: The inner city, the underclass, and public policy.* Chicago: University of Chicago Press.

Zaslow, M., Tout, K., Botsko, C., & Moore, K. (1998). *Welfare reform and children: Potential implications.* Washington, DC: The Urban Institute.

Zedlewski, S., & Alderson, D. (2001, March). Do families on welfare in the post-TANF era differ from their pre-TANF counterparts? *Assessing the New Federalism* Discussion Paper. Washington, DC: The Urban Institute. Cited in Weil, 2002.

6

Law and Procedure

Court Intervention with Children, Youth, and Families

Juvenile court history has again demonstrated that unbridled discretion, however benevolently motivated, is frequently a poor substitute for principle and procedure.
—Justice Abe Fortas, *In re Gault,* 1967, p. 18

CHAPTER OUTLINE

Introduction

Perhaps no social institution was founded with higher hopes for its contribution to justice for children than the juvenile court. In the last five decades, however, it has been a center of controversy. Its philosophy, procedures, and achievements have undergone scrutiny, challenge, and demands for radical change. At the heart of the controversy are differences over the proper purpose, focus, and procedures of the juvenile court.

The division of authority between courts and social agencies, particularly state child welfare agencies and the private child welfare agencies providing services under purchase-of-services arrangements with the public agencies, is a constant source of tension for the social worker. In the period of the juvenile court's history when its rules and procedures were informal, social workers were consulted for their expertise in "what's best for the child." Their opinions were given, generally with little questioning of the evidentiary bases for them, and the court acted with significant deference to those recommendations. As the juvenile court system became more structured to conform to legal requirements for admissibility of evidence, standards of proof, rights to attorney representation, and other procedural protections for children and their parents, the social worker's approach has had to adapt.

A constant source of conflict for social workers is that they are required to gather and act on both social evidence and legal evidence. Some situations of children and families do not yield clear legal evidence. Because the questions at issue in such cases are often not simple, social workers may rely on many sources of information, some of which is nonadmissible hearsay evidence or other information acquired informally. In such cases they look for repeated patterns of parent and child behavior and environmental influences. They may offer "voluntary" services to the family with the hope of resolving the concern. Frequently these offers of "voluntary" services are rooted in their knowledge that they have insufficient evidence to proceed to court intervention. This practice is receiving greater scrutiny and commentary within the social work and legal communities. Many argue that when the state intrusion and the treatment plan do not rest on a documented basis that could pass judicial scrutiny, social workers must carefully evaluate the reliability of any social evidence that in a way affects the rights of children and families and their ability to direct their own lives.

The challenge to social workers is to understand the nature of evidence and the court process, to become skillful in finding and organizing facts, and to integrate this knowledge and skill into their social work values and approaches to helping. In Chapter 2 we highlighted the major Supreme Court case decisions and their impact on the juvenile courts. In Chapters 3, 7, 8, 9, 10, and 11 we focus on the social work issues. In this chapter, we focus on the basics of the courts in the handling of abuse, neglect, and delinquency matters. Our intent is to orient the student to the structure and processes of the legal systems and their roles in them.

The Juvenile Court Movement

Juvenile courts were created by a legal and social work cooperative venture. In a spirit of mission, late nineteenth- and early twentieth-century social reformers enjoined the "child welfare" purpose to that of "youth correction." Historical factors in large measure account for the highly complex commingling of the child welfare system and the juvenile justice system that exists today: "The most significant fact about the history of juvenile justice is that it evolved simultaneously with the child welfare system. Most of its defects and its virtues derive from that fact" (Flicker, 1977, p. 27).

Philosophy and Purpose

From its inception, the juvenile court had high aims, combined with heavy responsibilities. Its purpose was conceived of as protection and rehabilitation of the child in place of indictment and punishment. It was based on a philosophy of "individualized justice," which directs the application of law to social ends by individualization, that is, by "dealing with each case as in great measure unique and yet . . . on a basis of principle derived from experience . . . developed by reason" (Pound, 1950, p. 36). The intent was a humanitarian one, based on the conviction that the individual child and his or her needs rather than an offense and its legal penalty should be the focus of consideration.

The concern of the juvenile court founders was directed toward the youthful law-breaker and children whose circumstances were likely to lead them into delinquency, rather than those who were grossly neglected or in need of other protections.

Judge Julian Mack, one of the early leaders in the juvenile court movement, described procedures prior to the passage of juvenile court legislation:

> Our common criminal law did not differentiate between the adult and the minor who had reached the age of criminal responsibility, seven at common law and in some of our states, ten in others, with a chance of escape up to twelve, if lacking in mental and moral maturity. The majesty and dignity of the state demanded vindication for infractions from both alike. . . . The child was arrested, put into prison, indicted by the grand jury, tried by a petit jury, under all the forms and technicalities of our criminal law, with the aim of ascertaining whether it had done the specific act—nothing else—and if it had, then of visiting the punishment of the state upon it. (Mack, 1909–1910, p. 106)

An early description of the aims and the humanitarian concerns of the new court will serve to draw the contrast between the old and the new philosophy:

> Emphasis is laid, not on the act done by the child, but on the social fact and circumstances that are really the inducing causes of the child's appearance in court. The particular offense that was the immediate and proximate cause of the proceedings is considered only as one of the many other factors surrounding the child. The purpose of the proceeding here is not punishment but correction of conditions, care and protection of the child and prevention of a recurrence through the constructive work of the court. Conservation of the child, as a valuable asset of the community, is the dominant note. (Flexner & Baldwin, 1914, pp. 6–7)

To implement such a philosophy, the juvenile court was of necessity a court of equity, one intended to temper the strict application of the law to the individual needs of the child. Its justice represented a departure from the concept of justice personified by the traditional symbol: a statue of a woman holding a balanced scale. In one scale, the crime is measured, and in the other, the punishment. When the two sides of the scale balance evenly, it was held, justice prevails. This symbol of justice wears a blindfold so that the wealth or poverty of the accused or other individual characteristics or station in life cannot influence her. She is blind to individual differences, all objective and evenhanded. There were historical reasons for this symbol. It marked a revolt against the tyranny and the inequities of earlier centuries when law was made and interpreted differently for nobles and peasants, rich and poor. It marked a claim of the ordinary person for equal treatment before the law.

But in the philosophy of the juvenile court, the blindfold was, in effect, stripped from the symbol of justice. The characteristics of the child became crucial to the judge, who was under obligation to examine the child and a particular situation with all its differences and to turn away from a scrutiny of the offense and its legal penalty. Julia Lathrop, one of the juvenile court's early founders, said that the outstanding contribution of the juvenile court was that "it made the child visible" (Lundberg, 1947, p. 119).

Founding

The first juvenile court in the United States was created in Illinois on April 2, 1899. The attainment of this significant and far-reaching piece of legislation came through cooperation among a group of discerning and energetic social workers in Chicago, lawyers for the Chicago Bar Association, and civic leaders from various organizations, particularly the Chicago Woman's Club.

The leading female reformer among those who assumed responsibility for securing the juvenile court was a social worker, Julia Lathrop. An early resident of Hull House, she had been challenged by the spirit and potentiality of youths and distressed at the careless and neglectful treatment of many of them.

In 1898, at the annual meeting of the Illinois State Conference of Charities, Julia Lathrop showed leadership in planning an entire conference program on the topic "The Children of the State." Different organizations were found to be considering legislative proposals for benefits to children. The various groups merged their efforts and appointed a committee to secure the cooperation of the Chicago Bar Association to bring about a draft of a juvenile court act. While there were many revisions, the bill that emerged was approved as a Bar Association bill and introduced into the state legislature (Lathrop, 1925, pp. 290–297). The task of proposing and testifying on behalf of the juvenile court bill was assigned to the lawyers, while the woman's club took responsibility for securing support for the bill (Rosenheim, 1962, pp. 18–19).

This initial piece of legislation, which served as a model for legislation in other states, was broadly entitled "An Act to Regulate the Treatment and Control of Dependent, Neglected, and Delinquent Children." Thereafter, children who violated laws or ordinances were classified as delinquents instead of criminals. The new act was considered a magnificent accomplishment, attained against the weight and opposition of tradition. Jane Addams believed that the new court brought such change that

> there was almost a change in mores when the Juvenile Court was established. The child was brought before the judge with no one to prosecute him and no one to defend him—the judge

and all concerned were merely trying to find out what could be done on his behalf. (Addams, 1935, p. 137)

Roscoe Pound said that the juvenile court represented "the greatest advance in judicial history since the Magna Carta" (National Probation and Parole Association, 1957, p. 127). The movement had strong appeal to individual citizens and to groups working on behalf of children. This exciting concept of justice for children and the new legal machinery for helping them was achieved during a period of support for social reforms generally and special interest in the needs of children, a factor that helped to speed the creation of juvenile courts in other states.

By 1945, all states plus the District of Columbia, Hawaii, Alaska, and Puerto Rico had enacted juvenile court legislation, and Congress had authorized similar procedures for use in the federal courts (Nutt, 1949, p. 270).

The Early Question of Constitutionality

Some opposition to the initial passage of the acts came from members of the bar who believed that the court procedures, although intended to protect children, actually took away their constitutional rights. Nevertheless, by finding that juvenile proceedings were not adversarial, the courts firmly established the constitutionality of the juvenile court statutes, substantially reinforcing and extending the doctrine of *parens patriae* to include juvenile delinquents. In all the leading test cases, the *parens patriae* tenet was called up and used to justify the state's authority in the new acts, even though this old doctrine had not been a direct antecedent of the juvenile court (Flexner & Oppenheimer, 1922; Lou, 1927). The first major test of the constitutionality of juvenile court procedures was that of the Pennsylvania Act of 1903. An excerpt from the decision is illustrative of the philosophy that prevailed.

> To save a child from becoming a criminal, or from continuing in a career of crime, to end in maturer years in public punishment and disgrace, the legislature surely may provide for the salvation of such a child, if its parents or guardian be unable or unwilling to do so, by bringing it into one of the courts of the state without any process at all, for the purpose of subjecting it to the state's guardianship and protection. . . . There is no probability, in the proper administration of the law, of the child's liberty being unduly invaded. Every statute which is designed to give protection, care, and training to children, as a needed substitute for parental authority and performance of parental duty, is but a recognition of the duty of the state, as the legitimate guardian and protector of children where other guardianship fails. No constitutional right is violated. (*Commonwealth v. Fisher,* 1905)

When the new juvenile court statutes were challenged on constitutional grounds, the state supreme courts successively upheld them on the basis that the juvenile court was not a criminal court and no child was brought before the juvenile court under arrest and on trial for a crime; hence, constitutional guarantees accorded defendants in criminal cases did not apply to juvenile procedures. The weight of decision was an overwhelming endorsement of the new laws.

Practically, this meant that the child or youth was brought under the power of the juvenile court without the legal safeguards claimed as a constitutional right by an adult accused of law violations. These safeguards are embodied in such procedures as open hearings, right to counsel, proof beyond a reasonable doubt, limitations on the use of hearsay evidence, protection against self-incrimination, and right to bail. This practice of failing to provide the minor with these constitutionally guaranteed protections eventually led to extensive criticism of the juvenile court, on the basis that the rights of the child should be no less highly regarded and no less strictly observed than those of an adult in any court. Over time, this philosophy was extended to child abuse and neglect cases.

Supreme Court Decisions: New Procedural Directions

The *Kent* and *Gault* decisions of the United States Supreme Court began the constitutional review of the juvenile court processes that had been the subject of heavy criticisms. Youth and their parents frequently were not informed of their right to counsel. The absence of suitable facilities had led to the use of jails for children who had been arrested but not adjudicated. The social investigation, designed as a basis for helping the judge make an informed decision, often was sparse or superficial, thus negating its purpose. Clear proof of charges was often lacking even though the result was undesirable labeling of the child, or loss of liberty through commitment to training schools. Frequently there had been no transcripts of court proceedings, or incomplete ones, which made an appeal to a higher court difficult (Ellrod & Melaney, 1950; Rubin, 1952; Beemsterboer, 1960; Elson, 1962; Handler, 1965). Too often there had been failure on the part of the state to provide true rehabilitative facilities following the removal of a child from parental custody, what Ketcham (1962) termed substitution of "governmental for parental neglect."

Supreme Court Justice Abe Fortas cogently pinpointed two of the major problems before the juvenile court, the lack of constitutional guarantees and the lack of rehabilitative treatment resources:

> There is much evidence that some juvenile courts . . . lack the personnel, facilities and techniques to perform adequately as representatives of the state in a parens patriae capacity, at least with respect to children charged with law violation. There is evidence, in fact, that there may be grounds for concern that the child receives the worst of both worlds: that he gets neither the protections accorded to adults nor the solicitous care and regenerative treatment postulated for children. (*Kent v. United States,* 1966)

The specific facts of the following cases are stated in Chapter 2 and will not be repeated here. The issue in the *Kent* case was the juvenile's constitutional rights during a transfer, or waiver, from the juvenile court to the adult criminal court. The decision specified that the juvenile court must hold a hearing on the matter of a waiver, provide the young person with counsel at this hearing, and make the juvenile court records available to his or her counsel. The second major United States Supreme Court decision in relation to procedural protections for juveniles was *In re Gault*. The issue in this case was the due process and equal protection requirements in juvenile court proceedings. While the Court made it clear that juvenile court proceedings on an adjudication of delinquency need not conform to all the requirements of a criminal trial, it held that such action must measure up to the essentials of due process and fair treatment guaranteed by the Fourteenth Amendment to the Constitution. Specifically, (1) the child and his or her parents must be given written notice of a scheduled hearing sufficiently in advance to provide opportunity to prepare for the hearing, and this notice must set forth the alleged misconduct "with particularity"; (2) the child and his or her parents must be notified of the child's right to be represented by counsel retained by them, or if they are unable to afford this, counsel will be appointed to represent the child; (3) the constitutional privilege against self-incrimination (the right to remain silent instead of admitting or confessing) is applicable in the case of juveniles as well as adults; and (4) the child or young person has a right to confront and cross-examine witnesses who appear against him or her (*In re Gault,* 1967).

Three other U.S. Supreme Court decisions are important in shaping the adjudication phase of a delinquency procedure. *In re Winship* (1970) established the principle of proof beyond a reasonable doubt as a requirement for a finding of delinquency (although not necessarily for finding a child "in need of supervision"). While *Winship* affirmed a required level of proof for minors, two other decisions, *McKeiver v. Pennsylvania* (1971) and *Schall v. Martin* (1984), were in the direction of limiting the legal rights of a minor. *McKeiver* held that the due process clause of the Fourteenth Amendment does not require jury trials for youths charged with delinquent acts that could result in incarceration, leading to the criticism that *McKeiver* "continues the tradition of conceptual oscillation when juvenile court procedure is at issue," resulting in "the extension of some rights and the denial of others" (Schultz & Cohen, 1976, p. 28). The *Schall* court decided that pretrial detention to protect an accused juvenile and society from the "serious risk" of pretrial crime is compatible with the "fundamental fairness" demanded by the due process clause. The interest of the state in promoting juvenile welfare is a *parens patriae* interest, and is what "makes a juvenile proceeding fundamentally different from an adult criminal trial" (*Schall v. Martin,* 1984, pp. 253, 263). Liberty can therefore be circumscribed by the power of *parens patriae.*

The doctrine of *parens patriae* found further expression in the first Supreme Court decision establishing a standard in the dispositional stage of juvenile proceedings. *Thompson v. Oklahoma* (1988) overturned the death penalty for a boy who was 15 at the time he participated in the brutal murder of his former brother-in-law. The Court's majority held that to execute a person who was under 16 at the time of committing a crime was cruel and unusual punishment and therefore unconstitutional. The court distinguished juveniles from adults in terms of a basic assumption of society about children as a class: "We assume that they do not yet act as adults do, and thus we act in their interest. . . . It would be ironic if these assumptions that we so readily make about children as a class—about their inherent difference from adults in their capacity as agents, as choosers, as shapers of their own lives— were suddenly unavailable in determining whether it is cruel and unusual to treat children the same as adults for purposes of inflicting capital punishment" (*Thompson v. Oklahoma,* 1988, p. 2693, n. 23).

These precedent-setting cases affirm that in instances of alleged delinquency, juveniles are granted legal rights differentiated from those of adults, and at the same time are afforded due process protections (see Box 6.1).

BOX **6.1**

Due Process in Juvenile Courts

These are the due process rights for parties in juvenile court matters:

- *Right to notice and opportunity to be heard.* This means they have a right to know in advance what the charges are; who is making them; what evidence there is to support the charges; the date and time for the court hearing; and the right to bring evidence in support of their side of the story.
- *Right to representation.* This means that parents charged with abuse or neglect and youth charged with delinquent offenses have a right to an attorney. If they cannot afford one, then they have a right to have one appointed at public expense. Children in neglect and abuse matters may or may not have a right to attorney representation, depending on the state statute. They do have the right to have someone speak on their behalf—often a guardian *ad litem.*
- *Right to remain silent or privilege against self-incrimination.* This means that parents and youth charged with delinquent offenses can choose not to speak on their own behalf and the court cannot interpret that as an admission of or presumption of guilt.
- *Right to confront and cross-examine witnesses.* This means that parents charged with abuse or neglect and youth charged with delinquent offenses have a right to challenge verbally and with documents the testimony and statements of any witness.

The Family Court Movement

The first family court was established in Cincinnati, Ohio, in 1914, just fifteen years after the founding of the juvenile court. Family courts, in general, have jurisdiction over a broad range of legal issues involving children and families. Specific jurisdictional issues include divorce; child support, custody, and visitation; paternity establishment; child abuse and neglect, including termination of parental rights; juvenile delinquency; guardianship; emancipation; and emergency medical and mental health treatment authorization. The underlying rationale is that family legal issues are not isolated. A family experiencing child abuse and neglect may already have custody and visitation orders that could conflict with orders arising out of the child abuse and neglect matter. Divorcing parents frequently charge each other with abuse or neglect. The family courts, having the comprehensive jurisdiction to adjudicate all matters arising out of the same situation, spare the parties the multiplicity of court appearances with their potential for conflicting results. One jurist knows all the facts and is responsible for the resolution of all the legal issues (Szymanski, 1995).

As of 1998, eleven states had statewide family courts; fourteen states had family courts in selected areas of the state; nine states had family courts planned or being piloted; and seventeen states had no plans for family courts. The subject matter jurisdictions of the courts vary, with only eleven states' family courts having jurisdiction over all family matters (Babb, 1998). Ross attributes these variations to the need to adapt the courts to the particular communities. She identifies four components necessary to classify a court as a "family court":

- comprehensive jurisdiction, that is, the ability to adjudicate a range of legal issues so that there is an integrated approach to the resolution of problems within the same family;
- efficient administration designed to support the concept of "one family, one team," that is, the provision of continuity in decision-makers so that individual solutions are crafted based in knowledge of the family and its total situation;
- broad training for all court personnel, that is, establishing mechanisms so that judges, lawyers, social workers, and other support personnel are trained in the social, medical, psychological issues that arise in connection with the legal issues;
- comprehensive services, that is, having a broad array of services available to the family that can be accessed as soon as the family assessment is completed. (Ross, 1998, pp. 15–28)

As the family court movement progresses, there is a need for critical evaluation of outcomes. In theory the decisions should be more timely with little, if any, conflicts in orders, and services should be available when needed and in the "dosage" required for the individual family situation. Mark Hardin comments

> If, in the end, it appears doubtful that the resources and organization needed to achieve excellence in child protection cases will be in place when a unified family court is established, then advocates will have to ask themselves whether the proposed unified family court will be an improvement for abused and neglected children or, if not, an improvement for children overall. Where the resources are not in place, advocates in some locations may ultimately choose to work for improvement through specialized juvenile courts. . . . In either event, child protection advocates should be aware of the significance of court reform to achieving change beneficial to abused children. (Hardin, 1998, p. 199)

The National Council on Juvenile Justice will publish a report on the Ohio family court outcomes in 2003.

The Criminal Court Movement

In the 1980s, the juvenile justice system was challenged with the "just desserts" or "adult crime–adult time" punishment approach. Under this approach, if juveniles were to commit certain statutorily enumerated offenses, generally the most serious offenses, they could be tried and sentenced in the adult criminal court system. It is the current policy approach for serious and/or chronic juvenile offenders.

This approach rests on the assumption that the juvenile court system has not been effective in deterring juvenile crime nor correcting juvenile offenders' behaviors. Clearly the data supported that conclusion; that is, there was a group of serious, chronic juvenile offenders who continued to commit increasingly more serious offenses while under the supervision of the juvenile courts and the juvenile justice treatment systems. Since the mid-1980s, all states have modified their juvenile codes to provide that juveniles could or would be adjudicated by the criminal courts and incarcerated in adult prisons if the crimes were serious enough. The crimes vary by state. In general, they include offenses found in Box 6.2.

BOX **6.2**

Offenses for Which a Juvenile May Be Tried as an Adult

Although states vary, in general youths from age 14 to 17 may be tried as adults for the following types of offenses:

- burning a dwelling
- assault with intent to commit murder
- assault with intent to commit great bodily harm less than murder
- assault with intent to rob—unarmed
- assault with intent to rob—armed
- attempted murder
- first-degree murder
- second-degree murder
- kidnapping
- criminal sexual conduct
- assault with intent to commit criminal sexual conduct
- armed robbery
- unarmed robbery
- possession, manufacture, or delivery of a controlled substance

Howell (1997) notes: "Once again, punishing the offense rather than the offender is the object of the current crime policy" (p. 23). Chapter 11 discusses in detail the prosecution and treatment of the serious, chronic juvenile offender in both the juvenile justice and criminal justice systems.

The Structure of the Legal System

The legal system is complex. Law is the body of rules set and enforced by the government. Its function is to provide order and stability to society. Laws are changed when the society, as a whole, determines that the changes are required to advance the goal of order and stability in an ever-changing society. Laws are established in federal and state constitutions, by statutes or ordinances passed by the legislative branch of federal, state, and local governments, by regulatory agencies in administrative rules and regulations, and by federal and state court case decisions.

The ultimate law of the land is the U.S. Constitution. No federal or state statute and no administrative rule or regulation that violates a provision of the U.S. Constitution will prevail when challenged on constitutional grounds and the federal courts find that the statute, rule, or regulation is in violation of the U.S. Constitution.

Assuming that a specific statute, ordinance, administrative rule or case decision is constitutional, when there is a conflict, the general rule is that

- federal law supercedes state law and administrative rules if the federal law provides a greater benefit;

- state law supercedes administrative rules and local ordinances; and
- administrative rules supercede agency policies.

Case decisions, that is, case law or decisional law, serve to clarify the intent and meaning of federal and state constitutions, statutes, and administrative rules as applied in a specific fact situation or to clarify legal principles if there is no existing statute. Once a higher court of appropriate jurisdiction has ruled on the matter, that ruling serves as the interpretation of the law that all lower courts within the jurisdiction covered by the deciding court must follow.

Trial and Appellate Courts

The court system is comprised of the federal and state courts. Different courts have different jurisdictions, that is, types of legal matters over which they have authority to hear and decide. A trial court is a court in which decisions are based on receipt, examination, and evaluation of witness testimony and evidence. Either a jury or judge makes decisions. An appellate court is a court in which decisions are based on receipt and review of the written record of the trial court. Parties can submit written and oral arguments identifying the alleged errors made at the trial court level. Appellate courts can overturn (*reverse*) or support (*uphold*) the decision of the lower court based on the record as submitted or can return the case to the trial court with specific instructions or orders (*remand*).

Different states have different statutes and court rules governing appeals. In general there are appeals of right and appeals by application and leave granted. An appeal of right is taken when a specific statute provides that the decision of a lower court can be appealed to and must be heard by the appellate court. If a specific statutory provision granting an appeal of right is not present, the appeal is taken "by leave granted," that is, petition to the appellate court with the court having discretion as to whether to hear the case. Very few abuse, neglect, and juvenile delinquency matters ever proceed beyond the trial court stage.

Jurisdiction

The **jurisdiction** of a court (that is, its legal authority to hear and decide a particular matter) is determined by state statutes. The judge's authority in decision making is limited to those situations authorized by the statute. In juvenile matters, the primary factors enumerated in the statutes are the subject matter, the maximum age of the children for original jurisdiction, the geographic boundaries of the court, and the matters in which the court has exclusive and/or shared or concurrent jurisdictions.

The **age** of the young person in question is a primary factor that enters into a decision as to whether a juvenile court has jurisdiction. For delinquency matters, in most states the maximum age for original jurisdiction is 17 years; in some states the maximum age is as young as 15. Most states allow the juvenile court to continue jurisdiction over juvenile offenders, once they are adjudicated, beyond the maximum age of original jurisdiction. For abuse and neglect matters, in most states the juvenile court now has original jurisdiction up to 18 years of age, and, if jurisdiction were assumed prior to 18 years of age, it could continue jurisdiction beyond 18 years of age when provided by statute. For status offenses and adoption matters, in most states the jurisdictional age limit is 18 years.

The **subject matter** jurisdiction of the juvenile courts, in general, includes four general areas: abuse, neglect, abandonment, and dependency; delinquency; wayward minor, status offender, and minor in need of supervision; and adoption. With the family court movement, the decisional capacities in many states have been expanded to include paternity establishment; child custody, support, and visitation; guardianship; and emancipation. The specific facts of the case determine the appropriate jurisdictional basis. It is not atypical for dependency, neglect, abuse, and delinquency to overlap in the same case: "Parental neglect can precipitate delinquent conduct and the delinquent child may have been subjected to hostility and child abuse in the home. The neglected child may also be a delinquent who has not yet been caught" (Brieland & Lemmon, 1985, p. 139).

Jurisdictional elements are state-specific. Refer to the specific statutes and court rules for the state in which you are practicing.

Evidence

Evidence includes the full range of information, written and verbal, provided to the court in support of the allegations or statements made. Rules of evidence direct the type of information and the method for presenting that information to the court. These rules are promulgated to ensure the fair administration of justice. You should review the rules for the state in which you will be practicing, specifically the rules related to hearsay, business records, and expert witness testimony. You should document cases and prepare for hearings or trials with these evidentiary rules in mind.

Standards of Proof

A **standard of proof** is the degree of evidence required for the party who has the burden of proof to present to the court in order to sustain its burden, that is, to prove what the party asserts. The standard of proof varies depending on the stage of the hearing process—adjudicatory or dispositional—and the type of case being heard.

The three standards of proof are preponderance of the evidence, clear and convincing evidence, and beyond a reasonable doubt.

Preponderance of the Evidence. This refers to the greater weight of the evidence or evidence that is more credible and convincing. In delinquency matters, this is the standard used in most states for dispositional phase. In neglect or status offense matters, which are not treated as delinquency cases, this is the standard used by most states for adjudicatory phase.

Clear and Convincing Evidence. This proof is beyond preponderance but less than beyond a reasonable doubt. Some say that this means proof beyond a well-founded doubt. This is the standard used in the adjudicatory phase for cases involving Indian Child Welfare Act cases and in termination of parental rights for all children except Indian children. In some states, this standard is used in delinquency matters when the recommended disposition is placement in a secure facility.

Beyond a Reasonable Doubt. This proof must satisfy a moral certainty, be entirely convincing; the facts proven must establish guilt. In delinquency matters, this is the standard used in adjudicatory hearings. It is also the standard used in termination of parental rights of children covered by the Indian Child Welfare Act.

Indian Child Welfare Act: An Example of Federal Law Superseding State Law

The Indian Child Welfare Act, P.L. 95-608, was passed in 1978. Its intent was to curb an excessive rate of placement of Indian children in non-Indian foster and adoptive homes. The legislation came about after years of agitation by Indian groups and other advocates of civil liberties who maintained that out-of-home placements contributed to disruption of tribal culture and to identity confusion on the part of Indian children and encroached on the sovereignty of tribes.

The federal legislation was a significant social policy development, unique in acknowledging and protecting cultural values and self-determination of a minority group within the larger American society. In passing the legislation, Congress stated that the policy of the nation was to promote the stability and security of Indian tribes and families by establishing minimum federal standards for the removal of Indian children from their families. The placement of such children in foster homes hereafter would reflect Indian preferences for placement in priority order: extended family; homes licensed by a nontribal entity; or institutions approved by an Indian tribe.

Tribal courts have exclusive jurisdiction over child custody proceedings involving most Indian children regardless of whether they reside on the reservation. This means that the state court has the responsibility to notify the tribal court that it has a custody matter involving an Indian child before it, and if the tribal court elects to take the case, the state court must transfer the case to the tribal court. Custody proceedings include all foster care or adoptive placements of Indian children resulting from abuse or neglect, termination of parental rights, or status offenses of running away, truancy, and curfew violation. The legislation provided for federal funding to assist tribes in developing and operating child and family service programs.

The United States Supreme Court has heard one case involving interpretation of the Indian Child Welfare Act, *Mississippi Band of Choctaw Indians v. Holyfield* (1989). That case involved twins born to an Indian mother who was a member of the Choctaw tribe and who lived on the reservation. The children were born off the reservation, and the mother and father released their parental rights to allow the Holyfields to adopt them. The Holyfields proceeded with the adoption, and the tribe brought a motion to vacate the adoption on the basis that the children were Indian children and the parents did not have the right to release them for adoption by non-Indian persons without tribal permission. The Court stated

> We agree with the Supreme Court of Utah that the law of domicile Congress used in the ICWA cannot be one that permits individual reservation-domiciled tribal member to defeat the tribe's exclusive jurisdiction by the simple expedient of giving birth and placing the child for adoption off the reservation. Since, for the purposes of ICWA, the twin babies were domiciled on the reservation when adoption proceedings were begun, the Choctaw tribal court possessed exclusive jurisdiction pursuant to 25 U.S.C. Section 1911(a). (Ibid., 490 U.S. 51, 1989, pp. 1610–1611)

The Court expressed its concern about the fact that the children had lived with the Holy-fields for three years while the case proceeded through the appellate process:

> We have been asked to make the decision as to who should make the custody determination concerning these children—not what the outcome of that determination should be. The law places that decision in the hands of the Choctaw tribal court. Had the mandate of the ICWA been followed in 1986, of course, such potential anguish might have been avoided, and in any case the law cannot be applied so as automatically to reward those who obtained custody, whether lawfully or otherwise, and maintain it during any ensuing (and protracted) litigation. . . . It is not ours to say whether the trauma that might result from removing these children from their adoptive family should outweigh the interest of the Tribe—and perhaps the children themselves—in having them raised as part of the Choctaw community. Rather, we must defer to the experience, wisdom, and compassion of the Choctaw tribal courts to fashion an appropriate remedy. (p. 1611)

The legislation and this decision should leave no doubt that matters involving Native American children that come to the attention of the state child welfare system should be immediately referred to the appropriate tribal authority. State systems have authority to act to protect these children from immediate harm while awaiting response from the tribal authority.

Legal Matters for the Child Welfare System

There are many legal matters involving children, including child abuse, neglect, abandonment, or dependency; juvenile delinquency; status offenses; adoption; guardianship; paternity establishment; support and visitation; child custody, support, and visitation; and emancipation. It is not atypical for a social worker in child welfare or juvenile delinquency to have a single case with a multitude of legal complexities involving the various issues identified.

Abuse, Neglect, Abandonment, or Dependency

The state's reporting law describes procedures for professionals and other citizens to use in reporting suspected instances of child abuse and neglect to the local child welfare agency and/or the local police department. After the report is received and investigated, the agency or police department decides whether to file a petition with the juvenile court. The factors that go into this decision vary. (See Chapter 7.) Important to note is that the child protection agency can find evidence of abuse, neglect, abandonment, or dependency and not bring the matter to the attention of the court.

The juvenile codes of the states typically provide for jurisdiction when it is alleged that the child

- lacks proper guardianship because his or her parents are minors, the parents' whereabouts are unknown, the parents are dead, or the parents are unable to provide acceptable care because of some established mental or physical incapacity; or
- has been physically, mentally, or emotionally abused by a parent or guardian; or
- whose basic needs for food, shelter, clothing, medical care, and education have not been met by the parent or guardian. (See Chapter 7.)

Once the court takes jurisdiction (adjudicates) due to abuse, neglect, or dependency, it has a number of dispositional alternatives, including leaving the child in the home; referring the child to a child welfare agency for placement in foster care, including foster homes (relative and nonrelative), group homes, or residential treatment facilities; and, in extreme situations, immediate termination of parental rights.

Social workers have a particularly important role in juvenile court cases involving abuse and neglect because their agencies usually have the following key responsibilities:

- determining when and whether to file a petition alleging abuse or neglect
- recommending that the child remain at home or be placed out of the home
- in the case of a recommendation for out-of-home placement, showing that the agency made "reasonable efforts" to keep the family together
- recommending a specific out-of-home placement, including placement with relatives, after investigating all possibilities
- establishing a treatment plan with the parent and monitoring progress
- reporting to the court on the parent's progress and recommending reunification or termination of parental rights
- monitoring and supporting reunification, if that is the plan
- preparing evidence to support a judicial decision for termination of parental rights, if it seems unlikely that the child can ever go home and can be adopted
- testifying in court

It is not an exaggeration to say that the extent to which the juvenile court successfully protects children while supporting continuity of family relationships for children depends to a large extent on the competence of the social worker and his or her knowledge of the case and of court procedures (Downs & Taylor, 1980). Continuous, meticulous documentation of all contacts with family members is essential if the social worker wishes to influence the decisions that courts make concerning children.

The following quotation, while over twenty years old, has no less relevance today than when made.

> *A primary, essential, unavoidable rule is document, document, document. Admittedly, the tedium of the practice is at times overwhelming, and if the parent improves and the children return home, it may not have been necessary. However, proper recording of the worker's activities is directly related to success in court. Depending on legal practices in your state, your case record may be submitted as an evidentiary exhibit. Any issue with possible controversy is secured by case recording and supporting correspondence. (A child welfare supervisor—Downs & Taylor, 1980)*

Juvenile Delinquency

Delinquency jurisdiction arises when a juvenile, as defined by the state or federal statute, is alleged to have violated any federal or state law, or municipal ordinance. States vary somewhat by excluding certain minor offenses such as vagrancy or loitering, by treating traffic offenses differently depending on whether they are heard in traffic court or juvenile court, and in how they define and handle status offenses, that is, those acts that are illegal because of the youth's age or status. However, the primary criterion in defining delinquency is whether the act would be a crime if committed by an adult.

Although delinquency matters account for only 2 percent of the juvenile court dockets nationwide, they receive the headlines and are perceived to be of significantly higher volume (OJJDP, 1996, 2000).

Nearly all states have some provision to permit a juvenile or, where appropriate, a family court to waive jurisdiction in the case of major offenses. This means that the juvenile or family court has the right to transfer a case to the criminal court for adjudication, following procedures delineated in the statutes or court rules that are consistent with those required by *Kent v. United States* (1966). In some states, the case may start in adult court, and it is up to the juvenile to prove that he or she is amenable to treatment in the juvenile system; in still others, the prosecutors have absolute discretion to file cases in adult court, without any hearing at all in juvenile court. (See Box 6.2 for the types of offenses that may be processed in criminal courts.)

Once the court adjudicates, the dispositional alternatives are similar to those it has in abuse and neglect matters. The youth can remain in the home, be placed in foster care—including foster homes, group homes, and residential treatment facilities—or be placed in a secure facility. The dispositional choice is based on the type of offense committed as well as social factors. Chapter 11 provides a detailed discussion of the juvenile delinquency services system.

The social worker or probation officer is charged with monitoring the treatment and rehabilitation process and making periodic reports to the court.

Status Offenses

Many states provide separate jurisdictional sections for status offenders, wayward minors, or minors in need of supervision within their juvenile codes. For most, jurisdiction arises when it is alleged that the youth is beyond the control of his or her parents or other guardians and displays patterns of conduct deemed incorrigible, uncontrollable, or likely to develop into more serious and dangerous behavior. These situations are often referred to as "status offenses" because the conduct that brings the youth before the court is held to be illegal only because of the youth's age and would not be regarded as illegal if he or she were not a minor. Examples of status offenses include truancy, running away, curfew violations, sexual promiscuity, undesirable companions, and disobedience to parents. Youth who commit status offenses may be referred to as persons (or minors or children) in need of supervision, with the corresponding acronym PINS, MINS, or CHINS. Maintaining status offenses within the jurisdiction of the juvenile court remains highly controversial. Some authorities challenge the wisdom and justice of authorizing the juvenile court to assume jurisdiction over youth who behave in ways encompassed under such general terms as *incorrigibility* and *in need of supervision*. Given the scope, vagueness, and equivocal language of the statutes in many states, almost any child could be brought within the jurisdiction of the juvenile court (Simonsen, 1991).

Concern is expressed that a too-ready transfer of responsibility to bureaucratic discretion is seriously weakening the traditional responsibility of the family for control of children's misbehavior. Within an increasingly adversarial context, some believe the juvenile justice system is being forced to deal with delinquents and status offenders in the same way, that is, to treat status offenses like delinquent acts (Simonsen, 1991). (See Chapter 11.)

Once the court adjudicates it has a number of dispositional alternatives, including leaving the youth in the home or placement in foster care, including foster homes (relative and nonrelative), group homes, or residential treatment facilities. (See Chapter 11.)

Adoption

Adoption is the full transfer of parental rights and responsibilities to persons other than the biological parents, after termination of parental rights or voluntary relinquishment of parental rights. The legal process of adoption, relatively speaking, is simple. A petition is filed, along with the appropriate verifications—original birth certificates, child-specific information as required by statute, an adoptive family home study—and the court may or may not hold a hearing. The court orders the placement with or without supervision, depending on the state's statutory requirements. (See Chapter 10.)

Guardianship

Custody, guardianship, and *in loco parentis* are frequently confused. *Custody* generally relates to physical/legal placement with a parent; *guardianship* generally refers to physical/legal placement with someone other than the parent, because parents are by law the natural guardians of their children; and *in loco parentis* generally refers to a designated individual having authority to engage in certain parental acts on behalf of a child through statutory authority or a specific court order, for example, foster parents.

There are important differences between the rights and responsibilities of parents and those of a court-appointed guardian. Guardianship through court appointment is subject to the continuing supervision of the court. Guardianship, unlike parenthood, does not involve the duty to support and educate the child, who is generally called a "ward," except from the economic resources of the child, that is, his or her estate. It does not carry the right to the ward's earnings and services. The parent of a child has the right to control incidental assets of the child such as income from gifts and typical childhood employment. Control over other assets of the child such as insurance settlements, lawsuit awards, distributions from wills and trusts, or income from professional employment during minority generally requires a specific appointment of the parent or someone else as guardian of the estate. This triggers court oversight of the management of the estate. Children under court-appointed guardianship have statutory rights to inherit from their parents should the parents die without a will (intestate succession); they do not have any statutory rights to inherit from their guardians. If the guardians want the ward to inherit from them, they must specifically identify them and what they wish them to have in the guardians' wills. Parents have the right to choose where their child shall live as long as the care given does not fall below the minimal standards demanded by the community. In contrast, a guardian of the person may or may not have the authority to independently change the ward's residence. Parents cannot independently transfer their rights of legal guardianship. Whether the transfer of guardianship is voluntary or involuntary, the state court having jurisdiction over guardianship matters must be involved, and that court remains involved, so long as the guardianship is in effect.

There are two basic types of guardianship: guardian of the person and guardian of the estate. The **guardian of the person** becomes responsible for the care and control of the child. Depending on the state law, the guardian can decide the kind of medical care, including permission for major medical, psychiatric, and surgical treatment; or decisions about education, employment, permission for marriage, and permission for entry into the armed forces; and the right to represent the child in legal actions. In certain instances, the guardian of person may have been invested by court action with the power to consent to the adoption of the minor when the parent–child relationship has been fully terminated by judicial decree. Guardians of the person do not have the right to receive and manage property that their wards may acquire unless specifically authorized to do so through a separate appointment as the guardian of the estate.

Guardian of the estate creates a means by which a minor can deal in the business world. Guardians of the estate have power to govern the estate and act for their wards in matters involving property. The guardian of the estate can mortgage, sell, or otherwise transfer property and make the resources available for the ward's needs during his or her minority. Guardians of estate are persons of presumed integrity and are subject to the continuing supervision of the court. In general, they must submit periodic accountings of the ward's assets and their transactions to the court. Unless the guardian of estate is also named guardian of person, the guardian does not have the right to interfere in personal affairs of the minor but must confine his or her activities to the management of the estate.

While state laws vary, parents in most states can provide for **standby guardians** and **testamentary guardians.** These options are particularly useful in effecting permanency plans in child welfare cases in which the parent has a terminal illness, such as HIV/AIDS. A standby guardian is a person named by the parent to assume guardianship of the child should the parent become disabled and/or unable to care for the child. A testamentary guardian is a person named by the parent in his or her last will and testament to assume guardianship of the person of the child on the parent's death. Both are voluntary, independent acts of parents. Both require court approval before the guardians assume their responsibilities. Only a legal parent can name a testamentary guardian, and the testamentary guardian does not automatically assume guardianship responsibilities if another legal parent survives the one designating the testamentary guardian.

Guardianship often has been insufficiently understood as a resource for children who are abused, neglected, or abandoned. Guardianship is a practice and a policy issue in child welfare practice. The use of guardianship arrangements instead of foster care for the substitute care of children has been acknowledged as a viable resource for children in the child welfare system by national standard-setting agencies. The Children's Bureau position, stated in 1961, remains unchallenged in principle to this date:

> All children are entitled to an individual guardian "by birth or adoption or a judicially appointed guardian." This guardian is responsible for safeguarding the child's interests, making important decisions in her or his life, and maintaining a personal relationship with the child. (Children's Bureau, 1961, p. 3)

The practice of guardianship placement in lieu of foster care or adoptive placement can, depending on the specifics of the state's guardianship statutes, raise significant due process issues for the children, the legal parents, and the guardians. It is not uncommon to see legal guardians charged with neglect or abuse of their wards. Nor is it uncommon to have legal guardians rescind their guardianships when the child becomes "unruly." In voluntary guardianship arrangements, the parent usually retains authority to return and demand physical custody of the child at any time. In involuntary guardianships, the parent's rights may be terminated if she or he fails to complete the agreed-upon plan in the specified time. Often courts do not provide supportive services to parents whose children are under guardianship arrangements, whereas those services are provided to parents whose children are under abuse or neglect jurisdictional arrangements. All of these concerns raise the fundamental issue of protection and permanency for the child. To minimize these concerns and ensure the best use of legal guardianship in child welfare cases, social workers should assess each case situation with these principles as guides:

- Children are individuals with the right to develop their fullest capacities in a stable, supportive adult–child relationship.
- Parents have the first right and responsibility to give care, protection, stability, and support to their children.
- When parental efforts fall short of society's minimum standards, the state has the authority and responsibility to provide substitute care and protection utilizing the jurisdictional basis that will provide the best due process, equal protections, and permanency for child and parent.
- The judicial review and oversight responsibility for legal guardianship should be no less than that imposed for abuse or neglect or dependency, that is, children under legal guardianship arrangements should be entitled to frequent judicial review of their status as wards and the quality of care provided by substitute caregivers.
- The choice of legal guardianship should not be made because the process is easier for the child welfare worker, but because it is in the best interests of the child.

Irrespective of whether the transfer of guardianship is voluntarily or involuntarily sought, the state court having jurisdiction over guardianship matters must be involved. Further, that court remains involved so long as the guardianship is in effect. (See Chapters 8 and 9 for additional discussion of the role of permanent guardianship in child welfare cases.)

Paternity Establishment, Support, and Visitation

If a child is born to unmarried parents, the paternity of the child must be established in order for the father to legally assume the privileges, benefits, and responsibilities of parenthood. State statutes govern the process for paternity establishment. In general, there are two procedures:

- acknowledgment voluntarily signed by the mother and father
- adjudication of parentage through a court process should either the mother or father object to a voluntary acknowledgment

Once paternity has been established, by whichever method, the parents' individual and collective abilities to support the child and the visitation rights, if the parents live apart, may be voluntarily agreed to or determined by the court.

The social worker should proceed with paternity establishment early in the processing of a child welfare case, because it is critical to case planning. From a legal perspective, the legal father and his family become potential care providers if identified early in the case processing, and furthermore proceeding to permanency through termination of parental rights requires identification of the father and termination of his rights. (See Chapter 9.)

Child Custody, Support, and Visitation

Most controversy over custody, support, and visitation arises with a divorce action. Divorce statutes in all states make provision for awards of custody of children of the marriage. When there are issues of child abuse and neglect or delinquency in the family, child custody, support, and visitation presents additional considerations. Specifically, unless the case is in a "family court" jurisdiction, at least two judges and two different courts will likely handle it. These judges and courts may or may not coordinate decision making, which may or may not result in conflicting orders with respect to the children's custody, support, and parental visitation.

Some jurisdictions no longer use the adversarial term *custody* and favor instead "allocating parental responsibilities" or "parenting plans following divorce." Many different options are available with respect to custody, support, and visitation. While custody with the mother had been the norm until the early 1980s, joint custody became the preference of many courts during the 1990s. This generally results from a court order or a court-approved agreement between parents that provides for joint decision making concerning a child's education, medical treatment, religious training, and care. In some joint arrangements, physical custody is also shared. Rarely does a court, in deciding child custody in a divorce matter, order custody of a child to a third party when the parent(s) are alive. When a child's best interests require it, most states provide for custody to be granted to someone other than one of the parents. Generally in such situations relatives or friends are given preference over social agencies.

The most frequent social work roles in custody actions arising from divorce are mediation with parents to arrive at the best plan for the child or, failing that, carrying out a family evaluation and recommending a particular custody or shared parenting time plan to the judge. Social workers handling child welfare matters may, from time to time, be confronted with conflicting court orders. The divorce order may grant custody to the father, whereas the child abuse/neglect order grants custody to the mother. In general, each state handles these conflicts by court rule. The social worker should know the rules and advise the juvenile court that a prior custody order exists.

Emancipation

Emancipation is the legal process by which a person younger than the age of majority, which is usually 18 years of age, is given the status and privileges afforded someone who is over the age of majority. State statutes specify the conditions under which emancipation can occur. Typically they provide that persons who marry or join the military are emancipated by operation of law, that is, automatically on execution of the marriage or joining the military. Otherwise a petition is required that must state the reasons for the emancipation and the young person's means of support.

Court Procedures

Processing the Abuse/Neglect or Delinquency Case in Juvenile or Family Court

An orderly process involving four steps is generally followed when a child or juvenile comes to the attention of the court: intake, investigation, adjudication, and disposition.

Initiating the Case.   Courts do not act as casefinders. Generally, a court concerns itself with children only when a complaint or petition is filed by law enforcement (delinquency matters), the designated child protection agency (neglect, abuse, and dependency matters), the parent or person acting *in loco parentis* (status offenses, and minors in need of supervision), or in some states the child through an adult acting for him or her (adoption, guardianship, emancipation, and termination of parental rights).

Depending on the state statute and court procedures, the police or child protective services agency files either a complaint or a petition. In filing the complaint or petition, the complainant or petitioner must allege sufficient facts to show that the case comes within the jurisdiction of the court. For example,

> John Brown, born October 1, 1990, was treated at the Children's Hospital for a broken arm. The parent's statement as to how the arm was broken was inconsistent with medical evidence. The hospital filed a complaint with the child protection agency. In addition to the hospital's report, the investigating worker interviewed the parent's mother, who stated that she saw the parent "yank the child by the arm." The worker submits that this is evidence of abuse within the juvenile code. Further, the child and his mother reside in Little Town within the jurisdiction of this Court.

or, if a delinquency matter,

> Susan Sharp is a 14-year-old residing in Midville. On July 3, 1998, she took a sweater from the Big Department Store located in Midville without paying. This act was recorded on security cameras. This act constitutes a violation of the Criminal Code Section 101.

The court clerk or another designated official determines if the complaint or petition meets the requirements for filing. If it does, a date is set for a hearing. The timing of the hearing date is provided in statute or court rules. The child's parents or guardians must be notified of the petition, the time of the hearing, and their right to be represented by counsel.

Preliminary Inquiry or Hearing.   Before the court can adjudicate the matter, it must first ensure that it has jurisdiction—that is, make clear the basis for the court's authority to hear and decide the case. The court does so by ascertaining certain facts, such as the age of the child, where he or she lives, where the alleged acts took place, and who committed the acts. If these established facts fit the kinds of situations over which the court has been given authority by statute, then it may proceed with the case. The court also makes a preliminary assessment of the evidence supporting the allegations and, consistent with state law or court rules, determines whether the child should remain with the parent or be removed pending the adjudication or whether the case should be diverted, dismissed, or authorized for adjudication.

Adjudication.   The adjudication is the fact-finding or trial phase of the processing of the case. Here the court weighs the facts, properly presented under the rules of evidence by both sides, and decides whether the child, under the law, is delinquent, neglected, or dependent; or is in need of supervision; or requires an award of custody or guardianship. In reaching a decision in a neglect, abuse, or dependency allegation, the judge is expected to determine whether a preponderance of the evidence presented supported the allegations. If it did, then there is basis for taking wardship. If it did not, then the case should be dismissed. In reaching a decision in a delinquency allegation, the judge is expected to determine whether the evidence presented proved beyond a reasonable doubt that this juvenile committed the alleged offense.

Disposition.   All court orders entered after the adjudication are dispositional. The disposition is, in essence, the decision as to how the child shall be treated—that is, what is to be ordered or arranged for him or her following the adjudication or case reviews. Judges have a great deal of discretion in the dispositional phase, in contrast to the adjudicatory phase in which they are bound by statutes and court rules. After a finding or plea that an act occurred within the statutory definition of abuse, neglect, delinquency, or status offense (adjudication), the judge must decide what to do to alleviate or remedy the condition(s).

If, at the conclusion of the adjudicatory hearing, the judge decides that there is sufficient evidence for the court to take wardship of the child, he or she may order a family and child assessment or social investigation to assist in the establishment of an appropriate disposition and treatment plan. The Adoption and Safe Families Act of 1997 requires courts to assume greater oversight in monitoring the case plan and services to the child and family to ensure permanency as soon as possible. Thus the social investigation and case plan become more important to the legal process as well as the social work intervention. (See Chapters 2, 7, 8, 9, 10 for a more detailed discussion of the Adoption and Safe Families Act of 1997.)

The social investigation may be carried out by the probation staff or by a social agency as a service to the court. Typically probation staff handles delinquency matters and social agencies handle all other matters. In some states, where the social agency also supervises delinquency wards, those agencies are expected to present the social investigation on youth already under their supervision who commit new offenses. In any case, it is important that the court have all the facts necessary to act properly in the best interests of the child and, if a delinquency matter, the promotion of public safety as well. The investigation presents facts and evaluations that help the judge determine what treatment plan is appropriate and what orders, if any, the court needs to make to ensure that the treatment plan is carried out in a timely manner.

Prior to the mid-1990s, judges had almost total discretion in dispositional alternatives. With increasing attacks on family preservation, children in foster care limbo, and community placement for juvenile delinquents, many states through statutory changes have limited the discretion of the judge. If a juvenile commits a certain offense, the disposition is prescribed in statute. If the abuse is so severe or is continuing and chronic, the disposition is prescribed in statute. The most common dispositions remain as follows:

- *Warn and dismiss.* No further action is needed and therefore the case is closed, as in instances of a single, minor delinquent act or status offense when it is believed that the family is able to prevent further misconduct on the part of the child.

- *Probation.* The child is found to be delinquent or guilty of a status offense and is placed on probation and permitted to remain in the community under the official supervision of the court.
- *Temporary wardship with in-home supervision.* The child is found to be neglected or abused and is allowed to remain at home under the protective supervision of a social agency.
- *Temporary wardship with out-of-home placement.* The child, whether delinquent, guilty of a status offense, neglected, abandoned, or abused, may be placed out of the home for protection, care, and treatment. Placements may be in foster homes, group homes, relatives' homes, an independent living situation if the youth is of appropriate age and maturity, institutions, or privately operated/state training schools or secure facilities.
- *Permanent wardship.* Increasingly, state statutes are providing for immediate termination of parental rights in serious abuse cases or where prior children have been removed and parental rights terminated. Further, all statutes provide specific conditions under which parental rights to a child who has been a temporary ward may be terminated.
- *Termination of court wardship.* This disposition is used when the child has exceeded the age limit for jurisdiction; the conditions that lead to neglect or abuse wardship no longer exist, or the juvenile has been rehabilitated and no longer poses a threat to public safety.

In delinquency matters, the juvenile court appears to be abandoning its historical tradition of basing its dispositional decisions on the individual characteristics of the juvenile and his or her need for rehabilitation, and moving toward a system of making dispositional decisions based on punishment, accountability, and public safety or offense-based dispositions (Office of Juvenile Justice and Delinquency Prevention, 1998, p. 32). The goals appear to be retribution and deterrence (Howell, 1997).

This change in the juvenile court processing of juvenile offenders is its acknowledgment of the increasing presence of serious, chronic juvenile offenders, the increasing use of drugs and alcohol by juvenile offenders within the system, and the need to hold juveniles accountable for their actions earlier in their delinquency careers in order to deter more effectively the tendency to continue and escalate their delinquent behaviors. The National Council of Juvenile and Family Court Judges endorsed a number of recommendations relating to the problem of serious juvenile crime in 1984, the first of which was this: "*Serious juvenile offenders should be held accountable by the courts.* Dispositions of such offenders should be proportionate to the injury done and the culpability of the juvenile and to the prior record of adjudication, if any" (National Council of Juvenile and Family Court Judges, 1984, p. x). The Council added that "the principal purpose of the juvenile justice court system is to protect the public," and qualified this position only by the statement, "Although rehabilitation is a primary goal of the court, it is not the sole objective and not always appropriate" (Heck, Pindur, & Wells, 1985, p. 29).

Review Hearings. Dispositional decisions are reviewed by the court at specific intervals established by statute or court rule or at any time on motion by the supervising agency, the prosecutor, the youth, or other person acting on his or her behalf. At review hearings, the situation is reassessed and a determination is made on whether to order a new disposition. For example, the judge might decide to send a child home from foster care if the conditions that lead to the child's removal had been alleviated to a degree that the child could be safe at home. In a delinquency matter, the judge could decide to move the youth from a secure to a nonsecure facility based on reports of the youth's progress in rehabilitation and the risk to public safety.

The review hearing is a monitoring mechanism to ensure that there is progress toward a permanent solution for the child. The review hearing can be used as a device to resolve controversies between the agency and parent when the agency has custody, such as a dispute over visitation or case planning. It can be used to clarify expectations of all parties and set a time certain for final disposition.

Termination of Parental Rights.   Termination of parental rights is the second most extreme action the legal system can take in abuse and neglect cases. The first, of course, is the initial intrusion into the family's autonomy with the removal of the child from the parent. In general, termination of parental rights is based on the following:

- Children need permanency and stability in their lives.
- The child before the court has been in out-of-home care for a statutorily specified time period.
- The conditions that lead to the removal have not been corrected.
- There is no reason to believe that they will be corrected in the foreseeable future.

Specific grounds for termination of parental rights are described in the statutes of each state. Pike, Downs, Emlen, Downs, and Case (1977) identified four overarching reasons for termination of parental rights that are present in some form in every state statute to this date: abandonment, desertion, parental condition, and parental conduct.

- *Abandonment and Desertion.* State statutes enumerate the failure of parents to identify the child, visit, establish paternity, contribute to the child's support, or maintain contact with the child's custodian for a prescribed period of time as grounds for termination of parental rights.
- *Parental Condition.* State statutes enumerate conditions such as mental illness, emotional illness, mental deficiency, narcotic or dangerous drug addiction, and alcohol addiction which have lasted or are expected to last for a certain period of time as grounds for termination of parental rights.
- *Parental Conduct.* State statutes enumerate conduct such as the chronic and continuing physical neglect of the child, serious physical abuse of the child or a sibling of the child, sexual abuse of the child or a sibling of the child and failure of parent to correct the conditions or conduct which lead to the child's removal as grounds for termination of parental rights. (Pike et al., 1977, pp. 5.1–5.8)

The social work issues related to a decision to seek termination of parental rights are discussed in greater detail in Chapter 9. The legal requirements are established in each state's statutes. A hearing to terminate parental rights is usually a formal proceeding like the adjudicatory hearing, even though it is a dispositional action. When contested, it can be lengthy and involve many elaborate, technical, legal procedures.

The burden of proof is clear and convincing evidence, a higher standard than preponderance of evidence but somewhat less stringent than the beyond a reasonable doubt standard. Another indicator of the seriousness of this state action is the attention to ensuring that any adult with possible parental rights to the child is notified and has the opportunity to present evidence in court. This is particularly salient in the case of unmarried fathers, whose rights were at one time disregarded. (See Chapter 2 for a discussion of U.S. Supreme Court decisions on the standard of proof and on the rights of unmarried fathers.)

How a Juvenile Offender Comes before the Criminal Court

The states vary as to the procedure used to effect these transfers—judicial waiver, prosecutor discretion, or legislative exclusion. In the judicial waiver situation, the case originates in the juvenile court, and prior to holding an adjudicatory hearing, the juvenile court, consistent with state statutory guidelines, determines that the nature of the offense, the age of the juvenile, and the juvenile's past history are such that the juvenile is unlikely to benefit from juvenile court intervention. Then the case is waived to criminal court.

In the prosecutorial discretion situation, the prosecutor—the official who brings the charge on behalf of the people of the state—has full authority to decide, consistent with the state statutory requirements, whether he or she will prosecute the juvenile in the juvenile court or in the criminal court.

If he or she originates the action in juvenile court, the juvenile judge has authority to waive the case. However, if he or she chooses to originate the action in criminal court, the criminal court does not have authority to return the case to the juvenile court in most states. In the legislative exclusion situation, certain crimes committed by juveniles of certain ages are automatically within the exclusive jurisdiction of the criminal courts, meaning only the criminal court can hear the case.

While the names of the different phases differ, the substantive processes are similar and the rights granted the juvenile are the same.

Processing a Juvenile Offender in Criminal Court

Again, the courts do not seek out cases. Cases are brought to them. In criminal offenses, the police usually receive a complaint from a victim or are called to the scene of a crime by an individual in the community. They investigate and apprehend or arrest the suspected offender. After investigation, they can choose not to file charges to divert the juvenile for other services. If they choose to go forward, the police submit their information to the prosecutor, who determines the specific crime to charge, based on the evidence submitted by the police, and files a complaint with the court.

Once it is determined that a juvenile offense is to be prosecuted in the criminal courts, the prosecutor must file a complaint. The matter is then scheduled for preliminary examination or probable cause hearing. When probable cause is found, it is scheduled for arraignment or bail hearing if these matters are not scheduled as part of the preliminary examination or probable cause hearing, and a date is set for trial. If the juvenile is found guilty at trial or pleads guilty, a sentencing hearing is scheduled.

The Complaint.   This complaint is similar to the complaint or petition filed in juvenile court in that it contains specifics about the offense, the law it violates, and the name, age, and address of the person alleged to have committed the offense. The prosecutor is given discretion to charge a crime less than the one supported by the evidence.

The Preliminary Examination or Probable Cause Hearing.   This procedure is a review of the evidence against the juvenile by the judge and results in a determination as to whether the evidence is sufficient to believe that this juvenile committed the charged offense, should be charged with a lesser offense, or should be diverted.

The Arraignment or Bail Hearing.   If the person has been arrested, he or she must be arraigned on the charges, that is, given an opportunity to appear in court and hear the charges and the evidence, enter a plea (guilty or not guilty), and have bail set (an amount of money to be posted with the court to guarantee appearance at the trial). Many states do not permit bail to be set if a serious crime such as murder or rape is charged. There is no proscription as to the maximum amount of bail that can be set. Thus many courts set high bails for juvenile offenders as a way of keeping them in custody until the trial. If the juvenile cannot post bail, he or she is held in jail. There is some debate as to whether a juvenile charged as an adult must be confined separately from adults.

The Trial.   The trial in criminal court is similar in form and process to the adjudication in juvenile court. The juvenile has a right to have the facts determined by a judge or jury. During the trial the evidence is presented in accordance with the state's rules of evidence. If the evidence does not prove beyond a reasonable doubt that the juvenile committed the crimes charged, he or she must be found not guilty and released. If the evidence proves beyond a reasonable doubt that the juvenile committed the crimes charged, he or she must be found guilty and the matter set for sentencing.

The Sentencing.   The sentencing is the phase in which the punishment is rendered. In some states sentencing guidelines require the judge to issue certain sentences for certain offenses. In other states, it is totally within the judge's discretion to determine the sentence. Most sentencing decisions are based on the crime, the juvenile's participation in the crime, the juvenile's past history, and any unique factors made known to the court in the sentencing report or by the juvenile.

Traditional sentences include

- probation
- suspended sentence
- fine
- community service
- restitution
- jail and probation
- periodic imprisonment (to permit the juvenile to continue employment while serving sentence)
- confinement in jail or prison
- death (Jacobs, 1995, 1997; Saltzman & Proch, 2000; Kramer, 2002)

The Role of the Social Worker in the Court Process

Social workers functioning as child welfare workers or juvenile probation workers provide social investigations, dispositional recommendations, and casework services for both the parents and the child until the court dismisses the case. In carrying out these responsibilities, the social worker must gather and document information to

- support the allegations in the petition
- advise the court on the actions taken to comply with previous court orders
- support the social worker's recommendations for dispositional actions
- present this information orally and/or in writing to the court when the case requires court intervention

Although many child abuse and neglect interventions occur without court involvement—that is, the parent acknowledges that the event occurred and agrees to voluntary interventions to ensure the child's safety—the practices suggested in this section ensure that the rights of all parties are protected and the facts are determined so as to promote appropriate interventions.

This section provides a brief summary of the critical elements in forensic interviewing, case documentation, court report writing, and oral testimony. The reader is directed to the references in the For Additional Study section of this chapter for materials providing comprehensive coverage of these areas.

Critical Elements in Forensic Interviewing

It is suggested that all investigations follow a forensic interviewing and documentation approach because this approach provides for an unbiased, multiperspective reporting of the incident from which the social worker can make an informed conclusion as to the truthfulness of the allegations and the most appropriate intervention.

Information is gathered through interviews with the child or juvenile, persons involved with the child and/or family, and a review of written documents pertaining to the child and/or family. Child welfare and juvenile justice investigations need to be conducted in ways that preserve the evidence and limit the attack on the social worker's methodologies in collecting that evidence. The interview process for court purposes is different from the interview for treatment purposes. In essence, the goal of interviews for court purposes, that is, forensic interviews, is to obtain descriptions of the events that occurred from people who experienced them from their experiential perspective as victim, perpetrator, observer, or professional interventionist. In these interviews, the social worker is attempting to determine what happened, when it happened, how it happened, and who was involved in the act (victim, perpetrator, and protectors/interveners). Having gathered this information from a variety of perspectives, the social worker then identifies the variances in the accounts and seeks to resolve these variances through additional interviews and review of written materials.

The fundamental elements of forensic interviewing follow.

- Create a nonthreatening environment by stating clearly your reason for wanting to talk with them, how the information they provide will be used, and ensuring that their comfort needs are met.

- Interview children outside the presence of parents or caretakers to the extent that it can be done without further trauma to the child.
- Determine the developmental and language/linguistic levels of all persons interviewed.
- Use simple, open-ended questions that encourage the person being interviewed to describe in his or her own words the who, what, when, how, and where of the incident under review.
- Ask clarifying questions for the purpose of ensuring that the interviewer understands what the interviewee has said or described, not to offer one's own assessment, judgment, or conclusion of what was said.

Interviews for investigative purposes occur throughout the case's history whenever the social worker wants to verify the accuracy or truth of the situation. For example, the agency receives a report from the emergency room of the local children's hospital. It alleges that a 3-year-old child required medical treatment for a burn. The mother told the hospital social worker that the child pulled a pan of hot water off the stove. The medical evidence does not support the mother's statements. The social worker's forensic interviews would focus on the following:

- Asking the mother to describe and demonstrate what happened in the place where the incident took place. She would then follow up on the mother's description and demonstration with clarifying questions of a nonjudgmental and nonconclusory nature to make sure she understands the mother's description of the incident.
- Asking the child to tell her and show her how he or she got burned after providing a protective environment for the child outside of the sight and sound of the mother. Again, follow-up questions consistent with the child's developmental and language skills would be asked to ensure that the social worker understands the child's description and demonstration of the incident.
- Asking medical personnel who took the mother's description of the incident and provided treatment to the child to describe the mother's presentation of the incident as well as her demeanor during the relaying of the incident. Further, the medical experts will be asked to provide statements as to why, in their opinions, the medical evidence is inconsistent with the mother's statement and the degree of certainty of their conclusion. Finally, the social worker will ask the medical experts for their opinions as to how the incident could have occurred based on the medical evidence.

After all interviews and written reports are gathered and reviewed, the social worker determines that court intervention is required, files the necessary petitions, and participates in the hearing process, which results in adjudication with dispositional orders requiring the mother to secure and submit weekly drug screening results to the agency, participate in an appropriate substance abuse treatment program, and participate in a parenting education program focused on the developmental appropriate disciplinary techniques. In providing ongoing services to the family after the court has adjudicated the case and entered specific dispositional orders, the social worker conducts similar fact-finding interviews and receives written documentation to determine the mother's compliance with the orders. If the orders have not been complied with, the social worker seeks to determine the specific reasons for noncompliance again through the fact-finding processes of forensic interviews with all involved parties. These facts are then used to assist the mother in achieving substantial compliance prior to the next court review and are reported to the court for its consideration in modifying the current orders.

Case Record Documentation

Case records, properly documented, are critical in the child welfare system's increasingly rapid march toward permanency for children. One of the unfortunate realities of the system is that staff turnover remains a major barrier to effective services for children and families. When workers leave and relevant information is not documented in the case file, the new worker loses much needed case intervention time in obtaining information that was known to the previous worker.

Each agency has its own case record documentation requirements. Much of the case record documentation is incidental to the reason the child and family are under the jurisdiction of the court, for example, eligibility determinations, computer system input forms, and supervisory case review forms. Other information, while helpful to ensuring the child's well-being and development, might be incidental to the court process unless it is connected to a reason the court took jurisdiction, for example, education reports and medical reports. Many times, the case plan and the court orders appear to have no connection with each other. A case record for a child that is under court jurisdiction and subject to the Adoption and Safe Families Act (ASFA) requirements for expedited permanency for children in out-of-home care should have a specific section in the original case plan stating the reasons the court took jurisdiction, the orders it entered, and the agreements between the parent, child, and agency stating the specific actions each will take and the projected time by which the actions will be taken to fulfill the orders of the court. Updated case plans would be completed based on contemporaneous documentation specific to dates and actions related to the previous case plan related to the progress of the parent, child, and agency in complying with previous court orders crafted to alleviate the conditions that brought the child and family to the attention of the court as well as modifications to orders based on subsequent findings of the court. Thus a very simplified case documentation structure for the legal aspects of the case plan, consistent with ASFA requirements, would include

- date of contact
- type of contact
- statement of the purpose of contact
- identity of persons participating
- location of contact
- description of what happened
- summary of actions to be taken and by whom as a result of the contact
- worker's signature and date of entry

Example: Case Documentation

On January 31, 2002, the court took jurisdiction of Rosie Jones and ordered, in part, that the mother get substance abuse treatment services from the Women's Substance Abuse Treatment Program, obtain weekly drug screens and submit the results to Child and Family Services, visit the child at the grandmother's home at least once a week, and attend weekly parenting education classes for parents with young children at the Parenting for Children Center.

The worker's documentation of a contact with the child's mother is shown in Box 6.3. As you can see, this contact documentation is factual and not filled with the worker's conclusions. This type of contact documentation, combined with others as well as the receipt and review of various reports from the involved agencies, provides the blueprint for the updated service plans and court reports. It minimizes lost information in the event of worker

---

B O X **6.3**

Rosie Jones Case Documentation

On March 4, 2002, I met with Mrs. Jones at the Child and Family Services offices to discuss the status of her participation in the substance abuse treatment program, weekly drug screens, weekly visitation with her child at the grandmother's home, and enrollment in the parenting education program as ordered by the court.

Mrs. Jones stated that she has been going in for weekly drug screens at the Drug Screening Center since the week after the court hearing. She signed a paper so they could send the results directly to me. She stated that she had not gone to the substance abuse treatment program. She did not give any reason for not going. She said she would go next week.

She said that she has been going to visit her child "just about every day." They read and play together while she is there. She said she frequently picks Rosie up from Head Start and walks her to her (Mrs. Jones's) mother's house.

I told Mrs. Jones that the agency has her on a waiting list for parenting classes. She would not be able to start the parenting classes until July 8. We reviewed the list of available locations and times for those classes. She picked Monday morning from 9 A.M. to 11:30 A.M. at the Jefferson Library on Jefferson and Dickerson. She told me that the library is down the street from the house where she is currently staying. She stated that she is living with her cousin, and the cousin says she can stay there until she finishes her treatment and her (Mrs. Jones's) mother lets her move back to her house. The address is 1201 Dickerson, MyTown 00014. Her phone number is (123) 456-7890.

Follow-Ups:
1. Mrs. Jones will go to the Women's Substance Abuse Treatment Program, enroll in the program, and fulfill the participation requirements. She will call me if she has any problems with this.
2. She will continue to get the drug screens weekly.
3. She will continue to visit Rosie as often as possible.
4. I will notify the Parenting for Children Center of the time and location she chose for the parenting education classes.
5. I will notify the court of her new address.

Signature: Charles W .Worker 03/04/02

turnover while helping to effect permanency for children by keeping the focus on what must be done to achieve that permanency through the court system. It ensures that case records do not subject the agency and its social workers to attacks from lawyers alleging that the social worker is biased or prejudiced against the mother, fails to assist the mother in obtaining needed services, is inexperienced or incompetent, and that the agency, through a stream of workers, provides inconsistent instructions or directions regarding the court's expectations.

Example: Court Report

Courts vary as to expectations about what is included in written court reports and when they are to be submitted to the court and parties. In addition, requirements will vary depending on the role the social worker has in the court process. A social worker providing child welfare services would be expected to focus his or her report on the status of the child and the parents with respect to the specific orders of the court. This report should provide the facts and be well documented by reports or testimony from those providing the direct service to the child and parent, as shown in Box 6.4.

A social worker providing mental health treatment would be expected to report on the nature of the mental illness or condition being treated, its impact on the parent's ability to perform parenting responsibilities in a manner sufficient to ensure child safety, the parent's degree of participation in treatment, the prognosis, and the expected length of time required for treatment before the parent is able to resume parenting responsibilities. Due to space limitations, an example of a mental health treatment report is not included here. The For Additional Study section has some excellent references for these professionals.

Testifying

In the court process itself, social workers are frequently called on to give testimony in addition to written progress reports, either as a fact witness or as an expert witness. A fact witness is one who gives information as to what he or she saw, heard, said, or did in relation to a specific issue before the court. An expert witness is one who is asked to give opinions or provide specialized knowledge on facts presented by others or themselves because they have specialized education, training, and experience. A social worker, depending on the circumstances, can function in both capacities (Dickson, 1995).

Although the thought of testifying may be terrifying to the beginning child welfare worker and a source of ongoing anxiety for the experienced child welfare worker, testifying becomes easier with advance preparation and documentation of evidence. Preparation requires knowing the law involved, knowing the facts of the case, and understanding how those facts and the law relate to one another. Documentation requires distinguishing fact from opinion. Fact, as supported by documents or witnesses, is evidence. Opinions that are based on the application of theoretical knowledge to the facts of the case are important, but opinions that are not based in fact or knowledge provide attorneys with the opportunity to totally discredit the social worker's testimony. If the social worker approaches testifying prepared with factual documentation and applicable theoretical knowledge coupled with a clear head, then the techniques used by attorneys in the examination and cross-examination processes should be immaterial.

B O X   **6.4**

Rosie Jones Court Report

ANY JURISDICTION FAMILY COURT
CHILD ABUSE AND NEGLECT DOCKET

Hearing Date: May 05, 2002

Case Name: Rosie Jones

Court File No: 2002-1050

Parent's Name: Anna Jones, mother
                       Father unknown

Progress Report for Review Hearing

On January 31, 2002, the court ordered Rosie Jones placed with the maternal grandmother, enrolled in Head Start, and provided a complete physical examination and required medical treatment. The mother was ordered to receive services from the Women's Substance Abuse Treatment Program, submit the results of weekly drug screens to Child and Family Services, visit the child at the grandmother's home at least once a week, and attend weekly parenting education classes for Parents with Young Children at the Parenting for Children Center.

Rosie was placed with the maternal grandmother, Sarah Jones, on February 1, 2002, and remains with her. This worker has visited Rosie in the home four times since the placement. She has her own room, several age-appropriate toys and books, and new clothing. She is an active child who loves to talk as long as her grandmother is in the room. Her grandmother calms her by hugging her and lifting her up to sit on her lap. Rosie does not attempt to break away from these hugs.

She was enrolled in Head Start on February 14, 2002, and remains enrolled. She shows intellectual and social development at or above age level. A copy of the Head Start report dated April 30, 2002, is attached.

She received a complete physical examination from Dr. Sarah Cooper on February 8, 2002. She received the necessary immunizations for Head Start enrollment on this date. On February 20, 2002, the grandmother received a call telling her that, based on the results of the blood work, additional screening for sickle cell trait or anemia was necessary. The grandmother scheduled a follow-up appointment with the recommended specialist for June 1, 2002. This was the earliest possible date for the appointment. A copy of Dr. Cooper's medical report is attached.

Mrs. Jones sought services from the Women's Substance Abuse Treatment Program (WSATP) on February 17, 2002. She was told to return on February 18, 2002, because she arrived too late in the day to be processed. She did not return to the agency until March 18, 2002. Mrs. Jones told this worker that she couldn't get a ride before then. She had not contacted the worker for assistance with a ride. She was enrolled in the program on March 18, 2002. The program required daily attendance for four hours in either the morning or the afternoon. Bus tickets were provided for each day of attendance. Between March 18 and April 30, Mrs. Jones attended 6 days according to WSATP. Given the infrequency of her attendance, WSATP has insufficient information to provide an assessment or recommendation regarding her ability to care for her child. A copy of the WSATP report dated May 1, 2002, is included with this report. Mrs. Jones had reported to the worker that she had attended most of the sessions. When asked to explain the difference in her statement of attendance and that of the agency, she said she didn't like the people in the group and just stopped going after the first week. When asked if she discussed this with WSATP staff, she said, "No." When asked if she understood that the court order required her to attend this program, she said, "Yes." When asked what she intended to do to comply with the court order, she said she did not know.

(continued)

BOX **6.4   Continued**

Mrs. Jones obtained weekly drug screens from the Drug Screening Center starting February 5, 2002. The center submitted written statements of the results directly to the agency each week. Mrs. Jones tested positive for cocaine in 35 percent of the screens. Copies of the weekly reports from Drug Screening Center are attached.

This worker sent the referral to the Parenting for Children Center on February 5, 2002, as required by its contract with Child and Family Services. Mrs. Jones is on a waiting list for parenting education services. The Parenting for Children Center will start a new class series in July.

Mrs. Jones visits Rosie just about every day according to Sarah Jones, the child's grandmother. She came to visit "high" on three occasions and Sarah Jones asked her to leave. The mother became loud and threatening, to which Sarah Jones said she just "stood my ground" and eventually Anna left. Generally, during the visits, Rosie and her mother read books, play with her toys, and prepare and eat a sandwich or dinner. The child is excited to see her mother. The grandmother says she is concerned that Anna will not acknowledge that she cannot handle her drug problem without help. The grandmother says she will help her in any way she can; but will not let her move back into the home until she stays in a treatment program.

Recommendation

Based on the progress to date, this worker recommends that Rosie be continued in placement with her maternal grandmother and continue to receive Head Start services. We recommend that the court continue the order for Mrs. Jones to participate in substance abuse treatment at WSATP. That agency has the best reputation for working with women who have children in foster care.

It appears that Mrs. Jones was attempting to blame her drug abuse on everyone else and not assume responsibility for her actions. When confronted by group members and staff, she just did not return to the group. Mrs. Jones needs to understand that the court expects her to take responsibility for her drug use and abuse and that her parental rights could be terminated in the next nine months if she fails to obtain the required substance abuse treatment services.

She has complied with the order for weekly drug screens and has, within the relapse expectations, maintained "clean" drug screens. She has complied with the visitation order and shows a genuine interest in her child's development. She has been unable to participate in the parent education program through no fault of her own. She is expected to enroll in the program in July and complete it in September.

The basic principles for giving testimony are as follows:

- Keep your temper. If you lose your temper, you discredit yourself and your testimony.
- Answer a question in the shortest possible way. The more you talk, the more likely you will provide the attorney an opportunity to find a small discrepancy in your testimony and use it to discredit you. Do not withhold information; but once you have responded to the question, be quiet.
- Always be willing to admit ignorance, or that your memory has failed you or that you are not sure. If you don't know the answer, say, "I don't know." To respond when you do not know opens you up to giving conflicting testimony.
- Never show partiality, or vindictiveness, to either party to the litigation. You have no personal interest in this matter. You represent the state. You are charged with provid-

ing facts and opinions based on those facts. If you waiver from the charge, you are subject to rigorous examination designed to show that you are not presenting facts but biased statements.

- Never show reluctance to concede a point in the opposition's favor. If the other side is right, it is better for you to recognize it and move on. To do otherwise exposes you to challenge as biased.
- Use short, simple language so that your point is immediately comprehensible. Avoid social work jargon. If you must use a specific social work term, explain what it means in plain English.
- Ask for a question to be repeated or rephrased if you do not understand it.
- Prepare ahead of time; but do not memorize your testimony. If you memorize testimony you may forget some parts of it under the pressure of testifying or could lose all memory of the facts. Your preparation should include knowing the pertinent facts and the applicable law so that you can correlate the two while testifying.
- Expect to feel nervous. You never know how you will be examined or cross-examined. Thus you will always feel tense until the process is completed.
- State the facts as you know them based on an unbiased, well-documented inquiry. Do not start with conclusions. The more you rely on facts that you have documented, the less likely you will be to get confused by an attorney's questions. Further, if the attorney engages you in a hypothetical ("what if . . .") discussion, you are able to differentiate the facts in the hypothetical from the facts in your actual case.
- If you are asked for an opinion or recommendation, first give the facts on which you base your opinion, then state your opinion or recommendation.
- Remain cool, calm, and collected. If you have prepared your case well and available evidence is not brought out by the attorneys or jurists, it is their fault not yours (Saltzman & Proch, 1990; Stein, 1991; Dickson, 1995; Stern, 1997).

Trends and Issues

Three specific trends identified in the previous edition remain important to watch over the next five years: establishment of family courts; increase in delinquency adjudications of children and youth who are already adjudicated abused or neglected; and the transfer of jurisdiction over juveniles who commit serious offenses to the adult court system. These trends have begun already but are in the infancy stage and should be carefully watched as they mature in the future. Family courts, that is, courts with broad jurisdiction to hear and decide all matters involving children, will continue to grow. It is hypothesized that this court structure will provide more efficient decisions. While preliminary data suggests that there are some benefits, it is not conclusive that this structure will be beneficial to children. The first comprehensive evaluation of the family court in Ohio had not been published at the time this book went to press, but is scheduled to be published in 2003.

For years studies have documented the negative impact of childhood maltreatment on youth development and correlated it with increased delinquent acts in adolescence. This trend requires a reexamination of the prevention and treatment interventions provided in the abuse and neglect system. Further, courts that previously have been reticent to hold abused and neglected children accountable for their delinquent behaviors until the behavior becomes more serious are beginning to reexamine that practice. Everyone agrees that it is necessary to look at the status of children and youth more holistically (Kelley, Thornberry, & Smith, 1997).

During the 1990s, the adult courts assumed greater responsibility for handling matters involving juveniles who committed serious offenses. It is anticipated that this trend will continue (Office of Juvenile Justice and Delinquency Prevention, 1998). (See Chapter 11.)

In addition as parental rights are terminated earlier and children remain "adrift in foster care" as legal orphans, expect to see increased specificity in court orders with respect to services for the child to ensure readiness for independence.

Chapter Summary

This chapter focused on the historical development of the juvenile court system, its transition from a benevolent system with full discretion given to the jurists to a system subject to rules providing for the protection of the parties in abuse, neglect, and delinquency matters. The movement toward family courts is growing throughout the United States. These courts have broader jurisdictions over the multiplicity of matters that arise when children are abused, neglected, or commit delinquent acts. It is hypothesized that family courts will provide administrative efficiency and ensure a consistent treatment of the various independent legal issues. Additionally, the adult criminal courts have been given more jurisdictional authority over juveniles.

The standard processing of a case through the juvenile court system has been reviewed, for both child abuse and neglect and delinquency cases. In addition, the processing of juveniles in adult criminal courts has been discussed. The role of the child welfare worker in the court system has changed as the juvenile court has become more "procedural." The social worker remains responsible for marshalling factual information to assist the court in determining the best plan for the child/juvenile and his or her parents; however, that information is now subject to more stringent examination by attorneys for the child and the parent. Child welfare and delinquency workers must understand the roles and responsibilities of their position and those of all the persons involved. This chapter provided a brief summary of these roles and responsibilities.

FOR STUDY AND DISCUSSION

1. Explain and evaluate the aims and guiding philosophy of the early founders of the juvenile court. Discuss ways in which the implementation of the juvenile court deviates from those aims and guiding philosophy.

2. Give arguments to support either the traditional rehabilitative model of the juvenile court or a model based on constitutional guarantees of due process and legal justice.

3. Obtain a copy of the juvenile court act in your state. Review it in these terms:

   a. What is the expressed intent of the act? How well does this intent reflect a modern juvenile court philosophy?

   b. Compare the act's definitions of classes of children who come under the jurisdiction with those discussed in this chapter.

   c. What does the statute provide with respect to the child's and parent's constitutional rights? Are there different provisions based on the type of case, that is, neglect or delinquency?

4. Read your state's statute and interview agency and court personnel to find out what the provisions are

in your state for termination of parental rights. How well does the statute protect the parent's rights and also provide for the child's need for permanency?

5. What is your assessment of the potential for family courts to provide for better administration of justice as compared with the juvenile court?

6. Distinguish the court process in your state from the standard process discussed in this chapter.

7. Why is paternity establishment so important in child welfare practice? How would you proceed to determine whether paternity had been established in one of your cases?

8. Identify a specific case that you will be testifying on in the next month. State the type of hearing for which testimony will be given. What information does the court need to accomplish the purposes of the hearing as stated in the statute? What information do you have? What are your sources for the information? What information are you lacking? How can you obtain the information you currently lack?

9. Should juveniles be prosecuted as adults for serious offenses? What factors should be considered in determining whether to treat them as adults or juveniles?

10. Review your state's statute for criminal prosecution of juveniles, and its impact.
   a. Compare the offenses for which a juvenile could be tried as an adult in your state with those listed in this chapter.
   b. Obtain data from your local juvenile and criminal courts for two years before and two years after the legislative change, on the number of juveniles adjudicated or convicted of each offense.
   c. Review media files' coverage of juvenile offenders during the same time period.
   d. How is the public safety better protected after the legislative change?

11. If you were designing the ideal court system for handling matters involving children and youth, what would it look like?

FOR ADDITIONAL STUDY

Ayers, W. (1997). *A kind and just parent: The children of juvenile court.* Boston: Beacon Press.

Besharov, D. J. (1990). *Combating child abuse: Guidelines for cooperation between law enforcement and child protective services.* Washington, DC: The AEI Press.

Bourg, W., Broderick, R., Flagor, R., Kelly, D. M., Ervin, D. L., & Butler, J. (1999). *A child interviewer's guidebook.* Thousand Oaks, CA: Sage.

Center for the Future of Children. (1996, Winter). *The Future of Children: The Juvenile Court, 6*(3).

Christian, S., & Ekman, L. (2000). *A place to call home: Adoption and guardianship for children in foster care.* Washington, DC: The National Conference of State Legislatures.

Davis, S. M. (1998). *Rights of juveniles: The juvenile justice system* (2nd ed.). St. Paul, MN: West.

Dubowitz, H., & DePanfilis, D. (2000). *Handbook for child protection practice.* Thousand Oaks, CA: Sage.

Epstein, L. (1992). *Brief treatment and a new look at the task-centered approach* (3rd ed.). New York: Macmillan.

Flango, C. R., Flango, V. E., & Rubin, H. T. (1999). *How are courts coordinating family cases?* Alexandria, VA: National Center for State Courts.

Haralambie, A. M. (1993). *The child's attorney: A guide to representing children in custody, adoption, and protection cases.* Chicago: American Bar Association.

Jacobs, T. A. (1995, supp. last updated 2002, June). *Children and the law: Rights and obligations.* St. Paul, MN: West.

Kramer, D. T. (1994). *Legal rights of children* (2nd ed.). Colorado Springs: Shepard's/McGraw-Hill.

Mather, J. H., & Lager, P. B. (2000). *Child welfare: A unifying model of practice.* Belmont, CA: Wadsworth, Brooks/Cole Social Work.

The National Abandoned Infants Assistance Resource Center. (2000, Fall). Legal permanency planning for HIV-affected families: The need to plan, current legal options, and future directions. In *The Source, Vol. 10,* no. 2. Berkeley, CA: National AIA Resource Center.

Pollack, D. (1997). *Social work and the courts: A casebook.* New York: Garland Publishing.

Poole, D. A., & Lamb, M. E. (1998). *Investigative interviews of children: A guide for helping professionals.* Washington, DC: American Psychological Association.

Shepherd, R. E., Jr. (1999). The "child" grows up: The juvenile justice system enters its second century. *Family Law Quarterly, 33*(3), 589–605.

Walker, A. G. (1999). *Handbook on questioning children: A linguistic perspective.* Washington, DC: American Bar Association.

INTERNET SITES

The following sites provide copies of statutes, case decisions, analyses, and commentary on legal issues affecting children in the juvenile and family court systems.

American Bar Association Center on Children and the Law.
www.abanet.org/child/home.html

Center for Law and Social Policy.
www.movingideas.org

Juvenile Justice Clearinghouse.
www.fsu.edu/~crimdo/jjclearinghouse

National Archives and Records Administration, Code of Federal Regulations.
www.access.gpo.gov/nara/cfr/cfr-table-search.html

National Clearinghouse on Child Abuse and Neglect Information.
www.calib.com/nccanch

National Council of Juvenile and Family Court Judges.
www.ncjfcj.unr.edu

THOMAS, Library of Congress.
http://thomas.loc.gov

United States of America, All federal governmental agencies.
www.firstgov.gov

INTERNET SEARCH TERMS

Family court
Forensic interviewing
Juvenile court
Supreme Court

REFERENCES

Addams, J. (1935). *My friend, Julia Lathrop.* New York: Macmillian.

Babb, B. A. (1998, Summer). Where we stand: An analysis of America's family law adjudicatory systems and the mandate to establish unified family courts. *Family Law Quarterly, 32,* 31–57.

Beemsterboer, M. J. (1960). Benevolence in the star chamber. *Journal of Criminal Law, Criminology, and Political Science, 50,* 464–475.

Brieland, D., & Lemmon, J. A. (1985). *Social work and the law* (4th ed.). St. Paul, MN: West.

Children's Bureau. (1961). Legislative guide for the termination of parental responsibilities and the adoption of children. (Publication No. 136). Washington, DC: U.S. Government Printing Office.

Commonwealth v. Fischer, 213 Pa. 48 (1905).

Davidson, H. A., & Gerlach, K. (1984). Child custody disputes: The child's perspective. In R. M. Horo-

witz & H. A. Davidson (Eds.), *Legal rights of children.* Colorado Springs: Shepard's/McGraw-Hill.

Dickson, D. T. (1995). *Law in the health and human services: A guide for social workers, psychologists, psychiatrists, and related professionals.* New York: Free Press.

Downs, S. W., & Taylor, C. (1980). *Permanent planning in foster care: Resources for training.* (DHHS Publication No. [OHDS] 81-30290). Washington, DC: U.S. Government Printing Office.

Ellrod, F. E., Jr., & Melaney, D. H. (1950, Winter). Juvenile justice: Treatment or travesty. *University of Pittsburgh Law Review, 11,* 277–287.

Elson, A. (1962). Juvenile courts and due process. In M. K. Rosenheim (Ed.), *Justice for the child* (pp. 95–117). New York: Free Press.

Flexner, B., & Baldwin, R. N. (1914). *Juvenile courts and probation.* New York: Century.

Flexner, B., & Oppenheimer, R. (1922). *The legal aspect of the juvenile court.* (Children's Bureau Publication No. 99). Washington, DC: Children's Bureau.

Flicker, B. D. (1977). *Standards for juvenile justice: A summary and analysis* (Institute of Judicial Administration and American Bar Association, Juvenile Justice Standards Project). Cambridge, MA: Ballinger.

Green, B. A., & Dohrn, B. (1996). Forward: Children and the ethical practice of law. (Proceedings of the Conference on Ethical Issues in the Legal Representation of Children). *Fordham Law Review, 64*(4), 1281–1323.

Handler, J. F. (1965). The juvenile court and the adversary system: Problems of function and form. *Wisconsin Law Review, 7,* 7–51.

Hardin, M. (1998, Summer). Child protection cases in a unified family court. *Family Law Quarterly, 32,* 147–203. Chicago: American Bar Association.

Heck, R. O., Pindur, W., & Wells, D. K. (1985). The juvenile serious offender/drug involved program: A means to implement recommendations of the National Council of Juvenile and Family Court Judges. *Juvenile and Family Court Journal, 36,* 27–37.

Howell, J. C. (1997). *Juvenile justice and youth policy.* Thousand Oaks, CA: Sage.

In re Gault, 387 U.S. 1 (1967).

In re Winship, 397 U.S. 358 (1970).

Indian Child Welfare Act, P.L. 95-608.

Jacobs, T. A. (1995, supp. 1997). *Children and the law: Rights and obligations.* St. Paul, MN: West.

Kelley, B. T., Thornberry, T. P., & Smith, C. A. (1997). *In the wake of childhood maltreatment.* Washington, DC: Office of Juvenile Justice and Delinquency Prevention.

Kent v. United States, 383 U.S. 541 (1966).

Ketcham, O. W. (1962). The unfilled promise of the American juvenile court. In M. K. Rosenheim (Ed.), *Justice for the child* (pp. 95–117). New York: Free Press.

Kramer, D. T. (1994, supp. 2002). *Legal rights of children* (2nd ed.). Colorado Springs: Shepard's/McGraw-Hill.

Lathrop, J. C. (1925). The background of the juvenile court in Illinois. *The child, the clinic, and the court.* New York: New Republic.

Lou, H. H. (1927). *Juvenile courts in the United States.* Chapel Hill: University of North Carolina Press.

Lundberg, E. O. (1947). *Unto the least of these: Social services for children.* New York: Appelton-Century-Crofts.

Mack, J. W. (1909–1910). The juvenile court. *Harvard Law Review, 23.*

McKeiver v. Pennsylvania, 403 U.S. 538 (1971).

Mississippi Band of Choctaw Indians v. Holyfield, 490 U.S. 51 (1989).

National Council of Family Law Judges. (1998). *Court appointed special advocates.* Reno, NV: National Council of Family Law Judges.

National Probation and Parole Association. (1957). *Guide for juvenile court judges.* New York: National Probation & Parole Association.

Nutt, A. S. (1949). Juvenile and domestic relations court. In *1949 social work yearbook* (pp. 270–276). New York: Russell Sage Foundation.

Office of Juvenile Justice and Delinquency Prevention. (2000). *Statistics.* Available: www.ojjdp.nc/rs.org/statistics.

OJJDP. (1998). *Juveniles in adult courts.* Washington, DC: Office of Juvenile Justice and Delinquency Prevention.

Pike, V., Downs, S. W., Emlen, A., Downs, G., & Case, D. (1977). *Permanent planning for children in foster care.* (No. OHDS 77-30124). Washington, DC: U.S. Department of Health, Education and Welfare.

Pound, R. (1950). The juvenile in the service state. In *1949 yearbook.* New York: National Probation and Parole Association.

Rosenheim, J. K. (Ed.). (1962). *Justice for the child.* New York: Free Press.

Ross, C. J. (1998, Summer). The failure of fragmentation: The promise of a system of unified family courts. *Family Law Quarterly, 32,* 3–30. Chicago: American Bar Association.

Rubin, S. (1952, November–December). Protecting the child in the juvenile court. *Journal of Criminal Law, Criminology and Political Science, 43,* 425–440.

Saltzman, A., & Proch, K. (1990). *Law in social work practice.* Chicago: Nelson-Hall.

Saltzman, A., & Proch, K. (2000). *Law in social work practice* (2nd ed.). Chicago: Nelson-Hall.

Schall v. Martin, 467 S.Ct. 253 (1984).

Schultz, L. L., & Cohen, F. (1976). Isolation in juvenile court jurisprudence. In M. K. Rosenheim (Ed.), *Pursuing justice for the child.* Chicago: University of Chicago Press.

Simonsen, C. (1991). Status offenders: An attempt to clarify the system. *Juvenile Justice in America.* New York: Macmillan.

Stein, T. J. (1991). *Child welfare and the law.* White Plains, NY: Longman.

Stern, P. (1997). *Preparing and presenting expert testimony in child abuse litigation: A guide for expert witnesses and attorneys.* Thousand Oaks, CA: Sage.

Szymanski, L. A. (1995). *Family courts in the United States.* Washington, DC: Office of Juvenile Justice and Delinquency Prevention.

Thompson v. Oklahoma, 487 U.S. 815 (1988).

7

Protecting Children from Neglect and Abuse

The little world in which children have their existence, whosoever brings them up, there is nothing so finely perceived and so finely felt, as injustice.

—Charles Dickens

To raise up and to restore that which is in ruin
To repair that which is damaged
To rejoin that which is severed
To replenish that which is lacking
To strengthen that which is weakened
To set right that which is wrong
To make flourish that which is insecure and undeveloped.

—Huisa M. Karenga, *Selections from the Huisa: Sacred Wisdom of Ancient Egypt*

CHAPTER OUTLINE

Case Example: A Protective Services Investigation

No case can stand as a typical example of a protective services investigation because of the great range of family situations that are reported. The alleged maltreatment may be categorized as neglect, physical abuse, sexual abuse, emotional maltreatment, other concerns about poor child care, or a combination of problems. The case presented here shows the protective services investigator "in action," as she attempts to understand the extent of a family's problems and the risk they represent to the children.

Jennifer Rogers, a protective services worker in a large midwestern city, received a call on a Friday morning from a concerned citizen who saw a mother crossing a busy street with her five children. The reporter stated that although the mother was carrying the youngest child and holding the hand of another, one of the smaller children was lagging behind. The mother screamed at the child to "hurry up" but then just kept walking. The child, whom the reporter thought was about 3, was almost hit by a car while the mother walked on ahead. Oncoming traffic had to stop while the child got across the street. The mother seemed unconcerned with the commotion and got into a car with the children. The reporter took down the license plate number and called CPS.

Jennifer, after speaking with her supervisor, decided to wait until the following week to investigate the case, as she had two other cases in which the children seemed at imminent risk of harm. She needed to speak with their caretakers that same day and perhaps take other action. Although the newly reported situation was clearly a risky one, there was no indication of injury or other maltreatment. Jennifer did, however, contact the police for a license check on the car.

The following Wednesday Jennifer received information on the name of the person who owned the car. It was Gloria Miles, a name Jennifer recognized immediately. Gloria was well known to CPS. She had five children, ages 7, 5, 3, 2, and 10 months. In a previous report to CPS last winter, Gloria had been seen in a public rest room with her children who were crying because they didn't have mittens and their hands were cold. Gloria was holding their hands under hot water trying to warm them up and yelling at them to be quiet. The woman who reported the situation had offered to help, but Gloria told her to mind her own business and left with the children. She left her purse in the restroom and thus her name became known. Gloria had also been previously reported by a neighbor, who had called to say she had gone to Gloria's door one night about 10 P.M. and there was no adult there. The 7-year-old answered the door. The neighbor said that Gloria didn't show up until the next morning. When CPS investigated that incident, they were told that an aunt had been sleeping in the house, which the aunt, when contacted, confirmed.

Gloria had been diagnosed in the past with schizophrenia and is supposed to be taking medication regularly. She has never liked taking this medication, feeling that it does "weird things" to her mind. When she does take it, she is able to provide for the children adequately. She keeps the children clothed, although they are often underdressed for the weather, and she keeps the house clean, although she has little furniture. The neighborhood is poor, with high unemployment. Although Gloria has a car, it often breaks down. She frequently uses the bus system, which is difficult to use with all the children. The children have been interviewed and examined; no injuries have been noted. They appear to mind Gloria and also to love her. She appears to be affectionate with them. She very much resents any outside interference in her life and frequently yells and screams at caseworkers to leave her alone and "get out of my life." Support services have been provided to help Gloria with her child care duties, but she is so unpleasant to the support providers that they do not remain. The children occasionally go to live with Gloria's sister when Gloria is "not feeling well," but the sister is not able to sustain care for the children for long periods of time due to her own family obligations. Gloria is poor, lives on food stamps, and has recently been placed on an employment program in order to earn her public assistance. Although she has not yet found employment, she is required to spend twenty hours a week at the income assistance/employment agency.

The CPS worker is very concerned about the children's welfare because of Gloria's continued marginal caretaking ability, now compounded by the work requirement. However, she knows that if Gloria has a work requirement, she also should be getting child care assistance. In thinking through options for this family, she is aware that a child care provider could help to provide a safety net for the children. Jennifer feels that the children are at continual risk. She decides to try to persuade Gloria to accept support services again, at least so that the children's condition can be monitored somewhat. However, she is aware that Gloria may refuse outside help, as she has in the past. A plan to engage the psychiatrist who is prescribing her medication might be in order. Perhaps a "case staffing" could be set up in an effort to work toward more consistency in Gloria's medication intake. Jennifer also decides to try Family Group Conferencing, in which family members and others who know the family convene to try to make a safety plan for the children. Jennifer decides to "substantiate" the case on the basis that the children are at continual risk of harm, which is a basis for substantiation in her state. She does not believe that the children are at imminent risk of serious harm and is aware that there is some extended family involvement, so she will try to keep the children in the home and provide supportive services to the mother. She also knows that, given Gloria's temperament and mental illness, family preservation services may not be able to help Gloria create a home that would provide for their ongoing nurture and safety.

This case shows how complex the world of children's protective services can be. The worker needs to continually balance concerns for the safety of the children with preservation of family bonds. Although there are clear-cut cases of abuse and neglect, often CPS cases are characterized by ambiguity and uncertainty about the dangers to children and the appropriate level of involvement of the agency. The CPS worker is also aware that there are limits to the services that can actually be offered to this client and the client's ability to use them effectively. This chapter will explore what constitutes abuse and neglect, the role of protective services, and the need for multisystem involvement in child maltreatment.

In child welfare and perhaps in all social services, there is no situation that raises such concern and outrage as does the neglect, abuse, or exploitation of children by parents or others responsible for their care. Fueled by media coverage of sensational instances of abuse and by considerable research and other scholarly attention, the last thirty years have witnessed a dramatic new concern for these child victims.

Incidence

No fully accurate figures are available to ascertain the incidence of child maltreatment. The primary source of data is the National Child Abuse and Neglect Data System (NCANDS), which is an aggregate of state reporting. Other sources are the National Incidence Study of Child Abuse and Neglect and the efforts of child welfare researchers. Researchers have used different methods at different times with different definitions, which have led to widely divergent results.

The National Child Abuse and Neglect Data System combines official reports of abuse and neglect made to child protective services agencies in each state and the District of Columbia. It is important to remember that the data include only *reported* cases, which is a serious underestimate of the actual incidence of child abuse and neglect. Probably less than half of all child maltreatment is reported to child protective agencies (Besharov & Laumann, 1996). It is also important to note that not all states report data in all the categories of abuse and neglect.

In 2000, states received almost 3 million reports of child abuse and neglect. Of these, only about one in four reports were confirmed, after investigation, as involving abuse or neglect, for a total of almost 879,000 children. The victimization rate has been declining since 1993, to a rate in 2000 of about 12 abused or neglected children per thousand children in the population as a whole.

Child neglect is the most common type of maltreatment and surpasses by far the incidence of child abuse. In 2000, children suffered the following types of maltreatment:

Neglect	63%
Physical abuse	20%
Sexual abuse	10%
Emotional maltreatment	8%

About 16 percent of victims suffered other types of maltreatment, such as abandonment, congenital drug addiction, and "threats to harm the child." Many states count victims in more than one category if more than one type of maltreatment has occurred, so the total of the percentages is more than 100 percent (U.S. Department of Health and Human Services, 2002).

The NCANDS data show that younger children are somewhat more likely to be maltreated than older children. Boys and girls suffer equal rates of maltreatment, except in sexual abuse, which is more likely to be inflicted on girls. About half of all victims are white, a quarter are African American, and 14 percent Hispanic. Most of the perpetrators are parents, though about 10 percent are relatives. Perhaps the most disturbing finding of the NCANDS data is that children who have been previously maltreated are three times more likely to suffer maltreatment again than are children without such history (U.S. Department of Health and Human Services, 2000a, 2002).

Other studies have also reported estimates of child abuse and neglect in the United States, usually much larger than the NCANDS data show. The most complete survey to date is the National Study of the Incidence and Severity of Child Abuse and Neglect, which collected data periodically from 1979 to 1994. Taking into account not only cases reported to child protective services but also cases known to other human service agencies such as hospitals and schools, the study estimated that over one and a half million children suffered maltreatment in 1993 (Sedlak & Broadhurst, 1996).

Surveys have been conducted of parents of victims of maltreatment, asking them questions concerning their participation in child abuse or neglect. Like the National Incidence Studies data, these surveys show higher rates of maltreatment than those reported to public agencies (Straus & Gelles, 1986; Finkelhor, Hotaling, Lewis, & Smith, 1990). In a 1995 Gallup poll, the self-reported behavior of parents led the researchers to conclude that about 3 million children suffered physical abuse from their parents, a rate that is sixteen times higher than that reported to public agencies. The same poll found that 23 percent of adults reported having been sexually abused as children by an adult or an older child, counting both contact and noncontact abuse (Gallup, Moor, & Schussel, 1997).

Although it is not possible to get fully accurate figures of the numbers of children affected by maltreatment, reporting methods have improved over the years. The slight decrease in reports of child maltreatment during the 1990s, reported by the NCANDS data, is encouraging. However, the incidence of child maltreatment remains unacceptably high, and the public child welfare system continues to be severely strained in its efforts to respond adequately.

Behind each statistic is a child, a child whose immediate safety, comfort, welfare, and future development are jeopardized or whose very life may be at stake. Parents also exist behind these numbers, parents who may have their child removed from their care or at least have their autonomy as parents eroded. For society, the costs are similarly high. Balancing society's desire to maintain and support the integrity of the family while protecting the welfare of its children is a complicated proposition requiring clarification of national values. The relative value society places on child safety or family sanctity and preservation changes from time to time and influences how resources will be allocated.

The majority of society's resources in the area of child maltreatment are spent after the fact, when the child has already been damaged by maltreatment. In allocating resources in this way, society misses the opportunity to address the underlying causes of maltreatment. Poverty and other social ills, many outside the ability of the family to change, "set the stage" for child maltreatment. Until they are addressed, maltreatment rates will continue to be unacceptably high. Maltreatment in childhood, in turn, is highly correlated with delinquency, substance abuse, crime, and other social problems that require large financial resources. Thus the case for effective intervention, beginning with an attack on child poverty, is not only a moral issue but a practical one as well (English, 1998; Jonson-Reid & Barth, 2000). (See Chapters 3, 4, and 5.)

Aims and Special Attributes of Child Protective Services

Child protective services are intended to reduce the risks to children's safety or well-being, prevent further risk of neglect or abuse, and restore adequate parental functioning whenever possible. If it does not appear that children will be adequately protected, steps are taken to remove children from their own homes and establish them in alternative living situations in which they will receive more adequate care. The Adoption and Safe Families Act (ASFA) now mandates that child safety, not family preservation, is to be the guiding force in decision making regarding service provision, placement, and permanency planning for children.

Protective services today reflect the conviction that many parents whose level of child care is unacceptable, can be reached on behalf of their children and can be helped to improve their parental functioning. The focus of child protective services is on both the investigation of reported maltreatment that initiates agency responsibility and on stabilizing and improving the children's own homes by helping parents to perform more responsibly in relation to their children's care. Protective services also are concerned with social planning to organize and coordinate collaborative efforts among community agencies involved in the child protection system (Melton & Barry, 1994).

Child protective services are characterized by certain distinctive features: (1) the way in which service is initiated; (2) the increased agency responsibility that accompanies work with parents of children at risk; (3) the kind of agency sanction or community authorization and (4) the balance required in the use of authority in relation to the rights of parents, child, and society.

1. *Child protective services are authoritative.* The protective agency initiates the service by approaching the parents about a complaint from some source in the community, such as police officers, school personnel, public health nurses, neighbors, or relatives. Because the protective service is frequently involuntary, the situation that justifies an agency's "intruding" into family life must strongly suggest that parents are not providing the basic care or protection a child needs for healthy growth and development.

2. *Child protective services carry significant social agency responsibility, because they are directed toward families in which children are at risk.* Children are highly vulnerable when their homes lack minimal levels of care or protection. Children cannot make effective claims by themselves for the enforcement of their rights. If appropriate and quick initiation of services does not follow a complaint from the community, lasting harm may result for a child who is being maltreated.

Social workers in the protective agency must act promptly; their decisions about the nature or seriousness of the complaint and objective assessment as well as subsequent actions, must be based on accurate fact-finding. Moreover, the social agency cannot withdraw from the situation if it finds the parents uncooperative or resistant to taking help, as it may in situations in which individuals have voluntarily sought help. Once protective services have been initiated, the agency can responsibly withdraw only when the level of child care in the home has improved to acceptable levels or when satisfactory alternative care has been arranged elsewhere, as in a relative's home or in foster care.

The protective agency, then, has a high degree of responsibility to the child at risk; to the child's parents, who are frequently experiencing great stress; and to the community, which charges the agency to act for it in the provision of child protection.

3. *Child protective services involve agency sanction from the community.* A child protection agency has been delegated responsibility by federal and state laws to receive reports about instances of unacceptable child care, to investigate them, and if necessary to initiate services for the family even though the parents have not requested help. Other social agencies expect and look to the child protection agency to act. The provision of child protective services is mandated by federal law as a fundamental public agency responsibility.

4. *Child protective services require a crucial balance in the use of the agency's authority.* Child maltreatment is both a social and a legal problem. The fact that the agency approaches a family about its problems without a request from the family itself denotes some invasion of privacy, however well motivated the services may be. Furthermore, an integral part of the protective agency's methods is to reserve the right to invoke the authority of the court by filing a petition alleging parental neglect or abuse if the parents do not improve their level of care. This "threat," implied or acknowledged, is recognized by the family and may be perceived as either subtle or overt coercion—pressure to cooperate or conform to other ways of child care. Today, protective services workers must operate within narrow time frames in treating families or petitioning for termination of parental rights. This sense of urgency may communicate to parents a message that their own concerns and problems are not important and that the agency expects them to fail.

The protective agency has the difficult task of maintaining a just and effective balance in its use of authority in relation to the child at risk, whose rights and protection depend on other persons; to parents, whose right to rear their children without outside intervention is being questioned; and to society, which has delegated a responsibility for the protection of children from neglect or abuse. These four attributes of child protective services will assume fuller meaning as we consider the specific social services that are extended to the family and the issues involved in doing so. But first it is important to look at the origins and subsequent growth of the protective services idea.

Historical Development of Protective Services

Early Attitudes toward the Treatment of Children

Accepted ideas on ways to rear children have undergone many changes through the centuries. We tend to lose sight of how recently the general public has strongly objected to indifferent parental care or to aggressive actions toward children by other members of society.

For many hundreds of years, history has recorded mistreatment of children. The Bible contains examples of cruelty to children, including Herod's order to slay "all the children that were in Bethlehem, and in all the coasts thereof, from two years old and under" (Matthew 2:16). Infanticide by different means was carried out in a number of societies to assure the survival of only strong, healthy infants who could become able to serve the state in combat, and to rid the society of "undesirable" offspring—females, out-of-wedlock children, or any infant who did not seem to be a promising child. Parents who were poor sometimes abandoned children, exposing them to weather and hunger, to escape the burdens of rearing them; richer parents often did the same to avoid dividing property into too many small parts.

During colonial times and even later, parents often enforced absolute obedience of children to the demands of adults in an attempt to "break their will" and free them from the evil disposition with which they supposedly had been born. Drugs, particularly laudanum (a form of opium), were given by parents and servants "almost indiscriminately" to infants to stop their crying (Sunley, 1963). Flogging and caning were used extensively and brutally by schoolmasters. Child labor was accepted and endorsed: "In colonial life, the labor of children was a social fact and a social necessity, not a social problem" (Cohen, 2000, p. 18).

Beginnings of Care for Neglected Children

After the Revolutionary War, various states passed legislation that recognized the needs of neglected children to the extent of authorizing the binding out, or commitment to almshouses, of children who were found begging on the street or whose parents were beggars. In 1790, the first public orphanage was established in South Carolina, which cared for and educated not only orphan children but also those whose parents could not afford to care for them (Abbott, 1938).

Homer Folks cited the year 1825 as the beginning of more general recognition and application of the principle that public authorities have a right and duty to intervene in cases of parental cruelty or gross neglect of children and "to remove the children by force if necessary, and place them under surroundings more favorable for their development" (Folks, 1911, pp. 168–169). Before the end of the nineteenth century, special laws were passed in nearly all states to provide for the protection of children from neglect or ill treatment by authorizing the courts to remove them from parents or guardians and commit them to some proper place of care.

Societies for the Prevention of Cruelty to Children

The new laws provided a legal basis for acting on behalf of maltreated children if they became objects of attention by a child-saving agency or a children's institution, or if the police chose to bring the situation to the attention of the court. However, there were no clear lines of responsibility among agencies or officials for *finding* neglected or abused children unless families were already requiring support from public or voluntary relief funds. As a consequence, societies for the prevention of cruelty to children (SPCCs) were established.

Examining the circumstances under which the first SPCC came into existence provides an aid to understanding the purpose and focus of the early societies. In 1873, Etta Wheeler, a church worker visiting tenement homes in New York City, heard the story of 9-

year-old Mary Ellen, who for two years had been cruelly whipped and frequently left alone, locked in an inner room during long days. The thin partitions between the tenement apartments let other occupants hear the child's cries and other evidence of the cruel treatment inflicted on her by the man and woman with whom she lived. They had obtained the child from an institution at 2 years of age, but institution personnel had made no inquiry about her well-being during the intervening seven years. Concerned neighbors had not known to whom to complain or how to get help for the child. The tenement visitor went to great lengths to investigate the report and establish evidence of the abuse and neglect. Then, when she sought advice as to how to obtain protection for the child, no one seemed to know of any legal means to "rescue" the child. Up to that time, the legal removal of children from cruel or neglectful parents was rare if not impossible.

Finally, Henry Bergh, who had founded the New York Society for the Prevention of Cruelty to Animals, arranged to file a petition to have the child removed from her custodians and placed with persons who would treat her more kindly. The abusing foster mother was sentenced to prison and Mary Ellen eventually gained loving parents. In 1875, the New York Society for the Prevention of Cruelty to Children was established.

The Mary Ellen case was not the sole cause of the emerging child protection movement. Large social movements rarely, if ever, are traceable to accidental causal beginnings. The emergence of the SPCCs is best explained by a coming together and fusing of various forces. Public awareness had been awakened by various stories about the lack of public response to the plight of children. Gaining in influence was the women's movement of the 1870s and its overarching influence on various thrusts toward social justice, one of which was the ideal of a protected childhood and cultural rejection of child abuse and punitive corporal punishment.

The formation of the New York SPCC triggered a rapid growth of other child cruelty societies. By 1898 more than 200 SPCCs had come into existence in the United States. Their primary function was to investigate cases of alleged maltreatment, present facts to the courts, and assist in the prosecution of adults responsible for the maltreatment (Costin, 1992).

Who Should Do Protective Work?

After the "discovery" of child abuse in 1874, child abuse seemed to disappear from public consciousness, only to be "rediscovered" in the 1960s. After the turn of the century, child welfare practice was marked by confusion and uncertainty as to which agencies should undertake the protective work. There was little public interest in creating a public agency with a mandate to intrude into the privacy of family life to protect children. The private agencies, for their part, continued to move away from child protection work. The use of authority, necessary in protective work, made social workers uncomfortable.

The Rediscovery of Child Abuse: The Battered Child Syndrome

The rediscovery of child abuse began in the 1960s, when Kempe and colleagues identified "battered child syndrome" (Kempe, Silverman, Steele, Droegemueller, & Silver, 1962). Advances in the technology of radiology made it possible for physicians to identify patterns of injuries, observable by X-rays, that were likely to have been inflicted rather than accidental. In the deluge of interest and publicity that followed this discovery, public interest in addressing child maltreatment was renewed. The interest quickly took the form of establishing official procedures whereby those who knew of instances of child abuse could report them to authorities.

The Child Abuse Prevention and Treatment Act

In 1974 the federal Child Abuse Prevention and Treatment ACT (CAPTA) was passed. The Act established a National Center on Child Abuse and Neglect, which was to be a clearinghouse for the development and transmittal of information on research in child protection. The Act also provided for grants to the states if they passed reporting laws, requiring certain groups of people, called "mandated reporters," to report alleged child maltreatment to the state child protective services agencies (Schene, 1998). See the section Reporting Child Maltreatment for more information on this law.

Shifting Priorities: Child Safety and Family Preservation

This history of children's protective services shows that society has changed from time to time in the mandate given to agencies to intrude into family life for the protection of children. Legislation in this country has reflected this uncertainty, swinging from an emphasis on child safety to an emphasis on family preservation and back to an emphasis on child safety. The Child Abuse Prevention and Treatment Act (CAPTA) was primarily concerned with child safety, and changes to it in 1996 reinforced this emphasis. In 1990, the Indian Child Protection and Family Violence Protection Act extended mandatory reporting to reservations (Earle, 2000).

However, other legislation reflects a priority of preserving families. The 1980 Adoption Assistance and Child Welfare Act encouraged agencies to serve children in their own homes. If removal were necessary for the children's protection, the Act encouraged family reunification if possible, even if it took years. Before removing a child from home, agencies were required to show the courts that they had made "reasonable efforts" to preserve the family by offering services to the parents. The Family Preservation and Support Act of 1993 increased the funding for family preservation efforts and for preventive services before maltreatment occurred. In 1997, the pendulum seemed to swing again, with the passage of the Adoption and Safe Families Act. While it expanded family preservation and support services, it clearly shifted the national priority to child safety. The Act clarified that child safety should not be jeopardized in order to meet the reasonable efforts requirement of earlier legislation. It also established clear and shortened time frames for deciding to terminate parental rights so the child could be placed in a permanent, adoptive home. It is too soon to tell whether this Act will improve safety to children, or whether we will find that child safety depends, ultimately, less on streamlined bureaucratic and judicial procedures, and more on improving the social and economic conditions in which children are raised. It is paradoxical that federal legislation, while mandating procedures to protect children, has consistently failed to provide the supports to families they need to keep their children safe. Legislation to protect children is necessary, but so are resources to help families raise their children in safety.

The Definitional Dilemma

There is no consensual definition of either child abuse or neglect. There is wide agreement that the type of extreme case most frequently reported by the media constitutes maltreatment, but such cases are relatively rare. The great majority of cases fall into more ambiguous categories in which complex sets of factors must be taken into account. The difficulty and the importance of developing clear definitions can be understood if viewed as society's attempt to establish minimum standards for the care of children. The development of research-based knowledge, treatment, and prevention of child abuse and neglect depends on a foundation of agreement on what constitutes child maltreatment. Legislative and judicial mandates must share in this foundation.

The Child Abuse Prevention and Treatment Act of 1974 (CAPTA), reauthorized in 1996, gave a national definition of child maltreatment:

Child abuse and neglect is, at a minimum:

- Any recent act or failure to act on the part of a parent or caretaker which results in death, serious physical or emotional harm, sexual abuse or exploitation; or
- An act or failure to act which presents an imminent risk of serious harm. (Child Abuse Prevention and Treatment Act, 1974, 1996)

This definition clarifies that only parents or other caregivers can be charged with abuse or neglect. Harmful behavior to children committed by other adults is considered assault and usually is handled by the criminal justice system. Note that the definition includes "emotional harm" as well as physical and sexual abuse and neglect. Also, it includes "endangerment" as a category of child maltreatment, through the use of the term *imminent risk* of *serious harm*. This means that child protective services could make a finding of abuse or neglect even though the child had not yet been observably injured, if the parent's threat to harm or extreme neglect seemed to represent a serious risk to the child. In the following section, we discuss these and other definitional issues in child maltreatment.

The CAPTA legislation left many specific details of defining abuse and neglect to the states, and states vary considerably in their definitions. For example, some states include educational neglect (caretaker's failure to ensure the child's school attendance) while others do not. Every state includes nonaccidental physical injury and sexual abuse in its definition of child abuse, but the definitions vary in how specific they are. Almost all states include neglect, emotional maltreatment, and sexual exploitation in their definitions, but some states do not distinguish between abuse and neglect. States differ on whether newborns who show signs of prenatal substance exposure must be reported. Some states, but not all, require reporting of suspected maltreatment in out-of-home placements such as foster care. Other states handle these situations differently (U.S. Department of Health and Human Services, 1999a).

Broad and Narrow Definitions

Harm comes to children from many sources and in many forms. The difficulty in defining child maltreatment is deciding what elements must be present in a situation for it to be officially considered parental maltreatment of a child, and not just one of the myriad hazards of childhood. One definitional problem is whether the motivation of the parent to harm the child is necessary for abuse to be said to have occurred. It is not always easy to differentiate between intentional and accidental behavior. Many times child abuse reflects a mixture of intentional and chance elements, as, for example, when harm to the child results from parental discipline. Another definitional controversy is whether to include endangerment in the definition of maltreatment, when the situation seems very risky but no actual harm has occurred. Related to this issue is the question of *cumulative harm.* This term refers to the cumulative effects of repeated moderate abuse or prolonged neglect, which are damaging in their cumulative effect, but do not cause a discrete injury. Examples of cumulative harm include ongoing verbal abuse or neglect to get medical care. These behaviors may not have an immediate effect on the child's development, but are damaging in the long run (Hutchinson, 1990; English, 1998).

Whether a broad or a narrow definition of child maltreatment is selected has implications for the policy and practice of child protective services. Proponents of a narrow definition would prefer to see only cases of observable harm, such as broken bones or burns, handled by child protective services. This policy would simplify the operation of protective services and provide clarity for all concerned—parents, those reporting maltreatment, and other professionals—on the scope and role of protective services in the community. Proponents of a broad definition, on the other hand, are concerned that many children suffering endangerment or cumulative harm would be left entirely unprotected and unnoticed if a narrow definition were adopted. They argue that the definition should include situations in which the child is at serious risk of suffering harm or negative developmental outcomes in the future.

Cultural Attitudes

In the culturally diverse society of the United States, differences among cultures in child-rearing practices and perceptions of acceptable parental behavior complicate the problem of providing clear definitions of child abuse and neglect (Giovanni & Becerra, 1979; Garbarino & Ebata, 1983; Ahn & Gilbert, 1992). Korbin (1994) points out the dilemma posed by cultural factors in determining whether a situation constitutes abuse or neglect: An extreme ethnocentric position, which disregards all cultural differences and imposes a single standard for child care on everyone, risks including situations that appear to constitute maltreatment but do not. On the other hand, an extreme position of cultural relativity runs the risk of ignoring situations that may in fact be harmful to children, even if accepted by the children's culture.

Korbin (1994) offers the example of "coin rubbing" among Southeast Asians to illustrate this dilemma. The practice of *cao gao,* believed to cure illness, involves pressing metal coins "forcefully on the child's body, leaving a symmetrical pattern of bruises" (p. 187). These bruises are, indeed, nonaccidentally inflicted and may leave a pattern of marks that appear more serious than the bruises resulting from being hit with a belt. An ethnocentric position would require that the case be reported for child abuse, even though the bruises were inflicted in a medical context. In fact, these cases are rarely reported because it is recognized as a cultural practice with good intentions. It should be noted though, that sometimes children involved in this procedure become very sick, not because of the procedure itself but because they did not receive standard medical care. In such a situation, some people might take the position that the child was discriminated against on the basis of ethnicity/race, because he or she did not receive the same level of protection as other children in American society.

Sometimes, a cultural practice acceptable within the community is taken to an extreme and then becomes a form of maltreatment. For example, a frequent cause for a child

neglect report among the Navaho Indians is that children have been left alone or unattended. Parents justify this behavior by pointing out that Navaho culture endorses sibling caretaking of younger children and entrusts children with a high level of responsibility. However, a survey of Navaho parents found that most mothers disapproved of leaving young children alone or with siblings who were not much older for overnight or other long periods of time. Many of the neglect cases were for children as young as 5. These situations could not be justified as culturally acceptable, but were in fact a departure from the cultural norms exacerbated by problems of poverty and alcohol (Korbin, 1994). Sibling caretaking as it was meant to be practiced within this culture should not be condemned, Korbin points out, but should be kept within acceptable limits.

Similarly Korbin suggests that culturally acceptable forms of physical discipline cannot always be considered as abuse. Within the culture, physical discipline may be considered appropriate and necessary if it does not harm the child. Child protective services workers tend to see only the cases in which children are left with bruises, welts, and other wounds, yet most physical discipline within the culture leaves the children without such marks. (For another point of view, see the discussion of corporal punishment in the Trends and Issues section of Chapter 3.)

Indeed, in an interesting study of African American child-rearing practices, parents and elders who were interviewed thought that physical punishment was a more effective form of discipline than the "reasoning" approach social workers often urged. They thought that a lack of physical punishment led to children who misbehaved, which then resulted in verbal abuse of children. It was this verbal abuse, "cursing and screaming," that they saw as child abuse, and not the physical discipline. The authors go on to argue that these children are no more at risk than other children and "as long as the child rearing methods are shared among members of a community, they should be respected as alternative cultural practices and not interfered with" (Mosby, Rawls, Meehan, Mays, Pettinari, 1999, p. 515).

In an acknowledgment of diversity in beliefs on acceptable child-rearing practices, the majority of states include provisions in their reporting laws stating that parental religious beliefs should be considered prior to a determination of abuse or neglect (U.S. Department of Health and Human Services, 1999b, p. 12).

As the following section on reporting child maltreatment shows, the lack of a clear, consensual definition of child maltreatment, understood and accepted by the community as a whole, has complicated the work of creating an efficient, effective, broadly endorsed, and humane child protection system.

Reporting Child Maltreatment

Since the passage of the Child Abuse Prevention and Treatment Act in 1974, every state and the District of Columbia have required reporting by physicians and other medical personnel, mental health professionals, social workers, teachers, and other school officials, child care workers, and law enforcement personnel. As of 2000, eighteen states require all citizens to report, and all states permit any citizen to report (National Association of Social Workers [NASW], 2000). Those required by statute to report suspected maltreatment are the state's "mandated reporters."

The last 20 years have witnessed radically improved performance in the reporting of suspected child maltreatment. The reporting process is strengthened by publicity campaigns, 24-hour hot lines, and administrative linkages between agencies likely to report, such as schools, welfare, and visiting nurses, and the legally mandated child protection agency in the community. Knowledge of the law is improving among those mandated to report, and they have increased their reports to state authorities. The rate of reported child maltreatment was ten cases per thousand children in 1976, while by 2000 the rate ranged from seventeen to eighty-six children per thousand, depending on the state (U.S. Department of Health and Human Services, 2002). As a result of improvements in reporting, many children have been saved from serious injury or death. Besharov and Laumann (1996) estimate that in the past 20 years, deaths from child abuse and neglect have fallen from about 3,000 a year to about 1,000 a year. New York State experienced a 50 percent reduction in child fatalities within five years of passage of a comprehensive reporting law.

Most reports of alleged maltreatment come from professionals, the "mandated reporters." Family members, the victims themselves, and neighbors and friends also make reports. About 20 percent of reports are done anonymously (U.S. Department of Health and Human Services, 2002). Figure 7.1 shows the sources of reports for 2000.

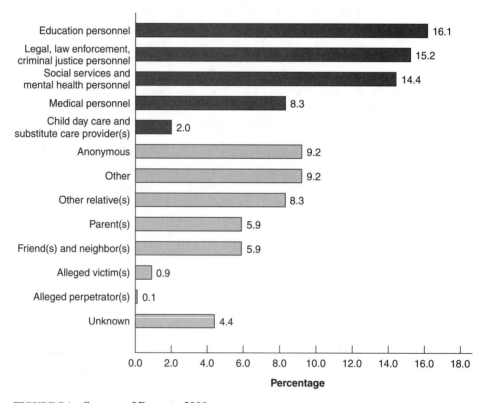

FIGURE 7.1   Sources of Reports, 2000

Source: U.S. Department of Health and Human Services (2002), *Child maltreatment 2000: Reports from the states to the National Child Abuse and Neglect Data System* (Washington, DC: U.S. Government Printing Office).

Problems with the Reporting Law

In spite of improvements in reporting, two major problems remain: the large number of cases that go unreported and the large number of unfounded reports. The plight of many vulnerable children continues to go unreported. Although legally mandated to do so, many professionals still do not report cases in which they suspect child maltreatment. Reasons for this reluctance to report include lack of clarity on which situations require reporting, concern about confidentiality and the effect of reporting on the therapeutic relationship, concern about lawsuits or reprisals from clients, reluctance to become involved, and a belief that reporting will not help the situation (Deisz, Doueck, George, & Levine, 1996; Warner-Rogers, Hansen, & Spieth, 1996).

A second problem is the large number of reports that, on investigation, are found to be without enough basis to warrant further action. These "unfounded" or "unsubstantiated" reports currently constitute almost 60 percent of all reports made to child protection agencies (U.S. Department of Health and Human Services, 2002). Figure 7.2 shows the disposition of child maltreatment reports for 2000. Very few of these unfounded reports are made by malicious people trying to cause trouble. Many are made by "nonmandated reporters," such as neighbors and relatives (U.S. Department of Health and Human Services, 2002), who may not know the definitions of child maltreatment used by the local child protection agency. However, there is a significant number of reports made by persons involved in child custody disputes.

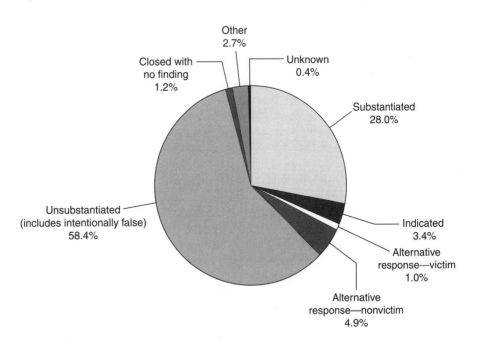

FIGURE 7.2   Investigations by Disposition, 2000

Source: U.S. Department of Health and Human Services (2002), *Child maltreatment 2000: Reports from the states to the National Child Abuse and Neglect Data System* (Washington, DC: U.S. Government Printing Office).

unfounded reports

Another reason for the large number of unfounded reports concerns agency policy regarding which kinds of situations to substantiate. As indicated earlier, states vary in the inclusiveness of their definitions of abuse and neglect, and local and county agencies also vary in what kinds of situations they believe warrant a thorough investigation or a decision to substantiate (English, 1998, p. 41).

Unfounded reports are of concern because of the possible conflict between a family's right to privacy and the state's interest in protecting children who may be abused or maltreated. A protective service investigation is intrusive. Workers must inquire into intimate details of family life. The children usually must be questioned and also friends, school personnel, day care workers, clergy, and others who know the family. The fact of the investigation is stigmatizing, even if the report is later unfounded. Justice Hugo Black pointed out that the parent "is charged with conduct—failure to care properly for her children—which may be viewed as reprehensible and morally wrong by a majority of society" (*Carter v. Kaufman,* 1971, p. 959). Critics question a system that infringes on the family's right to privacy without giving much assurance that the lives of children will be improved as a result of this infringement (Lindsay, 1994; Besharov & Laumann, 1996).

Another troublesome aspect of the large number of unfounded reports is that the agency resources are necessarily deployed to investigate reports while children already identified as abused are insufficiently served by the agency. The large increase in reports of child maltreatment has not been accompanied by sufficient increases in appropriations for child protection agencies, so staff must spend time investigating new cases rather than treating families already known to them.

Waldfogel (1998) offers strategies to address the dilemma of both underreporting (thus missing some serious cases) and overreporting (thus tying up caseworkers unnecessarily, which also results in missing serious cases). She urges that definitions provide more clarity about such contentious issues as severity, endangerment versus actual occurrence, type of maltreatment, type of caretaker, and burden of proof. "Reporting laws should clearly specify what constitutes reportable abuse or neglect, what should be looked for, and what counts as evidence. Current laws typically do not accomplish this" (p. 111). See the preceding section, The Definitional Dilemma, for a discussion of definitional problems. Waldfogel (1998) also suggests more training for mandated reporters and better communication between mandated reporters and the agency investigators. This could create a "feedback loop," giving investigators more information about a family and also educating reporters on what kinds of situations are likely to receive attention from the agency (p. 116). She also urges expanded and more thorough investigations, including interviews with members of the community and professionals who know the family situation. Other suggestions for reducing the number of unfounded reports involve dividing the most serious cases from the less serious, and treating less serious cases with support services rather than with full-fledged investigations (see Trends and Issues section).

Filing a Report

States include nearly every category of professionals serving children, such as teachers, social workers, day care workers, probation officers, and health care professionals, as mandated reporters who are required to report suspected abuse or neglect. Mandated reporters may face civil and criminal penalties if they fail to report, and have immunity from legal action by parents for reporting. They are also protected by confidentiality provisions in the reporting laws; the identity of the reporter is supposed to remain unknown to the parents.

Those reporting child abuse and neglect are not expected to have conducted an investigation to ascertain whether child maltreatment occurred. They are asked to report instances in which they have "reasonable cause to suspect" child maltreatment. Then child protective services will conduct the investigation. As indicated earlier, many professionals are confused about what types of situations are considered abuse or neglect by their local child protective agency. However, the general rule for mandated reporters is to report all cases in which they have "reasonable cause to suspect" child abuse or neglect, regardless of whether they believe that the child protective agency will act on the referral. By doing so, they are protecting themselves from any possible legal penalties as well as working to protect children.

The procedures for filing a report are quite simple in most states and are described in the state's reporting law. Generally, the reporter may make an oral report, such as a telephone call, to be followed by the agency writing a report within twenty-four hours. Reporters are encouraged to give as much information as possible, such as relevant names, addresses, and phone numbers, and specific information regarding the maltreatment, such as physical evidence and the statements of children or perpetrators. In some states, child protective services is required or encouraged to let the reporter know the results of the investigation.

An Ecological View of Child Maltreatment

Conditions leading to the neglect or abuse of children cannot be identified in simple, discrete terms. Multiple causes and conditions interact, reinforce each other, and generate new influences that lead to family malfunctioning. In general, child maltreatment results from the interaction of environmental stress, personality traits of the parent, and child characteristics. No one factor causes child maltreatment; rather the interaction among environmental, parental, and child characteristics creates situations in which child maltreatment is likely to occur (Belsky, 1993; English, 1998). (See Chapter 3.)

Community Deficits

Environmental conditions that contribute to child neglect and abuse often can be identified within a community's system of social services. There can be lack of early case-finding techniques, resulting in a pattern of providing social services only after a child is observed to be in an already dangerous situation, or when the care he or she is receiving finally reaches such a low level that it defies what a neighborhood or community can tolerate. A deficiency in "case accountability" is another factor, reflected in such practices as (1) giving inadequate or incomplete services, (2) failing to follow through on referrals for another service, (3) setting up barriers of communication or bureaucratic procedures that cut off some people from asking for or receiving help, (4) showing concern only about fragments of family life that present symptoms troublesome to the community, and (5) failing to develop an agency function that is an active part of a community-wide program of services. Preventive services may be unavailable to avert the onset of family problems. The situation in Miami, Florida, reported in 2002, in which a young child who was supposed to be under the oversight of the Department of Social Services, but instead could not be found, is an extreme example (and fortunately a rare one) of problems with case accountability.

Serious social problems abound in our communities today, and all of these, directly or indirectly, tend to increase the incidence of child neglect and abuse. Some of the most pressing social problems are a large-scale incidence of mental illness and substance abuse; escalating health costs and unequal medical services; poverty in the midst of affluence; lack of jobs for youth and heads of families; deplorable housing for large numbers of the population; high rates of delinquency; inadequate and irrelevant education for much of the nation's youth, with a lack of preparation for jobs, higher education, parenthood, and other aspects of adult responsibility; and a pervading sense that individuals lack the power of self-direction and are subject to the restrictive rules of bureaucracies or intangible outside forces that limit daily experiences for them and their children.

Societal Attitudes

We live in a culture saturated with images of violence. The media glamorize violence in movies, books, television, and music, and reinforce the widely held view that violence is a culturally approved way of resolving disputes. Toys and computer games for children glamorize "the thrill" of violent encounters. Child abuse must be viewed within the context of a society that accepts and too often condones violence in the domestic sphere and in the community. Physical force is still considered by many, including many school districts, to be an acceptable means to govern children's behavior.

Poverty

The relation of poverty to child maltreatment has been recognized at least since the nineteenth century. Research consistently shows a correlation between socioeconomic status and child maltreatment rate. In one national study, the poorest children were three times more likely to suffer maltreatment than were children in families with incomes between $15,000 and $29,000 and more than twenty-five times more likely to be maltreated than were children in the most affluent categories (Sedlak & Broadhurst, 1996). Of course, child abuse and neglect occur at all income levels. To some extent, the differences in rates between income groups may reflect differences in recognition of maltreatment rather than differences in occurrence. Although most states mandate that a petition alleging neglect be for reasons other than poverty, this distinction does not always get made in practice. Families of higher socioeconomic status may be able to conceal child maltreatment because of access to greater resources and less scrutiny by social services. It is also important to remember that most poor families do not abuse or neglect their children, and raise their children successfully in the face of great obstacles. Nevertheless, the magnitude and consistency of the difference in maltreatment rates among income groups makes clear that children in poor families are at greater risk of maltreatment.

Many factors work to increase the risk to poor children. Poor families frequently live in poor neighborhoods with few services. They face the ongoing stress of living in chronically poor conditions, and their children's safety is but one concern among many. Poor people may be less well informed about developmentally sound ways of disciplining their children than are middle-class families. The integral connection between poverty and all types of maltreatment (with the possible exception of sexual abuse) will become clearer in the sections describing each category of abuse and neglect.

Welfare reform, with its strict work requirements for families, may increase burdens on poor families and therefore increase the risk to their children of maltreatment. Families must be concerned with getting steady employment within specified time frames or be cut off completely from public welfare. Adequate child care may be very difficult to arrange. Convicted felons for drug use are ineligible to receive welfare at all. These factors may exacerbate already marginal care. In a review of recent research, Slack (2002) concludes that it is "too early to tell" whether welfare reform will affect the child maltreatment rate, but recommends increasing the safety nets and conducting longitudinal research on how children fare under welfare reform.

Race and Ethnicity

Some racial and ethnic groups are more likely to be reported for child maltreatment than others. As Figure 7.3 shows, African American children and Indian/Native Alaskan children have particularly high rates (twenty-five and twenty per thousand children in the population, respectively). White children are more likely than other races to be reported for sexual abuse (U.S. Department of Health and Human Services, 2000a). However, the relation of race to

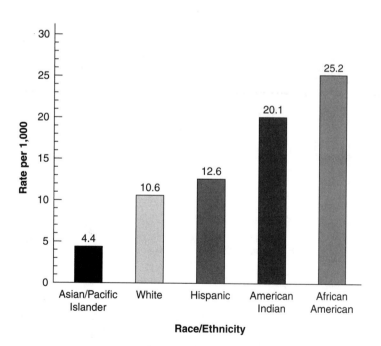

FIGURE 7.3   Victimization Rates by Race and Ethnicity, 1999

Source: U.S. Department of Health and Human Services (2002), *Child maltreatment 1999: Reports from the states to the National Child Abuse and Neglect Data System* (Washington, DC: U.S. Government Printing Office).

maltreatment is a complicated one. Misunderstandings about cultural beliefs and practices, such as those discussed earlier in this chapter, play a part in whether a situation gets reported. African American children are more likely to be reported, particularly if they are poor, because they are more likely to come to the attention of mandated reporters. It is difficult to separate out the distinct effects of race, poverty, and substance abuse, all closely linked to child maltreatment. Berrick, Needell, Barth, and Jonson-Reid (1998), after a major review of research, have concluded, in line with other researchers (Sedlak & Broadhurst, 1996; Ards, Chung, & Myers, 1998), that ethnicity by itself does not increase risk of maltreatment for children. It seems reasonable to conclude that race is often linked to a constellation of factors, including poverty and substance abuse that, together, represent increased risk to children.

Family Structure

Abuse and neglect are more likely to occur in single-parent households, as Figure 7.4 shows. Single parenthood is related to poverty and the additional risks that the difficulties

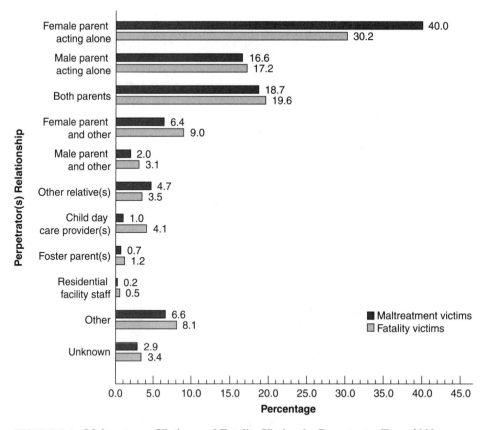

FIGURE 7.4   Maltreatment Victims and Fatality Victims by Perpetrator Type, 2000

Source: U.S. Department of Health and Human Services (2002), *Child Maltreatment 2000: Reports from the states to the National Child Abuse and Neglect Data System* (Washington, DC: U.S. Government Printing Office).

of living in poverty entail. Single parents, trying to fulfill both parental roles, may be more susceptible to stress, which can result in lashing out at children. They also have to try to handle the child care and other parenting tasks on their own, without a parenting partner. Another family characteristic related to abuse and neglect is the number of children at home; those with more children are at higher risk than are small families, probably due to increased demands on the parents (Sedlak & Broadhurst, 1996).

Substance Abuse

Drug abuse has increased tremendously in recent years, with devastating effects on the lives of adults and children. Substances such as alcohol, marijuana, cocaine, crack, PCP, and heroin are widely available. In 1997, a study of state child welfare agencies estimated that 67 percent of parents in the child welfare system required substance abuse treatment services (Child Welfare League of America, 2001). Parents who abuse substances, especially if they are addicted, are often unable to provide consistent, nurturing care that promotes their child's development. Feeding the addiction takes needed resources from the family, so that children may lack sufficient food and clothing and decent housing. Use of psychoactive drugs also increases the risk of abuse. Chemical substances lower inhibitions; an angry parent when drunk may become a physically abusive parent. Some parents recruit their children into selling drugs, prostitution, or other extremely damaging activities in order to obtain money to buy drugs or alcohol (Zuckerman, 1994).

Often addiction is related to a constellation of other problems that also affect the parent's ability to provide an adequate level of care for his or her children. Many women who are addicted experienced sexual or physical abuse as children. For them, use of drugs and alcohol may be an effort to dull the painful memories associated with these events. Domestic violence, depression, and substance abuse are interrelated conditions, which together compound the risks to children's healthy development (Zuckerman, 1994).

Although child welfare professionals have been aware for many years of a link between child maltreatment and drug and alcohol abuse, only recently have efforts been made to link the child protective and substance abuse service systems. In the past decade, professionals in both service systems have become more aware of the importance of an integrated approach, incorporating substance abuse treatment and help with parenting (Azzi-Lessing & Olsen, 1996).

One way that communities have attempted to assist those with substance abuse issues is through family treatment courts. These courts bring together legal services, social welfare services, and substance abuse services in the same courtroom with a permanently assigned judge to the case. Case managers whose task it is to link clients with services and monitor their use assist the judge. This close linkage of the judicial, social service, and substance abuse treatment arenas can help to keep everyone aware of progress and in compliance with time frames set out by ASFA (American Humane Association, 2002a). (See Chapters 8 and 9 for discussions of time frames and permanency planning for children of substance-abusing parents.)

Domestic Violence

Physical assault on children is much more common in households in which women are battered. Even if the children are not themselves abused, they may suffer neglect or psychological maltreatment associated with the abuse of a parent by another adult (Osofsky,

1999; Levandosky & Graham-Bermann, 2001). According to Barnett, Miller-Perrin, and Perrin (1997):

> Families where marital violence is occurring are generally experiencing high levels of stress. Children in such families are subject to self-blame, feelings of helplessness, neglect, abuse, and injury. Most likely, mothers in these families are psychologically unavailable for their children and are inconsistent in their parenting style. Fathers in violent families appear more irritable than other fathers and less likely to be involved in parenting. The children are traumatized by the threat of observing violence or becoming the object of physical assault. (p. 146)

Even very young children may be affected by violence in the home. Osofsky (1999) reported finding infants and toddlers showing "excessive irritability, immature behavior, sleep disturbances, emotional distress, fears of being alone, and regression in toileting and language. Additionally, some researchers have claimed that children may well suffer from PTSD and impaired development of trust and autonomy" (p. 36).

In spite of the clear link between children's development and domestic violence, professionals working in protective services and domestic violence services have often viewed themselves as having different mandates. Child protective services are highly regulated while domestic violence services generally operate with much less government oversight. Domestic violence workers generally are not named in state statutes as mandated reporters for child abuse and neglect and may view child protective services as indifferent to the needs of battered women or as punitively blaming them for their own abuse. CPS workers may view domestic violence as a failure of the mother to protect herself and her children.

Recently, federal legislation has addressed domestic violence, in particular, the Violence Against Women Act (VAWA) of 1994. States have started to enact legislation to require a connection between domestic violence services and CPS. Some states use child endangerment standards to prosecute batterers who attack their partners in the presence of the children. Approximately sixteen states now include children who witness acts of domestic violence in the category of children in need of protection. As with substance abuse, domestic violence treatment dynamics often conflict with decision-making time frames set out by ASFA.

Animal Abuse

Emerging research suggests that a link may exist between animal abuse and child abuse and other domestic violence. The American Humane Association's program, "The Link," looks at these possible connections. One study found that higher rates of animal abuse were found in homes in which physical abuse of children was substantiated (DeViney, Dickert, & Lockwood, 1983, cited in Ascione & Arkow, 1999). Garbarino (1999, cited in Ascione & Arkow, 1999) argues that professionals need to cultivate a "generic empathy for the victimized." Child protection investigators should be aware of the possibility for animal abuse while animal abuse officers should conduct a brief assessment of the children in households in which pets are abused. The state of Louisiana has mandated cross-reporting for animal humane officers and people who are investigating allegations of child abuse. California has legislation stating that county child and adult protective services workers may report animal abuse. Clearly, this is an area for further research and legislative intervention.

Parental Characteristics

Abusive and neglectful caretakers often have inappropriate expectations of their children. They may lack parenting skills and knowledge of child development, and are likely to have unreasonably high expectations of their children to care for themselves, to care for younger siblings, and to comply with parental demands. When these expectations are not met, the parent may assume the child is being willful or defiant and lash out physically. For example, a parent may believe that a 3-month-old infant who keeps on crying after being told to stop, just "won't mind" and needs a spanking.

Some parents have a very limited repertoire of techniques for guiding their children's behavior. They know how to spank a child but not how to use time-outs, explanations, negotiation, diversion, and positive reinforcement. Lack of knowledge of parenting skills, combined with lack of empathy and belief in authoritarian control can precipitate child maltreatment.

Maltreating parents may express more negative and neglectful feelings about their children than do other parents. Their interactions with their children are often limited, negative, controlling, and lacking in emotional nurturance. They may make many requests of their children but at the same time are unlikely to respond to requests from them.

Having been mistreated as a child puts a parent at greater risk of abusing and neglecting a child. Widom (1989), after reviewing research, estimates that about one-third of those who were abused as children will neglect or abuse their own offspring, and that two-thirds will not. Thus, the "cycle of violence" from one generation to the next does exist, but it is not inevitable.

The ability to form attachments is thought to depend on the quality of care the parent received as a small child, so failure to bond tends to get transmitted intergenerationally. Steele (1987) observed that parents who suffered massive emotional deprivation and physical abuse in early life often manifest a marked lack of empathy for their children. They seem unaware of and insensitive to their children's affective needs and moods, and are unable to respond appropriately. This deficit is observable in hospital maternity wards in the first interactions of the parent and child. The parent may seem cold, uninterested, and unwilling to attend to the newborn infant's needs. She may avoid eye or body contact with the child. Particularly when under stress, unempathic parents find the satisfaction of their own needs to be so compelling that they disregard those of the child (Erickson & Egeland, 1996).

Child Characteristics

Younger children, premature infants, children with developmental delays or physical or mental disabilities and disordered behavior, and children with irritable temperaments are at higher risk for abuse and neglect. Girls are at higher risk for sexual abuse. Infants, with fragile bodies, are more likely than other children to die of maltreatment (Berrick et al., 1998; English, 1998). Sadly, children already victimized are much more likely to experience recurrence of maltreatment than are children without a prior history of victimization (U.S. Department of Health and Human Services, 2001b).

Consequences of Child Maltreatment

Children experience disruptions to normal development as a result of maltreatment, leading to physical, psychological, cognitive, and social impairments. The extent of these effects varies depending on the age of the child when maltreatment occurred, the severity and duration of the maltreatment, the type of maltreatment suffered, and the individual makeup of the child. Effects on children of various kinds of maltreatment will be discussed in the individual section on categories of maltreatment. Here, we discuss two aspects that cut across categories: the tragedy of child fatalities and the phenomenon known as "the resilient child."

Child Fatalities

Each day three children in the United States die from abuse or neglect. In 2000, approximately 1,200 children died of these causes. The incidence of child fatalities due to maltreatment is probably underreported because some deaths officially listed as accidental death, homicide, or sudden infant death syndrome (SIDS) would be attributed more accurately to mistreatment (McCurdy & Daro, 1994). Fatalities reported in 2000 were more often due to neglect (35 percent) than physical abuse (28 percent), while 22 percent were due to a combination of both. Most child maltreatment fatalities occur to children under age 6, a fact that highlights the extreme vulnerability of young children (U.S. Department of Health and Human Services, 2002). (See Figure 7.5.)

To develop better community systems that can identify and monitor potentially lethal family situations, all fifty states plus Washington, DC, have established Child Fatality Review Teams. These teams are made up of representatives from health services, law enforce-

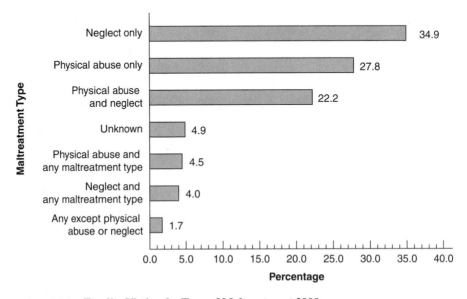

FIGURE 7.5   Fatality Victims by Type of Maltreatment 2000

Source: U.S. Department of Health and Human Services (2002), *Child maltreatment 2000: Reports from the states to the National Child Abuse and Neglect Data System* (Washington, DC: U.S. Government Printing Office).

ment, child protective services, the medical examiner's office, and the prosecutor. These multidisciplinary groups review the circumstances leading to the death, including the extent to which social and health agencies were involved with the family. The purpose of the reviews is to prevent future child death or serious injury, and many teams now focus on all injury or all child deaths, not just child maltreatment fatalities. They also develop and implement policies to improve the response of the community to endangered children (Daro & Mitchel, 1989; McCurdy & Daro, 1994; Durfee, Durfee, & West, 2002).

The Resilient Child

Some children seem to transcend seriously neglectful or abusive childhoods to become successful adults. It would be useful to know how this happens, as such knowledge could guide improvements in treatment interventions. Both environmental and personal factors seem to account for resiliency. Personal qualities of resilient children include good intellectual ability, a positive attitude toward others, physical attractiveness, enthusiasm, and an internal locus of control. External protective factors that may make a difference are the presence of caring adults outside the abusive family who take a strong interest in the child, and parents who, in spite of being abusive, are able to offer some family stability, expectations of academic performance, and a home atmosphere in which the abuse is sporadic rather than a constant, pervasive element. Additionally, such factors as access to good health care, education, social services, and other benefits of well-functioning communities also seem to promote resiliency in children (Starr & Wolfe, 1991; Fraser, 1997; Smith & Carlson, 1997).

Child Neglect

Physical Neglect

Physical neglect is the predominant form of child maltreatment in the United States. CPS agencies found over 500,000 children to have been neglected in 2000 (U.S. Department of Health and Human Services, 2002). Child neglect is more prevalent than physical abuse and causes more child fatalities. After many years in which professionals and policy makers tended to ignore child neglect, it is finally beginning to get the level of attention that corresponds to the seriousness of the problem. One reason for the "neglect of neglect" is that often it does not cause observable harm. Much of the damage from neglect accrues over time. It is the cumulative effect of malnutrition, lack of medical care, inattention to education, and emotional deprivation that has serious long-term consequences to the developing child. "Whether or not the child sustains physical injury, at the core of maltreatment is lasting damage to the child's sense of self and the resultant impairment of social, emotional, and cognitive functioning" (Erickson & Egeland, 1996, p. 5).

Some states define child abuse and neglect together as "child maltreatment" but most states provide separate definitions. Neglect is generally defined as "deprivation of adequate food, clothing, shelter or medical care." Some states make the distinction between parents who cannot financially provide for their children and those who fail to do so "for reasons other than poverty" with the latter group subject to investigation (U.S. Department of Health and Human Services, 1999a).

The condition of neglected children reflects the lack of attention they have received to even their most basic needs. Common signs of child neglect include chronic hunger, possibly manifested by a distended stomach; inappropriate dress, such as a lack of warm clothing in cold weather; poor hygiene, as shown by unclean clothing, hair, and possibly lice or other skin conditions; abandonment or lack of supervision; and unattended medical needs. Neglected children may display such behaviors as stealing and hoarding food; falling asleep at odd times or listlessness; frequent unexplained absences from school; self-destructive activity; and frequent reports that no caretaker is at home (Besharov, 1990a; American Humane Association, 1997).

Children's neglect may be directly observable in home conditions that affect them adversely, including dilapidated housing, insufficient material necessities for normal family life, overcrowding, and lack of privacy. Children may experience eviction and homelessness. A parent may maintain such low housekeeping standards that the family lives in squalor. Children may not have an adequate place to sleep. Young children may be left alone in the house or be left with persons who either cannot sufficiently care for them or actually threaten their safety. The home may contain physical hazards, such as poisons within reach of a young child, unsafe heating equipment, or unprotected stairways. Children may experience unwholesome or demoralizing circumstances at home—violence, excessive quarreling, substance abuse, cruelty to animals, or lack of love or concern for each other's welfare among family members (Helfer, 1987). In assessing neglect, it is important to be aware that poor home conditions may reflect lack of resources. Parents may be preoccupied with obtaining sufficient material resources for daily living. In these situations, caseworkers attempt to help parents get the resources before focusing on changing parental behavior. Often neglect reflects a combination of poverty and parental inattention, requiring a multifaceted approach to treatment.

Neglectful families are likely to be poor, to be headed by a single parent, most often the mother, and to have many children. They are often socially isolated, perhaps because they tend to be shunned by others rather than because they, themselves, avoid social contact. Other parental characteristics may include a lack of empathy, difficulty relating to others, impulsivity, and ineffective communication skills. They tend not to demonstrate nurturing behaviors to their children, and their interactions with the children lack warmth. Their lives often seem chaotic, with many conflictual relationships (Berrick, 1997). Neglectful parents tend to have a low opinion of their own competency and abilities, and lack a sense of well-being (Gaudin & Dubowitz, 1997).

Lack of Supervision

Lack of supervision (LOS) refers to situations in which children are without a caretaker or the caretaker is inattentive or unsuitable, and therefore the children are in danger of harming themselves or possibly others (American Humane Association, 1984). Also included are situations in which children are allowed to remain away from home overnight without the parents' knowing or attempting to find out the child's whereabouts, expulsion from home or refusal to allow the child to return home, and abandonment.

In a study of 375 LOS cases in New York State, Jones (1987) found that in many cases, the child was left unsupervised because the parent was engaged in some essential activity, such as school, work, or errands. In other cases, parents were socializing, engaged in illegal or irresponsible activity, or were hospitalized or incarcerated. About half of the parents believed that there was nothing wrong with what had happened. For example, a parent who left a child with a slightly older sibling may be convinced that the caretaker was competent. In most other cases, the parent did acknowledge a supervision problem but blamed someone else or said it was unavoidable.

Jones concluded that about half the families could have been helped with regular day care or as-needed baby-sitting. The other half of the cases were thought to need "supplementary child care . . . to shore up, stabilize, or enhance the caretaker's child care functioning," such as homemaker service, respite care, or foster care (Jones, 1987, p. 29). Day care alone would not have been enough to ensure the child's safety.

Unfortunately, the current welfare reform law with its emphasis on work for parents and insufficient funds for good-quality day care may exacerbate supervision problems for poor families. Lack of supervision may be unavoidable in many cases, particularly for older children whose parent(s) may not be able to afford or to find appropriate after-school care. Although parental education may be needed to inform some parents of minimally acceptable levels of supervision for children, this knowledge is meaningless unless good care is actually available. (See Chapter 4.)

Expelled and Runaway Youth

Adolescents told to leave home by a parent who has made no adequate arrangement for their care by others and who refuses to accept the youth's return may be labeled as expelled or "throwaway" youth. "Runaways" are adolescents who have left home with or without permission for an extended period of time. Although the circumstances of their departures vary, these teenagers may make up one homogeneous group who are characterized primarily by having extensive problems at home. Many have been chronically abused and neglected. The Family and Youth Services Bureau estimates that 1 million to 3 million children are expelled or runaways (U.S. Department of Health and Human Services, 2002).

Nonorganic Failure to Thrive

Nonorganic failure to thrive (NFTT) is diagnosed in infants when their height and weight are below the fifth percentile, if these measurements were once within normal ranges and if there is no apparent medical or organic cause for the condition. With organic causes ruled out, the assumption is that the parent(s) are failing to provide adequate physical, and perhaps emotional, care of the child (Wallace, 1996).

Results of NFTT can be serious. If untreated, it can result in permanent retardation, growth problems, and possible school failure. In extreme cases, the infant must be hospitalized and possibly later placed in foster care, where he or she can be monitored intensively until the medical condition is alleviated. In most cases the infant can be treated at home if the parents receive professional assistance. The first priority is to establish a reasonably successful feeding routine. Then, "the need for behavioral intervention should be addressed. . . . Mealtime must be relaxed, social, free of battles over eating, and without food being forced or withheld as punishment. Mealtime distractions should be minimal, and the caretaker should recognize the infant's cues for hunger, satiety, and food preferences" (Zanel, 1997, p. 378).

Skill and effort are required to establish the exact nature of the failure to thrive and its causes. A team of professional workers may be needed not only to diagnose but also to treat the ailment and manage the case at physiological, social, and psychological levels.

Case Example. The following case example shows how a health clinic social worker, in collaboration with a medical team, provided services to a family with a failure-to-thrive infant.

Mr. and Mrs. R brought their 8-month-old daughter, Miranda, to the hospital clinic on a referral from the pediatrician. Miranda weighed six pounds at birth and had barely doubled her weight. She did not roll over or sit alone and appeared listless. She was slow to respond to social stimulation and did not seek out attention. The medical social worker, Ms. G, reviewed the medical records and began exploring whether there was an environmental cause for Miranda's failure to grow and develop properly. While the social worker gathered family history and observed the family's interactions, physicians administered tests in search for organic causes.

Mr. and Mrs. R were in their early twenties and had not planned this pregnancy. They had been married eighteen months. Mr. R did not come home from work until late every evening although he worked an average number of hours. He did not account for his after-work activities and denied any alcohol or substance abuse. Mrs. R stayed home with the baby and was isolated from friends and family. She spoke quietly, without emotion, and avoided eye contact. Her appearance was unkempt although she was an attractive woman.

In the waiting room the couple did not converse or face each other. Neither attempted to engage Miranda or take her out of the car seat. When she cried, they gave her a bottle without interacting with her or removing her from her seat. During the initial interview, the parents were cooperative, but Mr. R made it clear that child care was his wife's domain and he did not feel he needed to be involved. He felt that Miranda's poor health was Mrs. R's fault.

Ms. G worked to establish a relationship with the family and engage them in the treatment process. She respected the stated family roles of the mother as being in charge of child care and reinforced her abilities to parent Miranda. She also emphasized the important role of the father in keeping his family healthy and functioning well, the importance of a male role model, and the special relationship fathers have with their daughters. Ms. G modeled how to hold Miranda closely and how to face her and make her smile. Then she gave Miranda to Mr. R and encouraged him to try to make her smile. As the parents interacted with Miranda, Ms. G praised their efforts, introduced new activities, and explained what Miranda was learning. At the end of the first session, Ms. G and the parents agreed that they would spend half an hour each day playing with Miranda.

In subsequent sessions, Ms. G continued to encourage the parents to stimulate Miranda socially. Mrs. R joined a community support group for full-time mothers and enrolled Miranda in a parent–tot swim class. A cycle began to develop in which Mr. and Mrs. R engaged Miranda, she would react, and the parents would be encouraged to interact again. Mr. R spent less time away from home and expressed pride in his relationship with his daughter.

As the family gained trust in Ms. G and self-confidence based on Miranda's progress, they were willing to discuss marital problems and other parenting issues. The family continued to strengthen as these core issues were addressed and the family developed a support system. The medical team continued to monitor Miranda's muscle tone and weight, which steadily increased. The parents were instructed in proper nutrition and exercise as well as child development. After several months of intervention, Miranda was approaching normal weight and had made developmental gains. Ms. G's intensive involvement with the family ended, but Mrs. R continues to attend her support group. (Gleason, 1994)

Medically Fragile Children

Disregard for Fetal Development.   Although it has been known for many years that pregnant women sometimes behave in ways that may harm a growing fetus, only recently have some of these behaviors been categorized as fetal abuse or neglect and come to the attention of child welfare agencies. Neglecting to get prenatal care and not acting on sound medical advice are ways that pregnant women might show insufficient care for the developing fetus. Reasons for maternal medical neglect include mental illness, particularly depression, mental retardation, and addiction to chemicals (Kent, Laidlaw, & Brockington, 1997).

Psychoactive substances used by pregnant women can affect the fetus's developing brain and cause learning disabilities and behavior problems. For example, pregnant women who use alcohol excessively may give birth to children who have fetal alcohol syndrome, a constellation of physical, psychological, and cognitive developmental disabilities. In 1999, the National Institute of Drug Abuse reported that over 5 percent of pregnant women used an illicit drug during pregnancy, resulting in approximately 220,000 babies who possibly had been exposed to drugs prenatally. The causal link between the mother's use of drugs during pregnancy and the condition of the fetus or newborn is not clear. One study found that 6 percent of children born to mothers who were dependent on heroin and 8 percent of children born to fathers dependent on heroin had significant neurological impairment and high incidence of hyperactivity, inattention, and behavioral problems. However, the developmental outcome of these children was greatly influenced by their environment after birth, suggesting that interventions should be offered not only during pregnancy but also during the children's developmental years (Ornoy, Michailevskaya, Lukashov, Bar-Hamburger, & Harel, 1996).

Scientific advances have made it possible to diagnose problems in the fetus and to treat the fetus directly, raising policy questions concerning the competing rights of the fetus and the mother. Judges and other policy makers are tempted to create laws that use restrictions or punishments to force pregnant women to adhere to medical advice as a way of protecting the fetus and ensuring its healthy development. Some women's advocates oppose such restrictions on the grounds that they constitute an impermissible infringement on the rights of women. Some states, such as Wisconsin, do allow custody of a pregnant woman with evidence of ongoing substance abuse and inability to control it.

Some state reporting laws require that newborns who test positive for drugs be referred to child protection agencies, though usually more evidence of ongoing drug use is required to trigger removal of the child from the home (Stein, 1998). States opting for statutes that require reporting of parents who use drugs during pregnancy should include safeguards against race and class bias in reporting. A county in Florida, which has mandated reporting for mothers known to have used alcohol or illicit drugs during pregnancy, found that African American women were reported at approximately ten times the rate for white women. Poor women were also more likely to be reported. The rates of substance abuse among all groups were quite similar, suggesting that race and class bias influenced the decision to report (Chasnoff, Harvey, Landress, & Barrett, 1990).

It is necessary to look at the reporting of fetal abuse in relation to the help such action will make available to the parents. If the purpose of such a report is to lay the groundwork for removing the child from the mother's custody immediately after the child's birth, mothers may become wary of using medical services for fear of this outcome. However, if the purpose of the report is to help the mother access services that would otherwise be unavailable, the report will further the effort to have a caring and capable parent for the arriving baby. "In examining the legal and social policy implications of fetal abuse, the question that must be asked is whether society's goal is control of the woman or protection of the baby. Ultimately, the child's interests will best be served by supporting the mother and providing the resources to meet her diverse needs" (Madden, 1993, p. 139). (See Chapter 2 for a discussion of the Supreme Court's decision in *Ferguson v. City of Charleston.*)

Children with AIDS.   AIDS is transmitted to children in several ways. Infected mothers transmit the disease to their children in utero, during labor and delivery, or postnatally through breastfeeding. Most of those who become infected prenatally have mothers who are intravenous drug users or are sexual partners of intravenous drug users. In addition to prenatal transmission of AIDS, children may become infected from blood transfusions, a particular risk if they have hemophilia. Adolescents are at risk for infection through sexual contact and intravenous drug use.

In 1994, the results of research were announced indicating that the drug AZT could reduce perinatal HIV transmission by as much as two-thirds in some infected women and their babies. For HIV-infected women and their infants to benefit optimally from AZT and other medical treatment, it is best for women to know if they are HIV infected early in pregnancy. They will then be able to seek out and receive the care they need for themselves and for reducing the chances of transmitting HIV to their infants (Public Health Service, 1995).

Many of the parents of children with AIDS or who are HIV positive are poor, are of minority ethnicity, lack medical insurance and health care, and are in ill health themselves. They are very likely to need the services of local child welfare agencies for help in caring for their children. Child welfare agencies are concerned, therefore, not only with the children's current well-being but also in testamentary planning for them after a parent's death (Stein, 1998).

Child Abuse

Each year in this country substantial numbers of children are physically injured by their caretakers in circumstances that cannot be explained as accidents. Moreover, their injuries usually result from recurring acts of violence rather than from a single expression of anger or loss of control by the adults who care for them. The severity of such injuries ranges from a mild form of abuse, which may not come to the attention of a doctor or other persons outside the home, to an extreme deviancy in child care resulting in extensive physical damage to the child or even death. After physical neglect, physical abuse is the most common type of child maltreatment. Boys and girls are about equally likely to be physically abused. Boys are more likely to be abused in the early grade school years, girls at the onset of puberty (U.S. Department of Health and Human Services, 2002).

Physical abuse includes such parental actions as hitting with a hand, stick, or other object and punching, kicking, shaking, throwing, burning, stabbing, or choking the child.

The primary symptom of child abuse is the evidence on the child of suspicious injuries that the parents cannot explain satisfactorily. Children often get bumped or bruised in the course of play and their daily activities, so not all injuries lead to a suspicion of child abuse. Physical indicators include unexplained bruises, welts, bite marks, bald spots, burns (especially cigarette-shaped burns or immersion burns in the shape of a glove or stocking), fractures, and lacerations. Some marks leave the shape of the object that was used to hit the child, such as belt buckles or hot irons (American Humane Association, 1997).

Abused children may also display behaviors that are suggestive of physical abuse. For example, they may be very aggressive or very withdrawn; they may complain of soreness, move uncomfortably, or wear inappropriate clothing to cover their body; they may be afraid to go home or continually run away.

Besharov (1990a) has identified a number of factors that lead to the suspicion that an injury was caused by abuse rather than by an accident. The location of the injury is important: Accidents cause injury to chins, foreheads, hands, shins, and knees, but injuries to other parts of the body, such as thighs, genitals, buttocks, and torso are often caused by physical assault. Corner or joint fractures are usually not caused by accidents but by violent shaking or twisting. Another indicator is the presence of old as well as new injuries. Although physical abuse can occur in a single episode, it is often a pattern of behavior that goes on over time. Children with injuries such as those described here should be reported to the child protection authorities. An accurate determination of the exact cause of the injury can then be made through medical diagnosis and social services investigation.

Physical Abuse and Reasonable Discipline

Society sanctions corporal punishment of children. Even though many people believe that any physical punishment of children is wrong and contributes to their emotional maladjustment, all states recognize the rights of parents to use physical force to discipline their children. The difficulty, for those concerned with reporting child abuse, is to differentiate between reasonable discipline and child abuse. Besharov (1990a) has provided guidelines for making this distinction. Discipline would be considered unreasonable if its *"reasonably foreseeable consequence was or could have been the child's serious injury.* This includes any punishment that results in a broken bone, eye damage, severe welts, bleeding, or any other injury that requires medical treatment" (p. 67). He points out that physical punishment of infants is always of concern because infants are not developmentally able to understand the reason for the physical assault on them and because their soft tissues make any physical violence dangerous. A forceful attack on the head of a child of any age is also dangerous and unreasonable punishment. In assessing cases of physical punishment, a number of factors should be considered, including "the child's age and physical and mental condition, the child's misconduct on the particular occasion and in the past, the parents' purpose, the kind and frequency of punishment inflicted, the degree of harm done to the child, and the type and location of the injuries" (p. 68). (See the Trends and Issues section, Chapter 3.)

Parent and Family Characteristics

Families of abused children tend to be larger than average. The caretakers tend to be young, with higher rates of abuse reported for parents under 27 years than for other age groups

(Connelly & Straus, 1992; Wolfner & Gelles, 1993). Poverty is strongly linked to child abuse, as families with low income and parents who are unemployed or lack a high school diploma are at greater risk of child abuse (Wolfner & Gelles, 1993).

Family structure also plays a part in child abuse. Single parents are more likely to abuse their children than are parents who live together. Abuse in single-parent families appears to be linked to poverty and may be explained by the stresses of living with very low income (Gelles, 1989).

Mothers' boyfriends are thought to increase the risk for abuse. Margolin's study (1992) supports this view. She points out that boyfriends have characteristics often associated with higher risk of abuse: being nongenetic caretakers, being male, and being located in a single-parent family. She suggests that the lack of an accepted, legitimate social role may put boyfriends on the defensive and make them more likely to react to perceived threats to their authority. Particularly if they are not supporting the family or fulfilling a parental role in other ways, they may be challenged by the children when they try to exercise authority and may then react with violence. Further, a mother's boyfriend may be in conflict with the children because both are competing for the mother's time, and the children may feel that the boyfriend is displacing their own father's role in the family.

Abusive parents are more likely than other parents to have suffered abuse themselves as children. They have learned negative behavioral models of parenting that they duplicate when they themselves become parents. Substance abuse or a psychiatric diagnosis of hostile or explosive personality are linked to higher rates of physical child abuse. Abusive parents tend to see their children in a more negative light than do nonabusive parents. They are apt to have inconsistent child-rearing practices, characterized by sporadic harsh coercion. Family members tend to communicate through arguments and other negative, hostile interactions (Kolko, 1996).

Shaken Baby Syndrome

Shaken baby syndrome occurs when a baby is violently shaken, which "repeatedly pitches the brain in different directions." Frequently, there are no physically evident signs of injury to the child's body, but the injury, on examination, is found in the child's head or behind the eyes. Injuries that can occur include "brain swelling and damage, subdural hemorrhage, mental retardation or developmental delays, blindness, hearing loss, paralysis, and speech and learning difficulties and death" (American Humane Association, 2002b). Shaken baby syndrome can be part of a pattern of abuse or the result of the caretaker's frustration with a young child. Sometimes caretakers simply play too roughly with infants, unaware of the infants' undeveloped neck muscles and fragile brain tissue.

Munchausen's Syndrome by Proxy

Munchausen's syndrome by proxy (MBP) is a rare and bizarre form of child maltreatment. The name is derived from Munchausen's syndrome, a condition in which a person, usually an adult, harms him or herself to induce symptoms of serious illness, followed by extensive and persistent involvement with the medical system. Munchausen's syndrome by proxy refers to the situation in which a parent induces such symptoms in his or her child. MBP has been defined as an illness that meets the following conditions:

1. Illness fabricated (faked or induced) by the parent or someone in loco parentis;
2. The child is presented to doctors, usually persistently; the perpetrator (initially) denies causing the child's illness;
3. The illness goes when the child is separated from the perpetrator;
4. The perpetrator is considered to be acting out of a need to assume the sick role by proxy or as another form of attention seeking behavior. (Meadow, 2002)

The incidence of MBP is less well established than other forms of maltreatment, partly because of difficulties with definition and categorization. Is it physical abuse or, as some claim, psychological abuse accompanied by physical abuse? Another problem is the difficulty of making the diagnosis and ruling out other organic causes of the child's symptoms of illness, and the likelihood that it has been concealed for years by parents who move children from doctor to doctor. However, increasing recognition of the problem suggests that it is more common than was previously thought.

A review of research on MBP identified fifty-nine articles on the syndrome, describing 122 cases from twenty-two countries (Feldman & Brown, 2002). In these cases, the mother was most often the perpetrator, and the majority of children were between the ages of 4 and 12. Over half (54 percent) of the children were male. The parents' methods of inducing the symptoms of illness in the child included "fabricating or inducing bleeding, administering harmful substances, falsely reporting seizures, and falsifying or inducing fever or failure to thrive" (p. 519).

The causes of MBP are not well understood, but seem to include both individual psychopathology and dysfunctional family interactions. To some extent, modern medicine provides a compatible environment for those with the syndrome to operate, with its invasive procedures, diagnostic testing, and medication trials, and with a lack of history taking, getting to know the family, and "expressions of empathy" (p. 519).

Psychological Maltreatment

The study and identification of psychological maltreatment, also referred to as emotional abuse and neglect or mental injury, has been hampered by the lack of a sound definition of the problem. In general, psychological maltreatment refers to a repeated pattern of behavior that conveys to a child that he or she is unwanted, worthless, valued only to the extent that he or she can meet others' needs, or is threatened with physical or psychological attack. Hart, Brassard, and Karlson (1996) developed an operational definition comprising six categories of behavior:

- *Spurning,* including belittling, degrading, shaming, ridiculing; singling out one child to do most of the household chores or to criticize and punish; and publicly humiliating
- *Terrorizing,* including threatening to hurt, kill, or abandon a child; placing a child in recognizably dangerous situations; and threatening or perpetuating violence against a child's loved ones or objects
- *Isolating,* including confining the child or placing unreasonable limitations on the child's freedom of movement or on social interactions with peers and adults in the community
- *Exploiting/corrupting,* including modeling, permitting, or encouraging such antisocial behavior as prostitution, performance in pornography, criminal activity, or substance abuse; encouraging developmentally inappropriate behavior such as parentification or

infantilization of the child; extreme overinvolvement or intrusiveness; and restricting cognitive development
- *Denying emotional responsiveness,* such as being detached and uninvolved, interacting only when absolutely necessary, and failing to express love and affection to the child
- *Mental health, medical, and educational neglect,* such as ignoring or refusing to provide for the child's needs in these areas (p. 74)

Psychological maltreatment is related to other forms of maltreatment; it is the psychological dimension of abuse, neglect, and sexual abuse. Terrorizing may be embedded in physical abuse; denying emotional responsiveness may be the psychological aspect of physical neglect. However, psychological maltreatment may also exist by itself, without other forms of maltreatment (Burnett, 1993).

It seems very likely that psychological maltreatment is underreported to child protection agencies. Although most states require reporting such maltreatment, the definitions given in state statutes are often vague or ambiguous. Psychological maltreatment is often difficult to prove, and generally must be tied to some observable harm to the child, such as "severe anxiety, depression, withdrawal, or untoward aggressive behavior, or as evinced by discernible impairment of the child's ability to function within a normal range of performance" (U.S. Department of Health and Human Services, 1999a, p. 10).

Children vary in how they respond to psychological maltreatment. Some children will direct their anger outward and become physically or verbally aggressive. Other children will turn their pain inward, becoming at risk for suicide, drug and alcohol abuse, and depression.

Children evidencing these behaviors have not necessarily been psychologically maltreated, so by themselves these signs of dysfunction are insufficient evidence that a child is suffering maltreatment. As a general guide for identifying a situation as psychological maltreatment, Besharov (1990a) suggests a two-tiered approach. For extreme acts of mistreatment, such as close confinement or torture, the parental behavior is sufficient evidence to ascertain that mistreatment has occurred. For less extreme forms, such as not allowing the child social and emotional growth or failure to provide a loving home, some relationship should be established between the parental behavior and the child's problems. Particularly important in a finding of psychological maltreatment would be the parent's refusal to accept help for the child's emotional problems.

Sexual Abuse of Children

Sexual abuse is defined in the Child Abuse Prevention and Treatment Act as

A. The employment, use, persuasion, inducement, enticement, or coercion of any child to engage in, or assist any other person to engage in, any sexually explicit conduct, or simulation of such conduct for the purpose of producing a visual depiction of such conduct; or

B. The rape, molestation, prostitution, or other form of sexual exploitation of children, or incest with children, under circumstances which indicate the child's health or welfare is harmed or threatened thereby. (Child Abuse Prevention and Treatment Act 42, as amended by P.L. 98-457, 98th Congress, 9 October, 1984)

Kathleen Faller, a noted expert on child sexual abuse, has defined sexual abuse as "any act occurring between people who are at different developmental stages which is for the sexual gratification of the person at the more advanced developmental stage" (Faller, 1988a, p. 11). This definition includes situations in which both the perpetrator and the victim are children as long as they are at different developmental stages. For example, an adolescent may abuse a latency or preschool-age child, or a child may abuse another child of the same age who is retarded. This definition assumes that sexual gratification plays a role in sexually abusive interaction. Even though other motivations may be involved, it is the sexual element that distinguishes this form of abuse from others (Faller, 1988a).

Sexual abuse includes various types of sexual behaviors, including oral, anal, or genital penetration; other forms of genital contact; the touching of intimate body parts; and inadequate or inappropriate supervision of children's voluntary sexual activities (Sedlak & Broadhurst, 1996). A definition may also include noncontact behaviors such as "sexy talk" or the perpetrator's exposure of intimate body parts to the victim. Often more than one type of behavior is involved (Faller, 1988a).

An unresolved definitional issue is when experimentation among children who are peers, or close to being peers, changes from exploration to abuse. A 17-year-old having intercourse with a 15-year-old may not be desirable, but may appear consensual with no ill effects that can be documented. Clearly, this is a different situation from one in which a 35-year-old is having sex with a 15-year-old.

Every year many children are sexually abused. Girls are more likely to be victims of sexual abuse than are boys and tend to be older when victimized; the median age of victimization for girls is 11; for boys, the median age is 8. In the last twenty-five years, studies have revealed that sexual abuse is much more common than people thought. Reports of sexual abuse have increased greatly since mandatory reporting began in the mid-1970s. This trend probably reflects increased willingness of the public to identify and report sexual abuse, not an increase in incidence (Berliner & Elliott, 1996). Unlike other more obvious forms of maltreatment, child sexual abuse can remain hidden unless the victim chooses to disclose it. In the past, victims very often chose to remain silent because they feared retribution from their attackers, because they were ashamed and blamed themselves for the abuse, or because they felt, often correctly, that they would not be believed. With increased understanding of the dynamics of sexual abuse, victims are more likely than in previous years to tell someone about the abuse, though it is still underreported.

Parent and Family Characteristics

Some family characteristics place children at greater risk for abuse. Although most stepfathers do not abuse their stepchildren, the presence of stepfathers in the home does increase somewhat the risk of sexual abuse for girls. Children in single-parent families and those in which the mother is disabled, dead, mentally ill, or out of the home for extensive periods are at somewhat higher risk than are other children, particularly if there are no other caring female adults for the child to confide in. Other parental characteristics associated with increased risk for children include reliance on punitive discipline, extreme marital conflict, social isolation, disorganized family life, substance abuse, and depression. Children from such families may be emotionally deprived and more susceptible to the ploys of child molesters who offer attention and affection (Finkelhor, 1993; Fleming, Mullen, & Bammer, 1997). Children with disabilities are more likely to be sexually abused than are other children (National Center on Child Abuse and Neglect, 1993). However, these characteristics are too general to be useful in identifying specific cases of sexual abuse. They are perhaps most helpful to social workers in selecting groups of children for prevention programs.

Sexual abuse that comes to the attention of child protective services is usually perpetrated by a family member, neighbor, or friend. The police handle cases of stranger rape and abuse. (See Chapter 4 for a discussion of sexual abuse in day care.) Patterns of sexual abuse vary widely. Multiple abuse episodes are common (Berliner & Eliott, 1996). In Faller's (1988a) clinical sample of 148 Michigan cases, on the average a given perpetrator victimized a child twenty-three times. Sexual contact was the most prevalent type of abuse, with noncontact abuse accounting for only 15 percent of the sexual acts. In more than half the cases, some form of force was used by the perpetrator to gain compliance. In cases in which force was not used or threatened, the children had a history of deprivation and abuse, and viewed sexual abuse as a way of receiving nurturance. Victims reported the abuse about three months after it began, on average. About half the perpetrators made some kind of admission or confession to the abuse (Faller, 1988a).

The vast majority of perpetrators are male, although women also commit sexual abuse. Perpetrators are characterized by a failure to control their sexual impulses toward children. They are likely to have suffered sexual abuse themselves as children (Sebold, 1987). As adults they often have ambivalent or hostile relationships with members of the opposite sex and have limited ability to develop intimate relationships or show affection. They also demonstrate excessive self-centeredness, strong dependency needs, and poor judgment (Bresee, Stearns, Bess, & Packer, 1986). Alcohol and drugs, which act as disinhibitors and also weaken guilt pangs, are frequently used by perpetrators.

Mothers of sexual abuse victims frequently have been abused themselves as children, or they were nonvictimized members of incestuous families (Faller, 1988a).

Case Example

The following protective services investigation concerns incestuous attacks by a father on his two young teenage daughters. It illustrates some of the dynamics of incest.

> The Smith family was referred to the agency by the police department. When Jill Smith was picked up for shoplifting earlier in the day, she informed the police that she shoplifted in order to get someone's attention. Her father had been making sexual advances toward her, and she was frightened. Jill indicated that the same thing had happened to her older sister, Nicki. [Nicki, Mr. Smith's daughter by a previous marriage, lives with her mother but saw Mr. Smith on visits.]
>
> When Mr. Smith was questioned by the police, he admitted that he made sexual advances toward both Nicki and Jill. The incident with Nicki occurred about two years ago when she was visiting the family for the summer. She was 13. Mr. Smith had removed her panties, touched her breasts and genital area, and penetrated her vagina with his finger. The incident with Jill occurred about a year later. Mr. Smith kissed her, putting his tongue in her

mouth, and he attempted to reach inside her blouse and touch her breasts. He did not try to undress her or convince her to do so.

Nicki returned to her mother's home immediately after her father made sexual advances toward her. She has not visited at her father's home since then.

According to Jill, her father had not made any other sexual advances toward her since that incident. However, he had begun to ask her to sit near him and to put his hands on her thighs even though she asked him not to do it. She described it as "creepy" and was afraid that he would try to become more intimate with her.

After questioning Jill and Mr. Smith, the police referred the case to the state attorney's office. The police also informed Mrs. Smith that she should not leave Jill alone with Mr. Smith under any circumstances.

[The CPS worker interviewed the family and learned that] the family consisted of Mr. Smith (age 39), a sales representative, Mrs. Smith (age 34), director of a day care center, and their daughter, Jill. Jill, age 13, is an eighth grader who is making satisfactory academic progress. The Smiths have been married for fourteen years. This is Mrs. Smith's first marriage and Mr. Smith's second.

Mr. Smith moved out of the home immediately after the police filed the report with the agency. He stated that he would continue to live away from home until the agency allowed him to return. He has scheduled an appointment with a psychiatrist at the local mental health center. He denies being sexually attracted to either Nicki or Jill, and he cannot offer any explanation for his sexual advances toward them. "It was just something that happened." He would like to resolve his problems and return to his wife and daughter.

Mrs. Smith cannot understand why her husband made sexual advances toward Nicki and Jill, and why neither girl had told her what had happened. She thought that she had a close relationship with them and that they trusted her. She is ambivalent about her husband; she did not feel that she could accept him as her husband again, but she hated the thought of living without him. She believes perhaps he did it when he was drunk and unable to control himself. Mrs. Smith expressed anger and concern over Jill's shoplifting. She thinks Jill told the police about her father not because she was afraid he would assault her but in order to elicit sympathy and get out of a sticky situation.

Jill reiterated the sequence and details of her father's sexual advances toward her to the child protection worker. She denies she told the police about his advances as a way of distracting attention from the shoplifting. She is adamant that she shoplifted purposely in order to have the opportunity to talk with someone. When asked why she did not simply call the police to report her concerns, she stated that she did not know that a report could be made by telephone. She hopes her mother will divorce her father. She said she hates him for what he did to her, for forcing Nicki to leave the family and therefore depriving her of a sister, and for the embarrassment his frequent intoxication caused her. (Proch, 1982, pp. 49–51)

Identifying Child Sexual Abuse

Child protective service workers may have great difficulty substantiating allegations of sexual abuse, unless the child or a witness discloses the abuse. Physical indicators include torn or stained underclothing, pain or injury in the genital area, difficulty walking or sitting, venereal disease, and frequent urinary or yeast infections (American Humane Association, 1997). Physical evidence exists in only a small percentage of cases (Rosenberg & Gary, 1988).

Sexually abused children may exhibit such behaviors as depression, excessive seductiveness, sudden massive weight loss or gain, substance abuse, suicide attempts, hysteria, sudden school difficulties, avoidance of physical contact, devaluation of self, and inappropriate sex play or premature understanding of sex (Browne & Finkelhor, 1986; Hibbard & Hartman, 1992; Chandy, Blum, & Resnick, 1996; Harrison, Fulkerson, & Beebe, 1997). Other symptoms can include enuresis, encopresis, fire setting, and cruelty to animals. By themselves, without physical evidence, these behaviors may not be enough for child protective agencies to substantiate sexual abuse (Oberlander, 1995).

Corroborating witnesses are a good source of evidence, but they rarely exist because sexual abuse usually takes place in secrecy. Perpetrators are likely to deny that they have engaged in sexual abuse, fearing rejection, shame, and criminal prosecution.

Children do not often make false allegations or misunderstand innocent behavior. However, interviewing sexual abuse victims requires specialized knowledge and techniques. Children making true allegations can usually give detailed information about the context in which the incidents occurred, and describe the sexual victimization and their own emotional state (see the following) (Faller, 1988b; Oberlander, 1995).

Legal Intervention

Legal entities that may intervene in sexual abuse cases include child protective services, law enforcement, the juvenile court, prosecuting attorneys, and the criminal courts. These agencies often are not well coordinated. Children who are sexual abuse victims may suffer additional trauma by having to describe the circumstances of their abuse to many investigators. If the case is criminally prosecuted, children face public court appearances, confrontation with their abuser, and cross-examination. The process may be even more painful if the accused is a family member rather than a stranger, because the child and others in the family may have mixed feelings about criminally prosecuting a close relative of the child. The child wants the abuse to stop but may not understand the need for legal interventions to stop it (Berliner & Barbieri, 1984). Decisions on whether to prosecute a sex abuse case through the criminal justice system depend on the plan that is developed to protect the child. (See Chapter 6 and the section in this chapter "Interviewing in Child Protective Services.")

Social Work Intervention

The first goal of intervention is to stop the sexual abuse. Victims need protection not only from further abuse but also from retribution from family members for disclosing the sexual abuse. Intervention possibilities include permanently removing the child from the home, criminal prosecution of the perpetrator, permanent exclusion of the perpetrator from the family unit, and reunification. Careful assessment of each parent is needed to guide case planning decisions. Nonoffending parents who are financially independent, or are able to become so, and who are loving and protective to their children can fruitfully be involved in a family rehabilitation plan. For perpetrators, key factors are their general level of functioning as providers and family members, the extent to which they acknowledge and feel guilty about the abuse they have inflicted on a child, and the duration, intensity, and frequency of the abuse (Faller, 1988c).

Individual and group treatment of sexual abuse victims can be effective in ameliorating the effects of abuse. Therapy is usually supportive and psychoeducational; topics include feelings about the abuse and the offender, education on sex abuse prevention, preparation for court appearances, and development of a support system. Treatment for victims with sexual behavior problems usually follows standard interventions for other types of child behavior problems, with a close focus on changing specific behaviors. Family therapy is often needed because the families function poorly; issues specific to the sexual abuse include helping parents work through their initial negative reactions to the disclosure and to the court procedures, and addressing the psychological distress of siblings, if incest was involved (Berliner & Elliott, 1996).

Cases of child sexual abuse raise particularly difficult issues for professionals in the human services. Many people are bewildered or repelled to learn that adults could have sexual feelings toward children. Discounting or disbelieving the child or rage at the perpetrator are understandable but unhelpful reactions, as are blaming the victim or the mother (Faller, 1988a). Another reason that sexual abuse cases are difficult to manage is that they require the specialized knowledge of several disciplines. As with other forms of abuse, the medical, legal, mental health, and child welfare fields each contribute needed knowledge to the resolution of sexual abuse cases. Multidisciplinary teams are an effective way for the community to respond to sexual abuse cases. Through a team approach the resources of the community can be effectively coordinated to arrange a case plan that is most likely to assist the victim's recovery (Faller, 1988a).

Survivors of Sexual Abuse

Children suffer in many ways from sexual abuse. The behaviors listed in the section Identifying Child Sexual Abuse show the powerful effects that these traumatic events can have on children's emotional and social functioning. Sexual behavior is common, manifested by excessive masturbation, sexual play with dolls, sexual statements, or behavior interpreted by others as seductive. These behaviors are the result, not the cause, of the abuse, and they do not imply acceptance of the sexual role by the victim (Faller, 1988a; Ryan, 1996). Many victims, particularly boys, become sexually aggressive, thus perpetuating the abusive cycle by victimizing other children (Burton, Nesmith, & Badten, 1997).

The effects of child sexual abuse can last into adulthood. Adults who were abused as children, in comparison to adults with no history of child sexual abuse, are more likely to have sexual disturbance or dysfunction, to report homosexual experiences, to have a diagnosable anxiety disorder, to show evidence of depression, to have difficulty expressing anger, and to have suicidal ideas and behavior. They are also susceptible to revictimization; they may be victims of battering, sexual assault, or rape. Women who have multiple personality disorder or borderline personality disorder often have child sexual abuse or physical abuse in their background. Male victims of sexual abuse are at risk for sexual dysfunction, gender-identity conflict, homosexuality, and an increased risk of becoming sex abuse perpetrators (Beitchman et al., 1992).

Persons who have suffered overwhelming trauma may develop posttraumatic stress disorder (PTSD), which is manifested by recurring memories of the traumatic events through flashbacks, nightmares, and intrusive thoughts. Studies show that between one-third and two-thirds of sexual abuse survivors suffer PTSD, particularly if the abuse was severe and of long duration (Berliner & Elliott, 1996).

Some survivors cope with the overwhelming pain of memories of sexual abuse through dissociation, including disengagement, depersonalization, psychic numbing, and amnesia. Clinicians and survivors report the phenomenon of an adult recalling traumatic abuse that occurred in childhood, after a period of not remembering these events. A controversy has arisen over whether these events did in fact ever happen, or if the adult is fantasizing (Loftus, 1993). Research in this area is still preliminary, but one recent study has found that many adult survivors of abuse report that they had periods in their lives when they could not remember their abuse, suggesting that it is possible for people to repress memories of traumatic events (Melchert & Parker, 1997). More research is needed to understand the relationship between memory and childhood trauma.

The effects of child sexual abuse on adult behavior vary; some survivors report very few symptoms, while others experience overwhelming difficulties. The severity of the adult survivor's problems are related to characteristics of the abuse she or he experienced. Serious, long-term adjustment problems are more likely to be reported by adult survivors who suffered abuse that was of long duration; was accompanied by violence, force, or threat of force; involved penetration; or was committed by a parent or stepparent rather than another member of the family or a nonrelative. Disclosure may increase the trauma to the child if it leads to the breakup of the family or to blaming the victim. Families that are supportive and have higher general functioning can help the victim's recovery. The ability of the mother to be warm, supportive, and caring makes a big difference in the long-term adjustment of her child to the abuse (Beitchman et al., 1992; Berliner & Elliott, 1996).

Ritualism and Child Sexual Abuse

Social workers helping families and children involved in sexual abuse may encounter, at some time in their practice, stories of bizarre, perverse, and sadistic sexual events. Descriptions of these events come from children and from adults recalling past abuse. These descriptions share some commonalities, including sadistic elements such as poking objects into body orifices; costuming, such as robes, masks, and animal paraphernalia; pornography; satanic rituals and belief systems; torture and sacrifice of animals and humans, including infants; and threats of extreme physical violence to ensure silence of the children. Events including these kinds of elements have been termed *ritualistic abuse,* defined as "abuse that occurs in the context linked to some symbols or group activities that have a religious, magical, or supernatural connotation, and where the invocation of these symbols or activities, repeated over time, is used to frighten and intimidate the children" (Finkelhor, Williams, & Burns, 1988).

Reliable estimates of the prevalence of ritualistic abuse do not exist, but the National Center for Child Abuse and Neglect surveyed professionals regarding their contact with such cases. In this survey, cases of religion-related abuse, such as abuse by clergy, corporal punishment to "beat the devil" out of children, and withholding medical care were included along with cases of ritualistic abuse. The study found that 31 percent of mental health professionals and 23 percent of prosecutors, law enforcement agencies, and child protection agencies who responded to the survey had encountered at least one case of ritualistic or religion-based abuse. The respondents overwhelmingly believed both the ritualistic abuse and the religion-related allegations (Goodman, Bottoms, & Shaver, 1994).

Reports of ritualistic sexual abuse usually involve multiple perpetrators and multiple victims, with males and females about equally likely to be victims (Kelley, 1996).

Therapists are aware of the extremely serious effects ritualistic abuse has on children. Affected children experience greater psychopathology than do other sexually abused children, with increased symptomatology and persistent fears related to their victimization (Jones, 1991; Kelley, 1996).

A central issue for therapists and law enforcement officials is the credibility of those who allege to have been abused. To date, most of the evidence for ritualistic practices comes from children and adults who claim they were abused as children. Very little evidence has come from police to corroborate these stories. Investigations of crime scenes have not found corpses or other physical evidence of violent murders (Lanning, 1991). More research is needed on this important topic before questions on the extent and effects of this phenomenon are understood.

The Practice of Child Protection

Public child welfare agencies have a number of functions related to the protection of children. They are best known for their work in investigating allegations of abuse and neglect within families. However, public agencies also have other programs that provide protection for children. In every state but Alaska, the protective services agency conducts investigations of abuse and neglect in licensed child care facilities, such as day care, group care, foster family care, and residential care. In this book, discussions of child protection in these settings are provided in the chapters on foster care and day care. In many states, the public agency is also responsible for investigating maltreatment allegations against nonfamily members such as strangers, clergy, school employees, coaches, and baby-sitters in nonlicensed facilities. However, many states have assigned responsibility for investigating nonfamilial maltreatment to law enforcement agencies (National Clearinghouse on Child Abuse and Neglect State Statutes, 2002).

Core Services of Child Protective Services

Child protective services in a democracy must provide safeguards for the rights of the child, the parents, and society; the development of clear standards and rules, as a basis for agency intervention; and the proper observance of legal provisions that will help to ensure that decision making is reasonable and based on relevant criteria.

Child protective service (CPS) agencies provide full geographic coverage throughout each state. These agencies vary in size and complexity, but they all should offer a basic set of services to protect children. Guidelines created by the National Association of Public Child Welfare Administrators (1988) emphasize that the purpose of CPS agencies is to assure the child's safety, but that "all decisions and activities should be directed toward enhancing the family's functioning and potential for growth. The agency's policies, procedures, and practices should reflect its focus on 'family based' child welfare" (p. 27). Figure 7.6 shows the

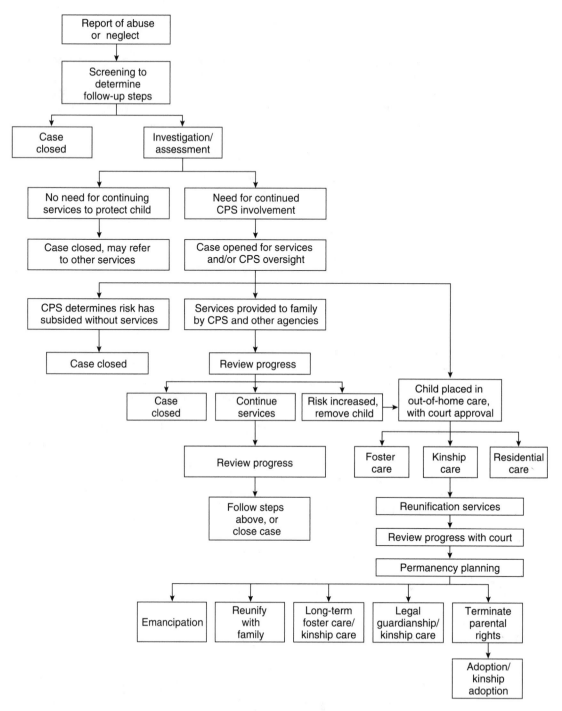

FIGURE 7.6 Overview of Steps Followed by Cases through the Child Protective Services and Child Welfare Systems

Source: P. Schene (1998), Past, present, and future roles of child protective services, *The Future of Children: Protecting Children from Abuse and Neglect,* 8(3). Reprinted with the permission of the David and Lucile Packard Foundation.

steps followed by cases through the child welfare system, beginning with a report of abuse or neglect.

All CPS agencies provide a basic set of core services, as follows.

Intake.   The intake service receives reports of abuse and neglect. When a member of the community makes a report to CPS, it is the function of intake to take the report and screen it for suitability for investigation (Wells, Stein, Fluke, & Downing, 1989). Agencies may screen out reports if the situation is not within the legally mandated mission of the agency, such as reports of delinquency, family eviction, or mental health problems.

Investigation.   The investigation involves the timely gathering of information, through contact with the child, the parents, and individuals who can provide collaborating information. CPS staff should be trained to conduct an investigation in an objective, thorough, but unobtrusive manner that is sensitive to the difficulties an investigation imposes on the family. The investigation should be done within specified time limits.

Disposition Determination.   The disposition determination involves timely decisions about the status of the abuse or neglect report and the need for further CPS action. In making the disposition, the agency should put the case in one of three categories:

1. *Unsubstantiated (not confirmed).* No or insufficient credible evidence of abuse or neglect has been identified.
2. *Substantiated (or confirmed).* Credible evidence has been identified that abuse or neglect has occurred.
3. *Critical sources of information not accessible.* For example, family moved, unable to locate; this category records the fact that the agency was unable to take action on the report.

The terms *unsubstantiated* and *not confirmed* are often misunderstood. They mean that the agency was unable to find credible evidence of maltreatment according to its definitions. However, it is quite possible that the family has some deficits in child rearing that are not serious enough to be labeled abuse or neglect but need attention. In this case, the families should be referred to agencies from which they can receive help on a voluntary basis.

Crisis Intervention.   Crisis intervention services should be available from CPS as needed during the time that CPS is engaged with the family, including the intake phase. These services should provide for immediate protection of the child and help families remain together during short-term emergencies. Crisis nurseries, domestic violence shelters, emergency housing, short-term placement with relatives, removal of the perpetrator, and twenty-four-hour emergency homemakers should be available to help stabilize families during a crisis (Gentry, 1994).

Case Planning and Coordination.   Case planning and coordination services are also the responsibility of CPS. For substantiated cases, the agency workers should design an individualized, goal-oriented case plan that clearly sets out what the agency expects parents to do in order to maintain children in the home. ASFA requires that parents be actively involved in developing the case plan and be aware of the time frames within which they must work.

Nature and Use of Authority

To make effective use of the authority essential to protective services, all those who provide these services must understand its nature and source, and convey it clearly and objectively; the parents, in turn, must be able to some degree to accept the authority if their child care and family functioning are to improve.

The CPS agency may provide the services listed on the case plan, or it may refer families to other service providers through purchase agreements. In either case, the CPS worker stays involved to monitor the parents' progress and coordinate the work of other agencies providing services to the family (Horejsi, 1996). (See Chapter 8.)

Discharge.   Discharge services are appropriate when the CPS agency determines that one of the following conditions exist: (1) The child is no longer at sufficient risk to warrant CPS involvement; or (2) the family is voluntarily receiving services from another agency to strengthen family functioning, and CPS involvement is not needed because the child is no longer at risk.

Central Registries.   A central registry is a centralized data system of child abuse and neglect reports maintained by states in compliance with their child maltreatment reporting laws. These registries are used to aid CPS agencies in their investigations and to maintain statistical information. In addition to CPS agencies, other individuals and organizations such as police officers, court personnel, and physicians may have access. Increasingly, registries are being used as screening devices for child care workers and foster parents. Central registries have come under criticism because the information is not always accurate or updated, and because of concerns about confidentiality for both the reported families and the reporter.

Although this is the model for most CPS agencies, it must be acknowledged that CPS is not always able to carry out these functions well. CPS suffers from high community expectations combined with insufficient resources. Staffing problems exist, including rapid turnover and low morale. Working with resistant, problem parents, with unsatisfactory care of children the pressing concern, is a heavy responsibility, requiring a range of knowledge and acquired competencies. Increased staff-development programs, lower workloads, improved relationships with the juvenile court, and skilled, available supervision are needed if CPS workers are to meet society's expectations of them.

Other considerations also interfere with the ability of CPS to meet the sometimes unrealistic expectations of society. It must be remembered that the job is complex, and most of the decisions are not clear-cut. Very few of the family situations are of the sort that make headlines; most are in the gray area of marginally adequate child care. Also, there is tremendous variation across jurisdictions in the staffing and organization of CPS. The values of court personnel and the workload of individual courts also significantly affect both service provision and length of involvement of children's protective services with the case. ASFA legislation, which requires greater court oversight and shorter time frames than formerly, can add to the difficulties of arriving at a fair and reasonable permanent plan.

These problems make it difficult to gain a consensus on what reforms are needed and what the appropriate focus of CPS should be. A further problem is that there are limits on the knowledge we have about how to intervene effectively in some families. Finally, a major difficulty for CPS is that it operates with conflicting values: On the one hand we are protecting children, but we also believe in the integrity and autonomy of the family. This conflict sometimes leaves CPS workers caught in a double bind and at best requires a careful weighing of factors before a decision is reached (Forsythe, 1987).

Sociolegal and Psychological Authority.   Authority is a complex phenomenon. It is the power to influence or command thought, opinion, or behavior. The key concepts—*power, influence,* and *behavior*—appear in definitions of authority, sometimes used in such a way as to result in a sociolegal emphasis, and in other instances, to focus more on the psychological aspects of authority.

Sociolegal authority stems from the authority of an office, or designated position, and the possession of this formal power is a legitimate one, a matter of right attached to the person who occupies a specified and socially endorsed position in the institutional structure of a society. Psychological authority, the power to bring about change through influencing behavior, is subject to another person's perception of authority and readiness to be influenced, directed, or controlled.

To be effective in protecting children from neglect and abuse, the worker must rely on and use both the sociolegal and the psychological aspects of authority. The worker who extends child protective services is given sociolegal authority by the law authorizing the agency to act in ways that will protect children from neglect and abuse. A caseworker's position and role in a publicly mandated child protective agency, then, embodies a legitimate and formal assignment of authority. This legal aspect of authority in child protection is expressed most centrally in the agency representative's duty to investigate complaints about the care of children, and if substandard care or maltreatment is found, to continue to visit the home until the level of care is improved or until the children are cared for adequately in another setting. Legal authority, then, brings what De Schweinitz and De Schweinitz refer to as the power "to be there" (1964, p. 288).

Although legal authority is a necessary element in protective services, it is not sufficient by itself. The power of someone else "to be there" can lead to an oppressive sense of restriction on parents that may only exacerbate their feelings of inadequacy and resistance to change. Whether the agency representative who exercises the authority "to be there" can then motivate neglecting or abusing parents to face their need to change—the first step toward improved child care—will depend in large measure on the extent to which the psychological aspect of his or her authority—that is, knowledge and skill in ways of helping people—is developed and used.

Psychological authority does not imply some intangible quality that a child protective worker may or may not happen to possess; it can be learned through study and experience. It encompasses an understanding of the law and administrative policies that relate to child protection, and of a community's standards in such areas as family life, health, and housing; the capacity to ascertain and evaluate relevant facts; a grasp of the nature of the protective worker's authority and an ability to use it constructively; sound judgment about the capacities of a particular parent; and an ability to develop, interpret, and implement a variety of treatment plans (De Schweinitz & De Schweinitz, 1964).

Use of Authority in Practice.   Authority need not be a necessary but negative part of protective services; it can be utilized as a factor to enable parents to fulfill their responsibility to
their children more satisfactorily. The social worker who presents authority skillfully can use
it to create a climate of communication that may motivate resistant parents toward change.

Certain difficulties commonly occur, however, and the social worker cannot expect
parents to be motivated simply because he or she comes to them representing an agency
with authority. This very action may tap a variety of negative feelings on the part of parents,
who probably already have had harsh and demeaning experiences with persons in an authoritative relationship. Parents who involuntarily become clients respond to the agency's
offer to help in varying ways, such as superficial compliance, hostility, passive resistance,
and belligerent defiance. Some parents are deeply distrustful of authority, while others may
welcome it as a means of escaping their burdens and responsibilities.

Whatever the parents' initial response, the social worker attempts to accept with empathy the basis for their feelings, but proceeds to identify objectively the areas of child care
that are of concern to the community and tells the parents the first concrete tasks they can
perform in using the service; for example, taking a child to a medical clinic, getting him or
her off to school each day, serving food regularly, following through on a search for employment, or applying for assistance.

One of the principal tasks of the social worker is to develop alternatives, or choices of
action, for the parents to consider, and to create opportunities for them to use their own
initiative to improve their situation. The social worker must convey that their freedom is restricted in only one direction—they are not free to neglect or abuse their children. Furthermore, the community endorses the right of the parents to receive help in improving their
level of child care before declaring them neglectful, and the social worker stands ready to
try to help them without resorting to legal action; but the community will not cease to be
concerned until the level of child care is improved, and the social worker "will not disappear or be denied" (Moss, 1963, p. 388).

The social worker in protective services cannot expect marked improvement immediately. The parents' problems are very great and their capacities are limited, so expectations,
although presented consistently, must be reasonable. Encouragement and endorsement of
even very minimal achievements toward improved family functioning are necessary.

In extending protective services, especially to very low-income families or families
with multiple and complex problems, one of the most difficult matters facing the agency and
its staff is the maintenance of proper balance in the use of authority. The families are difficult,
often exasperating, and defeating. The children are vulnerable and dependent on others for
improvement in their care. Citizens in the neighborhood and community are affronted by the
family and expect the social agency to act and effect improvement in the situation promptly.
Under such pressure, administrative actions that dangerously erode the right to direct one's
own life may come to be regarded as inevitable. It is important that administrative and legal
procedures be in place to safeguard the rights of the families, or these rights may be ignored
in an effort to respond to the problems they present to their children and to the community.

Informed Consent.   Recently, the issue of informed consent has arisen in relation to child
protective services. *Informed consent* means that "clients have a right to information about
the type of social work treatment they are about to receive and the efficacy of that treatment

in addressing their particular problem" (Regehr & Antle, 1997). However, when an agency needs to consider not only the interest of the client but also the interests of the community for information, an ethical dilemma can arise. Social workers need to be aware of the limits of confidentiality in child protective services practice and to inform their clients that information shared during the course of social service intervention may be used in court. See Chapter 12 for a further discussion of ethical issues in child welfare practice.

Decision Making in Child Protective Services

A number of factors influence the protective service worker's decision to substantiate a report of abuse and neglect (Jones, 1993).

Direct Evidence. Direct evidence of maltreatment includes physical evidence on the child and in the home; parental admission of maltreatment; the child's statements about the maltreatment; and the reports of witnesses. This evidence is valuable but is not always available. Sexual abuse in particular is often hidden; witnesses are not present, and parents have a powerful motivation to deny that the abuse occurred. Children may not be believed or may not be able to tell the story clearly. The nature and severity of the injury is often used as an indicator of abuse by investigators (American Humane Association, 1996). Medical research has provided useful information on differentiating between intentional injuries and accidents. However, workers may rely too heavily on the severity of the injury in substantiating abuse, and overlook more subtle evidence of chronic maltreatment (Jones, 1993).

Parental Response. The parent's response is often a key factor in the worker's decision to substantiate, particularly when direct evidence is not available. Workers assess the appropriateness of the parent's response to the situation and whether they can provide consistent and credible explanations of the child's injury. Workers are more likely to substantiate abuse if parents are uncooperative with the investigation. Assessing cooperation can be quite subjective; some families are uncooperative because of the way they perceive they are being treated by the agency; other families may be deemed uncooperative because of their appearance, because of their ability to verbalize feelings, or because of the worker's class or cultural biases. On the other hand, some parental responses are "red flags" of serious problems. In cases of obvious maltreatment, workers assess the extent to which the parents take responsibility for the maltreatment, express remorse, and acknowledge that the treatment the child received is harmful.

Child's Vulnerability. Workers are more likely to substantiate if the child is very young, has a serious mental or physical illness, exhibits unusual behavior problems, or is developmentally delayed. Other considerations are the interactions between the parent and child and the child's reaction to the parent, such as flinching or avoiding contact.

Assessing Risk and Safety

Risk assessment can be defined as "the systematic collection of information to determine the degree to which a child is likely to be abused or neglected at some future point in time" (Doueck, English, DePanfilis, & Moote, 1993, p. 442). Risk assessment, such as an investigation of a report of abuse or neglect, involves collecting information on the family. However, risk assessment is oriented toward the future; it attempts to establish the likelihood, or an educated prediction based on a careful examination of the data, that the child will be maltreated at another time. Risk assessment should be a process that continues throughout the course of CPS involvement, from time of initial screening of a report to discharge (National Association of Public Child Welfare Administrators, 1988). CPS agencies use risk assessment to prioritize cases for investigation and services, and to help determine the level of service that a family will receive. For example, a family rated as "high risk" would receive immediate and intense interventions, compared with a family rated as "low risk."

Items on risk assessment instruments are those that research and practice experience have shown to predict later maltreatment of a child, regardless of whether maltreatment has already occurred. The following is a list of risk factors compiled by the National Association of Public Child Welfare Administrators (1988).

- impact of parental behavior: CPS intervenes if behavior is serious and harmful even if harm to the child is not easily observed, such as psychological maltreatment or sexual abuse
- severity of abuse or neglect
- age and physical and mental ability of the child
- frequency and recency of alleged abuse or neglect
- credibility of the reporter
- location and access of child to perpetrator
- parental willingness to protect child and cooperate
- parental ability to protect

Risk assessment instruments hold promise of standardizing data collection and helping to make decisions more consistent within an agency, because all workers will collect the same areas of information on families and share, to some extent, a common understanding on how to assess the information collected (Schene, 1996). Risk assessment instruments are still under development and have received little validation so far when used under field conditions (Doueck, Bronson, & Levine, 1992). Proponents of risk assessment instruments emphasize that they are intended as an aid to worker judgment. They are not yet accurate enough to replace the experienced judgment of seasoned caseworkers and should not be relied on as the sole basis for case decisions (Doueck et al., 1993; Schene, 1996).

Protecting Children at Home or in Foster Care

A crucial phase of child protective work is the determination that children can be properly protected within their own home, or that they should be in foster care. The Adoption Assistance and Child Welfare Act of 1980 required agencies to make "reasonable efforts" to preserve families before placing children in foster care and encouraged the decision to leave the child in his or her own home. Social workers today generally hold that it is better to serve children in their own homes, whenever possible, and to extend social work effort to the strengthening of their family situations.

Nevertheless, not all children can remain at home, and some must be removed for their own safety and well-being. The Adoption and Safe Families Act of 1997 has specified situations in which "reasonable efforts" to prevent foster care are no longer required. These are

- parent subjecting the child to "aggravated circumstances" (e.g., abandonment, torture, chronic abuse, and sexual abuse);
- parent was convicted of (or involved in) murder or involuntary manslaughter of another child of the parent;
- parent was convicted of a felony assault resulting in serious bodily injury to the child or another child or the parent;
- or the parental rights of the parent to a sibling have been involuntarily terminated in the past. (U.S. Department of Health and Human Services, 2000b, p. 9)

In these situations, the agency may choose to place a child immediately in foster care.

Families that show only moderate child neglect are more hopeful in terms of preserving and strengthening the home as a place for the care of children. Parents in these families often have greater adequacy in their social functioning. They can be expected to respond in greater numbers to a constructive use of agency authority and social work services. Also, if a greater investment of the nation's resources is made to alleviate some of the serious social problems that impinge on these families, the outlook should be improved very considerably for strengthening not only these homes but also the level of child care so that foster placements need not occur. (See Chapter 8.) For a discussion of legal issues in maintaining children in their own homes under protective supervision, see Chapters 2 and 6.

Interviewing in Child Protective Services

Much of the evidence in a child maltreatment investigation comes from the statements of children and the families being investigated. Interviews for the purpose of gathering information are often termed *forensic interviews,* in contrast to therapeutic interviews, whose purpose is to alleviate difficulties of the client. Forensic interviews have an approach and practice methodology that are specific to their information-gathering function. (See Chapter 6.)

Particularly if the case goes to court, the information from interviews and the way that the interviews were conducted are essential considerations in the admissibility of evidence and the weight given to it. The quality of the interviews that investigators are able to conduct with concerned parties determines, to a great extent, whether the investigation will arrive at the truth concerning an allegation of abuse. The circumstances surrounding the interviews are often very difficult; the topics are ones usually considered taboo; children, particularly young ones, may not be able to explain events in a credible way; children of any age may not want to disclose the truth for many reasons or may recant earlier disclosures; parents may be hostile, fearful, defensive, and may be motivated to hide the truth rather than disclose it. For these reasons, social workers involved in interviewing families concerning neglect and abuse need to have expert interviewing skills and be able to use them in adverse circumstances.

Interviewing in child abuse and neglect requires the same basic skills that apply to all social work interviews. Suggestions for special techniques and considerations specific to forensic interviewing in child maltreatment are presented below, based on material from Wiehe (1996), Stattler (1997), and the American Humane Association (1992).

Planning the Interview

The interviewer should prepare for the interview by deciding its purpose, location, and who is to be interviewed, and making special arrangements for children.

Purpose.   It is important to have reviewed all available information prior to the interview and to have a clear idea of what issues are to be discussed. Usually the purpose of the interview is to obtain information on the allegations of maltreatment, and to assess the condition and safety of the child and the possible need for immediate protective intervention.

Interviewing Separately or Together.   In cases of maltreatment, the child victim is interviewed first, then the siblings, then the nonoffending parent, and finally the perpetrating parent. In cases of sexual abuse, it is necessary to interview the parents separately. In neglect cases, it may be more advantageous to interview the parents together, to obtain a more dynamic understanding of the family. Children should never be interviewed in the presence of the alleged perpetrator. Siblings should be interviewed separately. If the interview is in the client's home, neighbors or relatives may be present when the interviewer arrives. The parents should be consulted on the presence of others at the interview.

Age of Child.   Children under the age of 3 may not have sufficient language skills to be interviewed. Between the ages of 4 and 6 or 7, children can reliably recount events that they have witnessed, but the questioner must be careful not to influence the child's answers. The interview needs to be conducted at the child's developmental level, with consideration for attention span and special words for body parts and sexual terms (e.g., *pee-pee* for *vagina* or *penis*). Child-sized furniture and a home-like atmosphere will help to make the child comfortable.

Location.   The client's home may provide a convenient and comfortable setting for the family. Safety considerations, however, may indicate an office setting or a neutral meeting place, such as a neighborhood center, for the interview. Many initial interviews of children occur at the child's school.

Multidisciplinary Interview Centers.   If there are allegations of sexual abuse or severe physical abuse that may involve criminal charges of a perpetrator, it is recommended that children be interviewed in multidisciplinary interview centers. These settings provide a comfortable atmosphere for children, support staff who can answer parents' and children's questions about the investigative and legal processes, and the opportunity for prosecutors and police to observe the interview behind one-way glass or by TV monitor. This procedure will eliminate the need for children to undergo multiple interviews on the painful circumstances of their abuse.

Establishing Rapport

The interviewer attempts to create an atmosphere of calmness and mutual respect as a background for the exploration of the interview topics.

Respect.   Respect for those being interviewed is communicated through using titles, such as "Mr." and "Mrs." and explaining clearly the reason for the interview. "Hello, Mrs. Taylor, my name is Edna Mackenzie and I am from the county children's services agency. I am here because of a report the agency received concerning some burns on Robert. The agency has to look into the report."

Cultural Considerations.   Interviewers of the same ethnic/racial background as the person being interviewed may encounter fewer barriers to effective communication. Understanding the meaning of nonverbal communication, such as lack of eye contact, within the context of the interviewee's culture will reduce the likelihood of misinterpreting behavior. Non-English speakers should have an interviewer who can conduct the session in the interviewee's own language. Using a translator is a less desirable option.

Handling Resistance.   Acknowledging the interviewee's feelings may defuse the situation to some extent. If the client is angry, an approach might be, "I realize that my asking you these questions must make you angry." Passive, mute clients may be encouraged to talk if the interviewer acknowledges their difficulty: "I understand that it may be difficult to talk about such personal, private family matters." If possible, give the client an opportunity to vent anger, fear, and frustration before proceeding with the investigative questions. Ignoring hostility or fear will rarely make them disappear.

When interviewing a child, it is important to communicate respect for the parents, even if they have harmed the child. Children may depend on and be strongly attached to the parents, and become resistant if the interviewer appears to be trying to recruit the child into a conspiracy against them or to rescue the child from them. Children also need reassurance that they are not in trouble, and that the abuse is not their fault. If the child disclosed the abuse, they should be reassured that it was the right thing to do.

Types of Questions

The style of questions can shape the client's responses. Open-ended questions are more likely than other types of questions to elicit a full response from clients. With children, there is concern that the interviewer may lead the child to make up events or embellish them. Particularly if the content of the interview may become evidence in a court proceeding, it is important to ask questions that are unlikely to be challenged as having influenced the child's answers.

Open-ended questions and focused questions are preferable in forensic interviewing, because the children's answers are less likely to be influenced by the interviewer. In contrast, in multiple-choice and yes/no questions, the interviewer is providing information to the child that could influence his or her answers. Further, a child might select an answer in order to get the interview over with or for other reasons, but the answer may not reflect the reality of the child's experience. Sometimes, multiple-choice and yes/no questions are necessary, because more general questions may not elicit a response (Faller, 1990).

Particularly with younger children, interviewers use drawings, dolls, puppets, and other props as a means of communication. The use of anatomically correct dolls has been criticized as leading children into making statements, or implying sexual activity through their play, about sexual events that may not, in fact, have happened. In general, anatomically correct dolls should not be used in an interview until *after* the child gives indication of sexual abuse and is able to verbalize some specific details of the victimization (American Humane Association, 1992).

Another interview aid, anatomical drawings, are particularly useful with young children. Either the interviewer or the child may select the pictures. Children may draw on the picture (e.g., add or take off clothes, add or delete body parts). Anatomical drawings can be used in court as a visual record and have not been challenged as anatomical dolls have been (U.S. Department of Health and Human Services, 2001).

Aspects of Community Support and Influence

The way in which a protective agency discharges its responsibilities is influenced not only by the quality of its staff and its organization and structure, but also by factors within a community. Public attitudes and level of community support affect the responses of government, the professions, and voluntary associations to protect children from abuse and neglect.

Multidisciplinary Teams

An increasingly prevalent model for organizing community professionals in protective services is the multidisciplinary team. Teams consist of professionals from different fields, including social work, psychology, nursing, and law enforcement. Experience with the team approach shows that it is working in many areas across the country to provide consultation to child protective services agencies. Most teams have been involved in case planning, and some have also provided crisis service, case management, direct services to the family and child, public education, community organization and program planning, and advocacy. The team can work out of a hospital or be affiliated with a private or public child welfare agency (Bross, Krugman, Lenherr, Rosenberg, & Schmitt, 1988).

The use of a multidisciplinary team in relation to a particular case provides flexibility in the kinds of arrangements that can be made when a family crisis occurs. It helps to prevent a service from becoming wholly committed to traditional methods or narrow professional identifications because the variations in background, training, and special interests of the team members can be used to foster a climate that will stimulate innovation and response to newly perceived needs of families. It provides an opportunity for mutual support among staff members, which can lessen their need to receive some appreciation from a family or see some sign of progress prematurely. It can spread responsibility for crucial decision making—for example, for deciding when an infant can safely be left in the care of a parent who has injured him or her.

Advocacy Organizations

Tremendous public and media attention has been given to the plight of abused and neglected children since the reporting laws were passed in the early 1970s. Public concern for these children has found expression in a number of national advocacy groups. The Children's Trust Fund provides state revenue to fund programs to prevent child abuse and neglect, bypassing the traditional legislative appropriation process. Kansas was the first state to establish such a trust in 1980; currently, most states have established trusts. Revenues for the trust program are raised in various ways in the different states, including surcharges placed on marriage licenses, birth certificates, or divorce decrees, or voluntary checkoff plans using state tax refunds. The common feature of these methods is that they are separate from the ordinary state tax and revenue-collecting processes, and the money is earmarked especially for child abuse and neglect prevention.

The American Humane Association: Children's Division is a private, nonprofit organization located in Denver, Colorado. Founded in 1877 to protect children from abuse and neglect, its mission continues to be the protection of children and the prevention of child maltreatment. Its chief functions are to provide information on child maltreatment and to be an advocate for children and families in relation to effective service delivery systems in all communities.

The National Committee to Prevent Child Abuse is a volunteer-based organization dedicated to involving all concerned citizens in actions to prevent child abuse. Donna J. Stone, a Chicago philanthropist, founded the committee in 1972 out of concern for the number of infant deaths that appeared to be caused by inflicted injury. The committee's mission is to prevent child abuse through prevention programs, public awareness, education and training, research, and advocacy.

A backlash to child maltreatment investigations has developed in the formation of a citizen's organization called Victims of Child Abuse Laws (VOCAL), founded by people who stated that they were wrongly accused of abuse. It has lobbied state legislatures to drastically decrease the scope of child protective service investigations. The public also became aware of the possibilities of false accusations and false denials from caretakers, perpetrators, and sometimes children, particularly in the context of child custody disputes. However, these countertrends do not appear to have lessened public interest in reducing child abuse.

The National Center on Child Abuse and Neglect, though not an advocacy group, is included here because of the national leadership it provides in the area of child maltreatment. Established by the Child Abuse Prevention and Treatment Act of 1974, it is the primary federal agency with responsibility for assisting states and communities in developing capacity for child abuse prevention, identification, and treatment. The National Center allocates child abuse and neglect funds appropriated by Congress and coordinates federal child abuse and neglect activities. The National Center is located within the Department of Health and Human Services, Administration for Children, Youth, and Families.

The Child Welfare League of America (CWLA) is an association of more than 1,100 public and nonprofit agencies involved in the prevention and treatment of child abuse and neglect. CWLA establishes standards of excellence for child welfare practice and works to pass child welfare legislation. The staff publish child welfare materials, are available for consultation with public and private child welfare organizations, and convene conferences, seminars, and training sessions.

Trends and Issues

Appropriate Scope of State Intervention

What is the appropriate scope of state intervention into parental child-rearing practices? Some contend that neglect and abuse jurisdiction should be narrowed, giving a high degree of recognition to parental autonomy. They believe that, in the wake of large-scale public awareness campaigns, child protective service agencies have become overwhelmed with reports on relatively minor situations involving poor parenting practices. Besharov (1990b, p. 37) takes this view: "Many unfounded reports involve situations in which the person reporting, in a well-intentioned effort to protect a child, overreacts to a vague and often misleading possibility that the child may be maltreated. Others involve situations of poor child care that, though of legitimate concern, simply do not amount to child abuse or neglect." Current concern about the use of computerized central registries also relates to the issues of fairness, due process, and confidentiality for accused parents.

Others advocate extending the reach of child neglect and abuse laws. For example, Finkelhor (1990) disputes Besharov's view that the system is casting too wide a net. Rather, he says,

> The picture is of large numbers of seriously abused children, whose families and abusers have managed in past years to successfully evade detection, now finally being discovered by professionals and community members who have been sensitized to the problem. Many of these serious cases are still, for one reason or another, not getting into or are being rejected by the CPS system. The big overload of new cases does indeed make it difficult for CPS to work efficiently. But to deal with these problems, the system may need to be expanded rather than cut back. (p. 26)

Many social workers and juvenile court judges take a position somewhere between the views of Besharov and Finkelhor, often with considerable ambivalence. Clearly, some level of unsubstantiated reports is appropriate and necessary. The system depends on persons in the community calling in to report situations about which they have reasonable suspicions that child maltreatment has occurred. Only an investigation can reveal the truth of the situation, so it is reasonable to expect that some reports will turn out to be unfounded. There is agreement that the system could be improved in order to better protect children and become more proficient at targeting cases for intervention. Various reforms have been suggested that would help agencies and those reporting to become more expert at assessing situations and screening those cases that appear to need services. More education would help professionals identify cases appropriate for a report to child protective services. Clarification is needed on what kinds of evidence would justify a report, and on what kinds of situations can be considered abusive or neglectful, particularly in the area of psychological maltreatment. Agencies need to continue to develop procedures for prioritizing cases for investigation and for screening reports at intake, to ensure that potentially serious situations are responded to in a timely way.

Child Protective Services in a Comprehensive System

A problem related to the issue of defining the appropriate scope of child protective services is the one of configuring child protective services as a part of a comprehensive system of child welfare. Many are concerned that child protective services has absorbed a large proportion of resources available to child welfare, leaving gaps in services. Kamerman and Kahn (1990), in a survey of state child welfare agencies, found that the activities of public child welfare agencies focus on investigating allegations of abuse and neglect and on treating those families for whom maltreatment is substantiated. Families with less severe problems are not able to find help. Resources are also limited for needed foster care and adoption services for children whose families cannot maintain a minimally sufficient level of care.

Many forces have combined to create the current situation. The passage of the reporting laws in the 1970s caused a huge increase in child abuse and neglect reports. Public awareness campaigns contributed to the realization that many children lived in perilous or unnurturing environments in their own homes. At the same time, cutbacks in federal funding during the Reagan years caused services to families outside the child protection system to wither. During this same time period, social problems became exacerbated; the drug epidemic, AIDS, and a declining standard of living for young families increased the vulnerability of children to harm.

There have been a number of proposals for reconfiguring the child welfare system so that child protective services becomes part of a larger whole rather than the force driving the entire system. The National Association of Public Child Welfare Administrators (1988) has recommended that child protective services limit intake to a core of family situations, including physical and sexual abuse, serious psychological maltreatment, and physical neglect if the parent has the means to provide and refuses to do so. Under this plan, other service systems would be responsible for other family and child problems, in which help is clearly needed but not necessarily the authoritative approach of protective services. Situations that would be referred to other agencies include neglect cases in which the parent wants to provide for the child but has inadequate resources, and various child-centered problems, including status offenses and school truancy. The U.S. Advisory Board on Child Abuse and Neglect has called for a national child protection strategy that integrates the contributions of social service, mental health, and educational and legal professionals into a service delivery system offered at the neighborhood level (U.S. Advisory Board, 1993).

Jane Waldfogel (1998) suggests that a "differential response" is needed in the child protection system. In her proposed plan, levels and types of service would be available for different family and child needs. She recommends that informal helpers, such as relatives and neighbors, need to be more involved in preventing and intervening in child maltreatment. She points out that child protective services are not well integrated into the service system of the community. She cites family group conferencing as one very promising effort. In this approach, family members come together to make a plan for the protection of the child. If the plan works well, then the case may not need to move forward to court intervention. (See Chapter 8.)

Schene (2001) also recommends a two-tiered system, in which the most serious reports go to an "investigative track" while the less serious but still risky situations go on as "assessment track." The assessment track would include cases that are not substantiated. The alleged perpetrator's name would not go on the state child abuse and neglect registry. The important planning consideration for these families would be their level of need for services. This approach would allow ongoing assessment along with the provision of ameliorative services. A difficulty with the plan is that families would participate on a voluntary basis, which might cause some potentially very harmful situations to fall away from agency scrutiny.

Ultimately, the solution to enhanced child safety goes beyond the reorganization of child protective services. Clearly needed also is a renewed societal commitment to creating an environment in which children and their families can survive and flourish—a guaranteed, minimal level of income for all families that would provide adequate food, shelter, and medical care. Such a program would greatly reduce the stress on poor families and the child maltreatment associated with it. Sufficient long-term, effective programs for substance abusers would go a long way in reducing substance abuse–related child maltreatment, particularly neglect. School systems that are adequately staffed, with creative, energized personnel, can help to reduce children's problematic behaviors, which trigger some cases of maltreatment. A ban on the use of corporal punishment in schools would encourage parents and others in authority to learn other ways of managing children's behavior. A public backlash against the violence promoted by the entertainment industry would also encourage everyone to develop nonviolent strategies to resolve problems.

Staffing Child Protective Services

The quality of the staff in CPS is a critical factor in the quality and effectiveness of services provided to people whose lives are in turmoil, pain, and danger (Terpstra, 1992). Child protective service workers have an exceedingly difficult job. They deal daily with the misery and exploitation of some of society's most vulnerable members, children, and their families, who failed to protect them or who harmed them. They must confront the mistrust, hostility, and sometimes aggression of family members who may feel threatened by an investigative process that implicates them as having failed as parents. Workers function in a service system that is overstrained; hospital emergency rooms, the juvenile court, mental health agencies, and the public schools all may be overwhelmed with the seemingly insurmountable problems of those who need help.

The child protection agencies themselves usually have too few resources to help families or to provide the kinds of support the workers need to maintain a professional level of performance in their difficult work. The large increase in child protection cases has not been matched by increases in staffing. Many agencies report difficulty in recruiting staff because of low salaries and high caseloads. Lack of resources has forced some agencies to hire staff with no experience and, in some cases, without a college degree, even though the work they perform requires them to make accurate assessments about confusing and highly charged family situations (National Commission, 1990). Workers complain that they do not get the support they need, yet are blamed by the public and their own administrators if a child on their caseload is harmed in a situation which, in retrospect, seemed preventable.

A major challenge for the coming decade is to improve the quality of staff and the conditions in which they work. Some have called for a return of the close alliance between the social work profession, including social work education, and child welfare services. Social work is the conceptual parent of child welfare services, but "in recent decades that connection has largely been lost, as has much of the conceptual social work base" to child protective services (Terpstra, 1992). To remedy this situation, schools of social work are renewing their commitment to make social work education relevant to the needs of public child welfare services, and agencies are becoming increasingly committed to hiring staff with a social work education and to involving schools of social work in ongoing staff training (Briar, Hansen, & Harris, 1992). Using federal funds (Title IV-E), schools of social work have developed curricula specifically for child welfare workers at both the BSW and MSW levels, and in many cases are able to pay the tuition of students who are currently employed in child welfare agencies or plan child welfare careers after graduation.

These efforts, even when fully implemented, will not be enough to ensure a high quality of child protective services. Increased resources for agencies are needed as well, so they can hire qualified staff, assign them manageable caseloads, and offer competent supervision in well-managed agencies.

Chapter Summary

Media reports of abused and neglected children disturb us and make us aware of the appalling conditions in which many children live. Child protective services represents the organized response of each community to the circumstances of mistreated children and their families. Every year, about 3 million children come to the attention of child protective services, although only a percentage of the situations reported are "substantiated" or "confirmed" for abuse and neglect. Currently, the percentage of substantiated cases is about 25 percent. Child abuse and neglect are often hidden from the scrutiny of neighbors and professionals, and these cases are not reported, so the actual extent of child maltreatment is unknown. However, various surveys indicate that the number of cases reported to child protective services is only a small proportion of the total.

Types of maltreatment are neglect (including physical neglect, abandonment, lack of supervision, and medical neglect), which comprise more than half of all cases of mistreatment; abuse, comprising about a quarter of all cases of mistreatment; sexual abuse; psychological maltreatment; and educational neglect. Many times, more than one type of maltreatment is involved.

Violence toward children has been pervasive in American history. During the nineteenth century, concerned citizens formed societies for the prevention of cruelty to children, to investigate instances of child abuse and report them to the police. These societies (SPCCs) are the precursors of today's child protective services agencies. In the 1960s, the "discovery" of the battered child syndrome led to the passage of the Child Abuse Prevention and Treatment Act in 1974 and ushered in a new era of child protection.

Today all states have reporting laws, which require professionals to report all cases of suspected child abuse or neglect to CPS. However, the implementation of these laws is hampered by the lack of clear definitions of types of child abuse and neglect. Factors to be considered in definitions are the severity of the harm, the cumulative harm to the child over time, endangerment of the child even if the child has not yet suffered observable harm, intentional harm versus accidental harm, and cultural issues.

There are problems with overreporting and underreporting child maltreatment. About 30 percent of all reports are substantiated, which leaves many parents feeling that they have suffered an invasion of privacy and the stigma of having been the focus of a child abuse investigation. On the other hand, many cases of maltreatment are not reported because the potential reporters believe that reporting will not help the family and may make matters worse.

The causes of child maltreatment are complex and overlapping, and are best understood from an ecological perspective. No one factor causes abuse or neglect, but rather a combination of circumstances. Risk factors include social conditions, such as deprived, dangerous neighborhoods with few supports or social services and widespread societal tolerance for interpersonal violence. Poverty is highly associated with all forms of maltreatment and is the single most important risk factor for children. Race and ethnicity do not appear to be related to maltreatment, though people of color are more likely to be reported to CPS. Many family and parental characteristics and conditions are associated with abuse and neglect, including single parenthood, mental illness, substance abuse, domestic violence, social isolation, and a history of having been mistreated as children (though many children who are maltreated do not grow up to mistreat other children). Maltreating parents tend to lack empathy, express negative attitudes and hostility to their children, lack the ability to form attachments, and use the children to meet their own needs.

Children suffer in many ways from maltreatment, including death, permanent injury, and impaired physical, cognitive, social, and emotional development.

All child protective service agencies offer a set of core services, including intake, investigation, and case planning. While investigating families, the workers must also assess the current and future risk to the child, and take steps to remove the offender or child from the home when necessary. The preference is to maintain the child in his or her own home, if possible, by providing services to help the family. CPS workers have the legal authority to intervene in the lives of families and must develop strategies for using that authority to help parents achieve a minimally sufficient level of care.

A major issue today is the appropriate scope and authority of child protective services. One view is that CPS should be involved only for serious cases of child maltreatment and that less serious situations should be referred to other social service agencies. It is thought that this would protect families from needless intrusive investigations and free up resources for the most serious situations. Others believe that CPS should be expanded, because many abused and neglected children are not receiving any services and may, in fact, be unknown to any social service agency. Many policy makers believe that CPS must become more connected to the community, through partnerships with schools, police, and neighborhood groups, to form a comprehensive system for protecting and serving children.

FOR STUDY AND DISCUSSION

1. Discuss how the ecological approach is useful in understanding child maltreatment. What interventions using an ecological approach would be most effective for each of the different categories of child maltreatment?

2. Discuss how the historical development of children's protective services has resulted in the system we have today. What benefits do you see in today's child protection system? What are the disadvantages?

3. Discuss whether you think that some forms of child maltreatment are more serious than others and why.

4. Discuss whether the current ASFA legislation will benefit or hinder efforts to maintain the integrity of the family and to ensure the safety of children.

5. Discuss the feasibility of having two levels of definitions of child abuse and neglect: narrow definitions of the various categories of maltreatment for legal purposes and broad definitions for the purpose of determining the need for services. Give examples of narrow and broad definitions for one of the categories of child maltreatment.

6. In view of the characteristics of neglected and abused children as you have come to see them, make suggestions for new treatment approaches in direct work with such children.

7. Draw together what you regard as significant aspects of agency organization and community support if effective protective services are to be provided. Then study the protective service agency in your community in relation to these aspects.

8. Read transcripts or watch videotapes of interviews with children or adults in protective service investigations. Observe and comment on the techniques used by the interviewer.

9. Obtain a risk assessment guide or a protocol for a child maltreatment investigation from your local child protective services agency. Comment on its usefulness as a decision-making guide.

FOR ADDITIONAL STUDY

American Humane Association. (1996). *Guidebook for the visual assessment of physical child abuse.* Englewood, CO: Author.

Berrick, J. D. (1997). Child neglect: Definition, incidence, outcomes. In J. D. Berrick, R. Barth, & N. Gilbert, (Eds.), *Child welfare research review, vol. 2* (pp. 1–84). New York: Columbia University Press.

Briere, J., Berliner, L., Bulkley, J. A., Jenny, C., & Reid, T. (Eds.). (1996). *The APSAC handbook on child maltreatment.* Thousand Oaks: Sage.

Center for the Future of Children. (1998, Spring). *The future of children: Protecting children from abuse and neglect, 8*(1).

Faller, K. C. (1988). *Child sexual abuse: An interdisciplinary manual for diagnosis, case management, and treatment.* New York: Columbia University Press.

Helfer, R. E., & Kempe, R. S. (1987). *The battered child* (4th ed.). Chicago: University of Chicago Press.

Melton, G. B., & Barry, F. D. (Eds.). (1994). *Protecting children from abuse and neglect.* New York: Guilford Press.

National Association of Public Child Welfare Administrators. (1988). *Guidelines for a model system of protective services for abused and neglected children and their families.* Washington, DC: American Public Welfare Association.

Sedlak, A. J., & Broadhurst, D. D. (1996). *Third national incidence study of child abuse and neglect.* Washington, DC: U.S. Department of Health and Human Services.

Wiehe, V. R. (1996). *Working with child abuse and neglect: A primer.* Thousand Oaks, CA: Sage.

INTERNET SEARCH TERMS

Child abuse

Child neglect

Child protective services

Domestic violence

Sexual abuse

Substance abuse

INTERNET SITES

American Humane Association. This national advocacy organization for abused and neglected children has numerous resources on policy and practice in child protective services.

www.americanhumane.org

Children's Bureau, Administration for Children, Youth, and Families, U.S. Department of Health and Human Services. Contains information on federal initiatives in foster care and adoption and statistics, child abuse and neglect, and other programs.

www.acf.dhhs.gov/programs/cb

National Child Welfare Resource Center for Family-Centered Practice. The center helps child welfare agency managers and staff translate the tenets of the Adoption and Safe Families Act of 1997 into family-centered practices that ensure the well-being and permanent placement of children while meeting the needs of families. In particular, the center helps clients learn how to forge linkages among the child welfare system, other support systems for families, and the courts, especially in the areas of substance abuse treatment and domestic violence.

www.cwresource.org

National Child Welfare Resource Center on Legal and Judicial Issues. The center provides expertise to clients on legal aspects of child welfare, including court improvement, agency and court collaboration, timely decisions on termination of parental rights, nonadversarial case resolution, reasonable efforts requirements, legal representation of children, permanent guardianship, confidentiality, and other emerging child welfare issues.

www.abanet.org/child

National Clearinghouse on Child Abuse and Neglect Information.   This is a national resource for professionals seeking information on the prevention, identification, and treatment of child abuse and neglect, and related child welfare issues. The National Center for Child Abuse and Neglect may be accessed at this web site. The site contains numerous resources and links to other sites.

www.calib.com/nccanch

National Committee to Prevent Child Abuse.   This is the web site of a national advocacy organization whose purpose is to prevent and reduce child maltreatment. The site has numerous resources for advocates, including information packets, publications of statistics and trends, and lists of local chapters.

www.childabuse.org

National Resource Center on Child Maltreatment (NRCCM).   The NRCCM serves publicly supported child welfare agencies in developing effective and efficient child protective service organizational systems. Its objectives are to identify, develop, and promote the application of CPS practice models that are responsive to state, tribal, and community needs and to facilitate the connections that are essential for coordinated and integrated CPS service delivery.

www.gocwi.org/nrccm

National Resource Center on the Link between Violence to People and Animals.   This center, part of the American Humane Association, has the function of assisting professionals interested in preventing violence by providing resources and training regarding the connection between human violence and animal cruelty.

www.americanhumane.org

REFERENCES

Abbott, G. (1938). *The child and the state, vols. I & II.* Chicago: University of Chicago Press.

Ahn, H. N., & Gilbert, N. (1992, September). Cultural diversity and sexual abuse prevention. *Social Service Review, 66,* 410–427.

American Humane Association. (1984). *Trends in officially reported child neglect and abuse.* Denver: American Humane Association, Child Protection Division.

American Humane Association. (1992). *Helping in child protective services.* Englewood, CO: Author.

American Humane Association. (1996). *Guidebook for the visual assessment of physical child abuse.* Englewood, CO: Author.

American Humane Association. (1997). *Guidelines to help protect abused and neglected children.* Englewood, CO: Author.

American Humane Association. (2002a). Family treatment court: Significant results in recovery and reunification. *Child Protection Leader.* Englewood, CO: Author.

American Humane Association. (2002b). Fact sheet: Shaken baby syndrome. Available: www.americanhumane.org.

Ards, S., Chung, C., & Myers, S. (1998). The effects of sample selection bias on racial differences in child abuse reporting. *Child Abuse & Neglect, 22*(2), 103–115.

Ascione, F. R., & Arkow, P. (1999). *Child abuse, domestic violence and animal abuse.* West Lafayette, IN: Purdue University Press.

Azzi-Lessing, L., & Olsen, L. J. (1996). Substance abuse–affected families in the child welfare system: New challenges, new alliances. *Social Work, 41*(1), 15–23.

Barnett, O., Miller-Perrin, C., & Perrin, R. (1997). *Family violence across the lifespan.* Thousand Oaks, CA: Sage.

Barth, R. (2001a, March–April). Research outcomes of prenatal substance exposure and the need to review policies and procedures regarding child abuse reporting. *Child Welfare, 80*(2), 275–296.

Beitchman, J. H., Zucker, K. J., Hood, J. E., DaCosta, G. R., Akman, D., & Cassavia, E. (1992). A review of the long-term effects of child sexual abuse. *Child Abuse & Neglect, 16,* 101–118.

Belsky, J. (1993). Etiology of child maltreatment: A developmental-ecological analysis. *Psychological Bulletin, 114,* 413–434.

Berliner, L., & Barbieri, M. K. (1984). The testimony of the child victim of sexual assault. *Journal of Social Issues, 40*(2), 125–137.

Berliner, L., & Elliott, D. M. (1996). Sexual abuse of children. In J. Briere, L. Berliner, J. A. Bulkley, C. Jenny, & T. Reid (Eds.), *The APSAC handbook on child maltreatment* (pp. 51–71). Thousand Oaks, CA: Sage.

Berrick, J. D. (1997). Child neglect: Definition, incidence, outcomes. In J. D. Berrick, R. P. Barth, & N. Gilbert (Eds.), *Child welfare research review, vol. 2* (pp. 1–12). New York: Columbia University Press.

Berrick, J. D., Needell, B., Barth, R. P., & Jonson-Reid, M. (1998). *The tender years: Toward developmentally sensitive child welfare services for very young children.* New York: Oxford University Press.

Besharov, D. (1990a). *Recognizing child abuse: A guide for the concerned.* New York: Free Press.

Besharov, D. (1990b). Gaining control over child abuse reports. *Public Welfare, 48,* 34–41.

Besharov, D. J., & Laumann, L. A. (1996). Child abuse reporting. *Society, 33*(4), 40–46.

Bresee, P., Stearns, G. B., Bess, B. H., & Packer, L. S. (1986). Allegations of child sexual abuse in child custody disputes: A therapeutic assessment model. *American Journal of Orthopsychiatry, 56*(4), 560–569.

Briar, K. H., Hansen, V. H., & Harris, N. (Eds.). (1992). *New partnerships: Proceedings from the National Public Child Welfare Training Symposium, 1991.* Miami: Florida International University.

Bross, D., Krugman, R., Lenherr, M., Rosenberg, D., & Schmitt, B. (Eds.). (1988). *The new child protection team handbook.* New York: Garland.

Browne, A., & Finkelhor, D. (1986). Impact of child sexual abuse: A review of the research. *Psychological Bulletin, 99,* 66–77.

Burnett, B. (1993). The psychological abuse of latency age children: A survey. *Child Abuse & Neglect, 17,* 441–454.

Burton, D. L., Nesmith, A. A., & Badten, L. (1997). Clinician's views on sexually aggressive children and their families: A theoretical exploration. *Child Abuse & Neglect, 21*(2), 157–170.

Carter v. Kaufman, 8 Ca.App.3d 783, 87 Ca. Rptr. 678 (1970), *cert. denied,* 402 U.S. 964 (1971). (J. Black dissenting in separate opinion at 402 U.S. 954, 959).

Chandy, J. M., Blum, R. W., & Resnick, M. (1996). History of sexual abuse and parental alcohol misuse: Risk, outcomes and protective factors in adolescents. *Child and Adolescent Social Work Journal, 13*(5), 411–432.

Chasnoff, I. J., Harvey, M. D., Landress, J., & Barrett, M. E. (1990). The prevalence of illicit-drug or alcohol use during pregnancy and discrepancies in mandatory reporting in Pinellas County, Florida. *The New England Journal of Medicine, 322*(17), 1202–1206.

Child Abuse Prevention and Treatment Act, Public Law 93-247, 42 U.S.C.A. 510g (1974, amended 1996).

Child Welfare League of America. (2001). *Alcohol, other drugs and child welfare.* Washington, DC: Author.

Cohen, N. A. (Ed.). (2000). *Child welfare: A multicultural focus.* Boston: Allyn & Bacon.

Connelly, C. D., & Straus, M. (1992). Mother's age and risk for physical abuse. *Child Abuse & Neglect, 16*(5), 709–718.

Costin, L. B. (1992). Cruelty to children: A dormant issue and its rediscovery, 1920–1960. *Social Service Review, 66*(2), 177–198.

Daro, D., & Mitchel, L. (1989). *Child abuse fatalities continue to rise: The results of the 1988 annual fifty-state survey.* (Working Paper Number 808). Chicago: National Committee for the Prevention of Child Abuse, National Center on Child Abuse Prevention Research.

Deisz, R., Doueck, J. J., George, N., & Levine, M. (1996). Reasonable cause: A qualitative study of mandated reporting. *Child Abuse & Neglect, 20*(4), 275–287.

De Schweinitz, E., & De Schweinitz, K. (1964). The place of authority in the protective function of the public welfare agency. *Child Welfare, 43*(6), 286–291.

Doueck, H. J., Bronson, D. E., & Levine, M. (1992). Evaluating risk assessment implementation in child protection: Issues for consideration. *Child Abuse & Neglect, 16*(5), 637–646.

Doueck, H. J., English, D. J., DePanfilis, D., & Moote, G. T. (1993). Decision-making in child protective services: A comparison of selected risk-assessment systems. *Child Welfare, 72*(5), 441–452.

Duqette, D. N. (1988). Legal interventions. In K. C. Faller, *Child sexual abuse: An interdisciplinary manual for diagnosis, case management, and treatment.* New York: Columbia University Press.

Durfee, M., Durfee, D., & West, P. M. (2002). Child fatality review: An international movement. *Child Abuse & Neglect, 26,* 219–236.

Earle, K. A. (2000). *Child abuse and neglect: An examination of American Indian data.* Seattle: Casey Family Programs and NICWA.

Earle, K. A., & Cross, A. (2001). *Child abuse and neglect among American Indian, Alaska native children: An analysis of existing data.* Seattle: Casey Family Programs.

English, D. (1998). The extent and consequences of child maltreatment. *The Future of Children: Protecting Children from Abuse and Neglect, 8*(1), 39–53.

Erickson, M. F., & Egeland, B. (1996). Child neglect. In J. Briere, L. Berliner, J. A. Bulkley, C. Jenny, & T. Reid (Eds.), *The APSAC handbook on child maltreatment* (pp. 4–20). Thousand Oaks, CA: Sage.

Faller, K. C. (1988a). *Child sexual abuse: An interdisciplinary manual for diagnosis, case management, and treatment.* New York: Columbia University Press.

Faller, K. C. (1988b). Criteria for judging the credibility of children's statements about their sexual abuse. *Child Welfare, 67*(5), 389–401.

Faller, K. C. (1988c). Decision-making in cases of intrafamilial child sexual abuse. *American Journal of Orthopsychiatry, 58*(1), 121–128.

Faller, K. C. (1990). An approach to questioning children alleged to have been sexually abused. *The Advisor, 2*(2).

Fantuzo, J., & Mohr, W. (1999). Prevalence and effects of child exposure to domestic violence. *The Future of Children: Domestic Violence and Children, 9*(3).

Feldman, M. D., & Brown, R. (2002). Munchausen by proxy in an international context. *Child Abuse & Neglect 26,* 509–524.

Finkelhor, D. (1990, Winter). Is child abuse overreported? *Public Welfare, 48,* 22–29, 46–47.

Finkelhor, D. (1993). Epidemiological factors in the clinical identification of child sexual abuse. *Child Abuse & Neglect, 17,* 67–70.

Finkelhor, D., Hotaling, G., Lewis, I. A., & Smith, C. (1990). Sexual abuse in a national survey of adult men and women: Prevalence, characteristics, and risk factors. *Child Abuse & Neglect, 14*(1), 19–28.

Finkelhor, D., Williams, L. M., & Burns, N. (1988). *Nursery crimes: Sexual abuse in day care.* Newbury Park, CA: Sage.

Fleming, J., Mullen, P., & Bammer, G. (1997). A study of potential risk factors for sexual abuse in childhood. *Child Abuse & Neglect, 21,* 49–58.

Folks, H. (1911). *The care of destitute, neglected, and delinquent children.* New York: Macmillan.

Forsythe, P. (1987). Redefining child protective services. *Protecting Children, 4*(3), 12–16.

Fraser, M. W. (Ed.). (1997). *Risk and resilience in childhood.* Washington, DC: NASW Press.

Gallup, G. H., Moor, D. W., & Schussel, R. (1997). *Disciplining children in America.* Princeton, NJ: The Gallup Organization.

Garbarino, J., & Ebata, A. (1983). The significance of ethnic and cultural differences in child maltreatment. *Journal of Marriage and the Family, 45,* 773–783.

Gaudin, J. M., & Dubowitz, H. (1997). Family functioning in neglectful families. In J. D. Berrick, R. P. Barth, & N. Gilbert (Eds.), *Child welfare research review, vol. 2* (pp. 28–62). New York: Columbia University Press.

Gelles, R. J. (1989). Child abuse and violence in single-parent families: Parent absence and economic deprivation. *American Journal of Orthopsychiatry, 59*(4), 492–501.

Gelles, R. J., & Harrop, J. W. (1991). The risk of abusive violence among children with nongenetic caretakers. *Family Relations, 40*(1), 78–83.

Gentry, C. E. (1994). *Crisis intervention in child abuse and neglect.* Washington, DC: U.S. Department of Health and Human Services, National Center on Child Abuse and Neglect.

Giovannoni, J. M., & Becerra, R. M. (1979). *Defining child abuse.* New York: Free Press.

Gleason, B. (1994). Unpublished manuscript. Detroit, MI: Wayne State University, School of Social Work.

Goodman, G. S., Bottoms, B. L., & Shaver, P. R. (1994). *Characteristics and sources of allegations of ritualistic child abuse* (Executive summary of the final report to the National Center on Child Abuse and Neglect [Grant No. 90CA1405]). Washington, DC: National Center for Child Abuse and Neglect.

Harrison, P. A., Fulkerson, J. A., & Beebe, T. J. (1997). Multiple substance use among adolescent physical and sexual abuse victims. *Child Abuse & Neglect, 21*(6), 529–539.

Hart, S. N., Brassard, M. R., & Karlson, H. C. (1996). Psychological maltreatment. In J. Briere, L. Berliner, J. A. Bulkley, C. Jenny, & T. Reid (Eds.), *The APSAC handbook on child maltreatment* (pp. 72–89). Thousand Oaks, CA: Sage.

Helfer, R. E. (1987). Litany of the smoldering neglect of children. In R. E. Helfer, & R. S. Kempe (Eds.), *The battered child* (4th ed.). Chicago: University of Chicago Press.

Hibbard, R. A., & Hartman, G. L. (1992). Behavioral problems in alleged sexual abuse victims. *Child Abuse & Neglect, 16,* 755–762.

Horejsi, C. (1996). *Assessment and case planning in child protection and foster care services.* Englewood, CO: American Humane Association.

Hutchinson, E. D. (1990). Child maltreatment: Can it be defined? *Social Service Review, 64*(1), 60–78.

James, S., & Mennen, F. (2001). Treatment outcome research: How effective are treatments for abused children? *Child and Adolescent Social Work Journal, 18*(2), 73–95.

Jones, L. (1993). Decision making in child welfare: A critical review of the literature. *Child and Adolescent Social Work Journal, 10*(3), 241–262.

Jones, M. A. (1987). *Parental lack of supervision: Nature and consequence of a major child neglect problem.* Washington, DC: Child Welfare League of America.

Jones, P. H. (1991). Ritualism and child sexual abuse. *Child Abuse & Neglect 15*(3), 163–170.

Jonson-Reid, M., & Barth, R. (2000). From maltreatment report to juvenile incarcertion: The role of child welfare services. *Child Abuse & Neglect, 24*(4), 505–520.

Kamerman, S. B., & Kahn, A. J. (1990, Winter). If CPS is driving child welfare—Where do we go from here? *Public Welfare, 48,* 9–13.

Karenga, M. H. (1989). *Selections from the Huisa: Sacred wisdom of ancient Egypt.* Los Angeles: Sankore Press. Quoted in: Sullivan, M. (1996, Spring). An Afro-centric perspective on developing cultural identity. *The Prevention Report, 6.*

Kelley, S. J. (1996). Ritualistic abuse of children. In J. Briere, L. Berliner, J. A. Bulkley, C. Jenny, & T. Reid (Eds.), *The APSAC handbook on child maltreatment* (pp. 90–99). Thousand Oaks, CA: Sage.

Kempe, C. H., Silverman, F. N., Steele, B. T., Droegemueller, W., & Silver, H. K. (1962, July). The battered child syndrome. *Journal of the American Medical Association, 181.*

Kent, L., Laidlaw, J. D., & Brockington, I. F. (1997). Fetal abuse. *Child Abuse & Neglect, 21*(2), 181–186.

Kolko, D. J. (1996). Child physical abuse. In J. Briere, L. Berliner, J. A. Bulkley, C. Jenny, & T. Reid (Eds.), *The APSAC handbook on child maltreatment* (pp. 21–50). Thousand Oaks, CA: Sage.

Korbin, J. E. (1994). Sociocultural factors in child maltreatment. In G. B. Melton, & F. D. Barry (Eds.), *Protecting children from abuse and neglect: Foundations for a new national strategy* (pp. 182–223). New York: Guilford Press.

Lanning, K. V. (1991). Ritual abuse: A law enforcement view or perspective. *Child Abuse & Neglect, 15*(3), 171–173.

Levandosky, A., & Graham-Bermann, S. (2001). Parenting in battered women: The effects of domestic violence on women and their children. *Journal of Family Violence, 16*(2), 171–193.

Levine, M. (1996). Reasonable cause: A qualitative study of mandated reporting. *Child Abuse & Neglect, 20*(4), 275–287.

Lindsay, D. (1994). *The welfare of children.* New York: Oxford University Press.

Loftus, E. F. (1993). The reality of repressed memories. *American Psychologist, 48,* 518–537.

Madden, R. G. (1993). State actions to control fetal abuse: Ramifications for child welfare practice. *Child Welfare, 72*(2), 129–140.

Margolin, L. (1992). Child abuse by mothers' boyfriends: Why the overrepresentation? *Child Abuse & Neglect 16,* 541–551.

Matthews, M. (1999). The impact of federal and state laws on children exposed to domestic violence. *The Future of Children: Domestic Violence and Children, 9*(3).

McCurdy, K., & Daro, D. (1994). *Current trends in child abuse reporting and fatalities: The results of the 1993 annual fifty-state survey.* Chicago: National Committee to Prevent Child Abuse.

Meadow, R. (2002). Different interpretations of Munchausen syndrome by proxy. *Child Abuse & Neglect, 26,* 501–508.

Melchert, T. P., & Parker, L. (1997). Different forms of childhood abuse and memory. *Child Abuse & Neglect, 21*(2), 125–135.

Melton, G. B., & Barry, F. D. (Eds.). (1994). *Protecting children from abuse and neglect: Foundations for a national strategy.* New York: Guilford Press.

Mencher, S. (1960). The concept of authority and social casework. In *Casework papers, 1960.* New York: Family Service Association of America.

Mosby, L., Rawls, A. W., Meehan, A. J., Mays, E., & Pettinari, C. J. (1999, Summer). Troubles in interracial talk about discipline: An examination of African American child rearing narratives. *Journal of Comparative Family Studies,* No. 3, *489–521.*

Moss, S. Z. (1963). Authority—An enabling factor in casework with neglectful parents. *Child Welfare, 43*(8), 385–391.

National Association of Public Child Welfare Administrators. (1988). *Guidelines for a model system of protective services for abused and neglected children and their families.* Washington, DC: American Public Welfare Association.

National Association of Social Workers. (2000, July). *Social workers and child abuse reporting: A review of state mandatory reporting requirements.* Silver Springs, MD: NASW Press.

National Center on Child Abuse and Neglect. (1993). *A report on the maltreatment of children with disabilities.* Washington, DC: U.S. Department of Health and Human Services.

National Clearinghouse on Child Abuse and Neglect Information. (2002). *State statutes.* Available: www.calib.com/nccanch/statutes/civilstats.cfm.

National Commission on Child Welfare and Family Preservation. (1990). *Factbook on public child welfare services and staff.* Washington, DC: American Public Welfare Association.

National Institute of Drug Abuse. (1999). *Drug abuse and addiction research: The sixth triennial report to Congress.* Washington, DC: U.S. Department of Health and Human Services.

National Research Council. (1993). *Understanding child abuse and neglect.* Washington, DC: National Academy Press.

Oberlander, L. B. (1995). Psycholegal issues in child sexual abuse evaluations: A survey of forensic mental health professionals. *Child Abuse & Neglect, 19*(4), 475–490.

Ornoy, A., Michailevskaya, V., Lukashov, L., Bar-Hamburger, R., & Harel, S. (1996). The developmental outcome of children born to heroin-dependent mothers, raised at home or adopted. *Child Abuse & Neglect, 20*(5), 385–396.

Osofsky, J. (1999). The impact of violence on children. *The Future of Children: Domestic Violence and Children, 9*(3).

Polansky, N. A., Chalmers, M. A., Buttenwieser, E., & Williams, D. P. (1981). *Damaged parents: An anatomy of child neglect.* Chicago: University of Chicago Press.

Proch, K. (1982). *Child welfare case notebook.* Urbana: University of Illinois at Urbana Champaign, School of Social Work.

Public Health Service. (1995). *Questions and answers on PHS guidelines for HIV counseling and voluntary testing for pregnant women.* Atlanta: Centers for Disease Control and Prevention.

Regehr, C., & Antle, B. (1997). Coercive influences: Informed consent in court-mandated social work practice. *Social Work, 42*(3), 300–306.

Rosenberg, D. A., & Gary, N. (1988). Sexual abuse of children. In D. C. Bross et al. (Eds.), *The new child protection team handbook.* New York: Garland.

Ryan, K. (1996). The chronically traumatized child. *Child and Adolescent Social Work Journal, 13,* 287–310.

Schene, P. (1996). The risk assessment roundtables: A ten-year perspective. *Protecting Children, 12*(2), 4–8.

Schene, P. (1998). Past, present, and future roles of child protective services. *The Future of Children, 8*(1), 23–38.

Schene, P. (2001, Spring). Meeting each family's needs. *Best Practice, Next Practice,* 1–6.

Sebold, J. (1987). Indicators of child sexual abuse in males. *Social Casework, 68*(2), 75–80.

Sedlak, A. J., & Broadhurst, D. D. (1996). *Third national incidence study of child abuse and neglect: Final report.* Washington, DC: U.S. Department of Health and Human Services, National Center for Child Abuse and Neglect.

Slack, K. (2002). Assessing the influence of welfare reform on child welfare systems. *Focus, 22*(1), 98–105.

Smith, C., & Carlson, B. E. (1997, June). Stress, coping, and resilience in children and youth. *Social Service Review,* 231–256.

Starr, R. H., Jr., & Wolfe, D. A. (Eds.). (1991). *The effects of child abuse and neglect: Issues and research.* New York: Guilford Press.

Stattler, J. N. (1997). *Clinical and forensic interviewing of children and families.* Jerome N. Stattler, Publisher, Inc.

Steele, B. (1987). Psychodynamic factors in child abuse. In R. E. Helfer & R. S. Kempe (Eds.), *The battered child* (4th ed.) (pp. 81–114). Chicago: University of Chicago Press.

Stein, T. (1998). *The social welfare of women and children with HIV and AIDS.* New York: Oxford University Press.

Straus, M., & Gelles, R. (1986, August). Societal change and change in family violence from 1975–1985 as revealed by two national surveys. *Journal of Marriage and the Family, 48,* 465–479.

Sunley, R. (1963). Early nineteenth-century American literature on child rearing. In M. Mead & M.

Wolfenstein (Eds.), *Childhood in contemporary cultures.* Chicago: University of Chicago Press.

Terpstra, J. (1992). Foreword. In K. H. Briar, V. H. Hansen, & N. Harris (Eds.), *New partnerships: Proceedings from the National Public Child Welfare Training Symposium, 1991.* Miami: Florida International University.

U.S. Advisory Board on Child Abuse and Neglect. (1993). *The continuing child protection emergency: A challenge to the nation.* Washington, DC: U.S. Government Printing Office.

U.S. Department of Health and Human Services. (1999a). *Current trends in child maltreatment reporting laws.* Washington, DC: U.S. Government Printing Office.

U.S. Department of Health and Human Services. (1999b). Religious exemptions to criminal child abuse and neglect. *Child abuse and neglect state statutes elements, domestic violence.* (No. 41). Washington, DC: U.S. Government Printing Office.

U.S. Department of Health and Human Services. (2000a). *Child maltreatment 1999: Reports from the states to the National Child Abuse and Neglect Data System.* Washington, DC: U.S. Government Printing Office.

U.S. Department of Health and Human Services. (2000b). *Rethinking child welfare practice under the Adoption and Safe Families Act of 1997.* Washington, DC: U.S. Government Printing Office.

U.S. Department of Health and Human Services. (2001a). *Techniques for the child interview and a methodology for substantiating sexual abuse.* Washington, DC: U.S. Government Printing Office.

U.S. Department of Health and Human Services. (2001b). Child witness to domestic violence. *Child abuse and neglect state statutes elements, domestic violence* (No. 41). Washington, DC: U.S. Government Printing Office.

U.S. Department of Health and Human Services. (2002). *Child maltreatment 2000: Reports from the states to the National Child Abuse and Neglect Data System.* Washington, DC: U.S. Government Printing Office.

Waldfogel, J. (1998). *The future of child protection.* Cambridge, MA: Harvard University Press.

Walker, L. E. (1984). *The battered woman syndrome.* New York: Springer.

Wallace, H. (1996). *Family violence: Legal, medical and social perspectives.* Boston: Allyn & Bacon.

Warner-Rogers, J. E., Hansen, D. J., & Spieth, L. E. (1996). The influence of case and professional variables on identification and reporting of physical abuse: A study with medical students. *Child Abuse & Neglect, 20*(9), 851–866.

Wells, S. J., Stein, T. J., Fluke, J., & Downing, J. (1989). Screening in child protective services. *Social Work, 34*(1), 45–48.

Widom, C. S. (1989). Child abuse, neglect, and adult behavior: Research design and findings on criminality, violence, and child abuse. *American Journal of Orthopsychiatry, 59*(3), 355–367.

Wiehe, V. R. (1996). *Working with child abuse and neglect.* Thousand Oaks, CA: Sage.

Wolfner, G. D., & Gelles, R. J. (1993). A profile of violence toward children: A national study. *Child Abuse & Neglect, 17,* 197–212.

Zanel, J., Jr. (1997). Failure to thrive: A pediatrician's perspective. *Pediatrics in Review, 18*(11), 371–378.

Zuckerman, B. (1994). Effects on parents and children. In D. J. Besharov (Ed.), *When drug addicts have children* (pp. 49–63). Washington, DC: Child Welfare League of America and the American Enterprise Institute.

8 Family Preservation Services

Each family is so complex as to be known and understood only in part even by its own members. Families struggle with contradictions as massive as Everest, as fluid and changing as the Mississippi. . . . Yet when practical the preference should be for family.

—Maya Angelou

CHAPTER OUTLINE

Case Example: Using Intensive Family-Based Services to Prevent Placement

The following case example is one of countless family preservation efforts—each complex and unique—that successfully holds a family together when the events of that family's existence threaten a profound dislocation.

Amy is a 23-year-old mother of three young children. Jimmy, who is the father of Jeremy, age 6, and Tiffany, age 4, drifts in and out of their lives. When he is sober he visits and sometimes brings toys or food. When he has been drinking he becomes sullen and verbally abusive. Amy has learned to keep him from bothering them. Amy's youngest child, Ashley, is medically fragile—Amy was using crack heavily during her pregnancy.

Amy doesn't remember who Ashley's father might be. Amy's life has been a blur of misfortune in the last few years. She has been evicted from apartments twice for nonpayment of rent. They spent weeks going from homeless shelter to homeless shelter until her cousin took them in. Both Amy's stepmother and Jimmy have threatened to have the children taken from her. She struggles to stay free of crack. As a result of substance abuse treatment after Ashley's birth, Amy has had periods of nonuse and a brief relapse. Her nerves are frayed from the children's constant fighting and whining and Ashley's irritable, fretful crying. Amy tries to keep the children quiet because they annoy her cousin, who threatens to kick her out. She needs a drink or a joint to tolerate the children when they get out of control. Amy is frightened because she has been hitting the children in futile discipline attempts. She left bruises on Jeremy's buttocks and left arm after hitting him with a belt to show him that he couldn't hit his sister. When she took Ashley to the emergency room because the infant seemed very congested, a nurse noticed Jeremy's bruises and was concerned about Ashley's nutrition, as she was below the twentieth percentile. The hospital called child protective services.

Fifteen to twenty years ago, the children might have been placed in foster care. After a careful assessment of risk, the CPS worker referred Amy to a program that offers intensive, comprehensive, family-based services designed to preserve the family unit, protect the children, and keep the children out of care.

Carolyn, the family-based services worker, carries a cell phone so that she is available to Amy and the children around the clock, if needed. Because her caseload is limited to two or three families at a time, she is available, during the next six weeks, to work with the family. She will work to keep the family together by identifying and supporting their strengths, bringing in resources, teaching them problem-solving skills, and providing hope. She will engage Amy by helping her to locate housing and furniture, working with her at household tasks, and being an understanding, caring, and constant figure in her life. Carolyn will use a wide range of techniques and strategies, drawn from family therapy and social learning sources, to enable Amy to face and solve the problems that have led to the threat of child placement. She will also begin to put into place a safety net of ongoing community resources that will meet the children's developmental needs and Amy's needs during a long recovery process.

Controversy Concerning Family Preservation Philosophy and Services

Although social work has long been concerned with the family—the first direct practice journal was named *The Family*—historically the focus of child welfare has been on the child. However, in the 1980s the rapidly developing field of family therapy intersected with a strong government response to the problems of child welfare. Mandatory reporting of child maltreatment, combined with the substance abuse epidemic's devastating effect on families, had led to a great increase in the numbers of children identified as abused or neglected. However, services were inadequate or nonexistent to help their families improve the quality of their care (Sudia, 1981). It was clear to all that foster care was not the solution for every abused or neglected child, and that many families could be helped to retain their children at home if services were available to them. The 1980 Adoption Assistance and Child Welfare Act established mandates that "reasonable efforts" be made to keep families together. It gave federal support to state efforts to preserve the family before placing a child in foster care. The intent was to protect children from unnecessary separation from their parents and to encourage agencies to work with families in more than a cursory way.

The nation responded to the call to improve services to families and maintain children in their homes if possible. The U.S. Children's Bureau established a National Resource Center in Iowa to help agencies establish family preservation programs. Between 1981 and 1993, thirty states established statewide family-based programs, and twenty-seven state associations for family-based services were developed (Allen & Zalenski, 1993). The Family Preservation and Support Services Act of 1993 bolstered services that enhanced parental functioning; the child welfare field saw it as an opportunity to establish a continuum of coordinated, culturally relevant, family-focused services. An air of optimism stimulated the family and children's services system in the early 1990s. "That family preservation can be the catalyst for rehabilitating the entire service delivery system is the hope, already glimpsed and beginning to be realized, of its advocates" (Barthel, 1992, p. 75).

Soon, however, the concept of family preservation began to be called into question by professionals and media alike. Widely publicized failures to protect children from harm while they and their families were receiving family preservation services caused a growing backlash against family preservation (Hartman, 1993). Lindsey, writing for a professional audience, observed, "the risk with inappropriate removal of a child is that it may tear apart a family unnecessarily. However, the risk of leaving a child in an endangered home is a child fatality. Neither is acceptable, but protecting the child's life must always be paramount" (Lindsey, 1994, p. 279).

In response, Maluccio, Pine, and Walsh (1994) acknowledged that family preservation is viewed as competing with child protection and in particular cases these may be incompatible goals. However, they stated, "At the philosophical and policy levels family preservation and child protection are complementary rather than competing values. In essence, the best way to protect children is to preserve as much of their families as possible" (p. 295). Others argued that the goal of services to support families should change focus from placement prevention to child development and be part of a wide system of support services (Wells & Tracy, 1996). McCroskey (2001) noted that child welfare decisions involve weighing a complex set of factors: "These decisions are based on judgment calls and may not turn out always to have been justified, but no child welfare worker or agency wants to leave children in danger, even when they believe there may be some possibility of bringing the family together again" (p. 5). Professionals have acknowledged that family preservation services were originally oversold and that the backlash is to some extent a reaction to unrealistically high expectations about what family preservation could accomplish. Dennis (1997) pointed out that, in an effort to persuade legislatures to fund services to families, unrealistic claims were made about the cost-effectiveness of family preservation services. They were not given enough funding to meet the goals expected of them; many were short term and ill suited to the profound, systemic problems that the families presented.

The passage of the Adoption and Safe Families Act in 1997 culminated the philosophical and political shift away from some of the original tenets of family preservation. The act emphasizes child safety in the home, which reflects the public concern that the family preservation philosophy went too far in maintaining children at home, risking their safety in some cases. However, the act continues funding for preventive services to strengthen families (see Chapter 3) and for family preservation when children can be safely maintained at home. It increases treatment options for families, particularly for the problems of substance abuse, domestic violence, and homelessness. Even though the initial optimism that family preservation programs could reduce the need for foster care has diminished, family preservation remains a vital part of the child welfare service continuum.

Characteristics of Family Preservation Services

Principles of Family Preservation Services

Family-based services for the prevention of placement represent a philosophy that families are important, that they should be kept together, and that intensive, focused efforts will mobilize family strengths. As articulated by the National Resource Center on Family-Based Services, this philosophy is rooted in the belief that

- children need permanency in their family relationships in order to develop into healthy, productive individuals;
- families should be the primary caretakers of their own children; and
- social service programs should make every effort to support families in this function. (National Resource Center, 1994)

Common elements of intensive, family-based placement prevention programs include the following aspects:

- commitment to maintaining children in their own homes
- focusing on the entire family system rather than on individuals
- accepting for service only those families at actual risk of having children placed
- beginning service as soon as the referral has been made—no waiting lists
- seeing and working with families in their own homes
- maintaining flexible hours seven days a week, with round-the-clock response to family needs
- providing intensive service over a limited period of time (from one to five months)
- keeping caseload size small—often two to three cases at a time—enabling the worker to deliver intensive services
- providing comprehensive services meeting a variety of therapeutic, concrete, and supportive needs
- teaching family members skills

- offering counseling or therapy within the home
- basing services on client need rather than agency categories
- having access to flexible funding to support the case plan
- offering ongoing, in-service training and support to staff
- following up and evaluating family progress and program success (Edna McConnell Clark Foundation, 1985; Nelson, Landsman, & Deutelbaum, 1990; Whittaker, Kinney, Tracy, & Booth, 1990)

Theoretical Base

The conceptual frameworks for family-based prevention services draw from and integrate a number of theoretical sources. The ecological systems metaphor examines the transactions and exchange of energy and resources between the family and its environment, and views the family holistically in terms of interrelationships of systems. When children experience problems, for example, those difficulties need to be viewed in the context of the child's family, the family's community, and the community's involvement in the larger society.

Theories of coping and adaptation in both maturational and situational life transitions (Germain & Gitterman, 1980) are also applied, with the understanding that coping with ongoing conditions is part of family functioning. According to Bain (1978), the family capacity to cope is a function of the magnitude of the stress and the richness, relevance, and coherence of the "social container" within which the stress is experienced. The concept of the social container includes both the family's social networks and its formal institutional relationships. Such a view of family dysfunction suggests several options for intervening to enhance family coping, reduction of stress, facilitating the response of formal institutions, strengthening the social network, or enhancing the effectiveness of family members.

Another theoretical source for many family-based prevention programs is crisis intervention theory (Parad, 1965; Caplan, 1974). Families seen in family preservation programs are usually experiencing one of two crises: (1) Child protective services has said that the family is not providing adequate child care and is planning to remove one or more children, or (2) problems between parents and children have grown so severe that a parent is refusing to allow the child to continue to live at home, or the child is running away (Kinney, Haapala, & Booth, 1991). Crisis intervention theory postulates that people's familiar coping mechanisms break down during periods of high stress, so that they become more open to change. With competent intervention, the opportunity is created for healthier adaptation following resolution of the crisis.

Many family-based service programs, especially Homebuilders, integrate social learning theory into their approach. A key to understanding behavior is recognizing the rewards or penalties that follow the behavior and the antecedents that stimulate or trigger the behavior (Patterson, 1975). The expectations and cognitions about behavior also provide reciprocal influence with the behavior itself (Bandura, 1977). The clarity and specificity of cognitive-behavioral approaches fit with the focused intervention of most programs.

Family-systems theory, which takes note of family structure, family roles, family life cycle, multigenerational family issues, and the nature of family transactions, also undergirds a family-based services approach. It helps the social worker to understand the circular nature of interactions and behaviors that may jeopardize the safety of the child in his or her own home. The use of family-systems theory enhances the assessment of how the family "works." Many therapeutic techniques—such as eco-maps and genograms, increasing the clarity of communication, understanding the structure of the family, working with boundary issues, helping families change maladaptive roles, and establishing positive family rituals—come directly from family therapy sources.

Although many models of social work practice start with problems or pathology, the *strengths perspective* (Saleeby, 2002) emphasizes the strengths in people. The role of the social worker is framed as one of identifying and building on strengths. Noble, Perkins, and Fatout (2000) use the analogy of the athletic coach, who trains athletes to develop their muscles, to describe the role of the child welfare worker who trains clients to develop their strengths. In applying the strengths perspective to family preservation, they stress the importance of hope in the ability of people to change for the better and achieve success in areas of life such as housing arrangements, education, social support, leisure, relationships, health, personal care, and finances. The worker's optimism in the client's ability to achieve success must be balanced by good sense and realism.

Programs That Prevent Placement and Preserve Families

Currently, the federal government contributes to family preservation programs in all fifty states. While there is tremendous variety and diversity within the existing programs, they have in common a commitment to intensive, family-based services. Figure 8.1 shows the steps followed by cases through family preservation services.

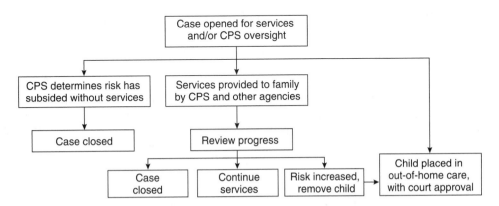

FIGURE 8.1   Overview of Steps Followed by Cases through Family Preservation Services

Source: Adapted from P. Schene (1998), Past, present, and future roles of child protective services, *The Future of Children: Protecting Children from Abuse and Neglect, 8*(1). Adapted with the permission of the David and Lucile Packard Foundation.

The Homebuilders Model

Homebuilders, an intensive in-home crisis intervention and education program for families, has pioneered concepts of family preservation since 1974. The families are referred by state workers when there is a child at imminent risk of placement. Workers serve only two families at a time, providing a wide range of services, including help with basic needs and counseling regarding family relationships. The Homebuilders philosophy includes several important assumptions: It is our job to instill hope; clients are our colleagues; people are doing the best they can (Kinney, Haapala, & Booth, 1991).

When a family is accepted into the program a face-to-face meeting takes place within twenty-four hours. Homebuilders therapists are on call to the client families and have flexible schedules so that they can meet with clients as needed, even on weekends, nights, or holidays. While much of the work takes place in the home, therapists also go where the problems are, whether that is a school or a teen hangout. The goal of all services is to enable families to resolve their own problems. Program goals are limited: to prevent out-of-home placement and to teach families the skills necessary to remain living together.

The therapist is involved in doing concrete tasks such as cleaning the apartment or driving to the grocery store with the family members. The therapist also uses a variety of educational and therapeutic techniques as the situation warrants, including teaching behavior-management skills, assertive skills, problem-solving skills, cognitive skills, and communication skills.

The brevity of the Homebuilders model, four to eight weeks, fits with a crisis-intervention theoretical foundation. The services are intense during the time-limited period, serving to keep therapist and family focused on the specific goals established by the family.

In addition to initiating the family preservation approach in 1974, Homebuilders has made several significant related contributions to the field. From its inception, an evaluation component was built into the model. This focus on accountability provided impetus for widespread adoption of Homebuilder concepts. It also convinced state legislatures that the program was cost effective and would save money if placement were avoided. Many states have family preservation programs based on the Homebuilders model.

Other Models

A model of family preservation services with two workers has been used in a number of places, from Maryland to Adelaide, South Australia. Advantages of having a staff pair to work with a family include the ability of the team to keep each other on target, to provide extra energy for difficult or complex tasks, and to keep a positive focus on family progress. The following case illustrates the need for teamwork:

> A family preservation team intervened in a situation in which the parent had allowed garbage and trash to pile up to the ceiling in the home. The media had photographed the housing inspector staring at the huge mounds of refuse and ran the photograph on the front page of the local newspaper with the headline "The Dirtiest House in the State." The mother was so shamed that it took three days before the family preservation team could go into the house. They met with the mother on the front porch and made cleanup plans. It took a contractor with three dumpsters to empty the house of rubbish, and a large group of relatives and

volunteers to scrub, clean, and paint. When the house had been restored to order and the mother engaged with mental health services in the community, the team members reflected on their success. They realized that it would have been much harder to counter the media criticism, ameliorate the depression and shame of the mother, and handle the overwhelming nature of the mess if they had been working singly, not as a team.

Typically such an arrangement consists of a professional social worker and a paraprofessional or case aide. The pair is usually part of a larger team that meets regularly to provide support and celebrate success.

A variation on the use of brief, intensive family preservation services was found in an experimental program in which IFPS workers were assigned to families at the front end of a child protective services investigation, before rather than after a CPS determination has been made. The family preservation workers assessed families in terms of strengths, and the CPS workers assessed risks in a collaborative decision-making process. The IFPS workers helped families establish a network of services for a strengthened environment, including informal support such as extended family members, friends, neighbors, and clergy. Families in the experimental group had fewer cases opened than did those in the control group and were more satisfied with the agency's services. By front-loading services to the time of CPS intake, child safety may be enhanced (Walton, 1997).

Family Preservation and Domestic Violence

Research and practice wisdom affirm that children in homes where partner abuse occurs are at risk of being battered by the adult abuser (Edleson, 1999). (See Chapter 7.) A collaborative model between the domestic violence and child welfare service delivery systems in Michigan (Findlater & Kelly, 1999) has shown that through policy development, resource sharing, and training, children can stay safe while remaining with their battered mothers. Family preservation workers help battered women and their children in a variety of critical areas, including establishing an independent home, safety planning, parenting issues such as supporting the mother's authority, and developing a social support network. They coordinate case services with domestic violence staff, who provide expertise on resources for battered women and consultation on the dynamics of abusive situations.

Family Preservation and Children's Mental Health Needs

Another form of services targeted at the prevention of placement addresses the needs of children and youth at risk of being sent from the community into costly residential care, or young people returning to family and community from a more structured setting. The "wraparound" approach, developed in Alaska by the former coordinator of Children's Mental Health Services, has been replicated in over 100 sites nationwide (Vandenberg, Grealish, & Schick, 1993). A wraparound service is developed by a community-based child and family team, which may include parents ("customers"), child welfare, mental health, juvenile justice, education, law enforcement, health, vocational rehabilitation, clergy, developmental disabilities, family advocates, and other concerned staff and community representatives. An individualized resource coordinator identifies those people already in the child's life and configures a wraparound team. This team, operating on the premise "never give up," develops culturally competent individualized services in the life domain of the child and family. Life domains include the basic human needs such as a place to live, family, social interaction, friends, psychological/emotional ties, safety, and so forth. Family strengths—"the good news about families"—are assessed, and problems are reframed. A family resistant to assistance might be commended for being a wise shopper for services, or an assaultive child might be reframed as someone who tries to stick up for himself. Creative approaches to meeting life domain needs might include hiring a college student who models acceptable behavior while keeping a youth from running away or doing destructive behaviors. Parent involvement is key to the wraparound approach. Wraparound services are funded through integration of funding streams for children's services and are cost effective in the prevention of expensive residential care or hospitalization.

Family Preservation for Substance-Affected Families

Models to coordinate substance abuse treatment with child welfare and maternal health services have been implemented in response to the epidemic of crack cocaine addiction.

Parental addiction is seen as "a chronic relapsing disorder" (Besharov, 1994, p. ix) that requires that current child welfare programs must be radically reoriented. Recognition of the severity of substance abuse and addiction—especially to crack cocaine—has led to a number of collaborative approaches that often involve health, substance abuse treatment, child development, and child care and child welfare services. Many of these initiatives involve longer-term case management than the typical family preservation, short-term, crisis-intervention program. While working with the family they may help to substantiate that there is a problem, help parents consider the need for treatment, help parents access treatment, and help develop structures for the child's safety.

Time-limited, intensive family preservation services are not adequate for substance-affected families. Such cases need ongoing services, including transitional housing for recovering parents, family-focused treatment, family planning services, and child care options. Recovering addicts should be trained to anticipate their own drug-using episodes and seek protection for their children before the crisis hits (Jones, 1994). Kinship care can be viewed as a form of family preservation that provides safe and supportive environments for children of addicts (Johnson, 1994). Barth (1994) proposes that intensive family preservation programs for drug users should be augmented by ongoing case management, shared family care, early childhood services, developmentally focused services, and child care to improve developmental outcomes while protecting children.

The National Council of Juvenile and Family Court Judges developed a "reasonable efforts" protocol for substance abuse cases. In examining the social service agency response to a substance-abusing parent, some of the questions to be asked are as follows:

> Has there been adequate intra-agency coordination to ensure that concrete services have been made available in a timely manner?
>
> Have all relatives been contacted and their ability to care for the child been assessed?
>
> How has the social service agency helped the substance-abusing parent obtain treatment?

Have referrals to treatment programs been appropriate . . . to programs experienced in treating women with the mother's particular addiction and problems with small children?

Has the availability of the following service programs been examined:

> family-centered drug treatment services
> intensive family preservation services
> emergency housing
> in-home caretaker
> out-of-home respite care
> teaching and demonstrating homemakers
> parenting-skills training
> transportation, etc.

(National Council of Juvenile and Family Court Judges, 1992, p. 19)

I was so scared that I'd lose my kids. I guess I might have deserved it because I'd been messing up and staying high for days at a time. If my worker hadn't gotten me into treatment I could be dead today. She gave us all a second chance, and we want to make it work. (A parent)

The Practice of Family-Based Services

The family-based services practitioner operates on values that form the bedrock of the family work. These values and beliefs enable the practitioner to enter a troubled family system effectively, engage family members, build hope, and begin the change process. One of the most important beliefs is that workers and clients are partners in change. Another belief is that a crisis is an opportunity for change. However, the most important belief is that the child's safety is paramount.

Family preservation programs generally focus on such practice components as engaging and building trust carefully; working in the clients' home whenever possible; providing concrete services; being available nights and weekends, with twenty-four-hour-on-call backup; deemphasizing diagnostic labeling; building on family strengths; setting specific client generated goals; and using client priorities (Kinney, Haapala, & Booth, 1991; Pecora, Whittaker, Maluccio, Barth, & Plotnick, 1992). The following case example illustrates the unique aspects of family-based services practice.

Case Study: Protecting Children from Sexual Abuse and Domestic Violence in a Rural Setting

Reason for Referral.   Tammie had fled with her children, Kelly, age 3, and Bethany, age 1, to a domestic violence shelter in another county after being beaten by Pete, the father of her children. At the shelter she and the staff discovered that Kelly's statements seemed to indicate sexual abuse by Pete. Fearing a referral to child protective services, Tammie left the shelter precipitously, moved in with a new boyfriend, Tom (who lived with several other men), and hid the children at her great-aunt's house so their father couldn't find them. She told her relative that she would get the children as soon as she found housing, but at the present time there was no room for them at Tom's place.

The great-aunt knew about the possibility of sexual abuse and was concerned about getting help for the children, so she called the local child protective services. The CPS worker was aware that Tammie had a previous referral in the county where the domestic violence shelter was located, and that her earlier living conditions had exposed the children to sexual and physical abuse. Other concerns were that Tammie's ability to protect the children was uncertain and that there appeared to be substance abuse in the mother's current living situation. Tammie needed to learn how to protect her children and to fulfill her parenting responsibilities, and she needed assistance in establishing a home. The case was referred to the local family preservation program.

Family Members.   Tammie, age 20, had run away from home at age 16 and lived on the streets of the nearest small city using drugs and occasionally trading sex for food or shelter. She was taken in by Pete, who fathered at least one of her two children. Tammie had left high school before her sixteenth birthday. As a young teen she had been sexually abused by her father when her mother was in a mental hospital. She left home before her mother returned from the hospital. Before the birth of her first child she tried to reach out to her parents, only to find that they had moved away and left word that they did not want her to try to follow them. She is ambivalent about her parents, alternately missing them and hating them. Tammie is petite, attractive, and looks much younger than her years.

Kelly is 3 years old. She appears healthy and strong for her small size although she eats mostly junk food. She resists going to sleep, but generally sleeps well with only occasional nightmares. She has had recurring bladder infections and is behind on her immunizations.

Bethany is 1 year old. She is quite small in size, which may be related to her mother's petite stature. She appears slightly developmentally delayed in motor skills in that she attempts to crawl but has not tried to stand yet. She appears attached to her mother.

Engagement and Developing Trust.   Elise, the family preservation services worker, met Tammie at the child welfare office. Tammie was angry with her great-aunt for calling child protective services, dismayed that she was "in trouble," and angry that she couldn't just pick up her children and move on. Elise drove Tammie to see the children and listened on the way to her tearful explanation of why she had left the children. Their father, Pete, had taken Tammie in when she was on the streets at age 16. When Tammie became pregnant by Pete, she realized that she was terribly dependent on him because her parents had moved away without her and she had nowhere to go. Before Tammie gave birth to Kelly, Pete became increasingly physically abusive to her. She tried working at a fast food restaurant to earn enough money to be able to leave Pete, but she was afraid to leave Kelly at home with him. She became increasingly depressed, quit her job, and was completely isolated. When she came home from the hospital after having their second child, Bethany, Kelly complained to her of a "sore bottom." Tammie wondered if Kelly had been sexually abused, but was too afraid and depressed to confront Pete, and too ashamed to ask for help. When she was ready to leave Pete, she took the children with her to the shelter, planning to leave the children with her great-aunt as soon as possible.

She felt lucky that Tom was taking care of her, but knew that it wasn't a good place to bring the children. She didn't know whether Tom or his friends could be trusted and Tom didn't want kids around anyway. Besides, she was just too upset to take care of them at the moment.

Elise listened quietly to the outpouring of despair as they drove to the great-aunt's home. She noted that Tammie was shaking and offered her a jacket to help keep her warm. She waited while Tammie visited with the children and observed that the little ones ran to their mother, clinging to her and kissing her. After the visit she dealt with Tammie's tears by asking how she could help and by reminding Tammie that the purpose of family preservation services was to keep families together. Tammie identified her first goal—finding housing—and her greatest fear—that Pete would find her or the children.

Assessment of Strengths.   Although Tammie had had a traumatic adolescence and appeared very young because she was physically petite, she showed maturity in her wish to be a good parent to her daughters and to locate housing. Tammie and the children appeared bonded to each other and showed appropriate emotion at their visit. Tammie is attractive, personable, and shows normal intelligence. She has made efforts to remove herself from a difficult situation, the first time when she tried to work so that she could leave Pete, and the second time when she actually left and found a safe place for the children. Tammie was excited that family preservation services would work with her to locate housing and establish a home for the children.

Goal Setting.   Tammie, with Elise's help, established four goals for the time they would be working together:

1. secure affordable housing and furnishings for the family that could be maintained over time
2. protect the children from further physical or sexual abuse and herself from Pete's violence
3. improve parenting and child management skills
4. improve her self-esteem regarding relationships with men and her ability to select men who would not be a danger to her and the children

Action Steps to Reach Goals.   Elise and Tammie worked together to locate a mobile home that could be rented reasonably. FPS flexible funding paid the security deposit and the first month's rent. Tammie applied for Temporary Assistance for Needy Families (TANF), food stamps, and WIC. Elise took Tammie to the distribution point for free commodities. They went grocery shopping together, and Tammie learned that nutritious snack foods such as apples and bananas are actually cheaper than potato chips and cheese curls. Elise referred Tammie to the county extension family nutrition program. They purchased a copy of "The Cheapskate's Gazette," a local bargain-hunter's newsletter, and scoured thrift shops in order to furnish the trailer and locate equipment such as a toddler car seat for Bethany. Tammie was also referred to the public assistance employment program with the goal of finding work that would fit her long-range goal of obtaining a GED or completing high school. Tammie and Elise talked about how to network with her new neighbors and barter goods or services such as child care or a ride to town. These action steps related to the goal of being able to live on assistance and maintain housing until she found adequate employment.

Legal action was begun for a restraining order to protect Tammie from Pete. According to the prosecuting attorney there was insufficient evidence to initiate criminal charges of sexual abuse against him. However, medical exams, and the great-aunt's report that Kelly was displaying the sexual behavior of "humping" with her toys, indicated that sexual abuse had in all likelihood occurred. Elise provided Tammie with several books and a videotape about protecting children from sexual abuse and discussed protection plans with her. They discussed sleeping arrangements for the children, who could be trusted with the children, and how to manage sexual acting-out behaviors. They also worked on other safety issues, putting all cleaning substances and other poisonous or hazardous supplies in high or locked cupboards, and generally childproofing the inside and the yard of the mobile home.

In preparation for the return of the children from the great-aunt's house, Elise began teaching Tammie child-management skills, including environmental controls, time-out, active listening, positive reinforcement, and natural and logical consequences. The children were returned to their mother several days after the mobile home was ready. Tammie and the worker spent many hours together as Tammie tried her new parenting techniques. One resource available in the rural community was a Head Start program that provided transportation and had a parent support group. Kelly was enrolled in Head Start after having been reunited with her mother for two weeks. Elise took Tammie to the first parent support group at the Head Start Center. The county nutritional aide began visiting. Tammie went to the county health department for the well-baby clinic and family planning services.

Tammie thought carefully about her dependency on men and the reasons she had gravitated to a relationship that would turn abusive to her and the children. Elise gently helped her see that she had characteristics, such as intelligence and sensitivity, that were as important as the "sexiness" that Tammie thought was her prime attribute. As her capacity to parent increased, Tammie realized that she had strengths of her own which meant she was not dependent on a male for survival. Tammie's relationship with her boyfriend Tom continued, but she began to look at how she might survive if the relationship should end. She began to examine this relationship for clues that Tom, too, might be abusive to her or the children. She listened to tapes on how to overcome past dysfunctional family rules in order to have healthier adult relationships. Elise coached Tammie on assertiveness-training skills.

Termination.   After five weeks the goals had been attained and the safety net of ongoing services was in place. The child protective services case would remain open. A public health nurse would make home visits, watch Bethany's development, and ensure that the children's immunizations continued. The nutrition aide would assist Tammie in meal planning and accessing commodities. Head Start and the parent support group would help her meet Kelly's developmental needs. The great-aunt would provide child care for brief periods if Tammie needed a break. Tammie could get transportation to town with a neighbor or her landlady. A restraining order against Pete would remain in effect, and Tammie's location remained a secret.

Elise had spent sixty-eight hours providing services to Tammie, including many hours of driving to services in the rural area. She had also spent slightly over $800 in flexible funds to cover initial costs of housing and furnishings plus some lunches and reading materials. Elise reflected in retrospect, "All that time I spent driving paid off. When Tammie and the kids were in the car with me we talked and interacted productively. When they weren't with me I used my recorder for dictation. Working in a rural area has its problems, like isolation and poverty, but you know all the key players in the helping system so you can get things done quickly. Besides, I appreciate the fresh air and wide open spaces."

Case Commentary.   Family preservation services adapts well to rural social work. The worker creates clinical interventions and brings them to the home, compensating for the lack or inaccessibility of services for a young mother isolated in a trailer in the hills with two small children. If Tammie had lived nearer to the battered women's shelter or had known earlier how to access that service system in the nearest city, she might have left an abusive relationship before her child was ever molested and would not have come to the attention of child protective services.

One might wish that a local sexual abuse survivors group or support group for women who had experienced battering had been available, so Tammie could continue to look at her dependent relationships with men. It is also clear that she has many unresolved family of origin issues. Perhaps she will be able or willing to address them as she matures; perhaps she will not. But Tammie is young and resilient. She has one family member in her support network who can help provide some stability. It is unfortunate that in this somewhat isolated county there is no children's play therapist available to work with Kelly regarding the trauma of sexual abuse, witnessing violence, and experiencing temporary separation from her mother. For the time being the family is together and has survived a crisis. Protective services involvement could be helpful in negotiating future developments with Pete or in financing other needed services. The short-term goals have been accomplished, and the family is stabilized. There are supportive services in place, as a step down from the intensive family-based services, which should help the family to stabilize further and begin working toward long-range goals. In the future as Tammie grows and pursues her goals there will be time for more changes.

This case illustrates the importance of providing concrete services to keep a family together and the use of multiple techniques to strengthen a parent's competence. The worker's reflections capture much of the essence and challenge of rural social work.

Culturally Competent Family Preservation Services

Family-based services for family preservation are congruent with the social work emphasis on cultural competence. (See Chapter 1.) Family preservation has been adapted successfully to serve families of diverse ethnic and racial backgrounds, including African American families (Gray & Nybell, 1990); Native American families (Cross, 1987; Mannes, 1993); Hispanic families (Sandau-Beckler, Salcido, & Ronnau, 1993); and lesbian families (Faria, 1994). Respecting clients' beliefs and culture, learning about the family's cultural context, sorting out differences between these beliefs and one's own values, advocating for clients, and dispelling stereotypes and myths are ways in which family preservation workers can operationalize social work knowledge, values, and skills about diversity.

Understanding the nuances of culture is a critical skill for family preservation workers engaging families across ethnic and cultural boundaries. Social workers need to ask about important traditions of the family of origin and country of origin. Culturally competent workers are sensitive to issues of shame in the family and the cultural prohibitions about discussing family business with an outsider (Sandau-Beckler, Salcido, & Ronnau, 1993).

Napoli and Gonzales-Santin (2001) discuss family preservation with Native American families living on a reservation. They place family preservation services within a Native American framework, which looks at the total ecology of the extended family network and understands wellness as a healthy connection to the land, the community, the spirit world, and the family. A team that includes representatives of the tribal community provides the family preservation services. To engage the family and increase trust, the team and family share personal stories while engaging in communal activities. Teams have successfully used a medicine wheel as an instrument to restore harmony and balance. They have also used cultural traditions such as the talking circle to frame engagement and intervention.

Like other models of social work practice, family preservation is most successful when adapted to the unique needs of a particular family. In a sense, each family has its own cultural stance and its own permutation of cultural origins. The family preservation worker is a cultural explorer, discovering traditions, meanings, values, and customs of the family in order to intervene most effectively.

Other Approaches That Help High-Risk Families

In addition to family preservation services, many other approaches also are used to protect the child and preserve the family. Children can be maintained in homes, and family life can be sustained, through a variety of programs, including family counseling, parent education, recreational groups, day treatment, drop-in or respite child care, homemaker services, parent aides, foster grandparents, employment and educational opportunities, and developmental early childhood education programs such as Head Start. These programs are used in a variety of combinations to work with families' diverse situations and family members' unique needs for nurture, stimulation, comfort, competence, contact, well-being, and protection. (See Chapters 3, 4, and 5.)

Many of the treatment approaches described here can be used with families and children regardless of whether the child has been removed from the home. In some cases they are part of a family reunification plan. (See Chapter 9.) These services constitute "reasonable efforts" to keep families together and are often offered as long-term follow-up after the intensive phase of family preservation services (about two months) has been completed.

Treating Loneliness

This phrase grew out of the observation that "among neglectful parents are many who make their circumstances worse by self-imposed aloneness, and who must thus deal with dreadful loneliness" (Polansky, Chalmers, Battenmeier, & Williams, 1981, p. 210). Although the roots of isolation may lie in circumstances of the parent's childhood, it can to some extent be remedied by providing parents the opportunity to be with people.

Group treatment of parents being served by CPS has been used to deal with individual problems, marital problems, and child-management techniques. An often-overlooked function of these groups, apart from other benefits, is that they give parents an opportunity to interact with other adults.

An example of groupwork with abusive parents is a twelve-week program designed to build social support networks for low-income abusive mothers who received training in conversational skills, self-protection, and assertion. In the first session women examined various types of friendships and were encouraged to identify features or patterns in their social networks. The term *friend* carried negative connotations—members reported being hurt and taken advantage of by persons they had considered friends. In the second session they identified danger signs of relationship problems, such as drug problems or lying. In the fourth session the right to feel safe was emphasized, with discussion of protective techniques. During the next few sessions participants focused on basic social skills such as initiating, maintaining, and ending conversations. In sessions eight through eleven, the women learned how to assert themselves and handle criticism. In the final session a shopping outing provided an opportunity for members to practice new social skills (Lovell, Reid, & Richey, 1992).

Treatment with individual parents can also incorporate the concept of strengthening social networks. Tracy, Whittaker, Pugh, Kapp, and Overstreet (1994) report that social network mapping used with family preservation clients yielded rich data about the importance of social support in helping families avert placement.

For example, the goals for one socially isolated abusive family were to teach basic child care skills and to capitalize on the support system that was in place. Family meetings were held to strengthen family relationships. The parents were encouraged to contact family or friends when they needed help (Tracy et al., 1994, p. 487).

Help with Reality Problems

For neglecting and abusing parents, actions usually speak louder than words. The disorganized daily living pattern of neglecting families means that family workers must relate to everyday problems and behaviors, and give direct help with pressing reality problems. These parents are not ready to deal with introspective questions.

Reality-oriented services are typically used when problems have been detected that are not quite serious enough to warrant removal of the children without an attempt to rectify the problem and meet the needs of the family and children. Each type of service can have multiple functions. In a "dirty house" case, a homemaker can mobilize the family to clean up the litter of dirty laundry, decaying food, animal feces, and dirt piles. The homemaker may also demonstrate housekeeping skills, teach basic techniques, model positive attitudes toward housecleaning, help the mother develop a cleaning routine, and break through the atmosphere of discouragement and depression surrounding the neglected home environment.

A parent aide can bring new input to an entropic situation of a young parent marooned with small children. She may provide transportation for shopping, set up recreational activities to stimulate and cheer a depressed mother, and counteract the isolation that heightened the risk of child maltreatment. Yet the success of a parent aide may depend more on intangible qualities of the relationship that develops between parent and aide than on activities. Kind and supportive comments by the aide may nurture the parent and provide role modeling of effective interaction, which can carry over into discipline of the children.

Head Start, which stimulates social and cognitive development to prepare preschoolers to succeed in school also has additional benefits for other family members, even as it is nurturing the child. Aside from the obvious respite it provides to stressed parents, it also offers adult socialization and learning opportunities, as parents engage in parent groups and programs. (See Chapter 4.)

Housing is an extremely important element of family preservation. In the past many children were at risk of placement due in part to homelessness or inadequate housing. The Family Unification Project is unique in that its central element is housing assistance. This program brings together child welfare agencies and housing agencies to make the needs of child welfare families and persons in domestic violence shelters a top priority (Doerre & Mihaly, 1996).

Evaluation of Family Preservation Programs

Family-based services present a number of problems to evaluation. Recently, Jacobs (2001) has enumerated some of the most troubling. The first, defining the mission of family-based services, must take into account the changes in mission that have taken place since they began in the 1980s. At the beginning, the goal was defined as preventing placement, but the mission has since been expanded to other goals, such as enhancing child development, improving family functioning, reducing child welfare expenditures, and enhancing collaborations across human service systems. The addition of new goals complicates the evaluation process. Second, the field lacks useful theories of change, making it difficult to show how or why a particular program produces desired results. Often, it is not clear whether change in family functioning that has been observed by researchers can be attributed to the interventions of the family preservation services. Third, there are numerous program models and definitions of the term *family preservation services,* making it difficult to compare evaluation results of different programs. Finally, there is a lack of good data due to poorly organized state management information systems, and a scarcity of instruments to measure progress in some outcome areas. A review of the history of evaluation of family preservation highlights these difficulties.

As the prototypical family preservation program, Homebuilders set an expectation for program evaluation. It used "prevention of placement" and "cost-effectiveness" as desirable outcomes. Working with a population considered to be "at imminent risk of placement," Homebuilders defined success as the prevention of placement at twelve months from the initiation of service. Using this measure, Homebuilders' success rate was over 70 percent of families served. The per-child cost of Homebuilders compared favorably with the average cost of placement, suggesting that family preservation could result in huge savings by avoiding foster care, group care, or psychiatric hospitalization of children (Kinney, Haapala, & Booth, 1991). Other early family preservation programs used the Homebuilders evaluation model, measuring success by the percentage of children served who did not end up in foster care. Estimated savings in foster care expenses suggested that the programs were very cost effective (Bergquist, Szwejda, & Pope, 1993).

However, a damper on these optimistic estimates of cost savings and placement prevention came in 1992, from an extensive evaluation of Illinois' Family First program. This study found that the risk of placement of children served by family preservation was actually quite low; most of these children were not expected to go into foster care even without family preservation services. This evaluation also found that the Family First program had no effect on subsequent reports of maltreatment by participating families after the program intervention was finished (Schuerman, Rzepnicki, & Littell, 1992). The media used this information to reach the simplistic conclusion that family preservation services didn't work.

Schuerman's research raised the issue that the program was not limited to those for whom it was originally intended, families with children at "imminent risk" of placement. Instead, the services were offered to a larger and more diverse group of families in the child welfare system. The researchers suggested that family preservation services should take place in a reformed, more expansive child welfare service system, because the families receiving services had great needs and the services were not necessarily being wasted (Schuerman, Rzepnicki, Littell, & Budde, 1992).

This research started a movement away from evaluations that looked only at placement rates. Courtney (1997) recommended that "service and support approaches should be developed for clearly defined subpopulations of families and children . . . one size simply doesn't fit all" (p. 73), and "a retreat from the unrealistic early objectives of the family preservation movement is reasonable" (p. 74). Recently, researchers have directed attention toward specific issues, including attempts to measure change in family functioning due to family preservation services intervention. Scannapieco (1993) found improved family functioning in 75 percent of families who had participated in a family preservation program.

Wells and Whittington (1993) studied family functioning among families with an emotionally disturbed child served by a mental health agency. They found that family functioning improved as a result of the services offered, and the children were able to remain in the home. However, the researchers questioned whether in some cases this was a desirable outcome. The families still had many difficulties, and it seemed possible that both they and the child would be better served if the child were admitted to residential treatment that could help him or her substantially.

Research has also addressed the question of what kinds of families can be helped by family preservation services. Bath and Haapala (1993) found outcomes less positive for neglectful than for abusive families. Neglectful families were affected by a greater range of environmental, social, and personal difficulties, and suffered the effects of poverty more than their abusive counterparts. Berry (1992) also found that neglectful families were less likely to be served successfully.

A key dimension of program evaluation in family preservation services is client satisfaction. Consistent with a family empowerment value orientation, most programs ascertain client perceptions of services given. Research has consistently shown that families are satisfied and even enthusiastic about this form of service delivery. In one typical study of family satisfaction, over 90 percent of families who responded to the family satisfaction surveys expressed high levels of satisfaction with the quality of the interaction with the worker and the willingness of the worker to listen to them and understand their situation. Over 80 percent reported positive behavioral change in family interactions as a result of the intervention in such areas as improved communication, appropriate discipline, and care of children (Berguist et al., 1993). An important result of the family preservation movement has been the endorsement by families, often labeled as "resistant," "multiproblem," and "hard to reach," of this form of service, with its focus on practical change in an empowerment and strengths-based framework. Not enough attention has been given to this quite remarkable discovery, considering the many years of "client blaming" and failure to engage clients that preceded the family preservation movement. For many families, this is their first positive experience with the social service system.

Recently, there have been calls for research to examine which models of family preservation are most effective and, particularly, to study the relationship of family preservation services to child cognitive, emotional, and social development outcomes (Heneghan, Horwitz, & Levanthal, 1996). Jacobs (2001) notes that "over the past five years or so, the number of evaluation reports . . . has tailed off quite dramatically, suggesting some loss of interest among funders and researchers alike in evaluating FPS [family preservation services]" (p. 4). Jacobs suggests that a combination of "evaluation fatigue," a spate of bad publicity, and renewed interest in other areas of child welfare, particularly adoption, are responsible for the scarcity of new research.

Kinship Care as Family Preservation

A tradition of mutual assistance within kinship networks is common to many cultures. From the villages of Africa and the clans of Scotland, our ancestors brought to the New World an understanding that the extended family cared for children when parents were incapacitated or unavailable. Despite widespread concern following the World Trade Center attack of September 11, 2001, no children affected by the disaster were placed in the foster care system. Most children who lost a parent continued with a surviving parent. The few who lost both parents were quickly absorbed into kinship care arrangements (Rabin, 2001). This example, drawn from a great tragedy, aptly illustrates that kinship care is normative in American society when the nuclear family cannot fulfill its child caring function.

In the field of child welfare, kinship care has become an integral part of family preservation practice. Kinship care can take either of the following forms:

- informal kinship care that takes place outside the child welfare system, as, for example, when a child goes to live with an aunt
- formal kinship care, made through the child welfare system, including kinship foster care, kinship guardianship, and kinship adoption

One could consider that *all* kinship placements of whatever type are a form of family preservation, if "family" is defined as the entire extended family network.

The Child Welfare League of America has affirmed the importance of kinship care: "Care of children by kin is strongly tied to family preservation. Family strengths often include a kinship network that functions as a support system. . . . The involvement of kin may stabilize family situations, ensure the protection of children, and prevent the need to separate children from their families and place them in the formal child welfare system" (Child Welfare League, 1994, p. 1).

The Cultural Tradition of Kinship Care among American Indian Families

It was through the efforts of the original people of the United States that concepts of kinship care were first enacted into child welfare law. The Indian Child Welfare Act of 1978, reversing a century of policies that intentionally or unintentionally separated large numbers of Indian children from their families, affirmed the extended family structure of Indian families as the primary resource for Indian children who could not live with their parents. Before the era of dominance by non-Indian influences, child rearing was shared within the extended family network and the community (Cross, 1986). (See Chapter 3.) The Indian Child Welfare Act highlighted the importance of kinship networks in child placement for the entire child welfare system and was a precursor of the family preservation movement. (See Chapter 6.)

Since implementation of the Indian Child Welfare Act, Indian child welfare programs have developed placement standards that are culturally sensitive to tribal traditions and living standards. Indian children and youth unable to live at home are now more likely to be placed with relatives or other Indian families than before the Act was passed. Non-Indian child welfare professionals sometimes mistakenly view these placements as foster care settings and are concerned about permanency planning for the child. However, from the point of view of many tribal child welfare organizations, these placements are made within the context of permanency planning and are considered to be legitimate long-term placements. To them, kinship care *is* family preservation, because their definition of "family" extends to a wide network of relatives. It should be noted that Indian child welfare organizations, in addition to using kin placements, also have intensive family preservation and reunification programs to work with the nuclear family (Mannes, 1993).

The Cultural Tradition of Kinship Care among African American Families

Kinship care, long a strength of the African American community, came into prominence in the child welfare system as a possible solution to the family breakdowns caused by the substance abuse epidemic of the 1980s. Kinship care in the foster care system had earlier been called "relative placement" and was used infrequently. By 1990, kinship care had been reconceptualized as a form of family preservation and was a recognized part of the child welfare system. The increase in status and acceptability of this form of care reflected new awareness of the importance of kinship ties to children and also the reality that the formal child welfare system lacked resources for protecting this new influx of children. (See Chapter 3.)

Although every ethnic group has felt the effects of the epidemic of crack cocaine in this country, it has had particularly noxious effects on many African American communities. A disproportionate number of African American children live with grandparents. Many of these arrangements are informal, as differentiated from formal placements made by the child welfare system. In informal situations grandparents, aunts, and other relatives simply assimilate into the household the children of mothers incapacitated by substance abuse or other difficulties. In some instances, the mother and the extended family caregivers may share a common household. "Recognizing the adaptive and healing power of the African American kinship network, and indeed the importance of kinship to all people, enriches the child welfare worker's ability to help the family develop creative solutions to child welfare issues" (Mills, Usher, & McFadden, 1999, p. 13).

Family Group Decision Making

Indigenous people in many countries have become aware of the Indian Child Welfare Act and its implications. In New Zealand, the Act influenced a movement of the indigenous Maori people to reform the child welfare system so that it would be more responsive to Maori culture and processes for protecting children. In turn, the New Zealand family decision-making model has evoked wide interest in the United States. It has been adapted by other Pacific Island peoples and in Australia.

New Zealand's Children, Young Persons, and Their Families Act of 1989 acknowledged the right of the Maori people to make decisions for their own families and to retain the child within the extended family network (Worrall, 2001). A key innovation of the New Zealand model is to return much of the decision-making power in child protective services to the extended family and to develop processes for mutual collaboration between the child welfare system and the family. The family and the child welfare bureaucracy are conceptualized as equal partners in this process.

In New Zealand, the family decision-making model involves a conference of extended family members following an investigation of child abuse by a child protection worker. The parents are asked to agree to involve their extended family in planning. The kinship network is then invited to participate; the child welfare system facilitates the transportation of family members from all over the two islands that constitute this country. The meeting takes place in a comfortable setting and may last for several days. During the conference, professionals share information about factors that place the child at risk. They leave the family alone to develop a plan for protecting the child, but are available for consultation if requested. The plan involves deciding on whom the child will live with and what supportive roles other family members will play. The conference coordinator, who is a child welfare staff member, records decisions and accesses resources needed for implementation of the plan (Smith & Featherstone, 1991).

Adapting the family decision-making model to an American setting raises many issues (Zalenski, 1994; Merkel-Holguin, 1998). Legal constraints around confidentiality, court processes, and liability make it difficult to involve the extended family in planning (Hardin, 1994). Yet the model is being transplanted to a number of states and communities in the United States.

In practice in the United States, the child protection worker investigating a case determines that the case will be referred to a family group conference coordinator. In most states families are referred voluntarily, although in a few locations such meetings may be court ordered. Merkel-Holguin (1998) identifies four distinct phases in the process:

Phase 1: referral to hold a family group decision-making (FGDM) meeting
Phase 2: preparation and planning
Phase 3: the family conference or meeting
Phase 4: follow-up

The coordinator prepares and plans for the meeting, a process that may take weeks. This involves working with the family; identifying concerned parties and members of the extended kinship network; clarifying their roles and inviting them to a family group meeting; establishing the location, time, and other logistics; and managing other unresolved issues. At the meeting the coordinator welcomes and introduces participants in a culturally appropriate manner, establishes the purpose of the meeting, and helps participants reach agreement about roles, goals, and ground rules. Next, information is shared with the family, which may involve the child protection workers and other relevant professionals such as a doctor or teacher involved with the child. If the program strictly adheres to the New Zealand model, the coordinator and other professionals withdraw from the meeting in the next stage, in order to allow the family privacy for their deliberations. (Some programs have adjusted the model to their local norms and allow the coordinator to remain in the meeting.) As a result of this process, the kinship network responds to several issues, including the safety of the child and the care of the child if it considers that protection is needed (American Humane Association, 1996). There is generally some type of follow-up involved to provide support to the designated caregivers and to plan for permanence when needed. It should be noted that the coordinator and/or child protection worker retain the right to veto a family plan if he or she believes the child will not be protected. In reality, this veto is rarely used.

Working with family group decision making requires a new approach to family-centered practice. The social worker must expand his or her ideas about the family to recognize the strength and centrality of the extended kinship network, particularly in communities of color. Use of the strengths perspective is critical. The worker must understand the greater investment of kin in the well-being of the child and should also understand that, even when parts of the kinship system may seem to be compromised or dysfunctional, the healthier kinfolk may effectively assess and deal with the problem. One of the greatest challenges for the American child welfare system is incorporating the sharing of power or returning of power to the kinship network (American Humane Association, 1998). Generally speaking, most FGDM workers welcome the opportunity to work in partnership with kin families and find it to be congruent with their values.

A comprehensive evaluation of family group decision making in one Michigan county found that it was a valuable addition to the child welfare service continuum; that children placed through family group conferences were less likely to have additional contact with children's protective services; that they moved less between temporary homes; that they were less likely to be placed in an institutional setting; that in two-thirds of cases children remained with their extended family members in legal guardianship; and that families "taking care of their own" is family preservation (Crampton, 2001).

The following case illustrates the implementation of the model within the child protection system of the United States.

Case Study of Mental Health Consumers

Judy and Ronnie R. are parents of a 7-year-old son, Chad. Judy and Ronnie had met in a community drop-in center for consumers of mental health services. Judy, the adopted daughter of Tom and Sandy J., had complex special needs, including developmental and learning disabilities, occasional seizures, and motor difficulties. Ronnie, the son of Mary Ellen R., was diagnosed with a mental illness. Both received SSI for their disabilities. When Judy's pregnancy became evident, both families supported the marriage of the young couple and became actively involved as grandparents for Chad. From time to time Judy and Ronnie would leave their child with paternal or maternal grandparents when they felt unable to cope. Several times Tom and Sandy had gone to the R.'s apartment to pick up Chad and actively intervene in his behalf. Gradually Judy and Ronnie began to isolate themselves from the extended family and refuse to allow Chad to have his regular visits with the relatives.

A referral was made to child protective services by Chad's teacher and the school social worker. Chad had missed twenty days of school in the first semester and appeared dirty and hungry when he was in school. He had difficulty focusing on his work, slept in class, and cried frequently. The school social worker had attempted to engage the parents but was not allowed into their apartment. Ronnie was threatening and belligerent to the school social worker and refused to let Judy speak.

When the protective service worker visited the home, he found it to be dirty to the point of being a health hazard. He noted that Ronnie appeared to spend much of his time locked in the bedroom, and Judy was absorbed in the TV. In a visual assessment of Chad he noted several bruises. The medical evaluation of Chad's condition was that he was suffering from malnutrition, was neglected, and that bruises on his back and buttocks were in the shape of handprints. In discussions with Judy, the protective service worker discovered that the grandparents had been involved with Chad before Judy and Ronnie had shut them out. Both parents indicated that they would rather have the grandparents reinvolved with Chad than risk the possibility of placement outside the family. Ronnie and Judy agreed to have a family group decision-making conference. Chad was allowed to stay temporarily with the paternal grandmother, Mary Ellen, while the case was referred to a family group conference coordinator.

The coordinator received the names and telephone numbers of both paternal and maternal grandparents. She met with Tom and Sandy, and also with Mary Ellen, doing genograms with each family to identify members of the kinship network. Both sets of grandparents helped contact other family members. The conference coordinator talked with each potential participant to explain the FGDM process and purpose.

The conference was held within two weeks of the initial referral, at the small grassroots agency where the coordinator worked. A number of persons attended the conference, including both sets of grandparents, Judy's two sisters and their husbands, her godparents, and her cousin. Ronnie's father, stepmother, and brother also attended. Ronnie and Judy chose not to attend the meeting. The coordinator explained the purpose of the meeting: to plan for the care and protection of Chad. After people became comfortable, with introductions and light refreshments, the coordinator invited the protective service worker to speak. He discussed the medical report, the teacher's concerns, and the condition of the apartment when he had called. The coordinator then asked the family to decide whether they thought Chad needed care and protection by his extended family. The professionals left the room, explaining that the family could have their discussion in private, but that the coordinator would be available as a consultant if they needed her. Within fifteen minutes, she was called back into the room by Tom, the maternal grandfather. The grandparents took turns speaking. First Tom stated that their family was aware of Judy's limitations and that they had tried hard to support her, until they found themselves shut out by Ronnie. They believed that Chad needed to live away from his parents in order to receive proper care. Mary Ellen, the paternal grandmother, stated that their family had been increasingly concerned about Chad over the past several years and that she knew from having Chad with her the past several weeks that he had not been properly cared for by his parents. Ronnie's father stated that everyone realized that Chad had been neglected and abused and that it was time for the family to step in decisively.

The coordinator then outlined several options and asked the family to develop a plan for caring for Chad. Again, the coordinator let the family plan privately. After an interval of about three hours, during which the coordinator worked in her office on other matters and lunch was brought in to the family, she was summoned back to the family meeting. This time, Judy's sister and brother-in-law, Marjorie and Ed, served as spokespersons for the family. They stated that the families had looked at many complicated issues, including Judy and Ronnie's disabilities, and had decided that in all likelihood Chad might need a home within the extended family for all of his growing-up years. Thus they reasoned that, while the grandparents wanted to remain strongly involved, it might be best for Chad to live with younger family members. Marjorie and Ed, who lived near both sets of grandparents, felt that they could raise Chad to adulthood, if needed, and could keep him in contact with both maternal and paternal relatives. Ronnie's father and brother stated that they would make sure Ronnie would not further abuse Chad or make trouble for Marjorie and Ed. Mary Ellen would provide day care for Chad on school holidays, and Tom and Sandy would provide respite care as needed. Marjorie and Ed would apply for guardianship of Chad. All grandparents would contribute to Chad's support through the purchase of clothing, furniture, and provision of money for allowance and incidentals. The family would try to work with Judy and Ronnie on cleaning up their apartment and using mental health services. Until the situation stabilized, the parents would have to visit Chad at the grandparents' homes. The family would make sure they continued to have a part in Chad's life.

This understanding was written down in a "family compact," which was approved by the coordinator and the protective service worker.

Case Commentary.   Not all family group decision-making cases are as easily resolved as this one. Both maternal and paternal relatives were able to reach a position of agreement and trust with each other. Both sets of kin had attempted to support the family and protect the child earlier. However, until empowered by protective service intervention, they were unable to overcome the barriers posed by the parents' isolation. Thus empowered, they promised to take specific roles in supporting the placement of the child and assisting the parents. This case illustrates the strengths and potential of a kinship network to develop a realistic plan based on the needs and situation of the child and family. It appears that both of the parents have conditions that will continue to affect their parenting. It should be noted that this family system had tried diligently to support the child prior to protective service intervention, but they were shut out by the parents. The protective service worker and family group conference coordinator empowered the extended family, enabling them to continue and intensify their efforts with the child.

Several key elements that contributed to the success of this family group conference were the consent of the parents, the strengths of the extended family members, the ability of the coordinator to enlist the cooperation of all members through careful planning, and the family's focus on the long-term needs of Chad. The signed family compact clarified the roles of all, the financial arrangements, the legal arrangement to be made, and the conditions under which protective services might have to be reinvolved.

Policy and Program Issues in Kinship Care

Kinship care, as a program alternative for children in need of child welfare services, spans various categories of child welfare programs and traditional legal arrangements: family preservation, foster care, guardianship, and adoption. The linkage of formal child welfare services and kinship care is congruent with current thinking on the importance of culturally competent human service delivery systems and on the psychosocial need of children for continuity and ongoing attachments.

However, there are a number of unresolved issues and concerns regarding the use of kinship care in the child welfare system. Legal and financial structures designed to define family relationships, protect children, and support families were not intended to apply to kinship care and are not suited to easy linkage with it in many cases (Johnson, 1994). There are also questions about whether to assess kinship homes for safety and as environments for child development in a different way from the assessment of nonkinship placements (Billing, Ehrle, & Kortenkamp, 2002).

The issues are complex and somewhat overlapping. One issue on which there is general agreement concerns the need of kin providers for social support and access to resources for themselves and their young relatives (Dubowitz, 1990; Berrick, Barth, & Needell, 1994; Terling-Watt, 2001; Ehrle & Geen, 2002). Children in relative placement may have very conflicted histories and present daunting behavioral, educational, and medical challenges. In addition to the aftereffects of abuse and neglect, the children may have serious diseases such as HIV/AIDS. Children with incarcerated parents are frequently in the care of relatives and are thought to have significant unresolved issues around separation and trauma (Hungerford, 1996; Slavin, 2000). Children with many different kinds of complex problems may need—in addition to the love, support, and sense of belonging they have in an extended family context—access to professional services of many types if they are to be helped and if the placement is to stay intact (Edelboch, Liu, & Martin, 2002).

Family caregivers also have needs. If employed, they may have concerns about continuing to work while undertaking new caretaking responsibilities. Older relatives, such as grandparents, may have health concerns for themselves or their spouse. Their lives may have grown to include interests and activities that conflict with child caring demands but which they are loath to put aside. They may need improved housing, respite care, support groups, and access to legal counseling.

Family dynamics in kinship arrangements may be complicated and volatile. For example, Warren (2001) notes that parent-absent adolescents may feel contempt for the parent who failed them, and they can turn their anger against themselves in depression or displace it onto grandparents who are raising them. Such situations require expert mental health services and family therapy (Minkler, Roe, & Price, 1992). One group of kin caregivers, adult siblings of children needing care, may have special issues of family dynamics and role conflicts. These arrangements often do not come to the attention of the child welfare system and very little is known about them.

Many child welfare and other organizations are increasing their efforts to help kinship caregivers. For example, the American Association of Retired Persons funds telephone "warm lines" for grandparents to use when feeling overburdened and at wit's end, grandparenting classes, and support groups (McFadden & Downs, 1995; Crumbley & Little, 1998; Jackson, Mathews, & Zuskin, 1999). However, overall, the service systems around the country to support kin placements are fragmented, lacking in many areas, and hard to access.

Financial and Legal Issues.   A serious unresolved problem is providing financial support to kin caregivers, and the problem is exacerbated by the linkage between legal status and eligibility for various forms of public support. One source of financial assistance is TANF, formerly known as public welfare. However, the financial support available for "child only" cases is extremely low. If the grandparent applies for funds on his or her own behalf, the grandparent is subject to the same work requirements as any other applicant, which may not be feasible or helpful to the child (Takas, 1993).

It is possible in some instances for kin providers to be licensed foster parents. These situations are often referred to as *formal kinship care* to distinguish them from *informal kinship care,* which takes place without changes of custody made through the child welfare system. In formal kinship care, the child is placed by the court in the legal custody of the child welfare agency; financial support for the care of the child is made through foster care payments if the kinship homes meet licensing or approval standards for foster parents; and the kinship caregivers are generally expected to comply with the foster parenting role, such as participating in training and cooperating with the agency in implementing a case plan. If they do not meet licensing/approval standards, then payments are made from TANF funds or special relative/kinship care funds.

Treating kin caregivers like foster parents allows them to receive foster care payments, much higher than TANF child only grants. However, many people, including many kin caregivers, have philosophical disagreement with classifying relatives as foster parents; they think that people should not get paid for taking care of their own. Agencies and caregivers alike may see conflicts between the foster parent role and that of relatives; foster parents are in some sense agents of the agency and answerable to it, whereas relatives may not feel that they are fundamentally accountable to the agency.

Problems with financial support, role conflict, and legal status also arise in permanency planning, if the preferred option for the child is a permanent living arrangement with relatives. Some kin caregivers are willing to make a home for a grandchild or other young relative on a permanent basis, but may be reluctant to legalize this arrangement through adoption (Thornton, 1991). Grandparents, in particular, may find it difficult to assume the parents' role and may be particularly reluctant to be part of a process in which their child's parental rights to his or her child are terminated so the grandparent can legally take that parent's place. Such an arrangement feels unnatural, is contrary to cultural expectations, and may mean a final relinquishment of hope that their adult child will recover from the problems that led to the placement of the children. For these caregivers, long-term foster care or guardianship might be a more workable permanency solution.

> *After all, he knows I'm his granny, I always was and I always will be. I'll always love him and I'll always take care of him. He knows we're permanent. We don't need no adoption to feel permanent. (A grandmother)*

If the grandparent is given guardianship and the case moves out of the system, the caregiver may lose the foster care pay rate as well as foster care support services. On the other hand, if the grandparent adopts the child, she will probably be eligible for an adoption subsidy. Proponents of kinship care suggest that subsidized guardianships may promote a new kind of permanency in formal kinship care (Child Welfare League of America, 1994). Others advocate for a new form of adoption—kinship adoption (Takas, 1993; Hegar & Scannapieco, 1999).

Assessment and Psychosocial Issues. An attitudinal barrier to the use of kinship care is expressed in the adage: "The apple doesn't fall far from the tree," indicating that the problems of the child's parents are related to their family of origin. A competent assessment of the relative's home is necessary to address safety and protection issues. A national body has developed the following list as factors to consider in kinship assessment (Child Welfare League of America, 1994, pp. 44–45).

- The quality of the relationship between the relative and the child
- The likelihood that the relative can/will protect the child from further maltreatment
- The safety of the kinship home and the ability of the relative to provide a nurturing environment (including presence of alcohol or drug involvement)
- The willingness of the relative to accept the child into the home
- The ability of the relative to meet the developmental needs of the child
- The nature and quality of the relationship between the birth parent and the relative, including the birth parent's preference about placement of the child with kin

Assessment of kin homes also requires that workers be aware of their own biases. Kin providers may be much older than the worker and of a different socioeconomic class and race (Dubowitz, 1990; Thornton, 1991; Berrick, Barth, & Needell, 1994). Workers may feel less comfortable working with kin caregivers and prefer working with established foster parents who are known to the agency, have more financial resources, and are better educated. In assessment, workers need to be aware of the possibility that their biases are affecting their perceptions.

A possible disadvantage of kinship care is that the maltreating parent could have too easy access to a child or the caregiver may have difficulty establishing boundaries with the parent. Although relatives may appear stable, they may also have some denial about the risk the parent represents to the child, or there may be undetected substance abuse or maltreatment patterns in the family system. It is reassuring that one research project found that children may be less at risk in relative care than in foster care (Zuravin & DePanfilis, 1997). However, there is also less monitoring of relative homes than of unrelated foster homes, raising the possibility of undetected maltreatment (Berrick, Barth, & Needell, 1993). One recent study reported that there was a higher rate of disruption among kin placements than with other types of permanent placements. Reasons for disrupted placements included health limitations of the caregiver, difficulties in the relationship with the children's parents, and difficulty in caring for special needs children (Terling-Watt, 2001). This finding highlights the importance of good assessment in making kin placements and of providing adequate levels of support after they are made.

In spite of these concerns, practice experience and research to date suggest that relatives are a viable resource for many children in the child welfare system who need safe, loving homes with people who think they are very special. The home of a relative can give a child a sense of belonging and promote the formation of cultural and personal identity. Kin caregivers may have more positive perceptions about children placed with them than do nonrelated family foster caregivers (Gebel, 1996; Berrick, Barth, & Needell, 1993). If the case plan supports it, the child can have easier access to parents for visiting and possible reunification. Children may be better able to address unresolved issues of loss and family trauma when placed in an extended family context (Crumbley & Little, 1997). More research is needed on effective strategies for strengthening kin placements and on the outcomes of children placed with relatives, including educational attainment, health status, and ongoing safety and protection.

Trends and Issues

Assessment of Family Functioning

Outcome research conducted in Los Angeles County with two voluntary agencies examined changes in family functioning during home-based family preservation services, as well as changes in child behavior, home environment, traits of parents, and placement outcomes for children (McCroskey & Meezan, 1997). The experimental program differed from the typical family preservation program in that the services provided were for a three-month period (as opposed to the four- to six-week crisis intervention model); the program provided less intensive service to a broader range of families than those with imminent risk of placement; and the program had different standards of program success than the avoidance of placement or cost savings. In many respects, the program appears to address significant issues raised by earlier evaluation (see Evaluation of Family Preservation Programs), especially with its approach to assessing family functioning.

The two agencies involved used a specially developed family assessment form (Children's Bureau of Southern California, 1997) that addressed family functioning in the following areas: (1) environment (physical environment, family finances, and social supports); (2) caregiver (caregiver's history, personal characteristics, and child-rearing ability); (3) family interactions (caregiver to children, children to caregiver, and caregiver to caregiver); and (4) children (developmental status, behavioral concerns, and child summary). It should be noted that studies of family preservation have used various tools to assess family functioning. For example, the Child Well-Being Scales (Magura & Moses, 1986) have been used in studies of family preservation with drug-exposed infants, while the Family Risk Scale (Magura, Moses, & Jones, 1987) was used in research (Thieman & Dail, 1997) on predictors of out-of-home placement.

The Family Assessment Form used in Los Angeles is a practice-oriented assessment protocol that allows the worker to monitor the progress of families. It has been used with families in many different program settings in agencies all over the world (Children's Bureau of Southern California, 1997).

Chapter Summary

Intensive family-based services, typically known as family preservation, have been demonstrated to be helpful to families struggling with multiple problems. These services are time limited and are provided primarily in the home and other environments within the family's ecosystem. Within an overall family-systems framework, a variety of approaches and techniques may be used, including but not limited to the following: cognitive-behavioral, crisis intervention, provision of concrete resources, parent education, mobilization of community supports, and operating from a strengths-based perspective. Flexible funds and the availability of the worker on a round-the-clock basis if necessary help to stabilize families in crisis and provide a wide range of resources for change. The approach is congruent with social work's historic concern and values about families.

While proponents of the services believe that they often prevent out-of-home placement of children and ensure the safety of children who remain in the home, program evaluations call into question the targeting of services to families at risk of placement and the concept of placement prevention. There is some agreement on the usefulness of the services to families, but researchers and practitioners alike call for further research on developmental outcomes for children, the effect of services on levels of family functioning and child safety, and the types of families for whom the family preservation approach is most effective. The trend appears to be toward a wider application of family-based services and greater flexibility in the area of time limitation.

Another important form of family preservation is the use of kinship care. Program approaches borrowed from New Zealand to involve the extended kinship network in the protection of children from abuse and neglect through family group decision making show promise.

A significant concern for proponents of kinship care is the lack of congruent policy and supports for kinship caregivers. Federal support and policy development for kinship care has been inconsistent.

FOR STUDY AND DISCUSSION

1. In your community, is there an intensive family-based services program that works for family preservation with families of children at imminent risk of placement? Visit the agency or invite a staff member to class to discuss assessment and safety issues. How does the agency operationalize the value "safety is our first concern"? How does it respond to attacks in the media? How is it evaluating the effectiveness of its program? What is the practitioner's role in evaluation?

2. Identify those agencies in your community providing support to relatives who are involved in kinship care. Are there support groups and/or advocacy groups? They may be framed as "grandparents raising grandchildren groups," forums for kinship caregivers, or parent-education classes for relative caregivers. Is there a "warm line" or information and referral service available to them? Talk to kinship caregivers and find out what they need.

3. Does your community have any community collaboratives for family support and family preservation? How do service delivery systems (mental health, child protective services, schools, and family preservation agencies) work together to identify needs, allocate resources, provide interdisciplinary team planning for wraparound services and coordinate the "step-down" services when a family moves from family preservation to community-based family support?

4. Talk with your child protection agency. Has your state or community piloted a project on family group decision making? Why or why not? If so, what involvement do the courts and child protection play in the process? What follow-up is available for assuring the children's safety and permanence?

5. Examine current media (newspapers, magazines, television, and talk shows) to identify issues being raised in your state and community about family preservation and safety of children. Do a simple content analysis to identify recurrent themes. Then research the evaluation of family preservation and write a letter to the editor or similar rejoinder to correct any media distortions.

6. Contact your local domestic violence, children's mental health, or HIV support agency. Inquire how it sees family preservation and what intensive, family-based services are being offered to its clientele.

7. Invite a family preservation social worker to speak to your class on the *specifics* of his or her job. How does he or she engage families? How does he or she provide hope? How do families respond to the worker's identifying strengths? What are the greatest challenges? What are the rewards?

FOR ADDITIONAL STUDY

Billing, A., Ehrle, J., & Kortenkamp, K. (2002). Children cared for by relatives: What do we know about their well-being? In *New federalism: National survey of America's families.* Washington, DC: The Urban Institute.

Ehrle, J., & Geen, R. (2002). Children cared for by relatives: What services do they need? In *New federalism: National survey of America's families.* Washington, DC: The Urban Institute.

Farrow, F. (2001). *The shifting policy impact of intensive family preservation services.* Chicago: Chapin Hill Center for Children at University of Chicago.

Jacobs, F. (2001). *What to make of family preservation services evaluations.* Chicago: Chapin Hall Center for Children at University of Chicago.

McCroskey, J. (2001). *What is family preservation and why does it matter?* Chicago: Chapin Hall Center for Children at University of Chicago.

McCroskey, J., & Meezan, W. (1997). *Family preservation and family functioning.* Washington, DC: Child Welfare League of America.

INTERNET SEARCH TERMS

Family preservation   Kinship care

INTERNET SITES

American Humane Association. This nationally recognized organization, known primarily for work in the area of child protection, provides references to publications specific to family group decision making.

www.americanhumane.org

Child Welfare League of America. This organization has a general child welfare site, with specific pages related to developments in family preservation and lists of topically related publications provided by CWLA.

www.cwla.org

National Family Preservation Network. The central coordinating point for a network of family preservation staff and programs.

www.nfpn.org

National Resource for Family Centered Practice. This federally funded resource center, which provides technical assistance and training to states and programs, has a comprehensive web site that includes lists of materials available, bibliographies, and *The Prevention Report.*

www.cwresource.org

REFERENCES

Allen, M., & Zalenski, J. (1993, Spring). Making a difference for families: Family-based services in the nineties. *The Prevention Report,* 1–3.

American Humane Association. (1998). *1997 National roundtable series on family group decision-making: Summary of proceedings, assessing the promise and implementing the practice.* Englewood, CO: Author.

American Humane Association. (1996). The practice and promise of family group decision-making. *Protecting Children, 12*(3).

Angelou, M. (1985). Introduction. In *Keeping families together: The case for family preservation.* Edna McConnell Clark Foundation.

Bain, A. (1978). The capacity of families to cope with transitions: A theoretical essay. *Human Relations, 31*(8), 675–688.

Bandura, A. (1977). *Social learning theory.* Englewood Cliffs, NJ: Prentice-Hall.

Barth, R. P. (1994). Long-term in-home services. In D. Besharov (Ed.), *When drug addicts have children* (pp. 175–194). Washington, DC: Child Welfare League of America, American Enterprise Institute.

Barthel, J. (1992). *For children's sake: The promise of family preservation.* Philadelphia: Winchell Company.

Bath, H., & Haapala, D. (1993). Intensive family preservation services with abused and neglected children: An examination of group differences. *Child Abuse & Neglect, 17,* 213–225.

Bergquist, C., Szwejda, D., & Pope, G. (1993, March). *Evaluation of Michigan's Family First program summary report.* Lansing, MI: University Associates.

Berrick, J., Barth, R., & Needell, B. (1994). A comparison of kinship foster homes and foster family homes: Implications for kinship foster care as family preservation. *Children and Youth Services Review, 16*(1–2), 33–63.

Berry, M. (1992). An evaluation of family preservation services: Fitting agency services to family needs. *Social Work, 37*(4), 314–321.

Besharov, D. (Ed.). (1994). *When drug addicts have children: Reorienting child welfare's response.* Washington, DC: Child Welfare League of America, American Enterprise Institute.

Billing, A., Ehrle, J., & Kortenkamp, K. (2002). Children cared for by relatives: What do we know about their well-being? In *New Federalism: National survey of America's families.* Washington, DC: The Urban Institute.

Caplan, G. (1974). *Principles of preventive psychiatry.* New York: Basic Books.

Child Welfare League of America. (1994). *Kinship care: A natural bridge.* Washington, DC: Child Welfare League of America.

Children's Bureau of Southern California. (1997). *Family assessment form: A practice-based approach to assessing family functioning.* Washington, DC: Child Welfare League of America Press.

Cimmarusti, R. (1992). Family preservation practice based upon a multisystems approach. *Child Welfare, 71*(3), 241–255.

Courtney, M. (1997). Reconsidering family preservation: A review of *Putting Families First. Children and Youth Services Review, 19*(1–2), 61–76.

Crampton, D. (2001). Making sense of foster fare: An evaluation of family group decision making in Kent County, Michigan. Dissertation, University of Michigan.

Cross, T. (1987). *Cross-culture skills in Indian child welfare: A guide for the non-Indian.* Portland, OR: Northwest Indian Child Welfare Association.

Cross, T. (1986). Drawing on cultural tradition in Indian child welfare practice. *Social Casework,* May, 283–289.

Crumbley, J., & Little, R. (Eds.). (1997). *Relatives raising children: An overview of kinship care.* Washington, DC: Child Welfare League of America Press.

Dennis, K. (1997). Advocate's narrative. In R. Golden (Ed.), *Disposable children* (pp. 169–172). Belmont, CA: Wadsworth.

Doerre, Y., & Mihaly, L. (1996). *Home sweet home: Building collaborations to keep families together.* Washington, DC: Child Welfare League of America Press.

Dubowitz, H. (1990). *The physical and mental health and educational status of children placed with relatives: Final report.* Baltimore: University of Maryland.

Edelboch, M., Liu, Q., & Martin, L. (2002). Unsung heroes: Relative caregivers in child-only cases. *Policy and Practice of Public Human Services, 60*(1), 26–30.

Edleson, J. L. (1999). The overlap between child maltreatment and woman battering. *Violence Against Women, 5*(2), 134–154.

Edna McConnell Clark Foundation. (1985). *Keeping families together: The case for family preservation.* New York.

Ehrle, J., & Geen, R. (2002). Chlidren cared for by relatives: What services do they need? In *New Federalism: National survey of American's families.* Washington, DC: The Urban Institute.

Faria, G. (1994). Training for family preservation practice with lesbian families. *Families and Society, 75*(7), 416–422.

Findlater, J., & Kelly, S. (1999, May). Reframing child safety in Michigan: Building collaboration among domestic violence, family preservation, and child protection services. *Child Maltreatment* (pp. 167–174). Thousand Oaks, CA: Sage.

Gebel, T. (1996). Kinship care and nonrelative family foster care: A comparison of caregiver attributes and attitudes. *Child Welfare, 75*(1), 5–18.

Gelles, R. (1996). *The Book of David: How preserving families can cost children's lives.* New York: Basic Books/HarperCollins.

Germain, C., & Gitterman, A. (1980). *The life model of social work practice.* New York: Columbia University Press.

Giarretto, H. A. (1982). *Integrated treatment of child sexual abuse.* Palo Alto, CA: Science and Behavior Books.

Gray, S. S., & Nybell, L. (1990). Issues in African-American family preservation. *Child Welfare, 69*(6), 513–523.

Hardin, M. (1994, May). Family group conferences in New Zealand. *ABA Journal and Child Welfare Law Reporter.*

Hartman, A. (1993). Family preservation under attack. *Social Work, 38,* 509–512.

Hartman, A., & Laird, J. (1983). *Family centered social work practice.* New York: Free Press.

Hegar, R., & Scannapieco, M. (1999). *Kinship foster care: Policy, practice, and research.* New York: Oxford University Press.

Heneghan, A., Horwitz, S., & Leventhal, J. (1996). Evaluating family preservation programs: A methodological review. *Pediatrics, 97*(4), 535–542.

Hungerford, G. (1996). Caregivers of children whose mothers are incarcerated: A study of the kinship placement system. *Children Today, 24*(1), 23–27.

Jackson, S., Matthews, J., & Zuskin, R. (1999). *Supporting the kinship triad: A training curriculum.* Washington, DC: Child Welfare League of America.

Jacobs, F. (2001). *What to make of family preservation services evaluations.* Chicago: Chapin Hall Center for Children at University of Chicago.

Johnson, I. (1994). Kinship care. In D. Besharov (Ed.), *When drug addicts have children,* (pp. 221–228). Washington, DC: Child Welfare League of America, American Enterprise Institute.

Jones, B. (1994). The clients and their problems. In D. Besharov (Ed.), *When drug addicts have children* (pp. 115–124). Washington, DC: Child Welfare League of America, American Enterprise Institute.

Kinney, J., Haapala, D., & Booth, C. (1991). *Keeping families together: The homebuilders model.* New York: Aldine de Gruyter.

Lindsey, D. (1994). Family preservation and child protection: Striking a balance. *Children and Youth Services Review, 16*(5–6), 279–294.

Lovell, M., Reid, K., & Richey, C. (1992). Social support training for abusive mothers. *Social Work with Groups, 15*(2–3), 95–107.

Magura, S., & Moses, B. (1986). *Outcome measure for child welfare services: Theory and applications.* Washington, DC: Child Welfare League of America Press.

Magura, S., Moses, B., & Jones, M. (1987). *Assessing risk and measuring change in families.* Washington, DC: Child Welfare League of America Press.

Maluccio, A., & Whittaker, J. (1997). Learning from the "family preservation" initiative. *Children and Youth Services Review, 19*(1–2), 5–16.

Maluccio, A., Pine, B., & Walsh, R. (1994). Protecting children by preserving their families. *Children and Youth Services Review, 16*(5–6), 295–307.

Mannes, M. (1993). Seeking the balance between child protection and family preservation in Indian child welfare. *Child Welfare, 72*(2), 141–152.

McCroskey, J. (2001). *What is family preservation and why does it matter?* Chicago: Chapin Hall Center for Children.

McCroskey, J., & Meezan, W. (1997). *Family preservation & family functioning.* Washington, DC: Child Welfare League of America Press.

McFadden, E. J., & Downs, S. W. (1995). Family continuity: The new paradigm in permanence planning. *Community Alternatives: The International Journal of Family Care, 7*(1), 44.

Merkel-Holguin, L. (1998). Transferring the family group conferencing technology from New Zealand to the United States. Paper presented at the twelfth International Congress on Child Abuse and Neglect, Auckland, New Zealand.

Mills, C., Usher, D., & McFadden, E. J. (1999, Fall). Kinship in the African American community. *Michigan Sociological Review, 13,* 1–16.

Minkler, M., Roe, K., & Price, M. (1992). The physical and emotional health of grandmothers raising grandchildren in the crack cocaine epidemic. *The Gerontologist, 32*(6), 752–761.

Napoli, M., & Gonzales-Santin, E. (2001). Intensive home-based and wellness services to Native American families living on reservations: A model. *Families in Society, 82*(3), 315–324.

National Council of Juvenile and Family Court Judges. (1992). *Protocol for making reasonable efforts to preserve families in drug-related dependency cases.* Reno, NV: National Council of Juvenile and Family Court Judges.

National Public Child Welfare Association and The National Resource Center on Child Maltreatment. (2001). *A research agenda for public child welfare.* Washington, DC: Author.

National Resource Center on Family Based Services. (1994). Project proposal. Iowa City, IA.

Nelson, K. (2000). What works in family preservation services. In M. Kluger, G. Alexander, & P. Curtis (Eds.), *What works in child welfare.* Washington, DC: Child Welfare League of America.

Nelson, K., Landsman, M., & Deutelbaum, W. (1990). Three models of family-centered placement prevention services. *Child Welfare, 69*(1), 3–21.

Noble, D., Perkins, K., & Fatout, M. (2000). On being a strength coach: Child welfare and the strengths model. *Child and Adolescent Social Work Journal, 17*(2), 141–153.

Parad, H. J. (Ed.). (1965). *Crisis intervention: Selected readings.* New York: Family Service Association of America.

Patterson, G. (1975). *Families.* Champaign, IL: Research Press.

Pecora, P., Whittaker, J., Maluccio, A., Barth, R., & Plotnick, R. (1992). *The child welfare challenge.* Hawthorne, NY: Aldine de Gruyter.

Polansky, N., Chalmers, M., Battenmeier, E., & Williams, D. (1981). *Damaged parents: An anatomy of child neglect.* Chicago: University of Chicago Press.

Rabin, R. (2001, November 18). What about the children? *Grand Rapids Press,* p. A13.

Ryan, P., Warren, B., & Weincek, P. (1992). *Removal of the perpetrator versus removal of the victim in cases of intra-familial child sexual abuse. Final report.* Ypsilanti, MI: Institute for the Study of Children and Families, Eastern Michigan University.

Saleeby, D. (2002). *The strengths perspective in social work practice* (3rd ed.). Boston: Allyn & Bacon.

Sandau-Beckler, P., Salcido, R., & Ronnau, J. (1993). Culturally competent family preservation services: An approach for first generation Hispanic families in an international border community. *The Family Journal, Counseling and Therapy for Couples and Families, 1*(4), 313–323.

Scannapieco, M. (1993). The importance of family functioning to prevention of placement: A study of family preservation services. *Child and Adolescent Social Work Journal, 10*(6), 509–520.

Schuerman, J., Rzepnicki, T., & Littell, J. (1992). *Evaluation of the Illinois Family First placement prevention program: Progress report.* Chicago, IL: Chapin Hall.

Schuerman, J., Rzepnicki, T., Littell, J., & Budde, S. (1992). Implementation issues. *Children and Youth Services Review, 14,* 193–206.

Slavin, P. (2000). Children with parents behind bars. *Children's Voice, 9*(5), 4+.

Smith, D., & Featherstone, T. (1991). Family group conferences—the process. In *Family Decision Making.* Lower Hutt, New Zealand: Practitioners Publishing.

Spake, A. (1994, November). The little boy who didn't have to die. *McCall's,* 142–151.

Sudia, C. (1981). What services do abusive and neglecting families need? In L. H. Pelton (Ed.), *The Social Context of Child Abuse and Neglect* (pp. 268–290). New York: Human Services Press.

Takas, M. (1993, December–January). Kinship care: Developing a safe and effective framework for protective placement of children with relatives. *Zero to Three,* 12–17.

Terling-Watt, T. (2001). Permanency in kinship care: An exploration of disruption rates and factors associated with placement disruption. *Children & Youth Services Review, 23*(2), 111–126.

Thieman, A., & Dail, P. (1997). Predictors of out-of-home placement in a family preservation program: Are welfare recipients particularly vulnerable? *Policy Studies Journal, 25*(1), 124–139.

Thornton, J. (1991). Permanency planning for children in kinship foster homes. *Child Welfare, 70*(5), 593–601.

Tracy, E., Whittaker, J., Pugh, A., Kapp, S., & Overstreet, E. (1994). Support networks of primary caregivers receiving family preservation services: An exploratory study. *Families in Society, 75*(8), 481–489.

U.S. General Accounting Office. (1997). States' progress in implementing family preservation and support services. Washington, DC: General Accounting Office, Health Education and Human Services Division.

Vandenberg, J., Grealish, M., & Schick, C. (1993). *Wraparound guidelines.* Lansing, MI: Michigan Department of Social Services.

Walton, E. (1997). Enhancing investigative decisions in child welfare: An exploratory use of intensive family preservation services. *Child Welfare, 76*(3), 447–461.

Walsh, R., Pine, B., & Maluccio, A. (1995). Essay, the meaning of family preservation: Shared mission, diverse methods. *Families in Society: The Journal of Contemporary Human Services,* 625–626.

Warren, D. H. (2001). Reaching for integrity: An Ericksonian life-cycle perspective on the experience of adolescents being raised by grandparents. *Child and Adolescent Social Work Journal, 18*(1), 21–35.

Wells, K., & Tracy, E. (1996). Reorienting intensive family preservation services in relation to public child welfare practice. *Child Welfare, 75*(6), 667–692.

Wells, K., & Whittington, D. (1993, March). Child and family functioning after intensive family preservation services. *Social Service Review,* 55–83.

Whittaker, J., Kinney, J., Tracy, E., & Booth, C. (1990). *Reaching high-risk families.* New York: Aldine de Gruyter.

Worrall, J. (2001). Kinship care of the abused child, the New Zealand experience. *Child Welfare, 80*(5), 495–511.

Zalenski, J. (1994). A new/old practice to care for children: New Zealand's family decision making model. *The Prevention Report* (pp. 11–14). Iowa City, IA: National Resource Center on Family Based Services.

Zuravin, S., & DePanfilis, D. (1997). Factors affecting foster care placement of children receiving child protective services. *Social Work Research, 21*(1), 34–42.

9 Foster Care for Children and Their Families

Children begin by loving their parents; as they grow older they judge them; sometimes they forgive them.

—Oscar Wilde

CHAPTER OUTLINE

With the passage of the Adoption and Safe Families Act of 1997, the American people, through their legislators, moved the issues of child safety, well-being, and permanency into the forefront of child welfare policy. Long intended as a "temporary" service for children and families, foster care—and the child welfare system—has become a way of life for too many children. Many children have not found permanency outcomes; in 2000, nearly a third of the 550,000 children in foster care had been in care for three years or more. About 130,000 children were identified as unlikely ever to return home and were awaiting a permanent plan. Minority children, who make up 55 percent of children in care, wait longer for permanent homes than do white children (AFCARS, 2002). To address the problem of too many children staying in foster care too long, the law expedites procedures and requires states to file termination of parental rights petitions for any child in foster care for fifteen of the most recent twenty-two months, unless the child is in the care of a relative or other possible compelling reasons.

The issue of safety was also of concern to policy makers. Of the thousand or so children who die of abuse and neglect each year, nearly half are known to child protection agencies (Pizzigati, 1998). Public concern has mounted as citizens read in their daily newspapers about children at risk in their families or in the systems designed to protect them. The new law addresses child safety by explicitly eliminating, in some dangerous situations, the requirement that child welfare agencies make "reasonable efforts" to preserve families before placing the child in care. To further protect children and promote quick permanency decisions, the law requires mandatory filing of termination of parental rights petitions in certain extremely dangerous situations: when there has been the murder of another child by the parent, abandonment of an infant, or felony assault resulting in serious bodily harm to a child. Criminal background checks for foster and adoptive parents are required. States must report annually to the federal government on their performance in protecting children.

Another aspect of the renewed focus on improving services to children themselves, apart from services to their families, is the requirement in the Act that agencies address the developmental needs of children. The Adoption and Safe Families Act requires the Department of Health and Human Services to prepare an annual report on state child welfare agency attainment of child well-being standards in health, mental health, education, and continuity of placement (Maza, 2000). This focus reaffirms that foster care should be a service focused on children's needs and should be accountable for how children fare while under state care. However, compliance may force states into hard choices concerning resource allocation for child services as opposed to family preservation services.

In another effort to address the problem of children remaining in care too long, in 1996 the U.S. Congress passed legislation requiring states to eliminate racial matching as a consideration in placement. The new law amends the Multiethnic Placement Act of 1994, which allowed agencies flexibility to give preference to same-race placements. The Interethnic

Adoption Placement Amendment of 1996 prohibited all race-based placement decisions in adoption and foster care. The policy of same-race placements had come under criticism as creating a possible barrier to permanency, as some children, mainly black, remained in foster care because a same-race home was not found for them, although a family of another race might have been available. American Indian children are not affected by this legislation, as the Indian Child Welfare Act continues to mandate that they be placed in Indian homes, unless the tribe approves a non-Indian home placement. This inconsistency in policy means that foster care today operates with two seemingly conflicting sets of principles regarding cultural diversity: Cultural values are paramount for the placement of Indian children, and nondiscrimination policies are paramount for the placement of all other children. This apparent conflict is resolved when we understand that federally recognized Indian tribes are sovereign nations within the United States. This means that they are the equivalent of a France, Germany, or England in some issues, such as holding jurisdiction in child welfare cases. Just as any of these countries establishes the laws regulating the adoption of its children, so too can Indian tribes establish laws regulating the adoption of their children.

How has a service that affects so many children and that has such a long-established position in child welfare become so burdened with highly complex problems? To shed light on this question, this chapter will trace the history of foster care, identify the components of the foster care system and the processes involved, describe the elements of the controversies, and detail the most promising strategies for improving the delivery of foster care services.

Case Example: Concurrent Planning in Foster Care

In foster care practice, as in all social work practice, each case situation is unique. Each family member has many strengths and compelling needs. Each family member in need of out-of-home care for children suffers from separation in his or her own way. Placement of a child in care is like major surgery for a family system—necessary, perhaps, in serious situations, but not to be undertaken lightly.

> The Denton children, Ricky age 3 and Elena age 5, were placed in foster care after they were found wandering in the street, unsupervised at 11 P.M. They told the children's protective service worker that "Mama's lost." After checking with neighbors, the CPS worker found that the mother frequently left the children alone while she was out "partying." Ms. Denton contacted the CPS worker three days later, claiming that she had just gone out for a drink with her boyfriend, but that she had ended up in the emergency room following a fight and an auto accident.
>
> The children had been placed with the Williams family, who made them comfortable, fed them, and reassured them. On the next day they took the children for a medical examination. The pediatrician informed the CPS worker that the children had skin conditions and signs of malnutrition consistent with a diagnosis of neglect. They also had several suspicious bruises, which they would not talk about.
>
> The CPS worker put Ms. Denton in touch by phone with the Williams home, so that she could share information about the children with the foster parents, speak with the children, and be reassured about their well-being. The next day the Williamses brought the children to the agency visiting room so that they could see their mother.

On an initial contact with Ms. Denton, the worker explored her family situation to see whether there was a potential relative placement. Ms. Denton stated that her mother was deceased and her father lived on the streets in another state. She did not know who was the father of Elena, and Ricky's father was serving time in prison for dealing controlled substances. Her only sibling was an unsuitable placement, she knew, as he had sexually abused her when they were children. She considered that the children were better off in the Williams foster home than with any of her friends.

At the court hearing, Ms. Denton acknowledged that her use of substances had caused her to leave the children home alone on more than one occasion and that her judgment had been impaired when she failed to return home on the dates alleged in the petition. The children were made temporary wards of the family court, and the judge instructed Ms. Denton that she must seek treatment for her substance use and be able to provide a home with proper supervision within legal time frames.

The case was transferred to Ms. Lee, foster care worker. Immediately Ms. Lee scheduled an appointment at the substance treatment center for an assessment on the effects of alcohol and other drugs on Ms. Denton's functioning and ability to parent. Ms. Denton was admitted for treatment, but checked herself out the following morning and once again could not be found. The foster care worker did a "differential diagnosis" based on information collected from a variety of sources. The prognosis for recovery and family reunification was not good at that point, so Ms. Lee began to implement a concurrent plan. The plan was still for family reunification (if Ms. Denton addressed the issues that had caused the children to be placed), but an alternative plan was also developed, to be used if the client defaulted on the plan.

Ms. Lee spoke with Mr. and Mrs. Williams on her second visit to the home to monitor the well-being of the children. The foster parents were experienced and well trained, so they were well aware of the deleterious effects of placement change on children. They committed to work intensively with Ms. Denton when she returned and to assist her in the reunification process. At the same time, they indicated they would be available as a resource for adoption if the children's mother did not follow through.

The next week, less than two weeks after the children had been placed in care, Ms. Denton reappeared, and Ms. Lee provided the mother with a full disclosure of the situation. She emphasized the urgency of the time lines required by federal law and stressed that Ms. Denton had a limited time in which to show the court that she was ready to be reunited with her children. Ms. Denton wept when confronted with the reality that she might lose her children and vowed to work hard for their return. A signed agreement was developed that specified the time lines of court review, the steps that Ms. Denton would undertake, and the resources and assistance that would be provided by Ms. Lee and the agency. That day she returned to the substance treatment center.

Mr. and Mrs. Williams brought the children to visit their mother frequently. They had learned in their training the importance of maintaining the parent–child bond. By sharing their observations of the children with the mother, they were able to show her how important she was to both Ricky and Elena. When Ms. Denton completed her inpatient stay, the Williamses brought her to their home for yet another visit. They also brought the children to the mother's apartment when the worker deemed the time for home visits had arrived.

Meanwhile, Ms. Lee was exploring the paternal claims to the children. Elena apparently had been the result of a "one night stand," and there was no knowledge of who the father might be. Corresponding with Ricky's father in prison, she ascertained that he was willing to relinquish parental rights in the event of an adoption. By attending to these details before the need to move to termination of parental rights and adoption, she was removing obstacles to timely permanency.

At the same time, the worker met with Ms. Denton's AA sponsor, who helped the newly recovering woman to attend frequent AA meetings to support sobriety. Ms. Lee also monitored other kinds of progress with the plan, including regular urine screens, enrollment in a parenting class, and the mother's use of appropriate discipline with the children. Mrs. Williams helped teach Ms. Denton to cook nutritious meals for the children when they visited.

After four months, the children were returned to their mother's care, and a family reunification worker supported Ms. Denton and the children with intensive family-based services (see Chapter 8). The family remained under foster care supervision for another six months. Occasionally, Ms. Denton would bring the children to visit with the Williams family when she needed a brief period of respite.

Had the reunification plan not succeeded, the children would have remained with the Williams family with whom they had made a good adjustment and were comfortable. When the case was dismissed from court jurisdiction, Ms. Denton confided to Ms. Lee that it was not until she was confronted with the reality that she might lose her children that she was able to move ahead to sobriety and learning to parent.

Basic Characteristics of Foster Care

As a service to children and their families, foster care has certain distinguishing characteristics:

1. Foster care is arranged by a public; private nonprofit; or private for-profit social agency.
2. Responsibility for children's daily care usually is transferred from the biological parents because of a serious situation—a complex set of interacting conditions or parental characteristics that makes the parents unable to care for their children properly and necessitates community assumption of responsibility.
3. Foster care is full-time care, twenty-four hours a day, outside the child's own home.
4. Foster care or out-of-home care may be given within a relative's home, a nonrelated family foster home, a treatment foster home, a small group home, a cottage setting, a larger residential care facility, or if the child is old enough, in his or her own residence with independent living program supervision.
5. In contrast with adoption, foster care is supposed to be a temporary arrangement, with the expectation that the child will return to the parents or extended family, be placed for adoption, or be discharged from care on reaching legal maturity.

Using social work methods, the social agency plays a major role in planning and carrying out the child's care. Typically the parents retain many of their rights even if the court has assumed temporary wardship of the child. Thus the agency shares the broad responsibility for the child with the court, the parents, and the community, even while the foster parents, house parents, or child care staff provide the day-to-day services for the child.

Children and youths who enter care have usually had difficult experiences, including the maltreatment and/or parental problems that necessitate care, and this is compounded by the painful separation from parents, siblings, kinfolk, and familiar environments. They may have unresolved conflicts in relation to their parents or divided loyalties between original family and substitute caregivers. Because of their life experiences—physical neglect, abuse, emotional neglect, sexual abuse, abandonment, or exploitation—young persons in care often have many unmet developmental needs. Consequently, for the foster care experience to be nurturing and successful, it must involve far more than a change of setting.

Underlying Principles

Certain generalizations or principles underlie contemporary foster care practice. Some have remained relatively stable during this century, while others have evolved:

1. The parent–child relationship and adequate parenting are of utmost importance to the child. Society's first responsibility is to try to preserve the child's own home. If that is not possible, the kinship network or extended family should be supported to provide the child continuity of relationships.
2. If parental care cannot be restored to a level that will protect children and provide at least minimally adequate care, and the kinship network cannot maintain the child, then family foster care can provide nurture within a family setting until a permanent family situation can be achieved for the child.
3. Different settings within the foster care system—family foster homes, specialized or treatment homes, group homes, and residential care—are an array of services from which the most appropriate placement service can be selected, based on the unique needs of the individual child and family.
4. In all settings the entire family is the identified client. The initial service goal is usually family reunification, with improved family functioning and safety and permanency for the child.
5. The foster caregiver (foster parent, houseparent, or child care staff) is an integral part of the service team. The caregiver participates in forming a permanency plan, serves as a role model to the family, aids in facilitating family reunification, and ensures that the child's health, dental and medical; mental health; and educational needs are met.
6. When decisions crucial to the future of the child are made, special consideration must be given to ensure that the legal rights of the child are protected. This must be balanced with attention to constitutional rights of parents and the rights of children to be part of a family and maintain family connections.

Historical Development

Indenture, Almshouses, and Institutions

In ancient times as throughout history orphaned children were usually cared for by their kinfolk through mechanisms embedded in clan or tribe and culture. Both Jewish and Christian religions made provisions for the care of children in family homes. Slingerland, in his treatise on foster care (1919), found no record of formal institutions for dependent children until about the end of the second century. These institutions have continued until very recently.

In England, the system of child placing for profit began under a system of indenture given national sanction in 1562. This system was imported into the American colonies, where it left a significant imprint on the development of child placing. By statute in many states, trustees of the poor were authorized to "bind out" to a master artisan a poor child, orphan, illegitimate child, or any other destitute child old enough to work. Such children would then become members of their master's household and be taught a craft or trade. In turn, the children were obliged to give their master obedience and labor, which was expected to pay for their keep and training by the time they reached maturity and the end of their indenture.

Indenture was seen as having two basic purposes: (1) to fix responsibility for the support and care of a dependent child on some person or family, and (2) to give training for work (it was a period of history when there was much work to be done for survival, and the growth of the country required most persons to acquire some skills or an occupation).

Homer Folks (1911) noted that the old-fashioned indenture or apprentice system passed largely into disuse and disrepute after 1874. The system had not been without merit and provided in varying degrees an experience of substitute family life for dependent children. However, changing industrial conditions in the nineteenth century tended to make the relationship of apprentice to master less intimate and kindly.

Not all poor children were indentured in the early years of this country. Sometimes "outdoor relief"—material supplied by the town to destitute parents in their own homes—preserved a child's own home. But punitive attitudes toward the poor made outdoor relief the least accepted form of care. When towns grew large enough to build almshouses, needy children were often sent to live in them. In 1842, Yates, then secretary of state of New York, surveyed the condition of paupers and strongly recommended the elimination of outdoor relief and that every county in the state maintain a poorhouse. The children of pauper inmates were to be educated and at a suitable age sent out for useful labor.

His plan was largely implemented in New York. However, thirty years after Yates's enthusiastic report on what the almshouse system would accomplish for children, an investigation of the poorhouses found them to be "most disgraceful memorials of the public charity" and "for the young . . . the worst possible nurseries" (*Report of Select Senate Committee,* 1857). Publicity about the poorhouse environment in which children were living led to the conviction that the placement of children there had been a serious mistake. As a result, various states began to remove children from the almshouse.

While the controversy was going on about outdoor relief, indenture, and almshouse care, some institutions for children apart from adults were being established. In the nineteenth century, public and private agencies set up institutions for special classes of children—the blind, deaf, mentally deficient, and delinquent—as well as orphanages for dependent children to protect them from neglect and abuse. While these institutions appeared to their founders as an improvement over the mixed almshouses (and many were), in some of the large congregate institutions there were problems of inadequate sanitation, poor medical care, inadequate diets, and epidemics of contagious disease from which many children died.

The trend toward orphanages grew, however, not only because of continuing dissatisfaction with the public almshouses but also because of the emerging practice of awarding assistance from the public treasury to voluntary agencies. Most of the orphan asylums were established under denominational auspices as various religious groups sought to provide for their own needy children and teach them their faith. Their programs combined religious duty with missionary zeal, lack of individualization of children, hard daily work for the children "to inure [them] to hardship and fatigue," and little chance for enduring relationships with particular adults. When children were received into care, the usual practice was to require parents to surrender their rights to their children. As they grew older and had been given some education, indenture was the means for moving them back into the community.

The vast majority of orphanages were operated by white people for white children. Many of the children were new immigrants whose families, migrating from Europe, had died or become separated during the migration process (Downs & Sherraden, 1983). By and large children of color were served by informal kinship placements, but in 1888 several African American women community leaders founded the St. Louis Colored Orphans Home. This agency evolved into the Annie Malone Children and Family Service Center, which still provides leadership in the African American service community today (Brissett-Chapman & Issacs-Shockley, 1997).

Orphan Trains and Free Foster Homes

Still another approach to the care of dependent children was the free foster home movement, best illustrated by the work of Charles Loring Brace, who in 1853 began the practice of taking needy or homeless children from the city in large parties to a rural locality, where they were placed in the homes of farmers and tradespeople. Brace was concerned about the increasing crime and poverty among the children of New York City and the plight of the many uncared-for, ignorant, and vagrant youth. In his book *The Dangerous Classes of New York,* he wrote that immigration "is pouring in its multitude of poor foreigners, who leave these young outcasts everywhere abandoned in our midst" (1872). The child "placing out" movement spearheaded by Brace took children from the cities by "orphan trains" to farm communities in the Midwest and South. Brace described his method as follows:

> We formed little companies of emigrants, and, after thoroughly cleaning and clothing them, put them under a competent agent, and, first selecting a village where there was a call . . . for such a party, we dispatched them to the place. The farming community having been duly notified, there was usually a dense crowd of people at the station, awaiting the arrival of the youthful travelers. The sight of the little company of the children of misfortune always touched the hearts of a population naturally generous. . . . The agent then addressed the assembly, stating the benevolent objects of the Society and something of the history of the children. The sight of their worn faces was a most pathetic enforcement of his arguments. People who were childless came forward. . . . Others, who had not intended to take any into their families, were induced to apply for them; and many who really wanted the children's labor, pressed forward to obtain it. (pp. 231–232)

Between 1853 and 1929, over 30,000 children were placed in family homes by way of the orphan trains (Thurston, 1930). Brace's movement attracted followers. It was bold;

many children did get good homes, and it provided a stimulus generally to the placement of children out of almshouses and into families. But there were critics as well. Some of the child welfare leaders of religious faiths different from Brace's had little enthusiasm for his program, as most of the homes in which children were placed were Protestant. By contrast, most of the children came from immigrant families, largely Catholic. Objections that children had been removed from the religion of their parents added a stimulus to the growth of sectarian agencies and to legislating religious matching as one determinant in the choice of foster or adoptive homes. Brace's experiment also revealed the problem of lack of ongoing supervision of placements once made.

The White House Conference on Children

By the last quarter of the nineteenth century, foster homes and institutions prevailed as fairly well-developed forms of care for dependent children. A philosophy of child care centered on the question "What does the child really need?" began to emerge. A consensus developed, articulated at the White House Conference on Children in 1909, that all children need families and that family care was the preferred environment to meet the needs of developing children.

Twentieth-Century Child Welfare Reforms

Family Foster Care, a Response to Institutional Care

From the White House Conference in 1909 through the 1960s, the main goal of the foster care program was to provide a safe, nurturing environment for children who could not live at home because of parental maltreatment or inadequacy. Child welfare practice focused on helping the child adjust to the foster home and helping the foster family with the child's development. The serious limitations of this phase were the lack of incentives within the system to work toward family reunification and the lack of recognition that the family of origin was important to the child in care. Because the main emphasis was on the child's well-being, it usually appeared safer to leave the child in care indefinitely.

The Permanency Planning Movement

A major impetus for reform was the growing recognition that although foster care had been intended as a temporary substitute for the child's own home, many children remained in foster care for years, sometimes moving through many different foster homes (Maas & Engler, 1959). The work of Bowlby (1969) and others (Geiser, 1973; Littner, 1975) lent theoretical weight to the notion that separations and disruption of emotional attachments would lead to difficulties in forming healthy attachments and would be damaging to children.

In response to these concerns, and because the critical mass of children in care had risen to over 520,000 by 1977, the 1970s saw the advent of permanency planning. *Permanency planning* is the "systematic process of carrying out, within a limited period, a set of goal directed activities designed to help children and youths live in families that offer continuity of relationships with nurturing parents or caretakers, and the opportunity to offer lifetime relationships" (Maluccio & Fein, 1983, p. 197). Moving children out of care into adoption became a desired goal. Throughout the 1970s the legal, attitudinal, and procedural barriers to moving children into adoptive families were systematically addressed through a variety of demonstration programs and national dissemination efforts (Pike, Downs, Emlen, Downs, & Case, 1977; Emlen, 1978; Fanshel & Shinn, 1978; Jones, 1978; Downs, 1981). In many states statutes were revised to make clearer the grounds for termination of parental rights, and to mandate case review and case planning. Underlying this phase was the belief that "no child is unadoptable" (Churchill, Carlson, & Nybell, 1979).

Family Preservation

As professionals demonstrated that the backlog of children in indeterminate foster care could be reduced, they promoted the understanding that some children would not have needed care in the first place if services had been available to their families. In the early 1980s, this awareness sparked practice strategies and legal reform to prevent family breakup (Nelson, Landsman, & Deutelbaum, 1990). Two major pieces of federal legislation, the Indian Child Welfare Act of 1978 and the Adoption Assistance and Child Welfare Act of 1980, gave federal support to state efforts to make diligent and focused efforts to preserve the family before deciding to place a child in foster care (Ratterman, Dodson, & Hardin, 1987). By 1984 the number of children in foster care (both foster family and group care) declined to 275,000 as a result of vigorous permanence planning and family preservation services. (See Chapter 8.)

Family Continuity and Kinship Care

By 1991, however, the number of children in care had climbed once again, in spite of permanency planning, family preservation, and adoption reforms. The onset of the crack cocaine epidemic, the spread of HIV/AIDS to women and children, and economic stressors were contributing factors to the fragmentation of families. Although the number of children entering care increased, the number of foster families prepared to receive them was in sharp decline, creating a placement crisis (U.S. General Accounting Office, 1989). The term *lobby bodies* referred to a growing phenomenon, children filling up the waiting room of the child welfare office waiting for a placement.

For these and other reasons, the focus has turned to the possibilities of placing more children with relatives. Although "relative placement" had been a possibility for many years, it now has become a more explicit agency policy. Kinship care provides continuity of family relationships for the child, and its use also has helped alleviate the foster home shortage crisis (Allen, Lakin, McFadden, & Wasserman, 1992; McFadden & Downs, 1995). See Chapter 8 for a discussion of kinship care.

Figure 9.1 outlines the phases of child welfare reform in the twentieth century.

FIGURE 9.1   Child Welfare Reforms in the Twentieth Century

Phase	Time	Reform	Focus	Cumulative Contribution to Field
One	1909–1970 White House Conference	Family Foster Care	Foster Family	Children belong in a family rather than an institution
Two	1970s	Permanancy Planning	Adoptive Family	Children belong in a permanent family; no child is unadoptable
Three	1980s Adoption Assistance and Child Welfare Act	Family Preservation	Biological Parents	Children belong with their biological parents; reasonable efforts must be demonstrated to maintain family
Four	1990s	Family Continuity	Extended/ Augmented Family	Children belong in a family network that continues relations over time

Source: E. J. McFadden & S. W. Downs (1995, April), Family continuity: The new paradigm in permanence planning. *Community Alternatives, 7*(1).

Why Children Are Placed in Care

Problems relating to parental characteristics and social conditions that precede foster care are in most instances very serious ones, which are not easily corrected by preventive, therapeutic, or family preservation services. In some instances they are so hazardous that these services are not attempted. The primary reason that children come into foster care is found in family breakdown or incapacity, exacerbated by severe environmental pressures. The breakdown reflects a cluster of critical and visible individual and environmental problems, in addition to the neglect or abuse of children, such as mental or emotional problems of parents, substance abuse, domestic violence, and chronic poverty.

Contrary to popular belief, children entering care are not orphans; at least, they have not lost their parents through death. Children in foster care usually have at least one living parent who may or may not visit and assume responsibility.

Family Characteristics

Children who enter foster care, particularly those who are likely to remain in care a long time, usually have parents who have a configuration of serious personal and environmental problems that have grown over time and the child does not have sufficient support from other adults. Nor has social services been able to help these families continue to care for their children in their own homes. Because almost all families whose children enter foster care have multiple problems and needs, it is difficult to identify a single principal reason for each placement. For example, a neglecting or abusing parent may also be mentally ill and trying to self-medicate with alcohol or other drugs. Some children come into care due to family homelessness or to the incarceration of the mother. A series of studies and reports over the last several decades indicate that the major problems bringing children into care are not their emotional or behavioral disorders, but *problems relating to parental functioning* (Phillips, Shyne, Sherman, & Haring, 1971; Jenkins & Norman, 1972; Jones, Magura, & Shyne, 1976; Besharov, 1994; Zuravin & DePanfilis, 1997; Semidei, Radel, & Nolan, 2001).

Since the 1980s, a major reason that children have come into care is the substance abuse of their parents, linked to other debilitating conditions (Horn, 1994; Groze, Haines-Simeon, & Barth, 1994). Addicted mothers of children in foster care are likely to be unemployed, have unstable housing, have dysfunctional families of origin, and have violent and unhealthy relationships. They often do not receive prenatal care and have many untreated health problems (Chasnoff, 1990). Children are *not* placed in care simply because their parent abuses drugs, but because they are abused or neglected (Wightman, 1991). However, the maltreatment that brings them into care may be related to their parent's substance abuse.

Parental drug use is related to another reason that children come into care: the presence of HIV/AIDS in the parent, the child, or both (Taylor-Brown & Garcia, 1995). About a quarter of children whose parents have HIV/AIDS are in the foster care system; the rest are in the care of their parents or relatives (Stein, 1998). Some of these children have HIV/AIDS themselves, transmitted to them prenatally; they may have developmental problems in addition to the illness and present a substantial caretaking challenge. Specialized foster homes have been recruited and trained to meet the complex needs of these children.

Standards for Decision Making

Child welfare decisions are made by caseworkers, supervisors, and jurists. These decisions occur when they apply agency guidelines, policies, or laws to the information gathered in a specific case. Important case decisions, including the decision to place, are being made by social workers with less specialized education and child welfare experience than in the past. Difficult tasks are often performed by persons who do not have the necessary skills and training. A majority of caseworkers in foster care lack professional graduate social work education. The situation is exacerbated by staff turnover.

The processing of information is influenced by contextual elements. Child welfare practitioners are forced to operate on a crisis-to-crisis basis, which limits the information collected and the time allowed for processing it. This can lead to decisions based on expediency. Another dimension of decision making is the range of persons involved in the process. Although the principal decision maker is usually the caseworker, this decision is rarely made unilaterally. There may be input from family members, other staff in the child welfare agency, and professionals within the community who have been working with the child and family. A preliminary decision to seek removal of a child from the family must be taken to the court and affirmed or denied through a legal process.

The decision about whether to place a child is influenced not only by the characteristics of the case and the decision-making context, but also by the criteria that have been established for such decisions. Standards for public agencies are promulgated through legislation and administrative rules. All states have statutes authorizing intervention to protect children. On a national level, the Adoption and Safe Families Act of 1997 set these standards:

1. Child safety is the paramount consideration in decision making regarding service provision, placement, and permanency planning. Reasonable efforts to preserve and reunify the family should be made except
   - where the parent has subjected the child to abandonment, torture, chronic abuse, sexual abuse or other exaggerated circumstances defined in state law;
   - the parent has been convicted of murder or involuntary manslaughter or aided another person in these acts against another child of the parent;
   - the parent has been convicted of felony assault to the child or another child; or
   - the parent has had parental rights to another child involuntarily terminated.
2. Foster care is a temporary setting and not a place for children to grow up. A permanency hearing must be held within twelve months of placement into foster care. A petition for termination of parental rights (TPR) must be filed for any child who has been in care fifteen of the last twenty-two months unless the child is safely placed with a relative, there is a compelling reason why TPR is not in the child's best interests, or the family has not, through no fault of their own, received the services that were part of the case plan.
3. Permanency planning efforts should begin as soon as the child enters care. Concurrent planning—that is, reasonable efforts to reunify and reasonable efforts to place for adoption/guardianship—can proceed at the same time.
4. The child welfare system must focus on results and accountability. Children are provided with quality services that protect their safety and health. Families are provided with quality services that increase their capacities to parent.
5. Innovative approaches are needed to achieve the goals of safety, permanency, and well-being, including helping states identify and address barriers to timely adoption placements; addressing kinship care; and identifying and addressing parental substance abuse. (U.S. Department of Health and Human Services, 2000)

Most states, in order to qualify for federal funds, have passed laws or administrative policies implementing these standards.

Characteristics of Children in Care

Age, Ethnicity, and Other Variables

Current data on foster care are available through the federal government's Adoption and Foster Care Analysis and Reporting System (AFCARS). Before AFCARS, the American Public Welfare System collected foster care program data from 1982 through 1990. However, not all states were able to provide all data requested, so the Voluntary Cooperative Information System (VCIS) data were considered "rough" national estimates. In 1986 the U.S. Congress provided for the establishment of a national mandatory data collection system for foster care and adoption of children from foster care, which became the current AFCARS system. Fifty-two jurisdictions (including the District of Columbia and Puerto Rico) participate in AFCARS.

In 2000, there were 526,000 children in foster care. The median age was 10.2. There are slightly more boys (52 percent) than girls. The racial composition of foster children was

Non-Hispanic black	40%
Non-Hispanic white	38%

Hispanic	15%
American Indian	2%
Asian	1%
Other	4%

Five percent of the children were of two or more races, or their race was unknown (AFCARS, 2002). The larger proportion of black children in care, compared to their proportion of the total population, reflects the greater vulnerability of families of color, due to social and economic disparity.

Working with the Placement Process

When a child is referred to a social agency because placement outside his or her own home is likely to be necessary, the agency must undertake a series of tasks. The use of a systematic placement process helps to assure that the agency meets its responsibilities for

1. trying to reunify the child with his or her family;
2. selecting an appropriate form of care;
3. helping the child separate from parents and move into the new child care arrangement;
4. helping foster parents or child care staff carry out their responsibilities successfully; and
5. seeing that a permanent home is provided for the child, either with her or his parents or relatives, or in a new permanent home through adoption, guardianship, or other forms of planned long-term care providing a stable living environment.

Parental Involvement

Removing children from their homes to place them into the foster care system is a very serious step with far-reaching consequences. It cannot be stated too often that this step should be undertaken only when it becomes clear that, even with outside help, the children's parents cannot provide for their safety.

To make the child's placement less traumatic, the social worker must reach out to the child's parents and try to understand them—their life experiences, the ambivalent feelings they may have about their child, and their strengths and weaknesses in parenting and how these affect the child. Parents should be involved in planning the placement to the greatest degree possible. Parents are to be viewed as partners (Maluccio & Sinanoglu, 1981) and as a valuable resource for the child in care (Blumenthal & Weinberg, 1983).

Parents are often the best source of information about the child's likes, dislikes, habits, and needs (McFadden, 1980; Ryan, McFadden, & Warren, 1981) and should communicate with the foster parents early in the placement process, preferably before the child goes to the foster home. The foster parent can answer the parent's questions about care and can benefit from detailed practical information about the child. Even if parents are in crisis, are angry about the removal of the child, or are highly negative about the child, the engagement process should be attempted by the foster care team at the earliest feasible time (Palmer, 1997).

When a child is in foster care, the court often orders parental visits and provision of child support. The social worker makes realistic plans with the parents about their contributions to the child's support as well as arrangements to visit the child under circumstances that will reinforce their affection and commitment to the child. It is important that parents be helped to understand their continuing rights and responsibilities. They need to know the short time frame they have to make substantial, measurable, progress, before federal mandates require a permanency planning hearing. It is essential that the social worker strive to help parents establish a realistically attainable plan to restore their home or, if this is not possible, to release the child for adoption. Because many of the children who enter foster care do not have adoptive homes made available to them, even though they are legally free for adoption, it is all the more important that whatever is of value in the parent–child relationship be supported.

Considerable attention has been given to the effects on children of separation experiences. In contrast, insufficient attention has been given to understanding the experiences of parents when their children enter foster care. The separation of children from parents is a crisis for the parents and for the whole family system. A parent whose children were placed following an episode of serious abuse recollected the impact of the separation on her:

> I had already lost my husband. Now I was losing everything, my self-respect, my children, I was losing myself. I felt like a piece of shit. My father had told me that I'd get no help from the family because I had disgraced them. I knew that I'd lose my financial assistance [AFDC]. Something was dying in me. I wanted to kill myself. Thank God my Parents Anonymous sponsor came down to the hospital emergency room while my children were being examined and taken away. She told me I shouldn't kill myself because if I killed myself I wouldn't get my kids back. I think I probably would have done myself in if she hadn't been there to help me at a time when I lost everything. (McFadden, 1984, p. 596)

Parents should be prepared with anticipatory guidance for the painful feelings surrounding placement. In acknowledging the difficulty of the separation, the worker can help the parent identify the supportive people in the environment who can assist them in the sad and anxious hours following the separation. The worker's skill in restating visiting plans and the plans made to achieve reunification may provide a needed element of hope, which can sustain the parent's motivation. For the parent to provide a verbal or written message to the child about the reasons for the separation and the hopes for the placement period, can be helpful to both parent and child.

Selecting the Placement

Figure 9.2 gives an overview of the steps followed by cases through the foster care system. Children are placed with relatives, in a nonrelative home, or in an institution. Their parents normally would be highly involved in reunification services, to help them correct the problems that brought their children into care.

Little empirical data exist to support decisions in selecting from a range of foster care facilities. Nevertheless, certain guidelines generally prevail in choosing among the different types of care for children.

Despite its difficulties, the foster home continues to be preferred for the majority of children if it appears that a child can participate in family life, attend community schools, and live in the community without danger to self or others. Especially for preschool-age children, foster homes are considered almost mandatory except for those with very severe problems requiring specialized service. Kinship foster care is often preferred because it enables the child to remain in an extended family network and lessens the trauma of separation.

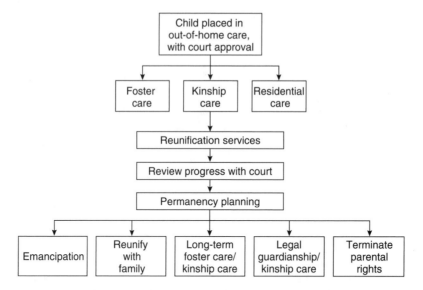

FIGURE 9.2   Overview of Steps Followed by Cases through the Foster Care System

Source: Adapted from P. Schene (1998). Past, present, and future roles of child protective services, *The Future of Children: Protecting Children from Abuse and Neglect, 8*(1), Adapted with the permission of the David and Lucile Packard Foundation.

Sibling groups should almost always be placed together, if possible, unless an older sibling abuses the younger one(s) and cannot be controlled. Children get comfort and stability from being placed with siblings (Rutter, 1985; Garbarino, DuBrow, Knostelny, & Pardo, 1992; Staff & Fein, 1992; Grigsby, 1994). For many children it may be very important to remain in their own school district so that their education is not disrupted and they can maintain their relationships with friends and teachers. For others, a complete change of environment might be more desirable and beneficial. About 25 percent of foster children are currently in kinship foster care, and 47 percent in nonrelative foster homes (AFCARS, 2002).

Treatment foster care is appropriate for children with emotional or behavioral problems that can be handled in a therapeutic family milieu. Specialized, highly trained foster homes take medically fragile children, such as those with HIV/AIDS, work closely with the hospital and medical team, and make it possible for these children to be in a home rather than a hospital (Hochstadt & Yost, 1991).

Group care is rarely used for young children and is generally considered to be appropriate for adolescents who are unable to tolerate the demands of family living. Many adolescents do well in general or treatment foster homes, and are desirous of having a positive experience with family life. For some adolescents, small or family-type group homes are a good solution. For others, group homes or cottages in which the child care staff are more role models than parent figures may be appropriate. In 2000, 8 percent of foster children were in group homes.

Children who cannot make use of family living are usually referred to institutions or residential treatment facilities; for example, troubled adolescents who are trying to free themselves of close family ties and for whom peer influences and group experiences may have greater value than family life. If youths have difficulty in forming relationships with substitute parenting figures because of past family experiences, they may fare better in a group setting. Some children have experienced successive replacements in poorly selected foster homes and can use the institution as a stable setting that provides continuity and physical, if not emotional, "roots" and a chance to seek out a few accepting or "safe" adult staff with whom to try to form ties.

Children and young persons who act out in aggressive ways dangerous to themselves or others or who display other behavior that the family or community will seldom tolerate are often served in a residential setting. Some children are cared for in residential facilities because their communities lack appropriate educational, medical, or psychiatric resources that they need. Usually a family setting is preferred for the first placement, based on the belief that children should be in the "least restrictive environment" possible, and moved to residential facilities if they cannot make a satisfactory adjustment to family life. The trend is to move the child back into a community setting as soon as possible. In 2000, 10 percent of children in care were in institutional settings (AFCARS, 2002).

Older foster children are being supervised in their own residences and provided independent living services to help them make the transition from foster care to productive adulthood. These youth are placed in their own residences by default (no other placement is available) or by plan (they have attained sufficient maturity to live without twenty-four-hour supervision by an adult. In 2000, 1 percent of children were in supervised independent living services (AFCARS, 2002).

The hope is that the child will experience only one placement or, failing that, the absolute minimum of placements possible. The first placement can be a very significant one for the child's future, as it may become his or her permanent home if the parents cannot resume care of the child and concurrent planning efforts have resulted in a plan of adoption or guardianship by the foster parents. Even though the first placement may become a permanent one and should, therefore, be made with special care, unfortunately there is rarely the time available to do a thorough assessment of the child and foster family, to ensure an appropriate match. The unfortunate reality is that choice of foster care placement is often determined by practical factors such as what is available; location of the home; and the constraints of agency contracts with other child placement agencies (Stein & Rzepnicki, 1984).

Meeting the Needs of Children in Foster Care

Attachment and Separation

Children who leave their own homes and enter foster care have experienced varying kinds and degrees of deprivation in parental care. Social workers have given considerable attention to assessing the likely long-term effects of poor parental care, particularly poor mothers, and to finding ways to help children with the distress they feel at separating from their parents, even neglectful or rejecting ones.

Assessing the child's attachment to parenting figures increases the worker's understanding of important relationships in the child's life. Attachment commonly refers to a close emotional bond that endures over time, beginning in infancy with the reciprocal relationship the child forms with the mother. As the child grows, he or she becomes attached to other family members as well. Children who have disordered, ambivalent, or anxious attachments may show some of the following behaviors: lack of comfort seeking when frightened, hurt, or ill; lack of warm and affectionate interactions or indiscriminate affection with unfamiliar adults; lack of compliance with caregiver request or, conversely, overcompliance; failure to check back with the caregiver in unfamiliar surroundings; and failure to reestablish interaction after separation (Levy & Orlans, 1998). Attachment problems create great difficulty in foster and adoptive homes, and later in life. Preserving the attachment to parents, siblings, and kinfolk is an important goal of contemporary child welfare practice (Bowlby, 1969; Goldstein, Freud, & Solnit, 1973; Fahlberg, 1991; Hegar, 1993; Grigsby, 1994).

Although each child's reaction to separation from parents is unique, certain painful feelings are common to the placement process. Children may be torn between conflicting feelings of love and anger toward their parents. No matter how appalling their homes might appear to others, the homes are familiar to children and they have developed ways of coping. In the situation of being separated from the parents for the purpose of placement, children almost inevitably feel powerless. Feelings of abandonment, rejection, helplessness, worthlessness, and fear are to be expected. They may feel shame or guilt about their "terrible" behavior that caused their parents to give them up or give up on them. These feelings can affect their self-concept and sense of reality and distort their interpretation of old and new environments (Freud, 1955; Littner, 1975).

The experience of repeated separations, as often happens in foster care, can elicit ever-increasing anger and related dysfunction. Attachment disorders underlie many of the clinical diagnoses that have been used traditionally to label extremely troubled foster children, such as conduct disorder (Delaney, 1991; Kools, 1997).

Children may also suffer from post-traumatic stress disorder (PTSD), characterized by intrusive imagery, somatic difficulties, sleep disturbance, hypervigilance, and inability to concentrate. A sound diagnosis is needed to identify PTSD.

Fahlberg (1991) summarized the factors that influence the child's reaction to separation:

- the child's age and stage of development
- the child's attachment to the parent
- the parent's bonding to the child
- the child's perceptions of the reasons for separation
- the child's preparation for the move
- the "parting message" the child receives
- the "welcoming message" the child receives
- the postseparation environment
- the child's temperament
- the environment from which he is being moved (p. 14)

These variables underscore the need for teamwork by worker, foster parents, and biological parents in the placement process and the treatment of the child.

Therapeutic Interventions

Therapeutic and socioeducational groups for children and young persons can help address the child's perceptions of the separation and assist in the child's adaptation to care (Palmer,

1990). One of the advantages of groupwork with children and youth in care is that they discover the similarity and normalcy of their feelings (Rice & McFadden, 1988). Another is that the faulty attributions and self-blame about the reasons for placement can be identified and resolved.

Individual treatment such as play therapy or counseling may also be helpful to the child making a transition into care. In working with the individual child to master past traumatic events, techniques such as bibliotherapy, puppet play, drawing, dollhouse play, or work with clay can help the child express hidden pain and reenact confusing or frightening events until some mastery is gained.

Mental health services are needed for an estimated 50 to 80 percent of children using the services of the foster care system. These services should be integrated into the service delivery system of child welfare agencies, should focus on prevention as well as dysfunction, and should be tailored to the various reasons for placement (Schneiderman, Connors, Fribourg, Gries, & Gonzales, 1998).

Many children coming into care have critical health care needs. The approach to providing health care to children in out-of-home care varies from community to community. Because children entering care suffer from a variety of conditions, including the effects of lack of preventive medical care and the sequelae of various forms of maltreatment, it seems imperative to develop comprehensive medical services targeted at their unique needs and situation. The mandate of the Adoption and Safe Families Act to focus on the developmental outcomes of foster children is calling renewed attention to educational, health, and mental health services for children in foster care.

Gay and Lesbian Youth in the Foster Care System

Gay and lesbian youth in out-of-home care are underserved (Child Welfare League of America, 1991). A significant factor among agencies that retards help to gay and lesbian youths is an inability to distinguish them from other youths. These young people have been socialized to fear admitting their sexual orientation and often have internalized societal homophobia. They need skilled help and understanding from caregivers who can accept them, and a safe environment in which they can talk about their concerns, meet peers and adults who can become role models, and learn skills that will enable them to live as a gay or lesbian adult in a straight society (NASW, 1993). For many of these young people, a gay or lesbian foster home can be the placement of choice. Unfortunately, agency staff may hold homophobic attitudes based on myth and stereotype, and may lack training on how to help gay and lesbian teens (Quinn, 2002). For more information on gay and lesbian families, see Chapter 3.

Family Reunification

Concurrent Planning

When the U.S. Congress passed the Adoption and Safe Families Act in 1997, several barriers to timely permanence for foster children were addressed. The law states that in certain serious situations the courts do not need to require "reasonable efforts" toward family reunification, but can move forward without delay with termination of parental rights. In such cases, a permanency planning hearing must be held within thirty days. Additionally, in those cases in which "reasonable efforts" for family reunification are being implemented, the law permits the use of concurrent planning. This means that states may plan to place a child for adoption or with a legal guardian at the same time that family reunification is tried. The two plans are being implemented simultaneously, so that an alternative plan is already in place in the event that family reunification fails (Katz, 1999). Concurrent planning requires that agencies and workers prepare for different outcomes at the same time, instead of sequentially. While at times this may seem to present the practitioner with an ethical dilemma, the goal of reunification can be in the foreground of practice efforts, with the goal of adoption in the background as a fail-safe option if the primary goal is not achieved. The parent must be fully informed from the beginning that the agency is starting work on an adoption plan, but only as a backup plan if reunification becomes very unlikely. The case example at the beginning of this chapter shows how the worker used concurrent planning in a way that was helpful to the parent.

Family-Centered Practice for Family Reunification

Family reunification, usually the preferred goal for permanency planning, is the "planned process of reconnecting children in out-of-home care with their families by means of a variety of services and supports to the children, their families and their foster parents or other service providers" (Pine, Krieger, & Maluccio, 1993, p. 6). Despite many system problems, most children in foster care do return home. In 2000, 57 percent of children exiting foster care were reunified with a parent or primary caregiver. Another 10 percent were living with relatives (AFCARS, 2002).

> *My kids is my life. There is not much in this world for me but my kids, and I do love them. I do not want my kids taken away from me. I do not like to be separated from them. (A parent—Marcenko & Striepe, 1997, p. 44)*

It is a fundamental goal of the foster care system to work with the parents so that they can resume care of their children. Unfortunately, there is no guarantee that foster care will improve, not exacerbate, the family situation. Parents may become immobilized by the grief of losing their children, and the parent–child attachment may be compromised, particularly if visits are infrequent.

A number of factors make reunification more likely. Marcenko & Striepe (1997) found that parental qualities of strong love for one's children, help of spouse or partners, success at drug treatment, belief in oneself, and spirituality were linked to reunification. Workers helping parents regain their children work with these strengths to motivate and encourage the parent. Some parental qualities present high barriers to reunification, notably serious ongoing parental drug use and severe mental illness (Hohman & Butt, 2001).

Parental ambivalence can be a barrier to reunification (Hess & Folaron, 1991). Some parents are able to verbalize mixed feelings. Others have difficulty expressing their concerns to the worker and appear to sabotage the case plan with their behavior. When workers engage the parents and open up honest communication about the permanency plan, parental ambivalence can be addressed more effectively. Some parents can be helped to articulate their need or desire to relinquish parental rights. Others can be supported to move toward reunification.

In addition to parental characteristics and attitudes, agency factors are also important in whether a family is reunified. Casey Family Services applied family preservation–type services to reunify families with multiple and serious problems. The project demonstrated that reunification is achievable if the agency has the resources to offer intensive services (Fein & Staff, 1993). Unfortunately, not all agencies have the necessary resources to provide intensive family reunification services. Particularly with chemically dependent parents, reunification may be difficult to achieve without sufficient resources. Children who are in care due to parental substance abuse tend to stay in care longer than other children and are less likely to return home (National Black Child Development Institute, 1989; Besharov, 1990; Walker, Zangrillo, & Smith, 1991).

Many agency services for restoration of family life are of insufficient strength and direction to have a sustained impact. The more effective programs include the following elements: (1) a wide variety of helping options; (2) a primary and continuing social work staff team; (3) small caseloads; (4) crisis intervention services around the clock; (5) use of natural helping resources in the neighborhood and the community; (6) intensive counseling services; (7) provision of transportation, health services, respite care and child care; and (8) availability and use of substance abuse treatment (Berry, 1988; Ten Broeck & Barth, 1986; Pecora et al., 1992; Besharov, 1994). Intensive family-based services—often the same services used to prevent placement—have been effectively used to reunify families in which placement has occurred (Walton et al., 1993; Gillespie, Byrne, & Workman, 1995).

Parent–Child Visiting

The overall purposes of visits are to maintain the parent–child bond and to move toward the permanency goal of reunification. Many studies have emphasized the importance of regular, frequent visits to attain these two goals. Children who receive visits have improved emotional well-being and fewer behavioral problems (Cantos, Gries, & Slis, 1997). Fanshel and Shinn (1978), in a classic study, concluded that, with few exceptions, parental visiting is linked to discharge from foster care and that this holds across ethnic and religious groups and is persistent over time. They found visiting patterns of parents—whether they visit and how often they visit their children in foster care—to be the strongest correlate of discharge from foster care. Other studies have also affirmed continuing visits by parents as central to family reunification (Weinstein, 1960; Mech, 1985; Proch & Howard, 1986; Milner, 1987).

Social workers have major responsibility for organizing and facilitating visits. In good foster care practice, every visit between parent and child has a plan and a goal. The immediate goal of a particular visit might be to work on an aspect of parenting such as behavior management; to reassure the child; to celebrate the child's birthday and show the child he or she is important; to demonstrate a skill such as comforting a tremulous, substance-affected child; or to learn to take pleasure and enjoyment from contact with one another.

In order to facilitate visits, social workers may need to arrange transportation and a meeting place that is satisfactory to all involved. Visits can occur at the agency when strict supervision is needed; at the foster home if the parent needs to see how and where the child is living; in a relative's home if the kinfolk are involved; in the parent's home to prepare for reunification; or at a neutral site such as a restaurant or park. Parents are often encouraged to attend a child's medical appointments, school conferences, sports events, and other important events in the child's life.

Foster parents are an important part of the team in making visits successful. Trained foster parents can use the time of the visit to help teach skills to parents and to facilitate joint visits to the school, doctor, and so forth. Their accepting and caring attitude to parents may encourage parents to work for reunification. Foster parents can help children prepare for the visit through making cookies, making a picture, and assembling their mementoes to show their parents. If parents fail to keep the appointment, trained foster parents can help the child deal with the disappointment not by blaming the parents, but by providing reassurance and support to the children.

Social workers have a responsibility to observe visits to assess attachment, parenting skills, and parent–child interaction. They may also need to coach parents and be supportive of foster parents.

Parent–Agency Service Agreement

Use of parent–agency service agreements (contracts) creates a sharply focused direction for practice (Stein, Gambrill, & Wiltse, 1977). It is an essential part of concurrent planning (Katz, 1999).

The contract typically relates to the allegations found on the petition leading to the court assuming jurisdiction over the child. If the court found that the parental home was filthy and unsafe, for example, and that the parents had neglected to feed or provide medical care to the child, then correcting those conditions would become key components of the contract. The contract spells out the permanency planning alternatives; the goal (usually return to the parents), what must be done to correct the elements of neglect found in the court petition, and who will do what to accomplish the goal. The contract might specify that the agency would provide homemaker services to assist the parent in cleaning up the filthy home; that the agency would refer the parent to nutrition classes; and that the parent would attend medical visits for the child.

The parent's responsibilities might include cleaning the home so that it would pass inspection by the health department, attending nutrition classes and demonstrating adequate food preparation skills, demonstrating an understanding of the child's medical needs, and participating in ongoing medical care. In contemporary practice, a frequent component of contracts is that the agency provide referral for substance abuse treatment and support group, and that the parent use treatment, attend the self-help group, and provide clean drug screens on a weekly basis. It is important to spell out in the contract what is an acceptable level of performance by the parent. Attending a parenting class does not necessarily mean that a parent will improve discipline techniques. The contract should show that attending parenting classes are related to the goal of using effective discipline without severe corporal punishment.

Case Review

Case review is a regular part of foster care programming. Its purpose is to ensure that time lines are being met in planning for permanency and that parent–child visits, efforts to help parents, and other necessary program components are occurring as planned. Case review exists at three levels: judicial, administrative, and citizen. Judicial reviews, mandated by federal law, occur at regular intervals at the juvenile or family court. They are the most authoritative and usually include testimony and a report from the social worker and testimony from the parents and other stakeholders. Administrative reviews are internal agency processes monitoring compliance with program goals and policy. Citizen reviews are conducted under the auspices of the court, an advocacy organization, or the agency, and are intended to provide oversight of the child welfare system by interested and knowledgeable citizens in the community (Jordan, 1994; Thoennes, 1996; National Association of Foster Care Reviewers, 1998). States vary in their use of each review method. Thoennes (1996) found that no single review model is decidedly superior in producing positive case outcomes and concluded that administrative and citizen reviews are advisable in systems that lack judicial resources to ensure regular, thoughtful review hearings.

Case Example: Family Reunification

Selena Q. had completed treatment for her addiction, attended a twelve-step support group, and was making steady progress in her recovery. Raymond, her estranged husband, was still using heavily and on the streets. Selena had returned to her earlier employment and located housing. She was responding to clear expectations spelled out in the parent–agency service agreement (contract). At first she had felt angry with the foster care worker for telling her what she had to do to get the children back, but now she appreciated the help she had gotten in working toward her goals. She felt shaky and anxious about maintaining sobriety, but had an NA sponsor and a relapse prevention plan. She knew that she could not reconcile with Raymond unless he stopped using and was in recovery. She wanted the children back but felt that she could not cope with all of them at once.

Her two middle children, girls aged 5 and 7, had been placed with her aunt in a kinship foster care situation, but her son, aged 14, was in group care for treatment, as he had been a sexual abuse perpetrator to his 5-year-old sister. The baby was in a specialized foster home because he had special medical needs. Selena had maintained contact with all four children through visits, although she had spent the most time with the two children placed with her aunt.

The worker and the mother decided together it would be wise to phase the return of the children. First, Selena stayed on the weekends with her aunt to resume care of her two middle children. Then the children returned to her new home, with the aunt providing day care while Selena worked. The family reunification worker was available to her around the clock, seven days a week, and met with her every evening to help her reconnect with the two girls who had been returned. The girls showed some anger and defiance, telling their mother that they only had to listen to Aunt Fay, and they didn't have to listen to her. The worker showed Selena how to set limits and have family meetings.

They then had a meeting with the reunification team, which included the parent, her aunt, the foster care worker, the foster parent, the group care worker, and her son's therapist. They developed a plan in which the baby would be returned next, and her son would start to visit in the home, with close supervision by the mother and the family reunification worker.

Selena and her aunt spent time with the foster parent learning the special techniques involved in baby Jeffrey's care. She and the mother went together to the doctor, the rehab clinic, and the public health department. The plan was that Jeffrey would visit first for long weekends, with the foster parent "on call" for problems. When the baby returned home,

Selena was able to reduce her work hours and still retain TANF eligibility. The first week that Jeffrey was at home, she called in her family reunification worker frequently, as she was feeling very stressed and found herself having cravings for her drugs. The worker and Selena's sponsor helped her get past the cravings, and the foster parent came in to provide respite so that Selena could get to more meetings of her twelve-step group. The sponsor, the reunification worker, and Selena developed a specific relapse prevention plan.

A serious concern was whether the return of Tyrone from group care would upset the precarious homeostasis and make Selena once again vulnerable to relapse. Selena was fearful that Tyrone might reoffend with the girls. She was also having flashbacks to her own sexual abuse as a child.

The family reunification worker helped Selena decide to get help for her survivor issues. She took Selena to a survivor's group and gave her some survivor workbooks. She helped Selena educate the girls about good touches and bad touches, the importance of "telling" and saying no. They decided that because Tyrone had completed the treatment program, it might be a good idea to bring him home while the family reunification worker was still involved.

The entire family, including Aunt Fay and the worker, went to a final treatment session at Tyrone's group facility. At this session, Tyrone got down on his knees in front of Jessica and apologized for his actions. He cried when he apologized to his mother for hurting one of the children. Aunt Fay promised to be the outside person who would monitor Tyrone's behavior to Jessica and Roshelle. Selena was helped to set very firm limits for Tyrone. Tyrone was to be enrolled in a new school and assigned an adult male mentor.

The first week Tyrone was back, Selena again went into crisis because Raymond, her estranged husband, showed up high, wanting money and demanding to take Tyrone with him for "some fun." The family reunification worker stepped in to support Selena in making Raymond leave and handling Tyrone's reactions to his father's visit.

Eight weeks after the first two children were returned home, the family was together, with the exception of Raymond, the father, who had not dealt with his addiction. Each of the older children had a support system, including school, Al-A-Tot or Al-A-Teen, neighborhood activities at a nearby church, and Tyrone's mentor. Their aunt was involved in their lives, and she was introducing them to other relatives who had distanced themselves earlier when Selena had been using.

Selena had good days and bad days. There were times when her cravings were hard to take. She used her twelve-step support group and her sponsor to deal with the urge to relapse. She attended the sexual abuse survivors group from time to time as painful feelings emerged. The family reunification worker got Selena on a waiting list for sexual abuse counseling at a local agency. Selena began to realize that part of her substance use had been to cover childhood pain. She also consulted an attorney about obtaining a divorce from Raymond. She was clear that she did not want to risk losing the children again. The family reunification worker ended her intensive services, although the family remained under supervision by the court and the foster care worker for another six months.

Case Commentary.   This case has been idealized to illustrate the strong points of contemporary foster care practice. The focus was family centered and involved the kinship network in planning and helping. Teamwork was essential, with active involvement by the foster parent, the group care facility, and community resources in implementation of the plan. The task of parenting was shared by the kinship caregiver, the parent, and the foster parent. The foster care worker and the family reunification worker used an empowerment focus, despite the strong element of social control underlying the child protection intervention. One limitation of the resolution of the case was that neither worker was able to reach Raymond, the children's father. They did, however, support and empower Selena in creating boundaries that would prevent his addiction from intruding into the reformed family in recovery. Special attention was paid to the realities of the recovery process, including development of a relapse prevention plan. The phased return of the children took into consideration the unique needs of the children and the mother's vulnerability to relapse. Although in some states there might be prohibitions against allowing Tyrone back into the home (certain statutes prohibit funding family reunification if there is a perpetrator in the home), he had completed a treatment program, and there was a plan for close supervision and monitoring of the sibling group.

Reentry into Foster Care

Reentry into foster care occurs when the reunification plan was unsuccessful, and the children are not safe in the family home. The reentry rate is not known, because many factors are involved, including whether the child is returning home from residential treatment or foster family care, and differences in state policies on reunification. Estimates are that between 3 and 25 percent of children returned home reenter the foster care system (U.S. General Accounting Office, 1991; Festinger, 1994). Families whose children reenter foster care are characterized by lack of parenting skills, limited social support networks, and drug addiction. The pressure to move children quickly out of foster care to meet federal mandates may result in agency decisions to return children to unsafe homes, and thereby create a revolving door for some, with the attendant problems of upheaval and lack of stability.

Permanency Planning

Options for Permanence

For children who cannot return home, options for permanence include long-term foster care, guardianship, kinship care, independence/emancipation, and adoption. Proponents of long-term foster care argue that when a child or youth has strong connections to the original family, adoption will not serve the young person's interests. Ensuring continuity of family relationships for these children may entail staying in the foster home where emotional ties have been formed and where the foster parents will facilitate ongoing connection to the original family, when possible (Bryant, 1994).

The use of guardianship, particularly in kinship care, is also an option for permanence that maintains the child's bonds to family or to long-term caretakers (Child Welfare League of America, 1994). However, there are many forms of guardianship, and some do not offer the level of permanence and protection that the family and the child need. (See Chapter 6.)

The preferred permanency option, once return to the original family has been ruled out and parental rights have been terminated, is adoption. Adoption offers an arrangement that is the legal equivalent of biological parenthood. Adoptions can be made in the context of family continuity, such as when long-term foster parents adopt a child, or when the child retains contact with parents or extended family members. (See Chapter 10.)

Termination of Parental Rights

Some families do not respond to services provided or have difficulties so pervasive that children cannot remain with them in safety. In these situations, federal and state law require that children not languish in an impermanent and temporary setting. Generally speaking, after a child has been in care twelve months without family reunification being accomplished, a permanency hearing is held. In order for a child to be legally free for adoption, parental rights must be terminated or relinquished voluntarily. If the child is in foster care for fifteen of the last twenty-two months, then termination of parental rights must be initiated.

For foster care workers, planning for termination of parental rights can be very challenging. It typically involves teamwork with attorneys, knowledge of legal procedures, gathering evidence in a format that is admissible in court, contacting witnesses, and locating absent parents who have a legal interest in the child. (See Chapter 6.)

Workers may have feelings of failure, sadness, and anger that they have not been able to help parents fulfill the terms of the parent–agency agreement for permanency planning. Some workers dread the adversarial court proceedings when they must testify against parents.

Types of Foster Care

Formal Kinship Care

Kinship care may be a preferred form of care for many children who must live away from their parents. Kinship care that takes place within the foster care system, in which the relative caregivers are licensed foster parents or the child is a court ward placed with the relative under the abuse/neglect provisions and the relative is not licensed, is called *formal kinship care* and is discussed in Chapter 8, in the section "Kinship Care as Family Preservation."

Family Foster Care

Family foster care (Figure 9.3) is a social system with many component parts and complex interrelationships between those parts. The foster child, the parents, the foster parents, the siblings, the foster siblings, the agency social worker, the court-appointed guardian or attorney—each party is an integral element of the whole. The foster home system has a set of external influences, which, added to the physical surroundings, makes up the care environment. These influences include such forces as the placing agency's supervisory and administrative structures, the court, the permanency planning laws, the licensing regulations of the state, the treatment resources within the community, the schools, and community norms about child caring.

Foster Parents and the Agency

The social agency responsible for the child in care has a continuing obligation to monitor the placement situation to see that proper care and treatment are given, and to consult with foster parents in a teamwork approach. The social worker has agency-constituted authority, as well as the influence derived from knowledge and competence. Consultation by the so-

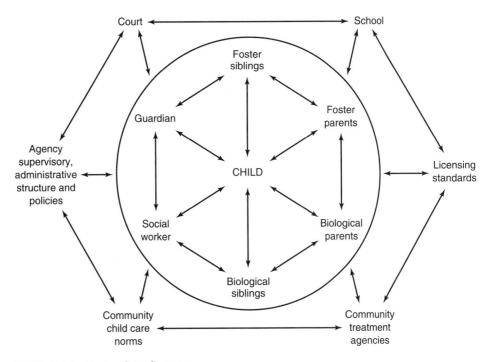

FIGURE 9.3   Foster Care System

cial worker about care of the child and work with the family augment the knowledge and skills foster parents have gained through training. Negotiation between social work and foster parents about specific tasks to be performed, and about clarification of roles, are part of the social work process with foster homes.

What kinds of problems arise in family foster care to which the foster parent and social worker must give attention? In undertaking the challenges of foster parenting, competent adults enter a new situation in which they risk failure. Fostering places increased demands to share relationship and possessions on the family, so problems of rivalry and jealousy come into play. Foster parents' own children may have difficulty coping with the loss implicit in the foster care situations (Twigg, 1995).

Foster parents may be unclear about their role or how to fill it appropriately. Foster mothers may see their roles more as "mothering" than providing care in a professional sense (Meidema & Nason-Clark, 1977). Foster parents may find themselves uncertain about actions to control behavior of the children, especially in light of agency discipline policies, which prohibit spanking and other child management techniques.

Being a foster parent is a demanding and intense experience that carries with it enormous pressure and expectations from the agency and the community. Despite the critical role foster parents play in the child welfare system, they are frequently neglected by agencies and social workers. One aspect of neglect is the low board rates paid to foster parents. Most states pay only enough to cover the actual costs of the child's care. In addition to monthly board payment, agencies cover the costs of medical and dental care (although it is hard for many foster parents to locate medical care providers who will accept Medicaid), clothing, and some incidental expenses. Most foster parents simply are not compensated for the services they provide (Downs, 1989).

A second aspect of the neglect of foster parents is their feeling that they do not receive the help they need from agencies. Very often agencies do not provide sufficient training for foster parents or opportunities for mentoring or support from other foster parents. Little help is given to workers on how to improve worker–foster parent communications. This neglect is highly related to the large turnover of foster parents. In a recent study of why they leave fostering, foster parents cited lack of agency support; poor communication with caseworkers; lack of input into plans for the child; and difficulties with the child's behavior. Those foster parents who continued to foster tended to have more advanced training, services to meet their needs, and support from other foster parents (Rhodes, Orme, & Buehler, 2001).

Factors Predictive of Foster Parent Success.   In a study of the maintenance of placements in the Casey Family Homes, Walsh and Walsh (1990) found four factors to be predictive of successful overall functioning of the foster family. These predictors related to the comfort of foster parents in their several roles; to their being motivated to take a foster child by a genuine liking for children; to the foster mother possessing strong emotional coherence; and to the ability of the family to tolerate unassimilated aspects of the child.

Foster Parent Recruitment.   Foster parents are selected by means of a home study and licensing/approval process. Licensing standards are set by states. Recruitment that is specifically targeted to finding families for the kinds of children the agency places is a more productive strategy than are generalized campaigns to interest as many families as possible. Agencies recruit new foster parents using multiple sources including newspapers, radio, television announcements, faith communities, current foster parents, service groups, and others. Consultation with community leaders is vital to vigorous recruiting of foster parents from minority racial and ethnic groups. Agencies must also assess the cultural competence of their agency and staff in approaching minority communities (Lakin, Whitfield, & Anderson, 1997).

Foster parents give multiple reasons for wanting to give care: liking children, identifying with abused and neglected children or unhappy children, a wish to provide a community service, and so forth. Even though some reasons appear promising and others may appear suspect, it is more important to focus on parents' skills and strengths in working with children than on their stated motivations. Orientation meetings and preservice training provide opportunities for foster parents to self-select as they learn more about the responsibilities of their role and allow the agency to continue the screening process.

Types of Family Foster Homes

Shelter Homes.   Family foster homes may provide temporary shelter for children during the period of initial assessment and determination by the court of a need for out-of-home care. Although children's agencies must have access to temporary shelter homes, assessment of children's need for placement can be made more reliably when they are still in their own homes rather than after they are abruptly separated from parents and placed in an unfamiliar temporary situation.

Long-Term Foster Homes.   Long-term foster homes are sought for children who have no chance to return to their parents, who need permanent family living, and who do not wish to be adopted or who have been denied adoption because no adoptive home could be found for them. Some foster parents may feel unable to assume guardianship for, or to adopt, children in their care but are willing to give a particular child a stable environment and the assurance of lasting relationship. The Casey Family Homes successfully provide well-resourced long-term care to young people with histories of multiple placements and other problems (Walsh & Walsh, 1990).

Specialized and Treatment Foster Care

Specialized family foster homes are used by some agencies for children who can profit from family living, although they may have emotional problems or developmental disabilities. Some homes specialize in adolescents and take a major role in preparing the youths for independent living. Remuneration is higher in specialized foster homes arrangements than in the usual family foster home arrangement.

Treatment Foster Care.   The last decade has witnessed a tremendous increase in the use of treatment foster care and the development of new programs.

The intensive service provided in the foster home distinguishes treatment foster care from regular foster care. Treatment foster care is "something of an adaptive hybrid combining elements of residential treatment programming and the foster family environment. . . . This model offers an alternative to both the family foster home and the institution for youngsters who are not appropriately or adequately served in either type of program" (Bryant & Snodgrass, 1990, p. 2). Treatment families have a high degree of training, with an emphasis on behavioral management theory and technique.

Shared Family Care

The newest form of out-of-home care is still at the stage of innovation and experimentation (Kufeldt & Allison, 1990). In this form of care, foster families foster both children and their parents. Types of families who have used shared family care include those in which the parents are teens, parents have developmental delays, substance-abusing parents are in recovery, parents are homeless, and parents have unstable physical or mental health.

This form of care has the potential to help some parents learn parenting and home management skills while the child is protected and the family stays intact (Barth & Price, 1999). A major challenge to the development of this form of care is that many states have funding policies that do not permit foster payments for adults in care. Another challenge is recruiting and adequately supporting foster parents.

Residential Group Care

Although all "institutions" have common characteristics, different types have been established to deal with particular sets of problems and serve distinct categories of children. These facilities may be under public or voluntary auspices and be administered by persons with a primary orientation to social welfare, education, medicine, psychiatry, or juvenile corrections.

Group care facilities include (1) residential group facilities for the care and protection of dependent and neglected children, including temporary shelters; (2) correctional institutions for delinquent and predelinquent young persons, including training schools, detention homes, and diagnostic reception centers; (3) treatment facilities for the emotionally disturbed, including psychiatric inpatient children's units, residential centers, and mental hospitals; (4) residential drug and alcohol programs; (5) facilities for developmentally disabled children and youth; and (6) private boarding schools.

Certain characteristics of the group residential care setting can be specifically useful in helping some disturbed children and young persons. These characteristics, which are different from those of the family home, in principle permit a controlled living process and a consciously designed therapeutic environment that can be varied to meet the needs of a particular group of children.

In contrast to a family home setting, young people in residential care can be freed from an obligation to form close personal relationships. The troubled child can keep relationships with others diluted so that there is less need to persist in old ways of reacting. Thus energy can be channeled into new learning processes. The group setting can allow greater variation in behavior than a family unit, and the impact of difficult behavior—"acting out"—may be less because it is diffused among a series of adults who work shifts, rather than being on duty twenty-four hours a day as parents and foster parents are.

The young person in group care has an opportunity for a variety of interpersonal relationships and patterns of behavior as he or she has access to more adult role models and other supportive relationships. The wider choice can permit the youth to remain relatively detached from relationships that in the past had been undesirably disturbing, but return to those relationships (parents, former foster parents, adoptive parents, mentors) that are rewarding, supportive, and productive. The peer group is an important resource and often a catalyst for constructive change. It offers an opportunity for interaction with others who share the same experience day by day.

A greater range of remedial and therapeutic programs and group activities can be brought together in a residential setting and made available for planning positive daily living experiences. The accessibility of the child to the staff facilitates diagnosis, observation, and treatment. Therapy for emotional problems, remedial programs for learning problems, and controls for behavioral problems can be integrated and related directly to the young person's daily life.

The consistent routine of group care may contribute to a disturbed child or youth's sense of continuity, regularity, and stability. Many young persons requiring group care have come from very disorganized home environments and need structure to facilitate impulse control.

Staff members in group care, by accepting formal employment conditions, assume an obligation for professional functioning and can be readily accessible to regular in-service training and supervision. They work in a context of backup and support from other professionals, which helps to minimize their reactivity to the problems of young residents in the facility.

These attributes of group care, which can create a therapeutic environment, are not automatically self-fulfilling. If not used with professional skill, each attribute could become a barrier to treatment. Depersonalizing influences can also penalize children and youths who need individual personalized attention. In group living there is always an implicit lack of privacy. Opportunities to make choices may be lost. Some children are overstimulated by the variety of relationships and activities in group care. Without appropriate supervision and controls, acting-out behaviors by young people in care can jeopardize other group members. Although institutional staffs are increasingly aware of the need to involve children and youths in the mainstream of community life, often the campus of the facility is geographically isolated from community influence. In the case of young people in trouble with the community, the isolation may be an advantage during the period in which new controls are being established, but a disadvantage when it becomes time to reintegrate the youth back into the mainstream of community life. Within the last few years, greater attention has been paid to the need for working with a child's or young person's family if therapeutic change is to be maintained. Wraparound services are being used to reintegrate young people back into their families or into the community in other family settings such as family foster care or kinship care.

The range of specific approaches to a planned therapeutic residential environment includes individualized psychotherapy, trauma therapy, behavior modification, play therapy, milieu therapy, group work, and positive peer culture. In all such approaches, the attempt is to use the everyday living environment as a therapeutic tool.

Group work approaches have emphasized social and peer supports and sanctions as a means of establishing new patterns of behavior. Youths are given selected responsibilities for the day-to-day operation of the unit and for governing their own and each other's behavior. The youth group assigns, schedules, and monitors the necessary chores, activities, and privileges. The use of recreational challenges, such as wilderness trips, high-ropes courses, and camp situations also strengthens young persons' perceptions of responsibility to the peer group goals. Staff act as facilitators or guides with the group interactions, as well as maintaining standards of expected behavior.

Behavior modification remains a dominant treatment approach in many settings. This approach is based on the idea that behavior is learned and is largely controlled or reinforced by its consequences. The staff has the tasks of making both the desired behavior and the consequences explicit to residents and of managing the system of consequence—rewards and punishments—to support and reinforce expectations. Familiar techniques in this approach include token economies, in which young people work for points or tokens to attain varied levels of privilege.

Agency Group Homes

The agency-operated group home has been mostly used with adolescents. The group home is typically a large single dwelling or apartment, either owned or rented by an agency or other organization, and located in a residential part of the community. Child care staff members are usually viewed as counselors rather than as foster parents. Some agency group homes have a married couple—group home parents—and child care staff, giving young people the benefit of family-like contact plus the additional opportunity to relate to child care staff as young adult role models. Other professional personnel serve the group home regularly—social workers, a psychiatric consultant, a psychologist, and perhaps at times other resource persons such as recreational therapists, special education consultants, or nutritionists. While the parent agency or institution has administrative and supervisory responsibility, however, the group home reaches out to the community for many activities.

Meeting the expectations of multiple constituencies is a problem for group homes. The constituencies include schools, police, the children or youths' families, and neighbors. Group homes are an open system, so interaction is frequent. Community relations functions are extremely important in the management of a group home. Use of community volunteers and community advisory groups is helpful in promoting positive transactions and community understanding of the needs of the young people in care.

Independent Living Services

Increases in the number of adolescents in foster care triggered a new challenge to the child welfare system—the necessity of preparing large numbers of at-risk foster adolescents for independent living, or *interdependent living,* a phrase that underscores the emancipating youth's need to continue to relate to family and community (Maluccio, Krieger, & Pine, 1990). In the past, young people who remained in foster care until the age of majority have been discharged into the community with the expectation that they could assume care for themselves. For many young persons exiting care, the lack of planning had disastrous results, and they ended up in homeless shelters with no place to go, no financial resources, and no families to fall back on. Many youths leaving foster care ended up on public assistance (Allen, Bonner, & Greenan, 1988).

The Independent Living Initiative, established by Congress in 1988, provides funds for services to emancipating youth. The legislative intent was to enable youths to seek a high school diploma, participate in vocational training, enroll in a program for life skills, and use individual or group counseling. Agencies were charged with integrating services for youth and making individualized independent living case plans (Allen, Bonner, & Greenan, 1988). The Foster Care Independence Act of 1999 and the John H. Chaffee Foster Care Independence Program amended the 1988 Act to improve independent living and transitional living services for youth in foster care or exiting foster care (P.S. 196-169).

Currently a wide range of programs exist, including special group homes that teach life skills, supervised apartment living, mentorship programs, group work for young people who are receiving in-home training from their foster parents, and specialized foster homes established to teach life skills and assist the emancipation process (Downs, 1990). A culturally specific African American rites-of-passage program teaches youth life care skills for the transition to adulthood using Afrocentric mentoring and ritual (Gavazzi, Alford, & McKenry, 1996).

> *He tells me, "You're going to move out on your own." No way, man, that's what I'll say. Not ready. Not ready. Not ready. (Young man in care, Martin & Palmer, 1997, p. 44)*

In addition to tangible independent living skills, young people emancipating from care often require assistance with the intangible aspects of emancipation, including reliving the original separation experience and confusion about their identity. Under the best of circumstances, emancipation can be a difficult process requiring a series of complex adaptations. The young person leaving placement often faces a double loss: leaving the foster home or group home and reexperiencing the original loss of the biological family (McFadden, Rice, Ryan, & Warren, 1989). The Chafee Program extended eligibility to all youth expected to remain in foster care to age 18 and those 18 to 21-year-olds who left foster care because they "aged out." It required youth participation in designing their independent living activities and accepting responsibility for achieving independence. Room and board payments could be made up to age 21. In addition, states could extend Medicaid benefits to eligible youth to 21 years (National Foster Care Awareness Project, 2000).

Professional Issues in Foster Care

Teamwork in Out-of-Home Care

Teamwork is necessary to achieve the purposes of out-of-home care. Social workers, primarily charged with implementing permanency plans, and the caregivers, who provide the day-to-day nurture that promotes development and healing of earlier trauma, must coordinate their activities with collateral professionals who also provide service to children and their parents. These professionals include educators, health care providers, mental health professionals, and others who are part of the overall plan. The team is part of a larger helping system brought into play by the social worker's brokering and coordinating functions. On a different level, there needs to be collaborative teamwork between the management of the child welfare agency, the courts, and the mental health and substance abuse treatment agencies (National Commission on Foster Care, 1991).

Today, there is particular interest in forming closer collaborations with the schools. Many have observed that the special education departments of public schools serve many of the same children as the child welfare system. Yet communication between these two systems is often nonexistent or adversarial. New approaches are needed to better coordinate these two service systems (Altshuler, 2003). Child welfare agencies are now accountable to the federal government for child development outcomes of the children they serve, which should encourage progress in these coordinating efforts. (See Chapter 1.)

Training Foster Parents, Child Care Staff, and Workers

Foster Parent Training.   Foster parents' roles are becoming more professional, such as the roles of group home "parents" or "counselors" or residential care staff who may fill roles of milieu therapists. In general, all caregiver roles in out-of-home care have evolved from less specialized to more specialized, from lay to paraprofessional or professionalized, and from strictly child focused to work with child and family.

The value of systematic training for foster parents is well established. Foster parent training has been shown to reduce the incidence of failed placements, increase the number of desirable placements, and encourage foster parents to remain licensed. Foster parent training is now mandated in most states. Training formats bring together experienced foster parents as mentors and trainers of those who are just starting, and offer time for foster parents to share experiences and offer support to one another in an informal setting. Topics that may be covered in training include emotional development of children in care, working with biological parents, handling destructive behavior of children, fostering sexually abused children, and working as part of a team.

Child Care Staff Training.   Many agencies and organizations have developed career ladders for child care staff, with comprehensive curricula focused on the emotional, social, and behavioral needs of children and youth in care. In addition, the content of training may include topics on teaching families and children practical skills to cope effectively with their environments, and working to enhance natural support networks for families. Staff must have skills of relating to young people of different ethnic groups and also to gay and lesbian youth.

Worker Training.   Foster care workers must be able to work across boundaries with many other disciplines. Training on legal issues related to permanency planning is necessary. Staff need to be grounded in legal terminology, understand legal processes related to permanency planning, know the legal basis of child welfare practice including constitutional rights of parents, be able to document all aspects of casework, be able to present effective testimony and prepare for court hearings, and be able to work collaboratively with attorneys.

The skills of casework, while still valuable for foster care workers, must be supplemented with the ability to do groupwork, to develop resources within the community, to be an internal organizational change agent, and to advocate for families and children at the level of social policy. They must be generalists in their skills but specialists in their knowledge of issues affecting families and children.

Protecting Children and Youth in Out-of-Home Care

When the community, through courts and agencies, intervenes in the life of a family, it has a moral and legal obligation to provide adequate care if the child is placed away from the family. The existence of maltreatment by caregivers and others in out-of-home settings is cause for serious concern and careful vigilance by foster care professionals. Long ignored, it has now been brought to national and professional attention mainly through class action lawsuits.

Agencies are now monitoring foster homes and institutions more closely. An unintended side effect of this increased scrutiny is that foster parents have felt that they were treated unfairly when allegations were brought against them and many have left fostering (Carbino, 1991). Agencies can reduce the chances of a child being maltreated in care through providing training, matching child with family, monitoring the child in the home, conducting a thorough initial home study, and decertifying a home known to be deficient. Some children are more at risk of maltreatment than others, including those with disabilities and severe emotional and behavioral problems, making it important to match children carefully with the specific capacities and strengths of foster parents.

Institutions for children are thought to place children at greater risk for abuse than foster care, although there is strong resistance to reporting abuse or believing that it can happen. Bloom (1992) recommends that institutions take the following steps when an allegation of abuse occurs: take allegations seriously, suspend the employee with pay during the initial investigation, reach out to the child's family, act to cut retribution by staff members or peers, and flood the child with support. He also urges treating the alleged perpetrator with respect and dignity during the investigation and finding ways of supporting the staff.

Trends and Issues

Managed Care

There is serious interest in applying the concept of managed care, which has been used in health care, to child welfare. The principles of managed care—having diagnostic categories with related lengths of stay or paying a flat fee for certain types of care, no matter how long it might take to achieve the permanency goal—come from the medical model, which does not seem clearly related to the way the foster care system has operated in the past. Managed care has been applied for some children and youths receiving mental health treatment services under Medicaid funding.

The Child Welfare League of America has established the Managed Care Institute to identify and describe current and potential changes in the way child welfare agencies are delivering services consistent with managed care principles. Some thirty child welfare administrators say they are implementing or planning to implement initiatives that include managed care features (Hutchins, 1997).

Managed care is related to the privatization of child welfare services. Kansas was one of the first states to move in this direction, when, in 1996 and 1997, three major child welfare services—family preservation, foster care, and adoption—were transferred to contracted private providers in a modified form of managed care. This involves a capitated case rate for each family or child. This case rate is expected to meet all of the crisis needs of the family and/or children for the duration of each of the services. While there was considerable agreement that the child welfare system had past problems and was in need of system change, not all reports on the new system have been positive. The Kansas chapter of the National Association of Social Workers enumerated concerns about the implementation of the new systems, and developed a set of recommendations, including:

- Develop community advisory boards.
- Adopt a set of best-practice standards to ensure child safety.
- Provide training for new case managers.
- Institute a grievance process.
- Create an ombudsman/advocate. (Kansas NASW, 1997)

Child welfare organizations are developing networks, partnerships, and mergers in order to successfully navigate the new managed care environment. Four key reasons for doing so are that they can provide more efficient and effective services, can have increased fiscal stability, and can increase their organizational control. Attention to leadership, economics, and qualitative improvements can develop strong organizations that can compete in the changing marketplace (Emenhiser, King, Joffe, & Penkert, 1998). As funding patterns are affected by managed care or become more flexible in order to move services toward the prevention end, foster care practice may see an increased emphasis on innovation such as shared family care, kinship care, family decision making for permanency planning, and other prospects that promote family continuity.

Legal Orphans

Maza has coined the term *legal orphan* to identify those children who remain in foster care for extensive periods after parental rights are terminated. Some of these children have adoption as the goal. Others do not. In any case, they are the "state's children"; that is, they have no individual person who has parental duties and obligations (Maza, 2000).

As ASFA's termination of parental rights provisions continue to be implemented, this group of children will swell the foster care rolls. The system should begin planning enhanced services to ensure their well-being while in foster care as they transition to independence.

Chapter Summary

Foster care is a service for children who cannot live with their parents due to parental incapacity. It is also a service to help parents resolve problems that led to placement so that they can resume care for their children. Foster care has a long and complicated history in the United States, evolving from nineteenth-century forms of care such as indenture, outdoor relief, almshouse care, orphanages and children's institutions, and free foster homes. During the twentieth century, foster care was established as the preferred form of care for most children, with institutions reserved for older children with serious problems. Foster care has changed from a program focused on stabilizing the child's placement to one emphasizing planning and movement of the child through the system and into a permanent home.

Only families with very serious limitations, often substance abuse related, are likely to lose their children to foster care. The placement process is recognized as very stressful for children and for parents, and social work services are necessary to help the whole family cope with separation. Reunification of the family is the first choice of permanency planning. Families receive services through a parent–agency service agreement, which structures what the agency and the parents will do in order for reunification to occur. Parent–child visiting is an essential component to family reunification efforts. If reunification is not possible or is tried and fails, the agency moves to alternative permanent plans, usually either guardianship or adoption. Adoption requires that the parents' rights to their child be terminated through a legal process. In making placement decisions, the agency takes into account the child's need for continuity of relationships established with parents, extended family, siblings, foster parents, and others, and also is attentive to the child's need for a cultural identity.

There are several different types of out-of-home care for children, including kinship care, family foster care, treatment foster care, group homes, and residential treatment centers. Adolescents aging out of foster care receive independent living services to help them make the transition to adulthood. Foster parents and child care staff are key members of the agency team in providing services to children and their families, though they tend to be underpaid and do not receive sufficient services to help them in their work. Most states require that foster parents receive ongoing training. Abuse of children in out-of-home care is a long-standing problem that was too long ignored; agencies are developing strategies and protocols for ensuring children's safety while in care. The field of foster care is now challenged to develop managed care as a way of financing placement services.

FOR STUDY AND DISCUSSION

1. Identify both positive and negative vestiges of the historical development of foster care practice that may be seen in current agency practice.

2. Talk with a placement specialist from a child placing agency to determine which options (shared family care, kinship care, family foster care, treatment foster care, group homes, and residential care) are available in your community. What criteria are applied for selecting a particular care option for a child and family?

3. Meet with a protective services supervisor to determine under what circumstances children in your community would be removed from their families and put into care. What are the critical problems or clusters of problems causing foster care placement?

4. Attend a foster parent association meeting and survey foster parents on their perceptions of social worker teamwork. Talk with foster care social workers about what they believe constitute characteristics of good foster parents. Compare points of convergence and discrepancies.

5. Invite a former foster child, or a panel of young adults who have been in care, to discuss their experiences with you in class.

6. Read more extensively on the needs and experiences of parents whose children are in care and talk with one in person.

FOR ADDITIONAL STUDY

Burns, B. J., & Hoagwood, K. (2002). *Community treatment for youth: Evidence-based interventions for severe emotional and behavioral disorders.* New York: Oxford University Press.

Children's Bureau. (1999). *Title IV-E independent living programs: A decade in review.* Administration for Children and Families. Washington, DC: U.S. Government Printing Office.

Fahlberg, V. (1991). *A child's journey through placement.* Indianapolis: Perspectives Press.

Hegar, R., & Scannapieco, M. (1999). *Kinship foster care: Policy, practice, and research.* New York: Oxford University Press.

National Foster Care Awareness Project. (2000). *Frequently asked questions about the Foster Care Independence Act of 1999 and the John H. Chafee Foster Care Independence Program.* Casey Family Program.

Pelzer, D. (2000). *A man named Dave: A story of triumph and forgiveness.* New York: Plume, Penguin Putnam.

Rehnquist, J. (2002a). *Recruiting foster parents.* Department of Health and Human Services, Office of the Inspector General. Washington, DC: U.S. Government Printing Office.

Rehnquist, J. (2002b). *Retaining foster parents.* Department of Health and Human Services, Office of the Inspector General. Washington, DC: U.S. Government Printing Office.

Simmons, D., & Trope, J. (1999). *P.L. 105-90 Adoption and Safe Families Act of 1997: Issues for tribes and states serving Indian children.* The National Indian Child Welfare Association, National Resource Center for Organizational Improvement. University of Southern Maine.

Walsh, R., Pine, B., & Maluccio, A. (1996). *Reconnecting families: A guide to strengthening family reunification services.* Washington, DC: Child Welfare League of America Press.

INTERNET SITES

Children's Bureau, Administration for Children and Families, Department of Health and Human Services, Adoption and Foster Care Analysis and Reporting System (AFCARS). This government site provides data on foster care.

www.acf.hhs.gov/programs/cb

Child Welfare League of America. This organization has a general child welfare site, with specific pages related to developments in foster care and lists of topically related titles by Child Welfare League of America Press.

www.cwla.org

Children's Defense Fund, Washington, DC. This site provides information on child care, current news as it relates to children, the black community, publications, and other related links. It also gives data on population and family characteristics, economic security, and federal program participation.

www.childrensdefense.org

International Federation of Social Workers. This organization has a central office in Switzerland, and links together social workers from around the globe. It is currently working with the United Nations on the Convention on Rights of the Child.

www.ifsw.org

International Foster Care Organization. This organization meets biennially for educational conferences. A youth in care network is part of IFCO. The organization links together child welfare agencies, nongovernmental organizations (NGOs), foster parent groups, and child care groups from many countries.

www.internationalfostering.org

National Foster Parent Association. Information on becoming a foster parent is available at this site. This site explains the purpose of the National Foster Parent Association and provides membership information. It offers a comprehensive site called KidSource, which addresses information on children, newborn through adolescence, as it relates to fostering.

www.kidsource.com/nfpa/index.html

National Resource Center for Permanency Planning. Provides information services, training, and technical assistance to ensure that children have safe families to grow up in. This site focuses on the following issues: permanency planning, kinship foster care, concurrent planning, family group decision making, and HIV/AIDS.

www.hunter.cuny.edu/socwork

REFERENCES

Adoption and Foster Care Analysis and Reporting System (AFCARS). (2002, August 7). Available: www.acf.hhs.gov/programs/cb/publications/afcars/report7. htm [2002, October 29].

Ainsworth, M. D. (1962). The effects of maternal deprivation: A review of findings and controversy in the context of research strategy. In *Deprivation of maternal care: A reassessment of its effects*. Geneva: World Health Organization, Public Health Papers (no. 14).

Allen, M., Bonner, K., & Greenan, L. (1988). Federal legislative support for independent living. *Child Welfare, 67*(6), 515–527.

Allen, M., Lakin, D., McFadden, E. J., & Wasserman, K. (1992). *Family continuity: Practice competen-cies*. Ypsilanti, MI: National Foster Care Resource Center.

Altshuler, S. (2003). From barriers to successful collaboration: Public schools and child welfare working together. *Social Work, 48*(1), 52–64.

Altshuler, S. J., & Gleeson, J. P. (1999, January–February). Completing the evaluation triangle for the next century: Measuring child "well-being" in family foster care. *Child Welfare, 78*(1), 125–147.

Altshuler, S. J., & Poertner, J. (2002, May–June). The Child Health and Illness Profile—adolescent edition: Assessing well-being in group homes or institutions. *Child Welfare, 81*(3), 495–514.

Bank, S., & Kahn, M. (1982). *The sibling bond*. New York: Basic Books.

Barth, R. (1986). Emancipation services for adolescents in foster care. *Social Work, 31*(3), 165–171.

Barth, R. P. (1999). After safety, what is the goal of child welfare services: Permanency, family continuity or social benefit? *International Journal of Social Welfare, 8,* 244–252.

Barth, R. P., & Blackwell, D. L. (1998, August). Death rates among California's foster care and former foster care populations. *Children & Youth Services Review, 20*(7), 577–604.

Barth, R. P., & Price, A. (1999, January–February). Shared family care: Providing services to parents and children placed together in out-of-home care. *Child Welfare, 78*(1), 88–107.

Battistelli, E. (1998). *The health care of children in out-of-home care.* Washington, DC: Child Welfare League of America Press.

Bazemore, G., & Terry, W. C. (1997). Developing delinquent youths: A reintegrative model for rehabilitation and a new role for the juvenile justice system. *Child Welfare, 76*(5), 665–718.

Berry, M. (1988). A review of parent training programs in child welfare. *Social Service Review, 62*(2), 302–322.

Besharov, D. (1990, July–August). Crack children in foster care: Re-examining the balance between children's rights and parents rights. *Children Today,* 21–25.

Besharov, D. (Ed.). (1994). *When drug addicts have children.* Washington, DC: Child Welfare League of America/American Enterprise Institute.

Billingsley, A. (1992). *Climbing Jacob's ladder: The enduring legacy of African-American families.* New York: Simon & Schuster.

Blatt, S., Saletsky, R., Meguid, V., Church, C., O'Hara, M., Haller-Peck, S., & Anderson, J. (1997). A comprehensive, multidisciplinary approach to providing health care for children in out-of-home care. *Child Welfare, 76*(2), 331–347.

Bloom, R. (1992). When staff members sexually abuse children in residential care. *Child Welfare, 71*(2), 131–145.

Blumenthal, K., & Weinberg, A. (1983). *Establishing parental involvement in foster care agencies.* New York: Child Welfare League of America Press.

Bolea, P. S., Grant, G., Burgess, M., & Plasa, O. (2003, March–April). Trauma from children of the Sudan: A constructivist exploration. *Child Welfare, 82*(2), 219–233.

Bowlby, J. (1969). *Attachment and loss.* London: Hogarth Press.

Brace, C. L. (1872). *The dangerous classes of New York and twenty years' work among them.* New York: Wynkoop and Hallenbeck.

Brissett-Chapman, S., & Issacs-Shockley, M. (1997). *Children in social peril: A community vision for preserving family care of African American children and youths.* Washington, DC: Child Welfare League of America Press.

Bromley, B., & Blacker, J. (1991). Parental reasons for out-of-home placement of children with severe handicaps. *Mental Retardation, 29*(5), 275–280.

Bryant, B. (1994). Panacea watch: Permanency planning. *The Review, 8*(3), 2–3.

Bryant, B., & Snodgrass, R. (1990). Therapeutic foster care past and present. In P. Meadowcroft and B. Trout (Eds.). *Troubled youth in treatment homes: A handbook of therapeutic foster care.* Washington, DC: Child Welfare League of America.

Cantos, A., Gries, L., & Slis, V. (1997). Behavioral correlates of parental visiting during family foster care. *Child Welfare, 76*(2), 309–329.

Carbino, R. (1991). Child abuse and neglect reports in foster care: The issue of foster families and "false" allegations. *Child and Youth Services, 15*(2), 233–247.

Cautley, P. W. (1980). *New foster parents.* New York: Human Sciences.

Charles, G., & Matheson, J. (1990). Children in foster care: Issues of separation and attachment. *Community Alternatives, International Journal of Family Care, 2*(2), 37–49.

Chasnoff, I. (1990). Maternal drug use. In *Crack and other addictions: Old realities and new challenges for child welfare* (pp. 110–120). Washington, DC: Child Welfare League of America.

Chernoff, R., Coombs-Orme, T., Risley-Curtis, C., & Heisler, A. (1994). Assessing the health status of children entering foster care. *Pediatrics, 93,* 594–601.

Child Welfare League of America. (1982). *CWLA standards for residential centers for children.* New York: Child Welfare League of America.

Child Welfare League of America. (1991). *Serving gay and lesbian youth: The role of child welfare agencies.* Washington, DC: Author.

Child Welfare League of America. (1994). *Kinship care: A natural bridge.* Washington, DC: Author.

Child Welfare League of America. (1995). *Standards of excellence for family foster care services* (rev. ed.). Washington, DC: Author.

Churchill, S., Carlson, B., & Nybell, L. (Eds.). (1979). *No child is unadoptable.* Beverly Hills, CA: Sage.

Colon, F. (1978). Family ties and child placement. *Family Process, 17,* 289–312.

Crumbley, J. (1999). *Transracial adoption and foster care: Practice issues for professionals.* Washington DC: CWLA Press.

Delaney, R. (1991). *Fostering changes: Treating attachment-disordered foster children.* Fort Collins, CO: Walter J. Corbett Publishing.

Downs, S. W. (1981). *Foster care reform in the 70s: Final report of the permanency planning dissemination project.* Portland, OR: Regional Institute for Human Services.

Downs, S. W. (1989). Foster parents of mentally retarded and physically handicapped children. In J. Hudson & B. Galaway (Eds.), *Specialist foster family care: A normalizing experience. Special Issue of Child and Youth Services Review, 12*(1–2). New York: Haworth.

Downs, S. W. (1990). Recruiting and retaining foster families of adolescents. In A. Maluccio, R. Krieger, & B. A. Pine (Eds.), *Preparing adolescents for life after foster care: The central role of foster parents.* Washington, DC: Child Welfare League of America.

Downs, S. W., & Sherraden, M. (1983). The orphan asylum in the nineteenth century. *Social Service Review, 57*(2), 272–290.

Emenhiser, D., King, D. W., Joffe, S., & Penkert, K. (1998). Washington, DC: Child Welfare League of America Press.

Emlen, A. (1978). *Overcoming barriers to planning for children in foster care.* Portland, OR: Regional Research Institute for Human Services.

Fahlberg, V. (1991). *A child's journey through placement.* Indianapolis: Perspectives Press.

Fanshel, D. (1975). Parental failure and consequences for children: The drug-abusing mother whose children are in foster care. *American Journal of Public Health, 65*(6), 604–612.

Fanshel, D., & Shinn, E. B. (1978). *Children in foster care: A longitudinal investigation.* New York: Columbia University School Press.

Fein, E., & Staff, I. (1993). Goal-setting with biological families. In B. Pine, R. Warsh, & A. Maluccio (Eds.), *Together again: Family reunification in foster care* (pp. 67–92). Washington, DC: Child Welfare League of America.

Festinger, T. B. (1994). *Returning to care: Discharge and reentry in foster care.* Washington, DC: Child Welfare League of America.

Fimmen, M. D., & Mietus, K. J. (1988). *An empirical analysis of the impact of joint training upon child welfare practitioners.* (DHHS Award No. 05CT1022/01). Macomb, IL: Western Illinois University.

Folaron, G. (1993). Preparing children for reunification. In B. Pine, R. Krieger, & A. Maluccio (Eds.), *Together again: Family reunification in foster care* (pp. 41–154). Washington, DC: Child Welfare League of America.

Folaron, G., & Hess, P. (1993). Placement considerations for children of mixed African-American and Caucasian parentage. *Child Welfare, 72*(2), 113–125.

Folks, H. (1911). *The care of destitute, neglected, and delinquent children.* New York: Macmillan.

Folman, R. D. (1998). I was tooken: How children experience removal from their parents preliminary to placement into foster care. *Adoption Quarterly, 2*(2), 7–35.

Foster Family-Based Treatment Association. (2001). *Annotations of research in treatment foster care.* Teaneck, NJ: Author.

Freud, C. (1955). Meaning of separation for parents and children as seen in child placement. *Public Welfare, 13*(1), 13–17, 25.

Garbarino, J., DuBrow, N., Knostelny, K., & Pardo, C. (1992). *Children in danger: Coping with the consequences of community violence.* San Francisco: Jossey-Bass.

Garnier, P. C., & Poertner, J. (2000, September–October). Using administrative data to assess child safety in out-of-home care. *Child Welfare, 79*(5), 597–613.

Gavazzi, S., Alford, K., & McKenry, P. (1996). Culturally specific programs for foster care youth. *Family Relations, 45,* 166–174.

Geiser, R. (1973). *The illusion of caring.* Boston: Beacon Press.

Gillespie, J., Byrne, B., & Workman, L. (1995). An intensive reunification program for children in foster care. *Child and Adolescent Social Work Journal, 12*(3), 213–228.

Gilligan, R. (1997). Beyond permanence? The importance of resilience in child placement practice and planning. *Adoption and Fostering, 21*(1), 12–20.

Golden, R. (1997). *Disposable children: America's child welfare system.* Belmont, CA: Wadsworth.

Goldstein, J., Freud, A., & Solnit, A. (1973). *Beyond the best interests of the child.* New York: Free Press.

Grigsby, K. (1994). Maintaining attachment relationships among children in foster care. *Families in Society, 75*(5), 269–276.

Groze, V., Haines-Simeon, M., & Barth, R. (1994). Barriers in permanency planning for medically fragile children: Drug affected children and HIV infected children. *Child and Adolescent Social Work Journal, 11*(1), 63–85.

Gurdin, P., & Anderson, G. R. (1987). Quality care for ill children: AIDS-specialized foster family homes. *Child Welfare, 66*(4), 291–302.

Hegar, R. (1993). Assessing attachment, permanence, and kinship in choosing permanent homes. *Child Welfare, 72*(4), 367–378.

Herczog, H., van Pagee, R., & Pasztor, E. M. (2001, September–October). The multinational transfer of competency-based foster parent assessment, selection, and training: A nine-country case study. *Child Welfare, 80*(5), 631–644.

Hess, P., & Folaron, G. (1991). Ambivalences: A challenge to permanency for children. *Child Welfare, 70*(4), 403–424.

Hochstadt, N., & Yost, D. (Eds.). (1991). *The medically complex child: The transition to home care.* New York: Harwood Academic Publishers.

Hohman, M. M., & Butt, R. L. (2001, January–February). How soon is too soon? Addiction recovery and family reunification. *Child Welfare, 80*(1), 53–70.

Horn, W. (1994). Implications for policy-making. In D. Besharov (Ed.), *When drug addicts have children* (pp. 165–174). Washington, DC: Child Welfare League and American Enterprise Institute.

Hudson, J., Nutter, R., & Galaway, B. (1994). Treatment foster family care: Development and current status. *Community Alternatives, 6*(2), 1–24.

Human Services Associates. (1998). *Finding our place: The inside story of foster care.* St. Paul, MN: Rummel Dubs & Hill.

Hutchins, H. (1997). Managing managed care for families. *Children's Voice, 7*(1), 28–29.

Jackson, H., & Westmoreland, G. (1992). Therapeutic issues for black children in foster care. In L. Vargas & J. Koss-Chioino (Eds.), *Working with culture: Psychotherapeutic interventions with ethnic minority children and adolescents* (pp. 43–62). San Francisco: Jossey Bass.

Jenkins, S., & Norman, E. (1972). *Filial deprivation in foster care.* New York: Columbia University.

Johnson, P., Yoken, C., & Voss, R. (1990). *Foster care placement, the child's perspective.* Discussion paper No. 036. Chicago: University of Chicago, Chapin Hall Center.

Jones, M. L. (1978). Stopping foster care drift: A review of legislation and special programs. *Child Welfare, 57*(9), 571–580.

Jones, M., Magura, S., & Shyne, A. (1976). *A second chance for families.* New York: Child Welfare League of America.

Jordan, C. (1994). Have external review systems improved the quality of care for children? Yes. In E. Gambrill & T. Stein (Eds.), *Controversial issues in child welfare* (pp. 136–140). Boston: Allyn & Bacon.

Kansas chapter. National Association of social workers. (1997). Kansas talk back: Early responses to the privatization of child welfare services. www.naswdc.org/PRAC/Kansas.htm.

Katz, L. (1999, January–February). Concurrent planning: Benefits and pitfalls. *Child Welfare, 78*(1), 108–124.

Klee, L., Soman, L., & Halfon, N. (1992, March–April). Implementing critical health services for children in foster care. *Child Welfare, 71*(2), 99–110.

Knutson, J. (1995). Pyschological characteristics of maltreated children: Putative risk factors and consequences. *Annual Review of Psychology, 46,* 401–431.

Kools, S. (1997). Adolescent identity development in foster care. *Family Relations, 46,* 263–271.

Kufeldt, K., & Allison, J. (1990). Fostering children—Fostering families. *Community Alternatives: International Journal of Family Care, 2,* 1–18.

Lakin, D., Whitfield, L., & Anderson, G. (1997). *Necessary components of effective foster care and adoption recruitment.* (Working paper). Southfield, MI: National Resource Center on Special Needs Adoption.

Lee, D., & Nissivoccia, D. (1989). *Walk a mile in my shoes: A book about biological parents for foster parents and social workers.* Washington, DC: Child Welfare League of America.

Leeds, S. (1992). *Medical and developmental profiles of 148 children born HIV-positive and placed in foster families.* New York: Leake and Watts Services.

Levy, T., & Orlans, M. (1998). *Attachment, trauma and healing.* Washington, DC: Child Welfare League of America Press.

Littner, N. (1975). The importance of the natural parents to the child in placement. *Child Welfare, 54*(3), 175–181.

Maas, S., & Engler, R. E. (1959). *Children in need of parents.* New York: Columbia University.

Mallon, G. (1977). Basic premises, guiding principles and competent practices for a positive youth development approach to working with gay, lesbian and bi-sexual youths in out-of-home care. *Child Welfare, 76*(5) 591–610.

Maluccio, A., & Fein, E. (1983, May–June). Permanency planning: A redefinition. *Child Welfare, 62*(3), 195–201.

Maluccio, A., Krieger, R., & Pine, B. (Eds.). (1990). *Preparing adolescents for life after foster care: The central role of foster parents.* Washington, DC: Child Welfare League of America.

Maluccio, A., & Sinanoglu, P. (Eds.). (1981). *The challenge of partnership: Working with parents of children in foster care.* New York: Child Welfare League of America.

Marcenko, M., & Striepe, M. (1997). A look at family reunification through the eyes of mothers. *Community Alternatives: The International Journal of Family Care, 9*(1) 33–47.

Martin, F., & Palmer, T. (1997). Transitions to adulthood: A child welfare youth perspective. *Community Alternatives, the International Journal of Family Care, 9*(2), 29–58.

Maza, P. L. (2000, September–October). Using administrative data to reward agency performance: The case of the federal adoption incentive program. *Child Welfare, 79*(5), 444–456.

Maza, P. L. (2002). The impact of ASFA on adoption. Presentation at National Conference on Child Abuse and Neglect.

McFadden, E. J. (1980). *Working with natural families.* Ypsilanti, MI: Eastern Michigan University.

McFadden, E. J. (1984). Practice in foster care. In A. Hartman & J. Laird (Eds.), *Handbook of child welfare.* New York: Free Press.

McFadden, E. J. (1985). *Preventing abuse in family foster care.* Ypsilanti, MI: Eastern Michigan University.

McFadden, E. J. (1991). The inner world of children and youth in care. Paper presented at the Seventh International Foster Care Organization Converence, Jonkopping, Sweden.

McFadden, E. J. (1996). Family-centered practice with foster parent families. *Families in Society, 77*(9) 545–557.

McFadden, E. J., & Downs, S. W. (1995). Family continuity: The new paradigm in permanence planning. *Community Alternatives: The International Journal of Family Care, 7*(1), 44.

McFadden, E. J., Rice, D., Ryan, P., & Warren, B. (1989). Leaving home again: Emancipation from foster family care. In J. Hudson and B. Galaway (Eds.), *Specialist foster family care: A normalizing experience.* New York: Haworth.

McFadden, E. J., & Ryan, P. (1991). Maltreatment in family foster homes: Dynamics and dimensions. *Child and Youth Services, 15*(2), 209–231.

Meadowcroft, P., & Grealish, E. M. (1990). Training and supporting treatment parents. In P. Meadowcroft & B. Trout (Eds.), *Troubled youth in treatment homes: A handbook of therapeutic foster care.* Washington, DC: Child Welfare League of America.

Mech, E. (1985). Parental visiting and child placement, *Child Welfare, 64*(1), 67–72.

Meidema, B., & Nason-Clark, N. (1977). Foster care redesign: The dilemma contemporary foster parents face. *Community Alternatives, the International Journal of Family Care, 9*(2), 15–28.

Milner, J. (1987). An ecological perspective on duration of foster care. *Child Welfare, 66*(2), 113–123.

Murphy, S., & Helm, M. (1988). Group preparation of adolescents for family placement. In J. Trisiliotis (Ed.), *Groupwork in adoption and foster care.* London: B. T. Batsford, Ltd.

National Association of Foster Care Reviewers. (1994). Court improvement project: The citizen review role. *The Review, 8*(3), 1–2.

National Association of Foster Care Reviewers. (1998). *Safe passage to permanency: Using third-party review to improve outcomes for children in foster care.* Atlanta, GA: Author.

National Association of Social Workers. (1993, April). *NASW News.*

National Black Child Development Institute. (1989). *Who will care when parents can't: A study of black children in foster care.* Washington, DC: National Black Child Development Institute.

National Commission on Family Foster Care. (1991). *A blueprint for fostering infants, children and youths in the 1990s.* Washington, DC: Child Welfare League of America Press.

National Foster Care Awareness Project. (2000). *Frequently asked questions about the Foster Care Independence Act.* Seattle: Casey Family Programs.

Nelson, K. (1992). Fostering homeless children and their parents too: The emergence of whole family care. *Child Welfare, 71*(6) 575–584.

Nelson, K., Landsman, M., & Deutelbaum, W. (1990). Three models of family-centered placement prevention services. *Child Welfare, 69*(1), 3–21.

Newton, R. R., Litrownik, A. J., & Landsverk, J. A. (2000). Children and youth in foster care: Disentangling the relationship between problem behaviors and number of placements. *Child Abuse and Neglect, 24*(10), 1363–1374.

Nowicki, S., & Duke, M. (1992). *Helping the child who doesn't fit in.* Atlanta, GA: Peachtree Publishers.

Ortega, R., Guillean, C., & Najera, L. (1996). *Latinos and child welfare/latinos y el bienestar del niño, voces de la comunidad.* Ann Arbor, MI: University of Michigan.

Oyserman, D., Benbenishty, R., & Ben-Rabi, D. (1992). Characteristics of children and their families at entry into foster care. *Child Psychiatry and Human Development, 22*(3), 199–211.

Palmer, S. (1990). Group treatment of foster children to reduce separation conflict associated with placement breakdown. *Child Welfare, 69*(3), 227–238.

Palmer, S. (1997). Training workers to include families in child placement. *Community Alternatives: The International Journal of Family Care, 9*(1), 49–70.

Pardeck, J., & Pardeck, J. (1987, May–June). Bibliotherapy for children in foster care and adoption. *Child Welfare, 66*(3), 269–278.

Pecora, P., Whittaker, J., Maluccio, A., Barth, R., & Plotnick, R. (1992). *The child welfare challenge.* New York: Walter de Gruyter.

Phillips, M., Shyne, A., Sherman, E., & Haring, B. (1971). *Factors associated with placement decisions in child welfare.* New York: Child Welfare League of America.

Phillips, S., McMillen, C., Sparks, J., & Ueberle, M. (1997). Concrete strategies for sensitizing youth-serving agencies to the needs of gay, lesbian, and other sexual minority youths. *Child Welfare, 76*(3), 393–409.

Pike, V., Downs, S. W., Emlen, A., Downs, G., & Case, D. (1977). *Permanent planning for children in foster care* (No. OHDS 77-30124). Washington, DC: U.S. Department of Health, Education and Welfare.

Pine, B., Krieger, R., & Maluccio, A. (Eds.). (1993). *Together again: Family reunification in foster care.* Washington, DC: Child Welfare League of America.

Pizzigati, K. (1998). Safety and permanence: New federal law reemphasizes both. *Children's Voice, 7*(3), 12–13.

Proch, K., & Howard, J. (1986). Parental visiting of children in foster care. *Social Work, 31*(3), 178–181.

Quinn, T. L. (2002, November–December). Sexual orientation and gender identity: An administrative approach to diversity. *Child Welfare, 81*(6), 913–928.

Ratterman, D., Dodson, D., & Hardin, M. (1987). *Reasonable efforts to prevent foster care placement: A guide to implementation.* Washington, DC: American Bar Association.

Raychaba, B. (1989). *We got a life sentence: Young people's response to sexual abuse.* Ottawa: National Youth in Care Network.

Redding, R. E., Fried, C., & Britner, P. A. (2000). Predictors of placement outcomes in treatment foster care: Implications for foster parent selection and service delivery. *Journal of Child and Family Studies, 9*(4), 425–447.

Reddy, L., & Pfeiffer, S. (1997). Effectiveness of treatment foster care with children and adolescence: A review of outcome studies. *Journal of American Academy of Child and Adolescent Psychiatry, 36*(5), 581–588.

Report of Select Senate Committee to visit charitable and penal institutions. (1857). (New York Senate Document No. 8). Reprinted in S. P. Breckinridge (1927). *Public welfare administration in the United States: Select documents.* Chicago: University of Chicago Press.

Rhodes, K. W., Orme, J. G., & Buehler, C. (2001, March). A comparison of family foster parents who quit, consider quitting, and plan to continue fostering. *Social Service Review,* 84–114.

Rice, D., & McFadden, E. J. (1988, May–June). A forum for foster children. *Child Welfare, 67*(3), 231–243.

Ricketts, W. (1991). *Lesbians and gay men as foster parents.* Portland, ME: University of Southern Maine, National Child Welfare Resource Center.

Robertson, R. (1997). Walking the talk: Organizational modeling and commitment to youth and staff development. *Child Welfare, 76*(5), 577–590.

Rutter, M. (1985). Resilience in the face of adversity: Protective factors and resistance to psychiatric disorder. *British Journal of Psychiatry, 147,* 598–611.

Ryan, P. (1995). Personal communication.

Ryan, P., McFadden, E. J., & Warren, B. (1981). Foster families: A resource for helping parents. In A. Maluccio and P. Sinanoglu (Eds.), *The Challenge of Partnership* (pp. 189–199). New York: Child Welfare League of America.

Saunders, E., Nelson, K., & Landsman, M. (1993). Racial inequality and child neglect: Findings in a metropolitan area. *Child Welfare, 72*(4), 341–354.

Schneiderman, M., Connors, M., Fribourg, A., Gries, L., & Gonzales, M. (1998). Mental health services for children in out-of-home care. *Child Welfare, 77*(1), 29–40.

Semidei, J., Radel, L. F., & Nolan, C. (2001, March–April). Substance abuse and child welfare: Clear linkages and promising responses. *Child Welfare, 80*(2), 109–128.

Shlonsky, A. R., & Berrick, J. D. (2001, March). Assessing and promoting quality in kin and nonkin foster care. *Social Service Review,* 60–83.

Slingerland, W. (1919). *Child placing in families.* New York: Russell Sage Foundation.

Staff, I., & Fein, E. (1992). Together or separate: A study of siblings in foster care. *Child Welfare, 71*(3), 257–270.

Staff, I., & Fein, E. (1995). Stability and change: Initial findings in a study of treatment foster care placements. *Children and Youth Services Review, 17*(3), 379–389.

Stein, T. (1998). *The social welfare of women and children with HIV and AIDS.* New York: Oxford University Press.

Stein, T. J. (2000, November–December). The Adoption and Safe Families Act: Creating a false dichotomy between parents' and children's rights. *Families in Society, 81*(6).

Stein, T., & Gambrill, E. (1977). Facilitating decision-making in foster care: The Alameda project. *Social Service Review, 51*(3), 502–513.

Stein, T., Gambrill, E., & Wiltse, K. (1974). Foster care: The use of contracts. *Public Welfare, 32*(4), 20–25.

Stein, T., & Rzepnicki, T. (1984). *Decision-making in child welfare services: Intake and planning.* Boston: Kluwer-Nijhoff.

Stokes, J., & Strothman, L. (1996). The use of bonding studies in child welfare permanency planning. *Child and Adolescent Social Work Journal, 13*(4), 347–367.

Stone, H. (1987). *Ready, set, go: An agency guide to independent living.* Washington, DC: Child Welfare League of America.

Tatara, T. (1993). *Characteristics of children in substitute and adoptive care.* Washington, DC: American Public Welfare Association, VCIS.

Taylor-Brown, S., & Garcia, A. (1995). Social workers and HIV-affected families: Is the profession prepared? *Social Work, 40*(1), 14–15.

Ten Broeck, E., & Barth, R. (1986). Learning the hard way: A pilot permanency planning program. *Child Welfare, 65,* 281–294.

Terling-Watt, T. (2001). Permanency in kinship care: An exploration of disruption rates and factors associated with placement disruption. *Children & Youth Services Review, 23*(2), 111–126.

Terpstra, J. (1997). Child welfare, from there to where. Unpublished paper.

Terpstra, J., & McFadden, E. J. (1993, Spring). Looking backward, looking forward: New directions in foster care. *Community Alternatives, 5*(1), 115–133.

Testa, M. F., & Rolock, N. (1999, January–February). Professional foster care: A future worth pursuing? *Child Welfare, 78*(1), 108–124.

Thoennes, N. (1996). Foster care review: Reducing delay and expense in the juvenile court. Alexandria, VA: State Justice Institute.

Thomlison, B. (1997). Risk and protective factors in child maltreatment. In M. Fraser (Ed.), *Risk and resilience in childhood.* Washington, DC: National Association of Social Workers Press.

Thurston, H. S. (1930). *The dependent child.* New York: Columbia University Press.

Tourse, P., & Gunderson, L. (1988). Adopting and fostering children with AIDS: Policies in progress. *Children Today, 17,* 15–19.

Twigg, R. (1995). Coping with loss: How foster parents' children cope with foster care. *Community Alternatives: The International Journal of Family Care, 7*(1), 1–14.

U.S. Department of Health and Human Services. (2000). *Rethinking child welfare practice under the Adoption and Safe Families Act of 1997: A Resource guide.* Washington, DC: U.S. Government Printing Office.

U.S. General Accounting Office. (1989). *Foster parents: Recruiting and preservice training practices and evaluation.* Washington, D.C.: Author.

U.S. General Accounting Office. (1991). *Foster care: Children's experiences linked to various factors; better data needed.* (HRD-91-64). Washington, DC: Author.

Walker, C., Zangrillo, P., & Smith, J. (1991). *Parental drug abuse and African American children in foster care: Issues and study findings.* Washington, DC: National Black Child Development Institute.

Walsh, J., & Walsh, R. (1990). *Quality care for tough kids.* Washington, DC: Child Welfare League of America.

Walton, E., Fraser, M., Lewis, R., Pecora, P., & Walton, W. (1993). In-home family-focused reunification: An experimental study. *Child Welfare, 72*(5), 473–487.

Weinstein, E. A. (1960). *The self-image of the foster child.* New York: Russell Sage Foundation.

Whittaker, J. K. (1987). Group care for children. In A. Minahan (Ed.), *Encyclopedia of social work* (18th ed.) (pp. 672–682). Silver Spring, MD: National Association of Social Workers.

Wightman, M. (1991). Criteria for placement decisions with cocaine-exposed infants. *Child Welfare, 70*(6) 653–663.

Wood, L., Herring, A. E., & Hunt, R. (1989). *On their own: The needs of youth in transition.* Elizabeth, NJ: Association for the Advancement of the Mentally Handicapped.

Wooden, K. (1976). *Weeping in the playtime of others.* New York: McGraw-Hill.

Zambrana, R., & Dorrington, C. (1998). Economic and social vulnerability of Latino children and families by subgroup: Implications for child welfare. *Child Welfare, 77*(1), 5–27.

Zuravin, S., Benedict, M., & Somerfield, M. (1993). Child maltreatment in family foster care. *American Journal of Orthopsychiatry, 63*(4), 589–596.

Zuravin, S., & DePanfilis, D. (1997). Factors affecting foster care placement of children receiving child protective services. *Social Work Research, 21*(1), 34–42.

In every child who is born, under no matter what circumstances, and of no matter what parents, the potentiality of the human race is born again and in him, too, once more, and each of us, our terrific responsibility towards human life.

—James Agee

Bandele. (Follow me home.)

—Swahili saying

CHAPTER OUTLINE

Case Example: Helping an Older Child Use Adoption

This case shows how a social worker, using an approach emphasizing continuity of family relationships, helped a child with a history of traumatic experiences move successfully through the adoption process. She supported him as he worked through his conflicting loyalty toward his birth family and his adoptive family, and his hesitancy to trust a new relationship after experiencing earlier rejection.

Ms. Franklin, an adoption specialist, met Grant when he was 10 years old and living temporarily in a residential center, where he had gone after his adoption of one year had disrupted. Her responsibility was to help Grant, if possible, to move into a new adoptive placement.

The first task was to get to know Grant well. She learned that he had entered the child welfare system at age 7, along with his older brother, Oliver. Their mother had been unable to manage the boys, who were often truant and were causing problems in the community. She had abandoned them at the child welfare agency and later voluntarily relinquished her rights. Their father was a gambler and involved in other illegal activities; during a period of time when the boys were in his care he had exposed them to "nightlife" and had not met their basic needs. He too relinquished his sons voluntarily.

Grant was originally placed in foster care with a single, middle-aged woman who had raised her own family. After a year, she adopted Grant. Initially, things went well, but Oliver, who had not wanted to be adopted and was living elsewhere, began to exert a strong influence on Grant. He let Grant know that "this is not your real family; I'm your real family." The more the adoptive mom put pressure on Grant to distance himself from Oliver, the more Grant felt a conflict of loyalties. His behavior began to reflect the conflict he was feeling and the adoptive mother decided she could not cope. So the adoption disrupted, and Grant was placed in the residential center. He had been there for several months when Ms. Franklin met him.

After assessing Grant's needs, Ms. Franklin felt he needed a home with a strong father figure, because he had had conflicts with two mothers. The family she found consisted of Mr. and Mrs. Robinson and their three children. Grant would be one of the middle children. Because Grant was an average student, Ms. Franklin was interested that the Robinsons did not put undue pressure on the children to excel in school but did expect the children to be conscientious students. Mr. Robinson had a steady job as a laborer, and Mrs. Robinson was a practical nurse. Ms. Franklin thought that this family would provide structure and guidance, and that Grant could meet their expectations.

The mother had a strong spiritual base and was active in church. Strong family networks on both sides, whose members were supportive of the placement, welcomed Grant as a cousin and grandson.

Because of Grant's previous experiences, Ms. Franklin and the Robinsons decided that Grant would feel less pressure if the placement started as foster care, which could develop into an adoption later if both sides wanted it.

Ms. Franklin visited the home twice a month for the next year to provide support and information about resources. During that time, Grant and the Robinsons, parents and children, decided to formalize the arrangement through adoption.

This decision made the adoption very real to Grant and he began to act out his anxiety over the upcoming change in his status. He started to cut classes at school and forged signatures to cover up his truancy. No matter what the parents did to establish consequences, Grant seemed unaffected. They began to question whether Grant wanted the adoption. Oliver reappeared at this time and encouraged Grant to refuse adoption. Also, at this time, Grant learned of his birth mother's whereabouts and visited her.

Ms. Franklin knew that finalizing an adoption can be very stressful for older children as it raises concerns they have over their earlier experiences. She had to help the family and Grant work through this difficult period so they would not rush into a decision during a time of crisis.

She went back over Grant's life history with the Robinsons and discussed how the earlier losses of a family might affect his attitude. She pointed out that both the birth mother and the previous adoptive mother had reneged on a commitment, so Grant was perhaps afraid that that would happen again once the adoption was finalized. She encouraged them to help Grant explore his feelings, and Grant was able to express that he was afraid of what his brother would say about the adoption.

Ms. Franklin helped the family develop several strategies to deal with the confusion everyone was feeling. One strategy was that the adoptive father, who had been from the first an involved and available parent, became more involved with Grant. He told Grant about some incidents from his own school days and how he had tried to resolve them, and took extra time to share activities with him. Another strategy was to keep an open line with the school to avoid an escalation of the crisis by having Grant suspended or expelled. The adoptive parents worked out an arrangement with the counselor and teachers so they all could work on Grant's truancy as a team.

To deal with the influence of Oliver, Mrs. Robinson spoke with him personally and reassured him that he would not lose his brother, and that he would be welcome in her home. She also let him know that the family loved Grant, wanted to take care of him, and would not harm him. She reassured him that they were not denigrating Grant's birth family. Mrs. Robinson also met Grant's birth mother and exchanged information with her. The Robinsons let her and Grant know that it was fine for them to stay in touch with each other. Grant himself was able to come to a decision that he wanted to live in the Robinson family. He seemed to understand that the new family would not replace his earlier family but could meet his current needs.

This period of uncertainty also gave the Robinsons a chance to clarify their own feelings about making Grant a permanent member of the family. After weathering this period, they came to believe even more strongly that "this is our kid."

After the adoption was finalized, Ms. Franklin gradually cut back her involvement with the family. She let them know that they were in charge and that the agency trusted them to take full responsibility for Grant's welfare. She continued to be a resource for information on services, and she assured them that she would be available to help them manage a crisis. She also worked to help Grant transfer his trust from the adoption worker to the adoptive parents. Though Grant is now grown, he still stays in touch with Ms. Franklin occasionally. He graduated from high school and is doing well.

The Changing World of Adoption

Adoption is a social and a legal process whereby the parent–child relationship is established between persons not so related by birth. By this means a child born to one set of parents becomes, legally and socially, the child of other parents and a member of another family, and assumes the same rights and duties as those between children and their biological parents. Adoption is a lifelong process of benefits to and adjustments by all members of the adoptive triad—the adopted person, the birth parents, and the adoptive parents. The complex legal framework for adoption reflects its importance to the families affected; it is the most drastic state intervention into families, as it creates new families from those not so related by blood.

Adoption has become one of the most dynamic arenas of child welfare practice. Change is occurring rapidly on all fronts, bringing controversy and uncertainty in its wake (Pertman, 2000). From being primarily a service matching white, healthy infants with traditional white middle-class families, adoption now is challenging long-held assumptions about the appropriate composition of families. Ideas about the qualities of people who might participate in adoption are rapidly expanding. Senior citizens, persons with AIDS, gay and lesbian couples, single adults, relatives, and people of a different race and culture from the adopted child are among the groups who are seeking to become adoptive parents and are publicly challenging traditional, untested assumptions about who should become a parent.

In contrast to earlier years when adoptive children were mainly healthy infants, today almost any child in need of a permanent home is considered a candidate for adoption, regardless of age, disabilities, or national origin. Many of these children are older and have lived with their biological parents, making the adoptive experience quite different from that of an adopted infant.

The role of biological parents in the adoption process is also changing. Biological parents may want a part in deciding who adopts their child and may wish some kind of ongoing connection to the child and adoptive family. The rights of biological fathers as well as mothers now must be considered in freeing children for adoption. The policy framework for adoption is more complicated than in earlier years. There is disagreement about who should handle adoptions, and there are also special issues that arise in international adoption.

A vivid example of how the concept of adoption has expanded to include adults and children who, until recently, would not have been considered a "family," is the story of Nasdijj, a migrant worker and adoptive father. "My 12-year-old Navajo son had AIDS. I knew he did when I adopted him last year. . . . I have wiped the tears of such children before. The disturbed and the vulnerable. The throwaways. . . . I was one of them, too. . . . I have been a migrant worker all my life. . . . This summer, I drifted with my son from Michigan to Florida, picking oranges, cherries, anything, as long as the farm boss paid me. . . . You are thinking, This man should not have had a child. But I did" (Nasdijj, 2001).

As adoption has expanded to involve many different types of family situations, the public has become increasingly aware of adoption. A national survey of adoption attitudes in 2002 showed that most Americans support adoption (94 percent of those surveyed) and have had either a family member or a close friend involved in adoption (64 percent). Given the rapid pace of change in adoption, it is not surprising that large numbers of Americans express confusion about adoption, with concerns about such issues as how adopted children turn out compared to birth children, and about the perceived costs of adoption. The survey found some attitudinal differences between races: Hispanics and African Americans were somewhat more likely than white respondents to state that they would seriously consider adopting a child (32 percent, 23 percent, and 16 percent, respectively) (Evan B. Donaldson Institute, 2002b).

The following section, briefly outlining the historical development of adoption, will help to explain the social and economic changes in this country and developments in our understanding of family dynamics that have impelled the transformations occurring in adoption policy and practice.

Historical Development

The adoption of children dates back to antiquity. References to adoption can be found in the Bible and in legal codes of the Chinese, Hindus, Babylonians, Romans, and ancient Egyptians. Its purpose has varied considerably by country and by period of time—for example, to make possible the continuance of family religious traditions, to provide an heir, to overcome difficulties in recognizing an out-of-wedlock child, or, more recently, to provide permanent homes for children in need of them.

Early Adoption Practices in the United States

The nature and social purpose of adoption as it is conceived today in many countries began to emerge in the United States during the latter part of the nineteenth century. Up to that time, inheritance had run through the history of adoptions so much more prominently than any other factor that its importance can hardly be overestimated (Witmer, Herzog, Weinstein, & Sullivan, 1963). Massachusetts in 1851 was the first to enact an adoptive statute in line with present concepts of the purpose of adoption. The Massachusetts law required a "joint petition by the adopting parents to the probate judge and the written consent of the child's parents, if living, or of his guardian or next of kin if the parents were deceased. The judge if satisfied that the adoption was 'fit and proper' was to enter the adoption decree" (Abbott, 1938, pp. 164–165). The state's new adoption statutes put adoptive status on a firmer legal ground by giving a state some control in adoptive situations before a contest arose, and they secured permanent status for the child in a new family as well as a right to an equitable share of the adoptive parent's estate.

Infant Adoptions

During the first half of the twentieth century, statutes reflected interest in secrecy, confidentiality, anonymity, and the sealing of records (Carp, 1995, 1998). Originally, these practices "were not designed to preserve anonymity between biological parents and adopters, but to shield the adoption proceedings from public scrutiny. These statutes barred all persons from inspecting the files and records on adoption except for the parties to the adoption and their attorneys" (Hollinger, 1991, p. 13). However, from the 1920s through the 1940s, states progressively amended their statutes to deny access of the records to everyone except on "a judicial finding of 'good cause' " (Hollinger, 1991, p. 13). The identities of the birth parents were to remain secret; the original birth certificate was sealed and a new one issued at the time the adoption was finalized (Sokoloff, 1993, p. 22).

During the early decades of the twentieth century, adoption became more and more popular, especially for infertile couples wishing to adopt infants. Previously, adoption was relatively rare, due in part to concern about "bad blood" associated with waifs and foundlings. Two developments that began to change the general reluctance to adopt were the wider availability of infant formula, making adoption of newborns more feasible, and the growing view that children were more profoundly influenced by environment than by heredity (Sokoloff, 1993).

After World War I, demand for infants grew rapidly, prompting the growth of black market adoptions by unregulated "baby brokers." In response, many states amended their statutes to require social investigations and a court hearing before a judge to finalize the adoption. During the 1920s, many specialized adoption agencies were founded to offer professional adoption services. Adoption services were used almost entirely by white couples to adopt white babies; adoption for children of other races rarely occurred through formal agency auspices and was more apt to be done informally, within the extended family network.

Social workers, supported by physicians, defined an "adoptable" child as one who was nearly perfect in health and development and, as far as could be determined by extended observation and examination, one who posed minimal risk to the adopting adults. Well into the middle of the twentieth century, infants released for adoption by their biological mothers did not go immediately after birth to adoptive parents. The newborn infant was usually placed first in a foster home for a three- to six-month period of observation. During this time, infants received physical examinations and intelligence testing. Many social workers made fine distinctions from the psychological report as to the intellectual qualities that should be sought in the infant's adoptive family. Eventually it was acknowledged that a careful "matching" of intellectual abilities or physical characteristics between parents and children, even were this possible, was no guarantee of a successful adoption.

By the 1940s, agencies were faced with having many more adoptive parent applicants than children to offer, a condition that influenced them to develop procedures to restrict the number of applicants. "Matching" of socioeconomic and religious background was common. Agencies placed restrictions on the age and financial status of the applicants, even though they acknowledged that many of the applicants they rejected would make good parents (Michaels, 1947).

The mismatch between the numbers of those desirous of adopting healthy, white infants and the supply available for adoption has increased throughout the latter half of the twentieth century. The rate at which women relinquish their infants for adoption has declined dramatically. Between 1982 and 1988, 3 percent of white women relinquished their children for adoption, dropping from 19 percent in the period between 1965 and 1972. The rate of relinquishment among black women and Latina unmarried women has been consistently at or under 2 percent. (Mosher & Bachrach, 1996.) The decrease of infants available for adoption can be attributed to a number of social developments of the 1960s: increasingly available, effective contraception; the rise in the abortion rate after abortion was legalized in 1973; and the increasing acceptability of single mothers keeping their infants rather than placing them out for adoption (Dukette, 1984). Families interested in adopting infants turned to transracial adoption and increasingly to international adoption. Also, "as advances in technology have permitted, couples have sought help through alternative means of reproduction including artificial insemination by donor, in vitro fertilization, embryo transfer, and most recently, surrogate parenting" (Sokoloff, 1993, p. 23).

Today, adoption of infants is often handled through private agencies or through *independent adoption,* the term for adoption outside of agency auspices, usually by individual professionals (doctors, lawyers, and social workers). This development has raised concern that private individuals, who stand to gain financially from adoption, may not be in the best position to help a pregnant woman make a decision to relinquish her child for adoption or to assess adoptive parents.

Adoption Today: Special Needs Adoption

At the same time that adoptive parents were unable to find infants, another trend was creating a different kind of mismatch: the increasing number of children without permanent families who were thought to be "unadoptable," particularly older children, children of color, and those with medical, emotional, or other handicapping conditions. Several developments led to an increase in the number of these children available for adoption. The abuse and neglect reporting laws, implemented in the 1960s and 1970s, resulted in many more abused and neglected children entering the child welfare system. Teenage pregnancy, the drug epidemic, racism, and poverty have also contributed to their growing numbers.

By the 1990s, adoption had split into two practice arenas: adoption for children with special needs and adoption of healthy infants. Special needs adoption has become primarily the concern of public child and family agencies and is often linked programmatically to foster care programs. Attention has turned to finding adoptive homes for these "special needs" children.

Adoption Today: The Cooperative Adoption Movement

In the 1970s and 1980s, *closed* (or *confidential*) adoption began to give way to a new *open* (or *cooperative*) adoption model. The notion that confidentiality was preferable for all three members of the adoptive triad—birth parents, adoptive parents, and children—came into question through the changes that have occurred in adoption during the last half of the twentieth century. As fewer infants became available for adoption, the birth mother found more leverage in the process of relinquishment and preferences about adoptive parents. Agencies learned that mothers might be less concerned with confidentiality than with helping to select the adoptive parents and with maintaining some kind of connection with the child after the adoption. Adults who had been adopted as infants, for their part, began assertively seeking to have their sealed records opened and demanded the right to know about their biological origins.

The movement to place children with special needs in adoption changed adoption practice dramatically. If older, these children have memories of their birth parents and siblings, and their foster, adoptive, and birth parents often have met one another. Adoptive applicants of children of color and of special needs children expressed the need for a shared partnership with the agency regarding selection and matching processes, leading to a trend toward open sharing of information with the prospective adoptive applicants so they could make an informed decision. Kinship adoption has become increasingly used as a permanent plan for children exiting foster care.

Many adoption agencies today have revised their traditional practices toward varying degrees of "openness" in the adoptive process. These changes take the form of planned communication between the adoptive parents and the biological parents prior to finalization of the adoption. All the parents may have face-to-face meetings before the birth of the child, at agreement for placement, or at various times after the birth of the child. The range of information that is exchanged may include ethnic and religious backgrounds, level of education, aspects of personality and interest, physical characteristics, genetic background, or other matters of common interest. These options are arrived at when birth parents and adoptive parents, with the help of an agency social worker, have agreed on the extent of "openness" in the present and future (Etter, 1997; Grotevant & McRoy, 1998).

Some Adoption Facts and Patterns

No aspect of child welfare practice has yielded such a short supply of accurate statistics as adoption. The U.S. government has collected comprehensive national data at various times, but has not done so since 1975. Since 1997 the federal government has required states to submit data on the number of children adopted from foster care as part of the Adoption and Foster Care Analysis and Reporting System (AFCARS), but this system does not include other common types of adoption such as stepparent, private, or international adoptions. Currently, the most recent complete picture of adoption is from the National Center for State Courts, whose researchers have compiled data from a variety of sources and published estimates of adoption up through 1992 (Flango & Flango, 1995).

- It is estimated that 1.5 million children in the United States live with adopted parents, about 2 percent of all American children (Fields, 2001).
- During the first half of the 1990s, about 120,000 to 127,000 children were adopted each year in the United States through foster care, international, private agency, independent, and stepparent adoption (Flango & Flango, 1994).
- The number of adoptions has fluctuated over time, due to a variety of social and economic factors. Adoptions increased from 50,000 in 1944 to a high of 175,000 in 1970 (Maza, 1984).
- Adoption of children from public agency foster care accounted for about 16 percent of all adoptions in 1992, for a total of about 20,000 children (Flango & Flango, 1994).
- Adoptions made by private agencies or through a facilitator such as a private attorney, accounted for about 38 percent of adoptions (47,600 children) in 1992. Note that this number does not include adoption by relatives (Flango & Flango, 1994).
- Children may be adopted by relatives either through a state child welfare agency or through a private agency or facilitator. In 1992, 42 percent of all adoptions were kinship or stepparent adoptions. The number of kinship adoptions has increased since 1980, as agencies increasingly formalize placements with relatives through adoption (Flango & Flango, 1994).
- Placement of children with families of a different race or ethnicity may be made by public child welfare agencies, a private agency, or a private facilitator, although the term usually refers to public agency adoptions. The most recent estimates, which include intercountry adoptions, are that about 8 percent of adoptions are transracial (Stolley, 1993).
- International adoption has increased substantially in the past decade. In 1991, there were about 9,000 international adoptions; by 2001, that number had increased to 19,000 (Evan B. Donaldson Institute, no date).

Agency and Independent Placements

In the earlier years of adoption as a social service, voluntary agencies arranged the majority of agency adoptions. This pattern has changed. As public agencies have assumed increasing responsibility for social services to children, public child and family services agencies and their private agency partners have substantially extended their adoption services, particularly for children with special needs—those with physical or mental handicaps, adjustment problems due to abuse, and older children and sibling groups. Children of color are often also included in the category of "special needs." They are disproportionately represented in foster care.

Placements by private individuals, termed *independent,* are of three types. *Direct placements* are those made by legal parents to someone known to them. Sometimes parents may gradually and informally relinquish more and more of their responsibilities for a child to a family friend or neighbor, and eventually adoption takes place. These placements are arranged within the state's legal framework and tend to work out satisfactorily for the child. Direct placements of this kind are legal except in three states.

Intermediary placements not for profit are arranged by a third person who is usually not seeking profit and may be well intentioned. Usually the adopting parents are unknown to the birth parents initially, though they may become acquainted if the adoption has some degree of "openness." An exchange of money may take place—for example, a standard fee for legal services or payment of the mother's medical or other living expenses during pregnancy—but the money exchanged is not disproportionate to real expenses and the placement is not motivated by a desire for profit. Such adoptions are legal in all but three states. A danger in this kind of independent placement is that the dividing line between paying legitimate expenses and paying for a child may be hard to distinguish and may facilitate "black market" adoptions (Hardin & Shalleck, 1984; Sullivan, 1998).

Intermediary placements for profit put children at great risk. These children are sold for adoption on the black market—that is, children are moved for profit, often across state lines. The intermediary in these instances usually charges what the traffic will bear. Sometimes these operations are carried out in connection with abortion counseling services by which vulnerable women or young adolescents are identified—those ambivalent about abortion or too far along in pregnancy for termination, or those who appear likely to give up the idea of abortion for an assurance of profit. In all instances of black market placement, the best interests of the child are given little or no consideration; the profit motive is primary. Such placements are illegal in all states, making it difficult to obtain accurate figures on the incidence. Reports suggest that such illegal placements are increasing because of the current shortage of white infants for adoption.

Underlying Principles of the Agency Adoptive Process

The social work profession relies on certain principles or generalizations in planning and extending adoption services. These are similar to guidelines for foster care but reflect greater attention to the permanency in the new parent–child relationship (National Association of Social Workers, 2002).

1. If a child has no long-term home and is legally free of parental ties (or could become so), society bears responsibility for action in his or her behalf; it is not a private mat-

ter. The formation of a new family unit, once an original one is broken, carries social responsibility and requires social and legal safeguards.

2. In most instances such homeless children should be provided with family life. Children of all ages need affection, security, continuity in relationships, and other kinds of care and guidance that are most feasibly and effectively provided within the family setting.

3. When adoption is contemplated, society has responsibility to give protection and service to three parties: the child, the biological parents, and the adopting parents. The child must be guarded against unnecessary loss of the biological parents and protected by the selection of new parents who give evidence that they can reasonably be expected to fulfill parental responsibilities. The child's first parents merit society's early help so they can utilize their strengths to establish and maintain a satisfactory home. When they cannot do so, they require protection from hurried decisions made under duress and sympathetic attention as individuals facing a critical life experience. Adoptive parents are entitled to counseling or guidance that may enhance the formation of a healthy parent–child relationship and an adequate assumption of parental duties.

4. Early placement of children who need adoption is desirable. Earlier placements generally are less complicated to carry out and offer a greater chance for success.

5. Adoptive parents are of first importance to the child. The social worker's primary task is to assess and enhance the applicants' capacities for parenthood, and enable them to assess and understand their own readiness to be parents of a particular child.

6. Despite the many basic similarities between biological parenthood and adoptive parenthood, and the fundamental needs shared by all children, adopting is different from having children by birth. All adoptive parents face the necessity of accepting the child's background and the adopted child's curiosity about her or his origins.

7. For the healthy development of their identity, children must be told that they are adopted and be helped to understand the concept of adoption. This prescription is universally endorsed by social agencies. Adult adoptees need access to information about their biological parents and siblings.

8. Children lacking their own permanent homes constitute the primary service group in an adoption program. Although understanding help is offered to birth parents and adoptive applicants, children and their need for family must be paramount in planning and extending adoption services. Social workers are increasingly committed to children who need permanent homes but who are denied them because they have certain less "marketable" characteristics.

9. Adoption services must be linked to other community social services and offered in ways that reflect cognizance of community attitudes and resources.

The Experience of Adoption

The Birth Parents

Birth parents interested in adoption are typically young, frightened, and confused about resolving an unplanned pregnancy. Most are unmarried, with varying levels of involvement of family, the father of the child, and friends. Agencies offering counseling to these young women, and sometimes to the prospective fathers and other family members as well, follow the general social work precepts of client self-determination and nonjudgmental attitudes. The decision on whether to place a child for adoption is fateful for the birth parents, and they need an environment in which they can make a voluntary and informed choice.

Agency services to help birth parents plan for the child should be comprehensive. They should be available to everyone in the community. In agencies operating from the principles presented above, the parents are informed of all options available to them in a nonjudgmental setting. They also receive information on all relevant community resources and are helped in accessing those resources. They receive a clear statement of their legal rights and responsibilities, and information on the legal process of relinquishment. Should they decide on adoption, the agency helps them through the relinquishment process and, very importantly, offers counseling and support to them as they cope with the grief, feelings of loss, and emotional conflicts that are inevitably aroused by permanent relinquishment of parental rights (Gritter, 1997).

> *The transfer of parental rights of a child should not be accepted until the birth parents have considered all alternatives, are sure of their decision, and are emotionally prepared to transfer these rights. (E. Jean Emery, former director of the Child Welfare League of America Adoption Program, in Emery, 1993, p. 141)*

Social workers counseling unmarried teenage birth parents need to communicate that the final decision is the parents' and at the same time help them face the reality of their situation and reflect on what will be in the best interests of the child. Some parents, through their young age, drug use, economic situation, lack of support from family, or other reasons, are unlikely to be able to provide a minimally sufficient standard of care for the child. The reality of an infant's incessant demands for care and the level of commitment he or she requires from competent caretakers need to be presented in concrete terms. Parents may be helped to see that in their current life situation they are unable to provide for the child the kind of care that they would like him or her to receive, and that relinquishment in such circumstances is an act of responsible parenting. Parents who face possible involuntary termination of parental rights in court may be helped to relinquish voluntarily, an option that preserves their dignity and sense of control. Under ASFA, a parent whose rights to a previous child have been involuntarily terminated is in jeopardy of losing rights to later born children as a matter of course, whereas if the parent voluntarily relinquishes rights, he or she is not exposed to this future loss.

With changing laws regarding privacy in adoption, it is important that agencies give complete and accurate information to birth parents concerning the limits to confidentiality of the adoption as well as their options regarding future exchanges of information with the child and the adoptive parents. Agencies vary widely in their policies regarding openness, with some arranging ongoing, personal contact between all parties in the adoption and others providing nonidentifying information only as necessary; most agencies fall between the two ends of the spectrum.

There is controversy on whether openness in adoption helps or hinders birth parents resolve their grief over the loss of their child. Proponents of confidential adoption suggest that openness hinders this resolution: "The increased knowledge and contact available through open adoption may encourage birth parents to avoid experiencing the loss, to postpone or prolong the separation and grieving process. Ongoing contact may serve as a continuous reminder of the loss, or as a stimulus for the fantasy that relinquishing a child is not really a loss at all" (Byrd, 1988, p. 20).

An opposing view is taken by those believing that openness promotes the resolution of grief, pointing out that loss of a child through relinquishment is different from loss through death. In death, "one can be certain that the lost person will never be encountered in earthly form again. In adoption, a parent knows that somewhere out there the child who has been relinquished still exists" (Watson, 1988, p. 27). Watson (1988) takes the position that "any attempt to make the adoption relinquishment a clean and total break denies the possibility of further contact and restricts the grief process from following its natural sequence. Openness, on the other hand, accepts the possibility of ongoing or subsequent contact and allows the relinquishing parent to face the real loss, the loss of the role of nurturing parent" (p. 27).

McRoy, Grotevant, and Ayers-Lopez (1994) interviewed 720 individuals, including 169 birth mothers, between 1987 and 1992 to ascertain their experiences with adoption. Those interviewed represented the full spectrum of adoption openness, including confidential adoptions, mediated adoptions, and adoptions with ongoing contact between birth mothers and children. The researchers found that mothers who were in adoptions in which information was shared with the adoptive parents generally felt positive about the experience. One mother stated: "Once she [the child] gets older, she won't think I just totally abandoned her, I didn't just give her up. She's gonna know I just did what I thought was best. . . . I didn't back out. . . . I'm just glad we keep in touch. It will help me I guess later, because I know she's gonna one day look me up" (p. 9). Some mothers expressed concern about ongoing contact with the child. For example, one mother with ongoing, mediated contact said: "I'm not sure how it will affect my other children. I haven't told them about Kerry. I'm not ready for them to know that I had a child as a teenager. I may have to stop seeing my birthchild when she gets old enough to ask to see my other children" (p. 9).

Whatever its policy on openness, the adoption agency has an obligation to remain available to parents whenever requested to do so, including after the adoption is finalized. A continuum of agency services may provide intermediary aids such as exchange of updated information with the adoptive family, open-ended support group meetings, individual or family problem-solving counseling, and counseling and go-between services in the event that contact of birth parent and child comes about through a "search."

The Child

Agencies have an obligation to arrange adoptions for children that are in their best interest. To this end, agencies undertake assessments of the child to ascertain his or her needs and attempt to find adoptive parents who are likely to meet those needs. They work to arrange adoptions as quickly as possible so that children are not left in the limbo of being without any family. Using strategies appropriate to the child's age, agencies also prepare children for adoption and support them through the placement process and afterward.

The adoption worker undertakes a sensitive assessment of the child's readiness for adoption. Most children will benefit from adoption with well-prepared, appropriate adoptive parents. However, older children may experience loyalty conflicts or fantasies about the future ability of the birth parent to care for them, which may hinder their ability to form new family relationships. Other children have been so severely traumatized by earlier experiences of harmful or inadequate parenting that they are not able to make an emotional attachment to a family. Information on the child's physical, social, cognitive, and emotional functioning, academic progress and school adjustment, and the kind of emotional traumas that he or she has experienced are important for assessment (McNamara, 1994; Edelstein, 1995). In making a thorough assessment of the child's readiness to use adoption, workers collect information from a variety of sources. Reports from teachers, previous foster parents, birth parents, and others who have known the child are very helpful. The child's view of these experiences must also be considered (Brown, 1989).

Life books have become a popular way to help older children make the transition to adoption. They consist of materials that help the child understand the narrative sequence of his or her life, such as photographs, school records, birth certificates, letters, and other memorabilia. Foster parents, birth parents, and workers can contribute valuable items to life books. Worksheets are available to help older children organize and make sense of their experiences of separation, loss, and attachment through a journey that may have included placements with foster families as well as birth parents and relatives (Schroen, no date).

In the case example at the beginning of this chapter, the social worker, Ms. Franklin, helped Grant to prepare for adoption in several ways. She collected extensive information about his past, including his birth family, the circumstances of his relinquishment, and his previous, failed adoptive placement. Analysis of the information led her to an assessment that Grant needed a home with a father, because he had experienced rejection from two mothers, and that he needed adults with realistic expectations for school achievement. Then she set out to find an adoptive family who would meet these criteria.

Once Grant was placed, she helped him and the adoptive family address Grant's loyalty conflicts by introducing the possibility that, to some extent, the birth family could be included in his new life as an adopted son, and by helping him see that the adoptive family "would not replace the birth family" but could provide him with the home and nurturing he needed now. She also helped the adoptive family to see that Grant's acting out was not a rejection of them or of the adoption, but was a reaction to the earlier family breakups.

The Adoptive Family

In contrast to earlier years, the process of selecting adoptive parents has become more open, engaging the applicants themselves much more in the process.

Today, agencies actively recruit adoptive parents for special needs children rather than wait for prospective families to approach the agency. Families interested in adoption are treated from the start as potential partners with the agency in the work of caring for children. Lakin (1992) describes the change in perception: "Agencies began to see adoptive parents as resources to be taught the skills necessary to meet the needs of these children, rather than to be ruled out if they did not meet certain age, income, housing, or other arbitrary criteria established to handle the supply and demand issues faced when couples approached the agency for healthy European American infants" (p. 4). When foster parents seek to adopt children in their care, they are given preference as the adoptive parent. More and more, in part because of concurrent planning and the understanding of the child's need for stability, foster home and adoptive home recruitment for children in the child welfare system are conducted as one integrated process.

Prospective adoptive parents are given much more information than in the past on the child's background. The current trend is toward full disclosure. The matching of a child to the home is no longer simply a worker decision. Rather, responsibility for the decision is shared with the adoptive parents, who will ultimately have full responsibility for the child. Drenda Lakin, director of the National Resource Center on Special Needs Adoption, explains:

> The worker does not abdicate responsibility. The worker has experiences, skills and knowledge to share with the family. It is the worker's job to share the child's history completely, explaining what happened, how the child may have interpreted what happened, and how earlier experiences are likely to affect the future. . . . No one can predict the future, but the worker can help the prospective adoptive parents anticipate challenges. . . . The worker can help the family develop plans to handle these anticipated challenges or identify those challenges they feel they cannot handle. (Lakin, 1994)

For adoptive parents, the issue of openness in adoption is related somewhat to the age of the child. Older children usually have memories of their birth families and possibly foster families as well. If the adoptive parents were also the child's foster family or are relatives, it is quite likely that they have a great deal of information about the birth parents and may know them well. The decision about how much contact there will be between the two families needs to be resolved sensitively and with the help of a skilled agency worker, in light of the individual circumstances of the case. Only a few states have laws enforcing postadoption visitation agreements. In the case example that introduced this chapter, the worker supported the adoptive mother's decision to meet with the birth mother and brother to help her adopted child resolve his loyalty conflicts over leaving the birth family for the adoptive one.

The Legal Framework for Adoption

The legal process of adoption is regulated by a myriad of state, federal, and international laws. For the most part, adoption law, like other laws dealing with families and children, is a state rather than a federal matter. The adoption laws in the states are not uniform and have not been applied consistently in the courts. Federal legislation exists in some areas, particularly the Indian Child Welfare Act, regarding the adoption of Native American children; federal immigration and naturalization laws affecting international adoptions; and the Adoption and Safe Families Act of 1997, providing for federal subsidies for families adopting special needs children. Other federal laws affect social security and taxes as they relate to adoptive families. A number of U.S. Supreme Court decisions have implications for adoption law. (See Chapter 2.) Depending on the legislation in a particular state, jurisdiction over adoption may be vested in juvenile courts, probate courts, or family courts within a district or circuit court system. The complexity of laws and jurisdictions has created great variation over even the most basic legal procedures such as obtaining parental consent and ensuring confidentiality. Hollinger (1993) has identified the legal framework for several related areas of adoption: parental consent or termination of parental rights; serving the child's best interests in making an adoptive placement; confidentiality; and permanence of adoption.

Parental Consent or Termination of Parental Rights

An essential condition for adoption is the consent of the biological parents or a judicial termination of parental rights so that the child is legally free for adoption. Courts will not grant adoption petitions unless the rights of the biological parents have been terminated either by consent or through involuntary termination, based on a finding that they have failed to exercise their parental responsibilities. This requirement is based on traditions of American law that give primacy to parental autonomy and privacy in rearing their children.

Parental rights are not dependent on marital status. The U.S. Supreme Court has indicated that unmarried fathers who have established a parental relationship with their child have rights that cannot be terminated without clear and convincing evidence of unfitness. (See Chapters 2 and 6.)

A number of areas of uncertainty currently exist regarding parental consent, which may call into question whether a particular child is in fact "free" for adoption. For example, do the rights of the birth mother to relinquish her child and of the child to remain with adoptive parents outweigh the rights of a birth father who has been unjustly thwarted in exercising parental duties through the actions of the birth mother or adoptive parents? Once consent has been given, should it be revocable, and if so, for how long? Another area of uncertainty concerns which parents have the right to consent to or block the child's adoption when the child has been created through artificial insemination or surrogate parenting.

Frequently a state statute specifies that when children to be adopted are of a certain age, perhaps 10, 12, or 14, their consent must also be given to the adoption. Children even younger than this age may have the opportunity to express their wishes. Should the children's wishes override those of the birth parent or agency (Hollinger, 1993)?

Serving the Child's Best Interests

There is agreement that the prospective adopters should be suitable parents and that the primary purpose of adoption is to provide children with permanent homes rather than to provide parents with adopted children. Traditionally, this has been accomplished by requiring that a social agency make the placement, except in adoptions by close relatives, or, if the adoption is done outside an agency, that the agency at least be involved to the extent of completing a home study of the adoptive family. Whether the adoption is arranged by an agency or independently, the completion of a home study and the judge's consideration of it are essential to adoption practice.

It is of current concern that the proportion of nonrelative adoptions arranged independently of a licensed child placing agency has increased. Where placements are made outside licensed adoption agencies, there is concern that the door is open for unscrupulous or misguided third parties to cooperate with or influence a mother to place her child for adoption. The third party may be a lawyer who stands to profit through a fee for legal adoption services even though he or she may technically stand free of the charge of procuring an adoption for profit.

Confidentiality

Adoptive parents have all the same rights to family privacy and freedom from state interference that biologically created families have. Traditionally, this principle of totally and irrevocably transferring parental rights and responsibilities from birth to adoptive parents has been reflected in the practices of sealing adoption records and issuing new birth certificates following the issuance of adoption decrees. With current recognition that children in the adoptive triad remain linked in fundamental ways to both birth and adoptive families, traditional practices in these areas are changing. Since the 1970s most states have required that agencies share with adoptive parents all nonidentifying information that is "reasonably available" to them about the child they are adopting. The statutes in these states also provide for the release of nonidentifying information to adoptees who request it after they reach adulthood.

Regarding confidentiality of adoptive records, there is general agreement that the records should be kept separate and withheld from public inspection, and that persons and agencies having a legitimate interest in the case should be able to have access to them. However, there is little agreement on how much access they should have or under what circumstances (Hollinger, 1993). A particularly controversial issue is the release of identifying information about biological parents to adoptive parents and adult adoptees. It is usually not available except for "good cause" or in situations in which the birth parents and the child have mutually consented to share it. Most adoptions of current adult adoptees took place under laws guaranteeing anonymity of all parties. Recognizing that over time anonymity may be less desirable to both adult adoptees and birth parents, states are changing their statutes regarding circumstances under which interested parties may have identifying information on one another (Hollinger, 1993).

Many states have implemented central adoption registries with which birth families can register their interest in being or not being contacted by a child (adult adoptee) they either voluntarily released for adoption or from whom parental rights were terminated. These registries are useful in the search process.

Permanence of Adoption

States require a period of time for the child to live within the proposed adoptive home under the guidance of a social welfare agency before the adoption is finalized. In some states the required period is six months; in others, twelve. Waiver provisions give flexibility so that the court can shorten the time if doing so is in the best interests of the child. Once the adoption is finalized, it is "for keeps" and cannot be abrogated because the birth parents wish to revoke their consent or because the adoptive parents decide that they do not want the child. Adoptive parents may lose their adopted children in exactly the same ways that pertain to biological parents: They may relinquish their rights to the child, and the state may remove the child from the home if it is found that the parents have abused or neglected the child. With the increase of adoption of children with special needs, more adoptions are dissolving, causing some persons to advocate the creation of humane ways to legally undo these placements so that the children can move on to more appropriate placements without feelings of failure (Hollinger, 1993).

Postadoption Services

Postadoption services have developed in recognition that "normally, adoptive families from time to time will need help with some of the complex changes in their lives. Such difficulties do not represent failure or a serious problem—only an understandable part of a special life situation" (Hartman, 1984, p. 2). Adoptive parents, particularly those of children with special needs, have found that mental health professionals did not always understand the unique needs of their family or their child. Adoption agencies, in response, have developed ongoing postadoption services that continue to support the adoption after finalization. These programs vary widely in design, but tend to be voluntary, be preventive as well as rehabilitative, make use of support groups with and without professional input, and offer specialized, intensive services if the placement is at risk of disruption (Festinger, 1996; Kramer & Houston, 1998; Kreisher, 2002). Although postadoption services were originally established mainly to prevent disruption of placements made from foster care, many postadoption service providers offer services to "all comers," including families who adopted infants or those with children from another country (Barth, Gibbs, & Siebenaler, 2001). To date, there have been no rigorous evaluation studies of the effects of postadoption services and the extent to which they might reduce adoption disruption, especially of children adopted from foster care. Recent research on the experiences of adoptive parents suggests that many parents find ongoing services to be helpful and would like to have them more widely available (Festinger, 1996).

The Jenkins Siblings: An Example of Postadoption Services

The following case illustrates several of the central issues in adoption that characterize the development of adoptive families and also the postadoption services offered by the agency social worker.

> Ms. Phillips first met the three Jenkins brothers when Antoine was 4, Samuel was 3, and Kareem was 2. They had been in the child welfare system for two years, having been picked up by the police because of the mother's absence from the home. The mother was a teenager who had a history of neglect. All the boys had different fathers. The mother continued to have five more children, all of whom where removed from her care shortly after birth because of her inability to provide a minimally acceptable level of care.
>
> While in the child welfare system, both Antoine and Samuel had had six or more separate foster placements; Kareem had been in one foster home. The foster mother who eventually took all three boys was in her early sixties, and the agency decided that she was too old to adopt them. They were placed in an adoptive home but were removed soon after when the agency discovered that the parents were using extreme physical discipline and not meeting the children's medical needs. Antoine had scoliosis. Samuel was a failure-to-thrive baby and was discovered to have a learning disability. Among them, they had a number of other developmental and medical problems as well.
>
> Ms. Phillips found an adoptive parent for the boys—a single, middle-aged mother, Ms. Martin, who had two teenage sons at home and two older sons who had left the home. The sons were all helpful with the young adoptive brothers; they were gentle with them and took the responsibility of socializing them to the family.
>
> Unfortunately, the placement got off to a bad start when on the first day, the boys destroyed the bedroom that the adoptive mother had prepared for them.
>
> Ms. Phillips worked closely with the adoptive mother. She helped her plan activities and devise strategies to manage the boys' behavior and set limits for them. Ms. Martin was a grandmother but she had to learn how to be a mother of young children all over again. Samuel required a great deal of medical attention. All the children needed help in school.

Samuel needed special education and Kareem needed to be admitted to an early intervention program. The adoptive mother needed coaching on how to deal with the medical and educational systems, because the problems of these children were very different from the ones she had experienced with her own children. Even with Ms. Phillips's help, she had difficulty organizing a medical schedule and maintaining collaboration with the schools.

Ms. Phillips began to wonder if this home was an appropriate setting for these children. Because the placement was still officially a foster home, she started looking for a new adoptive family. However, very few families expressed interest in three sibling boys, all of whom had special medical and educational needs. Finally, another family did come forward who seemed appropriate.

The advent of this new family seemed to mobilize Ms. Martin and helped her to clarify that she really wanted these children. Ms. Phillips had to make an agonizing choice: whether to place the children with the new family, who had a proven track record as capable adoptive parents, or whether to continue to work to strengthen the current placement and avoid another separation for the boys. To help her decide, Ms. Phillips worked with Ms. Martin to explore in detail her strengths and to understand where the gaps were. After this process, both Ms. Phillips and Ms. Martin came to the decision that she would be able to meet the needs of the children.

At about this time, Antoine had surgery for scoliosis. Ms. Martin, his adoptive mother, rose to the occasion and became aware of how much she had bonded with this boy. She organized her schedule and the family's so they could help Antoine. Ms. Phillips felt that she showed commitment to the children and decided to proceed with the adoption.

Ms. Phillips also worked to help the boys recover their past. They had been in so many foster homes that much of their history was missing. The adoptive mother developed a relationship with the foster mother who had had all three of them; the foster mother became a "grandma" for the boys. This foster mother was now caring for the younger siblings of the boys, born after they had gone into care. She had pictures to share of the boys when they were very young and knew more about the birth family than was contained in the agency's records. She arranged for the boys to visit their siblings who were in her care.

Antoine, Samuel, and Kareem are now 9, 8, and 7 and are doing well. The adoptive mother calls occasionally to let Ms. Phillips know how they are faring.

Dynamics in Adoptive Family Development

Child welfare practice was long in acknowledging that most adoptive families are different from other families in at least three ways: Adoptive parents go through a unique process, often without the kinds of supports and sanctions that accrue to biological parents; adopted children come into the family by means of a unique set of circumstances; and family dynamics are affected differently by adoption than by childbirth (Bourguignon & Watson, 1987; Silin, 1996; National Adoption Information Clearinghouse, 2000).

These differences between adoptive and biological families are apparent when the central issues of adoption are considered. Lakin (1992) has identified the following themes that characterize the adoption experience: entitlement; unmatched expectations; separation, loss, and grief; bonding and attachment; and identity formation.

Entitlement is a process that occurs before and during the time the child enters the family. It refers to the sense of the adoptive parent and child that they have a "right" to each other. Legal entitlement is granted with a court decree, but emotional entitlement is more complex and may take more time to appear. Until it develops, adoptive parents and children may hold back on their commitment to each other. In the Jenkins case, the entitlement issues are illustrated dramatically. The adoptive mother, who had been struggling with three special needs brothers, found when Antoine had surgery that she had become more attached to Antoine than she had realized. She told the social worker that she became aware that "This is my kid" when she saw him in the hospital. Recognizing that she had "claimed" the boys, she mobilized resources effectively to help him recover.

When adoptive children enter the family, both the parents and the children may be confronted with a discrepancy between the *expectations* they had and the reality of the situation. This can be especially troublesome for adoptive parents at the beginning of the placement. In the Jenkins case, the adoptive mother experienced disillusionment when the carefully prepared bedroom was trashed by the boys during their first day in the home. The process of giving up one's expectations and accepting other, alternative sources of satisfaction may take a long time. Another source of stress can occur around adapting to changed *patterns of everyday life.* Birth children may feel resentful about having to develop new family roles and modifying their family routines. Older adoptive children may resist adapting to the family's life patterns.

Feelings of *loss* are pervasive in adoption. Adopted children wonder, "Why did my parent give me up?" Infertile adoptive parents may need to grieve the loss of children they will never have. Before children and parents can make a commitment to the adoptive relationship, they must have resolved, to some extent, these earlier losses (Gritter, 1997).

Attachment refers to an emotional connectedness between two people. Infants and children who are denied the opportunity to form attachments with consistent, nurturing parental figures may not learn how to make meaningful attachments. Symptoms commonly seen in children with attachment problems are in the areas of conscience development, impulse control, self-esteem, interpersonal interactions, expression and recognition of their own and others' feelings, and a variety of developmental difficulties (Fahlberg, 1991; Lakin, 1992; Levy & Orleans, 1998). The Jenkins siblings had experienced many losses in their young lives. Learning more about their past and having contact with their siblings who were in another home helped them resolve some of their feelings about having been given up by their mother and by other families, so that they could invest emotionally in their new adoptive family.

Forming one's sense of self as a unique and valuable individual with boundaries is an essential developmental task of adolescence and beyond. *Identity* is rooted in the family history, nurtured through the natural processes of development, and shaped by individual and family dynamics (Lakin, 1992; Quinton, Rushton, Dance, & Mayes, 1998). Adopted children may feel that something is wrong with them or their birth parents would not have given them up, which lowers their self-esteem and affects their evolving sense of personal identity. An important step for some adopted children is to learn about their birth family and to incorporate that heritage into their sense of self. Incorporating the adoption into one's sense of self is a process that may go on well into young adulthood. Adolescent and young adult adoptees may benefit from support groups to process their evolving sense of personal identity (Grotevant, 1997; Brodzinsky, Smith, & Brodzinsky, 1998).

Survival Behavior

When adoptive families need help, it is essential to arrive at a good understanding of the nature of the problem, based on a thorough assessment of the situation. In addition to gathering information on the child and each adoptive parent, the social worker needs to clarify his or her own expectations about families. Families may have characteristics that are highly functional for adopting older children who have behavioral difficulties, but these same characteristics may not match the worker's unexamined expectations about "ideal" families. When working cross-culturally, social workers must be particularly aware of their own culture and how it may influence their interpretation of the family dynamics (Bourguignon & Watson, 1987; Lakin, 1992).

With older children, the problem may revolve around the child's "survival behaviors," which are rooted in earlier, traumatic experiences. For some children, the main issue is that they have "unfinished business" with their earlier family; they may experience loyalty conflicts or unresolved grief. For others, the problem may be difficulty in forming attachments to caring adults. A goal of the intervention in these situations is to increase the parents' competence and reduce anxiety by helping them understand the child's behavior in terms of the child's past experiences, and to show them strategies for how to anticipate the child's reactions to particular situations and then prepare appropriate responses. For the child, the goals are to help him or her feel secure and to establish trust with the adoptive family, and then help the child mourn past losses so that he or she can make a commitment to the present (Lakin, 1992).

It is not uncommon for postadoption services to occur during a crisis, when the family is not sure that it will actually stay together. Adoptive parents may be angry at the child, at themselves for perceived failure, and at the agency, which the family may see as not having fully disclosed information about the child. Child welfare workers may blame themselves for having made the placement. Experience has shown that successful crisis intervention with adoptive families should be quick and responsive, with clear lines of communication between family and worker, so that the family can reach help whenever it is needed. At the same time that the help should be timely and supportive, it is important that the worker not "overreact" and move the child precipitously.

Adoption Disruption

Although the large majority of adoptive placements prove to be successful for both children and adopted parents, in some instances and for various reasons the inability to establish stable family relationships may result in disruption of the placement. Adoption disruption refers to placements that end with the return of the child to the agency before legal finalization has occurred. Rosenthal (1993) estimates that from 10 to 15 percent of the adoptions of older children disrupt, in comparison with 1 or 2 percent for infants. A study of children adopted as adolescents showed a disruption rate of about 24 percent, over twice as high as that of other special needs children (Berry & Barth, 1990).

A number of factors affect the success of special needs adoption placements. The older the child, particularly past age 7 or 8, the more likely it is that the adoption will disrupt. Some studies show that boys are slightly more susceptible to having disrupted adoptions than girls. Developmental and serious medical disabilities do not appear to be major factors in disruption. However, emotional disabilities are strong predictors, especially aggressive, acting-out behavior. Other behaviors that place a child at risk for disruption are sexual acting out (a characteristic of children who have been sexually abused), stealing, vandalizing, threatening or attempting suicide, and wetting or soiling (Rosenthal, 1993; Logan, Morrall, & Chambers, 1998; Smith, Howard, & Monroe, 1998).

Various dimensions of adoptive family life can reduce or increase the risk of disruption. Families in which the adoptive parents expect and are prepared to accept behavioral and emotional problems resulting from the stress the child already has experienced and who can be flexible in family roles and rules have a better chance of succeeding than others. Unpredicted events in family life can severely affect the chance of disruption—for example, marital stress, financial difficulties, or serious illness of an adoptive parent or of another family member that brings long-term demands on the adoptive family. In such instances, if the new family stability has not yet been established or is tentative, the risk of disruption is keen (Rosenthal & Groze, 1992; Groze, 1996).

Adoptions by former foster parents are less likely to disrupt than those by new families, a finding that underscores the importance of thoroughly familiarizing the prospective adoptive parent with the child's situation. Research and the reports of adoptive parents have consistently shown that providing adequate background information on the child is an extremely important task that agencies must undertake to increase the chances that an adoption will be successful.

An adoption disruption does not necessarily result in continuing impermanence for the child. Many of these children are placed later in other adoptive homes, as the example of Grant, in the case study at the beginning of this chapter, shows. Pursuing homes for children through adoption requires that agencies be ready to take risks, so some disruptions are to be expected (Festinger, 1986).

Searches and Reunions

Some of the complex identity issues adopted children must resolve are now receiving more attention as adult adoptees in greater numbers have sought access to sealed court records or have returned to adoption agencies for information about their origins. Among adult adoptees who embark on a search of their past, some want only information—for example, the personal, social, or physical characteristics of their biological parents. They may believe such information will add to an understanding of themselves and their sense of identity. Practical considerations, such as obtaining security clearance for a job or obtaining medical history, may also cause adopted persons to seek more information about themselves.

Other adult adoptees want to locate their birth parents, meet them, and attempt to establish a relationship with them. Initially, agencies thought that only people who had unsatisfactory experiences in adoption wanted to seek out their birth parents. However, it is now recognized that many people from successful adoptions return to agencies to initiate a search. Despite confidentiality laws and regulations, most adult adoptees are successful in their efforts to seek out information on their past. Social workers should have information about the various regional and national networks for adoption searches. Some agencies offer intermediary services, contacting the birth mother to see if she wishes a reunion with her adult child who has initiated a search.

The following case vignette illustrates the way an agency helped a young man initiate a search for his birth family.

Ramon was 19 and in an agency-sponsored independent living situation when he telephoned the agency that had placed him for adoption when he was 3 years old. His relationship with his adoptive parents became conflictual as he grew older, and he was eventually placed in a residential setting. He now was interested in learning about his birth family and particularly about two siblings, a brother and a sister, whom he had heard were a part of his original family. He wanted to know if they had also been adopted and if he could find them. The agency representative made an appointment to see him, and, after checking the records, was able to give him information about his birth family. He actually had three younger siblings, two of whom had been adopted by one family; the youngest child had remained with the mother. Ramon was overwhelmed to meet the agency worker who had actually arranged the adoption. Through an intermediary, who contacted the other siblings and the mother, Ramon was able to reconnect with his family of origin.

Social workers have an important supportive role in helping adult adoptees or birth parents who are seeking reunions. Those searching may need help in preparing for the myriad of emotions they face as they undertake the search process. Persons searching often need assistance in creating realistic expectations about the type of relationship they envision once a reunion is effected. Searchers need to be aware that the person being found may have very different feelings from those of the searcher over the prospect of personal contact. A very real aspect of a successful reunion is that those involved are faced with negotiating a relationship with a stranger with whom they have a genetic tie, a bond, past issues to resolve, and current lives that are not usually congruent (Bourguignon & Watson, 1987).

Adoption of Children with Special Needs

The term *special needs adoption* refers to children who require special efforts to be placed in adoptive homes. They may have physical, mental, or emotional disabilities, but their primary shared characteristic is that they are wards of the public child welfare system and need planning services to be placed in permanent homes. Special agency services are needed to recruit, train, and support families who undertake adoption of these children (Neeley-Bertram, 2000).

Children Who Wait

Of great concern to child welfare policy makers are the large number of children in foster care who will never return home and require a permanent plan that will give them a stable family life and sense of belonging that will last throughout their childhood. These children are dependent on large, public child welfare bureaucracies and their private agency partners for their day-to-day maintenance and for planning their future. Caring and planning for these children is a serious, major public responsibility of both the federal and state governments. The number of children in foster care in need of an adoptive home is quite large, estimated at 131,000 in 2000. Of these children, less than half, about 51,000, were actually placed in adoption during that year. The majority of these adoptions were with the children's foster parents (61 percent). Kinship adoption, or adoption by relatives, accounted for

21 percent, and 18 percent were adopted by non-relative, new adoptive parents (Children's Bureau, 2002).

"Children who wait" share characteristics that may make adoption planning particularly challenging: They tend to be older (67 percent over age 5), to have been in foster care for a relatively long time (average forty-four months), to be of minority ethnicity (43 percent African American, 13 percent Hispanic), and are slightly more likely to be male (Children's Bureau, 2002). In addition, many of these children have behavioral problems that increase the complexity of planning for them. The drug epidemic has been a factor in bringing many into the public child welfare system, with the result that the children may have fetal damage due to the drug use of their mothers when pregnant, they may be infected with the HIV virus or have AIDS, and most have had early life experiences that have left them impaired emotionally, physically, and mentally.

Overcoming Barriers to Timely Adoption

In spite of increased foster parent adoption, children in the child welfare system still wait too long for adoption. Waits of three to seven years are not uncommon. Many children enter foster care as infants or preschoolers and reach grade school before they are referred to the adoption unit for planning. During their years in foster care, they may have experienced traumas that compounded whatever problems they had coming into care, making them even more challenging to adopt (McKenzie, 1993). Figure 10.1 shows the steps followed by cases through the child welfare adoption system.

In 1997, the U.S. Congress passed and President Clinton signed into law the Adoption and Safe Families Act, designed to expedite the progress of foster children who cannot return home into adoptive placements. Two key provisions of the Act are an Adoption Incentive Program that rewards states for increasing the number of adoptions, and a provision that promotes the termination of parental rights after children have been in care for a specified period of time. Implementation of the Act has resulted in overcoming identified barriers to adoption. For example, many states have started to do "concurrent planning," which means that they may plan to place a child for adoption or with a legal guardian at the same time that they are making "reasonable efforts" to reunify the child with his or her parents (Children's Defense Fund, 1997). Thus, concurrent planning provides for the simultaneous planning of both reunification services and, as a contingency, the preparation of an alternative permanent plan if reunification should fail (Katz, Spoonemore, & Robinson, 1994). The concern with

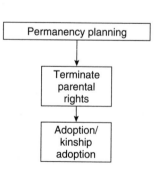

FIGURE 10.1   Overview of Steps Followed by Cases through the Child Welfare Adoption System

Source: Adapted from P. Schene (1998), Past, present, and future roles of child protective services, *The Future of Children: Protecting Children from Abuse and Neglect, 8*(1). Adapted with the permission of the David and Lucile Packard Foundation.

this innovation is that parents will feel that they are being betrayed by a process that, on the one hand, ostensibly is attempting to help them become reunified with their children while, at the same time, is moving ahead with termination of parental rights. This ethical dilemma can be avoided to some extent if the agency explains to the biological family from the beginning that the two planning processes are proceeding at the same time, while communicating the hope and expectation that family reunification is the plan of choice if possible. See Chapter 9 for a discussion and a case example of concurrent planning.

Another approach to reducing delays caused by the termination of parental rights process is "mediated adoption." Mediation procedures, involving the biological parents, the agency, attorneys for all parties, including the child, and the courts, are used instead of the traditional adversarial process to achieve termination of parental rights with abusive parents within a reasonable period of time. Although new, mediation programs hold promise to make the termination process both quicker and more humane to the parents, who do not undergo the public humiliation of a formal court procedure, in which all their shortcomings and failures are introduced as evidence (Heath, 1998).

The Act has had the result of speeding up adoption for many children; compared with the 15,000 children adopted from foster care in 1988, the year 2000 figure of 51,000 represents a substantial improvement (Maza, 2001). According to Maza's (2001) analysis, older children remain the greatest challenge in the effort to move children into timely adoptions. Although the large, public child welfare bureaucracies have made progress in moving children into adoption, too many children continue to wait for a long time for a permanent home. The movement to streamline the process, while retaining respect for the orderly legal safeguards of parental rights and for carefully matching the child's needs with the strengths of a possible adoptive family, continues to require close attention.

Adoption Subsidies

In 1980, the U.S. Congress passed legislation (the Adoption Assistance and Child Welfare Act) that for the first time provided federal funds for adoption subsidies and Medicaid insurance for special needs children. The subsidies are particularly helpful in allowing many foster placements to achieve permanent legal status through adoption, because they make it possible for the foster parents to give up foster payments in return for adoption subsidy and Medicaid.

In special needs adoption, the use of subsidies is very common, although some subsidies are set at a very low rate and are intended mainly to establish Medicaid eligibility. States vary in setting subsidy rates, with some providing only basic support and others including special services needed by children with handicapping conditions. States also vary in the kind of documentation required to obtain subsidy.

The adoption subsidy program is growing rapidly, as more and more special needs children are placed in adoption. To date, little research has been done to demonstrate the ways that subsidies support families, but anecdotal evidence from workers and adoptive parents suggests that subsidies are vital to the adoption of children with special needs, and that the current level of subsidy is not meeting the needs of many adoptive families (Barth, Gibbs, & Siebenaler, 2001). Even though current needs are not being met with adoption subsidy, it is a very expensive program and is getting more expensive each year. The rate of entry into the program far exceeds the rate of exit, which occurs when the adopted child reaches maturity and is eligible for other disability support programs. Escalating costs raise concern about the future costs of the program (Wulczyn & Hislop, 2002).

Adoption Resource Exchanges

A development in adoption practice designed to increase the likelihood of permanent homes for children who need them is that of national or regional "clearinghouses" by which agencies can cooperate more effectively in the location and use of adoption resources. Agencies having few contacts outside their own locality tend to be limited in the range of prospective adopters and children to be adopted. For some children with very challenging needs, it is useful to have a very broad-based recruitment strategy to identify the "one in a million" family whose caretaking interests and abilities match the child's needs. See the web site AdoptUSKids, whose URL is listed at the end of this chapter, for a view of the use of the Internet in adoption resource exchanges.

Kinship Adoption

Kinship care has become established as a sound placement choice for children in the child welfare system who cannot be reunited with their biological parents. Kinship placements promote family continuity, attachment to caretakers, and sense of belonging. The child adopted by kin has access to family history, a variety of familiar relationships, and a shared biological and cultural heritage. Questions of identity are more easily resolved within the context of family. Remaining within the extended family network reduces the effects of separation on children and minimizes the risk of "foster care drift" with multiple placements.

Questions have arisen about whether permanent placement with relatives requires legalized, formal adoption, or whether some other legal status might be more appropriate to provide an approved legal status to this family form. Children in kinship care are less likely to be adopted than children who are in nonrelative foster care settings. Although kinship caregivers usually express a commitment to and sense of permanency with the child, they may not see the need for adoption of someone with whom they already have an existing relationship (Thornton, 1991; Hegar & Scannapieco, 1994; Williams & Satterfield, 2000). See Chapter 8 for a discussion of the policy and legal issues in kinship care.

The following case example illustrates positive aspects of kinship adoption and demonstrates the importance of examining the extended kinship network for permanency options.

> Jametta and Kemal, ages 3 and 5 respectively, had been placed with their grandmother when their mother had left them unattended and they were found by a CPS worker in a filthy apartment with no food and no electricity. Their mother had been in a crack house for several days. Although substance abuse treatment services had been offered to their mother, she continued to use drugs. On several earlier occasions she had left the children alone when she was high.
>
> Supports were offered to the grandmother to assist her in working with the children. They had a variety of needs for developmental services, including speech therapy for Kemal's elective mutism and a play group for socialization. Ms. Jones, the grandmother, also lacked day care so that she could continue employment, and needed beds and dressers for the children, which the agency helped her to obtain. With support from the kinship care worker, the children had responded well to their grandmother's nurturing and the wraparound supports put in place.

When it became evident that Keisha, the children's mother, had not responded to treatment for her addiction and was unable to stabilize her living situation, a permanency planning hearing was held. The plan was for termination of parental rights followed by adoption planning. Ms. Jones was distraught, as she felt that her health problems (arthritis and a heart condition) might preclude her from raising the children to adulthood, but she was insistent that the children should not be placed for adoption outside the family.

The kinship care worker met with Ms. Jones to set up a family group meeting to plan for the children. They contacted Ms. Jones's sister, known to the family as Auntie Grace. Auntie Grace was the family communicator, who had the names and addresses of the kinship network, and was a central figure in "holding the family together." With the help of Auntie Grace, the kinship care worker and Ms. Jones invited a number of members from the kinship network and the pastor of their church to a family meeting. At the meeting, which was held in the social hall of the church, ten extended family members met to plan for the children. The social worker explained the family situation and the need of Jametta and Kemal for a permanent home. She commended Ms. Jones for the excellent care given to the children while the agency had tried to work with their mother toward reunification. Pastor Robertson then led the entire group in a prayer, asking for a blessing on the children and their deliberations about the future plans for the children. From this meeting, two families—one, a cousin and her husband; the other, an aunt who had several adolescent children—volunteered interest in providing a long-term home for the children.

Following the family group meeting, the kinship care worker visited and studied both families as possible kinship adoption resources. The cousin and her husband were childless and eager to take the children. However, they had serious concerns about possible interference from the children's mother. The aunt, a resourceful single parent, was not concerned about dealing with the children's mother, but had reservations about being able to provide adequately for the children as she was feeling financially stretched by the needs of her own teenagers. Both homes seemed suitable to the kinship worker. She reconvened another meeting in which the grandmother, the mother, and the two prospective adoptive families discussed the next steps. They arrived at a mutually satisfactory solution. The children would be placed with the cousin and her husband after a series of family visits by the grandmother and the children. Both the grandmother and the aunt's family would be involved in supporting the adoptive placement with respite care, family outings, and setting boundaries with the children's mother. If the children and their mother wanted to see each other, visits would occur at the aunt's home with the grandmother present. They made it clear to the mother that she was not to try to visit at the adoptive home and that she would not see the children if she were high. The children's mother was pleased that the children would remain within the family and gave them a positive message about the adoptive plan.

Adoption of Children of Color

The development of policy for the adoption of children of color has been characterized by debate and controversy. Until the middle of the twentieth century, children of color were generally ignored in adoption policy and practice, and very few were part of the formal adoption system. Beginning in the 1950s and 1960s, with the civil rights movement, the needs of children of color for child welfare services began to be recognized. Transracial adoption became an accepted practice for the placement needs of children of color. Attitudes concerning the importance of racial and cultural identity brought this practice into disfavor, and from the 1970s until very recently, the favored approach was same-race adoption. However, controversy continued, as many believed that children were being denied permanent homes because homes of the same race could not be found, while white homes were waiting and available to these children. These children tended to remain in foster care indefinitely. The Multiethnic Placement Act, passed by the U.S. Congress in 1994 and amended in 1997, has resolved the issue, at least temporarily, in favor of expediting permanency for children by prohibiting the delay of adoption for reasons of race of the child or adoptive parent. The tumultuous history of racial issues in adoption has varied with different ethnic and cultural groups. Examination of the events and issues of adoption of African American, Native American, and Latino children will elucidate some key themes and value conflicts in this area of child welfare practice.

African American Children

Traditionally, African American families have informally adopted children in their kin networks. The absorption of children who cannot live with their own parents into extended family systems has been a major strength of African American families (Hill, 1972; Prater, 1992). It has offered security and status as a member of a family to large numbers of children who otherwise would have been completely destitute.

No formal protections were available to children needing homes under slavery. After emancipation, very few formal adoption services were available to African American children. Until the 1970s, adoption agencies served mainly white, middle-class families. African American parents seeking to adopt tended not to use these services, due to both explicit and subtle practices of exclusion (Neal & Stumph, 1993).

Transracial adoption of children of color with white families occurred in the 1960s and 1970s, inspired primarily by the shortage of healthy white infants and by social activism emanating from the civil rights movement. The number of children adopted transracially was large; by 1972, about 10,000 African American children had been placed in white homes. More than one-third of all adopted African American children experienced transracial adoption (Klemesrud, 1972). Social workers, although not unanimous in their approval, for the most part seemed to endorse the practice as a means of providing homes for children who were otherwise likely to grow up in foster homes and institutions.

In the early 1970s, however, the climate of opinion about the appropriateness of transracial adoption began to change sharply as communities of color stressed the importance of racial and cultural identity. At its 1972 meeting, the National Association of Black Social Workers came out "in vehement opposition" to the practice of placing African American children with white families. Transracial placements were termed "a growing threat to the preservation of the black family" (Fraser, 1972). The practice of transracial placement of African American children fell off sharply and in some agencies virtually ended.

A major concern of those who opposed transracial adoption was that as children became adolescents they would face severe identity problems and that they would be vulnerable to attacks on their self-respect because they wouldn't have learned coping mechanisms to deal with racism in the larger society. A number of studies have addressed these concerns (Courtney, 1997). Some studies have tracked adopted children over time into adulthood, since they were first transracially adopted in the 1960s and 1970s (Feigelman & Silverman, 1984; Shireman, 1988; Simon, Alstein, & Melli, 1994). Other studies have used a retrospective design, collecting data during adolescence or young adulthood on children transracially adopted at a young age (McRoy & Zurcher, 1983). Rozenthal and Groze (1992) conducted a large-scale study of adopted children of color with special needs and compared those adopted inracially and transracially. The results of all these studies are quite similar. They show that, overall, there are no significant differences in outcomes of children adopted transracially from those adopted inracially. However, McRoy and Zurcher (1983) found that transracially adopted children may experience conflict over their racial identity and prefer Caucasian friends, while Rozenthal and Groze (1992) found that African American, inracial adoptive parents were somewhat more likely to report that the adoption's impact was very positive (58 percent) than were white, inracial parents (41 percent) or transracial adoptive parents (53 percent). Overall, the results of thirty years of research on this issue support both the viability of transracial adoption and the advantages of inracial adoption for African American children.

The Child Welfare League of America, in its Standards for Adoption Services, has reflected changing attitudes about transracial adoption in American society. The 1968 version of the standards stated that "racial background in itself should not determine the selection of the home for a child. It should not be assumed . . . that difficulties will necessarily arise if adoptive parents are of different racial origin" (p. 34). In 1972, the standard was amended to "it is preferable to place children in families of their own racial background." In 1988, the standards were again amended in an effort to recognize both the preference of minorities for inracial placements and the need for decisions that would not deny a child an adoptive home when one is needed. "Children in need of adoption have a right to be placed into a family that reflects their ethnicity or race. Children should not have their adoption denied or significantly delayed, however, when adoptive parents of other ethnic or racial groups are available" (Child Welfare League of America, 1988, p. 34). Today, with the policy instituted in the Multiethnic Placement Act, the adoption field is once again charged with finding homes that meet children's needs regardless of race.

Native American Children

Similarly to the situation with African American children, transracial adoption of Native American children occurred in the 1950s and 1960s. In the late 1950s, the Bureau of Indian Affairs and the Child Welfare League of America sponsored the Indian Adoption Project to find inracial and transracial homes for Native American children needing adoptive placement. About 400 children were placed, mainly transracially, during these years (Silverman, 1993).

By the 1970s, it is estimated that a quarter of all Native American children were not living with their families but were in boarding schools or foster or adoptive homes (Johnson, 1981). This was felt to be a great loss to Native American children of their cultural heritage and of their attachments and connections to family and tribe, and gave impetus to the passage of the Indian Child Welfare Act (ICWA) of 1978. This federal legislation was intended to restore and preserve Native American families.

The ICWA reaffirmed the right of tribal courts to assume jurisdiction over the placement of Native American children. Preference must be given to adoptive placements that are (1) a member of the child's extended family, (2) other members of the Native American child's tribe, or (3) other Native American families. Compliance with federal law has been enhanced over the past twenty-five years by the establishment of child welfare programs on many reservations. Large, urban child welfare agencies may have on staff a person whose function is to liaison with Native American jurisdictions when Native American children come into the child welfare system, and to facilitate placing the child under the jurisdiction of Native American courts, if the Native American court so chooses. The adoption of Native American children is unaffected by the Adoption and Safe Families Act, prohibiting the use of race as a factor in selecting adoptive homes. For the adoption of Native American children, the policies laid out in the ICWA continue to prevail. The Indian Child Welfare Act is described in Chapters 2, 3, and 7.

Latino Children

For many years, Latino children needing substitute care were "matched" not by placement with families of Latino culture but along color lines; dark-skinned Latino children with African American families and lighter-skinned children with white families. About 10 percent of children adopted each year are Latino (Jones, 1993), yet little research has been conducted to understand their needs in adoption or the extent to which they are being placed in Latino families. The evidence that is available suggests that many Latino children are adopted by white families (Gilles & Kroll, 1991; Benson, Sharma, & Roehlkepartain, 1994).

The Latino community has expressed concern about interethnic placement of Mexican American children with non–Mexican American parents. A survey of over 1,000 persons with Hispanic surnames in California revealed that around half of those surveyed agreed with one or more of the following statements: "(1) the child may have an ethnic identity conflict, (2) the child may forget his or her Latino background, (3) the child's participation in Latino cultural events may be limited, and (4) the child may not acquire the skills to cope with racism" (Bausch & Serpe, 1997, p. 136).

Elba Montalvo (1994), executive director of the Committee for Hispanic Children and Families, has identified a need for more Latino adoptive homes. She points out that Latinos are not monolithic; the major Spanish-speaking groups in the United States are Mexican American, Puerto Rican, and Cuban. These groups differ from one another culturally in many ways. She recommends the following to increase cultural competency in placement of Latino children:

- Welcome Latino families into adoption agencies with posters and handouts conveying the message "Bienvenidos Latinos." Recruitment efforts should make use of radio, particularly Spanish language stations. All written materials should be conceptualized and written in Spanish first, then translated into English.
- Hire Spanish-speaking staff, with attention to cultural congruence with the various Spanish-speaking groups in the area.
- Place Latino children, in order of preference: with relatives, with someone of his or her culture (i.e., Puerto Rican children in a Puerto Rican home), with a family of another Latino background.
- If a non-Latino home must be used, it should be evaluated for the family's ability to help the child learn about Latino culture and have contact with other Latinos.
- We agree with other child advocates that is preferable to provide a child the opportunity of a loving permanent home of any race or cultural background than to allow him or her to grow up without a permanent home and parents who care. (pp. 1–5)

Strengthening Multiethnic Placements

Today, policy and practice in adoption of children of color takes a two-pronged approach, working both to strengthen multiethnic placements and to develop innovative programs to reach out to communities of color regarding adoption of same-race children. The focus is on finding adoptive homes of any race for children who need them (Lakin & Malone, 2001). Note that currently the term *multiethnic* is often used instead of *transracial* when referring to the adoption of children by parents of a different race or ethnicity. As with other types of adoption, no reliable national statistics exist regarding the number of transracial adoptions. The most recent national survey, the 1987 National Health Interview Survey, found that only 8 percent of all adoptions included parents and children of different races (Stolley, 1993).

In 1994 the U.S. Congress reversed two decades of public policy that discouraged multiethnic placements with the passage of the Multiethnic Placement Act, which was made stronger by amendments in 1997. The current law prohibits public or private agencies receiving federal funds from delaying or denying adoption on the basis of race, color, or national origin of the child or the foster or adoptive parent. Its purposes are to decrease the length of time that children wait to be adopted, facilitate the recruitment and retention of adoptive and foster parents, and eliminate discrimination on the basis of the race, color, or national origin of the child or the prospective parent (Hollinger, 1998). In complying with the law, agencies, adoptive parents, and leaders of communities of color have cooperated in developing assessment tools and guidelines for families who are planning to adopt transracially. These materials emphasize the need for adoptive parents to hold positive views about the ethnicity of the child they are adopting and to be proactive in involving their families in the child's ethnic community, such as church or community center. They should be willing to help the child learn about his or her race's history and leaders, and in other ways to address the child's need for positive ethnic affiliation (Neal & Stumph, 1993; Smith, 1994; but also see Baden, 2001). Communities of color can also reach out to help families in multiethnic placements by welcoming multiethnic adoptive families into their communities and by preparing programs and materials especially for these families.

> *How do we help each other? For those of you who are white and whose children carry our color and the warmth of the sun in their genes, I believe we as black people can be of help . . . as you seek to give your children of color answers about their heritage, answers about the craziness of our world in relation to color. (Sidney Duncan, director and founder, Homes for Black Children, 1988)*

Culturally Competent Adoption Practice

While the controversy over transracial adoption continues, substantial efforts have been made to increase the number of same-race adoptive families available to children. Although many agencies have successfully developed their ability to recruit African American families and place children with them, the continuing backlog of African American children awaiting an adoptive home has impelled a redoubling of efforts. In 1990, the North American Council on Adoptable Children (NACAC) conducted a national survey to identify barriers to same-race adoption of children of color (Gilles & Kroll, 1991).

> *In hiring staff I look for good clinical skills, a sense of family, dependability, maturity, competence, and responsibility. . . . I want workers to know the strengths of black families, have pride in being black, appreciate cultural values, and love and appreciate black people and their differences. (Adoption agency director)*

The findings reveal that barriers still exist that were first identified thirty years ago (Billingsley & Giovannoni, 1972). Most (83 percent) of those interviewed said that they were aware of organizational or institutional barriers preventing or discouraging families of color seeking to adopt. The most frequently mentioned barriers were these:

- *Institutional/systematic racism.* Virtually all procedures and guidelines impacting standard agency adoption are developed from white middle-class perspectives. Whether conscious of this or not, agencies have come to espouse—and cater to those holding—distinctly middle-class views. Unfortunately, many families of color aren't familiar with or don't have a mind-set that allows them to access "middle-class agencies."
- *Lack of people of color in managerial positions.* Boards of directors and agency heads remain predominantly white.
- *"Adoption as business" mentality/reality.* Heavy dependence on fee income, coupled with the fact that supplies of healthy white infants are decreasing drastically, force many agencies to place transracially to ensure survival.
- *Historical tendencies of communities of color toward informal adoption.* Potential adopters of color question the relevance of formalized adoption procedures, many times wondering why such procedures are needed at all.

A very promising development over the past decades has been the effort by African American communities to recruit families, such as the One Church, One Child project located in many cities. A number of "specialist" African American adoption agencies located in African American communities have been created to emphasize their accessibility to African American potential adoptive applicants (Gant, 1984).

Intercountry Adoptions

Although U.S. families have adopted children from other countries in significant numbers since World War II, recently the number of adoptions has increased dramatically, as the forces of globalization affect more and more aspects of American life. Between 1971 and 2001, U.S. citizens adopted over 265,500 children from other countries. International adoptions have more than doubled since 1991, when 9,000 children were adopted, to over 19,000 in 2001. The number of countries sending children has also increased, with over 100 different countries sending children to the United States for adoption in 2001. However, a few countries predominate, with 95 percent of internationally adopted children coming from only 20 countries during 2001, mainly China and Russia, South Korea, Guatemala, and the Ukraine (Evan B. Donaldson Adoption Institute, no date). Figure 10.2 shows the number of children adopted from different countries by U.S. families in 2001.

In addition, the Convention on Protection of Children and Co-operation in Respect of Intercountry Adoption (commonly called The Hague Convention on Intercountry Adop-

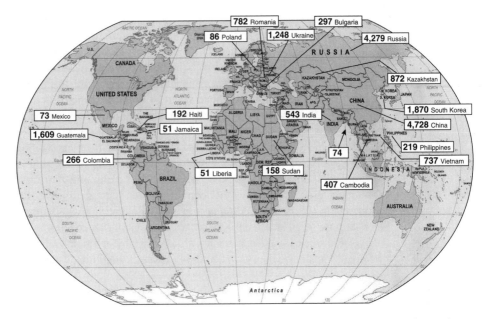

FIGURE 10.2   International Adoptions in the United States, 2001, Top Twenty Countries

tion) was adopted on May 29, 1993. This Convention ensures that the fundamental rights of children, their birth families, and their country of origin are protected. It requires the child's country of origin to certify that

- The child is adoptable.
- There is no possibility of adoption in the country of origin.
- Intercountry adoption is in the best interests of the child.
- The persons whose consent for the adoption is required have freely given that consent in writing in accordance with the laws of the country of origin.
- The consent was not induced by payment or compensation of any kind.
- The mother gave her consent after the child was born.
- The child, if of sufficient age and maturity, has been counseled.
- The child, if required, freely consents to the adoption.
- The child has not been induced by compensation or payment for his/her consent.

In addition, the receiving country must certify that

- The prospective adoptive parents have been determined eligible for adoption and suited to adopt the child.
- The prospective adoptive parents have been counseled as necessary.
- The child is or will be authorized to enter and permanently reside in the country. (The Hague Convention on Intercountry Adoption, 1993, Articles 4 and 5)

The Child Citizenship Act of 2000 and the Intercountry Adoption Act of 2000 provide additional supports to persons who wish to adopt children from abroad. The Child Citizenship

Act provides United States citizenship to any child under the age of 18 years who lives in the legal and physical custody of an American parent for whom the adoption has been finalized as of February 27, 2001. The Intercountry Adoption Act provides for implementation of the Convention and improves the ability of the federal government to assist U.S. citizens seeking to adopt children from abroad and residents from other countries who are signers of the Convention seeking to adopt children from the United States.

Agency reports suggest that, to some extent, intercountry adoptions are a means for matching the "surplus" of white homes in the United States seeking to adopt with the corresponding "surplus" of orphaned, nonmarital children in other countries for whom no families are available. Other factors contributing to intercountry adoptions include the mobility of families around the world; the greater ease of communication between countries; the continuing large numbers of American servicemen stationed abroad, many of whom seek to adopt children during their residence in another country or who father children out of wedlock with no means to care for them; and a humanitarian concern by many persons for the plight of refugee and other homeless children, many of whom are grossly neglected or discriminated against in their own country because of illegitimacy or mixed racial background.

> *[During] the summer of 1997, Carole and I traveled to Bosnia-Herzegovina as part of a humanitarian relief mission. I'll never forget standing in a small Sarajevo orphanage, surrounded by a dozen babies produced by rapes amid bombs and the nastiness of war. I was melted with compassion for these small lives. Who would love them? If I could, I'd have scooped up all of them my arms could hold to bring them home that day. (John Towriss, CNN journalist, 2001)*

The legal adoption of children from other countries requires compliance with laws in two or more countries. Islamic countries prohibit all adoption, foreign and domestic. Other countries prohibit or severely restrict international adoption. Many countries require that foreign adoptions follow the same procedures as domestic adoptions, which may necessitate that the adoptive parents come to the country to be screened. The United States has immigration rules that must be satisfied; and each state also has procedures governing adoption. The bureaucratic complexities are a significant barrier to international adoption, though adopters who work through established international adoption agencies may find that the procedures are no more complicated than those for domestic adoption. It may, however, be more expensive. Bartholet (1993) estimates that the costs "generally range upwards of $10,000, with many international adoptions costing $15,000 to $25,000" (p. 93). The finances involved in intercountry adoption are significant; Freidmutter (2002), in her testimony before the House Committee on International Relations, estimates that U.S. adoptive parents spent close to $200 million in 2001 for international adoption services.

Geographical distances and national boundaries create additional hazards to an adoption service. Sociolegal aspects of intercountry adoptions require special attention to parental consent, the child's status in matters of guardianship, citizenship, birth certificate, and assurance that the adoption is legally valid in both countries. With the recent explosion of interest in intercountry adoption, numerous service providers have emerged in many countries. The number of U.S. agencies involved in intercountry adoption has also increased; by the end of the 1990s, 80 U.S. agencies were active in Russia and 150 in China (Freidmutter, 2002).

A recent survey of American parents who have adopted internationally in the past five years identified problems in international adoption services as they are currently managed. In particular, parents expressed concern about the financial arrangements between agencies and families, and about the accuracy of information provided by agencies to the adoptive parents (Evan B. Donaldson Adoption Institute, no date). In her testimony to Congress, Cindy Freidmutter, executive director of the Adoption Institute (2002), recommended changes in U.S. policy regarding international adoption. She suggests that U.S. providers be directly responsible for all financial transactions, to do away with current practice in which American parents are urged to bring large amounts of cash to the sending country. These undocumented cash transactions create a climate in which unethical practices, such as baby selling, may flourish. (See, for example, the recent *New York Times* article on baby laundering in Cambodia; Corbett, 2002.) Friedmutter (2002) also recommends more explicit service contracts with foreign providers, clarifying services to be provided. Third, she recommends that prospective adoptive parents have access to objective information about overseas service providers and about the children referred to them.

The developmental and emotional problems of many intercountry adoptees have received widespread media attention (Talbot, 1998; Greene, 2000). Children may have physical problems that are not commonly seen in American medical centers, such as rickets (a nutritional deficiency), hepatitis, tuberculosis, and intestinal parasites, or have contagious childhood diseases. Children who spent years in orphanages before the adoption may evidence a syndrome of behaviors now identified as attachment disorder, in which children seem not to feel affection or bond to others in the family, no matter how much love and acceptance they receive. The behavioral problems associated with this disorder can be enormously challenging to parents (Talbot, 1998). In a few well-publicized cases, adoptive parents have been charged with child abuse of their adoptive child (Tuller, 2001). The extremely deprived environments that some children have experienced prior to their adoption seem to have left them unable to function normally in families and communities. Increased awareness of these problems has given impetus to improve medical and mental health postadoption services for intercountry adoptive families (Tuller, 2001), and to better procedures and oversight of overseas adoption agencies.

In spite of the tremendous difficulties faced by some adoptive parents and their adopted children from abroad, research shows that, overall, children fare well in international adoption. A 1994 study compared 199 Asian adoptees with 579 white adopted children and small numbers of American children adopted transracially. The sample of families was randomly selected from the records of forty-five public and private adoption agencies in the four states of Colorado, Illinois, Minnesota, and Wisconsin. The study participants, including adopted children who were adolescents at the time the study was conducted and their adoptive parents, completed extensive and confidential survey instruments containing a wide range of psychological and family measures. The study compared the Asian adoptions with same-race adoptions in regard to identity, attachment, family, and psychological health. The findings indicate that the Asian adopted adolescents were doing as well as their white counterparts in same-race families. In the important and controversial dimension of racial identity, 79 percent of the Asian children reported that "my parents want me to be proud of my racial background," and 66 percent stated that their parents actively try to promote racial pride. The study also found that most (80 percent) of the Asian children agreed with the statement that "I get along equally well with people of my own racial background and people of other racial backgrounds" (Benson et al., 1994, pp. 97–111). Other studies have also shown mainly positive outcomes for children of international adoptions, a surprisingly optimistic result considering that many of these children had negative experiences prior to adoption that might have been expected to affect their later adjustment (Tizard, 1991).

An important issue in intercountry adoption is the relation of the adopted child, and the host family, to the child's culture and country of origin (Benson et al., 1994). In earlier years, the emphasis was on assimilating the child into the culture of the United States and downplaying cultural or ethnic differences. Today, best practice suggests the importance of building connections for the child with the original home's culture. A well-developed program exists in some areas that offers summer "culture camps" to Korean adoptees, which may include group trips to South Korea. One mother, who sent her adopted daughter to Korea for a summer, explained, "Adoptive children face a lot of challenges. . . . Some of the questions that need to be answered are: who am I, where do I come from, what's my place in this world? I don't know how adoptive children can grow up to feel good about themselves without knowing their birth culture" (Zhao, 2002).

We really want Youjing to learn the language, . . . We want her to look Chinese and feel Chinese. (Paula Grande, intercountry adoptive mother, explaining why she placed her child in a school in which most of the students are children of Chinese immigrants; Zhao, 2002)

Trends and Issues

Gay/Lesbian Adoptive Parents

To what extent should sexual orientation of prospective adoptive parents be a factor in approving the home for adoption? This question is being asked with increasing frequency across the country in adoption agencies, courts, and state legislatures, and among gay/lesbian advocacy groups and individuals. They are arriving at very different answers. The debate concerns two somewhat separate but related types of adoption: stepparent adoption, now often referred to as "second parent adoption," in which the biological parent's partner legally adopts the child and thereby becomes legally the child's second parent; and adoption by other adults, such as occurs frequently in the adoption of children with special needs. Three states ban gay/lesbian adoption, seven permit them by law or court ruling, and elsewhere the status of such adoptions varies considerably (Goode, 2002). Social welfare agencies tend not to have formal policies on eligibility for adoptive parenthood of gay and lesbian adults, but there is usually a climate of opinion in the agency that favors or disfavors such applicants (Brooks & Goldberg, 2001). Depending on the laws of the state and the attitudes and policies of the adoption agency staff, gay and lesbian applicants may encounter a variety of responses to their request for approval as adoptive parents. They may find acceptance and help or they may have their application summarily rejected. They are quite likely to find the agency "overscrutinizing" their applications (Brooks & Goldberg, 2001). Some agencies suggest that gay/lesbian applicants hide their sexual orientation during the home study process. In some states, only one adult in the couple relationship may apply to become the adoptive parent, leaving the other partner with no legal rights to the child. In this situation, should the legal parent die or separate from the partner, the partner may have no legal means of maintaining a relationship with the child, even if he or she has filled the role of parent for a long period of time. Gay/lesbian adoptive applicants may find that they are considered qualified to adopt a child with multiple special needs, but would not be considered for one who would be easier to place. In short, policy and practice in regard to gay/lesbian adoptive parenthood is characterized by reliance on unexamined biases, expediency, and muddled half-measures, and has increased the risks of separation and instability in family relationships for children.

There is widespread belief that same-sex orientation and lifestyle disqualify people from receiving state sanction as parents, which occurs when the state approves an adoption. Concern may center on moral issues, but there is also genuine confusion over the effects on children of being raised in same-sex households. Those opposed to gay/lesbian adoptive parents express worries that the children may develop confused gender identities, or that they will be "recruited" into a same-sex lifestyle. There is concern that special needs children, who may already feel marginalized in society, will feel even more ostracized if their parents have a "deviant" lifestyle and will be subject to harsh taunts from their peers. Some people believe that gay/lesbian relationships are inherently unstable and may exacerbate the lack of permanency in the lives of the children they adopt.

These concerns and beliefs have not been tested by rigorous research on gay/lesbian *adoptive* families. However, an emerging body of research on gay/lesbian families has not found a difference in child adjustment or outcomes from heterosexual families. Recently, the American Academy of Pediatrics, citing the findings of two decades of research on this subject, issued a policy statement endorsing the adoption of children by the biological parent's partner (second parent adoption). The Academy said that such adoptions were in the best interests of the child, giving him or her the same safeguards that children have in families with opposite-sex parents. An important protection in second parent adoption is that, even if the biological parent leaves or dies, the child's ongoing relationship with the other parenting figure is ensured.

Increasingly, agencies are seeing gay/lesbian adoptive applicants as a potential resource for hard-to-place children, noting their financial security and their interest in caring for and raising children even though they may not have children of their own. Other strengths noted include strong family and friend networks, psychological stability, resourcefulness, and sensitivity to "difference," which can help them understand and cope with the challenges of parenting special needs children. In their qualitative study of agency attitudes toward gay/lesbian adoption, Brooks and Goldberg (2001) suggest that agencies help these adoptive parents develop strategies for acknowledging and explaining differences to their adoptive children and for preparing the children for expressions of discrimination and scorn. They also recommend further rigorous research on the question, "How does the degree to which gay and lesbian parents are open about their sexual orientation affect the adjustment of adopted and foster children?" (p. 155). The issue becomes, then, not a question of the inherent suitability of gay/lesbian adoptive parents, but the coping strategies for dealing with discrimination and the extent to which the couple have an accepting and open environment in which to raise children.

Open Adoption Controversy

The last three decades have seen the emergence of a controversy around the "search" phenomenon and the development of "openness" in present-day adoption practice. One result has been a recognition that the adoption experience has dimensions that were not acknowledged in closed adoption practice. The interest in various degrees of openness is in sharp contrast to the traditional viewpoint that normal well-adjusted individuals, although adopted, would not need nor want to know about their birth parents; the adoptive parents, the ones who raised them and brought them to maturity, would be sufficient. But we have learned that adoptees may at some point want access to a wider range of information that will give them a better understanding of themselves. These adoptees are not motivated by idle curiosity; they have specific questions related to their personal identity. Most searches stem from a lack of needed information (Gritter, 1997).

There is considerable acknowledgment that for birth parents and adoptive parents who freely and fully agree to ongoing contact, open adoption has the potential to bring about genuinely satisfying relationships for all concerned (Baran & Pannor, 1993). At the same time, questions have been raised as to the problems open adoption can bring and the need for various degrees of openness, and for some birth parents and adoptive parents, availability of some degree of closed adoption. Fears about too-rapid policy changes include these: Some families have more than one adopted child; what will it mean in family relationships if one has continuing contact with the birth mother and another does not? What of the risk of birth parents dropping out of the child's life after contacts have been in place? Young birth parents, however conscientiously they try to make the right decisions affecting their child at the time of adoptive planning, cannot foresee or judge future demands on their yet undeveloped capacities and the opportunities or disappointments that may follow. How will the task of helping children to understand the concept of adoption be further complicated by an active role of the birth mother in the child's life? Clearly the problem of role ambiguity is a serious and unresolved one in open adoption (McRoy et al., 1988).

Some professionals have observed that in discussions of open adoption, few benefits to the adopting parents are mentioned. There are concerns that because of a deeply felt need for a child, and the stated or unstated requirement in open adoption to satisfy the needs of the birth parents, the adoptive applicants may agree too quickly to proposed arrangements that may be to the detriment of their own needs and right to privacy.

There are repeated suggestions in the literature that adopting parents and birth parents should be allowed to choose participation in either open or closed adoption. The degree of acceptable and workable openness in any adoption plan is a highly individual matter, reason enough for caution about making drastic policy changes before research has been done.

Chapter Summary

Adoption is a social and legal process whereby the parent–child relationship is established between persons not so related at birth. By this means, a child born to one set of parents becomes, legally and socially, the child of other parents and a member of another family, and assumes the same rights and duties as those between children and their biological parents.

Adoption of children is an ancient practice, whose original purpose was to provide an heir for a family. In the United States, adoption became common in the twentieth century, to resolve the problem of out-of-wedlock pregnancies and to meet the demands of infertile couples for a child. More recently, the adoption of infants has declined, as abortion and contraception options have become available, and single parenthood has become more economically feasible and socially acceptable. At the same time, the adoption of children formerly considered unadoptable, including older children and those with special needs, has become more common. Today, adoption practice has split into two arenas, with private agencies and third parties such as lawyers handling most of the adoptions of healthy infants, and public agencies maintaining responsibility for the placement of special needs children who have become free for adoption after entering the child welfare system.

Adoption practice today faces many changes. During the last 40 years, the secrecy that surrounded both the legal and social aspects of adoption has been challenged by adult adoptees, who demand as a birthright information about their biological origins. Searching for biological family members separated by adoption has become common. Many agencies are now practicing various levels of openness in adoption, in which some measure of contact is maintained between the biological family and the adoptive family.

Protecting the right of unmarried fathers to be involved in adoption planning has required adjustments in adoption practice. As a result of U.S. Supreme Court decisions in the 1970s, the rights of unmarried fathers to their children cannot be disregarded in adoption planning. A problem arises when a father is not informed of his paternity until after the child has been adopted and then challenges the adoption. States have developed legislation to try to protect the rights of fathers while also ensuring the stability of the adoption.

Permanency planning, the policy of moving children out of long-term foster care and into permanent homes, has increased the number of older and special needs children who require adoption planning. This movement has challenged the child welfare system in several ways. Many children have waited for a long time in the child welfare system before being placed in a permanent, adoptive home, because of numerous delays in the system. Recently, new legislation, the Adoption and Safe Families Act, and amendments to the Multiethnic Placement Act, have reduced barriers to the timely adoption of children in the child welfare system. Increased recruitment efforts for adoptive parents in communities of color and more attention to kinship adoption have provided additional adoption resources.

In response to the challenges presented by the troubled histories of many children adopted after years in the child welfare system, postadoption services to children and families have expanded and developed a specialized knowledge base. Understanding children's survival behavior and accepting that children may have ambivalent feelings about permanently separating from their biological family and becoming attached to a new family, have helped social workers and adoptive parents better meet the needs of adopted children. Inevitably, some of the placements of older, emotionally troubled children break down, requiring agencies to develop sensitive practices to help the child recover from the disruption and move on to another placement.

Kinship adoption and intercountry adoption have been parts of the adoption arena for many years, but are taking on increased functions and visibility.

FOR STUDY AND DISCUSSION

1. Watch a movie with an adoption theme, such as *Secrets and Lies* or *Raising Isaiah*. Identify ways in which the movie illustrates and expands concepts in this chapter, such as transracial adoption, open adoption, postadoption services, and psychosocial adjustment to adoption.

2. Review the section on postadoption services and then answer the questions: Are there issues in adoptive family development so specific that they must be dealt with only by specialists in adoption? Or can they be adequately addressed by generalist family and individual therapists?

3. Prepare a presentation on some aspect of intercountry adoption. Possible topics include laws and administrative rules governing intercountry adoption; the experiences of children and their adoptive families in the finding, matching, and meeting of one another; and innovative programs to connect children adopted from other countries with their country of origin. Based on your research, make recommendations on ways that intercountry adoption could be improved to better meet the needs of children.

4. What position do you take on the issue of transracial placement as an alternative adoption practice?

State your reasoning on the question and compare it with that of others.

5. Consider and debate with others what you see as the benefits and the risks to open adoptions. On the assumption that some degree of "openness" in adoption practice is here to stay, state and describe a flexible policy that could best serve the needs and preferences of the three parties to the adoption triad.

6. Discover whether innovative programs exist in your area to recruit adoptive parents for special needs children. How are they working? Do they offer ongoing support to the family after the adoption?

7. Interview a family involved in kinship adoption. What kinds of supports and resources do they need from the child welfare agency? Do they have needs different from those of nonrelative adopters?

8. Read the novels *The Bean Tree* and *Pigs in Heaven* by Barbara Kingsolver, and analyze them in terms of the Indian Child Welfare Act. In what ways does the ICWA affect the adopted child, the biological mother, the adoptive mother, and the tribal nation involved?

FOR ADDITIONAL STUDY

Benson, P. L., Sharma, A. R., & Roehlkepartain, E. C. (1994). *Growing up adopted: A portrait of adolescents and their families.* Minneapolis, MN: The Search Institute.

Courtney, M. E. (1997). The politics and realities of transracial adoption. *Child Welfare, 76*(6), 749–779.

Groze, V. (1996). Successful adoptive families: A longitudinal study of special needs adoption. Westport, CT: Praeger.

Lakin, D. (1992). *Empowering adoptive families: Issues in postadoption services, reference and resource guide.* Southfield, MI: National Resource Center for Special Needs Adoption; and Baltimore: Baltimore City Department of Social Services.

Reitz, M., & Watson, K. W. (1992). *Adoption and the family system: Strategies for treatment.* New York: Guilford Press.

Rosenthal, J. A., & Groze, V. K. (1992). *Special needs adoption.* New York: Praeger.

Sorosky, A. D., Baran, A., & Pannor, R. (1989). *The adoption triangle: Sealed or opened records: How they affect adoptees, birth parents, and adoptive parents.* San Antonio: Corona Publishing.

INTERNET SEARCH TERMS

Adoption

International adoption

Multicultural adoption

INTERNET SITES

Adopt U.S. Kids. A national database of children awaiting adoption and families approved to adopt. The AdoptUSKids web site allows families to search for children and workers to search for families throughout the United States. The site also includes comprehensive adoption information for families and many features to assist social workers. AdoptUSKids is an initiative of the Children's Bureau, U.S. Department of Health and Human Services and is operated by the Adoption Exchange Association.

www.AdoptUSKids.org

Evan B. Donaldson Adoption Institute. Provides up-to-date information on research, policy, and practice in adoption.

www.adoptioninstitute.org

National Adoption Information Clearinghouse. Established by the U.S. Congress to provide information on all aspects of adoption, including infant and intercountry adoption and adopting children with special needs.

www.calib.com/naic

National Resource Center for Special Needs Adoption. The mission of the center is to assist states, tribes, and other federally funded child welfare agencies in building their capacity to ensure the safety, well-being, and permanency of abused and neglected children through adoption and postlegal adoption services program planning, policy development, and practice.

www.nrcadoption.org

REFERENCES

Abbott, G. (1938). *The child and the state, vol. 1.* Chicago: University of Chicago Press.

Adoptive Family Rights Council. (1996, April 3). Seminar on the Uniform Adoption Act. Harrisburg, PA: Author.

Baden, A. (2001, August). Psychological adjustment of transracial adoptees: Applying the cultural-racial identity model. Proceedings of 109th Annual Convention of American Psychological Association, San Francisco, CA.

Baran, A., & Pannor, R. (1993). Perspectives on open adoption. *The Future of Children, 3*(1), 119–124 (a publication of the Center for the Future of Children, the David and Lucile Packard Foundation).

Barth, R. P., & Brooks, D. (1997). A longitudinal study of family structure and size and adoption outcomes. *Adoption Quarterly, 1*(1), 29–56.

Barth, R. P., Gibbs, D. A., & Siebenaler, K. (2001). *Assessing the field of postadoption services: Family needs, program models, and evaluation issues.* U.S. Department of Health and Human Services. Available: http://aspe.hhs.gov/hsp/PASS/lit-rev-01.htm [2002, April 12].

Bartholet, E. (1993). International adoption: Current status and future prospects. *The Future of Children, 3*(1), 89–103 (a publication of the Center for the Future of Children, the David and Lucile Packard Foundation).

Bausch, R. S., & Serpe, R. T. (1997). Negative outcomes of interethnic adoption of Mexican American children. *Social Work, 42*(2), 136–143.

Bell, C. J. (1985). Consent issues in inter-country adoption. *Children's Legal Rights Journal, 6*(3), 2–8.

Benson, P. L., Sharma, A. R., & Roehlkepartain, E. C. (1994). *Growing up adopted: A portrait of adolescents and their families.* Minneapolis, MN: Search Institute.

Berrick, J., & Barth, R. (1994). Research of kinship foster care: What do we know? Where do we go from here? *Children and Youth Services Review, 16*(1–2), 1–5.

Berry, M. (1993). Risks and benefits of open adoption. *The Future of Children, 3*(1), 125–138 (a publication of the Center for the Future of Children, the David and Lucile Packard Foundation).

Berry, M., & Barth, R. P. (1990). A study of disrupted adoptive placements of adolescents. *Child Welfare, 69*(3), 209–225.

Billingsley, A., & Giovannoni, J. M. (1972). *Children of the storm: Black children and American child welfare.* New York: Harcourt Brace Jovanovich.

Blair, I. (2002). *Information packet: Indian Child Welfare Act.* National Resource Center for Foster Care and Permanency Planning. New York: Hunter College School of Social Work.

Bourguignon, J. P., & Watson, K. W. (1987). *After adoption: A manual for professionals working with adoptive families.* Post-Placement Post-Legal Adoption Services Project for Special Needs Children and Their Families: Federal Grant #90-CKO-02871. Chicago: Illinois Department of Children and Family Services.

Brieland, D. (1984). Selection of adoptive parents. In P. Sachdev (Ed.), *Adoption: Issues and trends* (pp. 65–85). Toronto: Butterworth.

Brodzinsky, D. M., Smith, D. W., & Brodzinsky, A. B. (1998). *Children's adjustment to adoption.* Thousand Oaks, CA: Sage.

Brooks, D., & Goldberg, S. (2001). Gay and lesbian adoptive and foster care placements: Can they meet the needs of waiting children? *Social Work, 46*(2), 147–157.

Brown, S. L. (1989). *Profile: Permanency planning assessment for children with developmental disabilities and special health needs.* Southfield, MI: Spaulding for Children.

Byrd, A. D. (1988). The case for confidential adoption. *Public Welfare, 46*(4), 20–23.

Carp, E. W. (1995). Adoption and disclosure of family information: A historical perspective. *Child Welfare, 74*(1), 217–239.

Carp, E. W. (1998). *Family matters: Secrecy and disclosure in the history of adoption.* Cambridge, MA: Harvard University Press.

Child Welfare League of America. (1968, 1972, 1988). *Standards for adoption services.* New York: Child Welfare League of America Press.

Child Welfare League of America. (1994). *Kinship care: A natural bridge.* Washington, DC: Child Welfare League of America Press.

Child Welfare League of America. (1995). *Child abuse and neglect: A look at the states.* Washington, DC: Child Welfare League of America Press.

Children's Bureau. (2002). *The AFCARS Report: Interim FY 2000 estimates as of August 2002.* U.S. Department of Health and Human Services. Available: www.acf.hhs.gov/programs/cb/publications/afcars/report7.htm [2002, November 7].

Children's Defense Fund. (1997, November). Summary of the Adoption and Safe Families Act of 1997. Available: www.childrensdefense.org/safestart.

Corbett, S. (2002, June 16). Where do babies come from? *New York Times Magazine,* pp. 42–47 ff.

Courtney, M. E. (1997). The politics and realities of transracial adoption. *Child Welfare, 76*(6), 749–779.

Curtis, C. M., & Alexander, R. (1996). The Multiethnic Placement Act: Implications for social work practice. *Child and Adolescent Social Work Journal, 13*(5), 401–410.

Curtis, P. A. (1986). The dialectics of open versus closed adoption of infants. *Child Welfare, 65*(5), 437–445.

Dukette, R. (1984). Value issues in present-day adoption. *Child Welfare, 63*(3), 233–244.

Duncan, S. (1988). *Healing old wounds.* Paper presented at the North American Conference on Adoptable Children, St. Louis, MO.

Edelstein, S. B. (1995). *Children with prenatal alcohol and/or other drug exposure: Weighing the risks of adoption.* Washington, DC: Child Welfare League of America Press.

Emery, L. J. (1993). The case for agency adoption. *The Future of Children, 3*(1), 139–145.

Etter, J. A. (1997). *A cooperative adoption workbook.* Washington, DC: Child Welfare League of America.

Evan B. Donaldson Adoption Institute. (1998). *Adoption in the United States.* Chicago: Author. Available: www.adoptioninstitute.org/research/ressta.html

Evan B. Donaldson Adoption Institute. (2002a, June). *Costs of adoption.* Available: www.adoptioninstitute.org/FactOverview/costs_print.html [2002, November 2].

Evan B. Donaldson Adoption Institute. (2002b, June). *National adoption attitudes survey: Research report.* Dave Thomas Foundation for Adoption and the Evan B. Donaldson Adoption Institute. Available: www.adoptioninstitute.org/survey/ [2002, November 2].

Evan B. Donaldson Adoption Institute. (no date). *International adoption facts.* Available: www.adoptioninstitute.org/FactOverview/international-print [2003, January 6].

Fahlberg, V. (1991). *A child's journey through placement.* Indianapolis: Perspectives Press.

Feigelman, W., & Silverman, A. R. (1984). The long-term effects of transracial adoption. *Social Service Review, 58,* 588–602.

Festinger, T. B. (1986). *Necessary risk—A study of adoptions and disrupted adoptive placements.* Washington, DC: Child Welfare League of America.

Festinger, T. (1996). *After adoption: A study of placement stability and parents' service needs.* New York: New York University, Ehrenkranz School of Social Work.

Fields, J. (2001, April). *Living arrangements of children.* (Current Population Reports, P70-74. U.S. Department of Commerce, Census Bureau). Washington, DC: U.S. Government Printing Office.

Flango, V., & Flango, C. (1994). *The flow of adoption information from the states.* Williamsburg, VA: National Center for State Courts.

Flango, V., & Flango, C. (1995, September–October). How many children were adopted in 1992? *Child Welfare, 74*(5), 1018.

Fraser, C. G. (1972, April 10). Blacks condemn mixed adoptions. *New York Times.*

Friedmutter, C. (2002, May 22). Testimony on "International Adoptions: Problems and Solutions" before the House Committee on International Relations. Washington, DC. Available: www.adoptioninstitute.org/policy/hagueregs.htm [2002, November 7].

Gant, L. M. (1984). *Black adoption programs: Pacesetters in practice.* Ann Arbor: National Child Welfare Training Center, University of Michigan School of Social Work.

Gilles, T., & Kroll, J. (1991). *Barriers to same race placement.* St. Paul, MN: North American Council on Adoptable Children.

Goode, E. (2002, February 4). Group backs gays who seek to adopt a partner's child. *New York Times,* p. A1, 21.

Greene, M. (2000, July 17). Annals of parenthood: The orphan ranger. *The New Yorker,* 38–45.

Gritter, J. L. (1997). *The spirit of open adoption.* Washington, DC: Child Welfare League of America Press.

Grotevant, H. D. (1997). Coming to terms with adoption: The construction of identity from adolescence into adulthood. *Adoption Quarterly, 1*(1), 3–28.

Grotevant, H. D., & McRoy, R. G. (1998). *Openness in adoption: Exploring family connections.* Thousand Oaks, CA: Sage.

Groze, V. (1996). Successful adoptive families. Westport, CT: Praeger.

Hardin, M. A., & Shalleck, A. (1984). Children living apart from their parents. In R. M. Horowitz & H. A. Davidson (Eds.), *Legal rights of children* (pp. 353–421). Colorado Springs: McGraw-Hill.

Haring, B. L. (1976). *Adoption statistics: Annual data, January 1–December 31, 1975: Submitted by 41 voluntary and 16 public agencies* (Publication No. X-9). New York: Child Welfare League of America.

Hartman, A. (1979). *Finding families: An ecological approach to family assessment in adoption.* Beverly Hills, CA: Sage.

Hartman, A. (1984). *Working with adoptive families beyond placement.* New York: Child Welfare League of America.

Heath, T. (1998, August). Qualitative analysis of private mediation: Benefits for families in public child welfare agencies. *Children and Youth Services Review, 20*(7), 605–627.

Hegar, R., & Scannapieco, M. (1994). From family duty to family policy: The evolution of kinship care. *Child Welfare, 74*(1), 200–216.

Hill, R. (1972). *The strengths of black families.* New York: Emerson Hall.

Hollinger, J. H. (1991). *Adoption law and practice.* New York: Matthew Bender.

Hollinger, J. H. (1993). Adoption law. *The Future of Children, 3*(1), 43–61.

Hollinger, J. H. (1998). *Adoption law and practice, vol. I* (1998 supplement). New York: Matthew Bender.

Hollinger, J. H., & the ABA Center on Children and the Law National Resource Center. (1998). *A guide to the Multiethnic Placement Act of 1994 as amended by the Interethnic Provisions of 1996.* Washington, DC: American Bar Association.

Hollingsworth, L. D. (1998). Promoting same-race adoption for children of color. *Social Work, 43*(2), 104–116.

Johnson, B. (1981). The Indian Child Welfare Act of 1978: Implications for practice. *Chlid Welfare, 60*(7), 435–446.

Jones, C. (1993, October 24). Role of race in adoptions: Old debate is being reborn. *New York Times,* p. 1.

Katz, L., Spoonemore, N., & Robinson, C. (1994). *Concurrent planning: From permanency planning to permanency action.* Seattle: Lutheran Social Services of Washington and Idaho.

Kim, C., & Carroll, T. G. (1975). Intercountry adoption of South Korean orphans: A lawyer's guide. *Journal of Family Law, 14*(2), 223–253.

Klemesrud, J. (1972, April 12). Furor over whites adopting blacks. *New York Times.*

Kraft, A. D., Palombo, J., Mitchell, D. L., Woods, P. K., & Schmidt, A. W. (1985). Some theoretical considerations on confidential adoptions. Pt. 1: The birth mother. *Child and Adolescent Social Work, 2*(1).

Kramer, L., & Houston, D. (1998). Supporting families as they adopt children with special needs. *Family Relations, 47,* 423–432.

Kreisher, K. (2002, November–December). Supporting loving families: After the adoption. *Children's Voice.* Available: www.cwla.org/articles/cv0211supporting. htm [2003, January 8].

Lakin, D. (1992). *Empowering adoptive families: Issues in post adoption services.* Southfield, MI: National Resource Center for Special Needs Adoption; and Baltimore: Baltimore City Department of Social Services.

Lakin, D. (1994). Personal communication. Southfield, Michigan.

Lakin, D., & Malone, S. (2001). Recruiting resource families. *The Roundtable: Journal of the National Resource Center for Special Needs Adoption, 15*(2), 1–3.

Lawrence, S. (1989, July 17). Personal communication. Philadelphia: Exchange Services, National Adoption Center.

Levy, T., & Orleans, M. (1998). *Attachment, trauma, and healing: Understanding and treating attachment disorders in children and families.* Washington, DC: Child Welfare League of America.

Lewin, T. (1997, November 9). U.S. is divided on adoption, survey of attitudes asserts. *New York Times,* p. 10.

Logan, F. A., Morrall, P. M. E., & Chambers, H. (1998, May–June). Identification of risk factors for psychological disturbance in adopted children. *Child Abuse Review, 7*(3), 154–164.

Magruder, J. (1994). Characteristics of relative and nonrelative adoptions by California public agencies. *Children and Youth Services Review, 16,* 123–132.

Mansnerus, L. (1989, October 5). Private adoptions aided by expanding network. *New York Times,* p. 1.

Maza, P. (1984). *Adoption Trends: 1944–1975.* Child Welfare Research Notes #9. Washington, DC: Administration for Chlidren, Youth, and Families.

Maza, P. (2001). The age factor in adoption. *The Roundtable: Journal of the National Resource Center for Special Needs Adoption, 16*(1), 1–3.

McDermott, M. T. (1993). The case for independent adoption. *The Future of Children, 3*(1), 146–152.

McKenzie, J. K. (1993). Adoption of children with special needs. *The Future of Children, 3*(1), 62–76.

McNamara, J. (Ed.). (1994). *Sexually reactive children in adoption and foster care.* Grennsboro, NC: Family Resources.

McRoy, R. G. (1998). *Special needs adoptions: Practice issues.* Garland Publishing.

McRoy, R. G., Grotevant, H. D., & Ayers-Lopez, S. (1994). *Changing practices in adoption.* Austin, TX: The Hogg Foundation for Mental Health, University of Texas.

McRoy, R. G., Grotevant, H. D., & White, K. L. (1988). *Openness in adoption: New practices, new issues.* New York: Praeger.

McRoy, R. G., & Zurcher, L. A. (1983). *Transracial and inracial adoptees. The adolescent years.* Springfield, IL: Charles C. Thomas.

Meezan, W., Katz, S., & Russo, E. M. (1978). Independent adoptions. *Child Welfare, 57*(7).

Michaels, R. (1947). Casework considerations in rejecting the adoption application. *Journal of Social Casework, 28*(10), 370–375.

Montalvo, E. (1994). Against all odds: The challenges faced by Latino families and children in the United States. *The Roundtable: Journal of the National Resource Center for Special Needs Adoption, 8*(2), 1–5.

Mosher, W. D., & Bachrach, C. A. (1996). Understanding U.S. fertility: Continuity and change in the National Survey of Family Growth. *Family Planning Perspectives, 28*(1), 4–12.

Nasdijj. (2001, September 16). Migrant father. *New York Times Magazine,* p. 80.

National Adoption Information Clearinghouse. (2000, April 2). Adoption statistics—A brief overview of the data. Available: www.calib.com/naic/pubs/s_over.htm [2002, November 7].

National Adoption Information Clearinghouse. (2000, August). Adoption and the stages of development. Available: www.calib.com/naic/pubs/s_over.htm [2002, November 7].

National Association of Social Workers. (1997, September). Adoption law raises questions. *NASW News,* 15.

National Association of Social Workers. (2002, March). Revised public and professional policies: Foster care and adoption/public child welfare. *NASW News,* 7–8.

National Committee for Adoption. (1982). *Children from other lands.* Unpublished mimeographed draft. Washington, DC: Author.

National Committee for Adoption. (1989). *Adoption factbook. United States data, issues, regulations and resources.* Washington, DC: Author.

Neal, L., & Stumph, A. (1993). *Transracial adoptive parenting: A black/white community issue.* Bronx, NY: Haskett-Neal Publications.

Neeley-Bertram, D. (2000). Making the connection: Are adoption matching parties good for kids? *Children's Voice, 9*(6), 16–18.

North American Council on Adoptable Children. (1995, Winter). The Multiethnic Placement Act. *Adoptalk,* 3.

Pertman, A. (2000). *Adoption nation: How the adoption revolution is transforming America.* New York: Basic Books.

Plantz, M. C., Hubbell, R., Barrett, B. J., & Dobrec, A. (1989). Indian child welfare: A status report. *Children Today, 18*(1), 24–29.

Prater, G. S. (1992). Child welfare and African-American families. In N. A. Cohen (Ed.), *Child welfare: A multicultural focus.* Boston: Allyn & Bacon.

Proch, K. (1981). Foster parents as preferred adoptive parents: Practice implications. *Child Welfare, 60*(9), 617–626.

Quinton, D., Rushton, A., Dance, C., & Mayes, D. (1998). *Joining new families: A study of adoption and fostering in middle childhood.* New York: John Wiley.

Reitz, M., & Watson, K. (1992). *Adoption and the family system: Strategies for treatment.* New York: Guilford Press.

Roles, P. E. (1989). *Saying goodbye to a baby.* Washington, DC: Child Welfare League of America.

Rosenthal, J. A. (1993). Outcomes of adoption of children with special needs. *The Future of Children, 3*(1), 77–88 (a publication of the Center for the Future of Children, the David and Lucile Packard Foundation).

Rosenthal, J. A., & Groze, V. K. (1992). *Special-needs adoption: A study of intact families.* New York: Praeger.

Schroen, S. (no date). *Here I am: A lifebook kit for use with children with developmental disabilities.* Southfield, MI: Spaulding for Children.

Shireman, J. F. (1988). *Growing up adopted: An examination of major issues.* Chicago: Chicago Child Care Society.

Siegel, D. H. (1993). Open adoption of infants: Adoptive parents' perceptions of advantages and disadvantages. *Social Work, 38*(1), 15–23.

Silin, M. W. (1996). The vicissitudes of adoption for parents and children. *Child and Adolescent Social Work Journal, 13*(3), 255–269.

Silverman, A. R. (1993). Outcomes of transracial adoption. *The Future of Children, 3*(1), 104–118 (a publication of the Center for the Future of Children, the David and Lucile Packard Foundation).

Simon, A., Alstein, H., & Melli, M. S. (1994). *The case for transracial adoption.* Washington, DC: American University Press.

Smith, A. (1994). *Transracial and transcultural adoption.* The National Adoption Information Clearinghouse. Available: www.calib.com/naic/pubs/f_trans.cfm [2003, January 10].

Smith, S. L., Howard, J. A., & Monroe, A. D. (1998). An analysis of child behavior problems in adoptions in difficulty. *Journal of Social Service Research, 24*(1–2): 61–84.

Sokoloff, B. Z. (1993). Antecedents of American adoption. *The Future of Children, 3*(1), 17–25 (a publication of the Center for the Future of Children, the David and Lucille Packard Foundation).

Sorosky, A. D., Baran, A., & Pannor, R. (1989). *The adoption triangle: Sealed or opened records: How they affect adoptees, birth parents, and adoptive parents.* San Antonio: Corona Publishing.

Spencer, M. E. (1987). Post-legal adoption services: A lifelong commitment. *Journal of Social Work and Human Sexuality, 6*(1), 155–167.

Stolley, K. S. (1993). Statistics on adoption in the United States. *The Future of Children, 3*(1), 26–42 (a publication of the Center for the Future of Children, the David and Lucile Packard Foundation).

Sullivan, A. (1995, Winter). The uniform adoption act: What price uniformity? *The Children's Voice, 4*(2), 25–26.

Sullivan, A. (1998). *Adoption and privatization.* Washington, DC: Child Welfare League of America.

Takas, M. (1993). *Kinship care and family preservation: A guide for states in legal and policy development.* Washington, DC: American Bar Association Center on Children and the Law.

Talbot, M. (1998, May 24). Attachment theory: The ultimate experiment. *New York Times Magazine,* pp. 24–30 ff.

Tatara, T. (1993). *Characteristics of children in substitute and adoptive care: A statistical summary of the VCIS national child welfare data base.* Washington, DC: American Public Welfare Association.

Thornton, J. (1991). Permanency planning for children in kinship foster homes. *Child Welfare, 70*(5), 593–601.

Tizard, B. (1991). Intercountry adoption: A review of the evidence. *Journal of Child Psychology and Psychiatry, 32*(5), 43–56.

Towriss, J. (2001). Our hearts are ready. *CNN.Com In-Depth Special, the New Americans.* Available: www.cnn.com [2001, November 14].

Tuller, D. (2001, September 4). Adoption medicine brings new parents answers and advice. *New York Times,* p. D7, D10.

U.S. Department of Health and Human Services. (1997, February). *Adoption 2002: A response to the Presidential executive memorandum on adoption.* Washington, DC: Author. Available: www.acf.dhhs.gov/programs/cb/special/2002toc [1997, February].

U.S. General Accounting Office, HEHS Division. (1998). *Foster care implementation of the Multiethnic Placement Act poses difficult challenges.* Washington, DC: U.S. Government Printing Office.

U.S. Immigration and Naturalization Service. (1991). *Statistical yearbook of the Immigration and Naturalization Service, 1991.* Washington, DC: U.S. Government Printing Office.

U.S. Senate Committee on Children and Youth. (1975). Hearings before the Subcommittee on Labor and Public Welfare. *Adoption and foster care.* Washington, DC: U.S. Senate, 94th Congress, First Session.

Vick, C. (1995, Winter). The 1994 Uniform Adoption Act: The wrong model for positive change. *Adoptalk,* 4–5.

Vonk, M. E. (2001). Cultural competence for transracial adoptive parents. *Social Work, 46*(3), 246–255.

Watson, K. W. (1988). The case for open adoption. *Public Welfare, 46*(4), 24–28.

Williams, M., & Satterfield, M. (2000). Kinship care: Is adoption the best option? *Children's Voice, 9*(6), 20–22.

Witmer, H., Herzog, E., Weinstein, E. A., & Sullivan, M. E. (1963). *Independent adoptions: A follow-up study.* New York: Russell Sage Foundation.

Woods, M. (1989). Adoptive planning for American Indian children. *The Roundtable: Journal of the National Resource Center for Special Needs Adoption, 4*(2), 3.

Wulczyn, F., & Hislop, K. (2002). *Growth in the adoption population.* Chapin Hall Center for Children. University of Chicago. Available: http://aspe.hhs.gov/hsp/fostercare-issueso2/adoptin/index.htm [2003, January 10].

Zhao, Y. (2002, April 9). Immersed in 2 worlds, new and old. *New York Times,* p. A27.

11 Juvenile Delinquents

The Community's Dilemma

But the Constitution does not mandate elimination of all differences in the treatment of juveniles.

—*Schall v. Martin*, 1984, p. 269

CHAPTER OUTLINE

Case Example

Peter is 15 years old. He became a temporary ward of the court when he was 4 years old. His mother had repeatedly beaten him with an extension cord. The last time he was beaten, he ran out of the house and into the street. His mother, in a drunken stupor, chased after him with the extension cord in her hands. Neighbors kept him from her and called the police.

After being taken to the hospital, he was placed in a foster home. Over the next two years, his mother visited twice. When the foster parents sought to adopt him after he had been with them for two years, the agency told them that they were working on placing him with an aunt. The foster parents questioned this plan, because no family member had visited the child and he had not mentioned an aunt. The agency told the foster parents that it had located the aunt in another state. A home study had been completed and she would be coming to meet Peter in the next month. The aunt came and took Peter home with her.

Peter began to wet the bed immediately. The aunt thought he was having some initial adjustment problems, so attempted to console him when it happened. About eight months into the placement, he began to urinate on and hit other children at home and at school. The aunt became worried. The school social worker recommended that she get counseling for him. He was seen by the child guidance agency for two years. The urinating behavior stopped and the hitting behaviors were significantly reduced. Services were terminated.

At 10 years of age, Peter stole a bicycle from a garage. His aunt made him return it, spanked him with a belt, and told him he would not be allowed to play outside for a week. The next day, Peter told the teacher that his aunt had beaten him with a belt and he did not want to go back to her house. The teacher called child protective services. Child protective services talked with Peter and the aunt. Both confirmed that the aunt had hit him with a belt. The aunt said she would just as soon he not come back to her house because he had been a constant problem since he was placed with her. He was placed in a shelter.

The home state was contacted to arrange for Peter's return. After two weeks, a worker came to pick him up and took him to a shelter in the home state. The agency sought a foster home placement. As they were preparing to move him to a foster home, the shelter reported that he had been found having sexual intercourse with an 8-year-old girl in the shelter. The agency told the prospective foster parents of this incident, and they declined to have him placed in the home because they had younger children. He remained in the shelter for six months and was eventually placed in a small group home for children with sexually aggressive behaviors. He remained in this placement for two years.

Peter had to leave the group home because it could keep children only until their twelfth birthday. He moved from one group home to another. A fight with another youth that Peter had allegedly started precipitated each move. No delinquency charges were filed in any of these incidents. He is now in the juvenile detention facility charged with forcible rape of a 12-year-old girl.

This case example highlights an issue of great concern in child welfare, that children who originally come to the attention of the child welfare system because of neglect, abuse, or abandonment later appear in the juvenile justice system (Kelley, Thornberry, & Smith, 1997). Their reappearance as juvenile delinquents suggests that the earlier interventions of the child welfare system were not successful in reversing the negative effects of their maltreatment.

Jonson-Reid and Barth (2000) conducted an exploratory study of the school-age children who had been in the California child abuse and neglect foster care system to determine their rate of entry into the California juvenile justice system. A sample of approximately 79,139 children who had been in foster care during the period 1970 to 1984 was drawn. Only 0.75 percent, or 590, of these children later entered state juvenile justice services. However, the significant findings regarding these children are informative with respect to improvements in foster care policy and service delivery. Children most likely to enter the juvenile justice system had been

- reunited with their families following their first entry into foster care;
- had spent more time in reunification than in foster care;
- had multiple foster care entries; and
- had their first foster care entry between the ages of 11 and 14 years.

In addition, African American and Hispanic children who were reunited with their families were more likely to enter juvenile justice services than were white children (Jonson-Reid & Barth, 2000).

Jonson-Reid and Barth (2000) state

> Reunification rates are considered a positive indicator of child welfare agency performance. . . . If certain home and neighborhood environments are not conducive to healthy development, however, then policy makers and practitioners must weigh these factors in the prioritization of the best interests of the child. (p. 512)

Perhaps the conclusion is not to question the value of reunification as a policy preference, but to address the intensity of after-care services for families reuniting after foster care, particularly those with adolescent children, as well as comprehensive community development services to remove the challenges in the communities where these families must live. Irrespective, these findings do suggest that we need to explore the nature of services provided to early adolescents during foster care placement in particular.

Juvenile Offender Categories

Juvenile delinquency policy and practice addresses two distinctly different categories of juvenile offenders: the juvenile who commits an act that violates a criminal statute, and the juvenile who commits an act that violates a law or ordinance designed to regulate his or her behavior because of his or her age or status.

Within the first category of delinquents, those who commit violations of criminal statutes, there are two subgroups. The first are those who commit violent crimes, including murder, forcible rape, robbery, and aggravated assault. These are the juvenile offenses that receive the most media attention and public discussion. Yet these offenses accounted for less than 5 percent of all juvenile offenses reported in 1999. For example, the total number of violent crimes by juveniles reported (103,900) was much less than the number of juvenile runaways (150,700) (Synder, 2000). In spite of the relatively small number of violent juvenile offenders, the failure of the juvenile justice system to effectively address them sparked the "adult crime–adult time" movement, which holds that the juvenile who commits certain categories of offenses should be tried and sentenced as an adult.

The second subgroup of delinquents who commit violations of criminal statutes, are minors whose offenses include property crimes such as burglary, larceny-theft, motor vehicle theft, arson, receiving or possessing stolen property, embezzlement, fraud, drug manufacture, possession, or sale, and the nonviolent personal crimes such as sexual offenses and nonaggravated assault.

Within the second category of delinquents are those who commit acts that are deemed status offenses, such as truancy from home, truancy from school, failure to obey the reasonable commands of the parent or guardian, and violating curfew. In some states, these juveniles are called children in need of supervision, persons in need of services, status offenders, or wayward minors. A status offense is an act that is an offense only when committed by a juvenile. A continuing controversy among policy makers is whether status offenders should be removed from juvenile court jurisdiction and their problems dealt with by noncoercive, community-based services. Those who hold this view are concerned that the traditional responsibility of the family to control children's misbehavior is being seriously weakened by a too-ready transfer of responsibility to bureaucratic discretion. There is also concern that the juvenile justice system is being forced to treat delinquents and status offenders alike, without distinction for their different statuses, in an increasingly adversarial and bureaucratic context (Howell, 1997).

This chapter explores the historical development of a separate system of justice for juveniles, the current trend toward treating juveniles who commit the more serious offenses in the adult criminal system, the risk factors for delinquency, and the range of prevention and treatment strategies used to address the multiple problems of juvenile delinquents and their families.

Scope of the Problem

The data inform us that, in spite of negative publicity, relatively few children come before the juvenile court. Of the 24 million youths aged 10 through 17 in the United States in 1999, only 2.5 million, or less than 10 percent, were arrested for delinquent acts, including status offenses. Violent crimes (murder, forcible rape, robbery, and aggravated assault) accounted for 4 percent of all juvenile arrests. The ages of youths at the time of arrest for all crimes were as follows: 23 percent were 17 years of age, 68 percent were 13 through 16 years of age, and 9 percent were less than 13 years of age. The racial composition was 69 percent white, 28 percent black, 1 percent Native American, and 2 percent Asian. Males make up about 73 percent of all delinquency arrests (Snyder, 2000).

Butts (1997) completed an analysis of the arrests and juvenile court dispositions for crimes committed by juveniles under the age of 15 years in response to the perception that younger juveniles are committing more serious offenses and in increasing numbers. This perception is, in part, the basis for the push to lower the age at which juveniles can be tried as adults and for more serious punishment for juvenile offenders. They concluded:

> This study suggests that today's serious and violent juvenile offenders are not significantly younger than those of 10 or 15 years ago. Yet many juvenile justice professionals, as well as the public, would assert the opposite. What explains this discrepancy? The authors of this study believe several factors are at work.
>
> First, overall growth in the number of violent juvenile offenders has drawn increased attention to the problem of young offenders in general. . . . Second, the nature of delinquency cases involving juveniles age 12 or younger has changed. Person offenses, which once constituted 16% of the total court cases for this age group, now constitute 25%. . . . Third, delinquency caseloads have doubled nationwide since 1970. . . . Fourth, justice professionals tend to accumulate memories of exceptional cases. . . . Finally, the news media have increased their reporting of crime, especially violent crimes by the very young. . . . The

growing publicity about these cases may suggest to the public that they are occurring more frequently, even if juvenile crime trends indicate otherwise. (1997, p. 11)

A National Center on Juvenile Justice study found that female arrests had increased by 50 percent and juvenile court cases involving females had increased by 54 percent between 1986 and 1995. Once in the juvenile court system, cases involving females were more likely to receive probation than those involving males charged with the same offenses (Poe-Yamagata & Butts, 1996). Between 1995 and 1999, female arrests decreased by 9 percent (Snyder, 2000).

The Office of Juvenile Justice and Delinquency Prevention is the best source of data on juvenile crime. Its most recent comprehensive report, *Juvenile Offenders and Victims: 1997 Update on Violence* (1997), provides the following trend data:

- "The juvenile crime arrest rate declined in 1995 following a ten-year period of constant increases." (p. 18)
- "The number of juvenile murderers increased steadily from 1984 through 1994 and dropped by 17 percent in 1995." (p. 13)
- "The juvenile murderer was likely to be co-defendant with an adult in 32 percent of the murders." (p. 12)
- "The victims of juvenile murderers were predominately family members and acquaintances (64 percent) as opposed to strangers (36 percent)." (p. 12)
- "Juvenile murderers used a gun in 79 percent of all murders." (p. 12)
- "The issue of school-related crime is growing in significance—10 percent of high school students completing the 1995 Youth Risk Behavior Survey stated that they had carried a gun, knife, or club to school within the last thirty days; 8 percent reported that they had been threatened or injured at school by a student using a weapon, and 5 percent stated that they had not gone to school because they were afraid either at school or traveling between home and school." (pp. 14–15)
- "Official records indicate that there are more chronic (defined as four or more juvenile justice system referrals) offenders and that they are proportionately responsible for more of the juvenile offenses." (p. 25)
- "Fifty-seven percent of all juvenile crimes are committed on school days." (p. 26)

Regarding the processing of juvenile cases, the report found that:

juveniles in all states can be tried as adults in criminal courts. The states vary as to the procedure used to effect these transfers—judicial waiver; prosecutor discretion or legislative exclusion covers the categories. In juvenile waiver states, the juvenile court must decide to transfer the case to the criminal court. In prosecutor discretion states, the prosecutor chooses to file in juvenile or criminal court. In legislative exclusion states, the state statute specifically identifies the offense categories that are excluded from juvenile court jurisdiction. (p. 29)

There has been a trend toward increasing the proportion of cases waived to adult court. The Office of Juvenile Justice and Delinquency Prevention reports an estimated 7,500 cases were waived in 1999 (Puzzanchera, Stahl, Finnegan, Tierney, & Snyder, 2002). This number does not represent the total number of juveniles prosecuted in the adult system. Those filed in the adult system under prosecutorial discretion or legislative exclusion are not included in this count. There are no reliable data sources for these cases.

In 1994, according to Butts (1997), of the 15 million cases handled by the juvenile courts, 55 percent were processed by formal petition in juvenile court, with 33 percent of those handled by waiver of jurisdiction to the criminal court. It is important to note that the data are not conclusive, but are estimates based on information supplied by 1,800 jurisdictions to the National Juvenile Court Data Archive. These reporting jurisdictions represent 67 percent of the juvenile population. These figures support some policy and practice perspectives and not others.

Historical Development of Juvenile Delinquency Services

From Adult Criminal Court to Juvenile Court

Historically, juveniles over the age of 7 years—the age recognized under common law as the age at which one could form criminal intent—who committed crimes enjoyed no special privileges due to their age. They were arrested, detained, tried, and sentenced in the same manner as an adult would be for the same crime. The Society for the Reformation of Juvenile Delinquents (the Society), organized in 1823, called for removing juveniles from adult jails. Their organizers saw this removal as a way to save these youth from the negative influences of adult criminals. Their basic belief was that prisons did not reform adult criminals, and by exposing juvenile offenders to adult criminals, the juveniles would most likely develop into better criminals (Finestone, 1976).

In 1825, the Society opened the New York House of Refuge, designed to provide an environment that would ensure the positive development of youth by focusing on meeting their basic needs, instilling in them the value of work, providing education, and overseeing their moral development. Finestone (1976) commented, "So certain were its founders of the righteousness of their mission that they showed little concern with the civil rights of the children they institutionalized: admissions included homeless children and convicted juvenile offenders indiscriminately" (p. 7).

Nonetheless, this movement caught on and spread throughout the United States (Dean & Reppucci, 1974). During the period from 1825 until the founding of the juvenile court system at the end of the century, these reform, industrial, or training schools (as they were known in various localities) continued to increase in number. Unfortunately they became sources of constant scandals rather than the incubators of positive youth development as first envisioned. They were overcrowded, used excessive disciplinary methods, experienced significant violence, and provided a custodial rather than a treatment environment (Howell, 1997).

Charles Lording Brace at the New York Children's Aid Society challenged the institutionalization of children and youth in reform schools. He promoted relocating children from the inner cities to families in the Midwest and West. (See Chapter 9.) Concurrently, Jane Addams, Julia Lathrop, and Lucy Flower were undertaking a movement in Chicago to establish settlement houses to address the impact of increasing urbanization and poverty on families and children. They chose to work with the family and child within the neighborhood. Both initiatives focused on helping the child develop within the context of a family environment rather than an institutional one.

Out of this grew the interest of the Chicago Women's Club in improving the conditions of juveniles who were institutionalized. Their work resulted in the establishment of the first juvenile court. Their vision was that this court would treat those who committed delinquent acts as children in need of firm direction and support, not as criminals deserving of punishment. The judge was given full discretion to determine what was the best course of intervention for the child, with the input of social workers and others. It is interesting to note that the Illinois statute, while precluding placing juveniles in adult prisons and providing for alternatives in dispositions such as family placement and probation, did not preclude placing them in the same reform schools that were the source of significant scandal at the time (Jacobs, 1997).

A complete discussion of the juvenile court's operation and the subsequent attacks on it is described in Chapter 6. The reader is reminded that the challenge to the juvenile courts' operations was that its "benevolence" often took precedence over the due process rights of the juvenile. These attacks on the juvenile court system operation emanated out of its informal, individualized handling of juvenile delinquency matters. Specifically, the U.S. Supreme Court decisions *In re Gault* and *Kent v. United States,* decided in 1966, marked the beginning of the juveniles' right to due process (Kramer, 2000). What had been designed as a benevolent system to handle child abuse, neglect, and delinquency and to protect children from the trauma of the adult legal system was found to be constitutionally deficient.

In the *Kent* case, the law of the District of Columbia provided that a person 16 years of age or older charged with an offense that would be a felony if committed by an adult could be waived to the adult court for trial after a full investigation by the juvenile judge. Kent, who was charged with robbery, rape, and breaking and entering, was waived. He challenged the waiver on the grounds that he was not afforded a hearing, no reasons for the waiver were provided to him, and his lawyer was denied access to his records. The Court held that under the due process clause, a juvenile was entitled to a hearing, full access to records and reports used by the court in arriving at its decision, and a statement of the reason for the juvenile court's decision (*Kent v. United States,* 1966).

Gault was a 15-year-old Arizona teenager charged with making a lewd telephone call to a neighbor. He was on probation at the time of the call. He was arrested without notification to his parents, detained, not provided counsel, and never afforded a formal hearing. He was found delinquent and committed to the state training school until the age of majority. He challenged the proceedings. The Court, in reversing the decision of the Arizona Supreme Court, established the due process requirements for juvenile delinquency hearings: (1) notice of sufficient detail to mount a defense; (2) right to be represented by counsel and, if necessary, right to court appointed and paid counsel if child and parents could not afford counsel; (3) privilege against self-incrimination; and (4) right to review evidence and cross-examine witnesses. Justice Fortas made two statements in this decision that challenged the basic foundation of the juvenile court system and signaled the scope of constitutional protections for juveniles

> . . . neither the Fourteenth Amendment nor the Bill of Rights is for adults alone. (*In re Gault,* 1967, p. 13);

and

> . . . juvenile court history has again demonstrated that unbridled discretion, however benevolently motivated, is frequently a poor substitute for principle and procedure. (Ibid., p. 18)

Subsequent U.S. Supreme Court decisions went on to place the rights of juveniles in the juvenile court system on par with the rights granted adults in the criminal system in most respects. The Court held that the standard of proof in a delinquency case is "beyond a reasonable doubt," the same standard required in adult criminal proceedings (*In re Winship,* 1970). It held that a transfer to adult court for prosecution after an adjudication of delinquency in the juvenile court violates the Fifth Amendment protection against double jeopardy (*Breed v. Jones,* 1975).

The Supreme Court has not required that the juvenile court operate like the adult criminal courts in all respects. It has supported variations in the treatment of juveniles in the juvenile court system. In *McKeiver v. Pennsylvania* (1971) it held that the fundamental fairness standard in fact-finding procedures for juvenile proceedings as developed by *Gault* and *Winship* did not require a jury trial. The 1984 *Schall v. Martin* decision, in which the Supreme Court upheld a New York statute that provided for pretrial detention, reflects the continuing balancing of juvenile rights and differential treatment provided by the juvenile courts. The Court stated

> There is no doubt that the Due Process Clause is applicable in juvenile proceedings. "The problem," we have stressed, "is to ascertain the precise impact of the due process requirement upon such proceedings. . . ." We have held that certain basic constitutional protections enjoyed by adults accused of crimes also apply to juveniles. . . . But the Constitution does not mandate elimination of all differences in the treatment of juveniles. . . . The State has "a *parens patriae* interest in preserving and promoting the welfare of the child," . . . which makes a juvenile proceeding fundamentally different from an adult criminal trial. We have tried, therefore, to strike a balance—to respect the "informality" and "flexibility" that characterize juvenile proceedings, . . . , and yet ensure that such proceedings comport with the "fundamental fairness" demanded by the Due Process Clause. (*Schall v. Martin,* 1984, p. 263)

In summary, then, for juveniles charged with delinquent or criminal offenses, the Court has clearly established that they must be afforded due process rights equal to those afforded adults and that the states can, provided the fundamental fairness tests are met, maintain some flexibility and informality in its juvenile court processes to ensure the benevolent treatment of juveniles.

Federal Government Leadership

The federal government began an active involvement in juvenile justice policy in the 1960s. As is the norm, it established policies and influenced state action, acceptance, and implementation of these policies by linking federal funding to adoption and implementation of the federal policies.

The White House Conference on Children and Youth of 1960 was followed by the 1961 establishment of the Crime Committee on Juvenile Delinquency and Youth Crime. The Crime Committee combined the efforts of several federal departments to focus on delinquency prevention projects. The Juvenile Delinquency and Youth Offenses Control Act of 1961 funded demonstration projects for delinquency prevention.

The Juvenile Delinquency Prevention and Control Act of 1968, which was renamed the Juvenile Delinquency Prevention Act in 1971, provided federal support to states for delinquency services.

In 1974, the Juvenile Justice and Delinquency Prevention Act (JJDPA) signaled the beginning of a new era in juvenile justice policy reform at the federal level. This act was the result of several reports articulating juvenile court failures, namely lack of due process for juveniles before the court, crowded training schools, excessive use of detention of children in jails, increasing juvenile crime rates, and ineffective interventions (Empey & Stafford, 1991). The act called for, among other things, diversion of minor offenders from the juvenile court, separation of juvenile offenders from adult offenders in detention, the removal of status offenders from secure detention facilities and the establishment of non-secure alternatives for them, and the establishment of the Office of Juvenile Justice and Delinquency Prevention (OJJDP). The act was especially significant in that it required compliance with these provisions as a condition for states to receive federal funding (Howell, 1997, p. 33).

Over the course of the twenty-nine years since its initial passage, the act has been amended several times. These amendments have provided exceptions to some of the original mandates and expanded others. For example, the adult–juvenile separation mandate progressed from total sight and sound separation to total removal of juveniles from adult jails to delineation of specific instances in which juveniles can be detained with adults. Additionally, status offenders can be ordered into secure facilities if there is sufficient evidence to show that they have violated a court order and secure detention is found to be the only way to contain them. This option can be used for a limited period of time. The 1988 amendment called for states to pursue reductions in the disproportionate representation of minorities in the system. This provision was made a mandate in 1992 (Howell, 1997).

Monitoring reports suggest that all eligible states and territories are participating, with fifty-five of the fifty-seven governmental bodies in full compliance with the mandates. Howell (1997) states, "These accomplishments are unprecedented in the history of federal social legislation. . . . Excepting the creation of reform schools and juvenile courts, these are the most significant changes in the history of juvenile justice in the United States" (p. 38). The reasons he gives for this success are

- professionals and advocacy organizations joined together
- required infrastructure to monitor compliance at the state level
- prevention and intervention program focus
- Department of Justice legal support for compliance
- JJDP Act's promotion of progressive programming (pp. 39–41)

Back to the Criminal Court

Despite the successes of the Juvenile Justice and Delinquency Prevention Act and the Office of Juvenile and Delinquency Prevention in administering it, the juvenile justice system is being challenged with the "just deserts" or "adult crime–adult time" punishment approach. This approach rests on the assumption that the juvenile court system has not been effective in deterring juvenile crime nor correcting juvenile offenders' behaviors. Clearly the data support that conclusion and have been used by those who wish to eliminate the juvenile court system. According to the proposed reform, juveniles would be adjudicated by the criminal courts and incarcerated in adult prisons if the crimes were serious enough. Howell (1997) notes: "Once again, punishing the offense rather than the offender is the object of current crime policy" (p. 23).

Risk Factors for Delinquency

Many factors contribute to delinquency. Hawkins and Catalano (1992) have summarized the research findings from longitudinal studies that have identified risk factors within the community, the family, the school, and the individual that contribute to adolescent problem behaviors of substance abuse, delinquency, teenage pregnancy, school dropout, and violence. Figure 11.1 summarizes those risk factors and the adolescent problem behaviors likely to result from those risk factors.

FIGURE 11.1 Communities That Care: Risk Factors for Adolescent Problem Behaviors

Risk Factors	Adolescent Problem Behaviors				
	Substance Abuse	Delinquency	Teen Pregnancy	School Drop-Out	Violence
Community					
Availability of drugs	✔				
Availability of firearms		✔			✔
Community law and norms favorable toward drug use, firearms, and crime	✔	✔			✔
Media portrayals of violence					✔
Transitions and mobility	✔	✔		✔	
Low neighborhood attachment and community disorganization	✔	✔			✔
Extreme economic deprivation	✔	✔	✔	✔	✔
Family					
Family history of the problem behavior	✔	✔	✔	✔	✔
Family management problems	✔	✔	✔	✔	✔
Family conflict	✔	✔	✔	✔	✔
Favorable parental attitudes and involvement in the behavior	✔	✔			✔
School					
Early and persistent antisocial behavior	✔	✔	✔	✔	✔
Academic failure in elementary school	✔	✔	✔	✔	✔
Lack of commitment to school	✔	✔	✔	✔	✔
Individual/Peer					
Alienation and rebelliousness	✔	✔		✔	
Friends who engage in a problem behavior	✔	✔	✔	✔	✔
Favorable attitudes toward the problem behavior	✔	✔	✔	✔	
Early initiation of the problem behavior	✔	✔	✔	✔	✔
Constitutional factors	✔	✔			✔

This conceptualization of the risk factors of delinquency has influenced the development of a model of delinquency prevention and intervention called Communities That Care, which is being implemented in many communities. Essentially, the conceptualization and model suggest the following (Hawkins & Catalano, 1992; Howell, 1995):

- The greater the number of exposures to risks, the higher the likelihood of the juvenile engaging in the undesired behaviors.
- Because risks are found in multiple domains, multiple strategies must be used concurrently to reduce the risks.
- There is consistency in risk factors across races and cultures, although the levels of risk vary.
- Some common risk factors are predictive of the different problem behaviors, which indicates implementation of prevention strategies that can address multiple problems.
- Protective factors can reduce the impact of exposure to risk factors.
- Communities have a significant number of resources that can provide the protective factors.
- Communities must take charge of the prevention and intervention of juvenile delinquency by engagement in a strategic process that identifies the risks and resources within the community and targets intervention with specific programs that have been proven to be effective in reducing or eliminating the identified risks.

Juvenile Delinquency Prevention and Intervention Strategies

In the past fifteen years, the concepts of "graduated sanctions," "balanced and restorative justice," and "adult crime–adult time" have become the guiding philosophies in juvenile justice policy and practice. It is expected that they will remain so for the foreseeable future. All rest on the principle that juveniles should be held accountable for their antisocial or criminal behaviors. Shepherd (1999) states

> In sum, the trends of the past decade have all been in the direction of transforming the juvenile court from an institution that still resembled the rehabilitative model envisioned by the founders at the turn of the twentieth century into a criminalized institution that more closely resembled the adult criminal court disdained by the founders. (p. 599)

Graduated sanctions in juvenile justice means that a juvenile receives some "punishment" for each adjudicated offense. The nature and severity of the sanction is determined by the nature of the offense and the juvenile's offense history. For example, a juvenile with no prior juvenile offense record steals a CD and is adjudicated. An appropriate sanction would be to pay for the CD and apologize to the owner. Three months later, he steals another CD. An appropriate sanction would be to pay for the CD, apologize to the owner, and perform ten hours of community services. Another juvenile robs an elderly woman at gunpoint. This is his first offense. Given the nature of the offense and the vulnerability of the victim, an appropriate sanction would be more severe, such as detention until trial and, after adjudication, secure residential placement as well as supervised community services.

Balanced and restorative justice means that the juvenile is held accountable for his behavior and has a responsibility not only to repair the harm caused the victim through restitution but also to repair the harm caused the community through constructive community service. It encourages victim and community engagement in the rehabilitation process for the juvenile. The second offense sanction for stealing a CD in the earlier example and the first offense sanction for armed robbery in the example above are applications of balanced and restorative justice concepts.

Adult crime–adult time means that juveniles, of certain ages with reasoning capacities, who are convicted of committing violent offenses, differently defined in state statutes, should experience the same punishments that adults would experience for the same offenses. The assumption is that the offenses are so reprehensible and the success of the juvenile system in preventing future crimes by violent offenders so low, that protection of the community dictates severe punishment.

Practices developed under graduated sanctions and the balanced and restorative justice philosophies have provided an opportunity for the juvenile court and the juvenile justice system to demonstrate that rehabilitation and community protection can coexist. Shepherd (1999) states

> Since youth are developmentally different from each other, the correction of juvenile delinquents through services that are expressly designed to treat their behaviors and problems in an individualized fashion is best capable of preventing future offending. (p. 601)

Juvenile delinquency prevention and intervention strategies developed and implemented over the last thirty years with federal funding assistance include parenting training, early education, school behavior management, conflict resolution and violence prevention, mentoring, intensive family preservation services, gang prevention, recreation and leisure activities, vocational training, community services, policing strategies, out-of-home placement continuum, and incarceration. All of these strategies have been shown to be effective with some juveniles and not with others.

The three sections that follow present the research findings for the types of interventions that work to prevent and treat juvenile delinquency. The discussion is divided into prevention and early intervention strategies effective with status offenders, with nonchronic offenders, and with chronic or serious juvenile offenders. A chronic or serious offender is one who commits four or more crimes and/or who commits at least one violent offense (Butts, 1997).

Prevention and Intervention with Status Offenders

Status offenses are acts that are only an offense because of the juvenile's age; they would not be offenses if committed by an adult. Examples of status offenses are truancy from home, truancy from school, failure to obey the reasonable commands of the parent or guardian, violating curfew, and underaged drinking. In some states, juveniles who commit these acts are also classified as juvenile delinquents. In other states, these juveniles are called children in need of supervision, persons in need of services, status offenders, or wayward minors (Kramer, 2000). According to the U.S. Department of Justice, juvenile courts processed over 162,000 status offense cases in 1996 (Office of Juvenile Justice and Delinquency Prevention, 2000); about 28 percent of these involve underage drinking; about 20 percent relate to truancy; the remaining cases include "ungovernability" or incorrigibility (12 percent), runaway cases (16 percent), and other offenses such as curfew violations, smoking tobacco, and violations of court orders (18 percent). More than half of all status offenders are 15 or younger. Females accounted for 41 percent of status offense cases processed. Females were most likely to be charged with running away from home and truancy, whereas males were more likely to be charged with liquor offenses and incorrigibility. Black youth had higher case rates than white youth in all categories except liquor offenses.

Less than 4 percent of status offenders are held in secure detention facilities. For the most part, those in secure detention are placed there after a hearing in which it was determined that secure detention was necessary for the youth's safety until appropriate placement could be arranged (Sickmund, 2003).

A continuing controversy among policy makers is whether status offenders should be removed from juvenile court jurisdiction and their problems dealt with by noncoercive community-based services. "It has been urged that only juveniles whose acts would result in criminal prosecutions if they were adults be handled in the juvenile justice system and that status offenders should be kept from contact with the juvenile justice system and cared for by alternative agencies" (Simonsen, 1991, p. 449).

The issue of jurisdiction over status offenders is complicated by research findings on the question of whether status offenders are more similar to than different from delinquent youth. So far, the weight of evidence strongly suggests that youth tend to be concurrently involved in both delinquent and status offense behavior. Such findings imply that it is not possible at this time to differentiate involvement in status offenses from involvement in delinquency, at least in less serious delinquency. "There seem to be two major categories of illegal involvement . . . one is petty illegal behavior which includes status offenses and less serious delinquency, and the other is serious delinquency" (Weis, Sakumato, Sederstrom, & Seiss, 1980, p. 99; OJJDPS, 1997).

Such findings suggest that the juvenile justice system should treat the two categories of petty and serious offenders differently. Some recommend that jurisdiction over status offenders, as well as over less serious delinquents, should be restricted or perhaps abandoned. Appropriate dispositional decisions by the court and treatment alternatives in the community for status offenders and for less seriously delinquent youth may well be the same (Weis et al., 1980).

As the juvenile court approached its one hundredth anniversary, youth policy planners questioned whether any quasi-legal means of regulating childhood can take the place of the family as the primary source of nurture and support for the child. The juvenile justice system, many contend, has been vested with overwhelming and sometimes quite unrealistic expectations. Its institutional limitations must be acknowledged and efforts made to reeducate the public about the responsibilities the family and the community must accept, particularly in relation to children in need of supervision (Smith, Berkman, Fraser, & Sutton, 1980, p. 160; Schwartz & Orlando, 1991; Ayers, 1997).

For the most part, status offenders commit no offenses except against themselves. Their actions are often a response to neglect, abuse, alcohol and substance abuse, or other family dysfunctions, but they are treated as if they were guilty of some very serious wrongdoing. Some of them do come within the province of the delinquency system; however, their offense is more likely to be running away, truancy, substance abuse, or being ungovernable or incorrigible. Children who run away from home, foster homes, or residential placements, for the most part, can cite credible reasons. Some understand that their lives would be in danger if they did not run away. Many have been rejected by their families and thrown out of their homes. Unhappily, many have had bad experiences with social welfare agencies and other would-be helpers who wished to help but unwittingly made matters worse. In such cases, the activities of these children should be seen as urgent signals to look into the causes. For some advocates this suggests that the family or the child welfare agency is not the caring and supporting environment that others contend, and, in those situations in which the parental actions do not rise to the level of abuse or neglect under the statute, status offenders should have a quasi-legal system to protect children from the actions of their parents.

Arguments cited in support of removing status offenders from the legal system usually focus on the misapplication of judicial power and the injustice that often results when the punishment is out of proportion to the offense—for example, truancy or being on the streets after curfew. The proponents of policy change also cite the harm done to youths by the stigma of having participated in the judicial process. They maintain as well that the juvenile justice system clearly lacks the capability to resolve individual behavior problems typical of minors in need of supervision. On the other hand, juvenile court judges in many states strongly oppose the proposal to remove status offenders from their authority. In their view, there is no other system with any control power over the juvenile. Further, they cite the fact that over 52 percent of all status offender cases are brought to juvenile courts by parents or persons acting in *loco parentis* (NCJJ, 2000).

The status offender problem is persistent despite the efforts of the National Institute of Juvenile Justice and Delinquency Prevention (NIJJDP) and the various states to improve the handling of minors in need of supervision. An assessment by the NIJJDP of the current state of knowledge concerning status offenders found that they continue to be involved in a significant portion of juvenile arrests, intake and court procedures, and detention homes and other institutional placements. Wide variation in state status offense legislation exists, negating any assumption that decisions are being made on uniform principles and procedures. Dealing with noncriminal adolescent behavior is a significant issue in most states (Smith et al., 1980; Kramer, 1994; Jacobs, 1995, supp. 1997; Howell, 1997).

Figure 11.2 provides the dispositions for status offense cases referred to juvenile courts. The status offender is generally first treated as a nonchronic offender with respect to dispositional alternatives. However, a disproportionate number of status offenders receive detention or residential placement because of family refusal to have them in the home. Juveniles who have multiple status offenses—particularly those who run away from home or foster care placements, are truant from school, or are incorrigible—challenge current intervention

Of every 1,000 petitioned status offense cases handled in 1996, 308 resulted in formal probation and 72 resulted in residential placement following adjudication

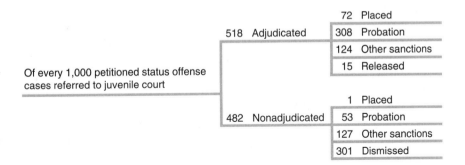

Of every 1,000 petitioned status offense cases referred to juvenile court

518 Adjudicated	72 Placed
	308 Probation
	124 Other sanctions
	15 Released

482 Nonadjudicated	1 Placed
	53 Probation
	127 Other sanctions
	301 Dismissed

1,000 petitioned runaway cases

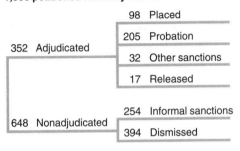

352 Adjudicated	98 Placed
	205 Probation
	32 Other sanctions
	17 Released

| 648 Nonadjudicated | 254 Informal sanctions |
| | 394 Dismissed |

1,000 petitioned truancy cases

569 Adjudicated	66 Placed
	423 Probation
	60 Other sanctions
	19 Released

| 431 Nonadjudicated | 96 Informal sanctions |
| | 335 Dismissed |

1,000 petitioned ungovernability cases

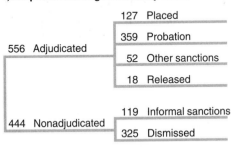

556 Adjudicated	127 Placed
	359 Probation
	52 Other sanctions
	18 Released

| 444 Nonadjudicated | 119 Informal sanctions |
| | 325 Dismissed |

1,000 petitioned liquor law violation cases

553 Adjudicated	38 Placed
	321 Probation
	185 Other sanctions
	10 Released

| 447 Nonadjudicated | 260 Informal sanctions |
| | 187 Dismissed |

FIGURE 11.2   Dispositions on Petitioned Status Offense Cases

Note: Cases are categorized by their most severe or restrictive sanction. Detail may not add to totals because of rounding.

Source: H. Snyder and M. Sicklund (2000), *Juvenile Offenders and Victims: 1999 National Report* (Washington, DC: Office of Juvenile Justice and Delinquency Prevention).

options. The future success of reducing the number of status offenders in the courts appears to lie with early intervention programs involving parents and children and early intervention with academic difficulties.

Prevention and Early Intervention
with Nonchronic Offenders

The objective of prevention and early intervention programs is to reduce risk factors, increase protective factors, and achieve prosocial behavior. While no intervention has proven to be completely successful with all children and youth, in the last twenty years, many programs have been implemented that are designed to reduce the number of youth who engage in delinquent behaviors and/or reduce the number of youth who have been adjudicated delinquent who commit subsequent offenses (recidivate). The prevention programs are aimed at populations identified as at-risk because of the presence of risk factors discussed above. Early intervention programs are aimed at children who have had a nonserious offense contact with the police or who have exhibited problem behaviors that, if not corrected, could lead to delinquent behaviors.

Parenting Programs.   Provide parents with developmental information, so that they are better able to direct the behaviors of their child and themselves in relation to the child. Most focus on both parent and child factors. For example, a program provides education and training for the mother's employment as well as information of developmental needs of the child and modeling parental approaches to problem behaviors. These programs have proven successful for general prevention in at-risk populations and with the nonchronic status offender and nonviolent offender.

Early Education Programs.   Academic achievement or lack thereof is a significant risk factor for problem behaviors. Early education programs focus on providing the child with a head start cognitively and socially. If children enter school ready to learn and knowing how to interact with others in a socially appropriate, nonaggressive way, they are more likely to succeed. These programs are targeted to at-risk populations.

Early Elementary School Programs.   Focus additional training on social development for children identified as at risk because they engage in antisocial behaviors. In addition, many school districts provide general health promotion instruction for all children to encourage positive development. Mentoring and after-school leisure and recreation programs are added interventions.

Middle and High School Programs.   Focus specifically on substance abuse education and alternatives; sex education; gang prevention; social conduct and peer relations, for example, peer mediation and counseling. Mentoring and after-school leisure and education programs continue in importance.

Specific Interventions.   Focus on juveniles who have committed nonserious offenses. They are designed to specifically address the underlying issues that precipitated the offense with the expectation of "turning the juvenile around." Interventions include mental health counseling, substance abuse treatment, teen issues groups focused on providing general awareness and alternative approaches, intensive family preservation services, placement outside the parental home if that environment is found to contribute to the youth's problem behaviors, remedial education, vocational training, and supported employment.

Intervention with Chronic or Serious Juvenile Offenders

As stated previously, although the number of chronic or serious juvenile offenders is relatively small, they have been and continue to be the focus of both the public's and the policy makers' discourse. In 1993, OJJDP proposed a graduated sanctions model to address this issue. Specifically, this model combines treatment and rehabilitation with reasonable, fair, humane, and appropriate sanctions, and offers a continuum of care consisting of diverse programs. The continuum includes the following:

- immediate sanctions within the community for first-time, nonviolent offenders
- intermediate sanctions within the community for more serious offenders
- secure care programs for the most violent offenders
- after-care programs that provide high levels of social control and treatment services (Howell, 1995)

In implementing the graduated sanctions philosophy over the last ten years, practitioners have focused on risk assessments and interventions based on the juvenile's likelihood to re-offend based on the risk assessments. It is too early in the process to provide conclusive statements as to the effectiveness of this approach. To support graduated sanctions philosophy, several new program interventions have been added to the traditional group homes or institutions/training schools. They include boot camps, wilderness/survival programs, intensive community supervision, work-study-home detention, and individual mentoring. These programs are designed to give immediately more severe consequences to the youth with the hope that the youth will see that all behaviors have consequences (graduated sanctions). Some commentators suggest that the system was out of control because juveniles did not see any immediate consequences for their behaviors and continued to escalate until they had to be incarcerated because of the nature of the offenses. If the behaviors receive progressively more severe consequences, then escalation might not occur (Torbet, 1996). The prevention and early intervention programs discussed earlier are critical to the continued decrease in the number of youth who commit serious or violent offenses because early antisocial behavior is generally documented in case histories of youth who commit these acts. Increasingly, interventions at the later childhood years are recognizing the need for multidimensional, integrated interventions instead of simply targeting the children and youth with school-based programs (Wasserman & Miller, 1998).

The Female Juvenile Offender

In previous editions of this book, we have addressed "gender issues" within the Trends and Issues section. In this edition, we decided to bring female juvenile offenders into the mainstream of our discussion of juvenile offenders. Clearly, the juvenile justice system remains male offender dominated. However, the concern of policy makers and practitioners is that females are experiencing much higher increases in arrest and adjudication than are males and females' proportion of arrests for serious, violent crimes is increasing. Between 1990 and 1999, males experienced a 5 percent decrease in arrests for aggravated assaults; females experienced a 57 percent increase. Males experienced a 7 percent decrease in arrests for weapon offenses; females experienced a 44 percent increase. Males experienced a 13 percent decrease in arrests for vandalism while females experienced a 28 percent increase. In other offense categories in which males and females trended in the same, females increased more or decreased less than males (Snyder, 2000, p. 4).

Females accounted for 27 percent of all juvenile arrests in 1999. Females accounted for

- 17 percent of arrests for murder, forcible rape, robbery, and aggravated assault
- 59 percent of arrests for running away
- 54 percent of arrests for prostitution and commercialized vice
- 48 percent of arrests for embezzlement
- 38 percent of arrests for offenses against family or children
- 37 percent of arrests for forgery and counterfeiting
- 36 percent of arrests for theft (Snyder, 2000, p. 2)

The research to date does not inform us as to why this trend has developed and continues (Sickmund, 2003). From these data, it is clear that female offenders are found within all categories of offenders: status offenders, nonchronic offenders, and serious or chronic offenders.

In the 1996 edition of this text, we stated that juvenile delinquency in the United States is largely a male phenomenon: "Males under the age of 18 account for the overwhelming majority of arrests, the bulk of the referrals to juvenile courts, and the largest proportion of young people in detention centers and training schools across the country." Nevertheless, large numbers of girls enter the juvenile justice system each year, and some are inappropriately sent into institutions because few if any community-based programs have been provided for delinquent females. For the most part, these girls have been confined because of relatively minor delinquent acts. Follow-up studies have not produced clear evidence that locking girls into institutions has been helpful to them in any clear way. Instead, it appears that "most young female offenders can be managed and treated in their own community without compromising public safety." Nevertheless, troubled and delinquent girls continue to be neglected amid policy-maker preoccupation and public concern about violent juvenile crime, primarily committed by male adolescents (Schwartz & Orlando, 1991).

In the 2000 edition of this text, we stated that a 1996 study by Poe-Yamagata and Butts, *Female Offenders in the Juvenile Justice System,* found that juvenile female arrests for violent crimes increased 131 percent compared to juvenile male arrests for violent crimes, which increased by 66 percent between 1986 and 1995. Furthermore, juvenile female arrests for property crimes increased 38 percent while juvenile male arrests for property crimes increased only 1 percent. With these increases, females accounted for 20 percent of the juvenile violent crime arrest growth and 89 percent of the growth in property crime arrests. Since that report was issued, NCJJ has issued these additional findings:

- 702,200 juvenile females were arrested in 1995.
- By 1995, the ratio of male to female arrests for violent crimes was 6 to 1 and for property crimes was 3 to 1, down from 8 to 1 and 4 to 1, respectively, in 1986.

- The female proportion of all juvenile court cases increased from 19 percent to 21 percent between 1985 and 1995.
- In 1994 delinquency cases involving females were less likely to be adjudicated once petitioned (52 percent versus 56 percent), and females whose cases were processed formally were more likely to receive probation and less likely to be in detention or out-of-home placement. (National Center for Juvenile Justice, 1997)

The potential for change is contained in the Juvenile Justice and Delinquency Prevention Act (JJDPA). Federal funds are available for developing alternative programs for juvenile offenders. The act states specifically that assistance must be made available to "all disadvantaged youth, including . . . females." Young female offenders have some special needs that, for the most part, are not addressed in the juvenile justice system. They are frequently victims of sexual abuse and can see only one way to safety—to run away. In such instances they soon learn that there is no safety for them on the street. Access to crisis intervention services, shelter care, day treatment, therapeutic foster care, independent living arrangements, and, not to be overlooked, access to continued education are much needed.

The 1992 reauthorization of the JJDPA required states to include

> An analysis of gender specific services for the prevention and treatment of juvenile delinquency, including the types of such services available and the need for such services for females; and a plan for providing needed gender-specific services for the prevention and treatment of juvenile delinquency.

The negative trending of female offender data, as well as the desire to assist states in meeting the requirements of the 1992 amendment to the JJDPA, led to a comprehensive report, *Juvenile Female Offenders: A Status of the States Report* (Maniglia, 1998). After a thorough review of national and state efforts, the author concludes

> When the entire range of services is available for young women and when each individual program is developed with the young women's critical needs in mind, the system is more likely to be able to provide appropriate and effective placements, no matter what a young woman's level of involvement. (p. 38)

The report identifies the following "elements of a female continuum":

1. *Prevention services:* including services such as prenatal care for pregnant women, early childhood education, family living skills, comprehensive health and sexuality information, education, career development and life skills, and parenting skills.
2. *Early intervention and diversion services:* including gender-specific counseling; education; substance abuse education and intervention if necessary; skills in assertiveness in handling everyday life challenges such as domestic violence and abuse; alternatives to family placement: shelters, group homes, respite residential placements; single gender support groups.
3. *Juvenile justice intervention services:* including all female treatment homes; specialized homes depending on her needs; staff-secure halfway houses or residential facilities

with range of intervention services for nonchronic, nonviolent offenders; secure facilities with range of intervention services for chronic or violent offenders; transition
services; after-care reintegration.

The report concludes

Although States have put forth a deliberate effort, the goal established by Congress to develop and adopt policies that prohibit gender bias and ensure that female youth have access
to a full range of services remains a challenge. Policymakers, service providers and juvenile
justice professionals have begun to realize the need for change in providing services to girls.
What is required now is the commitment to evaluating services that work and implementing
the necessary policies to warrant provision of effective programs for this too often ignored
population. (Ibid., p. 58)

Trends and Issues

Although the juvenile justice system has changed greatly since passage of the Juvenile Justice and Delinquency Prevention Act in 1974, the issues that have plagued it since the early
1970s continue to remain of concern. Specifically, the nation's provisions for juvenile offenders have not yet resolved the following issues: overrepresentation of minorities; alternatives to the use of secure detention; school violence; death penalty for juveniles; and the
community's readiness to support alternative programs. These concerns reflect the increasing severity of mental health and substance abuse problems of juvenile offenders.

Overrepresentation of Minorities

Overrepresentation means that a particular racial or ethnic group is represented in a greater
percentage in the juvenile justice system than it is represented in the general population. For
example, if black youth are 15 percent of the general youth population and they are 25 percent
of the juvenile justice system population, they are overrepresented in the juvenile justice system. However, if they were only 12 percent of the juvenile justice system population, they
would be underrepresented.

African American and Latino youth are overrepresented in every phase of the juvenile justice system. A recent study found that, compared to white youth who commit the
same type of offense, they are more likely to be arrested and less likely to be released while
awaiting trial. A Florida study found that "Florida courts were three times as likely to transfer an African-American or Native American charged with delinquency to adult court than
they were to transfer his or her white counterpart. The impact on African Americans was
particularly disproportionate, and they were far more likely to be sentenced to detention by
a juvenile court" (American Bar Association, 1993, p. 62).

As stated previously, a 1992 amendment to the Juvenile Justice and Delinquency Prevention Act requires states to reduce the number of minority youth in detention, but the federal government has not enforced this provision in the law. The ABA Presidential Working
Group on the Unmet Legal Needs of Children and Their Families (American Bar Association, 1993) recommended that communities develop culturally sensitive training for police

and judges and increase the representation of minority staff at the juvenile court. They also recommended that effective grievance procedures be instituted for situations in which the police use excessive force or other situations relating to ethnic, racial, or gender bias.

In 2000, the Office of Juvenile Justice and Delinquency Prevention reported that African American juveniles, who comprised 15 percent of the juvenile population in 1996, accounted for 28 percent of all juvenile arrests; 58 percent of murder arrests; 45 percent of forcible rape arrests; 60 percent of robbery arrests; 42 percent of aggravated assault arrests; 38 percent of motor vehicle theft arrests; 42 percent of fraud arrests; and 77 percent of gambling arrests. Additionally minority youth, including African Americans, Hispanics, Asian/ Pacific Islanders, and Native Americans, who were 32 percent of the youth population in 1996, made up 68 percent of the detention center population on the day in time chosen. Further, they represented 68 percent of the juveniles in public long-term facilities (Snyder & Sickmund, 2000).

Despite addressing this concern for over twenty years, we cannot provide a definitive explanation. Research to date has presented inconsistent findings. Since 1970, research has focused on the effects of race, race and gender, and race and family status on decisions at all stages of the juvenile justice system. The findings have been inconsistent (Leiber & Mack, 2003, p. 35). Recent data analyses and studies show that blacks' overrepresentation in the juvenile justice system was greater in 1996 than in 1987. Overrepresentation occurs at all stages of the juvenile justice system: referrals to juvenile court, detention, adjudication, probation, and residential placement (Snyder & Sickmund, 2000).

Leiber (2002) conducted an analysis of state and federal efforts based on compliance reports submitted to OJJDP. He concluded that OJJDP's weak enforcement of the 1992 JJDPA requirement that the states reduce disproportionate minority youth confinement (DMC) and its lack of direction to the states produced identification and assessment reports fraught with weaknesses and incapable of generalization. Within the last two years, OJJDP has taken a more active role and Leiber (2002) submits,

> OJJDP has begun to address these deficiencies and the benefits of these efforts may result in a greater number of states becoming more committed to DMC and information to better inform strategies to reduce the disproportionate representation of minority youth in our juvenile justice system. (p. 6)

Leiber and Mack (2003) argue that race alone may not be the determining factor for overrepresentation of minority youth in the juvenile justice system. They suggest that race, gender, and family considerations must be evaluated in combination to discern the reason for the overrepresentation. Research studies had examined each of these variables independently; none had attempted to examine the interactional effects. Leiber and Mack (2003) took a random sample of cases in four Iowa jurisdictions over a twelve-year period, 1980 to 1991. They concluded, "Being African American interacts very little with gender and family status to influence juvenile justice outcomes . . ." (p. 58).

Alternatives to the Use of Secure Detention

Criteria established by the National Council on Crime and Delinquency for admission of children and youth into secure detention emphasize that detention should not be used "unless failure to do so would be likely to place the child or the community in danger" (Pappenfort & Young, 1980, p. 99). In all jurisdictions, courts are faced at times with children who, after arrest or some other form of intake, cannot be returned home. In such instances, secure detention is often misused. The reasons given in justification are numerous: (1) A child's psychiatric and neurological problems require attention, and no alternative to detention is available. (2) Neglected and dependent children are sometimes classified as children in need of supervision and detained, pointing up in another way the common characteristics of status offenders and other children before the court. (3) Some youth must be detained to prevent the chance of their committing a delinquent act or engaging in incorrigible behavior while awaiting adjudication. (4) Some children go into secure detention only because there is no other place for them to stay. (5) Some children who present little or no danger to themselves or the community go into detention so that they can be readily referred into services that otherwise would not be available to them (Pappenfort & Young, 1980).

Many jurisdictions are attempting to avoid inappropriate use of detention by developing strict criteria for its use, by reviewing early the detention decisions by a juvenile court judge, and by developing nonresidential and residential alternatives. Home detention is one such alternative. Youths are released to their parents to await court hearings with supervision by a youth worker attached to the court's probation department (Howell, 1997). Residential group homes also are used as alternatives to detention and are frequently directed toward runaway children, a type of status offender generally considered to be troublesome to deal with effectively. Another alternative to detention is found in some jurisdictions in which foster parents are paid an annual salary to make their homes available for youths on a short-term basis. The foster parent role is to provide care and supervision as well as companionship to troubled youth awaiting court hearings.

The Annie E. Casey Foundation supported the Juvenile Detention Alternatives Initiative in Sacramento County, California, Cook County, Illinois, and Multnomah County, Oregon, from 1993 through 1997. Two other sites, New York City and Milwaukee, Wisconsin, terminated involvement quite early in the project. The Initiative's objectives were to reduce unnecessary or inappropriate detentions; to minimize the number of youth who do reoffend pending adjudication or fail to appear for court hearings; to redirect public funds to reform strategies; and to improve conditions of confinement (Annie E. Casey Foundation, 2003). Preliminary results show that detention admissions dropped in all three counties until 1997, when they went up in all counties. Youth failure to appear at court hearings decreased and youth arrested again before trial remained the same. In addition, courts reduced their case processing times.

These results occurred by

- specifying the offenses for which detention would be required, typically the violent, person offenses, and those that would be subject to review using a risk assessment tool for alternative assignment. This was a necessary prerequisite to calm the anxieties of both the law enforcement/juvenile justice professionals as well as the community. Judge William Hibbler, presiding judge of Cook County Juvenile Court, said

    With everybody out there talking about how we need to lock more kids up, you don't want to go around wearing a button that says, "I'm for detention alternatives." You need an educational process to let people know that this is not a crazy idea. (Stanfield, 2000, p. 9)

- developing alternatives: including house arrest with electronic monitoring bracelets; day and evening reporting centers; graduated sanctions, that is, violate and automatically given detention; nonsecure foster and group home placements.
- developing comprehensive, collaborative approaches with law enforcement, education, mental health, and substance abuse programs.

Casey Foundation funding for the projects ended in 1999. All the projects were continued. The lessons learned from these projects have been shared with many other jurisdictions. It is expected that many more jurisdictions will see reductions in unnecessary and inappropriate detentions over the next five years. The repeat status offender is presenting ongoing challenges to alternatives to detention. Many jurisdictions are using an approach of warning them at disposition that they will be placed in detention if they absent themselves from home or community placement, fail to attend school, or use liquor or drugs. It is too early to determine whether this approach will reduce the number of repeat status offenders who are detained in secure facilities.

School Violence

Because of several high-profile cases, attention to school violence issues has increased tremendously. Fatal crimes against students occurring on school property, at school events, or going to and from school are relatively rare. During the 1998–1999 school year, 50 deaths occurred while the student (34) or adult (4) was at a school. Of these, 38 were murders, 9 were suicides, 1 was an accidental shooting, and 2 were killed by law enforcement officers, responding to the call for assistance. Theft, rape, sexual assault, robbery, aggravated assault, and assault crimes occurred at the rate of 101 per 1,000 students. In 1998, 58 percent of all crime at school was theft. All school-related crime indicators continue to decrease according to the data available. However, there are significant gaps in the data that must be addressed if we are to have a truly accurate statistical description of the scope of school and school-related violence (Small & Tetrick, 2001).

Pollack and Sundermann (2001), citing a 2000 report from the U.S. Department of Education and the U.S. Department of Justice, state: "Although some may perceive schools as dangerous, schools remain the safest place for a child to be" (p. 14). They suggest that creating safe schools includes having comprehensive prevention and intervention strategies; an emergency response plan; a positive, respectful environment; partnerships with law enforcement, mental health, and social services; and encouraging parental and community involvement. While the incidence of violence at schools or school-related events is comparatively small, schools are seen as a natural site to educate children in alternatives to violence.

Death Penalty for Juveniles

The Supreme Court of the United States has decided that the juvenile's age at the time of the offense is critical to whether the imposition of the death penalty violates the Eighth Amendment of the U.S. Constitution's cruel and unusual punishment protections. It has held that imposition of the death penalty on juveniles less than 16 years of age at the time of the offense violates the Constitution (*Thompson v. Oklahoma*, 1988). It also has held that imposition of the death penalty on juveniles who commit the offense when they are 16 or

17 years of age does not violate the Constitution (*Stanford v. Kentucky,* 1989; *In re Kevin Nigel Stanford,* 2002).

A total of 164 death sentences were imposed on juveniles between January 1, 1973, and October 31, 1998. Twelve juveniles have been executed. All those executed were legal adults within the statutory guidelines for the state where the offense occurred, that is, at least 17 years of age, at the time of their offenses. Their ages at the time of execution ranged from 24 years to 38 years. Six were white; five were black; and one was Hispanic. States where their capital offenses occurred were Texas (7), South Carolina (1), Virginia (1), Missouri (1), Louisiana (1), and Georgia (1). Of the juveniles sentenced to death, 82 had their sentences reversed. Of those who had had their death sentences reversed, 12 had them reinstated. One of those had his death sentence reversed and reinstated four times. As of October 31, 1998, 76 persons who committed death sentence crimes as juveniles were on death row. All were male. Approximately 62 percent were minorities (Snyder & Sickmund, 2000, pp. 211–212).

Thirty states and the federal system specify minimum ages for imposition of the death penalty. Twelve states specify age 16, four states specify age 17, and fourteen states and the federal system specify age 18. Eight states do not specify an age (Ibid., p. 212).

Community Readiness to Support Alternative Programs

The term *community-based* implies an intention to enable troubled youth to retain their ties to persons in the community, to move about and communicate freely within the community, and to experience some degree of acceptance from others in the community. Yet community residents often object to plans for alternative programs. Such proposals, especially for residential programs, often bring prompt and vigorous opposition on the assumption that the kind of youth served would be a danger to the surrounding neighborhood. Somewhat paradoxically, professional interests and federal guidelines that favor community-based alternatives came at a time when many citizens were expressing intense fear about delinquency and crime, and state legislatures were enacting more restrictive laws affecting the handling of law offenders generally. Those statements are as accurate today as when stated by citizens in 1996. There is some hope of community support, as evidenced by the expansion of diversion and early intervention programs for less serious offenders. But, as to the serious and chronic offender, community support for community-based alternatives does not exist (Howell, 1995, 1997).

Chapter Summary

This chapter has focused on juvenile delinquency. The chapter gives voice to juveniles involved in delinquency activities and discusses delinquency within the scope of child welfare and family services. Historically, U.S. society has addressed these youth separately from abused, neglected, and abandoned youth. Increasingly, society is seeing that they are the same or that some children in the same family carry abuse or neglect labels while others carry juvenile delinquent labels. If society is to develop effective child, family, and community interventions to prevent and treat child abuse, neglect, and delinquency, we must begin to look at children and families holistically.

The November, 2002, Amendments to the Juvenile Justice and Delinquency Prevention Act recognizes the interconnection between the child welfare and the juvenile justice systems. States are required to implement policies across systems to ensure sharing of case information necessary for treatment planning and services, and require case plans and review policies and procedures for federally funded (Title IV-E) delinquency cases similar to those required for abuse and neglect under Title IV-E.

This chapter provided an overview of the scope of the problem, the types of offenses committed by juveniles, the processing of juveniles in the juvenile court and criminal court systems, some persistent issues, and some promising interventions.

FOR STUDY AND DISCUSSION

1. Explain and evaluate the aims of the juvenile justice system. How do they differ from those of the adult corrections system?

2. Give arguments to support either the traditional benevolent-rehabilitative model of the juvenile court or a model based on constitutional guarantees of due process and legal justice.

3. Obtain a copy of the juvenile court act in your state or some other. Evaluate it in these terms:
   a. What is the expressed intent of the act? How well does this intent reflect a modern juvenile court philosophy?
   b. Compare its definitions of classes of children who come under its jurisdiction to the categories discussed in this chapter.

c. What indications are there in the statute that the child's and parent's constitutional rights shall be respected?
   d. How adequate are the act's provisions in regard to personnel and services of the court?

4. What are some of the principal differences between children and youth who are (a) neglected or abused, (b) delinquent, or (c) guilty of a status offense? What are some of their similarities?

5. How would you design an "ideal" juvenile delinquency program? What would be its features? Why? How could stigma be averted?

6. Review the data discussed in the Scope of the Problem section. Is delinquent behavior as serious as the media projects? Explain your answer.

FOR ADDITIONAL STUDY

Behrman, R. E. (Ed.). (2002, Summer–Fall). *Children, youth and gun violence. The Future of Children, 12*(2).

Breckenridge, S., & Abbott, E. (1912). *The delinquent child and the home.* New York: Russell Sage Foundation.

Butt, J. A., & Harre, A. V. (1998). *Delinquents or criminals: Policy options for young offenders.* Washington, DC: The Urban Institute.

Fass, S. M., & Pi, C. (2002). Getting tough on juvenile crime: an analysis of costs and benefits. *Journal of Research In Crime and Delinquency, 39*(4), 363–399. Thousand Oaks, CA: Sage.

Gottfredson, D. M. (Ed.). (2000). *Juvenile justice with eyes wide open: methods for improving information for juvenile justice.* Pittsburgh, PA: National Center for Juvenile Justice.

Heide, M. (1999). *Young Killers—The challenge of juvenile homicide.* Thousand Oaks, CA: Sage.

Humm, S. R., Ort, B. A., Anbari, M. M., Lader, W. S., & Biel, W. S. (1994). *Child, parent, and state: Law and policy reader.* Philadelphia: Temple University Press.

Kelly, B. T., Huizinga, D., Thornberry, T. P., & Loeber, R. (1997, June). *Epidemiology of serious violence.* Washington, DC: Office of Juvenile Justice and Delinquency Prevention.

Loeber, R., & Farrington, D. P. (Eds.). (1998). *Serious and violent offenders: Risk factors and successful interventions.* Thousand Oaks, CA: Sage.

National Juvenile Court Data Archive, Juvenile Justice Clearinghouse, Rockville, MD.

Nelson, K. E. (1990). Family based services for juvenile offenders. *Children and Youth Services Review, 12*(3), 193–212.

Office of Juvenile Justice and Delinquency Prevention. (1996). *Creating safe and drug free schools: an action guide.* Washington, DC: U.S. Department of Justice, Office of Juvenile Justice Programs, Office of Juvenile Justice and Delinquency Prevention.

Office of Juvenile Justice and Delinquency Prevention. (1998). *Guide for implementing the balanced and restorative justice model.* Washington, DC: U.S. Department of Justice, Office of Juvenile Justice Programs, Office of Juvenile Justice and Delinquency Prevention.

Office of Juvenile Justice and Delinquency Prevention. (1999). *Promising strategies to reduce gun violence.* Washington, DC: U.S. Department of Justice, Office of Juvenile Justice Programs, Office of Juvenile Justice and Delinquency Prevention.

Office of Juvenile Justice and Delinquency Prevention. (2000a). *The incredible years training series.* Washington, DC: U.S. Department of Justice, Office of Juvenile Justice Programs, Office of Juvenile Justice and Delinquency Prevention.

Office of Juvenile Justice and Delinquency Prevention. (2000b). *Second chances; giving kids a chance to make a better choice.* Washington, DC: U.S. Department of Justice, Office of Juvenile Justice Programs, Office of Juvenile Justice and Delinquency Prevention.

Office of Juvenile Justice and Delinquency Prevention. (2000c). *From the courthouse to the schoolhouse: making successful transitions.* Washington, DC: U.S. Department of Justice, Office of Juvenile Justice Programs, Office of Juvenile Justice and Delinquency Prevention.

Office of Juvenile Justice and Delinquency Prevention. (2001). *Blueprints for violence prevention.* Washington, DC: U.S. Department of Justice, Office of Juvenile Justice Programs, Office of Juvenile Justice and Delinquency Prevention.

Scalia, J. (1997, January). *Juvenile delinquents in the federal criminal justice system.* Washington, DC: Office of Juvenile Justice and Delinquency Prevention.

Szymanski, L. (1999). Parental responsibility for the delinquent acts of their children. *NCJJ Snapshots 4*(7). Pittsburgh, PA: National Center for Juvenile Justice.

Szymanski, L. (2001). Parental support obligation of institutionalized delinquents. *NCJJ Snapshots 6*(5). Pittsburgh, PA: National Center for Juvenile Justice.

U.S. Department of Education and U.S. Department of Justice. (2000). *2000 annual report on school safety.* Washington, DC: Authors.

Urban Health Initiative. (2000). Safe Passages targets middle schools to reduce violence. *Helping Communities Work Smarter for Kids Fall 2000 Newsletter:* Seattle, WA: Urban Health Initiative.

INTERNET SEARCH TERM

Juvenile justice

INTERNET SITES

These Internet sites offer a broad range of legal, statistical, program, and policy information.

American Bar Association Juvenile Justice Center.
www.abanet.org

National Center for Juvenile Justice.
www.ncjj.org

National Council of Juvenile and Family Court Judges, Inc.
www.ncjfcjunr.edu

Office of Juvenile Justice Delinquency Prevention.
www.ncjrs.org/ojjhome.html

U.S. Department of Justice, Bureau of Justice Statistics.
www.ojp.usdoj.gov/bjs

REFERENCES

American Bar Association. (1993). *Unmet legal needs of children and their families.* Chicago: American Bar Association.

Annie E. Casey Foundation. (2003). *Juvenile detention initiatives.* Available: www.aecf.org/programs.

Ayers, W. (1997). *A kind and just parent: The children of the juvenile court.* Boston: Beacon Press.

Bazemore, G. (2001). Young people, trouble, and crime: Restorative justice as a normative theory of informal social control and social support. *Youth and Society, 33*(2), 199–226. Thousand Oaks, CA: Sage.

Breed v. Jones, 421 U.S. 519 (1975).

Butts, J., & Mears, D. P. (2001). Reviving juvenile justice in a get-tough era. *Youth and Society, 33*(2), 169–198. Thousand Oaks, CA: Sage.

Butts, J. A. (1997, April). Prosecuting juveniles in criminal court. *National Center for Juvenile Justice in brief vol. 1* (No. 4). Pittsburgh, PA: National Center for Juvenile Justice.

Dean, C. W., & Reppucci, N. D. (1974). Juvenile correctional institutions. In D. Glasser (Ed.), *Handbook of criminology* (pp. 865–894). Chicago: Rand-McNally.

Empey, L. T., & Stafford, M. C. (1991). *American delinquency: Its meaning and construction* (3rd ed.). Belmont, CA: Wadsworth.

Finestone, H. (1976). *Victims of change.* Westport, CT: Greenwood.

Flexner, B., & Baldwin, R. N. (1914). *Juvenile courts and probation.* New York: Century.

Flowers, R. B. (2002). *Kids who commit adult crimes.* Binghamton, NY: Haworth.

Hawkins, J. D., & Catalano, R. F. (1992). *Communities that care.* San Francisco: Jossey-Bass.

Heck, R. O., Pindur, W., & Wells, D. K. (1985). The juvenile serious habitual offender/drug involved program: A means to implement recommendations of the National Council of Juvenile and Family Court Judges. *Juvenile and Family Court Journal, 36,* 27–37.

Heide, K. M. (1999). *Young killers: The challenge of juvenile homicide.* Thousand Oaks, CA: Sage.

Howell, J. C. (1995). *Guide for implementing the comprehensive strategy for serious, violent, and chronic juvenile offenders.* Washington, DC: Office of Juvenile Justice and Delinquency Prevention.

Howell, J. C. (1997). *Juvenile justice and youth policy.* Thousand Oaks, CA: Sage.

In re Gault, 387 U.S. 1 (1967).

In re Kevin Nigel Stanford, 537 U.S. _____ (2002).

In re Winship, 397 U.S. 358 (1970).

Jacobs, T. A. (1995, supp. 1997). *Children and the law: Rights and obligations.* St. Paul, MN: West.

Jonson-Reid, M., & Barth, R. P. (2000). From placement to prison: The path to adolescent incarceration from child welfare supervised foster or group care. *Children and Youth Services Review, 22*(7), 493–516.

Kelley, B. T., Thornberry, T. P., & Smith, C. A. (1997, August). *In the wake of childhood maltreatment.* Washington, DC: Office of Juvenile Justice and Delinquency Prevention.

Kent v. United States, 383 U.S. 541 (1966).

Kramer, D. T. (1994, supp. 2000). *Legal rights of children* (2nd ed.). Colorado Springs: Shepards/McGraw Hill.

Leiber, M. J. (2002). State responses to disproportionate minority youth confinement. *The Prevention Report, 2002* (1). Iowa City, IA: The National Resource Center for Family Centered Practice.

Leiber, M. J., & Mack, K. Y. (2003). The individual and joint effects of race, gender, and family status on juvenile justice decision making. *Journal of Research in Crime and Delinquency, 40*(1), 34–70. Thousand Oaks, CA: Sage.

Loeber, R., & Farrington, D. P. (Eds.). (1998). *Serious and violent offenders: Risk factors and successful interventions.* Thousand Oaks, CA: Sage.

Maniglia, R. (1998). *Juvenile female offenders: A status of the states report.* Washington, DC: Office of Juvenile Justice and Delinquency Prevention.

McKeiver v. Pennsylvania, 403 U.S. 538 (1971).

Miner, M. H. (2002). Factors associated with recidivism in juveniles: an analysis of serious juvenile sex offenders. *Journal of Research in Crime and Delinquency, 39*(4), 421–436. Thousand Oaks, CA: Sage.

Muck, R., Zempolich, K. A., Titus, J. C., Fishman, M., Godley, M. D., & Schwebel, R. (2001). An overview of the effectiveness of adolescent substance abuse treatment models. *Youth and Society, 33*(2), 143–168. Thousand Oaks, CA: Sage.

National Center for Juvenile Justice. (2000). *NCJJ in brief.* Pittsburgh, PA: National Center for Juvenile Justice.

Office of Juvenile Justice and Delinquency Prevention. (1997). *Juvenile offenders and victims: 1997 update on violence: Statistics summary.* Pittsburgh, PA: National Center for Juvenile Justice.

Pappenfort, D. M., & Young, T. W. (1980, December). *Use of secure detention for juveniles and alternatives to its use: A national study of juvenile detention.* Office of Juvenile Justice and Delinquency Prevention. Washington, DC: U.S. Government Printing Office.

Poe-Yamagata, E. (1997, March). *Detention and delinquency cases, 1985–1995* (Office of Juvenile Justice and Delinquency Prevention Fact Sheet #56). Washington, DC: Office of Juvenile Justice and Delinquency Prevention.

Poe-Yamagata, E. (1997, February). Female participation in delinquent behavior is on the rise. *NCJJ in Brief, 1*(2). Pittsburgh, PA: National Center for Juvenile Justice.

Poe-Yamagata, E., & Butts, J. A. (1996). *Female offenders in the juvenile justice system.* Washington, DC: U.S. Department of Justice, Office of Juvenile Justice and Delinquency Prevention.

Pollack, I., & Sundermann, C. (2001). Creating safe schools: A comprehensive approach. *Juvenile Justice, 7*(1), 13–20.

Puzzanchera, C., Stahl, A., Finnegan, T., Tierney, N., & Snyder, H. (2002). *Juvenile court statistics 1999.* Washington, DC: Office of Juvenile Justice and Delinquency Prevention.

Saltzman, A., & Proch, K. (1990). *Law in social work practice.* Chicago: Nelson-Hall.

Schall v. Martin, 467 U.S. 253 (1984).

Schwartz, I., & Orlando, F. (1991). *Programming for young women in the juvenile justice system.* Ann Arbor: University of Michigan, Center for the Study of Youth Policy.

Shepherd, R. E., Jr. (1999). The child grows up: The juvenile justice system enters its second century. *Family Law Quarterly, 33*(3), 589–605.

Sickmund, M. (2003). *Juveniles in corrections.* Washington, DC: Office of Juvenile Justice and Delinquency Prevention.

Siegel, J. A., & Williams, L. M. (2003). The relationship between child sexual abuse and female delinquency and crime: A prospective study. *Journal of Research in Crime and Delinquency, 40*(1), 71–94.

Simonsen, C. (1991). *Status offenders: An attempt to clarify the system. Juvenile justice in America.* New York: Macmillan.

Small, M., & Tetrick, K. D. (2001). School violence: An overview. *Juvenile Justice, 7*(1), 3–12.

Smith, C. P., Berkman, D. J., Fraser, W. M., & Sutton, J. (1980). *Jurisdiction and the elusive status offender: A comparison of involvement in delinquent behavior and status offenses.* U.S. Department of Justice, Law Enforcement Assistance Administration, Office of Juvenile Justice and Delinquency Prevention. Washington, DC: U.S. Government Printing Office.

Snyder, H. N. (2000, December). *Juvenile arrests 1999.* Washington DC: Office of Juvenile Justice and Delinquency Prevention.

Snyder, H. N., & Sickmund, M. (2000). *Juvenile offenders and victims 1999 national report.* Washington, DC: Office of Juvenile Justice and Delinquency Prevention.

Stanfield, R. (2000). *Pathways to juvenile detention reform: The JDAI story: building a better juvenile detention system.* Baltimore, MD: Annie E. Casey Foundation. Available: www.aecf.org/publications/pdfs/pathways8.pdf.

Stanford v. Kentucky, 482 U.S. 361 (1989).

Thompson v. Oklahoma, 487 U.S. 815 (1988).

Torbet, Patricia, et al. (1996). *State responses to serious and violent juvenile crime.* Washington, DC: Office of Juvenile Justice and Delinquency Prevention.

Wasserman, G. A., & Miller, L. S. (1998). The prevention of serious and violent juvenile offending. In R. Loeber & D. P. Farrington (Eds.), *Serious and violent juvenile offenders: Risk factors and successful interventions.* Thousand Oaks, CA: Sage.

Weis, J. G., Sakumato, K., Sederstrom, J., & Seiss, C. (1980). *Reports of the national juvenile justice assessment centers: Jurisdiction and the elusive status offender: A comparison of involvement in delinquent behavior and status offenses.* U.S. Department of Justice, Law Enforcement Assistance Administration, Office of Juvenile Justice and Delinquency Prevention. Washington, DC: U.S. Government Printing Office.

12 Professional Responsibilities

Ethics and Advocacy

*Vision without action is merely a dream. Action without vision just passes the time.
Vision with action can change the world.*

—Joel Arthur Barker, *The Power of Vision*

CHAPTER OUTLINE

Case Example: Balancing Client Advocacy and Ethical Requirements

Susan Smith is a child welfare worker for the Big County Children's Services Agency (BCCSA). She has worked in child welfare for two years since receiving her MSW from Big State University. She has had approximately eight days of program-specific training and attended a one-day conference on permanency planning since employment. She is a member of the National Association of Social Workers (NASW). She began employment in BCCSA in the protective services program and moved into the foster care program approximately six months ago.

Last week Susan received the Blue case. There are three children, Mary (4 years old), Michael (2 years old), and Joseph (2 weeks old). The case came to protective services on a complaint from the hospital that Joseph was born drug addicted. The protective services worker recommended that a petition be filed and all children be removed from the home.

Susan's initial assessment, based on the materials in the files, was that the children should not have been removed from the home. The case file stated that the mother denied using cocaine on an ongoing basis. She stated that she went to a party about two weeks before Joseph's birth and smoked cocaine for the first time. Susan confronted the protective services worker in the staff lunchroom and they engaged in a loud, heated argument about their different assessments of the case. Her final statement to the protective services worker was "You are so ignorant! I'm going to bring this case to the attention of the administration. You ought to be fired."

Susan proceeded to tell her supervisor that this was the third case that she had received from this protective services worker. In all three cases, there had been inadequate documentation to justify a removal under the agency's policies. It appeared to her that this protective services worker and her supervisor did not accept the agency's family preservation policies and were intentionally harming children and families because of this bias. She stated that, in one of the cases, after she gave her testimony, the judge stated that BCCSA administration needed to "do something" with this worker and supervisor. She forgot to pass the information on to administration at the time.

Susan is concerned that other workers might not be as vigilant as she in defending families against the misjudgments of this worker. She wants administration to intervene so that no family has to suffer the trauma of separation due to worker bias, inadequate and incomplete investigations, and the general incompetence of the worker.

After this communication with her supervisor, Susan interviewed the mother. She told the mother that the file did not contain sufficient documentation to warrant removal of the children from the home. Susan told her that she wanted to work with her to get the children returned as soon as possible. To help her determine the approach to presenting her recommendation, Susan asked Ms. Blue to tell her everything she needed to know about the one instance of drug use. Ms. Blue stated that she had used cocaine during the entire pregnancy and that she had used cocaine for about three years. The downstairs neighbor would check on them several times a day and would take Mary and Michael to her flat when she found Ms. Blue too high to care for them. The neighbor had called protective services once when she did not come home for two days, but Ms. Blue arrived before protective services came out, and the neighbor had called protective services back and told them she made a mistake.

Ms. Blue had been in a substance abuse treatment program, but services were terminated because she had received the full thirty days of services for which she was eligible under Medicaid. Ms. Blue stated that she loved her children and that she knew it was stupid to continue to use cocaine while she was pregnant. She knew it was stupid to deny to the protective services worker that she was an ongoing user, but she did so because she knew the protective services worker was against her from the beginning.

Ms. Blue said she would like the children returned to her as soon as possible and she would do whatever Susan required because she felt Susan understood her. Susan became concerned and asked her to talk more about her drug use. As the story unfolded, Susan told Ms. Blue that she would have to reconsider her recommendation due to Ms. Blue's admissions of long-term and continuing drug use. Susan needed to discuss the matter with her supervisor. Ms. Blue became enraged that Susan would "worm her way into her confidence with false promises." She asked Susan to leave immediately.

Case Commentary

While Susan Smith seems to have the right credentials for child welfare practice—several years of child welfare experience, the appropriate advanced degree, membership in a professional organization, and some training—she has apparently had a lapse in judgment and then committed an ethical violation in the course of her work on the Blue case. One wonders why her credentials did not better prepare Susan in the area of sensitivity to ethical practice. The most obvious ethical violation was her public criticism of a colleague. But the lapse in judgment was potentially more problematic. Without having interviewed the new client, Susan decided, based only on materials in the file, that the children should not have been removed from the home. This placed her in the awkward position of appearing to promise to return the children from foster care soon. On discovering that the parent did have a long-standing history of substance abuse, Susan had to reevaluate her earlier position, which was now completely invalidated by her new knowledge.

In all likelihood Susan is a conscientious professional who would be shocked and upset to think that she had violated part of the NASW Code of Ethics and that she did not use sound professional judgment in her interactions with her client. If she is as busy as most foster care workers are, she may not even have time to reflect on her actions. Yet if she is to develop her professional potential, it is imperative that she understand the implications of her actions. Failure to do so could result in damaged relationships with clients, an ethics complaint, or even, at some point, litigation. Child welfare workers operate under difficult conditions. Many are not as well prepared as Susan.

This chapter addresses several issues that on the surface appear disparate: professional responsibility, liability and malpractice, confidentiality and privileges, forensic interviewing, risk management and duty to warn, the client's right to treatment in a managed care environment, testimony, and advocacy. The common thread is the social work profession's mission, ethics, and values. "The primary mission of the social work profession is to enhance human well-being and help meet the basic human needs of all people, with particular attention to the needs and empowerment of people who are vulnerable, oppressed, and living in poverty" (National Association of Social Workers, 1999, p. 1).

Child welfare practice presents many ethical dilemmas. These dilemmas result from the challenges of serving multiple clients—parents and children—in multiple organizational environments (public and private child welfare, mental health, substance abuse agencies, schools, hospitals, mental health facilities, and juvenile and family courts) subject to multiple legal and regulatory requirements that are not consistent and/or compatible. In previous chapters, we have discussed legal and regulatory issues. In this chapter, we raise and discuss several common dilemmas within the context of the NASW Code of Ethics (the Code). The Code is liberally cited and case examples are used to help you recognise some of the dilemmas and the alternate considerations. Reamer (1995) states "there is no precise formula available for resolving ethical dilemmas. Reasonable thoughtful social workers can disagree about the ethical principles and criteria that ought to guide ethical decisions in any given case" (p. 64). He suggests a seven-step process in resolving these dilemmas:

1. Identify the ethical issues and the conflicts.
2. Identify individuals, groups, and organizations who might be affected by the decision.
3. Identify all courses of action and benefits and harms to each party.
4. Examine the reasons supporting or negating a particular course of action.
5. Consult with supervisors, administrators, and attorneys.
6. Decide and document how you came to that decision.
7. Monitor impact of decision. (Ibid., pp. 64–65)

Professional Responsibility

Professional responsibility is an ominous term. It embraces the concept that a person who has attained the education and training necessary for entry into a profession has a responsibility to maintain the integrity of that profession. The integrity of the profession is maintained if its individual members are accountable to the general public for individual execution of the values and standards that the profession has established for itself or that have been established by various state statutes and regulatory schemes.

National Association of Social Workers Code of Ethics

The National Association of Social Workers (NASW) is the largest professional organization of social workers in the United States. It adopted its first code of ethics in 1960 (Reamer, 1995). There have been several revisions, the latest in 1999. Codes of ethics are adopted by professional organizations to establish norms and standards for the operation of the profession. If the professions themselves adopt these norms and standards, then it is less likely that outside administrative organizations will find the need to do so. In addition, these codes provide objective criteria for adjudicating misconduct (Reamer, 1995). Operationally, they are not as black and white as this might lead you to believe. The NASW Code of Ethics has been revised several times since its original adoption in 1960. Those revisions have occurred in response to developments in the profession and in the NASW. In this chapter, we use the latest revision, adopted in 1999.

The Code sets out the mission, values, ethical principles, and ethical standards for social work professionals in the United States. Other countries have different codes, which reflect the interplay of the social work profession within the context of their societies. The Code identifies six purposes to be served: to identify the core values of the profession; to provide a summary of the core values and standards to guide practice; to assist in resolving professional conflicts or ethical uncertainties; to provide notice to the general public of the expectations of the profession; to socialize new practitioners to the profession; and to give standards by which the profession can regulate itself (NASW, 1999).

The challenge to the professional is found in this statement:

> The Code offers a set of values, principles, and standards to guide decision making and conduct when ethical issues arise. It does not provide a set of rules that prescribe how social

workers should act in all situations. Specific application of the Code must take into account the context in which it is being considered and the possibility of conflicts among the Code's values, principles, and standards. (NASW, 1999, pp. 2–3)

Space does not permit us to discuss all the principles and standards stated in the Code. We discuss only those principles that raise ethical dilemmas for child welfare practitioners most often: that social workers should respect the inherent dignity and worth of the person; that social workers should recognize the central importance of human relationships; that social workers should behave in a trustworthy manner; that social workers should practice within their areas of competence, and develop and enhance their professional expertise; and that social workers should challenge social injustice.

It should be noted that the National Association of Social Workers has an established procedure for dealing with violations of the Code of Ethics—the Committee on Inquiry, a professional peer review process. When a request for review (formerly known as a complaint) is filed with a state chapter or the national office, it is screened to determine whether the issue involved would constitute an ethical violation if it had actually occurred. If so, the matter is reviewed by a Committee on Inquiry, which hears the requester or complainant and the social work respondent. There are a number of sanctions for social workers who have been found to have breached ethics, ranging from a recommendation by NASW for professional supervision to publication of the offense and suspension of membership. This process is used only for ethical violations—actions that go against the professional code of conduct—and is different from the legal process set in motion through the courts when a social worker has committed bad practice and violated professional standards of practice—malpractice.

Professional Malpractice and Liability

Malpractice is the failure to meet the standards of the profession in the provision of professional services. A person is held legally responsible for the consequences of his or her actions or inactions if the suing party has sufficient evidence to prove all of the following factors:

- The person against whom the suit is brought owed the suing party a duty.
- The person breached that duty.
- The person's breach was unreasonable—that is, a reasonable person of like education and training, under the same or similar circumstances, would not have acted in the same way.
- The suing person suffered injury or damages.
- The breach was the proximate cause of the injury or damages.

In child welfare practice, federal and state laws, administrative policies, rules, and regulations create duties, case decisions, and standards adopted by the profession. Previous chapters addressed the duties created in decisional and statutory law and administrative policies, rules, and regulations. Such issues as who can consent to entry into the home, interviewing children without parental permission, visual inspections of children's bodies, medical examinations without parental permission, failure to adequately monitor care provided in parental homes after abuse or neglect has been found, failure to adequately monitor care provided in foster homes and institutions, and failure to ensure permanency have been litigated. In this chapter we focus on the ethical duties created by the Code. The question becomes whether the social worker's behaviors were within the ethical standards of the profession.

The first section of the Code of Ethics addresses the ethical responsibility for competent practice. This may feel problematic to child welfare workers, who often feel overwhelmed by the responsibilities of being entrusted with decisions that can affect children's lives. Like Susan Smith in the case study at the beginning of this chapter, child welfare social workers may have the right credentials but still have difficulty learning the fine points of child welfare practice. Code Section 1.04 states

(a) Social workers should provide services and represent themselves as competent only within the boundaries of their education, training, license, certification, consultation received, supervised experience, or other relevant experience.

(b) Social workers should provide services in substantive areas or use intervention techniques or approaches that are new to them only after engaging in appropriate study, training, consultation, and supervision from people who are competent in those interventions or techniques.

(c) When generally recognized standards do not exist with respect to an emerging area of practice, social workers should exercise careful judgment and take responsible steps (including appropriate education, research, training, consultation, and supervision) to ensure the competency of their work and to protect clients from harm. (NASW, 1999, pp. 8–9)*

Section 4.01 states

(a) Social workers should accept responsibility or employment only on the basis of existing competence or the intention to acquire the necessary competence.

(b) Social workers should strive to become and remain proficient in professional practice and the performance of professional functions. Social workers should critically examine and keep current with emerging knowledge relevant to social work. Social workers should routinely review the professional literature and participate in continuing education relevant to social work practice and social work ethics.

(c) Social workers should base practice on recognized knowledge, including empirically based knowledge, relevant to social work and social work ethics. (NASW, 1999, p. 22)

Child welfare, as a field of practice, is one of the most complex in the field of social work. Its complexity lies in the multiplicity of the knowledge base and intervention techniques required, as well as the ever-changing public attitudes that translate into federal and state policies. Child welfare practitioners, as a whole, do not hold degrees in social work, yet are characterized as social workers or caseworkers in the minds of the general public. Those who have degrees in social work frequently are in need of supplemental education and training specific to child welfare practice. The demands on child welfare workers are such that frequently they lack the time to engage in the further education and training necessary. Thus the dilemma. See Figure 12.1 for specific activities of child welfare work that may raise liability issues.

*Copyright 1996, National Association of Social Workers, Inc.

FIGURE 12.1   Areas of Risk of Liability*

Activity	Level of Risk
Failure to report	Moderate
Failure to accept report for investigation	Moderate
Failure to adequately investigate report	Moderate**
Failure to remove child from home	High**
Failure to protect child once returned home	Moderate–High**
Wrongful reporting	Low
Defamation/slanderous investigation	Low
Negligent, overintrusive investigation	Low–Moderate
Malicious initiation of a child abuse or neglect proceeding	Low
Breach of confidentiality	Low
Wrongful removal	Moderate
Failure to adequately protect child from harm in foster care	High**
(e.g., due to inappropriate placement, inadequate supervision,	
failure to revoke license, etc.)	
Negligent diagnosis or treatment	Moderate
Sexual impropriety	Moderate
Failure to provide services leading to return of child	Moderate
Failure to warn of child's dangerousness	Moderate–High
Fraud (e.g., in adoptive placement)	Moderate

Source: American Bar Association (1991), *Liability in child welfare and protection work* (Washington, DC: Author). Reprinted by permission.

*This list was developed as a starting point for evaluating levels of risks nationwide. It is unlikely that it will reflect accurately the situation in a particular jurisdiction but serves instead as a model for the process of identification and evaluation of the risks of liability.

**The level of risk in federal court actions may be different.

Child welfare practice is, for the most part, an involuntary service. Even when there is no court intervention, the parents' general belief is that they must do what the worker and the agency expects or risk having their children removed from their custody. It is the rare parent who comes to a child protection agency requesting assistance. Many parents seek assistance from mental health agencies or juvenile or family courts when their children are exhibiting behavioral difficulties. Some receive this assistance and some do not or do not receive it in the manner necessary to resolve the difficulties. The latter group generally receives involuntary services through the abuse or neglect or delinquency systems. The involuntary nature of the system, coupled with the dual client problem, raises many ethical issues. Code Section 1.03 states

   (a) Social workers should provide services to clients only in the context of a professional relationship based, when appropriate, on valid informed consent. Social workers should use clear and understandable language to inform clients of the purpose of the services, risks related to the services, limits to services because of the requirements of a third-party payer, relevant costs, reasonable alternatives, clients' right to refuse or withdraw consent, and the time frame covered by the consent. Social workers should provide clients with an opportunity to ask questions. . . .

(b) . . .

(c) In instances when clients lack the capacity to provide informed consent, social workers should protect clients' interests by seeking permission from an appropriate third party, informing clients consistent with the clients' level of understanding. In such instances social workers should seek to ensure that the third party acts in a manner consistent with clients' wishes and interests. Social workers should take reasonable steps to enhance such clients' ability to give informed consent.

(d) In instances when the clients are receiving services involuntarily, social workers should provide information about the nature and extent of services and about the extent of clients' right to refuse service.

(e) . . .

(f) Social workers should obtain clients' informed consent before audiotaping or videotaping clients or permitting observation of services to clients by a third party. (NASW, 1999, pp. 7–8)

In general, children lack the capacity to give informed consent. In general, it is the role of the parent or guardian to give consent on behalf of the child. In child welfare practice, however, the interests of the parent and child may conflict. Should the social worker inform the parent that he or she will request court intervention in those situations in which, in the social worker's judgment, the parent's decision is not in the child's best interests? Should the social worker inform the parent that he or she will report statements made by the client to the court? What does the social worker tell the child client? Consider this case situation.

David, an autistic child with extremely self-injurious behaviors, has not been helped by a number of behavioral programs designed to control head banging and self-mutilation. An expert that the parents consulted independently recommends that the child be sent out of state to a private treatment setting that uses electric shocks as a deterrent to the behavior. This treatment center claims outstanding results in reduction of self-injurious behavior and maintenance of the non-self-injurious state, through an ongoing program of intermittent shocks when the child first begins to display the undesired behavior.

Understandably, the parents feel quite desperate. They have stated to you that their marriage is in jeopardy due to the stress from this child. The mother is not willing to have the child placed in group care or an institutional setting. The father is stating that his wife's constant preoccupation with David's needs is damaging the well-being of their other two children. Jenny, the younger sister, appears depressed. Donny, the eldest child, has been failing in school. Clearly the whole family is in a lot of pain. Their minister has counseled them to take the advice of the expert, who seems to be highly regarded within their denomination.

In order to be admitted to the program, the family must be recommended by their minister and by a child and family therapist. They plead with you to make the referral for them. They believe it is David's last chance, and the family's last chance to remain intact.

Confidentiality and Privileges

Confidentiality and *privilege* are frequently used interchangably, but they do not mean the same thing. *Confidentiality* refers to the statements made by a client with the expectation that they will not be shared with persons other than those to whom they are spoken unless the client authorizes otherwise. *Privilege* refers to confidential communications that are protected by statute from being disclosed in legal proceedings. The rationale for privilege statutes is that confidentiality is necessary to ensure and establish a trusting relationship so that the client divulges information necessary in the intervention process that he or she might not otherwise divulge if he or she thought the information might be passed on to someone else without her or his knowledge or consent (Gothard, 1995).

Child welfare communications may or may not be privileged, depending on individual state statutes and the specific evidence contained in the confidential communication. Even where states provide for social worker–client privilege, there are generally exceptions to absolute privilege—that is, disclosure only with client consent—that provide that confidential information can be disclosed by order of the court under certain circumstances delineated in the statutes. Remember that the confidence and the privilege belong to the client and not the professional. While the professional can state that the communication is confidential and/or privileged, the client is the one who must assert the privilege—that is, consent or not consent to the release of the information—and in the final analysis, the court will determine if it should overrule the client's decision not to consent.

You should review the privilege statute for the state(s) in which you are currently practicing or intend to practice.

The Code provides direction and dilemma on this issue. Section 1.07 states

(a) Social workers should respect clients' right to privacy. Social workers should not solicit private information from clients unless it is essential to providing services or conducting social work evaluation or research. Once private information is shared, standards of confidentiality apply.

(b) Social workers may disclose confidential information when appropriate with valid consent from a client or a person legally authorized to consent on behalf of a client.

(c) Social workers should protect the confidentiality of all information obtained in the course of professional service, except for compelling professional reasons. The general expectation that social workers will keep information confidential does not apply when disclosure is necessary to prevent serious, foreseeable, and imminent harm to a client or other identifiable person or when laws or regulations require disclosure without a client's consent. In all instances, social workers should disclose the least amount of confidential information necessary to achieve the desired purpose; only information that is directly relevant to the purpose for which the disclosure is made should be revealed.

(d) . . .

(e) Social workers should discuss with clients and other interested parties the nature of confidentiality and limitations of clients' right to confidentiality. Social workers should review with clients circumstances where confidential information may be requested and where disclosure of confidential information may be legally required. This discussion should occur as soon as possible in the social worker–client relationship and as needed throughout the course of the relationship.

(f) . . .

(g) . . .

(h) . . .

(i) Social workers should not disclose confidential information in any setting unless privacy can be ensured. Social workers should not discuss confidential information in public or semipublic areas such as hallways, waiting rooms, elevators, and restaurants.

(j) Social workers should protect the confidentiality of clients during legal proceedings to the extent permitted by law. When a court of law or other legally authorized body orders social workers to disclose confidential or privileged information without a client's consent and such disclosure could cause harm to the client, social workers should request that the court withdraw the order or limit the order as narrowly as possible or maintain the records under seal, unavailable for public inspection.

(k) Social workers should protect the confidentiality of clients when responding to requests from members of the media.

(l) Social workers should protect the confidentiality of clients' written and electronic records and other sensitive information. Social workers should take reasonable steps to ensure that clients' records are stored in a secure location and that clients' records are not available to others who are not authorized to have access.

(m) . . .

(n) . . .

(o) . . .

(p) Social workers should not disclose identifying information when discussing clients for teaching or training purposes unless the client has consented to disclosure of confidential information.

(q) Social workers should not disclose identifying information when discussing clients with consultants unless the client has consented to disclosure of confidential information or there is a compelling need for such disclosure. (NASW, 1999, pp. 10–12)

Section 1.08 states

(a) Social workers should provide clients with reasonable access to records concerning the clients. . . . Social workers should limit clients' access to their records, or portions of their records, only in exceptional circumstances when there is compelling evidence that such access would cause serious harm to the client. Both clients' requests and the rationale for withholding some or all of the record should be documented in the clients' files.

(b) When providing clients with access to their records, social workers should take steps to protect the confidentiality of other individuals identified or discussed in such records. (NASW, 1999, p. 12)

Section 3.04 states

(a) Social workers should take reasonable steps to ensure that documentation in records is accurate and reflects the services provided.

(b) Social workers should include sufficient and timely documentation in records to facilitate the delivery of services and to ensure continuity of services provided to clients in the future.

(c) Social workers' documentation should protect clients' privacy to the extent that is possible and appropriate and should include only information that is directly relevant to the delivery of services. (NASW, 1999, p. 20)

The Code encourages protection of client's privacy while at the same time acknowledging that there are instances in which the client's privacy must give way to the sharing of the information with or without client consent. In child welfare practice, there are many instances in which the confidentiality of clients may be compromised. For example, when a child with HIV is placed in a foster home, the foster parents will need to know about the child's medical condition in order to work as part of a health care team. Or if a parent, believing that he has a confidential relationship with a child welfare worker, confides in the worker that he did indeed molest his child, this information could be used in criminal proceedings against that parent.

Under the law, social workers are required to report abuse and neglect. Yet in doing so, the social worker may face angry accusations of betrayal from a parent or other client who dared to trust. Social workers also have an affirmative responsibility to act to prevent murder or suicide. It is important in all professional relationships to discuss the limits of confidentiality when first engaging a client.

Child Client Confidentiality. The ever-present questions for the child welfare practitioners is what information provided by the child the social worker may share and with whom. The social worker also faces the dilemma of needing to confirm the child's information without revealing the source. Consider the following case situation.

> Hank, age 13, was in a residential treatment setting. His foster care worker was making a routine visit to monitor Hank's progress, when Hank confided that he was being "beat up" by other youths in the program who made fun of him and harassed him after lights out. Hank said he had a secret that he would only share if his worker promised not to tell anyone. Janice, his worker said, "I won't tell anyone unless it is absolutely necessary to protect you." After some hesitation, Hank confided that he couldn't take it any more and had developed a plan to commit suicide.
>
> Janice moved quickly to inform child care staff and Hank's therapist of the suicide threat and to put necessary precautions in place. Hank was very angry and told Janice he couldn't trust her any more. Janice reminded him that she had said she would not tell anyone unless it was necessary to protect Hank. "Hank, this time it was necessary. It could have been a matter of life and death. Your well-being is my first concern."

Working with Other Professionals

Child welfare practice involves engagement with many different professionals. Given the diversity of professionals, it is not atypical for professional disagreements to arise. Code Section 2.01 provides guidance to the social worker on how to handle referrals and the disagreements that may result from these referrals. It states

> (b) Social workers should avoid unwarranted negative criticism of colleagues in communications with clients or with other professionals. (NASW, 1999, p. 15)

Section 2.04 states

> (a) Social workers should not exploit clients in disputes with colleagues or engage clients in any inappropriate discussion of conflicts between social workers and their colleagues. (Ibid., p. 16)

Section 2.06 states

> (a) Social workers should refer clients to other professionals when the other professionals' specialized knowledge or expertise is needed to serve clients fully or when social workers

believe that they are not being effective or making reasonable progress with clients and
that additional service is required.

(b) Social workers who refer clients to other professionals should take appropriate steps to
facilitate an orderly transfer of responsibility. Social workers who refer clients to other
professionals should disclose, with clients' consent, all pertinent information to the new
service providers. (Ibid., p. 17)

Special Issues in Child Welfare Practice

Treatment in a Managed Care Environment

Managed care is gaining momentum in child welfare practice. It became a standard in mental health and substance abuse services during the 1990s. For many of the parents, and increasingly for many of the children, these services are critical to successful outcomes in child
welfare. Historically, the lack of availability of appropriate mental health and substance
abuse services in the appropriate "dosage" have been identified as barriers to permanency for
children in out-of-home care and as underlying conditions for referrals to children's protective services and juvenile justice services. Managed care practice exacerbates the problem
(Field, 1996; Kowal, 1996; Institute for Human Services Management, 1996; U.S. General
Accounting Office, 1998; Stroul, Pires, Armstrong, & Meyers, 1998).

In addition, managed care potentially raises ethical dilemmas for the social worker.
Section 1.16 of the Code states

(a) Social workers should terminate services to clients and professional relationships with
them when such services and relationships are no longer required or no longer serve the
clients' needs or interests.

(b) Social workers should take reasonable steps to avoid abandoning clients who are still in
need of services. Social workers should withdraw services precipitously only under unusual circumstances, giving careful consideration to all factors in the situation and taking care to minimize possible adverse effects. Social workers should assist in making
appropriate arrangements for continuation of services when necessary. (NASW, 1999,
pp. 14–15)

Given the complexity of child welfare cases, it is highly unlikely that they will be
conducive to a managed care model that limits the number of sessions provided or the time
period in which service eligibility exists. Several states are experimenting with the concept
of managed care in the child welfare environment to determine its applicability to child
welfare practice and any necessary modifications to the model for implementation to child
welfare practice (National Community Mental Healthcare Council, 1997).

A related ethical problem is raised within the policy and financing context demonstrated in the following case situation.

You are employed by a foster care agency to provide treatment for abused and neglected
children and adolescents. You have been working with an 8-year-old girl who, after six
months of treatment, has begun to trust you enough to disclose sexual abuse by both her parents. She has been placed in a kinship care situation with an aunt, who is due to receive

guardianship as a permanence plan. (Parental rights were terminated earlier.) Because the permanence plan is about to be completed, the agency is preparing to close the case. The agency's service contract, which funds you, provides funding for treatment of foster children. It does not, however, provide funds for children in guardianship situations. This means that you as therapist will no longer be funded to provide treatment. Thus you have been advised by agency management to terminate treatment within the next two weeks.

You have seen the child's reaction as she began to play out sexual abuse themes. You can honestly describe the child as having been in a state of terror at that time. You are also aware of her dissociative episodes and are beginning to speculate as to whether the child may have a multiple personality disorder. You are of course concerned about the possible potential of the child to perpetrate against other children. You have strong clinical indications that it is essential for you to continue treatment at this critical point.

You have suggested that the agency continue the child's foster care status so as not to disrupt treatment. The agency management is not willing to do so, as such an action would violate their funding contract by prolonging foster care when a permanence option was available. Your supervisor suggests that the aunt could take the child to the local community mental health agency, or even that she could bring the child to your agency's private-pay family counseling branch, and pay the sliding scale fee herself. The problem as you see it is that changing therapists at this point would jeopardize the child's progress in treatment at the most critical point, when the child's defenses are down and she has just started to trust.

The supervisor has suggested tactfully to you that you may perhaps be emotionally overinvolved with the child, as you are having problems "letting go." The supervisor is also concerned that if you press your point with the aunt she may be reluctant to assume guardianship. She feels her niece is "a normal kid who just needs a lot of love." You think that to terminate prematurely for reasons related to agency funding patterns constitutes the ethical violation of client abandonment.

Child welfare practice is inherently a process of risk evaluation and risk taking. Advocates have long argued that to be effective, child welfare practitioners need to have a comprehensive knowledge and skills base coupled with a range of supportive resources and interventions that could be utilized, based on their comprehensive initial assessment and continuous reassessment of the family, its individuals and its environment. Managed care is a system based on the principle that the majority of cases and conditions fall within a prescriptive intervention that can be delivered in a certain time period or number of sessions. Child welfare policy has advanced the concept of permanency through the adoption of specific time frames, although not absolute time frames, for returning the child to the home or termination of parental rights. This policy is based on research addressing the child's needs for stability in relationships, not on research on the effectiveness of service delivery systems in meeting the complex needs of multiproblem child welfare cases.

Duty to Warn and Report

All states now have statutes that require certain professionals to warn third parties, generally through law enforcement agencies, of threats to their physical safety made by clients receiving treatment from the professional that the professional believes the client has the intent and means to carry out (Dickson, 1995). In addition, all states require social workers, as well as other specifically identified professionals, to report instances of suspected child abuse and neglect (National Clearinghouse on Child Abuse and Neglect Information, 1998). Code Section 1.07 (e) states

> Social workers should discuss with clients and other interested parties the nature of confidentiality and limitations of clients' right to confidentiality. Social workers should review with clients the circumstances where confidential information may be legally required. This discussion should occur as soon as possible in the social worker–client relationship and as needed throughout the course of the relationship. (NASW, 1999, p. 11)

Forensic Social Work Practice

Child welfare matters, including juvenile delinquency, frequently result in court intervention. *Forensic* means "belonging to or connected with a court" (Black, 1992). Juvenile court procedures have changed substantially since their inception as a court of benevolent and discretionary decision making. Court decisions, discussed in Chapter 2, have resulted in greater formalities in the decision-making processes to ensure constitutional safeguards for children, juveniles, and their parents. These formalities have resulted in the need to conduct child welfare investigations in ways that preserve the evidence and limit the attack by opposing attorneys on the child welfare worker's methodology in the collection of the evidence.

The goal of a forensic interview with a child "is to obtain a statement from the child, in a developmentally-sensitive, unbiased and truthseeking manner, that will support accurate and fair decision-making in the criminal justice and child welfare systems" (Michigan Governor's Task Force on Children's Justice, 1998, p. 1). The process of forensic interviewing has been discussed in Chapter 6. Here we are concerned with the ethical dilemmas raised when you know that you are interviewing to gather information for use in a legal proceeding. Section 1.07 of the Code states

(a) Social workers should inform clients, to the extent possible, about the disclosure of confidential information and the potential consequences, when feasible before the disclosure is made. This applies whether social workers disclose confidential information on the basis of a legal requirement or client consent. . . .

(e) Social workers should discuss with clients and other interested parties the nature of confidentiality and limitations of clients' right to confidentiality. Social workers should review with clients circumstances where confidential information might be legally required. This discussion should occur as soon as possible in the social worker–client relationship and as needed throughout the course of the relationship. . . .

(j) Social workers should protect confidentiality of clients during legal proceedings to the extent permitted by law. When a court of law or other legally authorized body orders social workers to disclose confidential or privileged information without a client's consent and such disclosure could cause harm to the client, social workers should request that the court withdraw the order or limit the order as narrowly as possible or maintain the records under seal, unavailable for public inspection. (NASW, 1999, pp. 10–11)

The dilemma is that, by informing the client of the possible uses and consequences of disclosures in advance of those disclosures, you limit the information available for assessment and intervention. This could result in improper intervention and decision making. On the other hand, if you do not inform the client in advance, you are not complying with your ethical duty.

Testifying in Administrative and Judicial Proceedings

The principles of testifying were discussed in Chapter 6. Here the focus is the dilemmas raised by Section 1.07 (j) of the Code:

> Social workers should protect confidentiality of clients during legal proceedings to the extent permitted by law. When a court of law or other legally authorized body orders social workers to disclose confidential or privileged information without a client's consent and such disclosure could cause harm to the client, social workers should request that the court withdraw the order or limit the order as narrowly as possible or maintain the records under seal, unavailable for public inspection. (NASW, 1999, p. 11)

How do the terms *to the extent permitted by law* and *could cause harm to the client* apply in child welfare practice? The social worker is engaged with the child and family to carry out a public function, that is, the protection of vulnerable children and/or the protection of society from the actions of wayward or delinquent children. Which client do you protect—the adult or the child? Perhaps even society is your client. Whose interests are paramount? Should you consider the potential harms to yourself and your agency? The child welfare worker must be aware of federal laws, such as strict confidentiality with respect to federally funded recipients of substance abuse services, that supercede state laws with respect to what information the court can order divulged.

Child Advocacy

The history of the social work profession is rich with initiatives focused on advocacy for the poor and vulnerable. Over the years, the profession has shifted focus to individual, group and community practice and, in the view of some commentators, has lost sight of its roots in social reform (Fink, Anderson, & Conover, 1968; Bailey & Brake, 1975; Richan, 1991; Netting, Kettner, & McMurtry, 1998; Chambers, 2000; Haynes & Mickelson, 2000). While advocacy efforts for some disadvantaged groups may have diminished, it is clear that child advocacy efforts continue to grow and achieve significant gains at the federal, state, and local levels (Ness, Pizzigati, & Stuck, 2002).

Responsibility for Advancing Social and Economic Justice

The social worker's ethical responsibility to engage in advocacy efforts is delineated in Section 6 of the Code. The responsibilities are broad-based and rooted in the concept of advancing social and economic justice. Section 6.01 states

> Social workers should promote the general welfare of society, from local to global levels, and the development of people, their communities, and their environments. Social workers should advocate for living conditions conducive to the fulfillment of basic human needs and should promote social, economic, political, and cultural values and institutions that are compatible with the realization of social justice. (NASW, 1999, pp. 26–27)

Section 6.02 states, "Social workers should facilitate informed participation by the public in shaping social policies and institutions" (Ibid., p. 27). Section 6.04 states

   (a) Social workers should engage in social and political action that seeks to ensure that all people have equal access to the resources, employment, services, and opportunities they require to meet their basic human needs and to develop fully. Social workers should be aware of the impact of the political arena on practice and should advocate for changes in policy and legislation to improve social conditions in order to meet basic human needs and promote social justice.

   (b) Social workers should act to expand choice and opportunity for all people, with special regard for vulnerable, disadvantaged, oppressed, and exploited people and groups. (NASW, 1999, p. 27)

    Many child welfare workers and supervisors are intimidated by the mention of "advocacy." They think that it involves skills beyond their grasp. They have no idea about where to start once the advocacy involves more than advocating for a particular client for a particular service or benefit from a particular agency responsible for providing that service. However, as you can see from Box 12.1, clinical practice and case/policy practice and advocacy share common general problem-solving steps: definition of the problem; data collection and analysis; choosing an appropriate intervention; continuous reevaluation and

---

B O X   **12.1**

Comparison of Clinical Practice and Policy Practice/Advocacy Steps

Clinical Practice Steps	**Policy Practice/Advocacy Steps**
1. Get client's view of problem	1. How does society define the problem? How does the advocacy group define the problem? What are the points of differences in the definitions?
2. Collect data to confirm client's definition or revise it (psychosocial history)	2. Complete needs assessment (scope of problem; who is affected; current policies and programs; regulations)
3. Diagnose or assess	3. Identify appropriate site of intervention (legislative, executive, or judicial) and stage (policy formulation, implementation, or evaluation)
4. Develop treatment plan	4. Develop intervention strategy options
5. Execute treatment plan	5. Execute chosen strategy
6. Evaluate and modify treatment plan	6. Evaluate and modify chosen strategies
7. Achieve desired outcome	7. Achieve desired outcome

Source: Adapted from K. S. Haynes and J. S. Mickelson (2000), *Affecting change: Social workers in the political arena* (Boston: Allyn and Bacon).

modification of the chosen interventions based on new information or changed circumstances; and finally goal attainment. Certainly, the individual techniques used will vary. We will discuss techniques and skills useful at all levels of child advocacy in the rest of the chapter. We want to assure the reader that these techniques and skills are within the grasp of each reader through building on and adapting micro skills.

Advocacy in the Local and Global Context

"Think globally, act locally" should be the mantra of the child welfare advocate. All children, irrespective of geographic, political, and cultural origins are entitled to adequate nurturance to ensure the maximization of their emotional, cognitive, social, moral, and spiritual development. What this nurturance looks like varies from place to place, but the essential end is that all children are free from abuse or neglect at the hands of their immediate caretakers as well as their governments and are provided care and nurturance to guarantee survival and development in all domains.

The United Nations' Convention on the Rights of the Child has fifty-four articles specific to the rights children all over the world should be ensured by their governments. The following summarizes the major rights identified in those articles. Children shall have the right to

- care and protection necessary for his or her well-being including life, survival, and development.
- know and be cared for by their parents and the right to live with their parents absent a judicial determination that separation is in the best interests of the child.
- maintain contact with their parents, if separated, even across political jurisdictions.
- freedom of thought, expression, conscience, and religion, and to voice opinions and desires freely if capable of forming their own views and to have their views given weight in accordance with age and maturity.
- receive care and services in facilities and from programs that meet minimum standards in the areas of health, safety, and staff competency and sufficiency.
- respect given to the responsibilities and rights of their parents, extended family, and community in caring for them.
- a name, a nationality, a registered birth, and a right to preserve this identity as well as ethnic, religious, cultural, and linguistic background.
- intercountry adoption only if the child cannot be placed in a foster or adoptive home in his or her country of origin.
- special care for any disabilities and access to education, training, health care services, rehabilitation services, preparation for employment and recreation opportunities in a manner conducive to achieving full potential.
- access facilities for primary health care, illness treatment, and rehabilitative health care.
- a standard of living adequate to physical, mental, spiritual, moral, and social development.
- compulsory, free primary education in a humane environment.
- be protected against economic exploitation and from performing hazardous work, drug trafficking, and sexual prostitution including pornographic performances.

- be free from torture, degrading treatment, and unlawful detention.
- not be required to engage in armed conflicts if they are 15 years of age or younger.

The Convention is the one document that all advocates can look to as the organizing framework for global advocacy. All nations, except the United States and Somalia, have signed it as of this writing implying agreement with its assurances. Thus those signatory nations conceptually are committed to implementing those rights for all children within their political jurisdictions.

Clearly, none of those signatory states has met the prescribed standards. So, much global advocacy is necessary. The complexity of actual advocacy in a country—and in some countries a region—other than that of the advocate's residence is beyond the scope of this text. However, that does not preclude all child advocates from

- voicing concern over the plight of children in other countries,
- providing support to the advocates in those countries attempting to secure the rights their governments' promised their children upon signing the Convention, and
- encouraging our government to use our resources of influence and affluence to influence how those governments treat their children.

Further, we must remain mindful that the United States of America, despite its influence and affluence, does not ensure that every child has adequate economic support, nutrition, health care, education, behavioral/mental health services, family support services, protective services, out-of-home care services, independent living services, or permanency and adoption services. In advocating for and securing universal services for all of our children, we can demonstrate to other nations and advocate that it is possible to ensure that all children and their families have the supports they need to reach adulthood with maximum capabilities for citizenship and personal fulfillment.

What Is Advocacy?

In 1981, the Child Welfare League of America defined child advocacy as "the process of sensitizing individuals and groups to the unmet needs of children and to society's obligation to provide positive response to these needs" (p. ix). This definition emphasizes the educational role inherent in all advocacy efforts. But the League also recognized the definitional dilemma by stating: "Whether one talks in terms of advocacy, or influencing public social policy, or engaging in social action or promoting institutional change makes no essential difference" (p. 1). It is interesting to note that persons who viewed advocacy as a large part of their work defined it as "intervention on behalf of a client or client groups with an unresponsive system" (Epstein, 1981, p. 8). Mickelson (1995) has advanced the following definition: "In social work, advocacy can be defined as the act of directly representing, defending, intervening, supporting, or recommending a course of action on behalf of one or more individuals, groups, or communities with the goal of securing or retaining social justice" (NASW, 1999, p. 95).

Jansson (1999) differentiates policy practice and policy advocacy. Policy practice includes efforts to change policies at all levels and stages of policy development and implementation, whereas policy advocacy is a specific policy practice common to the social work profession in that it is directed toward helping the powerless and disenfranchised individual or group by securing benefits and services (Jansson, 1999, pp. 10–11).

While case and class advocacy are the two broadest conceptual categories of child advocacy, this text discusses case, class, and policy advocacy as three distinct types of child advocacy. This is done because in the context of the child welfare worker's and supervisor's experience, they are more accustomed to case advocacy being done for individual clients within their agency or with another agency to obtain a service for the individual; class advocacy being done for a group of named individual clients within the context of their agency or other administrative agencies or through litigation in the courts; and policy advocacy being done to change public policy on behalf of a targeted service population within the context of the political arena.

Historical Background.   The practice of child advocacy takes different forms as the needs of children and the organizational environments responding to those needs change. Present-day child advocacy has its origins in 1899 with the juvenile court movement, the 1910 White House Conference on Children, and the establishment in 1912 of the Children's Bureau at the federal level. Among the forces that helped to produce interest in child advocacy in more recent times were the new visibility given to

- poverty and delinquency in the 1960s and the government programs intended to reduce the number of children and families living under seriously inadequate economic conditions;
- child protection, the protection of juvenile offenders, and permanency for children in foster care in the 1970s;
- family preservation, family reunification, and getting tough on juveniles who commit serious offenses in the 1980s;
- child safety as the "paramount concern" over family preservation or reunification; permanency through adoption for children in out-of-home care; expanding the adult crime–adult time approach to juvenile offenders; and "work, not welfare" in the 1990s extending into the 2000s.

From the Mobilization for Youth project came the concept of "client advocacy," defined as intervention "on behalf of a client with a public agency to secure an entitlement or right which has been obscured or denied" (Cloward & Elman, 1967, p. 267). In later sections, this type of advocacy is called "case advocacy." Mobilization for Youth was an inner-city youth project developed by a multidisciplinary social agency on New York City's Lower East Side. Its focus was on the need for broad social, economic, and institutional reform. Delinquency was viewed as the result of a lack of congruence between a young person's aspirations and opportunities. A range of services was offered—employment, legal, educational, psychological, and social. The community action programs under the Economic Opportunity Act were largely modeled on the Mobilization for Youth experience. The "War on Poverty" launched by the Economic Opportunity Act produced the principle of "maximum feasible participation" on the part of clients affected by the new antipoverty programs, challenged the conventional and sometimes complacent service delivery methods, and persistently questioned the processes that led to institutional decisions about poor families and children.

Another set of influences that moved the idea of child advocacy forward came from attention to problems in public school education. The 1960s brought a stream of studies, evaluations, and opinions with provocative titles, such as *How Children Fail, Death at an Early Age,* and *Crisis in the Classroom,* about inadequate educational facilities and the failure of the schools to educate children, especially children of the poor and children with special needs—for example, physically and mentally handicapped children and children in need of bilingual education (Holt, 1964; Kozol, 1967; Silberman, 1971). Out of the controversy came attempts to create new approaches to education by modifying school conditions and practices.

Successful demonstrations in the late 1960s of the gains to be made for children through the use of the judicial system constituted another influence on the development of the child advocacy movement. The *Kent* and *Gault* decisions affirmed due process rights of juveniles alleged to be delinquent. A significant court case in Pennsylvania questioned the constitutionality of school policies that resulted in the exclusion of handicapped children (*Pennsylvania Association,* 1971). Similar suits followed and eventually played an important part in congressional enactment of the Education for All Handicapped Children Act of 1975. Another major litigation challenged conditions in juvenile correctional institutions and resulted not only in an order for changes in such institutions but also in the creation of a community-based system of alternative forms of care and treatment (*Morales v. Turman,* 1974). These and other demonstrations of ways in which litigation can be used to advance child rights not only led to change in service procedures and methods but also helped to establish important principles inherent in the concept and practice of child advocacy.

Another development begun in the 1960s was also related to the emergence of interest in child advocacy. Ralph Nader's consumer advocacy efforts have been focused on the obligations of corporations to respond to consumer interests and on the failure of government regulatory authorities to monitor the activities of industry adequately. Knitzer (1976) pointed out that, unlike the participatory model of antipoverty activists, Nader's strategies are "overtly elitist, both in choice of staff and in the processes by which issues are selected" (p. 207). Nevertheless, she acknowledged, Nader and his staff have been highly successful in researching and focusing attention on systemic problems—an accomplishment that has not been lost on proponents of child advocacy.

Illustrations of avant-garde child advocacy programs are found in the records of the U.S. Children's Bureau in the years between the progressive era and the enactment of the Social Security Act in 1935 and in the contemporary Children's Defense Fund. In each instance far-thinking and daring women committed to social justice for women, children, and young families are credited with successful leadership. Julia Lathrop was the first and Grace Abbott the second chief of the Children's Bureau; Marian Wright Edelman is the founder and president of the Children's Defense Fund. All three have records that encompass the following:

- effective definition of problems that require social action
- development and maintenance of diverse constituencies
- building and supporting coalitions
- conceptualizing and implementing systematic studies of the problem and the forces affecting it
- disseminating findings in strategic forums
- astutely recognizing political factors that control the targeted problem
- applying sound judgment as to where and when pressure can be effective.

Children's Defense Fund.   Following the new surge of advocacy in the 1960s, attempts were made to develop national child advocacy organizations, most of which had limited success (Steiner, 1976). One that has survived as an effective and dynamic advocacy unit is the Children's Defense Fund (CDF), a nonprofit organization committed to long-range systematic advocacy to bring about reforms in behalf of children. Marian Wright Edelman, who founded the organization in 1973 and has provided its leadership since then, is recognized as a dynamic and highly effective advocate for children in the complex and competitive arena in which social policies and legislation are influenced.

Carefully defined goals in relation to children and their unmet needs seemed to Edelman an effective focus for broadening the base and building a coalition for social change. Edelman sought to cut through race and class barriers by addressing the needs of children throughout the country.

> *What scares me is that today people don't have the sense that they can struggle and change things. In the sixties, in Mississippi, it just never occurred to us that we weren't going to win. We always had the feeling that there was something we could do, and that there was hope. (Marian Wright Edelman—Tomkins, 1989, p. 74)*

The CDF set out to protect effective programs already in existence and work for new programs that would emphasize parental involvement and community change. The selection of targets for reform activity was made on the premise that effective advocacy must be specialized, not global, in its approach to change, and that the issues should be ones that affect large numbers of children, that are easily understood by the public, that are subject to attacks at local, state, and federal levels, and that give promise of being affected by a combination of strategies. The early issues the CDF chose to pursue included the following:

- the exclusion of children from school
- classification and treatment of children with special needs
- the use of children in medical (particularly drug) research and experimentation
- the child's right to privacy in the face of computerization and data banks
- reform of the juvenile justice system
- child development and child care
- children in foster care. (Beck & Butler, 1974)

Over time, CDF has broadened its areas of interests to include other issues such as child neglect and abuse, children's health care, early education/Head Start, homelessness, poverty, youth violence, and teenage pregnancy and parenting. The wide dissemination of findings from CDF studies by means of publications, testimony before congressional committees, and presentations in a variety of public forums has been highly effective in securing interest and action for change.

On the assumption that some groups that may not support a general effort may come together around a children's issue that affects their special interests, the CDF relies on specialized coalition building as a primary strategy. Issues for reform activity are selected not only for their importance to children and families but also for their potential for building coalitions and constituencies. Other specialized strategies and activities include litigation, drafting and pushing legislation, monitoring administrative agencies, providing public education, and organizing local groups who work with children and offering them technical support.

Case, Class, and Policy Advocacy

The types of situations and issues that indicate the need for child advocacy have been discussed in each chapter of this book: poverty; poor nutrition; inadequate housing; homelessness; lack of proper health care; and the failure to provide educational programs that succeed in preparing young people for the basic skills that are required for entry into the world of work. Specific to the field of child welfare are issues of the application of due process guarantees in the juvenile courts; the definitions of child abuse and neglect; the meanings of reasonable efforts, permanency, family preservation, and child protection; the jailing or secure detention of youth prior to adjudication; sexism and racism in the dispositional decisions of child welfare agencies and the courts; the provision of legal representation for children and parents in adjudications directly affecting them; and the question of the scope of constitutional protections for children.

Advocacy on behalf of children is needed now as much as it has been in the past. All of these situations, and others as well, call attention to the necessity of monitoring legislative, administrative, and budgetary processes and, at times, the professional behavior of persons charged by society to act on behalf of children. The approach to advocacy for a specific issue can include techniques focused on resolution of the issue for an individual client (case advocacy) or techniques focused on resolution of the issue for all persons now affected or who may be affected in the future (class advocacy). Class advocacy can be undertaken within agencies (the administrative/executive level), through litigation (the judicial level), or through the political process in the form of policy change (the legislative level). Because of the potential impact of policy advocacy on child welfare service delivery, it will be discussed separately from class advocacy occurring in the context of litigation or named individuals currently harmed by an existing policy or practice. Through elaboration of the facts in the case example presented at the beginning of this chapter, we will illustrate how you might undertake case, class, and policy advocacy.

Case Advocacy.   Case advocacy is focused on an individual child in order to bring about resolution of some barrier to the child's receiving a needed service or concrete benefit. A child may need a service that is not available in the community, or is in such short supply as to be unavailable to this particular child. Sometimes the service exists, but parents do not know how to find and use it, and sometimes children are denied service without any defensible rationale. In other instances, services may be given, but in a form that is seriously inadequate or inappropriate. In situations like these, someone directly concerned usually initiates advocacy action for the child—a social worker or other professional, or a paraprofessional, such as a health aide or teacher's aide.

Other situations that invite case advocacy are readily illustrated—a child is unfairly detained in jail; a child is inappropriately or unfairly placed outside the mainstream of the school learning structure; a child is denied an adoptive home because no one in the foster care system has initiated or followed through on a positively oriented review of his or her suitability for adoption; or a child is repeatedly suspended from school without a hearing by school personnel to determine whether the child is persisting in the offending behavior for reasons over which he or she has little or no control.

Class Advocacy.   If these individual case advocacy issues appear over time to involve the same policy, practice, or agency, then the effective advocate will shift to class advocacy techniques. This approach is more efficient when the problem is widespread, in that class advocacy maximizes the current benefit to all children who should receive the benefit or who should not be subjected to the sanction. When successful, it results in changes in policies, practices, or agency administration. For example, the advocate may involve a citizen's group in examining the conditions that lead to children's being held in the community's jails, or, with a group of parents, the advocate may endeavor to bring change in school practices in relation to suspensions or placement of children in special education classes. These actions may not be adversarial nor require legal action. They may rather be aimed at supporting school or court personnel in the development of corrective measures to advance generally approved goals for children.

If there is a need for litigation, Rule 23 of the Federal Rules of Civil Procedure (1998) provides that a class action can be advanced if these four conditions exist:

- The class membership is so numerous that to join all members in the court action is impracticable.
- The legal issue or problem common to the class predominates over any legal issue or problem affecting members as individuals.
- Claims of the representative members are typical of the claims of the class.
- The representative members will fairly and adequately protect the interests of the class.

Action on behalf of a class of persons is done primarily for the purpose of efficiency. Progress on a case-by-case basis takes too long and does not necessarily bring change for others. Nor does case advocacy provide the political leverage that helps to bring change for children generally in related problem areas.

Policy Advocacy.   When these organization's practices are inconsistent with governmental policies, then case or class advocacy through administrative processes or litigation are appropriate strategies. However, when these organizations are constrained by policies or practices imposed by governmental units and these policies or practices are inconsistent with the service needs of the targeted client population, then policy advocacy is the appropriate level of advocacy.

Policy is defined as

> statements that prescribe courses of action in organizations. They govern the internal functioning of organizations, their external relations, and the way they attain their goals. They are codified in documentary form and facilitate standardized decision-making. (Midgley, Tracy, & Livermore, 2000, p. 3)

Public policy, also called social policy, is all the policies of government that define its responsibilities to its citizens and its citizens' responsibilities to their government and one another. As we have discussed throughout, public child welfare as we know it today is driven by federal and state policies in the form of statutes/public laws, administrative rules and regulations, and judicial decisions interpreting those statutes/public laws or administrative rules and regulations. Public policies are not stagnant. The major child welfare legislations summarized in Chapter 2 and discussed in Chapters 3, 4, 5, 7, 8, 9, 10, and 11 have been amended several times since original passage of the enabling legislations. These amendments occur because some group or groups, typically external to the government itself, determine that the current policies are not achieving the desired goals or the current policies are no longer desirable within the value or knowledge context of the group or society. This is policy advocacy. To simplify the distinction, case and class advocacy, as discussed above, always involve attempts to resolve policy implementation disputes for named individuals. Policy advocacy focuses on advocacy for a particular approach to an issue that affects unnamed children and their families now alive and yet to be born.

Nevertheless, efficiency and political leverage are by no means the central reason for child advocacy. Protecting the rights of the individual child is the central purpose of all child advocacy efforts. Although for child advocacy to be successful individual needs must often be grouped and classified, the needs and the rights of the individual are the heart of advocacy at any level and for any group of persons. Case, class, and policy advocacy are inseparably related.

Common Assumptions.   Writing from the perspective of the highly effective advocacy programs of the Children's Defense Fund, Knitzer (1976) identified some underlying assumptions common to all forms of advocacy:

1. Advocacy assumes that people have, or ought to have, certain basic rights.
2. Advocacy assumes that rights are enforceable by statutes, administration, or judicial procedures.
3. Advocacy efforts are focused on institutional failures that produce or aggravate individual problems.
4. Advocacy is inherently political.
5. Advocacy is most effective when it is focused on specific issues.
6. Advocacy is different from the provision of direct services. (p. 205)

Child advocacy, then, is primarily concerned with seeing that existing organizations and services work for children.

Components of Child Advocacy

Child advocacy projects vary in significant ways. Within the diversity, however, there appear to be features that are fundamental to all projects: auspices, sanction for intervention, target selection, and basic tasks, strategies, and techniques.

Auspices.   The question of auspices for a child advocacy program is a significant one. Auspices determine certain basic characteristics of a project: who authorizes it, who pays for it, and who runs it.

Early debate about who should authorize and fund child advocacy centered on the question of whether child advocacy should be separate from any governmental system to avoid the inhibitions that might result from risks in challenging high-level officials. But private funding can also pose constraints. In practice, the necessity of locating and competing for funds has meant that both public and private funds have been used for child advocacy projects.

As child advocacy has developed, advocacy projects have come to include these types, classified according to their auspices:

- Projects authorized and paid for by a governmental body made up of citizens. These projects are mandated by local, county, state, or federal governments. For example, if the state elects to receive federal funding for child abuse and neglect, foster care, and adoption programming, it is required to establish and staff Citizen Review Panels, Children's Justice Act Task Forces, and Juvenile Justice Task Forces to oversee the state's policies and practices in the areas of children's protective services, foster care, adoption, and juvenile delinquency/juvenile justice.

- Projects authorized and operated within a governmental body, often at the state level, with staff members who are employees of government. For example, the federally mandated State Protection and Advocacy organization is mandated to provide advocacy services for persons with mental illnesses, emotional disturbances, and developmental disabilities.

- Projects independent of government and funded by private foundations, by memberships, or by individual contributions; for example, the Children's Defense Fund and the National Association of Child Advocates.

The auspices of a project can be a crucial determinant of what can be undertaken and accomplished. But, as Knitzer (1976) pointed out, any advocacy effort involves risks, and important as the auspices are, the energy, commitment, and political know-how of the advocates are equally important.

Who Is the Advocate? The question of who is best equipped to be an advocate for children continues to be debated. Some have argued for a more limited role for professionals. In fact, the renewed interest in child advocacy was largely based on a mistrust of professionals and the organizations they operate. The fear was that professionally directed advocacy efforts would be weighted more toward professional self-interest than toward the needs of children. This has led to a demand for a significant degree of citizen and paraprofessional participation in advocacy projects.

In many cases, an effective advocacy effort involves multiple groups of professionals, scholars, citizens, and the youth themselves. Many advocacy efforts are complex, requiring a variety of roles to be filled, depending on the situation. Successful child advocacy programs have employed, in various configurations, different kinds of personnel, including college students, social scientists, parents, citizens, lawyers, and other professionals. There is obviously not a single answer. What is most clear, however, is that the welfare of children is best served when increased numbers of people from all stations of life become actively involved.

Sanction for the Right to Intervene. Child advocacy requires sanction. Responsible child advocacy means that persons who attempt to intervene in society's institutions must be sure that their assertive or adversarial stance is justified.

In view of all that has been said about the injustice to children and the unmet needs for social services, one may well question why individuals should be required to justify their right to try to improve the status of children. But when an advocacy group decides that an individual agency or institution is not responding adequately to the children for whom it carries responsibility, then that advocacy group is usually attempting to bring about some significant change in an institution or agency, such as making the target agency more flexible in its approach to child needs, increasing budget allocations, undertaking new programs, or reassigning control of programs.

But on what basis can child advocates establish their right to intervene? Kahn, Kamerman, and McGowan (1972) gave the following guidelines for validating the right to advocate:

1. A sanction for child advocacy exists when children have justifiable rights, that is, "legislatively specified benefits for which administrative discretion is quite circumscribed and which can be adjudicated in the courts when administrative agencies do not deliver." In such instances there is a clear-cut entitlement to a benefit or a specific service, such as survivors' benefits under Social Security, or an appropriate educational program in the least-restrictive environment for a handicapped child. In such cases, the child advocate's sanction to act is clear-cut. Other instances in which the right to advocate is easily recognized include those where there is strong indication that some children or families are being treated differently from others in a similar situation, perhaps because agencies and personnel are ignoring their own policies and procedures or are acting carelessly or in a discriminatory way. For example, the right to advocate is clear if a children's agency mandated by law to receive and investigate all reports of child abuse and neglect attempts to manage a heavy workload by deciding to respond to reports of neglect only when those reports carry an indication of physical abuse as well, or if a juvenile court makes sure that middle- and upper-income parents are present and informed of their right to counsel when hearings affecting them and their children are held, but fails to do the same for parents who are very poor.

2. A sanction for child advocacy exists when the effort is intended to expand the boundaries of legally governed child rights. For example, it is generally held that the parent–child relationship remains intact, with parental rights primary, unless serious abuse, neglect, or unfitness on the part of parents is established. But a question arises as to whether continued state intervention is justified if it is merely an exchange of governmental neglect for parental neglect. If a child's parents make the difficult but often necessary decision to institutionalize their child and only a simple regime of enforced custodial care is given— not treatment that is appropriate and adequate in light of present knowledge—then the issue of a right to treatment emerges.

   In situations like these, advocates for children may choose to work for an extension of child rights beyond what is already clearly established in law. Sometimes the sanction to do so rests on a series of lower court decisions or inconclusive actions, or simply on statements of some authoritative body that has spoken out on the issue.

3. A sanction for child advocacy may exist even when no specific right or statement of principle appears in law. The right to intervene may be validated in a number of ways, which Kahn et al. (1972) identified:

   a. Available professional knowledge and expertise about dangers to child development may provide backing for child advocacy.
   b. The joining of knowledge and values may bring about agreement on a "social minimum" that finds support in professional and community norms and thus gives validity to the child advocacy effort.
   c. Sometimes groups such as parents of disadvantaged or handicapped children articulate their own needs, and in doing so provide a sanction for child advocacy. Even

though this sanction rests on self-definition and personal experience, it is often enough for advocacy to proceed.

d. Sometimes the view people have of society, social justice, and acceptable priorities in the use of resources leads them to study social indicators of the status of children and to collect data about families and children in relation to such critical factors as school attendance and achievement, health and illness, and nutrition. Their analysis of such data then becomes a sanction for child advocacy. (pp. 70–75)

Selecting the Target for Advocacy.   The target for advocacy is the system or organization that is the locus of the service or disservice to the child(ren) or their family(ies). In some child advocacy projects, the target is only one system—for example, the school system. The individual caseworker or supervisor and the advocacy group attempt to deal with a range of school situations whereby children or families are affected, such as suspension, corporal punishment, education for children with disabilities, and the use of drugs for control of pupil behavior. Other projects may at various times attack issues involving a number of agencies or institutions. Often a project that starts out with only one organization or system as the target begins to uncover negative effects of other organizations or systems on children, and so its advocacy efforts are expanded. For example, dealing with advocacy issues in a public school often raises questions about the mental health system, and attention to the mental health system may lead in turn to concern about the juvenile justice system. Further, advocacy initiatives that begin as case or named-class advocacy frequently lead to policy advocacy concurrently or subsequently.

Tasks, Strategies, and Techniques.   All advocates, irrespective of the type or level of advocacy undertaken, use four basic skills:

- analytical,
- political,
- interactional, and
- value clarification or ethical reasoning.

Analytical skills are needed to gather, synthesize, and evaluate the interrelationship of various data elements central to the issue under review and develop alternative action strategies or recommendations. Political skills are needed to develop feasible action strategies, to help identify people of influence to assist in advancing the message, and to help develop political strategies. Interactional skills are needed to develop and facilitate networks and coalitions to assist in realizing the advocacy goal. Value clarification or ethical reasoning skills are needed to ensure that the means taken to realize the advocacy goal are not inconsistent with the goal itself or higher principles are not compromised to achieve the end (Jansson, 1999). Maryann Mahaffey, a social worker and president of the Detroit City Council, said

> A social worker brings to the political process something that's unique, that no one else has. . . . What the social worker brings is a value system that, if implemented, along with the skills, makes the difference. (Haynes & Michelson, 2000, p. 40)

Advocates use a range of specific techniques—suggestion, negotiation, education, consensus building, persuasion, pressure, demands, confrontation, legal action, legislative testimony, pickets, providing data for media exposes, and the like—in case, class, and policy advocacy projects.

Child advocacy sometimes is an adversarial process, but, as Knitzer (1976) remind us, "it is also a problem solving process that requires keen attention to problem definition and analysis" (p. 208). There are four major tasks for all advocacy projects:

1. fact-finding
2. development of strategies to secure remedies or solutions
3. implementation of the strategies
4. monitoring for results

Once a constituency is settled on, whether that constituency be an individual child or a group of children sharing a similar condition, such as mental illness, teenage parenthood, being adrift in foster care, waiting for a permanent home, or being subjected to given corporal punishment at school, then the advocate or advocacy group must turn its energies to fact-finding. Both client-centered and organization-centered or system-centered data that are relevant to the need for advocacy must be collected, organized, studied, and assessed—data such as the identified characteristics, needs, and legal rights of clients; societal and institutional perceptions of the client group; the responsibilities and resources of the organization or system; the location of the sources of power in the organization or system; and the nature of the decision-making process in the organization or system.

Gaps in services and obstacles to the utilization of services must be identified, such as barriers posed by insufficient or inappropriate allocation of staff resources, untrained staff, or failure to develop alternative practices—for example, alternatives to the use of secure detention for juvenile status offenders. The problem that is causing the trouble—the difficulty in the child–environment transactions—must be documented and analyzed before remedies can be developed and effective intervention can take place. Frequently this procedure requires becoming informed on substantive matters that affect the workings of the target organization or system; the nature of law and the judicial process; the knowledge about foster care that has been verified through research; the curriculum content of a public school program and what school administrators and teachers consider to be major curriculum issues; or the organization's or system's sources of funding and the legal constraints on its budgeting processes.

Political factors that affect or control the situation of concern must be assessed. These could include the positions taken earlier by key persons in the organization or system target or the points at which pressure is likely to be effective or to intensify resistance.

Once the problem has been defined and analyzed, then comes attention to what Knitzer terms "the heart of advocacy," that is, *the development of strategies and remedies.* "Without attention to strategies and remedies, fact-finding alone would be nothing more than an exposé" (Knitzer, 1976, p. 308). The advocate may rely on a single strategy or a range of interventions.

You have essentially asked and answered these questions during fact-finding:

- What specific service do I want this organization or system to provide for my child?
- If I cannot get this service, what service would be acceptable?

- Does this organization have a mandate to provide this desired or acceptable service?
- Does my child meet the eligibility criteria for this service as stated in the organization's policies?

Having determined that the organization is mandated to provide the service to children with conditions like your child has, the next step is to get the organization to provide the service. The strategy to do this may be benign or adversarial. A benign strategy is recommended when you know that the organization's mandate is to provide the desired or acceptable service. In some situations, the organization's policies include an internal dispute resolution or appeal process to a caseworker's decision. If the organization has such a policy, follow it!

An adversarial strategy, particularly if it involves administrative tribunals or courts, can take many years to resolve the conflict. However, even in a benign strategy, there is adversity if there has been a prior contact and services have been denied or the organization is overwhelmed by the volume of children needing the service and encourages screeners to apply narrow readings of the organization's policies to individual referrals. In this situation, you would confirm the decision with the person making the decision, attempt to understand the basis for their decision, provide additional information as necessary, discuss your understanding of the organization's policies as applied to your child's situation, and, if you cannot resolve the matter with him or her, advise that you wish to speak with the supervisor. Then you or your superiors convey the same message to people in that organization at progressively higher levels within the organization until you get the desired or acceptable service, or you have talked with the top person in the organization with no positive response. It is at this point—a final decision from the organization has been received—that an external adversarial strategy is pursued. This can be administrative or judicial in nature. For example, during fact-finding you identified the organization's source of funding, so you contact the funder requesting assistance in resolving the matter, or your agency or an advocacy organization files a lawsuit on behalf of the child alleging that the agency denied services to a child who met the eligibility criteria for services as stated in the agency's policies. Another increasingly useful strategy in situations in which organizations or systems are failing to meet their responsibilities is the media exposé. This will be discussed in more detail in the policy advocacy example that follows. The critical component in benign or adversarial strategies is that the advocate has facts and documentation that support the advocate's position. Enthusiasm, compassion, and a sense of mission are not enough. Box 12.2 summarizes the essential steps in a case advocacy project. See this chapter's For Additional Study and References sections for references on advocacy skills.

While case advocacy, class advocacy, and policy advocacy share many of the same steps as those stated in Box 12.2, class advocacy projects on behalf of named individuals and public policy advocacy projects include strategies infrequently used in individual case advocacy projects. The primary strategy of all such projects is the development of coalitions of different groups of people, sometimes quite diverse, who have an interest in the problem or the proposed remedy. Steiner (1976) has emphasized the significance of involving groups with a self-interest and joining them with social altruists as a driving force in the children's cause. As an example he cites the national school lunch program. A powerful coalition of political forces came together to produce a greatly expanded national school lunch program. Lobbyists for agricultural interests and congressmen from rural states wanted to

---

B O X   **12.2**

Steps in Case/Class Advocacy

1. Identify the specific child or children with the unmet need.
2. Define the specific problem to be resolved.
3. Determine the desired and acceptable resolutions.
4. Identify the barrier(s) to accomplishing your objective policy, practice/procedure, or person.
5. Determine who has the authority to eliminate the barrier(s)—start with the lowest person in the chain of command.
6. Assess options in approaching authority—who has the greatest potential to get them to agree to your position?
7. Implement approach strategy.
8. If unsuccessful, proceed through chain of command until final decision is received.
9. If no internal resolution, evaluate litigation option on behalf of an individual child or on behalf of a group of children who have similar unmet needs.

Source: Content adapted from Jansson, 1999; Chambers, 2000; Haynes & Mickelson, 2000; Mather & Lager, 2000; Midgley, Tracy, & Livermore, 2000.

---

maintain an outlet for surplus farm products. Welfare-oriented congressmen were responsive to the nutritional problems of children in poor families. The school lunch program was a convenience for middle-income groups, and the middle-income subsidy it provided was popular with some lawmakers in Washington. Lobbyists for various nutrition groups and others interested in children's learning problems saw hungry children as unable to learn at school. Proponents of the War on Poverty viewed school lunches as an acceptable relief program. The American School Food Services Association, an association that exists in all fifty states, had a self-interest in an expanded universal program rather than one for poor children only. The association is made up of school lunch directors, supervisors, and line workers, and their organizational intent is to maintain job opportunities and improve wages and working conditions. A group of social altruists—an ad hoc Committee on School Lunch Participation—made up of five women's organizations, each with a religious orientation, set out to learn why relatively few children were participating in the school lunch program and why it was failing to meet the needs of poor children. As a result of their inquiry, they came out on the side of a universal program. An expanded program also had the support of another lobby, the Children's Foundation, an antihunger organization made up of social altruists and functioning independently of governmental funds. The result was a social benefit that is almost universally available in schools. Aside from public education itself, Steiner noted, no social welfare program provides public benefits to more children than the national school lunch program (Steiner, 1976).

As important as coalition building is, so is the *maintenance of coalitions.* Keeping a coalition together can be difficult and sometimes impossible, particularly when advocacy efforts at the peak of their consensus and influence meet powerful opposition.

A strategy that has been used successfully by advocacy groups as a way to increase the cadre of advocates and give them a self-interest in bringing about reform is to *reach out to and co-opt groups of volunteers.* "The volunteer-as-participant invariably becomes the volunteer-as-partisan" (Steiner, 1976, p. 249).

Box 12.3 summarizes the steps in policy advocacy. Box 12.4 summarizes the steps in developing a movement to effect policy change when it is necessary to develop interest in an issue to expand the number of participants in the coalition or to get people of influence to support your position with the legislative body.

Most policy advocacy occurs in the political arena. To be effective in that arena, child advocates must understand the difference between educating a legislator about a specific issue and lobbying for the introduction, passage, or defeat of a specific bill pending before the legislature. Education is permissible without limitations whereas lobbying is not. Lobby

---

B O X 12.3

Steps in Policy Advocacy

1. Define the problem.
2. Establish your desired outcomes—remember that policy making is a compromise process—know when to hold them and when to fold them.
3. Identify other organizations and individuals who have an interest in the issue, and share your concerns and desired outcomes with them.
4. Establish a coalition of individuals and organizations willing to pursue policy advocacy consistent with your values, principles, and objectives/outcomes.
5. Identify the policy-making branch and people within it who have the authority to change policies/programs to achieve the desired outcomes: legislative, executive, or judicial.
6. Determine the formal/informal systems for decision making in the appropriate policy-making branch.
7. Determine what actions will persuade public policy makers to implement changes (the strategy).
   - Documentation
   - Testimony
   - Expert witnesses
   - Written communications
   - Face-to-face communications
   - Client empowerment
8. Develop an advocacy plan acceptable to all coalition members including desired outcomes, strategies, and techniques.
9. Implement the advocacy plan with continued reassessment and modification until you achieve your desired objectives.
10. Achieve your advocacy objective and establish a monitoring system to ensure implementation.

Source: Content adapted from Jansson, 1999; Chambers, 2000; Haynes & Mickelson, 2000; Midgley, Tracy, & Livermore, 2000.

B O X   **12.4**

Steps in Developing a Movement to Effect Policy Change

1. Identify one or two people who share your interest, establish a leadership structure, define the problem, and establish desired outcomes.
2. Develop awareness of the need or problem by completing thoroughly researched policy briefs with executive summaries no longer than three pages.
3. Distribute the executive summary to targeted individuals or groups that have similar advocacy or policy interests. Tell them a policy brief is available if they wish more detail. Ask for their perspectives on the issue.
4. Utilize frequent and persistent contact, written and verbal, to educate these individuals and groups on the importance of the issue to children and to their overall concerns.
5. Increase presentation of issue to more groups, organizations, and individuals to increase awareness as well as expand options for potential solutions and advocacy strategies.
6. Encourage open discussion of the issue and mediate conflicts as the various solutions and strategies emerge.
7. Use fact-finding to resolve conflicts as well as to analyze potential strategies and solutions and develop a compromise position.
8. Use print and broadcast media to bring the issue and possible resolutions to the attention of the general public.
9. Continue with steps 4–10 listed in Box 12.3, Steps in Policy Advocacy.

Source: Content adapted from Jansson, 1999; Chambers, 2000; Haynes & Mickelson, 2000; Midgley, Tracy, & Livermore, 2000.

---

is "an attempt to influence legislation at the local, state, or federal level" (Internal Revenue Code, 26 CFR Section 1.501 (c) (3)-1(c) (3)). Many child advocates employed in private, nonprofit organizations and governmental units believe that they cannot engage in any lobbying activities. That is incorrect. Nonprofit organizations and their employees can lobby, but with restrictions as to what funds may or may not be used and how much of the organization's total resources, cash and in kind, can be used. Prior to engaging in lobbying activities, the advocate, if employed by a nonprofit organization or governmental unit, must review his or her organization's policies on lobbying.

A child advocate working in the political arena on a consistent basis must have technical knowledge about government structures, budgeting, legislatures, and official program and policy guidelines as well as skills in political negotiation. It is not enough to know how to reach and influence major officials: The advocate must also be well informed on substantive issues. These advocates are generally from advocacy organizations with full-time staff for this purpose, such as the Child Welfare League of America, Children's Defense Fund, and National Association of Child Advocates. A child advocate who becomes active with a legislative body around a specific issue or pending legislation generally does so to provide information through letters and written or oral testimony. Haynes' and Mickelson's book, *Affecting Change: Social Workers in the Political Arena,* Fourth Edition, is an excellent resource for practical tips on legislative letter writing (campaigns or individual efforts) and testimony (oral and written).

Another important part of successful advocacy is *monitoring*—maintaining contact with persons in a position to watch over the conduct of those who serve children. Monitoring, or follow-through, is essential if advocacy is to be more than a one-time exposé. Monitoring is a way to assure continuous community awareness and presence. It is particularly important in class action litigation in order to make sure that the process of implementing court decisions gets under way. It has also been used successfully in assuring that federal agencies implement legislation or that state agencies observe federal program guidelines.

Case Example: Using Different Advocacy Strategies and Skills.   This case example will highlight advocacy at the case, class, and policy levels. Due to space limitations, it will not demonstrate each step in the processes nor every skill. It is designed primarily to show how these different levels of advocacy are interrelated and how a single caseworker carrying out her day-to-day case management responsibilities can be the conduit for system change. Further, it demonstrates that child advocacy in child welfare includes parent advocacy. The case is intentionally designed to raise issues for disagreement and discussion. Disagreement, discussion, and compromise are the hallmarks of most advocacy projects. As we all know, there are no easy answers nor is there one resolution to any given set of facts in child welfare. This case is also designed to raise ethical considerations; for example: Should an employee request a court order mandating that her employer provide a needed service for a client?

> The Blue case, discussed at the beginning of this chapter, was brought to the attention of children's protective services because 2-week-old, Joseph, was born drug addicted. There are two other children, ages 4 and 2. All children are in foster care. The mother, Ms. Blue, admitted to using cocaine during her entire pregnancy and for about three years overall. She reported that her neighbor took care of the children when Ms. Blue was too high to do so. She also reported that she had been in a substance abuse treatment program, but services were terminated because she had received the full thirty days of services for which she was eligible under Medicaid. Let us look at this case from three advocacy approaches: case, class, and policy advocacy. Our goal in this case is to return these children safely to their mother as soon as possible.
>
> Common to all the approaches is fact-finding. Considering the facts necessary for a case advocacy approach, you know that there are three children under the age of 5 years and a mother who admits to ongoing substance abuse. Further you know that she is sometimes too high to care for the children. Based on your knowledge of substance abuse and child development, you know that children of these ages require constant adult supervision and attention and that the use of cocaine inhibits the ability of Ms. Blue to meet these needs. Ms. Blue told you that a neighbor took care of the children when she was too high to do so. You need to verify that with the neighbor. You need to know how she knows when Ms. Blue is too high. You need to know her level of commitment to caring for these children on an ongoing basis because we know that substance abuse is an addiction subject to relapse at any time. You need to determine Ms. Blue's behaviors toward the children when she is and is not on drugs. You need to know what substance abuse services are available to Ms. Blue and the cost for those services. The results of your fact-finding follow:
>
> ■ The neighbor, Mrs. Green, who lives in the downstairs flat, is an older woman who is retired with income from social security and a pension. She owns the house and has rented to

Ms. Blue for about five years. She reported that she had checked in on Ms. Blue two or three times a day while she was pregnant. She reported that Ms. Blue was really too high "maybe twenty times in nine months." Prior to Ms. Blue's pregnancy, she would check in with her if she heard a lot of noise from the children or saw Ms. Blue come home "looking funny." In addition, she saw Ms. Blue and the children most afternoons on the porch or in the backyard. Sometimes Mrs. Green would be gardening while the children were playing outside. She had previously taken care of the older children while their mother was receiving in-patient substance abuse services. Further, she took care of the older children most afternoons while their mother was pregnant. Mrs. Green said that she had told the protective services worker that she was willing to be licensed as a foster parent for the children when the worker came to remove the older children from the mother's home after the baby was born. She remains committed to helping Ms. Blue and the children "in whatever way she can."

■ Ms. Blue has had no previous reports of child abuse or neglect. Despite the fact that Ms. Blue said she had used drugs for about three years, the 2-year-old child was not born addicted to drugs based on the hospital birth records. You confirmed that Ms. Blue completed a thirty-day in-patient drug treatment program and was discharged because her Medicaid would pay for only thirty days. You were told that people with private insurance generally remain in the program for sixty days. She was placed on a waiting list for community-based services at discharge, has been on the waiting list for four months, and "probably would be in services in a month or so" according to the substance abuse treatment agency.

■ During a visit, you observe Mrs. Green and Ms. Blue interacting with the children and with one another. Mary, the 4-year-old, easily goes back and forth between her mother and Mrs. Green to show off her drawings and to get help building a Lego toy. Michael, the 2-year-old, after some quiet play with the trucks, throws one at Mary. His mother comes over and tells him "don't throw things." About a half hour later, he runs around the room, falls over a truck, and lies on the floor crying. Mrs. Green goes to him, picks him up, sits in the rocking chair and rocks him, saying, "Is Granny's baby tired? Let's rest." Michael calms down. Joseph, the baby, wakes up. Ms. Blue checks his diaper, asks Mary to bring his bottle, and then sits beside Mrs. Green and starts feeding the baby.

How do these facts help your decision? You know that Mrs. Green is supportive and has been for the entire period Ms. Blue has lived upstairs. You know the children have a bond with her. It appears that Mrs. Green and Ms. Blue have a good relationship with one another and have a coparenting relationship with the children. You know that Ms. Blue was honest about her substance abuse treatment and is willing to continue with community-based services when "her turn comes up." From this, you conclude that there is no serious risk of harm to the children if they are returned home now. The supervisor is a little concerned because of the length of time the mother has used drugs and the lack of information as to when, why, and with whom she uses; but says to go ahead with the recommendation at the court hearing. The judge orders the children returned to the mother only if Mrs. Green agrees to provide daily contact with Ms. Blue and the children. Mrs. Green and Ms. Blue readily agreed to this stipulation. Further, the judge ordered weekly visits by the worker to include face-to-face contacts with all the children, the mother, and Mrs. Green. Finally, he orders the agency to get Ms. Blue into substance abuse treatment services this week because he is "tired of all these families waiting for months to get service." He wants you back in court next Tuesday to report that the order has been carried out.

Now your challenges begin. You have both a case advocacy and a potential class advocacy issue. The case advocacy issue is getting Ms. Blue into a substance abuse treatment program in one week when she is not scheduled to enter services for "a month or so." The judge, in his order and comments, identified a potential class advocacy issue: the long delay in getting parents of children in foster care into drug treatment services. You know that this issue is real because on your caseload alone you have five parents on waiting lists for substance abuse treatment services. This problem has been raised at staff meetings for the last year, and the supervisor says that higher-ups are meeting with the substance abuse agency to try to get more services. To your knowledge, this is the first time the judge has ordered the agency to get the parent services immediately.

You go to your supervisor and show her the order. She directs you to contact the substance abuse treatment agency and report that you have a court order requiring you to get Ms. Blue into services by next Monday. She takes a copy and says she would bring the matter to the attention of her superiors.

You contact the substance abuse treatment agency. You are told that there is no possible way Ms. Blue can get into services next week. There are thirty people on the waiting list before her. The court ordered your agency not the treatment agency to get her into services. You say that the only agency you can refer to is this agency because it is the central screening agency for all substance abuse services in the county. The screener says that is true, but she cannot make a decision to move someone up on the waiting list. You ask her for the name of the person who could make that decision. She gives you the name and phone number of her supervisor, Mrs. Yellow. You call her and leave a voice mail message. You tell your supervisor, and she says to keep her informed. She has shared the order with her supervisor, who, in turn, sent it to your legal affairs office. Your supervisor says, "This might be just what we need to bring this problem to a head." You are thinking about standing before the judge next Tuesday and the perspiration starts.

You get no call back before the end of the day, so you call Mrs. Yellow again. Her voice mail message now says she is out of the office until Thursday. Your supervisor is gone for the day. You have a sleepless night. The next morning, you contact the screener again and ask for someone above her supervisor. She gives you Mr. Brown's name and phone number. You call and leave a message in his voice mail. You then tell your supervisor the new developments. Also, you let her know that you have to replace a teen today, and it will take all day because you are moving him to a residential facility across the state. Your anxiety is high. She sees it and says she will follow up with Mr. Brown. You go. You have another sleepless night.

You return to the office hoping to see a message from your supervisor telling you that the problem is resolved. There is no message. Your supervisor, along with all the managers, is in a meeting out of the building until noon. You call Mr. Brown. He tells you quite angrily that he told your supervisor yesterday that he would have to discuss the matter with the agency's executive director because granting an exception in this case could lead this judge to order all the parents of children in foster care to be serviced by his agency immediately, which would create total chaos. You thank him. You remain anxious.

You call Ms. Blue to let her know the status. She says she is scared the judge will take the kids away from her if she is not in a program by next Tuesday. She says she talked to some women who were in the residential program with her. They meet at the church down the street from her each day—just them, no professionals—to support each other. She could join their group. Would that work? You tell her that you are not sure, but to go ahead and attend their meetings and ask if some of them would come to the hearing next Tuesday. You will talk with your supervisor about it this afternoon.

Your supervisor finally gets to the office. You tell her what has happened. She says you made a good decision in telling Ms. Blue to go ahead with the voluntary group because things did not look hopeful with the substance abuse treatment agency. Later that day, her supervisor tells her that there is a meeting of the executive directors of your agency and the substance abuse agency this afternoon. You get no feedback from the meeting by the end of the day. You rest a little better knowing that the executives had met and it is no longer just your problem.

It is Friday at last! You go to court on another case before the same judge. You hope he does not ask about Ms. Blue's situation. He does not, but he does order the agency to get the mother in this case into drug treatment within a week. You are on the treadmill again!! You immediately tell your supervisor. She had good news about Ms. Blue. She is to start in the program on Monday. However, she thinks this new order will upset the executives. It appears that you are the only worker who has been getting these orders. Are you asking for them? You tell her that you would have to be out of your mind to bring this kind of stress on yourself. You become quite upset that she would even ask the question. You tell the other workers what happened with your supervisor. They say they will start asking the judges to give them the specific orders on their cases that have been waiting for substance abuse and mental health services for long periods of time. They say: "It is about time somebody does something about this problem. The executives have known about it for years and done nothing. It is unfair to the children, their mothers, and the workers!!!" The movement begins.

You call Ms. Blue to tell her where to go to begin services on Monday. She tells you she will go. She will also continue with the self-help group and will bring two of them to the court hearing on Tuesday. Mrs. Green will take care of the children while she is gone.

At the hearing on Tuesday, you and Ms. Blue report that she is in substance abuse treatment. She talks about the self-help group. The judge listens to one of the women from the group and tells you that these self-help options should be considered by your agency instead of just letting the mothers stay on waiting lists indefinitely. He commends you and Ms. Blue for your creativity. He could see this approach as very cost effective and helpful to parents after agency services end to reduce relapses. He says he knows his orders have created quite a stir in both agencies because they have requested a meeting with all the judges to discuss the problem. He hopes this signals a reexamination of how the systems are structured so that children, families, and workers have an easier time getting the services that so many families need in order for the children to safely return home. Your opinion of him begins to change!

You immediately report to your supervisor. She appears troubled by the judge's comments. She tells you that you both must meet with the executive director tomorrow to discuss why you are the only one getting these orders. You are anxious and angry. You go back to your desk and see copies of five other court orders that other workers have gotten on their cases. These orders required your agency to start substance abuse or mental health treatment services for these mothers within seven to ten days. The anxiety and anger eases as you think, "I am not in this alone."

Over the course of the next two months, the executives of child welfare, substance abuse, and mental health and the judges meet and develop a plan accepted by all to increase the responsiveness of all systems to the children and parents served by the child welfare system whether under court order or not. This plan is shared with the workers. It looks as though the system will be more responsive. A group of workers met after reviewing the plan in detail. They discovered in reviewing the plan that there were federal funding requirements that mandated mental health and substance abuse services be provided and that priority be given to families with children in out-of-home care. These requirements had been in place for years. They concluded that they needed to work together on an ongoing basis to make sure that they knew what the regulations were and that they monitored their agency's implementation of the regulations on an ongoing basis. They had had too many sleepless nights and anxious days trying to get needed services that should have been readily available for children and families.

Trends and Issues

Media attention to problems of children, youth, and their families will continue to play a significant role in elevating the needs of children to public exposure, discussion, and debate. Television, newspapers, opinion journals, popular magazines, and films publicize in different ways the problems of poverty, teenage pregnancy, juvenile crime, youth drug use and sales, increased HIV infection and AIDS in children and adolescents, multiple foster care placements, sibling separations, adoption drift (legally available children languishing in foster care because adoptive homes are not available), inadequate mental health services, and homelessness. Much of the publicity has drawn attention to the inadequacies of the child welfare system, among others. Currently, and historically, media publicity often focuses on the inadequacies of the systems and individuals charged with the responsibility to provide services to these children. Effective use of these media stories as advocacy tools requires, in the author's opinion, less defensiveness on the part of the systems and individuals attacked and greater readiness to objectively analyze the weaknesses and strengths of the system and make constructive changes. The College of Journalism at the University of Maryland has established the Casey Journalism Center for Children and Families as a national resource for journalists who cover children and their parents. It promotes careful and thorough examination of issues by reporters and supports this with conferences that expose journalists to national policy and research experts on a range of issues affecting disadvantaged children. This type of engagement promotes, within the journalism profession as a whole, reporting that provides more "good news" stories in which the systems or individuals are effective and more evidence based, specific target stories in which the systems or individuals are ineffective (Casey Journalism Center for Families and Children, 1998).

Federal and state legislation on behalf of children does not come easily. The 1990s saw continued shrinking of resources and a concomitant increase in competition for those that are available. This trend continues. Without doubt, many decisions in the next decade will be reached on the basis of finances. Specifically, we are moving into an age of managed care. In such a milieu, the need for case, class, and policy advocacy on behalf of children (illustrated repeatedly throughout this text) will be critical. An essential piece of advocacy in the 2000s will be data. Outcome data on organizations and programs currently serving the population will be a requisite to enter the executive and legislative hallways. Once in the doors, advocates must clearly articulate how their proposals will enhance those outcomes. Suggesting and monitoring legislation, building coalitions, testifying in Congress and state capitals, securing and maintaining presence on executive agency policy-making and advisory committees, and becoming active in political campaigns will be necessary. Parents, youth, and other citizens need encouragement to express their views about the status of child and family life, the risks they see, and the changes they want in order to strengthen and maintain strong family life and maximum opportunity for children and youth.

The qualifications and training of child welfare workers continues to receive public scrutiny. Most child welfare workers are not professionally trained in social work. Few receive the depth and breadth of in-service or on-the-job training and supervision necessary to effectively manage the responsibilities of their positions. Many professionally trained social workers do not have child welfare–specific expertise. This presents challenges to the profession as well as to the individual worker. The community as a whole views all child welfare workers as "social workers." Bad practice is attributed to the profession, irrespective of the training of the child welfare worker involved. The National Association of Social Workers has undertaken the professionalization of child welfare workers as a strategy to alleviate the current situation (National Association of Social Workers, 2002). Liability exposures with resultant legal judgments or settlements in cases involving "bad practice" could persuade public officials to join with NASW in this effort.

Chapter Summary

In discussing professional responsibility, this chapter has provided a broad set of issues to consider as you undertake child welfare practice: confidentiality and privacy; liability and malpractice; confidentiality and privileges; forensic interviewing; risk management and duty to warn; clients' rights to treatment in a managed care environment; testimony; and advocacy. Its purpose was to show the range of responsibilities attributed to the professional and the dilemmas inherent in these responsibilities. Many of the dilemmas have no conclusive answer that the child welfare worker can rely on in every case. Decisions require balancing interests and consequences as applied to the current case situation. On the other hand, some are clearly resolved by statutory requirements that supercede ethical principles and standards, such as reporting suspected child abuse or neglect. A methodology has been provided to assist the worker in resolving the dilemmas and pursuing change for children through case, class, and policy advocacy.

FOR STUDY AND DISCUSSION

1. Apply Reamer's seven steps for resolving ethical dilemmas to the following case situation. Kevin, age 16, has run away from his adoptive home. You have been working with the adoptive parents and Kevin concerning his adjustment to the family's expectations (he was adopted two years ago), his poor academic performance and acting out behaviors in school (he was recently expelled for bringing a knife to school), and his sometimes explosive anger. You have identified several critical issues in your individual work with Kevin. He has never processed his grief over the termination of parental rights prior to his adoption. He yearns to find his birth family and has threatened to run away to look for them. He is frightened of some of the other male students at his high school and has verbalized that they might do "terrible things" to him, although he refuses to say more on the topic. His self-esteem is, as Kevin himself says, "so down in the pits it couldn't be lower." Kevin's perception is that he will never fit into his adoptive family because they are "so good and so religious."

You are awakened from a deep sleep at 2 A.M. by your agency on-call service. Kevin is in crisis and needs to talk to you immediately. You call the number given. Kevin is so upset that the conversation is disjointed and rambling, and it takes your best skills to keep him talking and get the facts: Kevin ran away in search of his birth parents, whom he could not locate. He is calling from the home of his (biological) uncle. While at his uncle's house he used some drugs (he does not specify what) and allowed his uncle to have anal intercourse with him, hoping to please his uncle so that he could find out what happened to his parents. He has been having what he describes as "flashbacks" about "nasty things that I did when I was a kid." He is afraid that he is gay and is in a panic. He wants to meet with you to talk, but will not do it unless you promise that you will not tell his adoptive parents you have had contact with him. If you try to contact his parents (or the police) he says he will either run away and never come back, or kill himself. He will not tell you where his uncle's house is or what his uncle's name is. He offers to come to your house to see you now or to meet you in some place away from the agency in the morning.

2. Which should take precedence when the needs of the child, the family, the agency, or society in general are in conflict? Are we ever justified in violating the law to help a client?

3. Joe is a 10-year-old child who entered foster care after his mother had broken his arm for the third time. He wants to go home with his mother. Does he have a right to self-determination? Why or why not? How do you explain your answer to him?

4. Joan is the 8-year-old daughter of the mayor of Big City. She has been referred to you by her teacher because she appears unusually anxious. Joan told you that her father has been rubbing the inside of her leg next to her vagina each night since school started. She thinks he should not be doing this and she wants to tell her mother, but she does not want her mother to get mad at her. You tell her that her father should not be doing this and you will help her. You report this to your supervisor and tell her that you will make the mandated report to the child protective services agency. She

tells you not to make the report. She will make the report after she has discussed the situation with "administration." What do you say?

5. How can children and youth be given an opportunity to help define the problems and issues that are advocated in their behalf?

6. Methodically apply the advocacy steps outlined in this chapter to the case example given. Identify from that process the knowns and unknowns or places where additional facts must be gathered and alternative strategies devised.

7. Select a problem facing a group of children or youth in your state or community. Apply the steps of advocacy described in this chapter to the problem.

8. Debate the merits of a variety of persons acting as children's advocates. Include lawyers, social workers, college students, parents, and teachers. A list of qualifications for advocates should emanate from such a discussion.

9. Discuss the limits on the extent to which agency child welfare workers can act as advocates for children on their caseloads and children not on their caseloads who are served by the agency.

10. Responsibility for the neglect of today's youth is broadly shared. Discuss ways in which society could reshape its attitudes and priorities to help children and youth with their problems.

FOR ADDITIONAL STUDY

Barker, R., & Branson, D. (1993). When laws and ethics collide. In *Forensic social work.* New York: Haworth.

Bussiere, A., English, A., & Teare, C. (1997). *Sharing information: A guide to federal laws on confidentiality and disclosure of information for child welfare agencies.* Chicago: American Bar Association.

Children's Defense Fund. (2002). *Congressional workbook 2002: Basic process and issue primer.* Washington, DC: Author.

Cooper, P. J., & Newland, C. A. (Eds.). (1997). *Handbook of public law and administration.* San Francisco: Jossey-Bass.

Gustavsson, N. S., & Segal, E. A. (1994). *Critical issues in child welfare.* Thousand Oaks, CA: Sage.

Hardin, M. (2001). *Privacy and information sharing in child abuse and neglect cases.* Chicago: American Bar Association.

Jansson, B. (1994). *Social policy: From theory to policy practice.* Pacific Grove, CA: Brooks Cole.

Kirst-Ashman, K. K. (2000). *Human behavior, communities, organizations and groups in the macro social environment.* Belmont, CA: Brooks/Cole Social Work.

Linden, R. M. (1998). *Workbook for seamless government: A hands-on guide to implementing organizational change.* San Francisco: Jossey-Bass.

Meredith, J. C., & Dunham, C. M. (1999). *Real clout: A how-to manual for community-based activists trying to expand healthcare access by changing public policy.* Boston: The Access Project.

Myers, J. E. B. (1992). *Legal issues in child abuse and neglect.* Newbury Park, CA: Sage.

Myers, J. E. B. (1994). *The backlash—Child protection under fire.* Thousand Oaks, CA: Sage.

Netting, F. E., Kettner, P. M., & McMurtry, S. L. (1998). *Social work macro practice* (2nd ed.). New York: Longman.

Rothman, J., Erlich, J. L., & Tropman, J. E. (1995). *Strategies of community intervention* (5th ed.). Itaska, IL: F. E. Peacock.

Sedaka, J., Ketchum, J., Kowal, L., & Bocella, I. (1997). *Engaging the media: A toolkit for responding to public concerns about child protection.* Washington, DC: Technical Assistance and Training Corporation.

Specht, H., & Courtney, M. E. (1994). *Unfaithful angels: How social work has abandoned its mission.* New York: Free Press.

Thomas, J. C. (1995). *Public participation in public decisions: New skills and strategies for public managers.* San Francisco: Jossey-Bass.

Urban Health Initiative. (2000, Spring). *Helping communities work smarter for kids.* Seattle, WA: Robert Wood Johnson Foundation's Urban Health Initiative.

INTERNET SEARCH TERMS

Advocacy

Confidentiality

Professional ethics

INTERNET SITES

There are several sites that provide competently researched policy and data for child welfare advocacy use.

Administration for Children & Families.
www.acf.dhhs.gov/programs/acyf

American Academy of Pediatrics.
www.aap.org

American Public Human Services Association.
www.apwa.org

Annie E. Casey Foundation.
www.aecf.org

Center for Law and Social Policy.
www.epn.org/clasp.html

Children, Youth and Family Education and Research Network.
www.cyfernet.mes.umn.edu/index.html

Children's Defense Fund.
www.childrensdefense.org/index.html

Child Trends.
www.childtrends.org

Child Welfare League of America.
www.cwla.org

Families & Work Institute.
www.familiesandworkinst.org

Family Life Development Center.
http://child.cornell.edu/fldc.home.html

Juvenile Justice Clearinghouse.
www.fsu.edu/~crimdo/jjclearinghouse/jjclearinghouse.html

Kids Count.
www.aecf.org

National Association of Child Advocates.
www.childadvocacy.org

National Association of Social Workers.
www.naswdc.org

National Center for Children in Poverty.
www.cpmcnet.columbia.edu/dept/nccp

National Center on Child Abuse and Neglect Clearinghouse.
www.calib.com/nccanch

National Child Welfare Resource Center for Organizational Improvement.
www.muskie.usm.maine.edu/helpkids

*National Child Welfare Resource Center
on Legal and Judicial Issues.*
www.abanet.org/child/reljc.com/research

*National Clearinghouse on Child Abuse
and Neglect Information.*
www.calib.org

National Data Archive on Child Abuse and Neglect.
www.ndacan.cornell.edu

*Office of Juvenile Justice and
Delinquency Prevention.*
www.ncjrs.org/ojjhome.html

United States Congress.
www.firstgov.gov

U.S. General Accounting Office.
www.gao.gov
www.firstgov.gov

Urban Institute.
www.urban.org

REFERENCES

American Bar Association. (1991). *Liability in child welfare and protection work.* Chicago: Author.

Bailey, R., & Brake, M. (Eds.). (1975). In *Introduction: Social work in the welfare state.* New York: Pantheon Books.

Beck, R., & Butler, J. (1974). An interview with Marian Wright Edelman. *Harvard Educational Review, 44*(1), 1–12.

Black, H. C. (1992). *Black's law dictionary* (8th ed.). St. Paul, MN: West.

Casey Journalism Center for Children and Families. (1998). *The children's beat.* University of Maryland College of Journalism: College Park, MD.

Chambers, D. E. (2000). *Social policy and social programs: A method for the practical public policy analyst* (3rd ed.). Boston: Allyn & Bacon.

Child Welfare League of America. (1981). *Statement on child advocacy.* New York: Author.

Cloward, R. A., & Elman, R. M. (1967). The storefront on Stanton Street: Advocacy in the ghetto. In G. Brager & F. P. Purcell (Eds.), *Community action against poverty.* New Haven, CT: College and University Press.

Dickson, D. T. (1995). *Law in the health and human services—A guide for social workers, psychologists, psychiatrists and related professionals.* New York: Free Press.

Epstein, I. (1981, Summer). Advocates on advocacy: An exploratory study. *Social Work Research & Abstracts.*

Field, T. (1996, Summer). Managed care and child welfare—Will it work? In *Public Welfare.* Washington, DC: American Public Welfare Association.

Fink, A. E., Anderson, C. W., & Conover, M. B. (1968). *The field of social work.* New York: Holt, Rinehart and Winston.

Gothard, S. (1995). Legal issues: Confidentiality and privileged communication. In *Encyclopedia of social work, vol. 2* (19th ed.) (pp. 1579–1584). Washington, DC: National Association of Social Workers.

Haynes, K. S., & Mickelson, J. S. (2000). *Affecting change: social workers in the political arena.* (4th ed.). Boston: Allyn & Bacon.

Holt, J. (1964). *How children fail.* New York: Pitman.

Institute for Human Services Management. (1996). *Managed care and child welfare: Are they compatible? Design issues in managed care for child welfare.* Bethesda, MD: Author.

Jansson, B. S. (1999). *Becoming an effective policy advocate: from policy practice to social justice* (3rd ed.). Pacific Grove, CA: Brooks/Cole.

Kahn, A. J., Kamerman, S. B., & McGowan, B. G. (1972). *Child advocacy: Report of a national baseline study.* Washington, DC: U.S. Children's Bureau.

Knitzer, J. E. (1976). Child advocacy: A perspective. *American Journal of Orthopsychiatry, 46*(2), 200–216.

Kowal, L. W. (1996). *Keeping the focus on kids: Outcomes, ethics and partnerships in a managed care environment.* Paper presented at the American Humane Association's roundtable in Vail, Colorado.

Kozol, J. (1967). *Death at an early age.* Boston: Houghton Mifflin.

Mather, J. H., & Lager, P. (2000). *A unifying model of practice.* Belmont, CA: Brooks/Cole.

Michigan Governor's Task Force on Children's Justice and Family Independence Agency. (1998). *Forensic interviewing protocol.* Lansing, MI: Family Independence Agency.

Mickelson, J. S. (1995). Advocacy. In *Encyclopedia of Social Work, vol. 1* (19th ed.) (pp. 95–100). Washington, DC: NASW Press.

Midgley, J., Tracy, M. B., & Livermore, M. (2000). *The handbook of social policy.* Thousand Oaks, CA: Sage.

Morales v. Thurman, 380 F. Supp. 53 E. D. Tex. (1974).

National Association of Social Workers. (1999). *Code of ethics.* Washington, DC: Author.

National Association of Social Workers. (2002). *Social work speaks.* Washington, DC: NASW Press.

National Clearinghouse on Child Abuse and Neglect Information. (1998). *State statute series.* Washington, DC: Author.

National Community Mental Healthcare Council. (1997). *Child welfare and managed care briefing.* Rockville, MD: Author.

Ness, M., Pizzigati, K., & Stuck, E. (2002). *A child advocacy primer: experience and advice from service providers, board leaders, and consumers.* Washington, DC: Child Welfare League of America.

Netting, F. E., Kettner, P. M., & McMurtry, S. L. (1998). *Social work macro practice* (2nd ed.). New York: Addison Wesley Longman.

Paul, J. L. (1977). *Child advocacy within the system.* Syracuse, NY: Syracuse University Press.

Pennsylvania Association for Retarded Citizens v. Commonwealth of Pennsylvania, 334 F. Supp. 1257, E. D. Pa. (1971).

Reamer, F. G. (1995). *Social work values and ethics.* New York: Columbia University Press.

Richan, W. C. (1991). *Lobbying for social change.* New York: Haworth.

Rule 23 Federal Rules of Civil Procedure.

Silberman, C. E. (1971). *Crisis in the classroom.* New York: Random House.

Specht, H., & Courtney, M. E. (1994). *Unfaithful angels: How social work has abandoned its mission.* New York: Free Press.

Steiner, G. Y. (1976). *The children's cause.* Washington, DC: The Brookings Institution.

Stroul, B. A., Pires, S. A., Armstrong, M. I., & Meyers, J. C. (1998). The impact of managed care on mental health services for children and their families. *The future of children: Children and managed mental health care, 8*(2).

Tompkins, C. (1989, March 27). Profiles: Marian Wright Edelman: A sense of urgency. *New Yorker,* 48–50.

United States Government General Accounting Office. (1998). *Child welfare: Early experiences implementing a managed care approach.* HEHS-99-8. Washington, DC: U.S. Government Printing Office.

NAME INDEX

SUBJECT INDEX